The Danse Macabre

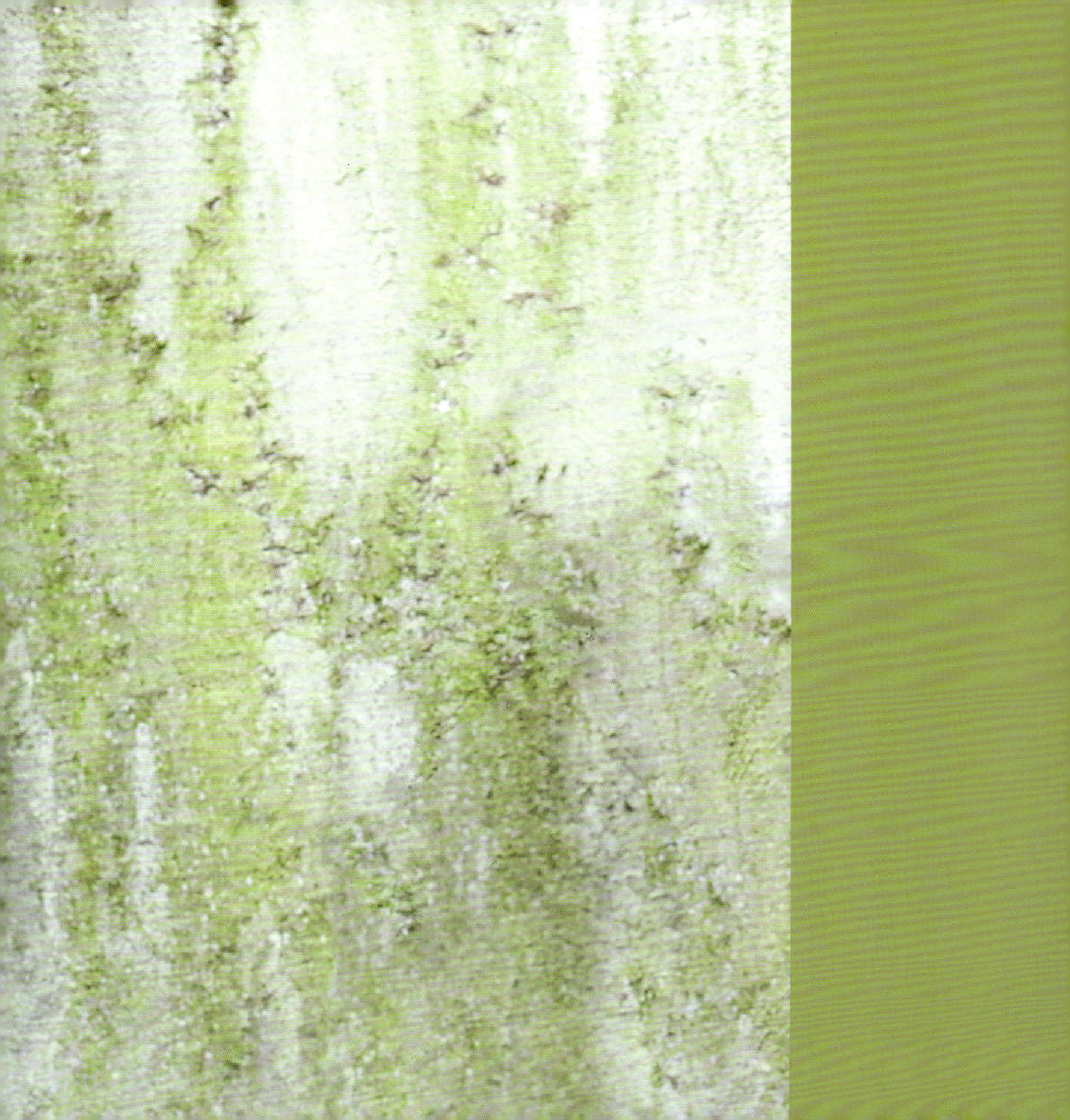

THE DANSE MACABRE

CELEBRATION AND SURVIVAL IN NEW ORLEANS

CHERYL GERBER

FOREWORD BY
MAURICE CARLOS RUFFIN

LOUISIANA STATE UNIVERSITY PRESS BATON ROUGE

Published with the assistance of the V. Ray Cardozier Fund

Published by Louisiana State University Press
lsupress.org

Manufactured in China
FIRST PRINTING

LSU PRESS PAPERBACK ORIGINAL

DESIGNER: Mandy McDonald Scallan
TYPEFACE: Chaparral Pro
PRINTER AND BINDER: Reliance/Martin Book Management

COVER PHOTOGRAPH: Austin Feldbaum participates in the Krewe de Mayahuel's
Día de los Muertos parade, 2022. Photo by Cheryl Gerber.

PAGE 260: "Down In New Orleans" from *The Princess and the Frog*
Music and Lyrics by Randy Newman
© 2009 Walt Disney Music Company
All Rights Reserved. Used by Permission.
Reprinted by Permission of Hal Leonard LLC

LIBRARY OF CONGRESS CATALOGING-IN-PUBLICATION DATA
Names: Gerber, Cheryl, author, photographer. | Ruffin, Maurice Carlos,
    writer of foreword.
Title: The danse macabre : celebration and survival in New Orleans / Cheryl
    Gerber ; foreword by Maurice Carlos Ruffin.
Other titles: Celebration and survival in New Orleans
Description: Baton Rouge : Louisiana State University Press, [2024]
Identifiers: LCCN 2023035253 | ISBN 978-0-8071-8099-0 (paperback)
Subjects: LCSH: New Orleans (La.)—Pictorial works. | New Orleans
    (La.)—Social life and customs—Pictorial works. | City and town life—
    Louisiana—New Orleans—Pictorial works. | Photography, Artistic.
Classification: LCC F379.N543 G4584 2024 | DDC 976.3/3500222—dc23
LC record available at https://lccn.loc.gov/2023035253

I will dance and resist and dance and persist and dance.

This heartbeat is louder than death.

—SUHEIR HAMMAD, AMERICAN POET

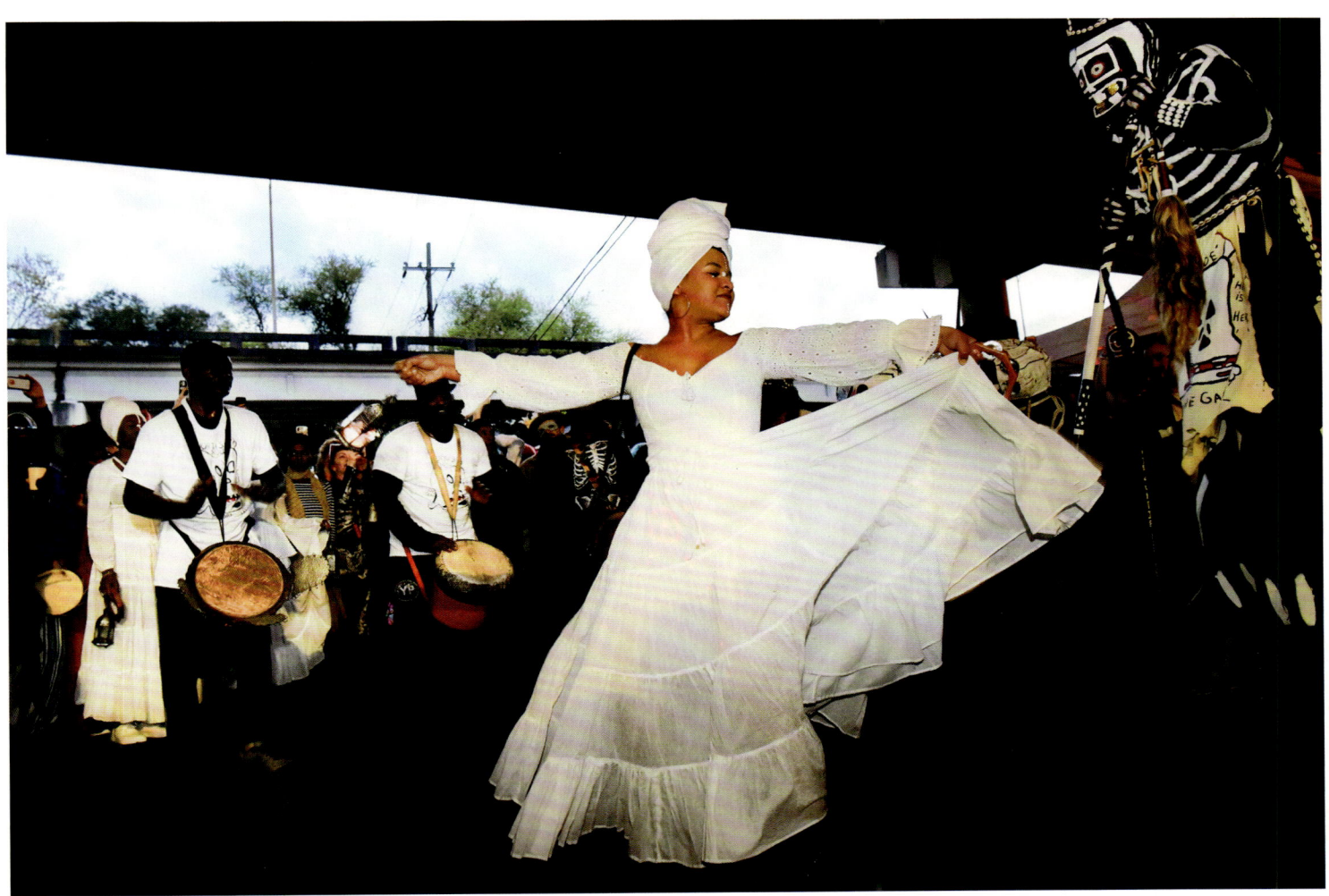

A member of the Mystic Seven Sisters dances with the North Side Skull and Bone Gang on Mardi Gras morning, 2020.

CONTENTS

FOREWORD City of Life

Man stands face to face with the irrational. He feels within him his longing for happiness and for reason. The absurd is born of this confrontation between the human need and the unreasonable silence of the world.

—ALBERT CAMUS

What I remember most about returning to New Orleans in 2005 just over a month after Hurricane Katrina was the silence. My shotgun house was on a narrow lot barely a stone's throw from an elementary school. During the school year, standing in my driveway, I might hear my neighbor's stereo blasting '70s R&B from his balcony as a young student walked along the sideway and a mosquito bit my arm. I realize now, through the lens of time, that this was a kind of happiness. Did I always want to hear that music vibrating up the street? Did I like finding a bag of blazing-orange corn puffs on the ground near my steps? Did I like the mosquitos, roaches, mutts, and mice that sometimes visited my little plot? No, no, and no. But I loved them all.

When I bought that house, after signing the deed, I walked outside and scooped up a handful of dirt and smelled it. But post-Katrina, the gorgeous dark-brown soil had taken on a pallor like the stuff that accumulates around one's mouth when we're sick. That film was left over from the floodwaters—waters filled with motor oil, lead, pesticides, dissolved medications, and, most grievously, the leavings of the dead. That film was evidence of what ran off the stray dogs, killed the bugs, dislocated my music-loving neighbor, and banished the children. For a time, there were virtually no children in New Orleans because the schools were obliterated. New Orleans, land of brass and feathers, was as sonically cold and gray as one of our above-ground cemeteries.

But death is not as shocking in New Orleans as it is most of the United States.

The North Side Skull and Bone Gang who have dressed as skeletons for hundreds of years and wandered the streets remind us that, as the text of this book says, "Get your life together, (because) next time you see us, it's too late to cry."

Life and death live cheek to cheek in my city. It doesn't mean we're morbid. It just means that we see the larger picture. As in any major city, someone's life ends every day, but hardly a week passes without a festival within the city limits, if not nearby: Mardi Gras, Jazz Fest, Voodoo Fest, LUNA Fête, and on and on.

New Orleans is threatened by climate change with its attendant rising sea level. For whatever reason, fate has destroyed our city by fire and flood and plague more often than one would expect. This may be something that gives a resident a unique perspective on endings. Like ball-turret gunners in World War II, astronauts and cosmonauts in spacecraft built by the lowest bidder, and deep-sea divers with half-empty oxygen tanks, New Orleans people understand precarity, vulnerability, exposure. Perhaps this is why we live how we do. We dance, we sing, we eat, we drink.

Gerber is a keen observer of our native exuberance. Her camera's eye observes our people in the throes of ecstasy and in our most difficult moments. Often these moments are captured in a single frame. Throughout this book, the gorgeous photos of our singularity capture the incredible sweetness and humanity of life in New Orleans. Gerber has a sense of juxtaposition and humor too. See how a picture of a trio of New Orleans Saints fans dressed as bishops lays next to a picture of a trio of ordained clergy at St. Louis Cathedral. Or peruse the photos of recently deceased jazz legends next to lovingly homemade depictions of them in public spaces. Pride, cheekiness, and honor are all hallmarks of our culture, a culture Gerber captures with verve.

—MAURICE CARLOS RUFFIN

ACKNOWLEDGMENTS

Taking the photos that appear in this book was the fun and easy part. Assembling them to tell the complicated story that is New Orleans, night after night in a tiny dark office, was a tedious and profoundly lonely task. Were it not for the support of my husband Mark McGrain, who nourished me physically and mentally throughout the process, I am not sure I could have finished a project of this magnitude. Thank you, Mark, for always making sure I had the time, space, and advice I needed to see this thing through. And thank you for the martinis that would magically appear at just the right time.

I first met Maurice Carlos Ruffin nearly twenty years ago while on assignment for a story about attorneys who assisted our most vulnerable citizens, the unhoused. When I arrived at St. Jude Community Center on N. Rampart Street, Maurice was in a suit and tie, counseling a woman wrapped in a blanket, while a dozen other clients waited their turn to be advised *pro bono*. I knew at that moment that he was a special human being. Back then, I had no idea how remarkable he would become as a writer and author. His books and essays speak volumes about his humanity. I will forever be grateful for the wisdom and insight he brought to this project.

I would also like to thank my editor Jenny Keegan and the staff at LSU Press for their invaluable feedback and guidance, which helped make this the best book it could be. During times of contentious debates surrounding the banning of books, I am forever appreciative of the freedom LSU Press gave me to include photographs that otherwise might never see the light of day; they are essential to portraying the full picture.

Most of all, I would like to thank all the extraordinary people of this remarkable city who opened their souls to me every time I clicked the shutter. The people of New Orleans have taught me so much about perseverance and what it means to be part of the most interesting community in the world. Without each one, there would be no *Danse Macabre*.

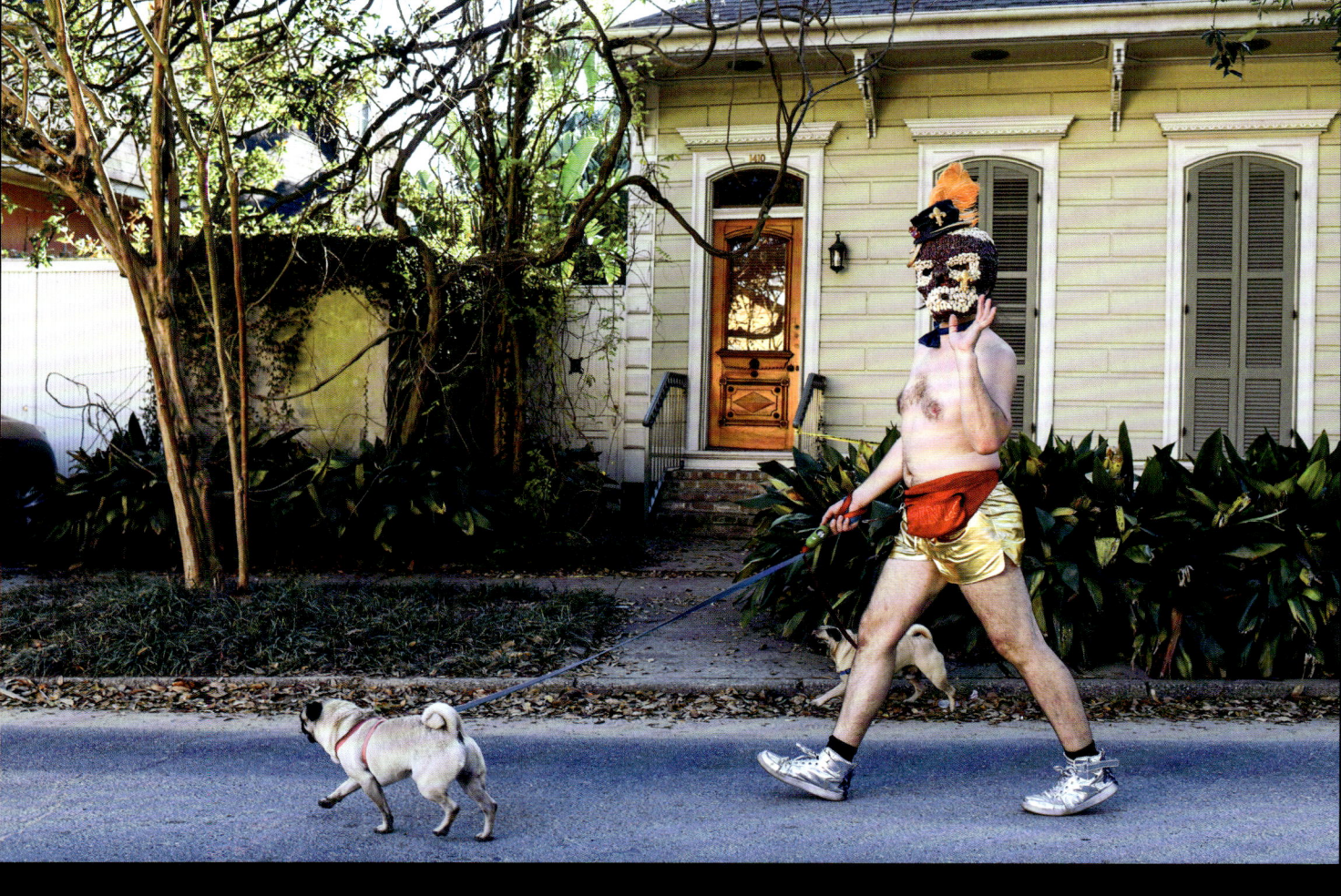

A man costumed for the Dead Beans parade walks his dogs through Tremé, 2022.

INTRODUCTION

This city wears two faces. Just like the Mardi Gras masks, tragedy and comedy.
— **DEB "BIG RED" COTTON,** writer and video blogger, as quoted
in Jason Berry's documentary film, *A City of a Million Dreams*

Exactly sixteen years to the day that Hurricane Katrina wrecked New Orleans, my husband and I rode out Hurricane Ida in our historic shotgun house in the Faubourg Marigny. We were prepared for the storm, but not for the flood of emotions it unleashed.

As the first furious outer bands of Ida's winds arrived, the house began to creak. They say that when one faces death, their life flashes before their eyes. In my case, facing a Category 4 storm barreling toward our fragile coast, images of Katrina-ravaged New Orleans made their way to the forefront of my psyche.

I recalled photographing cars under houses, houses atop trees, families mucking through mud in search of heirlooms, and ghost-like streets with concrete steps to nowhere. The haunting images of death and destruction inundated me with thoughts of worst-case scenarios and doubts about my native city's survival.

Then, as the green lightning lit up the sky, I remembered an image that I had happened on in the aftermath of Katrina while photographing the devastation. There was not a soul on the streets. In the distance, orange and beige feathers blowing in the wind caught my eye. Hanging on the front porch of a flooded-out house in the Eighth Ward was a Black Masking Indian feathered crown with a handwritten message scribbled on a satin bib: "I'll be Back, Wild Man Loco." The rust-colored waterline on the wall behind the suit belied such optimism.

Yet, nearly fifteen years later, on Super Sunday 2019, there was Jaime "Wild Man Loco" Cooper; now in a wheelchair, he was surrounded by Indian chiefs from other tribes rattling tambourines, as together they sang "We won't bow down," the defiant line from the anthem of the Indian nations, "Indian Red." Wild Man Loco came back, and so did New Orleans.

Even as some around the country were debating whether New Orleans should be rebuilt, signs of resurrection began to pop up everywhere. Colorful murals appeared all around the city, breathing new hope into our apocalyptic landscape. The culture not only thrived but also evolved with an explosion of new marching krewes, including the Baby Dolls, who emerged as one of our strongest cultural traditions after a half-century hiatus. And a new generation of young musicians like those in the Big 6 Brass Band led thriving Sunday second lines, assuring us that the good times would keep on rolling.

Perhaps there was something to Louisiana author Walker Percy's well-documented "hurricane theory" that suggests that moments of existential crisis are a remedy for "the malaise": a hopelessness associated with the feeling that you are not connected to the world or the people in it. "Have you noticed that only in time of illness or disaster or death are people real?" Percy wrote in *The Moviegoer,* his 1961 debut novel that won the National Book Award.

Maybe that explains why New Orleanians are stitched together by common threads that make us all part of the fabric of the most interesting city in the nation. We celebrate life and death unlike any other place on Earth.

In its more-than-300-year history, New Orleans has been resurrected from ruin many times over. The seemingly eternal city has survived and recovered from the Great Fire of 1788, the Civil War and Reconstruction, yellow fever and smallpox, and Hurricanes Betsy and Katrina. And in the face of recent catastrophes and conflicts, that renaissance continues.

In 2021, New Orleans was spared a direct hit from Ida, but the city languished in the weeks following the storm that devastated our neighbors to our west: our hearts are with them as they rebuild. Many New Orleanians were without power for weeks. We waited in extremely long lines for gasoline, and we suffered the stench of garbage after weeks of no trash pickups.

But in good times and bad, New Orleanians just "roll with it," as the popular Rebirth Brass Band song goes. Neighbors helped neighbors, sharing food, gas, and even generated power to help charge phone batteries. But it was the ubiquitous tongue-in-cheek humor expressed in those difficult weeks that makes me love this city even when I think I cannot endure another day.

Disgusted with the growing piles of trash left on our curbs, a group of frustrated residents gathered for a "Trash Parade," marching to City Hall with their garbage. The pouring rain did not dampen the spirits of protesters who had costumed appropriately for the parade's theme. One protester decorated her umbrella in trash, sporting a sign reading, "Y'all Trashy." Another costumed as Oscar the Grouch in a garbage can, with a lid to protect from the downpour. But the one that really caught my attention was a woman dressed like Marie Antoinette (whom New Orleanians often satirize for her excesses and corruption), in a billowing dress crafted from plastic garbage bags and carrying a sign that read "Let Them Eat Trash." It reminded me of the first parade after Katrina when I had photographed a Phunny Phorty Phellows reveler dressed as "MRE Antoinette," referring to the military ready-to-eat meals distributed when we had no power or gas to cook.

New Orleans's long tradition of cultural and political satire is not limited to hurricanes and disasters. Irreverent, decadent, and politically incorrect, the city's Carnival culture is shaped by historical events such as colonization and slavery. Take Zulu for instance. One of the most anticipated parades of Mardi Gras, Zulu began in the early 1900s as a parody of the oppressive white political establishment that staged early Carnival; its members wore, and continue to wear, blackface and grass skirts. Although some condemn the predominantly African American krewe's practice of wearing blackface, Zulu members defend the tradition as their way of expressing their Black identity.

Mardi Gras has historically empowered marginalized people to publicly communicate shared experiences of injustice, trauma, and disaster. In recent times, the LGBTQ+ community has adopted that uninhibited and unabashed spirit in the annual Southern Decadence celebration, the largest gay event in the South, in which men parade in tutus, elaborate dresses, or barely anything at all.

For a first-time visitor, it can be overwhelming. In a city where Voodoo converges with Catholicism, where a French and Spanish heritage merges with African and Caribbean culture, the intoxicating and paradoxical nature of New Orleans can compel even the meekest small-town tourists to participate in wild, sometimes obscene, behavior.

On the flip side, many conservative religious protesters show up every year during Mardi Gras and Southern Decadence to try to save us from our wicked ways. I have heard it said that New Orleans is where God shook hands with the devil so the party could go on.

I guess that saying is true: New Orleans welcomes saints and sinners alike, much to the chagrin of many of our fellow Americans. Case in point: in the days after Katrina, some religious leaders suggested that the hurricane was God's wrath for the Southern Decadence parade that had been scheduled for the following weekend. But in true New Orleans style, several dozen scantily clad gay men found their way through the devastation to Bourbon Street and led a parade under their tattered rainbow flag.

New Orleans may not be the first place one thinks of when conjuring images of Americana, but New Orleanians exercise their American freedoms to the fullest. There is a sense of acceptance here that does not exist anywhere else in the Deep South.

As a study in contrasts, New Orleans is unparalleled. During my thirty-year career, I have peered through the lens not only at the rich ways that New Orleanians celebrate life but also at the many dichotomies that make living in the "Big Easy" so damn hard.

New Orleans is also called the "City of the Dead" because of our many above-ground crypts and cemeteries: life and death are inextricably tied together in this city. We have all danced with death at some time on the streets of New Orleans during our abundant traditional funeral processions, colloquially referred to as "jazz funerals." In recent years, they have taken place all too frequently. While young musicians such as Trombone Shorty and Jon Batiste have brought New Orleans music to the world stage, an entire generation of cultural legends has passed. Between 2012 and 2022, thousands gathered in the streets for memorial second lines and funerals celebrating the lives of musicians Allen Toussaint, Dr. John, Fats Domino, Pete Fountain, and Dave Bartholomew, to name a few.

And if all those deaths were not enough, they were compounded by yet another existential crisis.

Unlike a hurricane, we did not see this one coming.

Just before dawn on a Tuesday morning in 2020, I ventured into the heart of Tremé, the historic African American neighborhood adjacent to the French Quarter, to photograph the North Side Skull and Bone Gang, whose members continue the 200-year-old tradition of Black Masking that kicks off Mardi Gras. Skeletons wearing larger-than-life papier-mâché skulls walk door to door to wake up neighbors with a macabre message that is the very essence of Mardi Gras: life is as precious as it is fleeting. "Get your life together, (because) next time you see us, it's too late to cry," they sang.

We danced and partied in communal merriment, oblivious to the lethal contagion circulating among us like glitter in the wind.

Three weeks later, Mayor LaToya Cantrell ordered a citywide shutdown in response to the COVID-19 pandemic, which was growing in strength throughout the city and the world. Mardi Gras had been a super-spreader, making New Orleans the nation's epicenter of the disease.

Just like after Katrina, I walked the eerily empty streets of the city, making images of a ghost-like Bourbon Street, a hauntingly empty Café du Monde. The global pandemic stopped us in our tracks, quieting the constant roar of New Orleans and leaving us to face an uncertain future once again.

For many, that future would never come.

Icons such as jazz patriarch Ellis Marsalis, culture bearer Ronald Lewis, and actress Carol Sutton succumbed to the virus. We mourned our beloved, our neighbors, and our friends, in isolation.

Normally, one and all would have been honored with huge second lines and sendoffs befitting New Orleans royalty. But with COVID threatening everyone, they were laid to rest quietly, with only a handful of socially distanced mourners. New Orleanians in drive-by caravans waved goodbye.

In the months that followed, the pandemic death rate slowed but not before several more surges and many more deaths, although not all were related to COVID. In an ironic twist, the seemingly immortal Mr. Mardi Gras himself, Blaine Kern, the float builder credited for turning Mardi Gras into a world-renowned event, quietly passed away. Masked mourners, though wearing surgical and not Carnival masks, bid him farewell during a small celebration of his enormous life at Gallier Hall.

By the time the next Mardi Gras rolled around, the virus was still raging, and the city decided to shut down all parades for the 2021 season. But even a deadly virus could not kill the enduring spirit of Mardi Gras. The "Krewe of House Floats," a phenomenon that spread to every corner of the city, saved the season. People decorated their homes to replace the missing parade floats, paying homage to those we had lost and to all things wonderful about New Orleans. That edgy creativity and resilience that New Orleanians are known for were on full display.

"We Won't Bow Down" has become a de facto motto for the city, long before the NBA Pelicans adopted it as a slogan for their marketing campaign.

For more than a century, nearly every Sunday thousands of descendants of enslaved Africans take over the streets for four hours, dancing and weaving their way through neighborhoods in second lines, complete with brass bands. These street parades, now organized by social aid and pleasure clubs, carry on a tradition deeply rooted in defiance.

During the historic Women's March of 2017, thousands of women and their partners marched to fight for women's rights and issues with unique New Orleans flair. A year later, strippers and their supporters stormed Bourbon Street in an Unemployment March after ATF agents shut down clubs, an act that many women saw as an expression of a conservative agenda. And thousands of fans of all ages and backgrounds staged the Boycott Bowl parade in 2019 when a referee's bad call cost our beloved Saints a trip to the Super Bowl.

But none have been more emblematic of a fired-up citizenry than the protests and counter-protests surrounding the controversial removal of four Confederate monuments, as neo-Nazis and white supremacists from around the country swarmed the city and clashed with Black Lives Matter and Take 'Em Down NOLA protesters.

There had been death threats to our mayor, Mitch Landrieu, who in 2015 had called for removing the monuments. A protester brandished an assault rifle at the foot of the Jefferson Davis statue. Someone had fire-bombed a contractor's car. But on May 19, 2017, men wearing black masks to protect their identities removed the statue of Confederate general Robert E. Lee from the tallest pedestal in the city, where it had stood for 133 years.

It was a day of jubilation for New Orleanians. People of all ages and races danced side by side in the street during the day-long celebration that had the atmosphere of a block party, ending a three-year contentious battle between those seeking to preserve what they saw as their southern heritage and those demanding to tear it down.

After a two-year hiatus caused by the pandemic, I returned to Tremé to photograph the North Side Skull and Bone on Mardi Gras Day in 2022; they had moved to the Little People's Place after the Backstreet Cultural Museum was destroyed by Hurricane Ida.

I arrived at 5:30 a.m. but was already too late to get close to the skeletons. Thousands of people clambered onto the streets, celebrating the city's revival after such devastating loss. It was a magical day. New Orleans was reborn yet again.

As I write this, New Orleans is facing several existential threats. Gentrification and the proliferation of short-term rentals are increasing homelessness. A shrinking police department is leading to rising crime. And rising seas and insurance rates threaten our way of life. But we have danced with death before, or, should I say, in defiance of death.

New Orleanians are a tight-knit people. We march to the beat of our own drums and toot our own horns. We twirl our umbrellas when it is not raining and wave white handkerchiefs in the air, not as a surrender but in celebration and sometimes in rebellion.

Though racial and class divisions still linger, one thing is certain. No matter our stations in life, no matter our dark and cruel history, we know that disaster and death unite us all.

Hope springs eternal in New Orleans. *We won't bow down. Don't know how.*

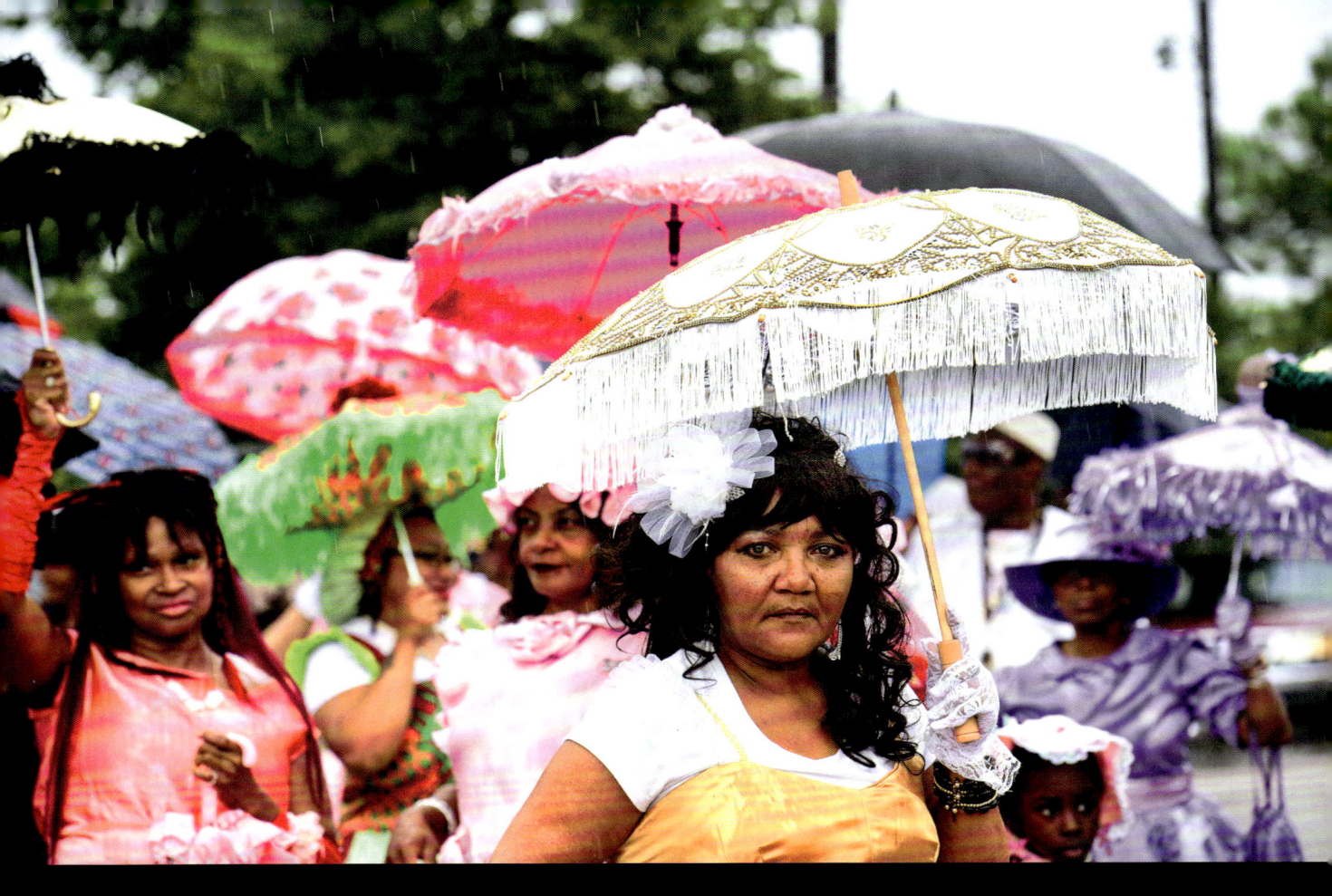

Carol "Baby Doll Kit" Harris leads the N'awlins D'awlins Baby Dolls during a procession
in the rain at the funeral for musician Art Neville of The Neville Brothers band, 2019.

PHOTOGRAPHER'S NOTE

I made every effort to include the names of the subjects, but many are missing because I failed to get them during the event or to protect their privacy.

In Part I, I arranged the photos much like one might see New Orleans for the first time—as colorful, fun, and decadent. But as one peels back the mask, images of problems begin to emerge until there is no way to avoid the issues of homelessness, crime, and insolence. I committed Part II to the "saints and sinners" and their overlapping nature. Part III is dedicated to our dearly departed, and Part IV is devoted to the defiance and spirit of New Orleanians.

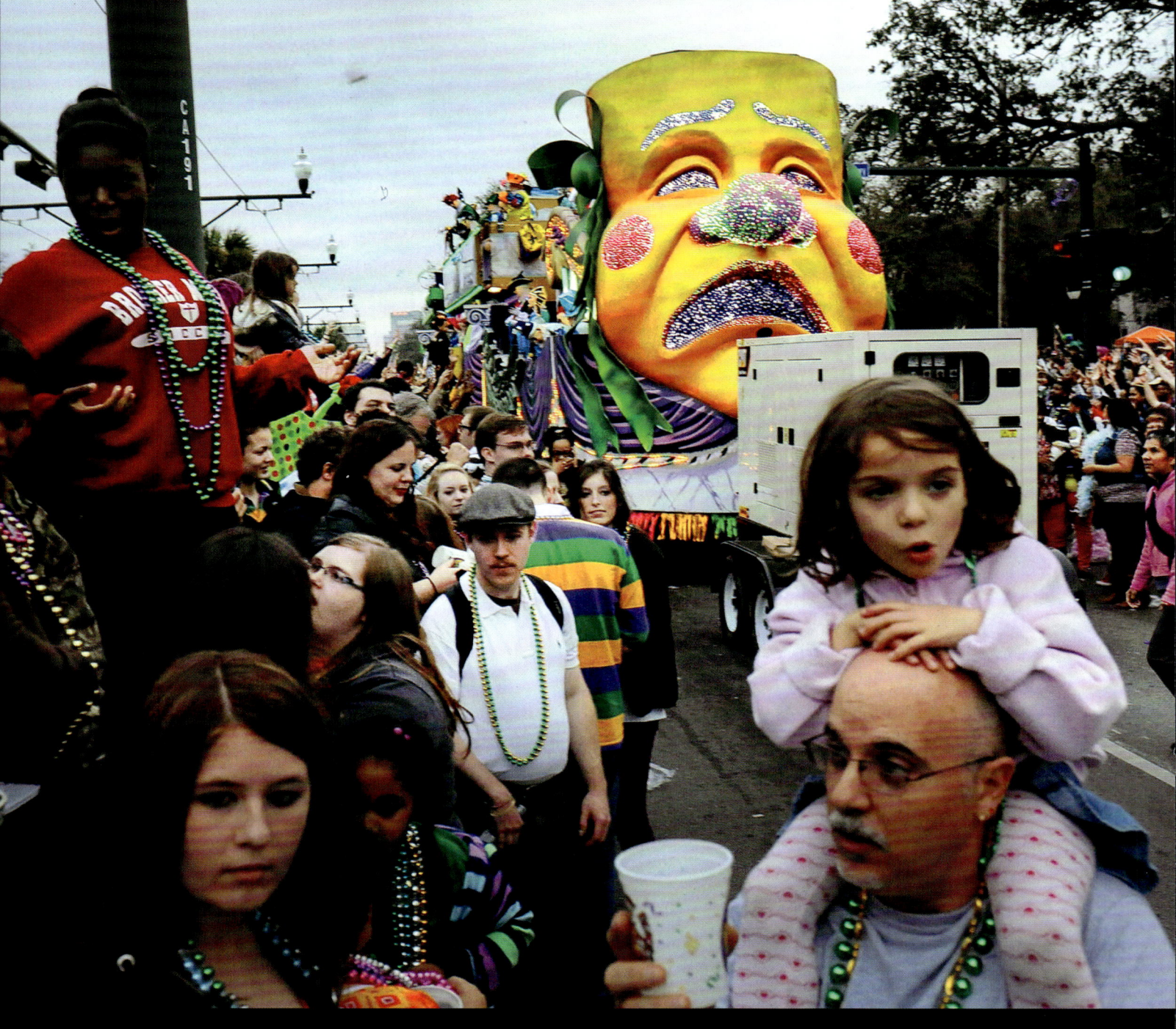

Joseph and Gianna Furnari in the wake of Endymion's signature title float during the krewe's parade, 2013.

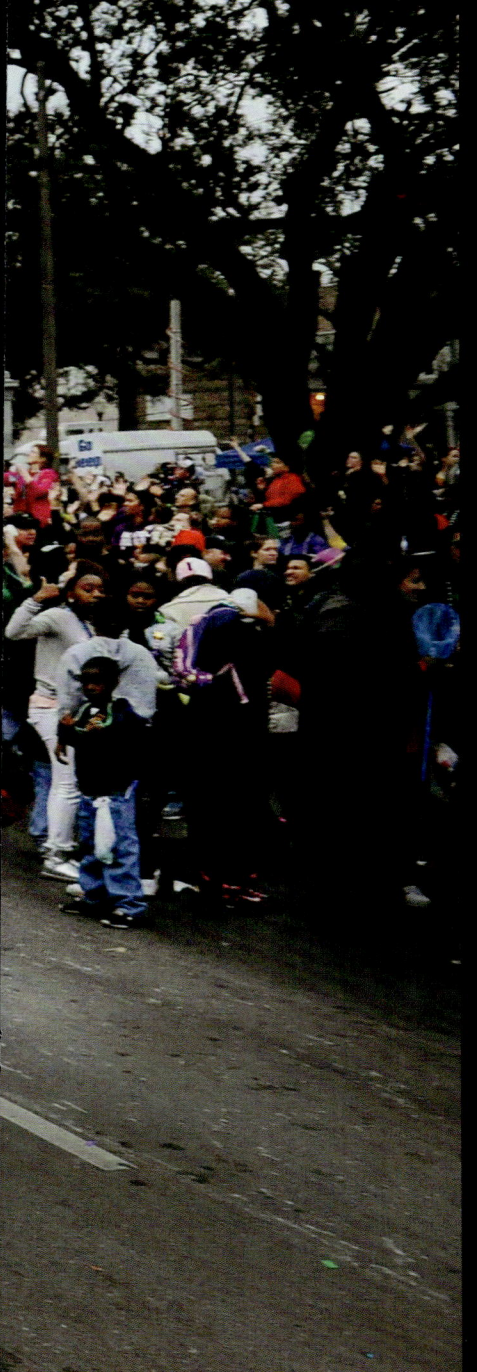

PART I

The Good Times Rolled

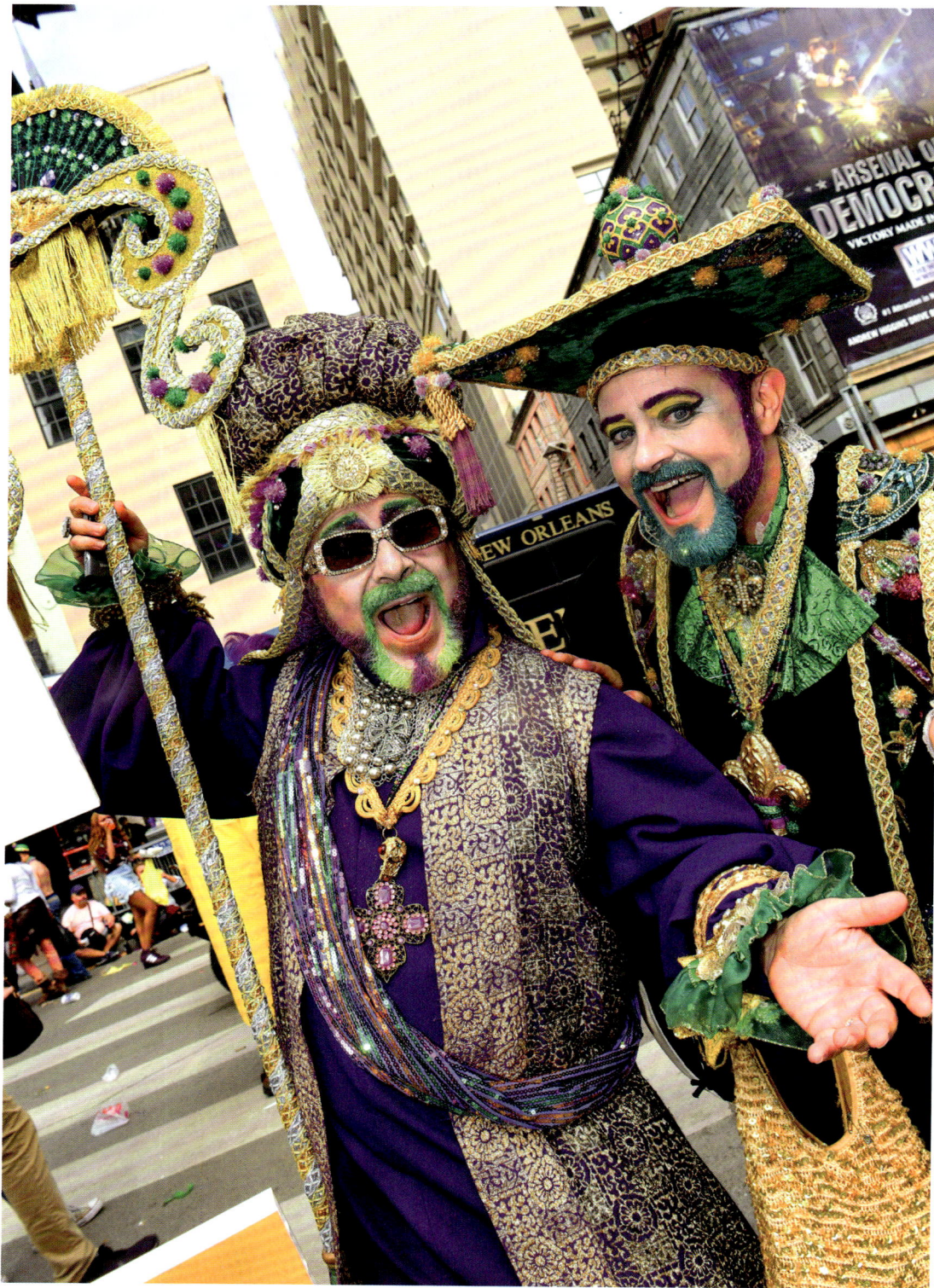

Award-winning actors and designers Edward Cox and Vatican Lokey, known as "Grand Marshal Marty Graw" and "Professor Carl Nivale," parade together on Mardi Gras, 2018. The married couple had celebrated their thirty-second anniversary on January 6, also known as Twelfth Night, which kicks off the Carnival season.

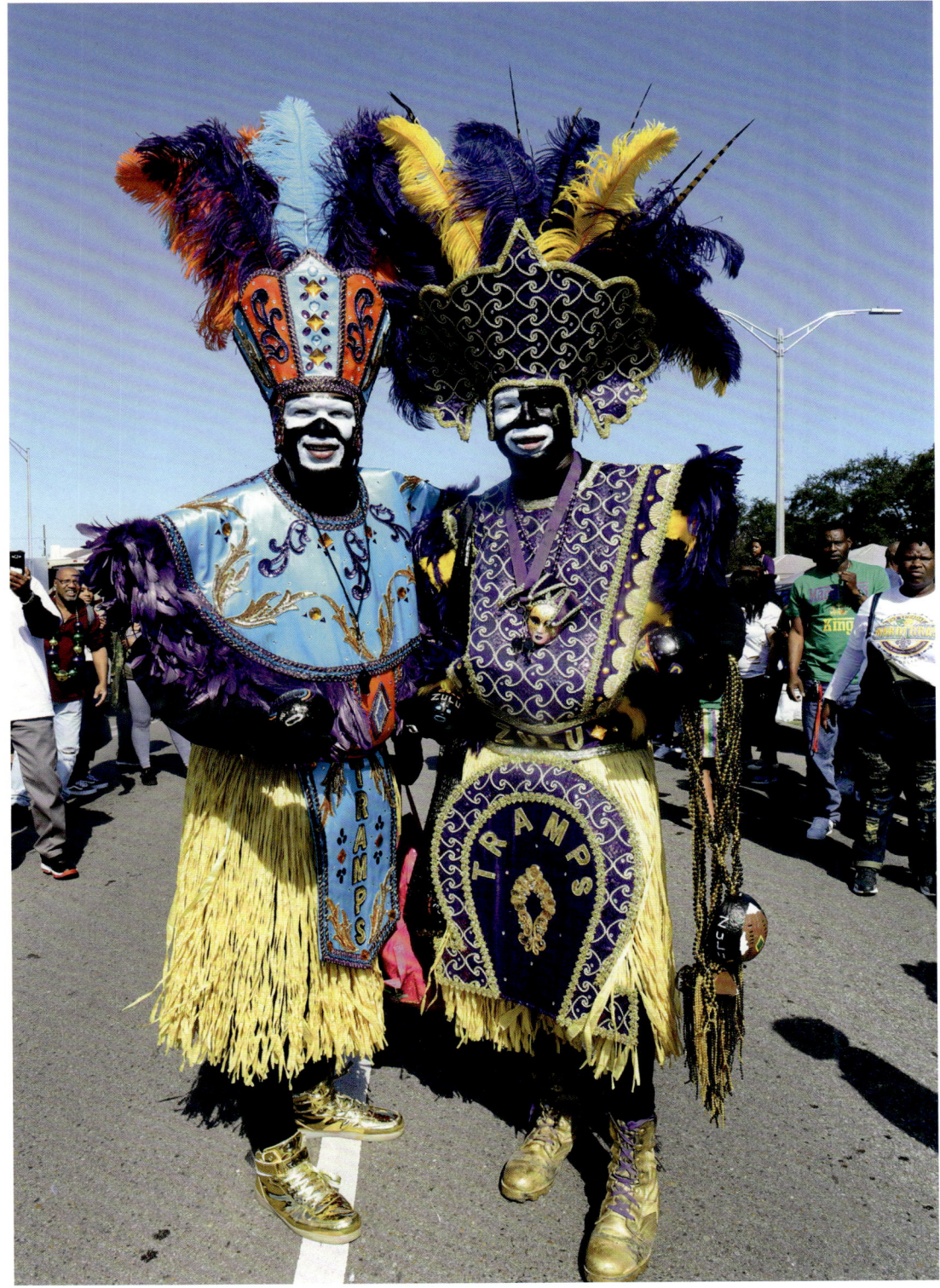

"Zulu Tramps" Brian Trotter and Shawn McCoy show off their coveted hand-painted coconuts during the Zulu parade on Mardi Gras, 2018. Zulu is New Orleans's largest predominantly African American Carnival organization; some say it was founded in response to racism that prohibited African Americans from parading. They are known for wearing blackface and grass skirts, a tradition that dates to the early 1900s. Some are disturbed by Zulu's tradition of blackface, but the organization defends it as their right to express their Black identity, with or without makeup.

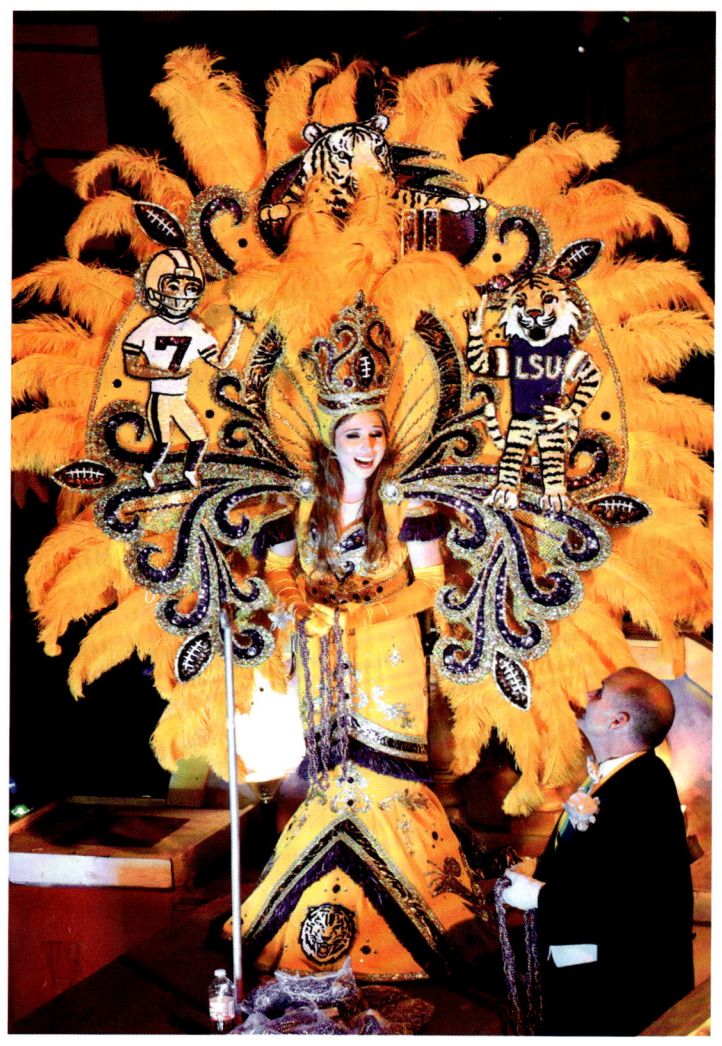

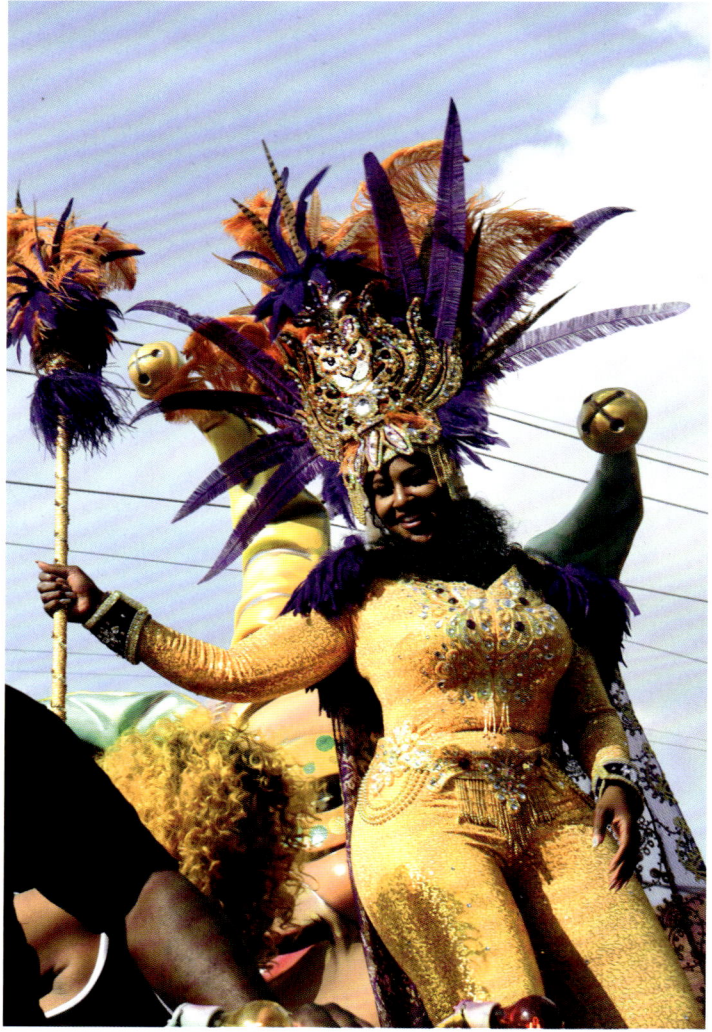

Representing the jazz classic "Tiger Rag," Amanda Gerrets rides as a maid in the royal court in the Endymion parade, 2018. Endymion, founded in 1967, is one of three superkrewes with more than three thousand members; it parades on the Saturday before Mardi Gras with a celebrity Grand Marshal. It is the only parade on the Mid-City route, ending with the "Endymion Extravaganza," a huge concert event usually held at the Superdome.

2017 Queen Beaunka McGee of the Treme Sidewalk Steppers Social Aid and Pleasure Club rides in the club's annual parade, 2018. The Treme Sidewalk Steppers club holds one of the largest annual second lines through the Sixth and Seventh Wards and has been second-lining for thirty years.

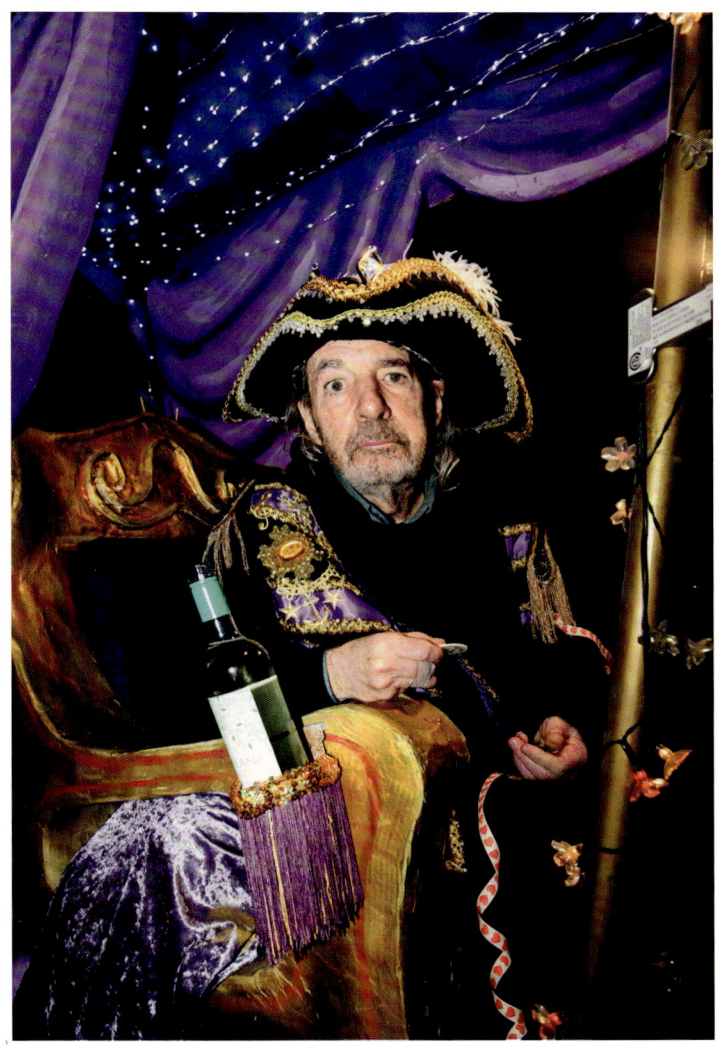

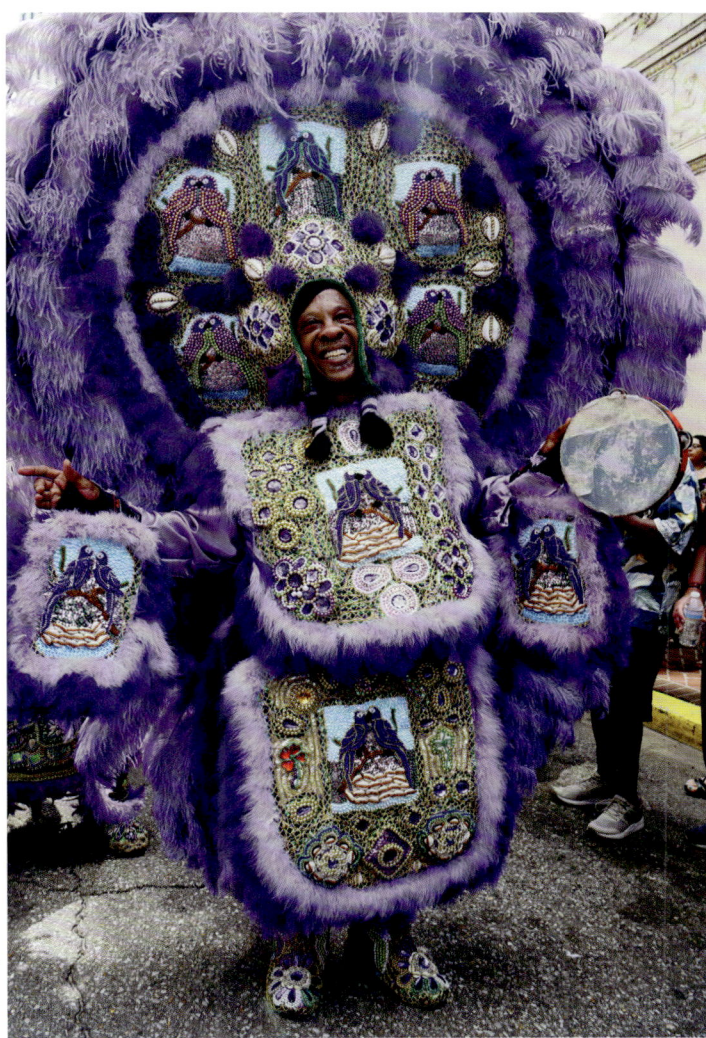

Actor Harry Shearer reigns as "King Plenipotentiary and Captain of New Orleans" in the satirical parade of krewe*delusion*, 2020. Shearer is an Emmy Award–winning and Grammy-nominated actor, comedian, writer, musician, radio host, director, and producer best known as a cast member of *Saturday Night Live* and an actor in several movies and TV shows, including *This Is Spinal Tap* and *The Simpsons*. He and his wife have made New Orleans their home and perform an irreverent annual benefit Christmas show called "Christmas Without Tears."

Albert Polite Jr., Spy Boy of the Spirit of Fi Yi Yi and the Mandingo Warriors, a Black Masking Indian tribe, leads the funeral procession for Malcolm John Rebennack Jr., better known as the musical artist Dr. John, 2019.

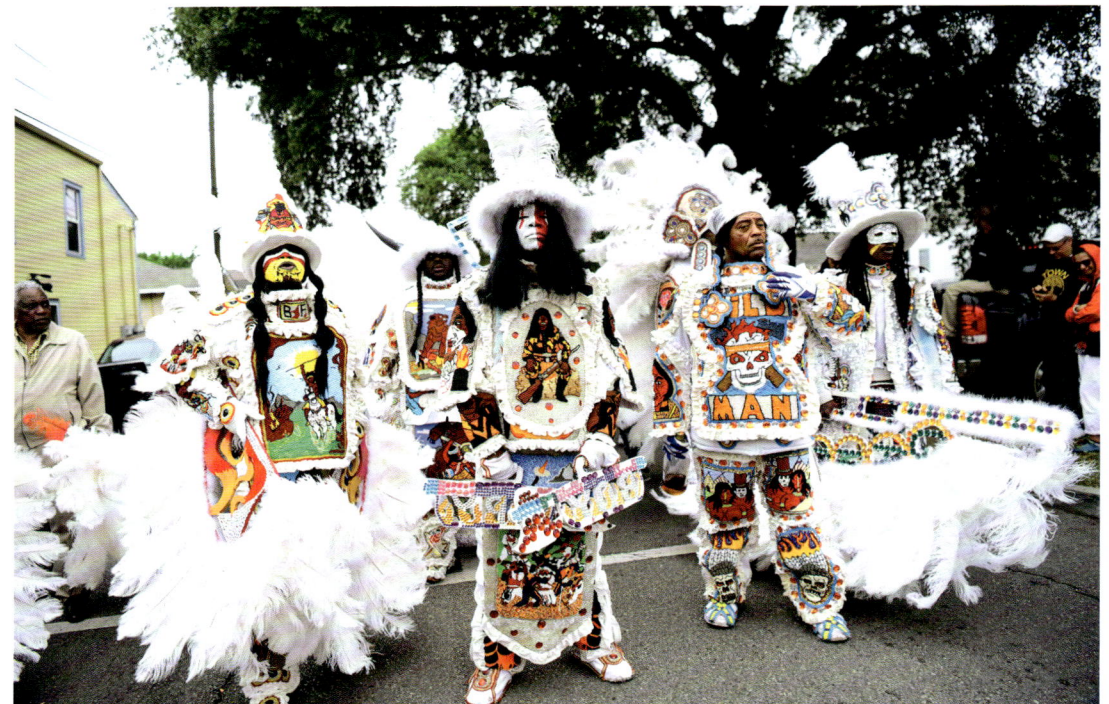

Black Masking Indians inaugurate their tribe Black Flame Hunters, led by Big Chief Jeremy "Black" Lacen, on Super Sunday, 2018.

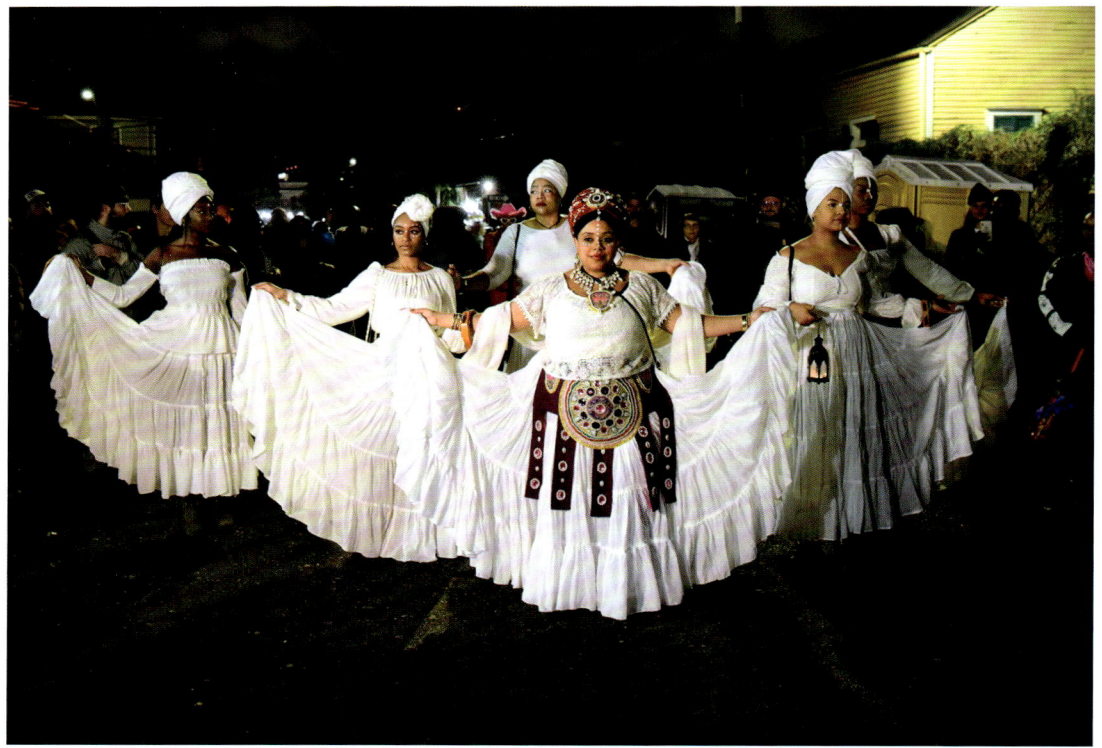

The Mystic Seven Sisters join predawn rituals in Tremé on Mardi Gras morning, 2020. The group of women, led by Voodoo Queen Kalindah Laveaux, was formed with the purpose of bringing the healing traditions of wise women to street culture.

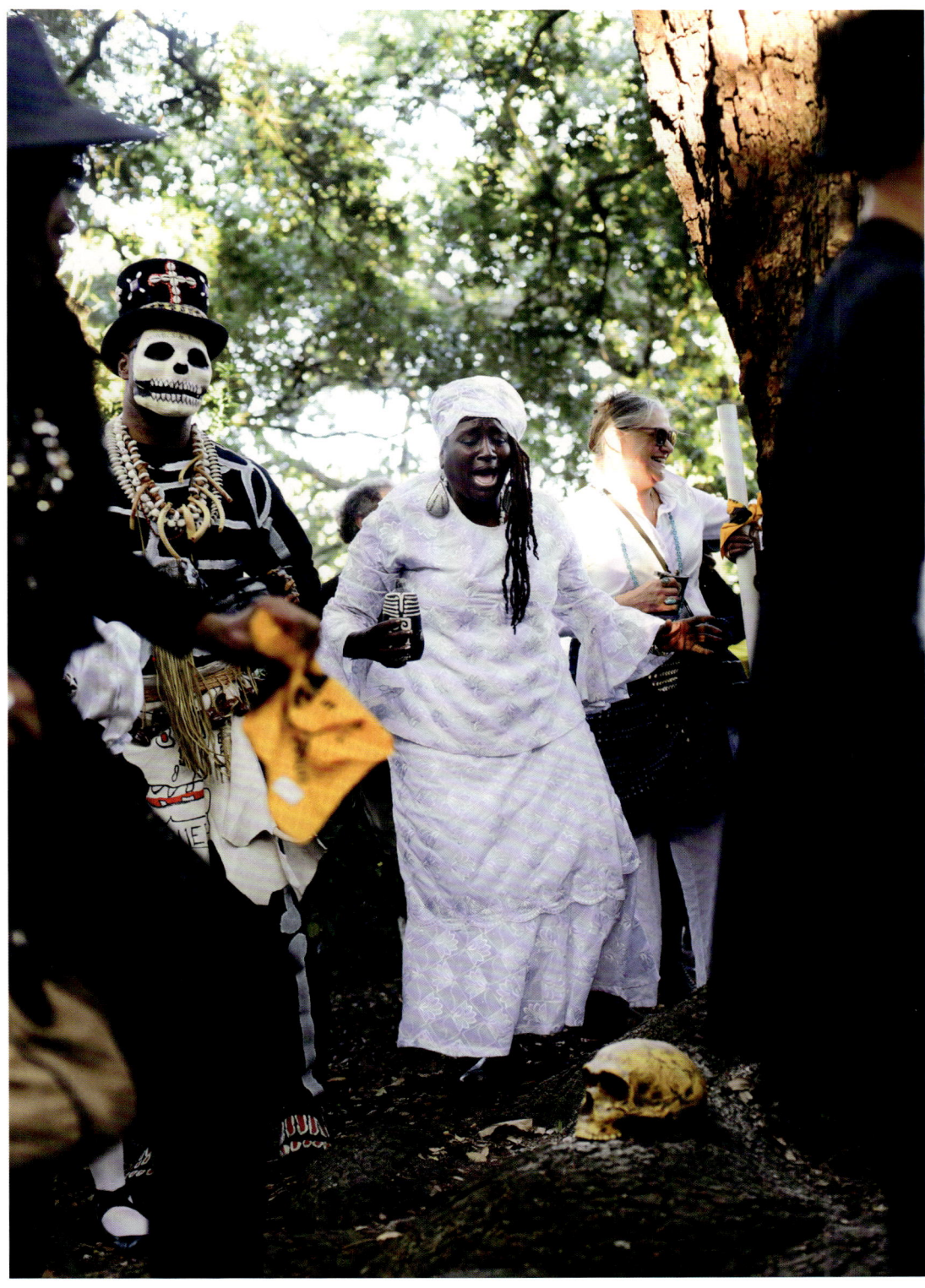

Ausettua Amor Amenkum—activist, educator, and Big Queen of the Washitaw Nation Black Masking Indians—sends prayers for Royce Osborn's safe passage to the ancestral plane, 2017. Osborn, who passed away at the age of fifty-eight, was a writer and producer of film documentaries about New Orleans culture; he is best remembered for *All on a Mardi Gras Day*, the 2003 PBS film about Black Carnival.

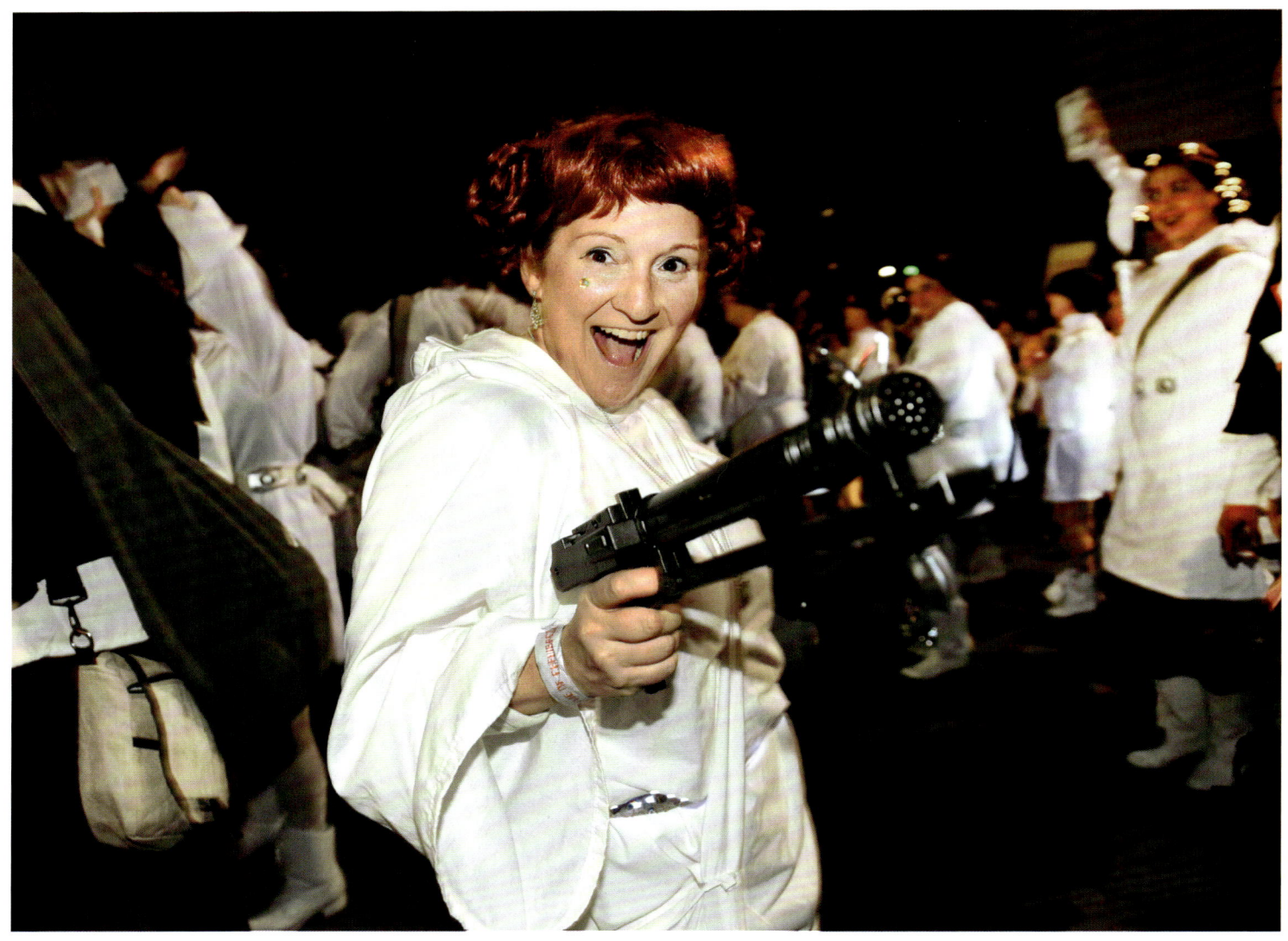

Elizabeth Pearce dances with the Leijorettes, a marching group honoring Princess Leia, in Chewbacchus, a science fiction parade, formally known as the Intergalactic Krewe of Chewbacchus, 2018.

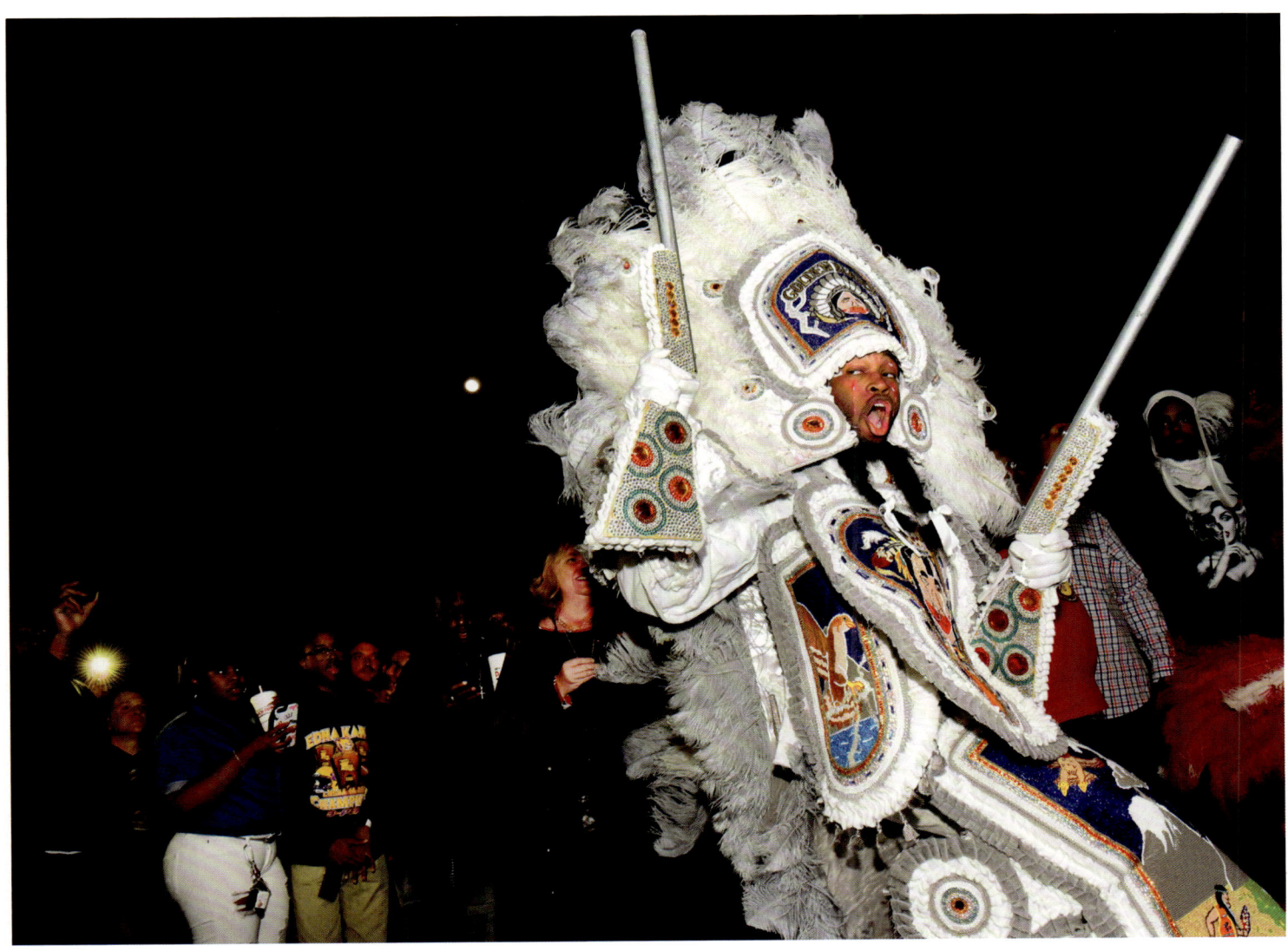

Alphonse Feliciana IV, Spy Boy of the Golden Blades Black Masking Indians, chants to signal to his tribe that he sees other Indians approaching on St. Joseph's Night in Central City, 2019.

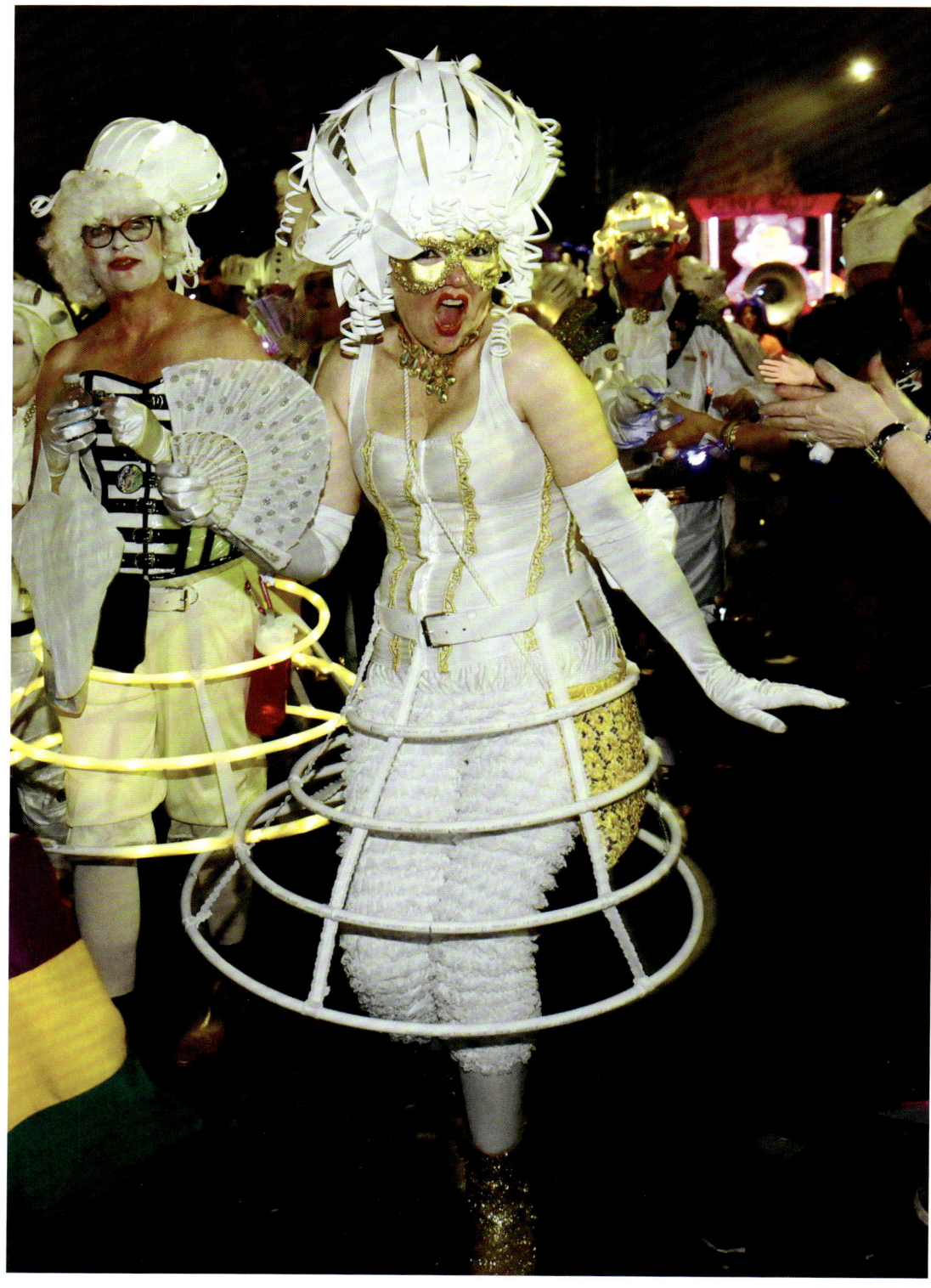

Costume designer Tracy Thomson masks as Ruling Crass in the Krewe du Vieux parade themed "Crass Menagerie," 2017. Krewe du Vieux, established in 1987, parades through the Faubourg Marigny and meanders through the French Quarter. One of the earliest parades on the Carnival calendar, it is noted for wild satirical and adult themes.

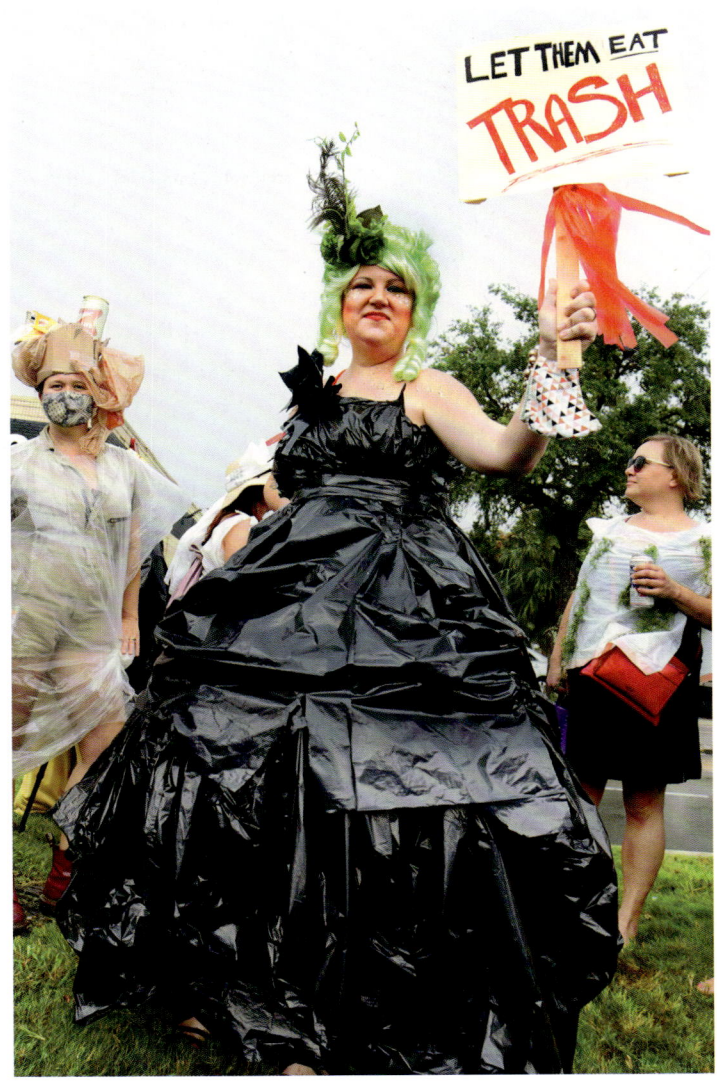

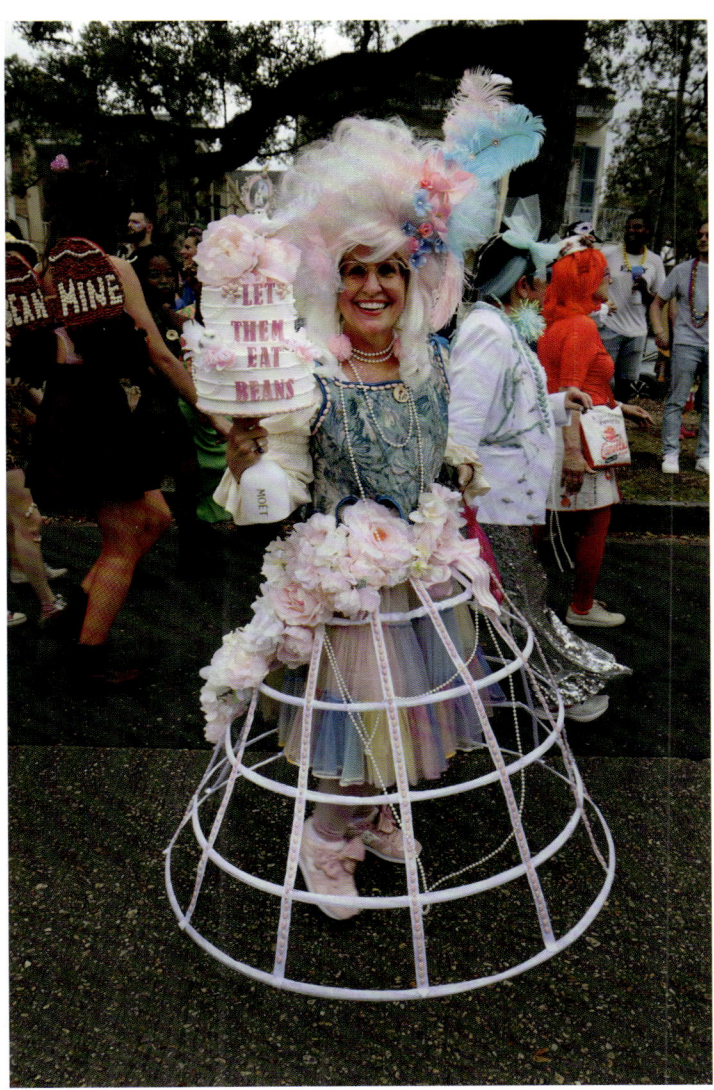

Heather Stephenson costumes as Marie Antoinette, a symbol of excess who is as often celebrated as she is satirized in New Orleans. The "Trash Parade" formed as a protest after uncollected garbage sat on the curbs for several weeks after Hurricane Ida, 2021.

Samra Smith costumes as Marie Antoinette with her sign "Let Them Eat Beans" in the Krewe of Red Beans parade on Lundi Gras, 2023.

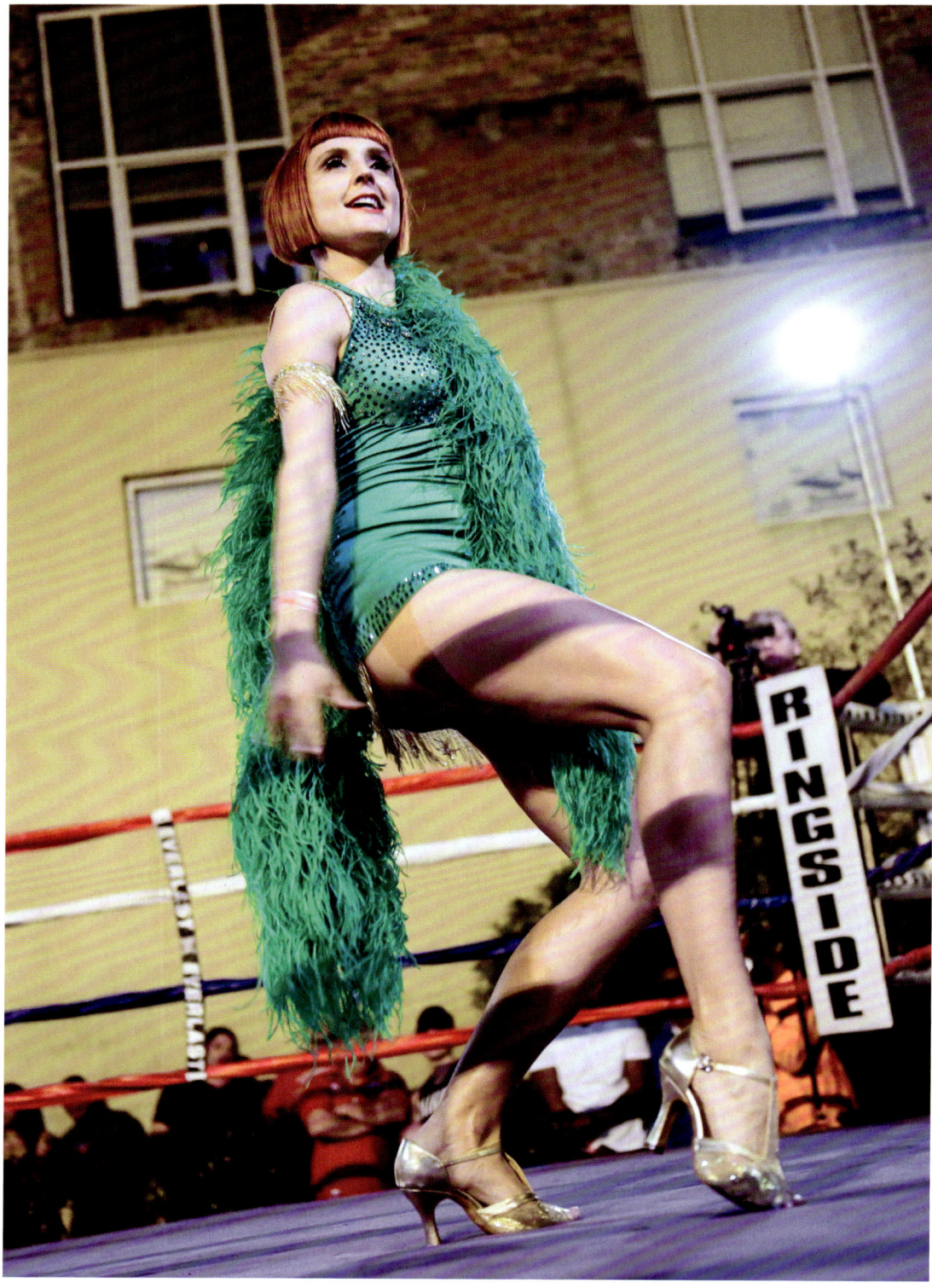

Burlesque artist and model Roxie Le Rouge performs at Friday Night Fights amateur boxing in Central City, 2017. The amateur boxing event, created by Central City gym owner Mike Tata, features novelty acts and audience participation.

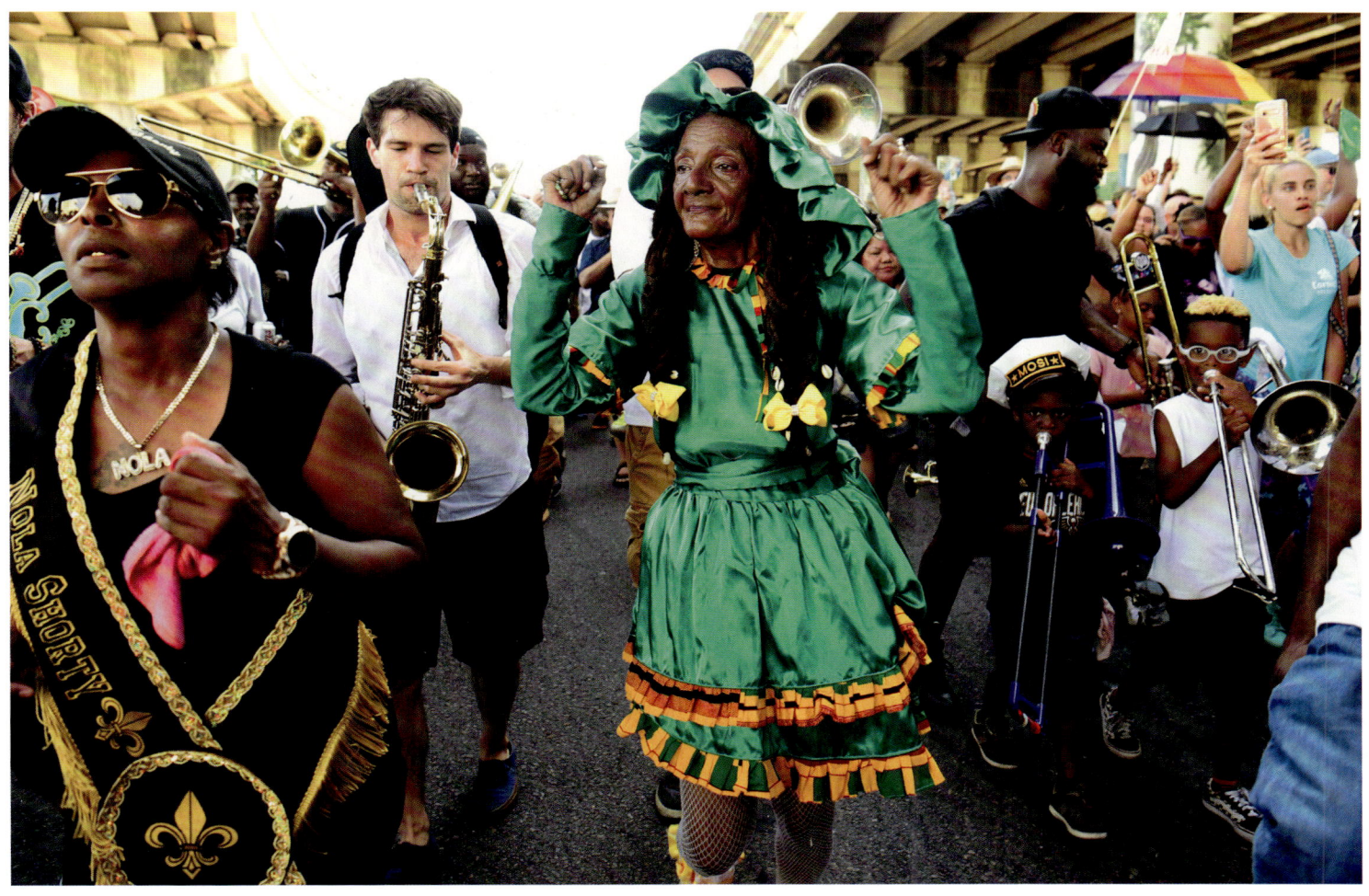

Baby Doll Merline Kimble walks in a memorial second line for musician Dr. John in Tremé, 2019. Kimble, founder of the contemporary iteration of the Gold Digger Baby Dolls, helped revive the Black Masking tradition that dates to around 1912. The Baby Dolls were one of the first women's organizations to mask and perform during Mardi Gras, tracing their origins to Storyville-era brothels and dance halls.

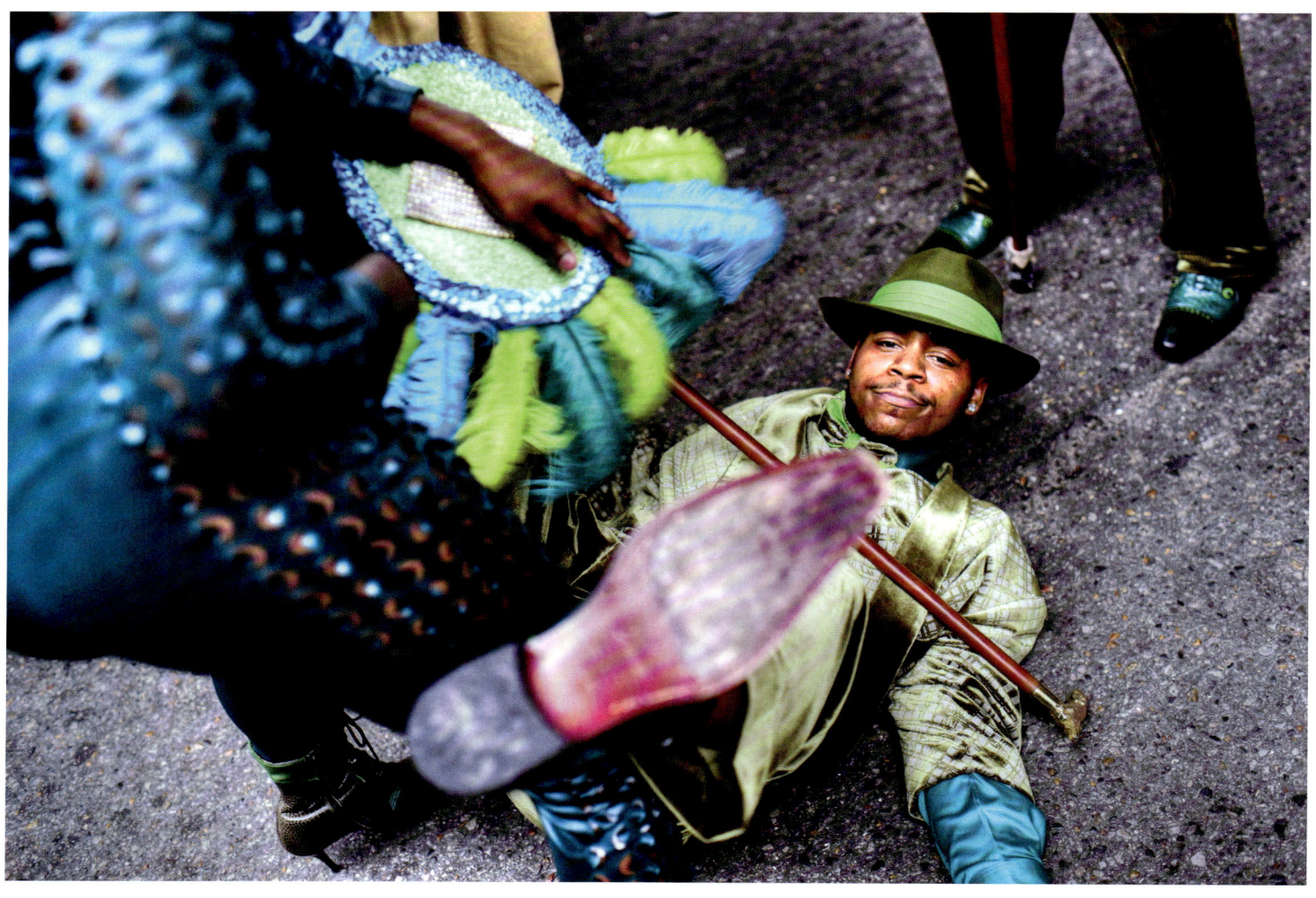

A club member dances on the pavement during the Undefeated Divas and Gents Social Aid and Pleasure Club's annual second line parade, 2017.

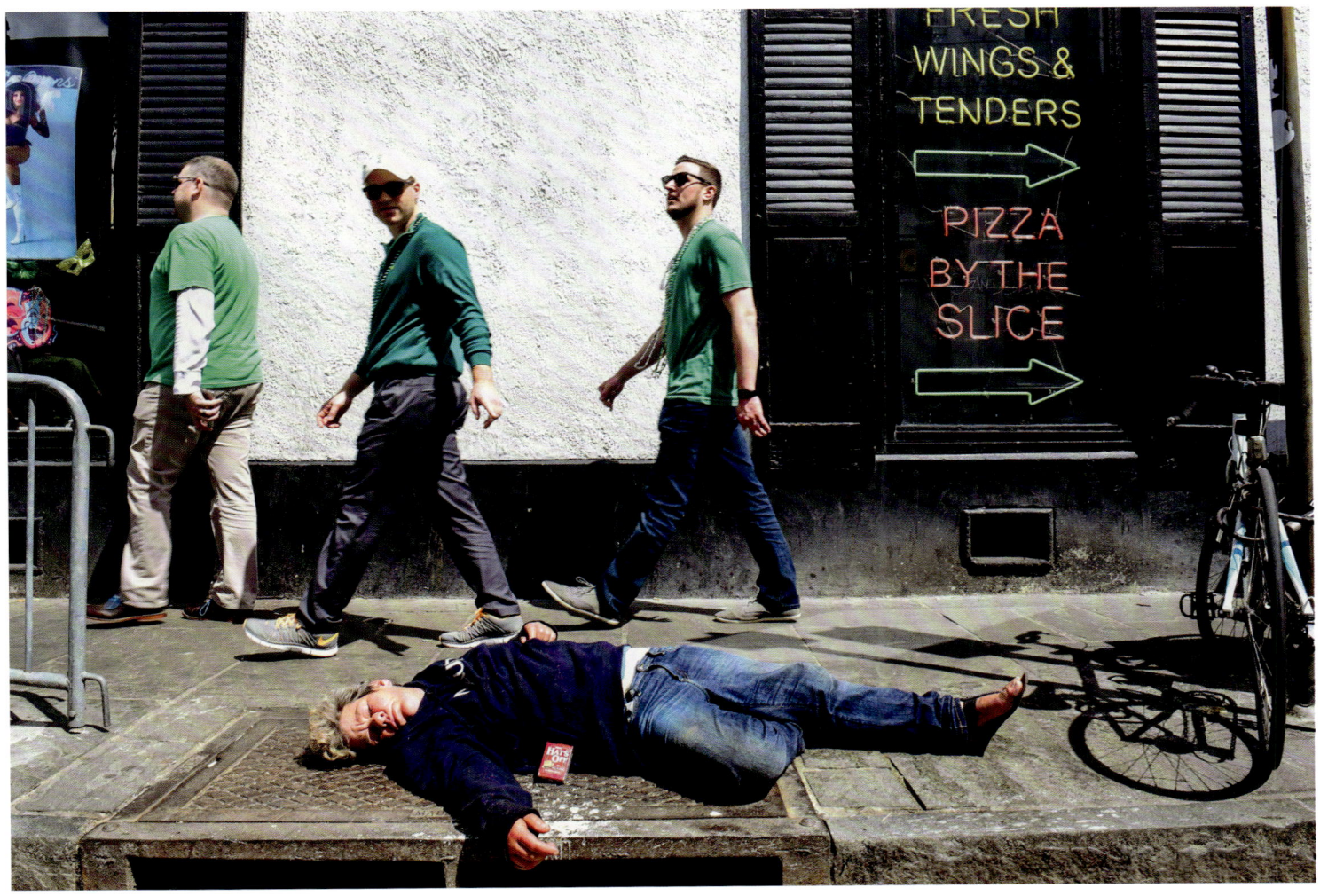

Tourists walk by someone passed out on the curb on St. Patrick's Day in the French Quarter, 2017.

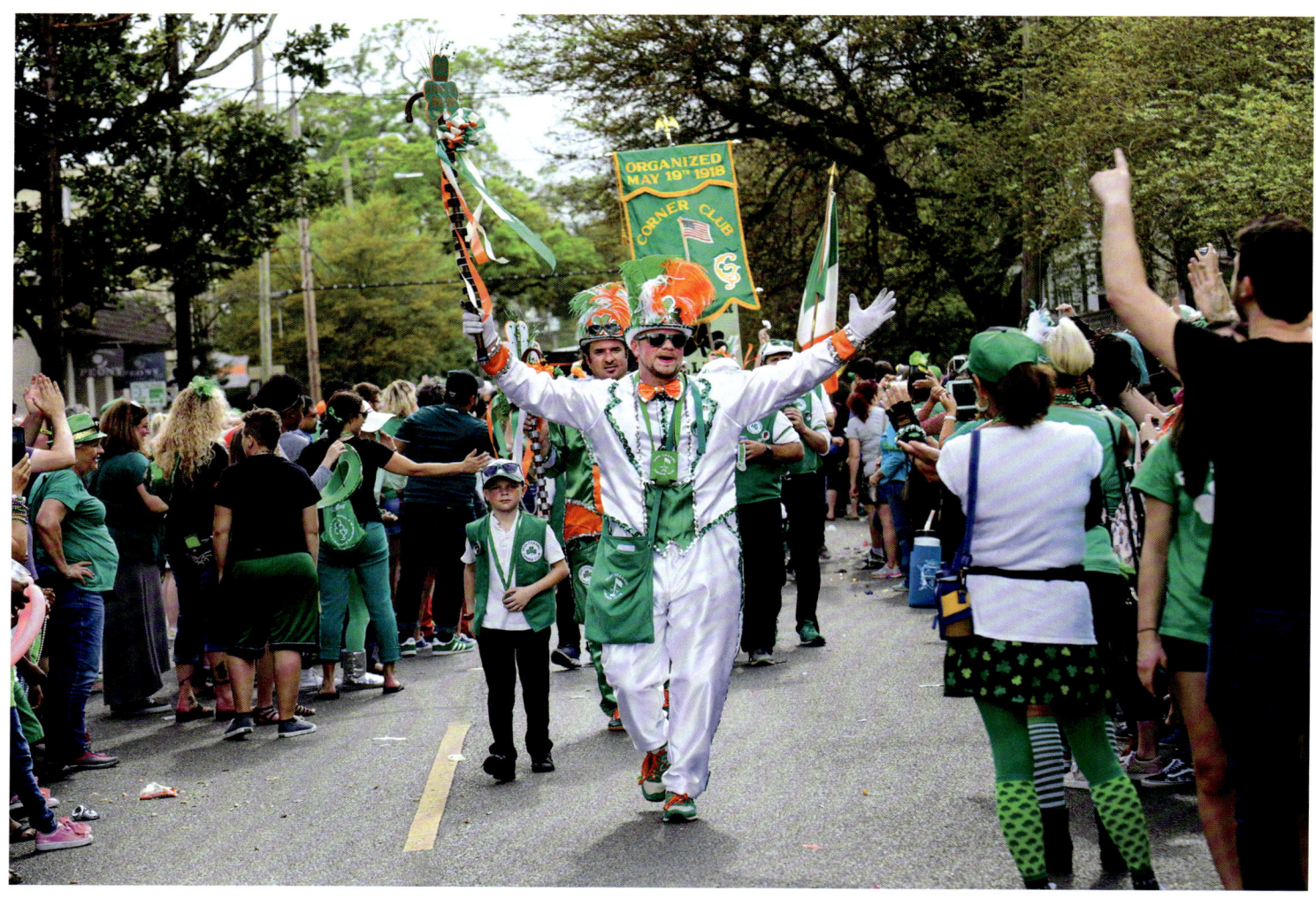

Seann Halligan, Grand Marshal of the Corner Club, marches in the annual Irish Channel St. Patrick's Day Parade, celebrating the club's one hundredth year, 2018. The Irish Channel Corner Club was organized in May 1918 by a group of seven men on the corner of Third and Rousseau Streets in the Irish Channel, an Uptown neighborhood originally settled largely by immigrants from Ireland in the early nineteenth century.

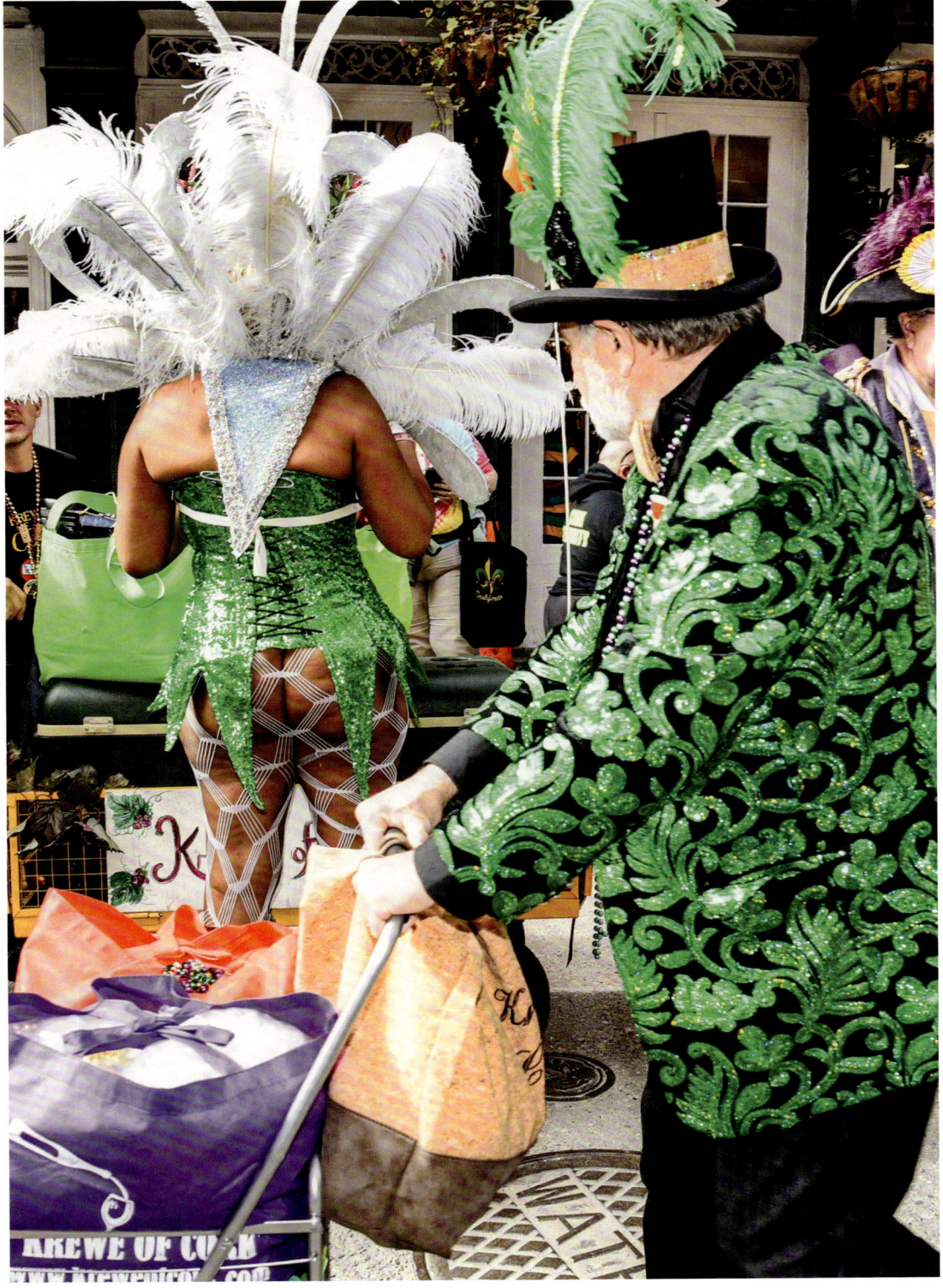

A member of the Krewe of Cork marching club takes a gander at a scantily costumed reveler while lining up to parade, 2022. The Krewe of Cork, a marching club with four hundred members that was founded in 2000 to celebrate wine, food, and fun, strolls through the French Quarter during Carnival.

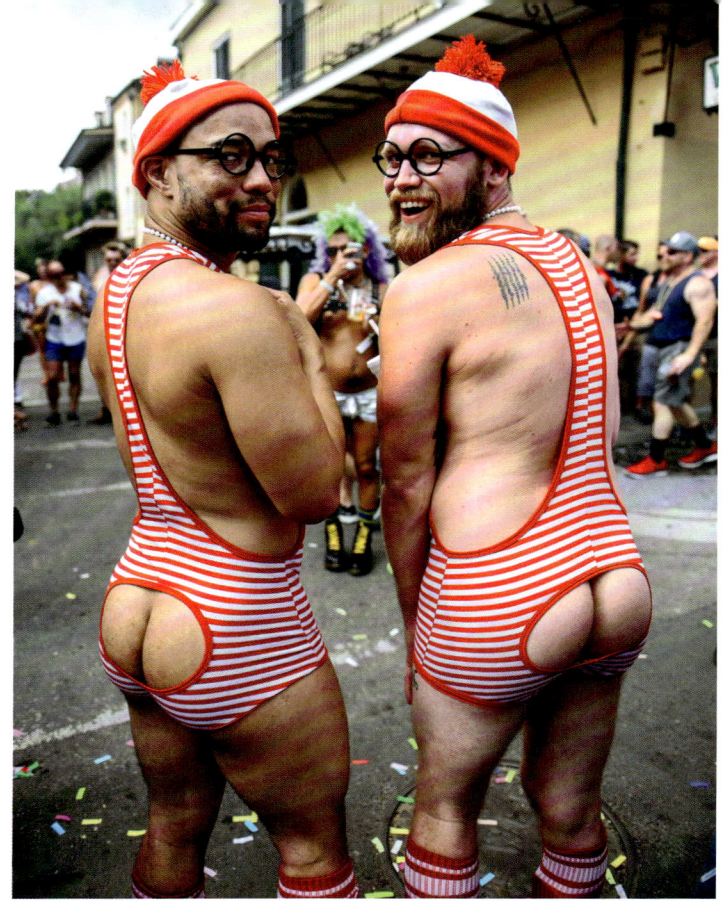

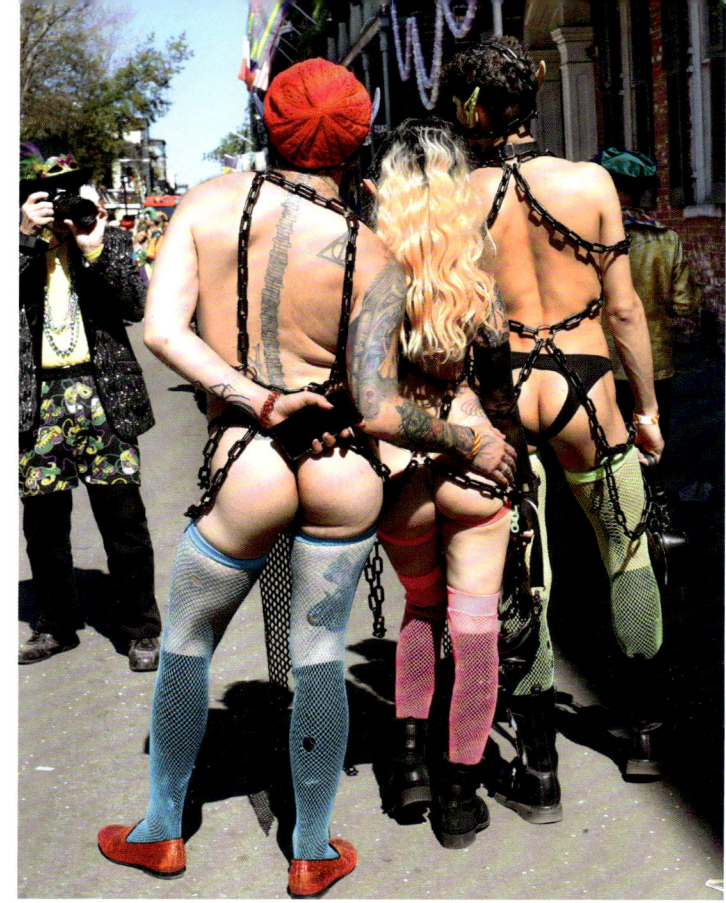

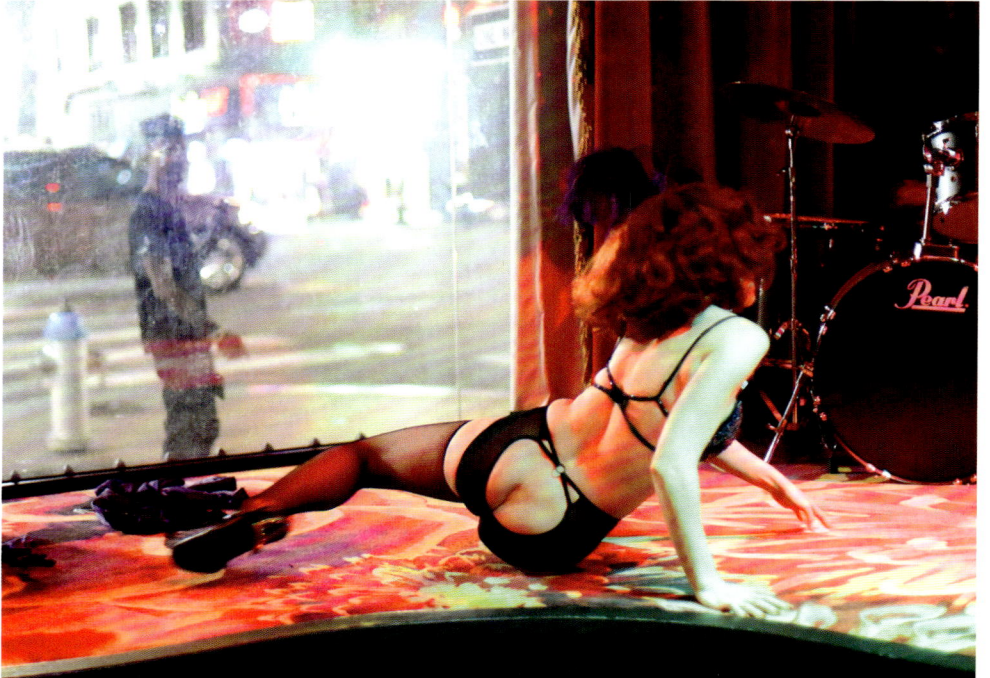

above left "Tongue-in-cheek" revelers partake in adult fun at the Southern Decadence parade, an annual marching parade that celebrates the LGBTQ+ community, 2015.

above right Mardi Gras Day revelers pose for a photo, 2022.

left Burlesque artist Cherry Bombshell performs at the Saint Hotel on Canal Street, 2018.

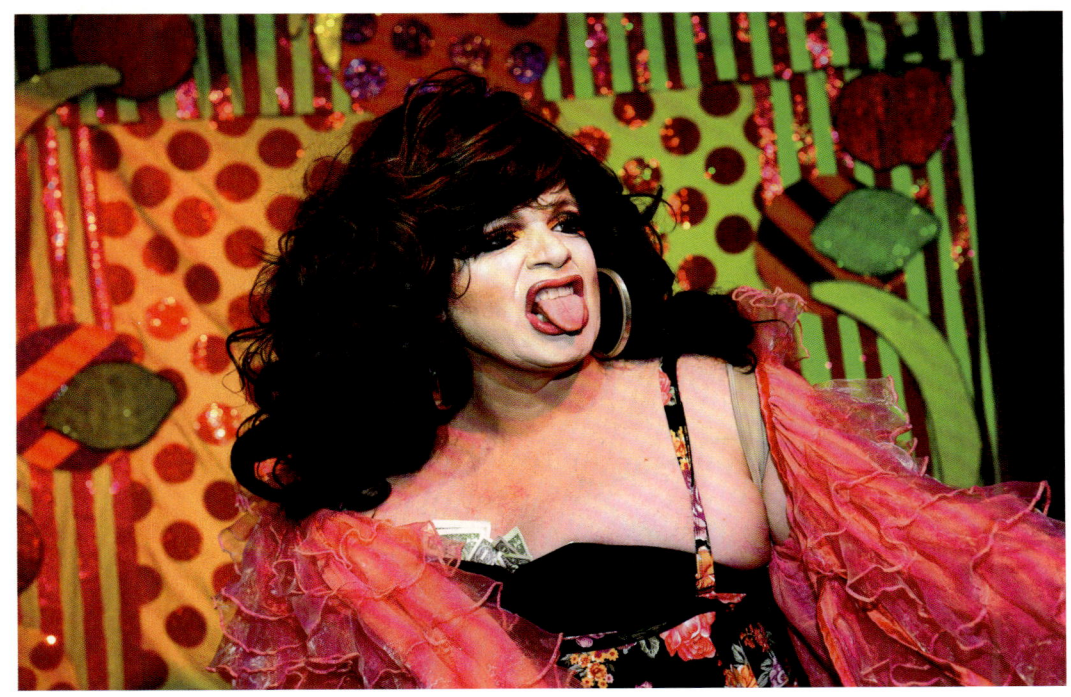

left Arthur Severio performs in drag as "Reba Douglas" at the Golden Lantern Bar, 2020.

below left Flag Boy Charles Dillon of the Mohawk Hunters Black Masking Indians shows off his beaded suit on Super Sunday, 2018.

below right Tarriona "Tank" Bell, the lead singer of Tank and the Bangas, performs at Jazz Fest, 2018.

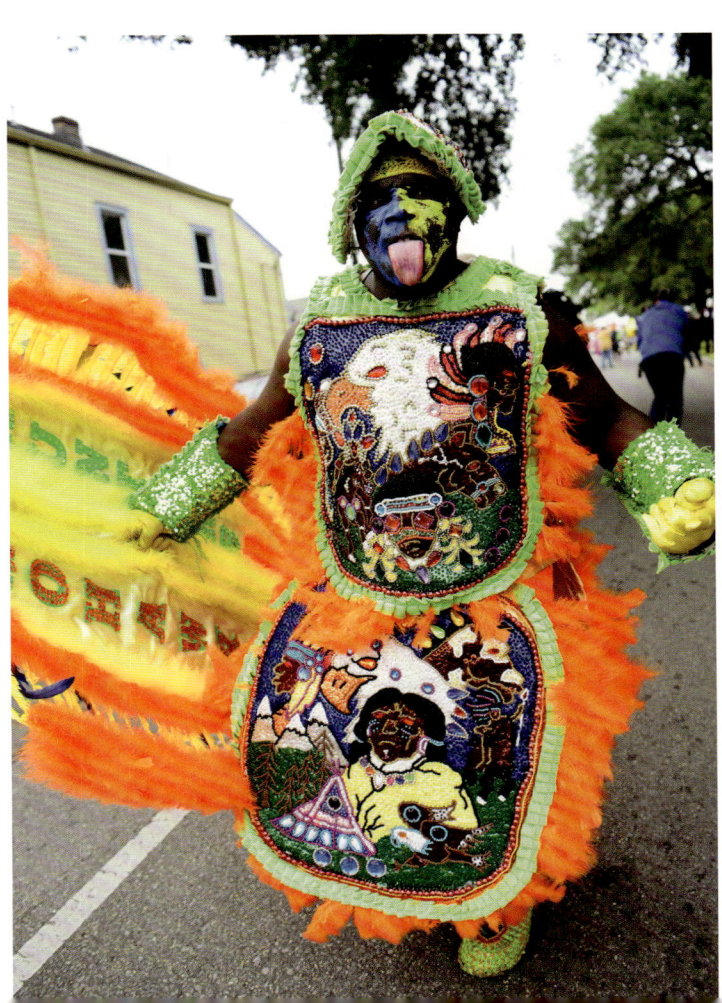

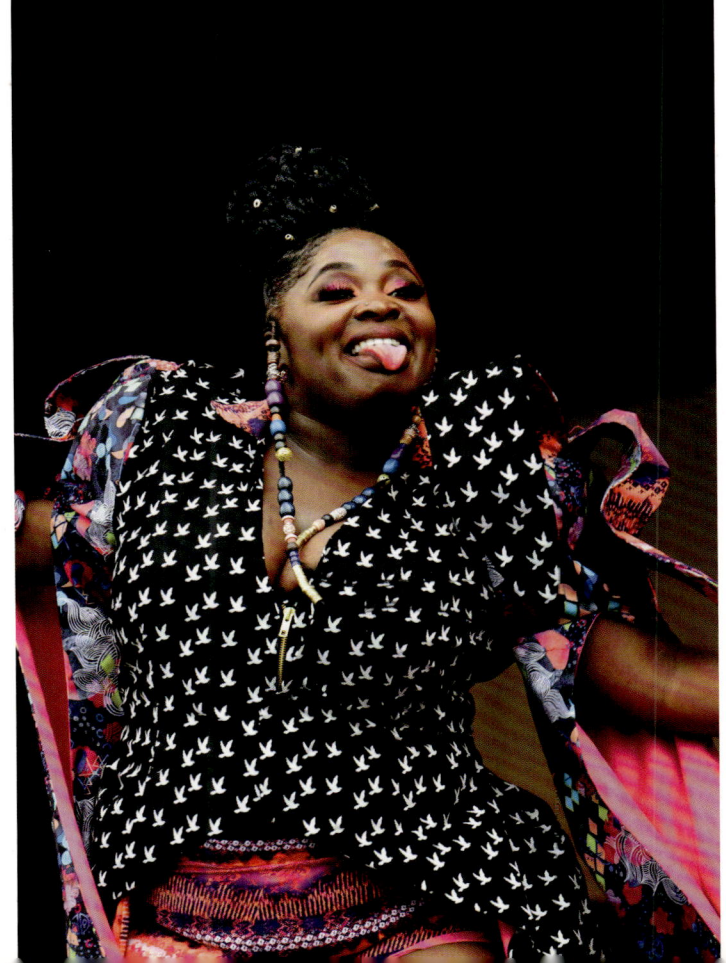

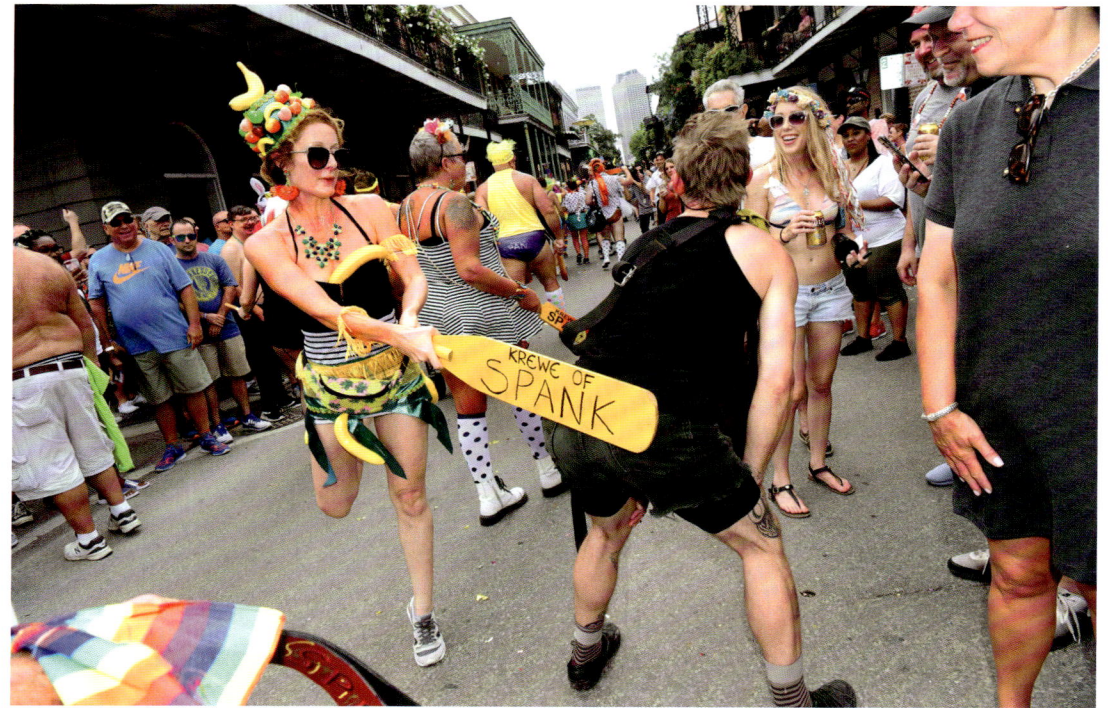

A member of Krewe of Spank, formed in 2012 as a subkrewe of Krewe du Vieux, paddles a willing participant in the French Quarter, 2019.

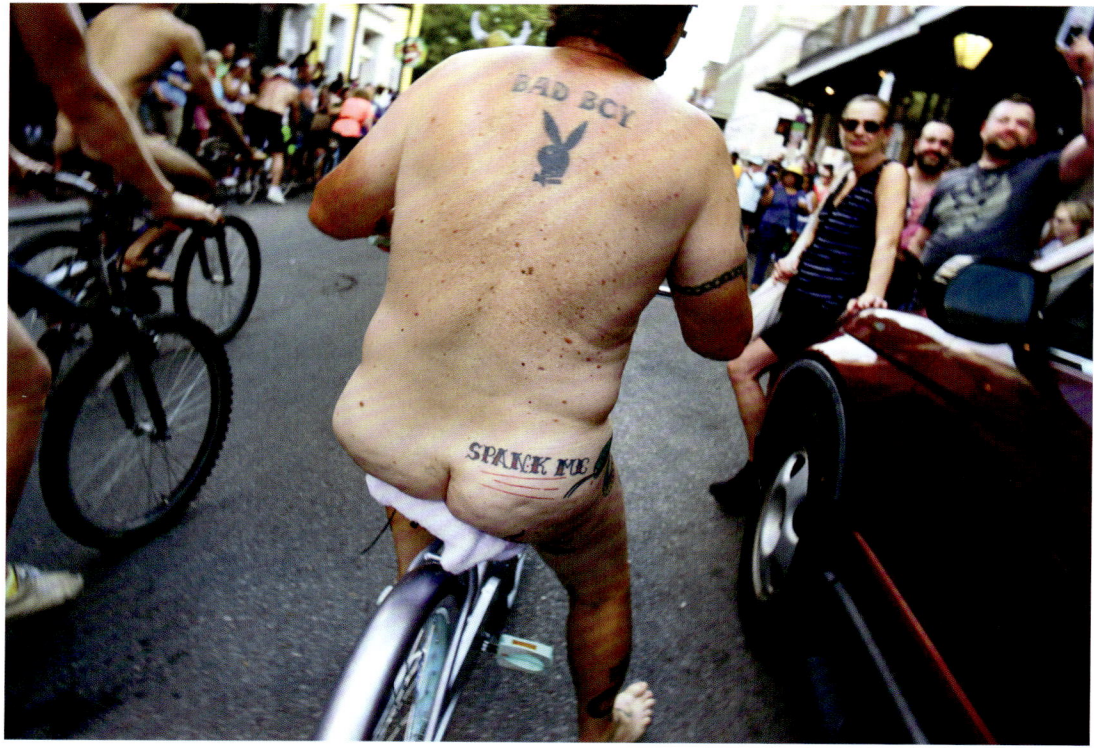

A participant in the World Naked Bike Ride, an annual event to promote cycling awareness and the benefits of biking, bares all in the French Quarter, 2019.

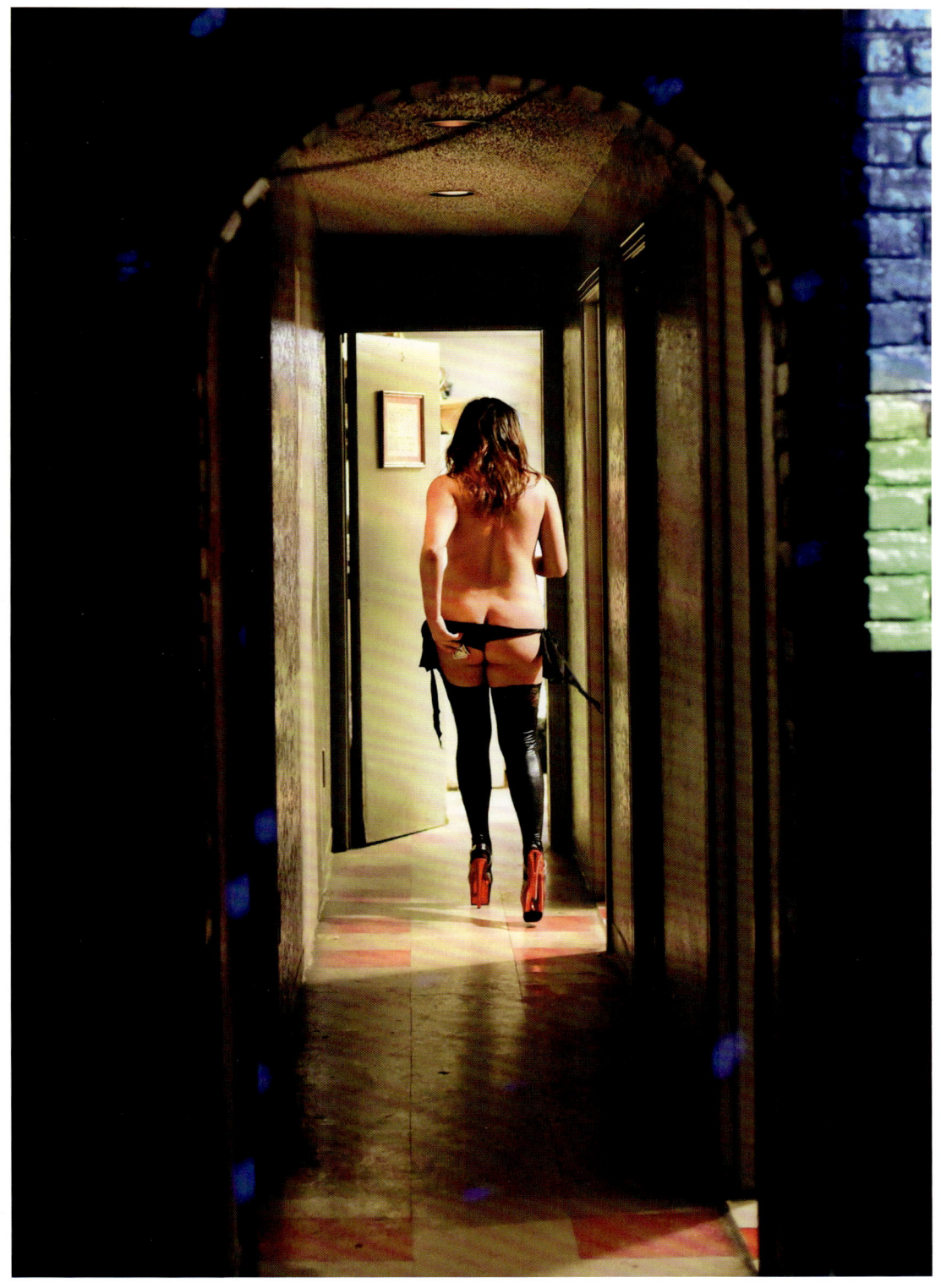

A stripper at Poor Boys Bar walks backstage while collecting her tips from her G-string, 2018.

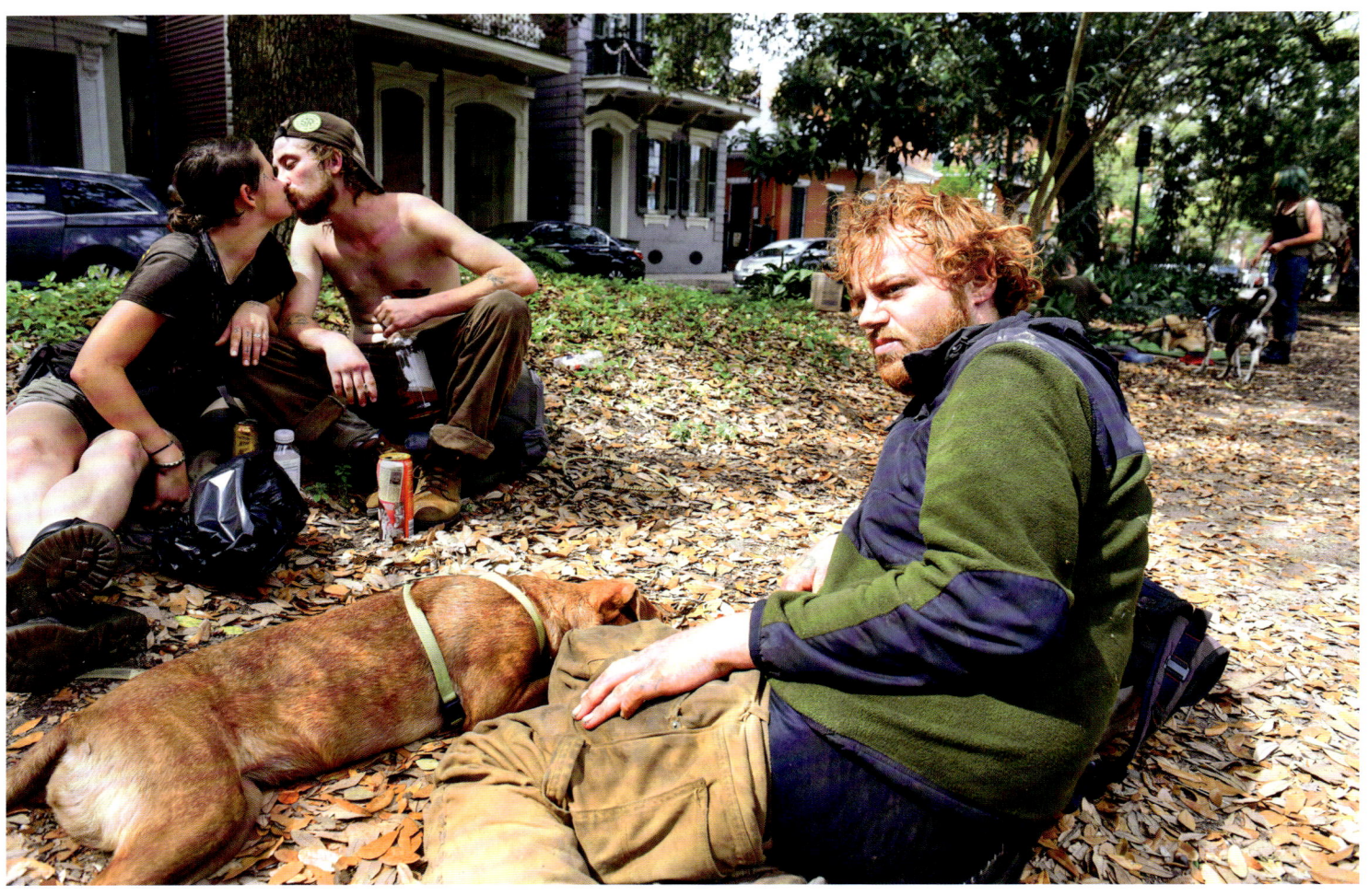

Self-proclaimed "Travelers," also known as "gutter punks" and "crusties," share a kiss and whiskey while camping out on the Esplanade Avenue neutral ground, 2017. The subculture is often associated with a lifestyle of voluntary homelessness, squatting, and panhandling.

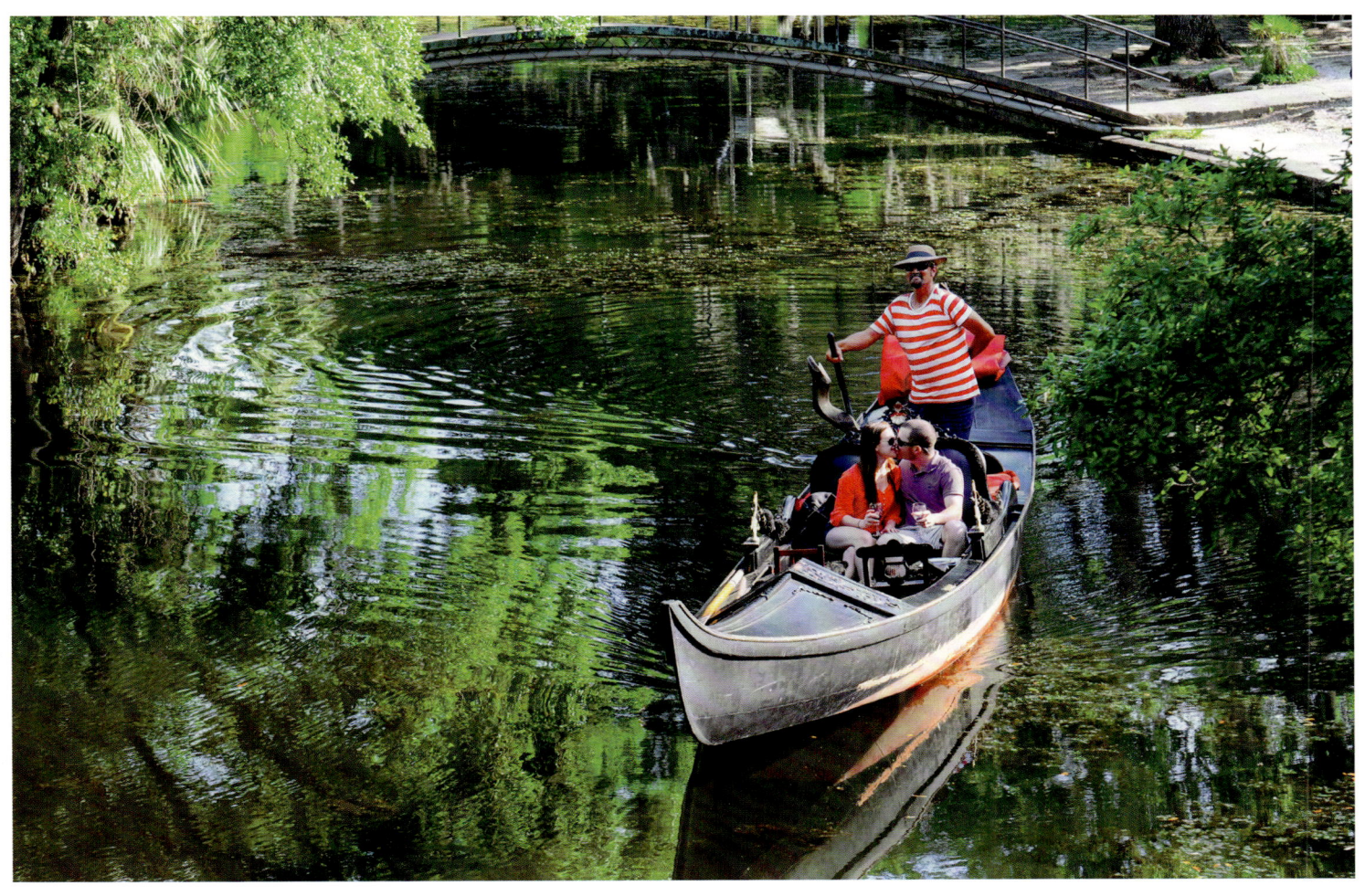

Gondolier Robert Dula steers a kissing couple around the lagoons of City Park, 2015.

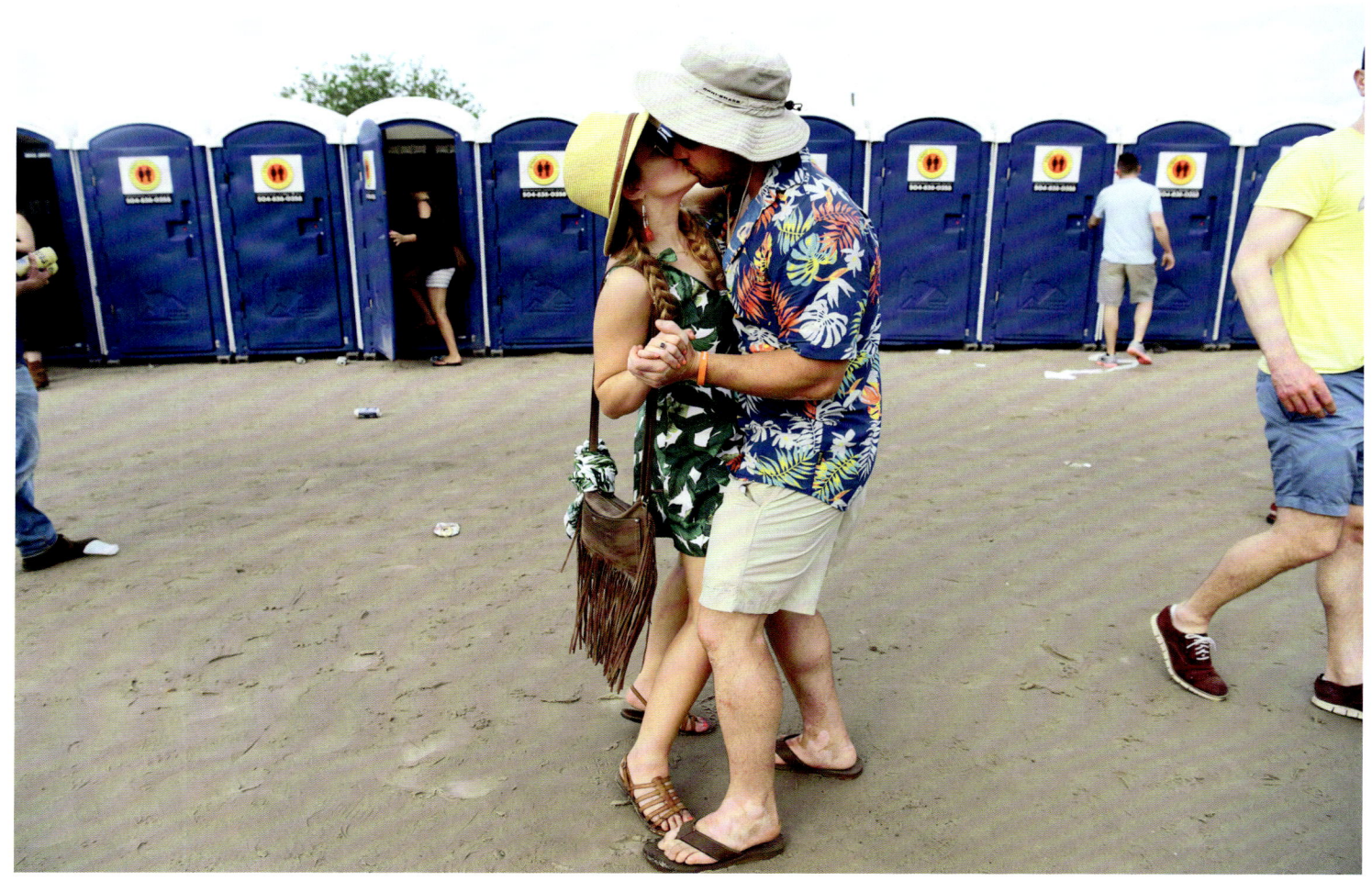

A couple kisses while dancing outside the portalets on the racetrack at Jazz Fest, 2018.

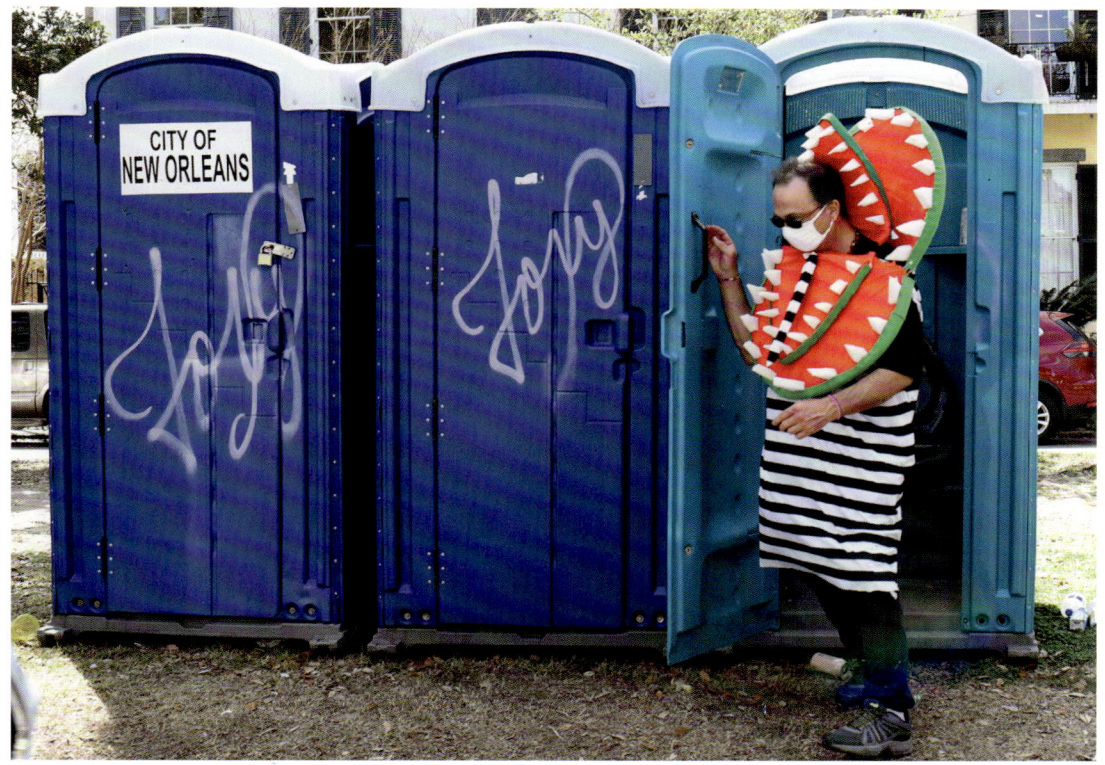

A Mardi Gras costumer uses a portalet on the neutral ground, 2022.

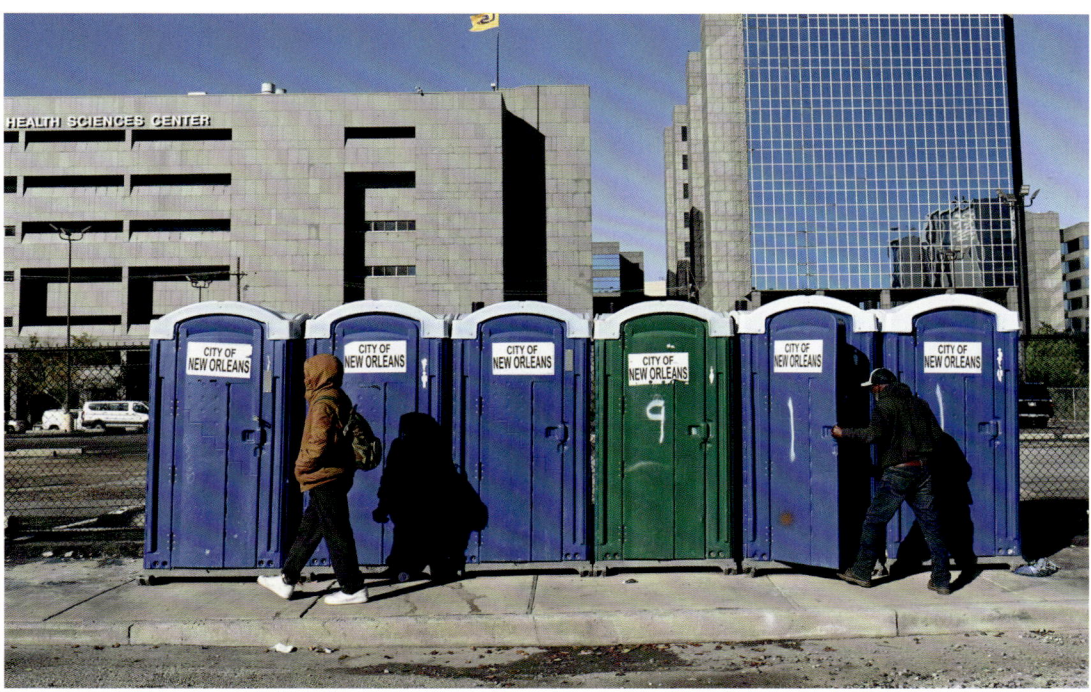

Portalets placed near homeless encampments downtown get steady use, 2022.

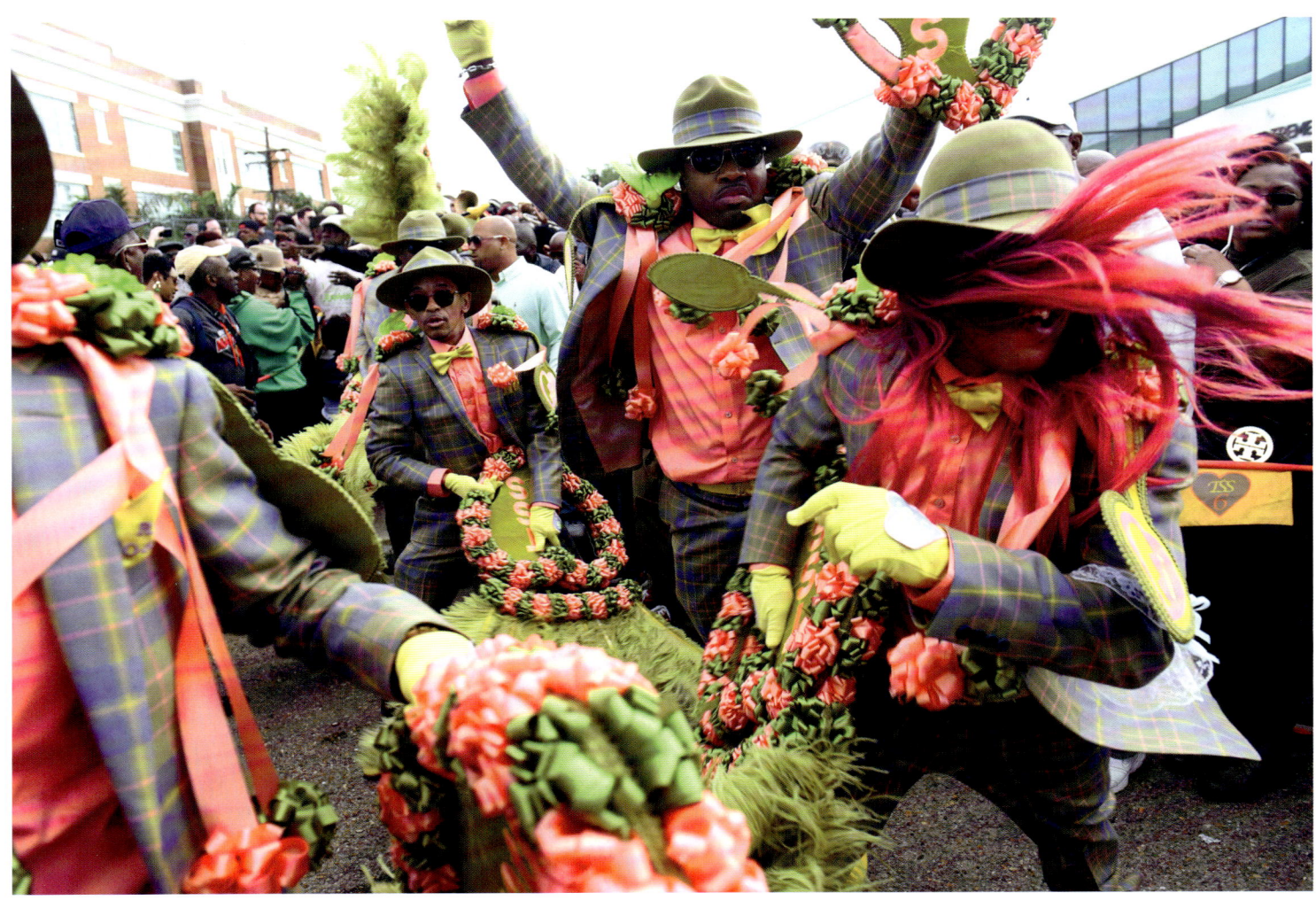

Club members dress in pink and green during the Treme Sidewalk Steppers Social Aid and Pleasure Club's annual second line parade in Tremé, 2016.

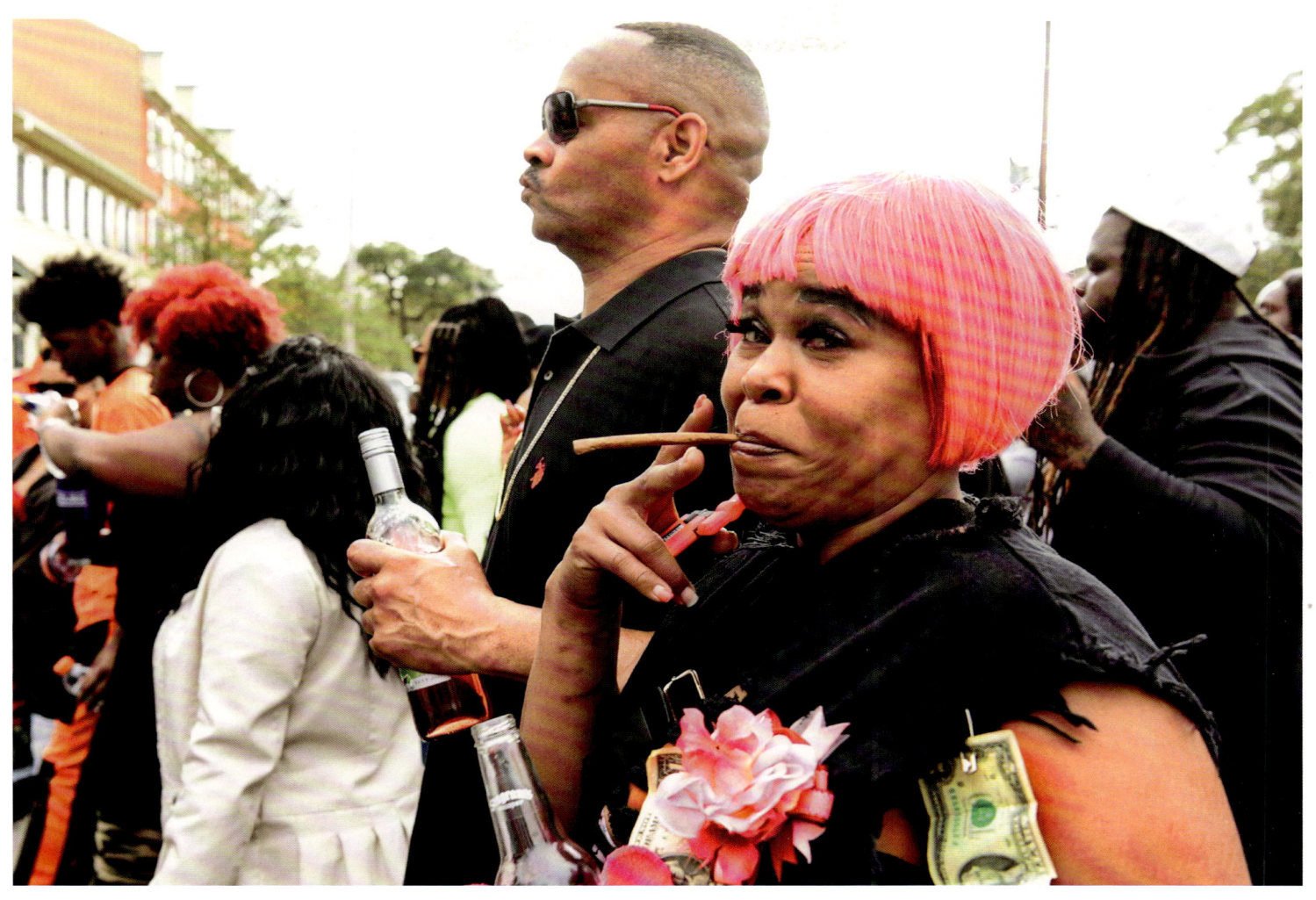

A birthday girl pinned with cash, a New Orleans tradition, celebrates during her jaunt in a second line, 2020.

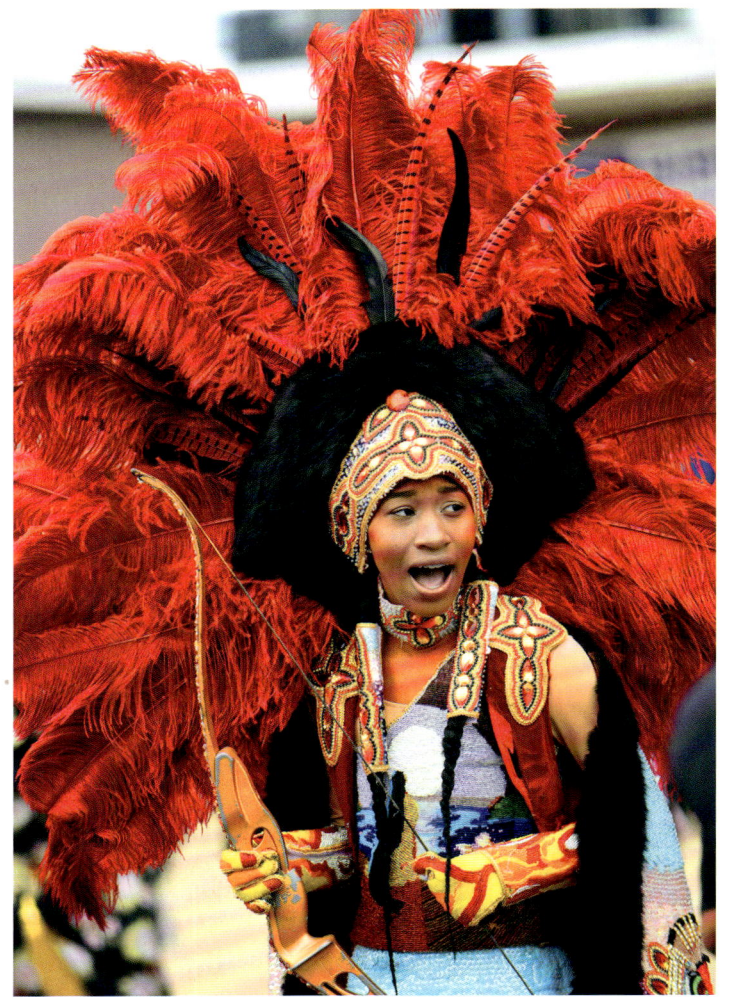

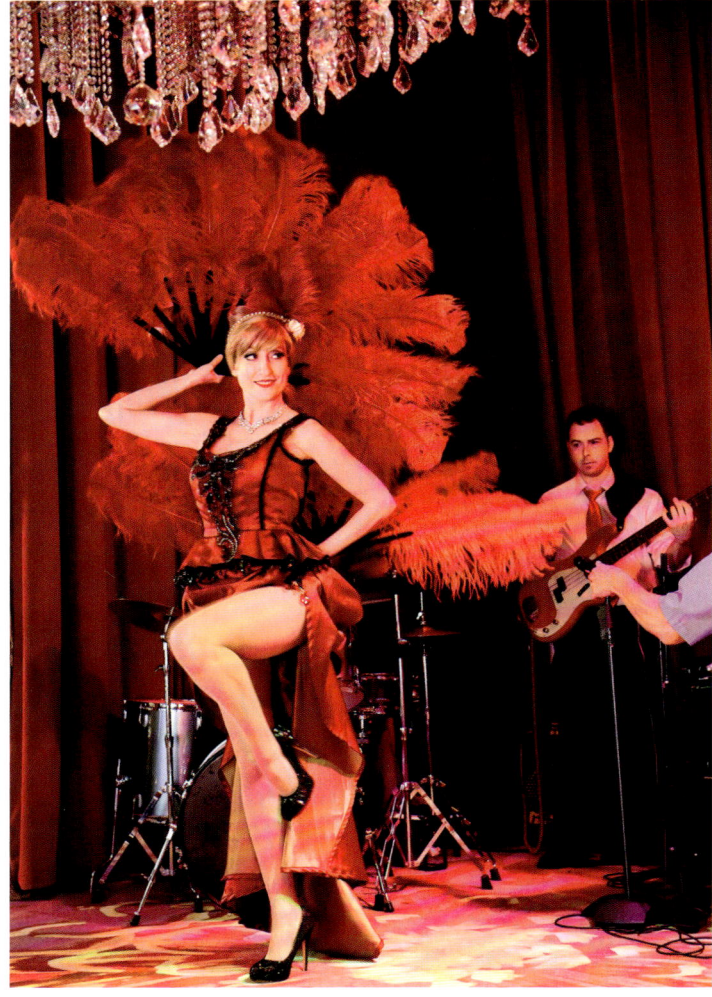

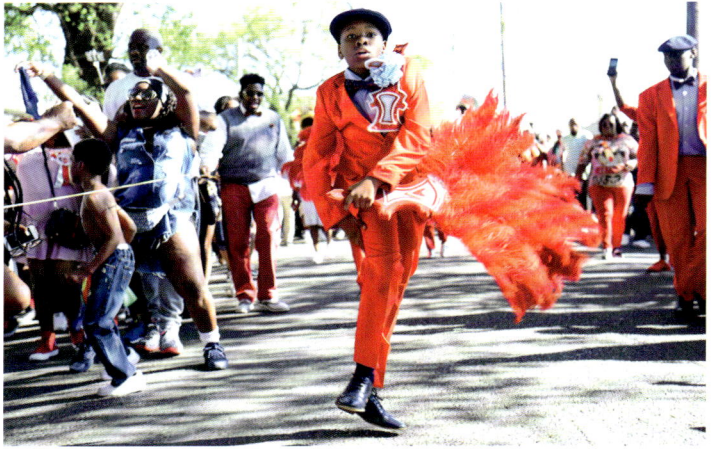

above left Queen Tahj Williams of the Golden Eagles Indian tribe on Super Sunday, 2018.

above right Burlesque artist and entrepreneur Trixie Minx, 2018.

left A young club member in the VIP Ladies and Kids second line parade, 2018.

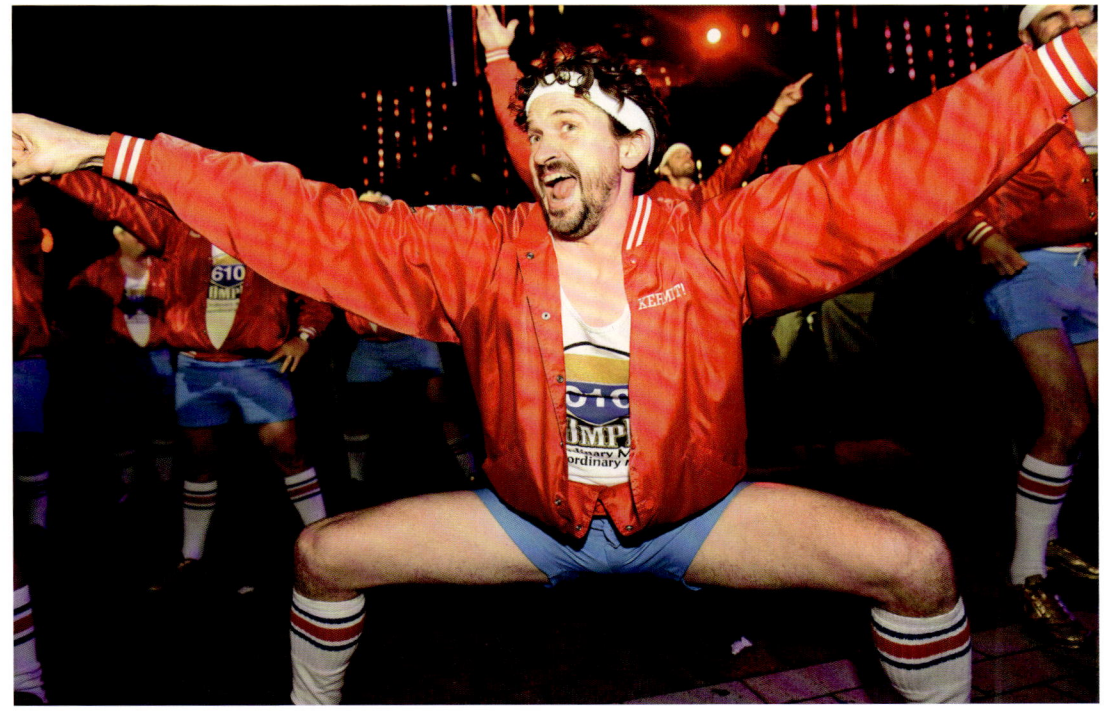

Chris "Kermit" Dalbom performs with the 610 Stompers at a charity event, 2018. The 610 Stompers are New Orleans's first all-male dance troupe with the motto, "Ordinary Men with Extraordinary Moves"; it was formed in 2009.

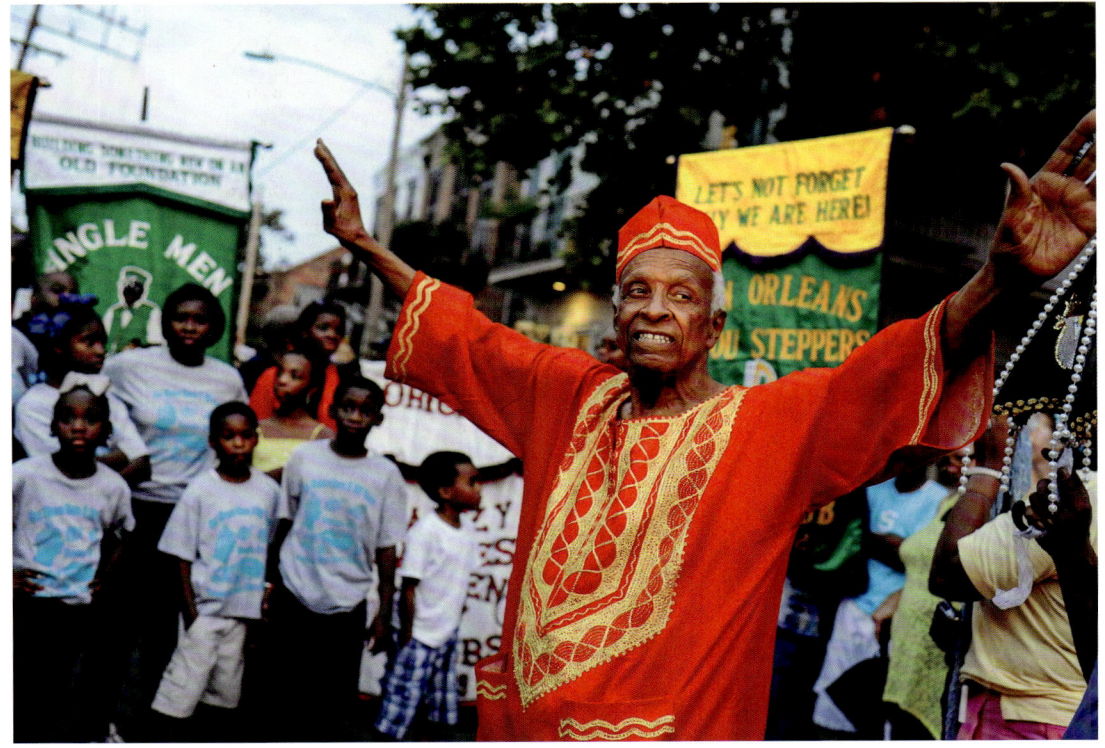

Father Jerome LeDoux, the longtime priest at St. Augustine Catholic Church in Tremé, established by free people of color and said to be the oldest Black Catholic parish in the United States, marches with the Bayou Steppers Social Aid and Pleasure Club at a Silence Is Violence protest in 2012. He was known for his activism and ministry, especially after Hurricane Katrina when his congregation was widely displaced. Father LeDoux passed away in 2019.

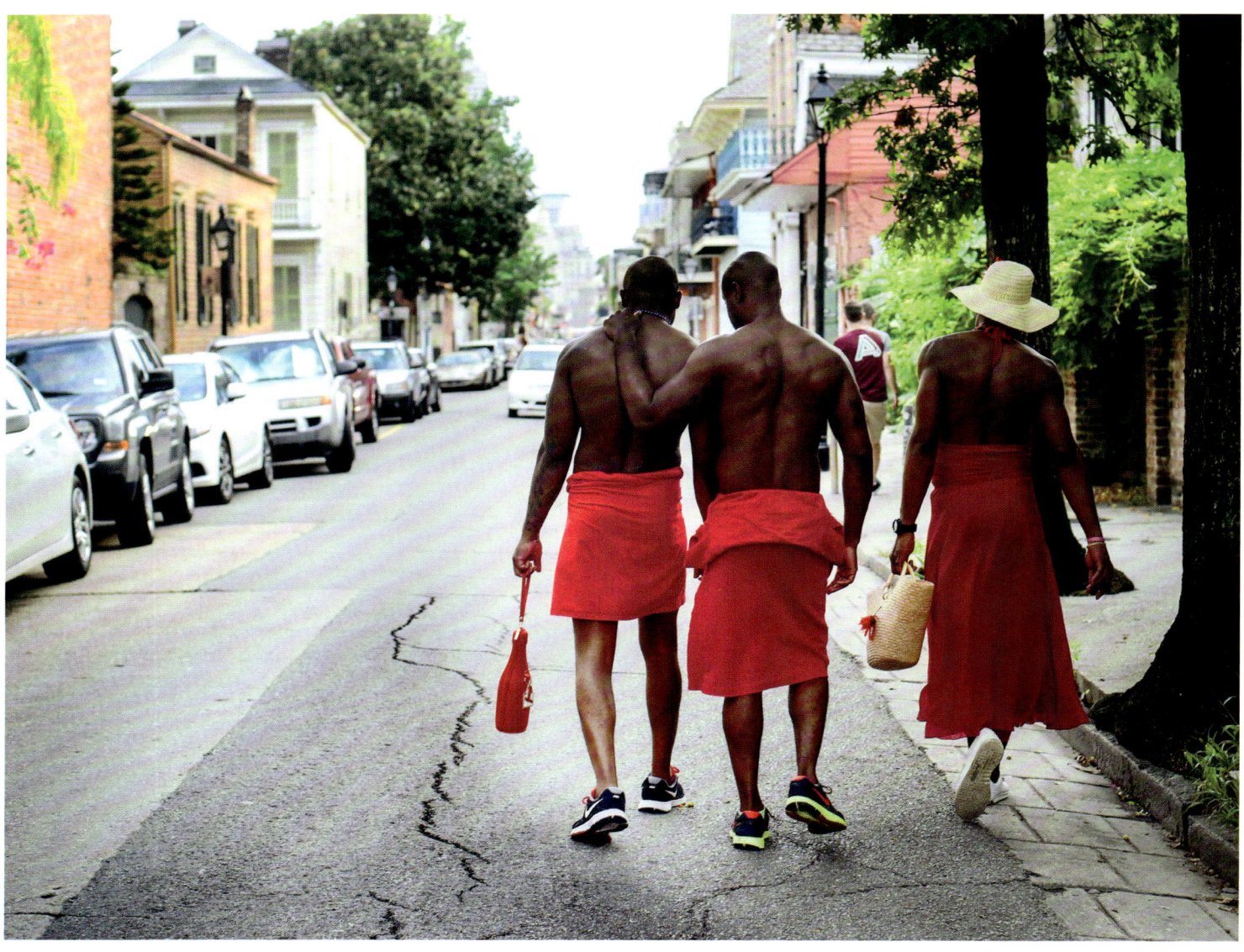

Men seen after the annual Red Dress Run (RDR) in the French Quarter, 2016. The RDR is sponsored by the Hash House Harriers, a "drinking club with a running problem." It winds through the French Quarter and downtown in August, raising funds for local charities.

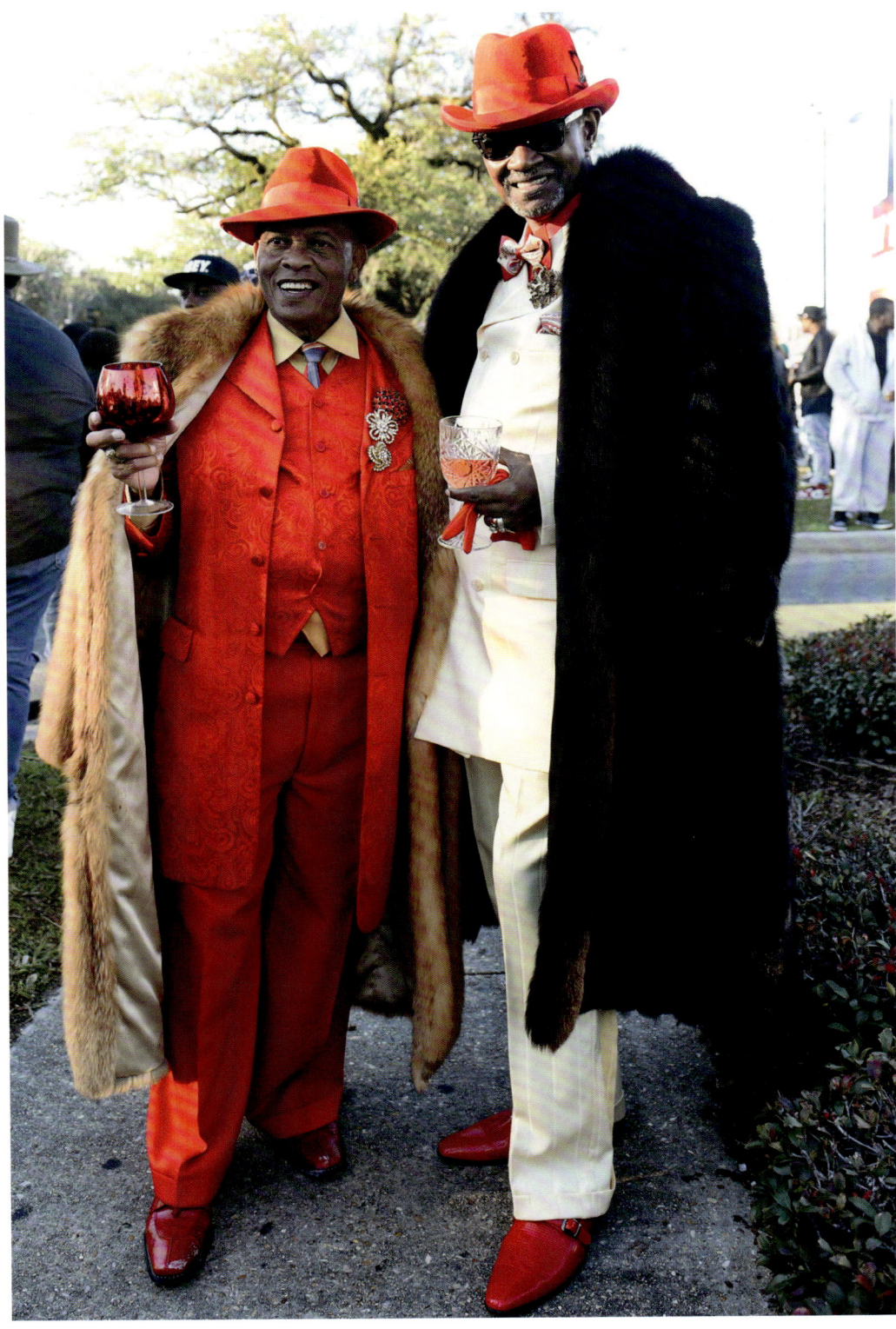

Elegantly dressed men seen during the Undefeated Divas and Gents' annual second line in the Seventh Ward, 2016.

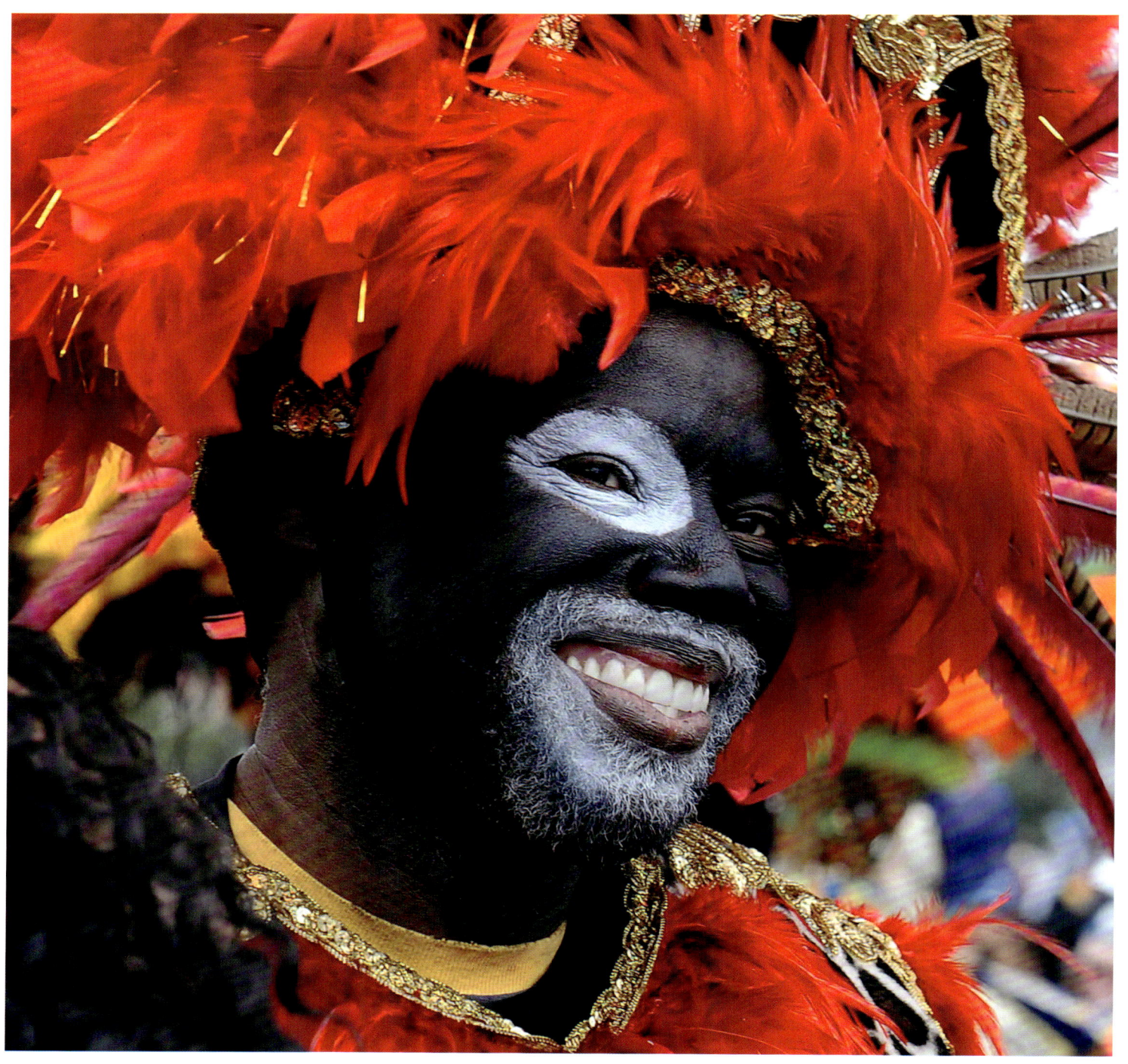

Zulu parade reveler Ronald Lewis, 2015.

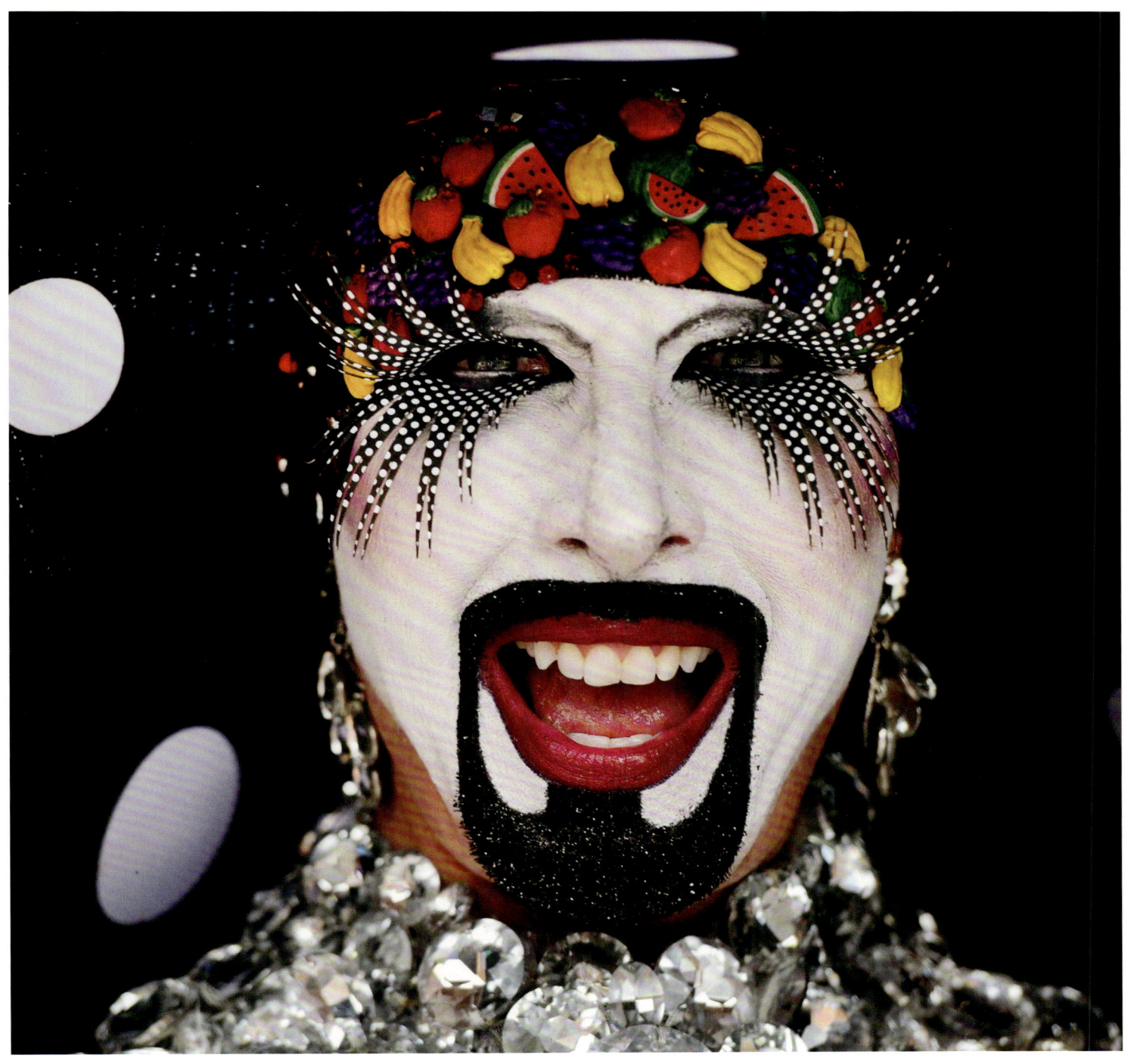

Southern Decadence reveler William H. Anderson, 2019.

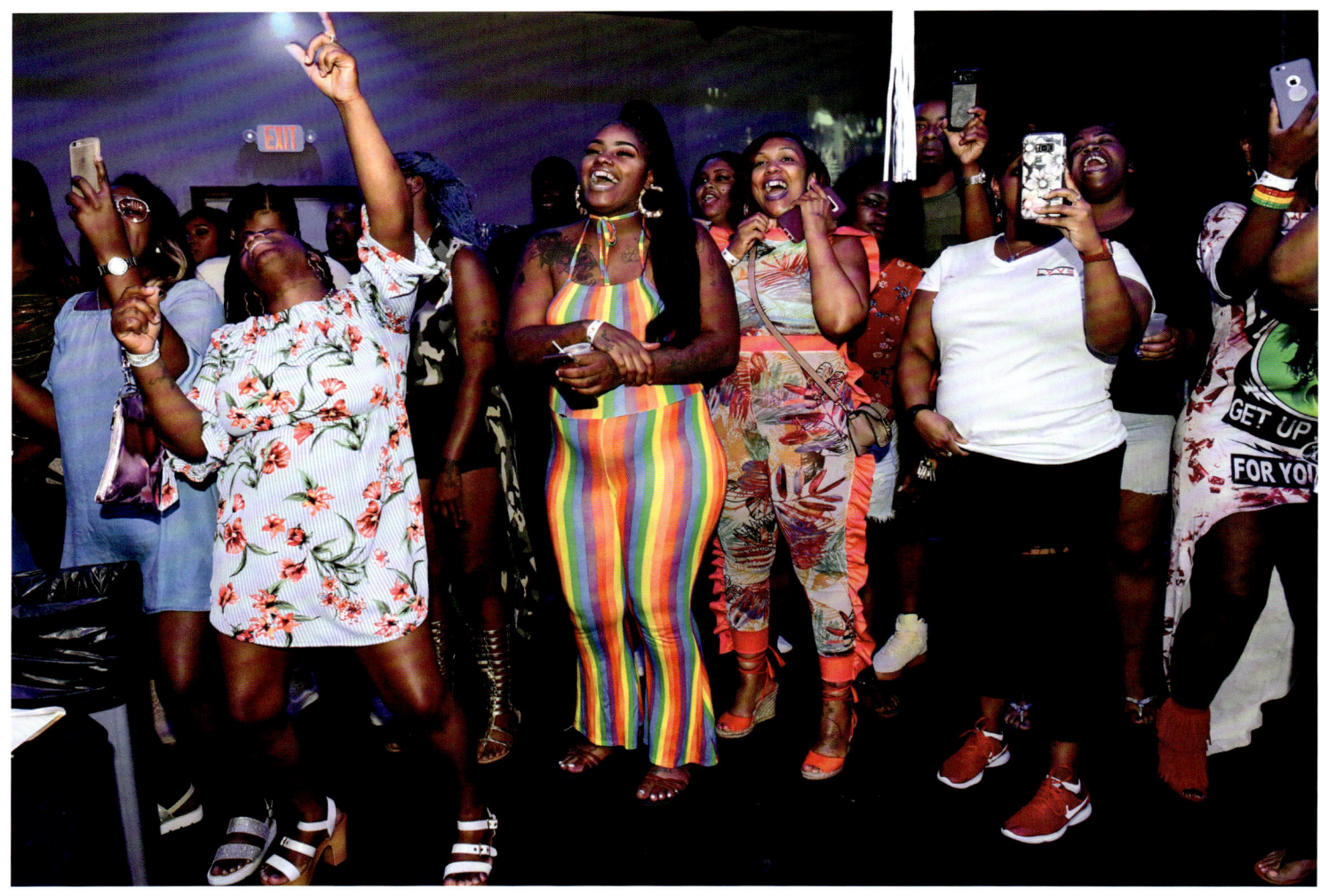

Fans of rap artist Cheeky Blakk cheer at the first annual Mama Fest for Mother's Day at Lyve Nightclub, 2018. Blakk, born Angela Woods, is a popular hip hop artist who debuted in 1993 as one of the first female rappers to embrace bounce music, along with Ms. Tee and Magnolia Shorty.

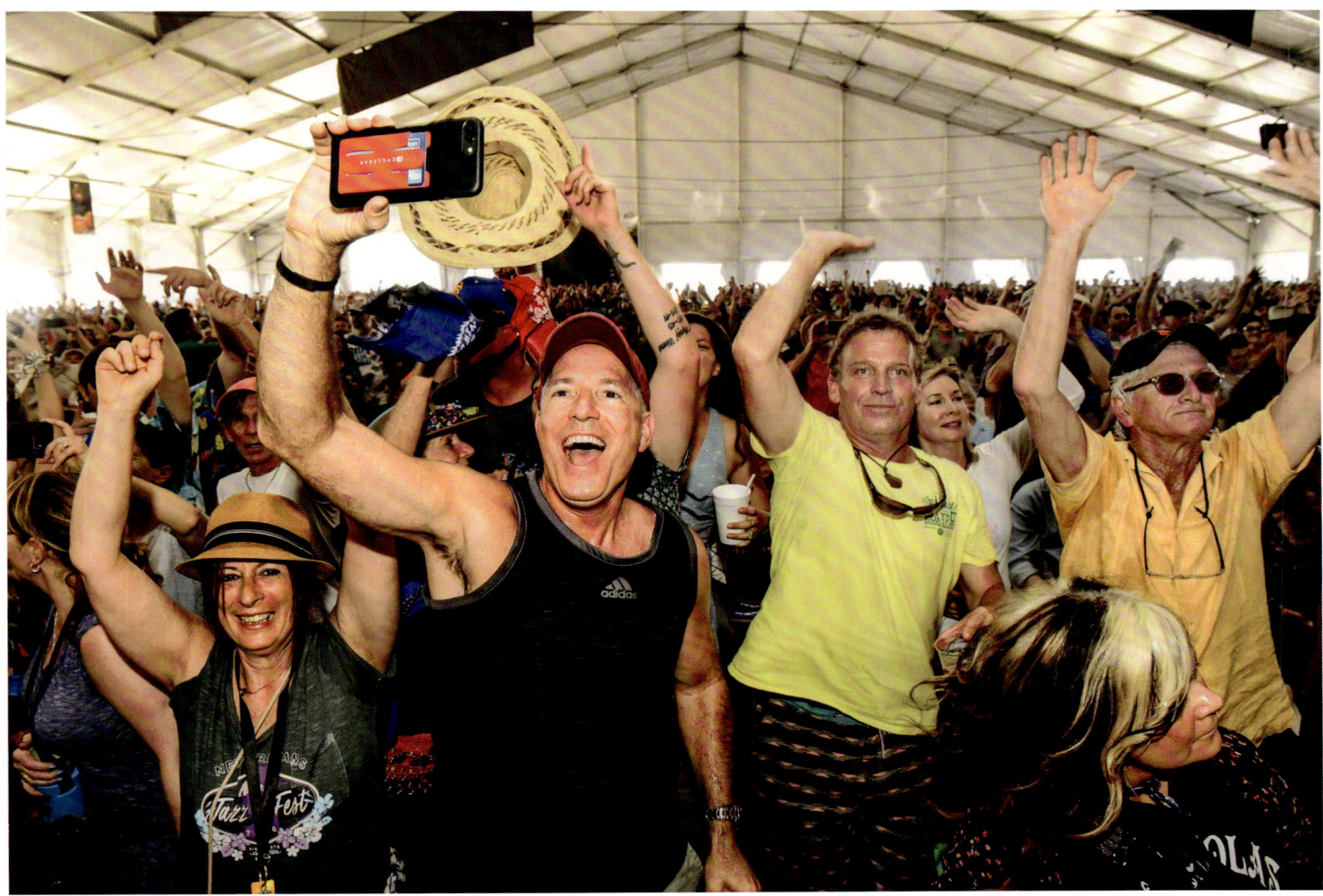

Fans of trombonist Glen David Andrews cheer in the Blues Tent at Jazz Fest, 2018. Andrews is a native son of the famous Andrews family and has been touring the world with various brass bands since he was fourteen years old. He now headlines festivals with his own ensemble, bringing jazz, gospel, blues, and funk to the world stage.

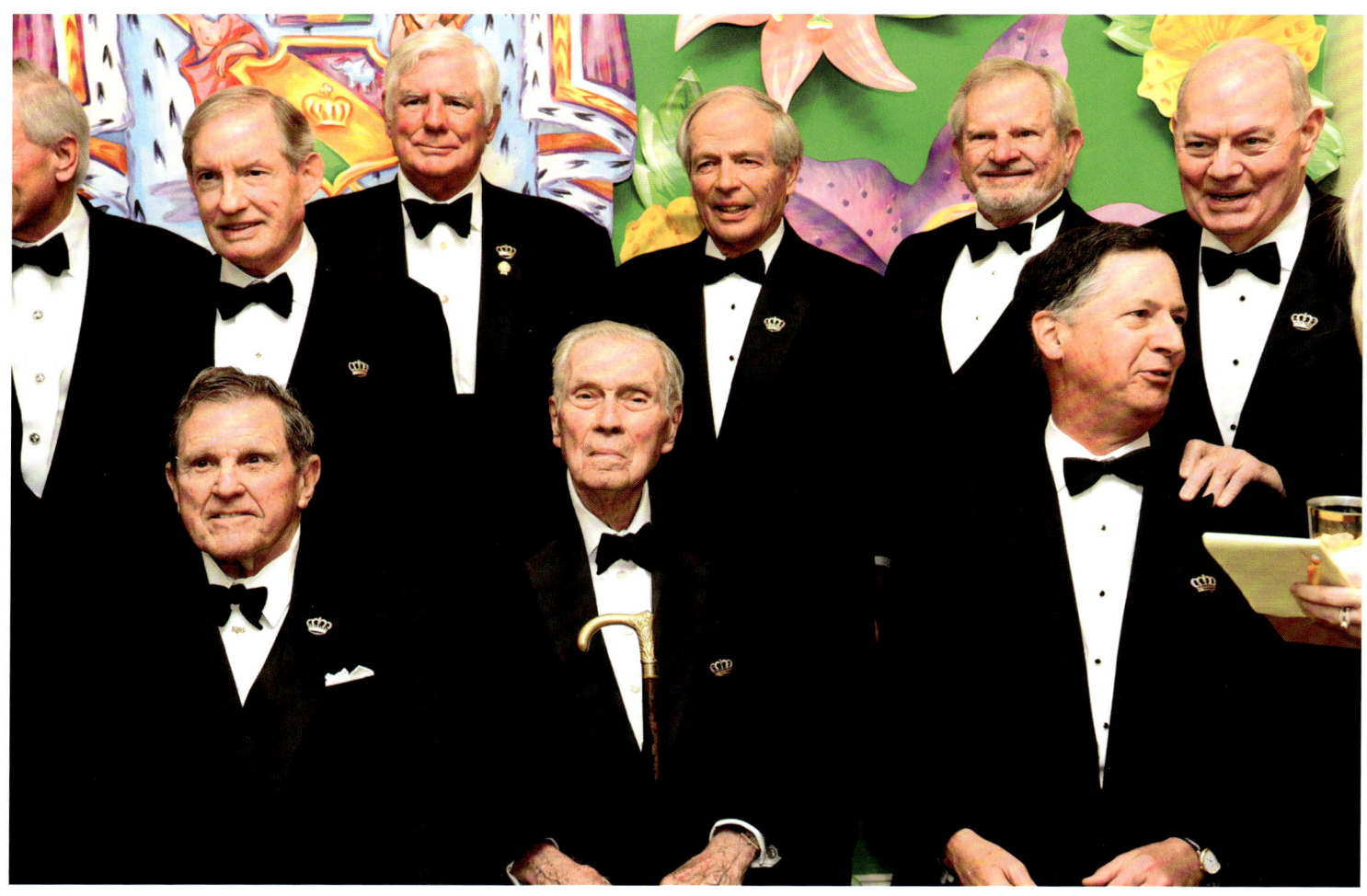

Former kings of the Rex organization wear black tie to celebrate the 150th anniversary of the School of Design at the Louisiana State Museum's Presbytère, 2022. Rex, founded in 1872, is a Carnival krewe that stages one of the city's most-celebrated parades on Mardi Gras Day in which one member reigns as "King of Carnival."

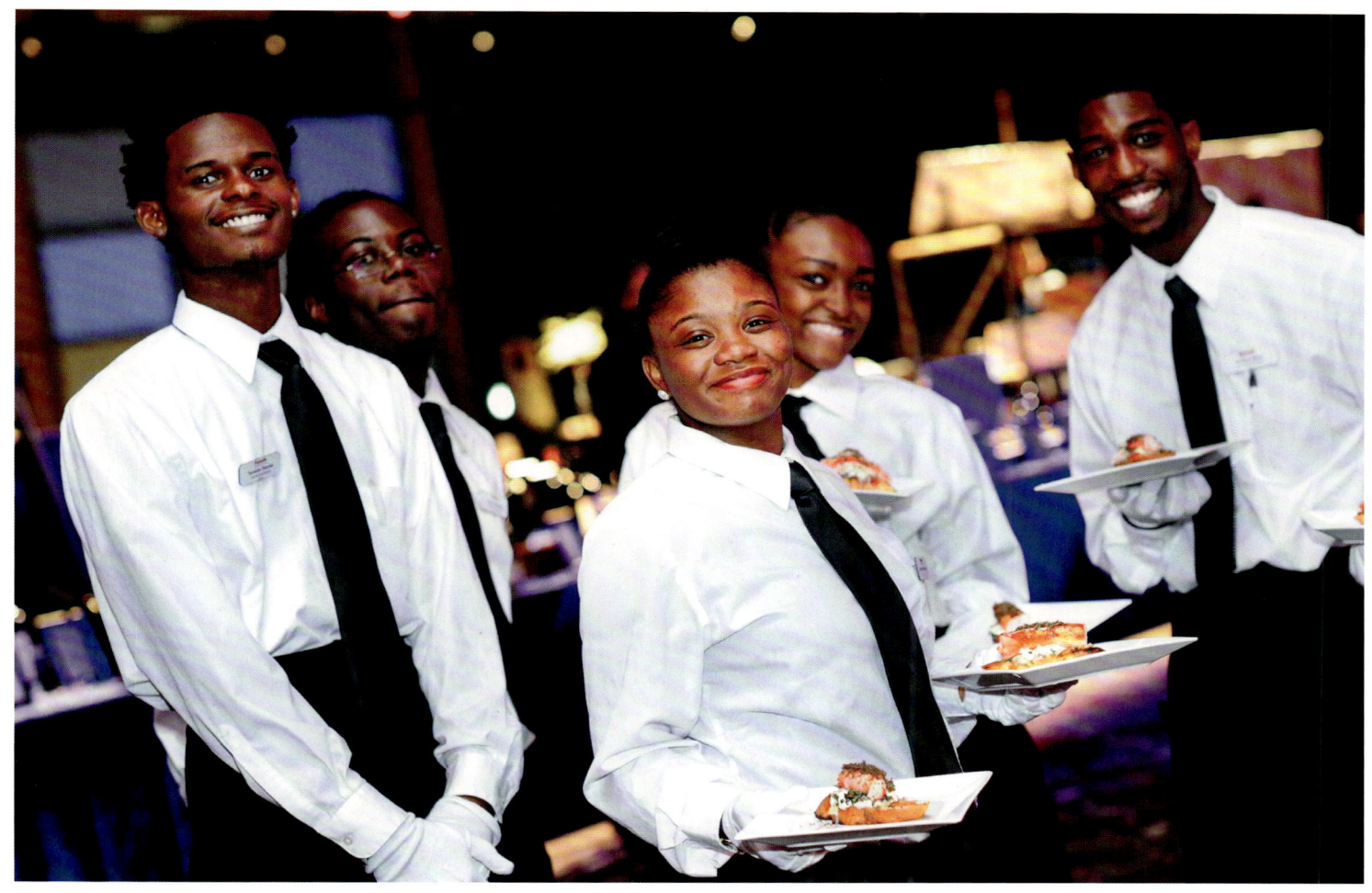

Waiters get ready to serve patrons at Emeril Lagasse Foundation's annual fundraiser, Carnivale du Vin, 2014. The foundation was established in 2002 by celebrity chef Emeril Lagasse and his wife Alden; it has raised millions of dollars to benefit youth through culinary, nutrition, and arts education.

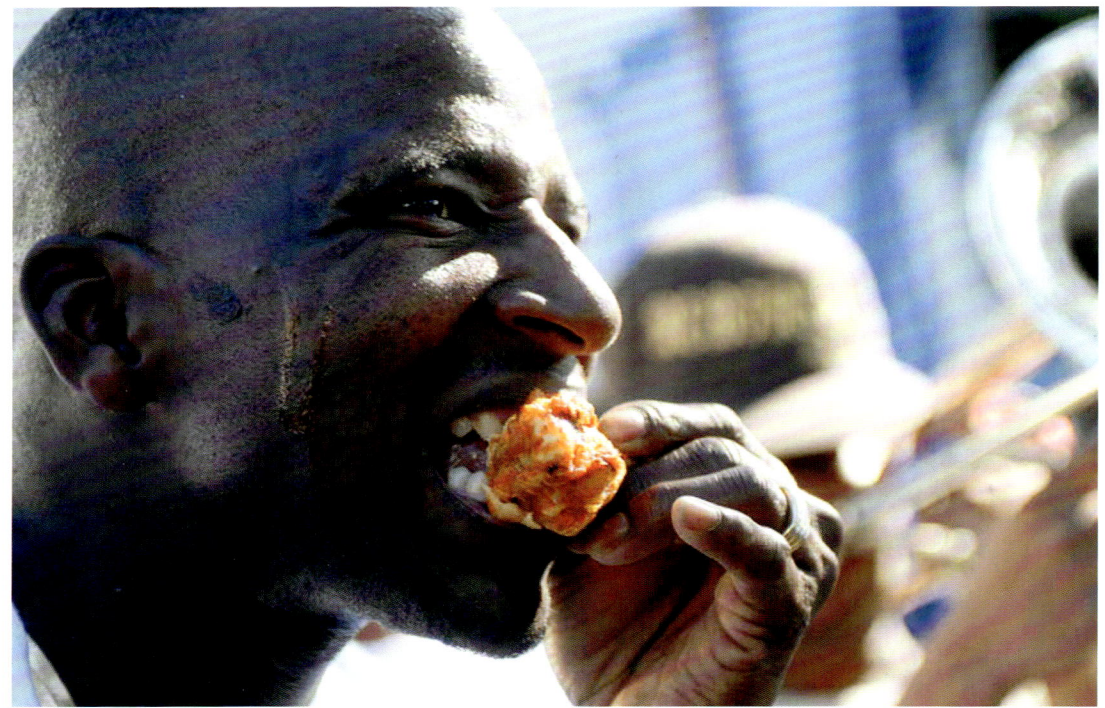

A second-liner eats a chicken wing, 2016.

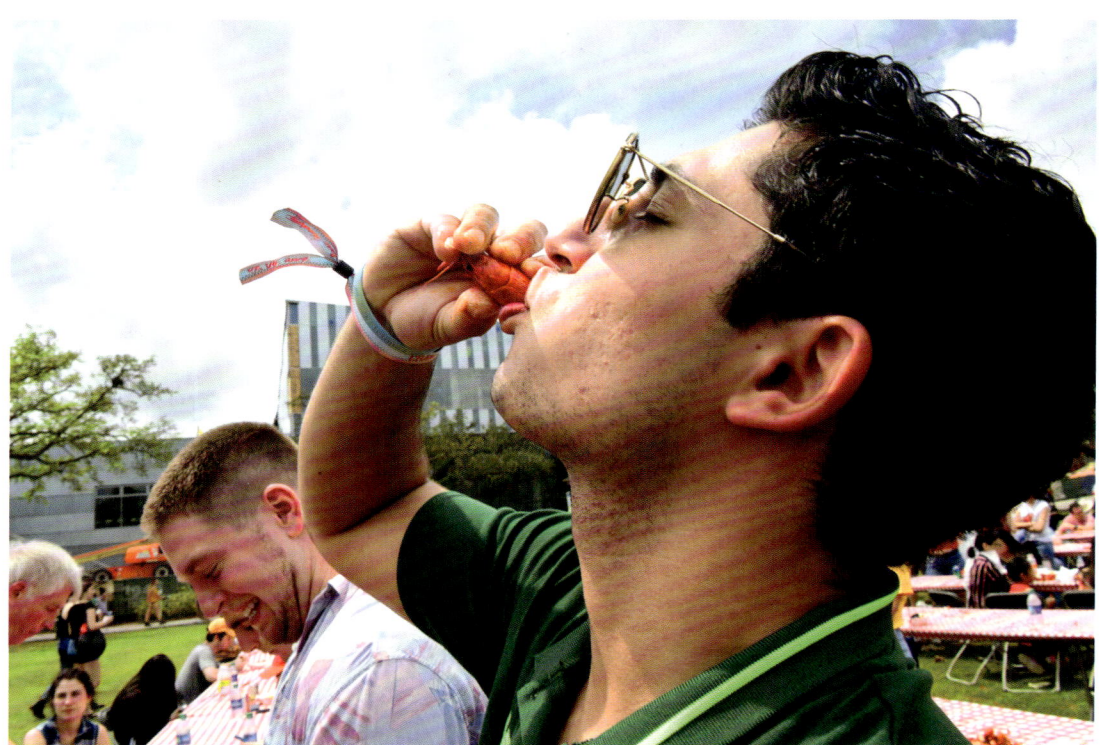

A Tulane student sucks a crawfish head at Crawfest, a student-run music, food, and arts festival held annually on the university's campus to celebrate Louisiana crawfish, 2019. The phrase "eat, drink, and be merry, for tomorrow we die" has been used for centuries throughout literature and is a way of life in New Orleans.

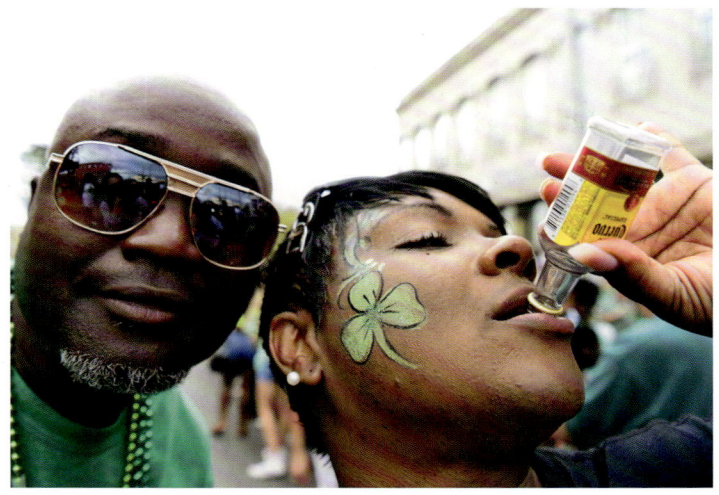

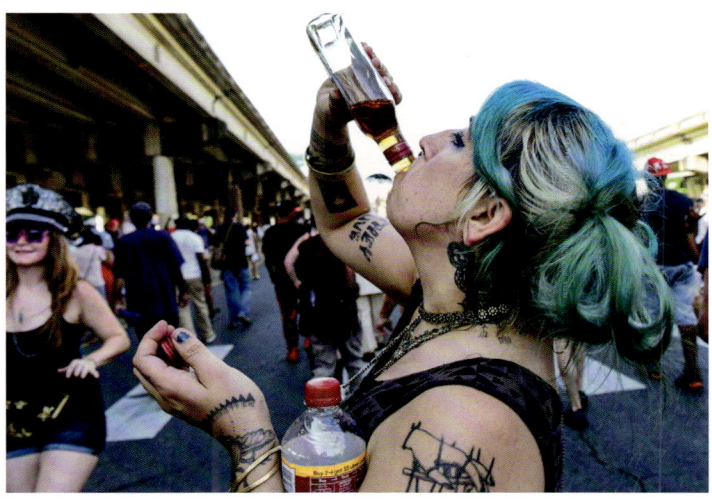

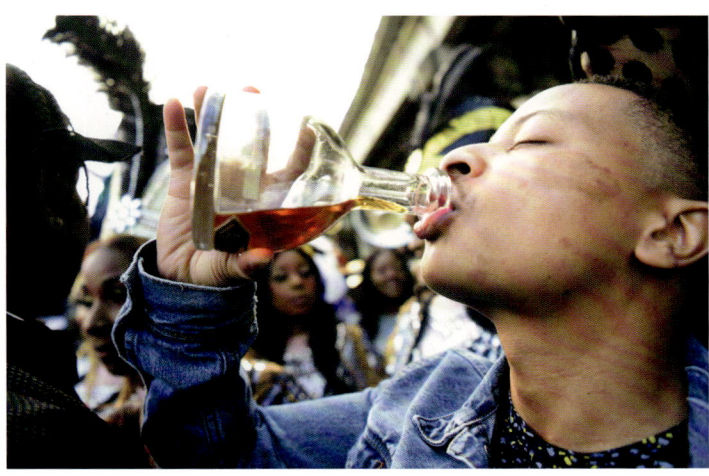

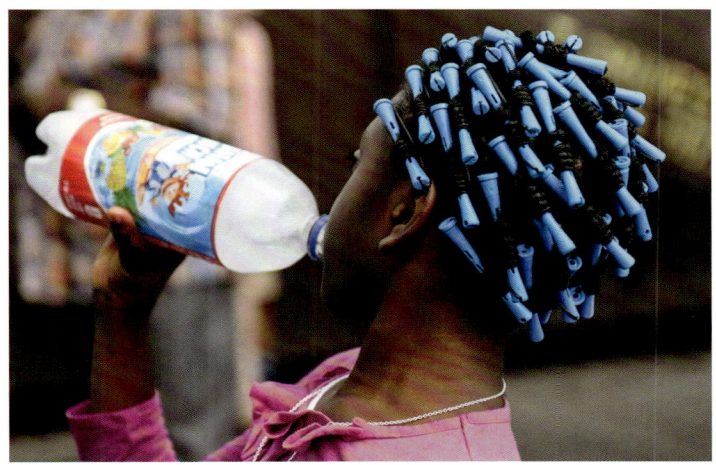

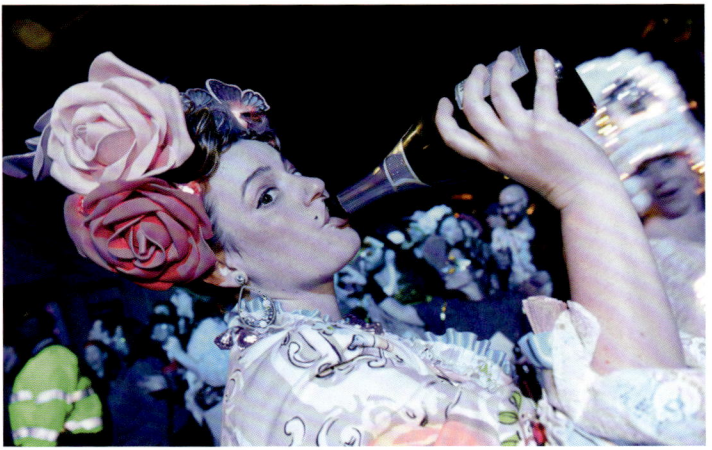

Imbibing and parading from Uptown to Downtown (**clockwise**): St. Patrick's Day in the Irish Channel, 2018; Second line, 2019; A girl in Central City, 2017; A member of the court of the Merry Antoinettes, a cheeky and glamorous marching krewe, 2018; Second line, 2019.

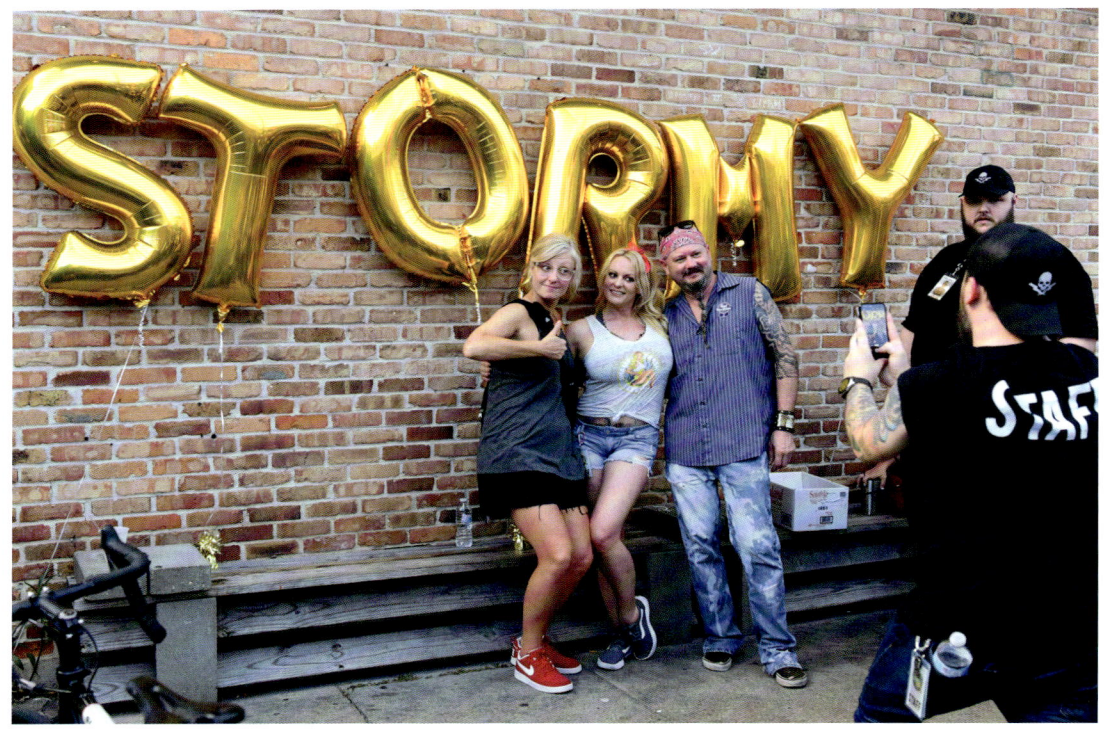

Stormy Daniels (*center*) poses with fans at her "Swamp Trash Block Party" in the Bywater neighborhood to benefit the Abortion Fund, 2019. Daniels, born in Louisiana in 1979 as Stephanie Gregory Clifford, is an American pornographic film actress and director known for accepting $130,000 in hush money in 2016 to stay silent about an affair she alleges she had with Donald Trump.

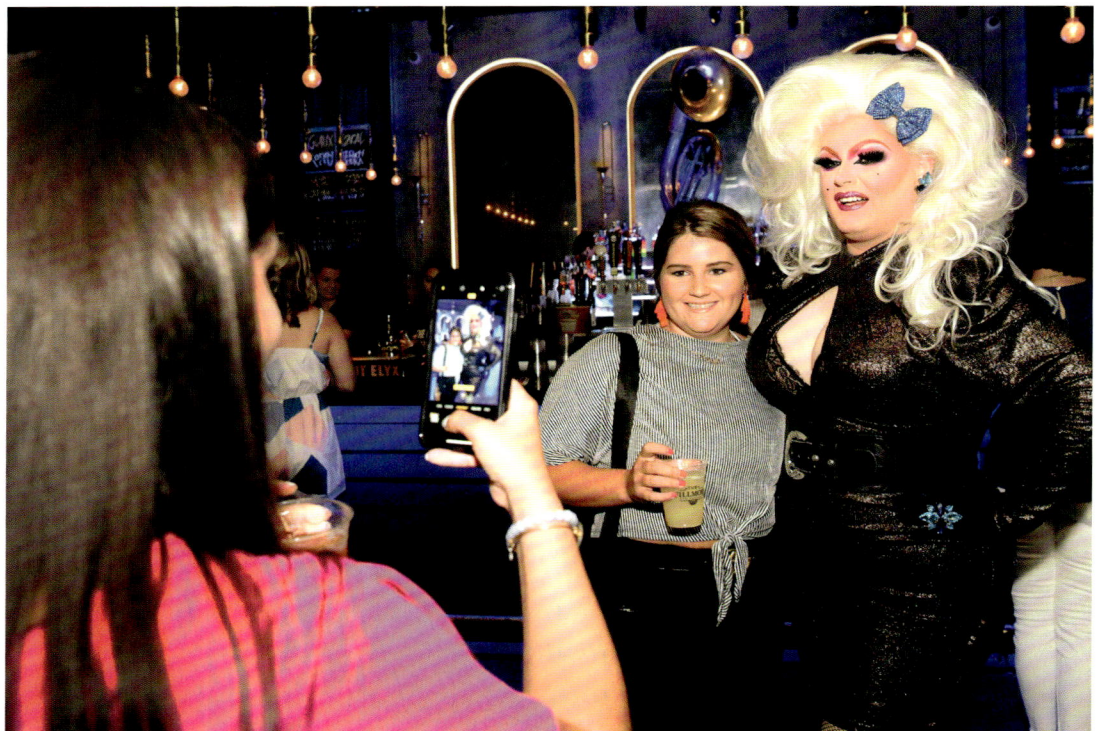

Lana O'Day, an entertainer who performs as a drag queen and female illusionist, poses with fans for photos at the Fillmore's Sunday Drag Brunch, 2019.

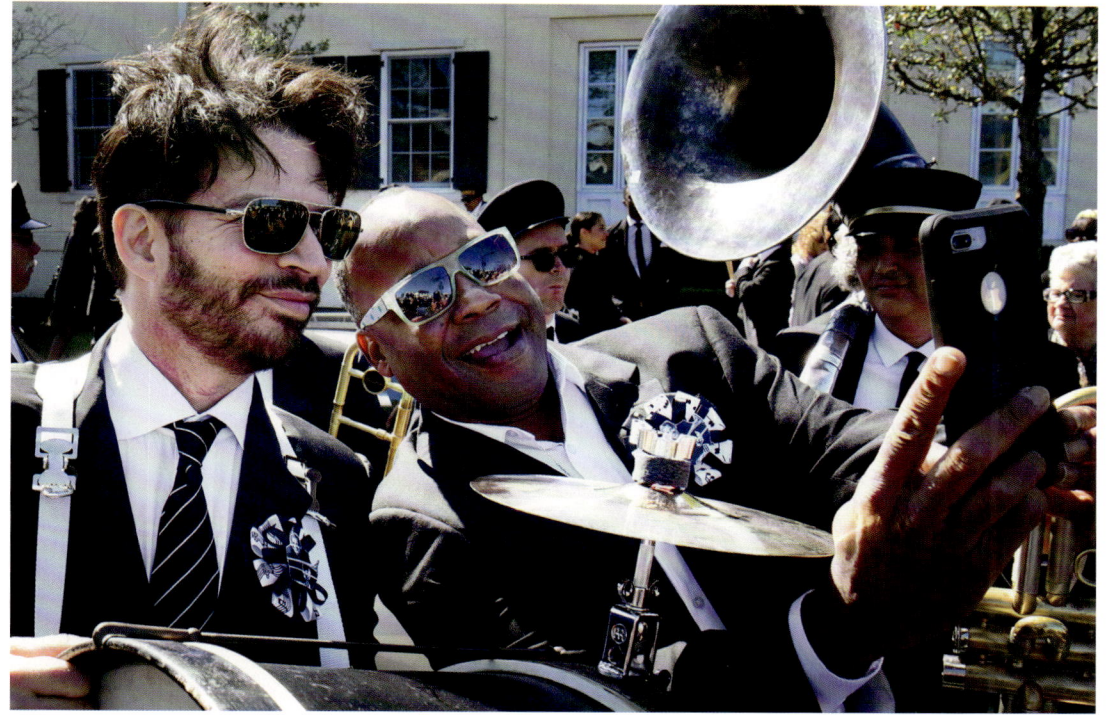

Musicians Harry Connick Jr. and James Andrews pose for a selfie before the funeral for musician Lucien Barbarin, 2020.

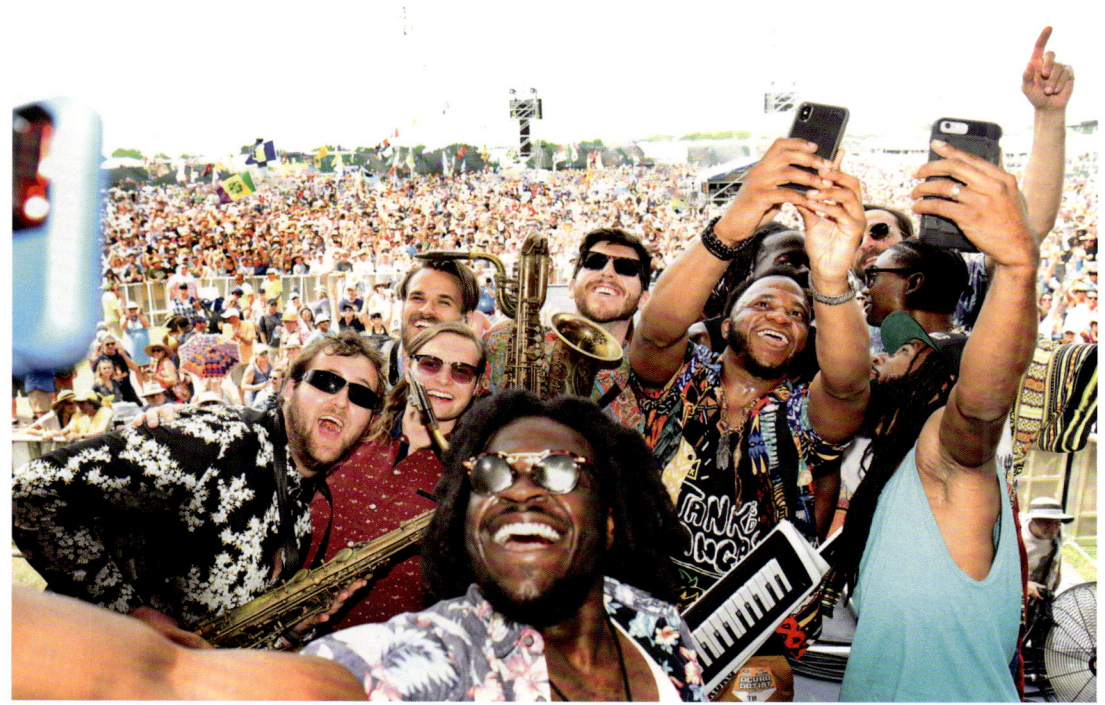

The Bangas, of Tank and the Bangas, take selfies after their Jazz Fest performance, 2018.

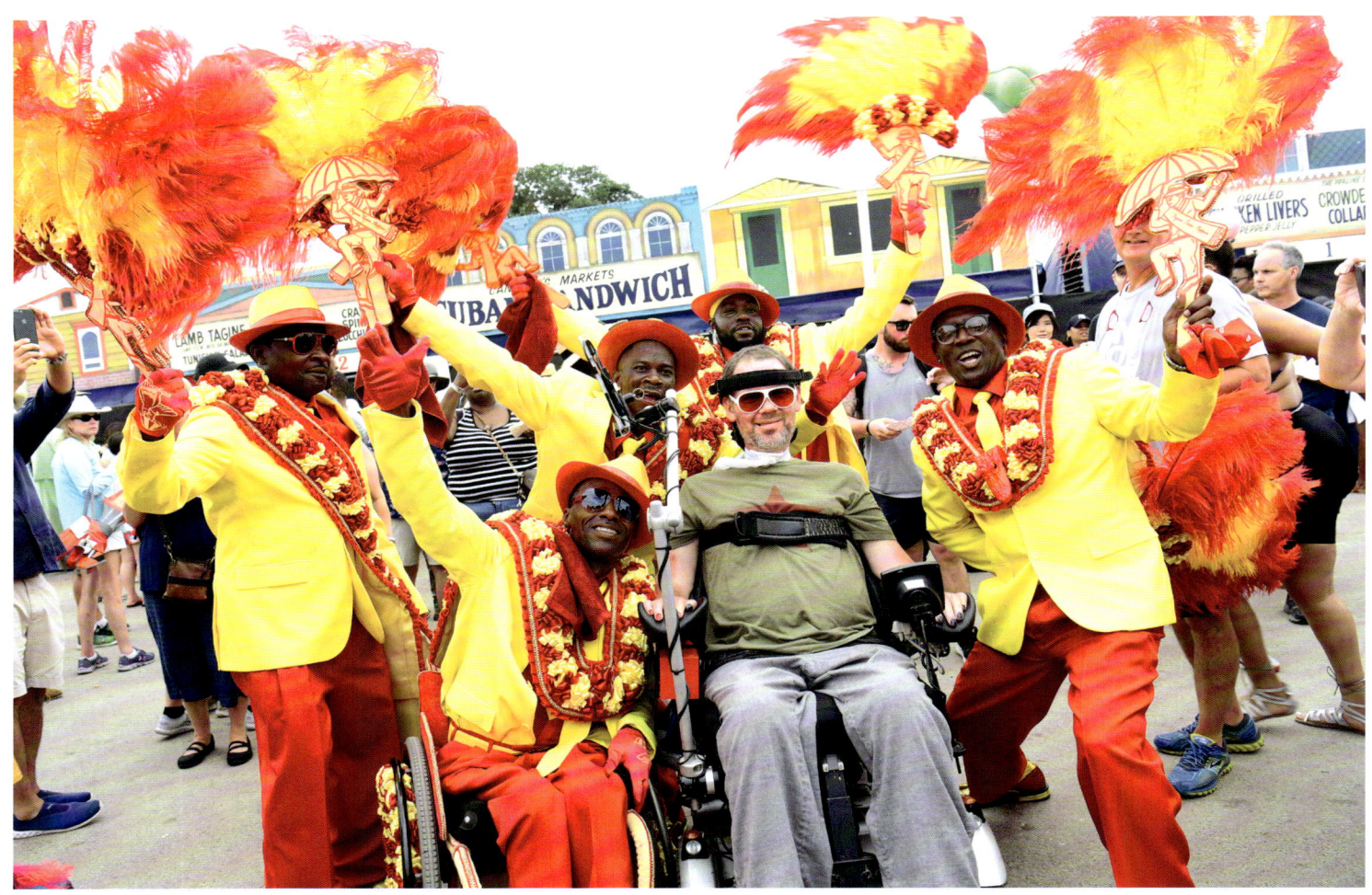

Former New Orleans Saints player Steve Gleason is spotted and surrounded by the Pigeon Town Steppers Social Aid and Pleasure Club at Jazz Fest, 2018. Gleason played football for the Saints from 2000 to 2008 and will always be remembered for sparking the city's "rebirth" with his blocked punt against the Atlanta Falcons on *Monday Night Football* in the Louisiana Superdome, in the first football game held there after Hurricane Katrina. He was diagnosed with ALS in 2011, and as his health declined, he founded Team Gleason, raising awareness and money and advocating for legislation and technology to help those with the neuromuscular disease. The documentary film *Gleason*, released in 2016, covers five years of his struggles.

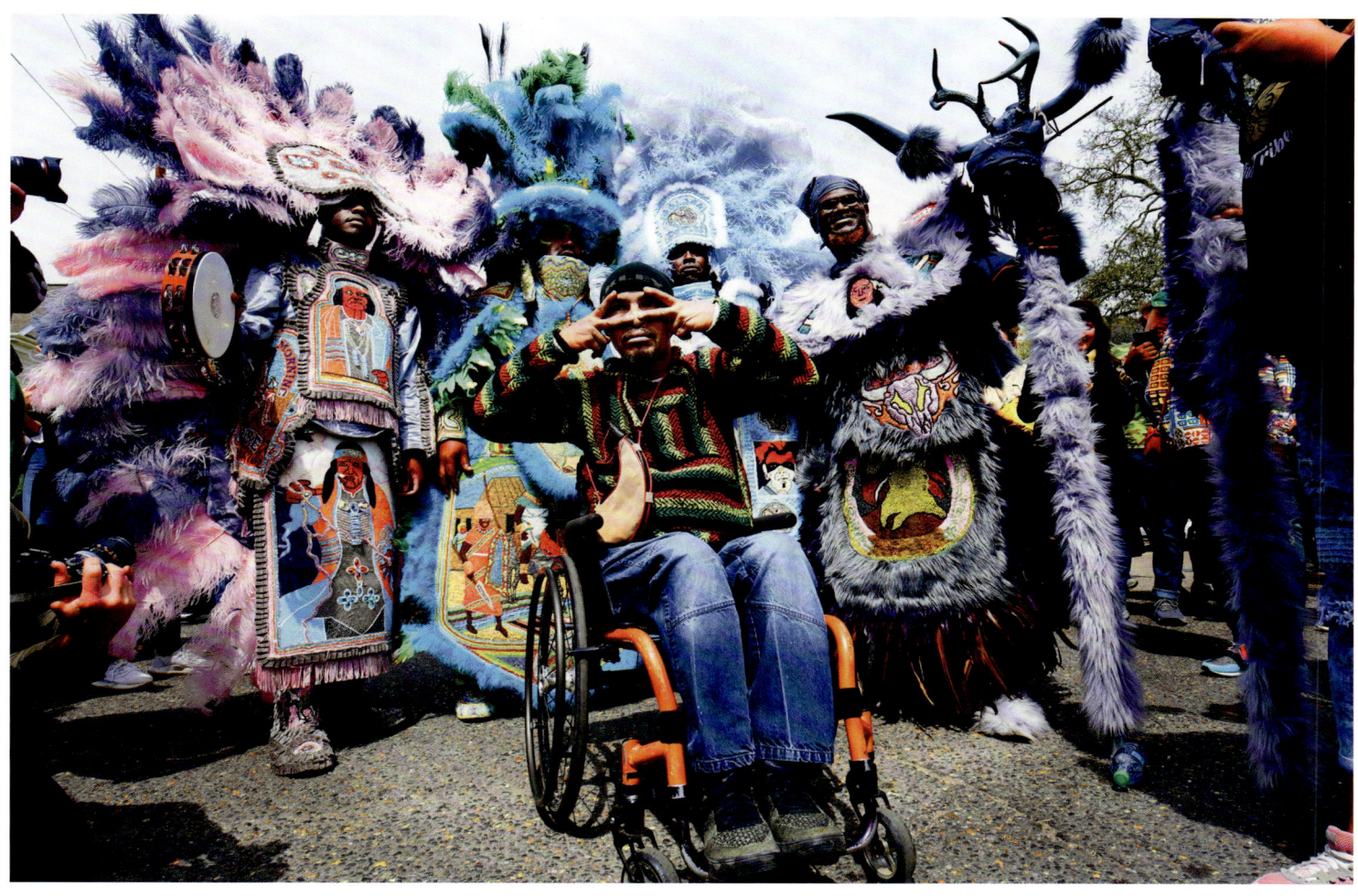

Jaime "Wild Man Loco" Cooper poses with Black Masking Indians on Super Sunday, 2019. Cooper became disabled after Hurricane Katrina: while working on the Mississippi River docks, ten tons of cargo fell on him. Despite his disability, he continues to participate in Black Masking traditions.

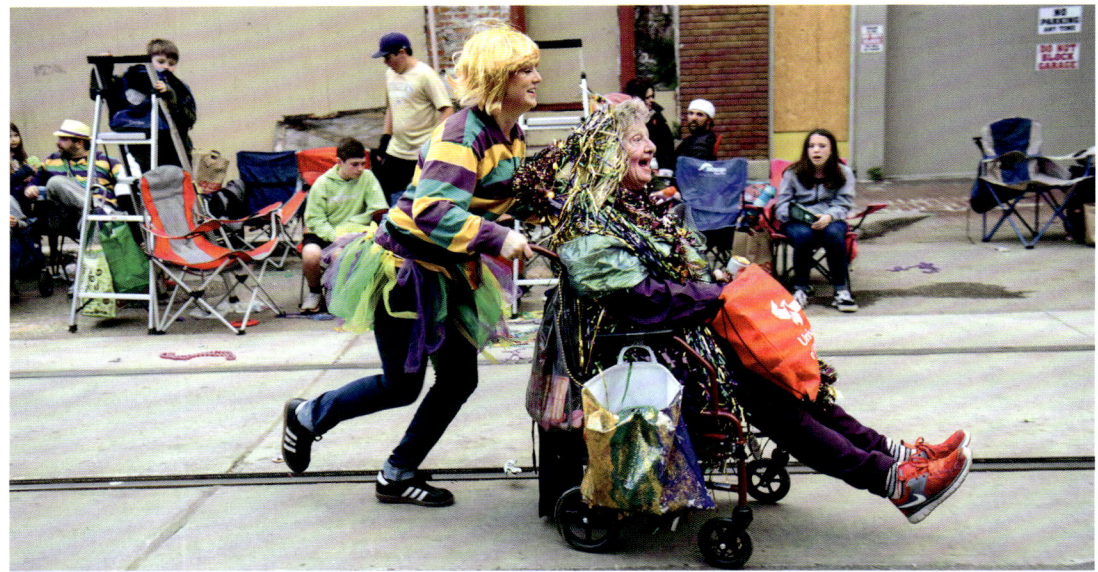

Debra Walden Julian gets a push in her wheelchair during Mardi Gras, 2020.

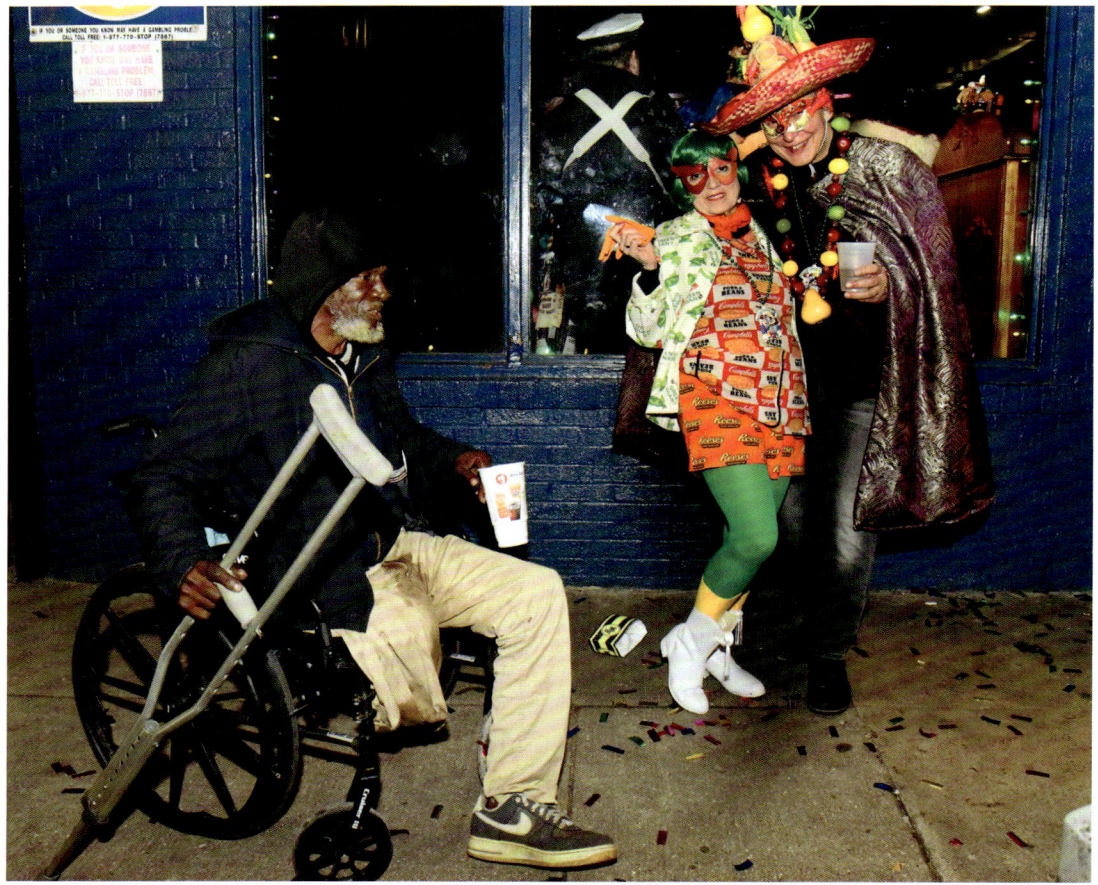

A disabled man approaches Claudia Baumgarten and Mark McGrain as they pose for photos outside the ball for the Carnival krewe Société des Champs Elysée, a social aid and benevolent krewe dedicated to feeding the unhoused, 2019.

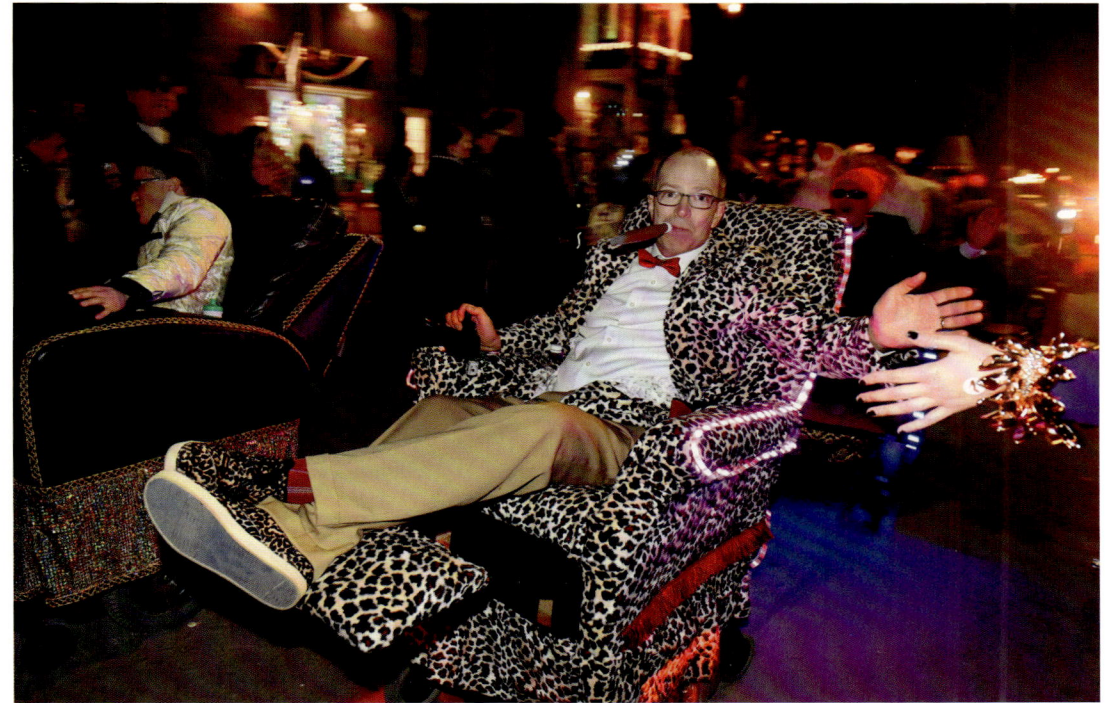

Michael Tisserand of the Laissez Boys Social Aid and Leisure Club, founded in 2013, lays back in his electric-powered recliner during the Muses parade, 2016.

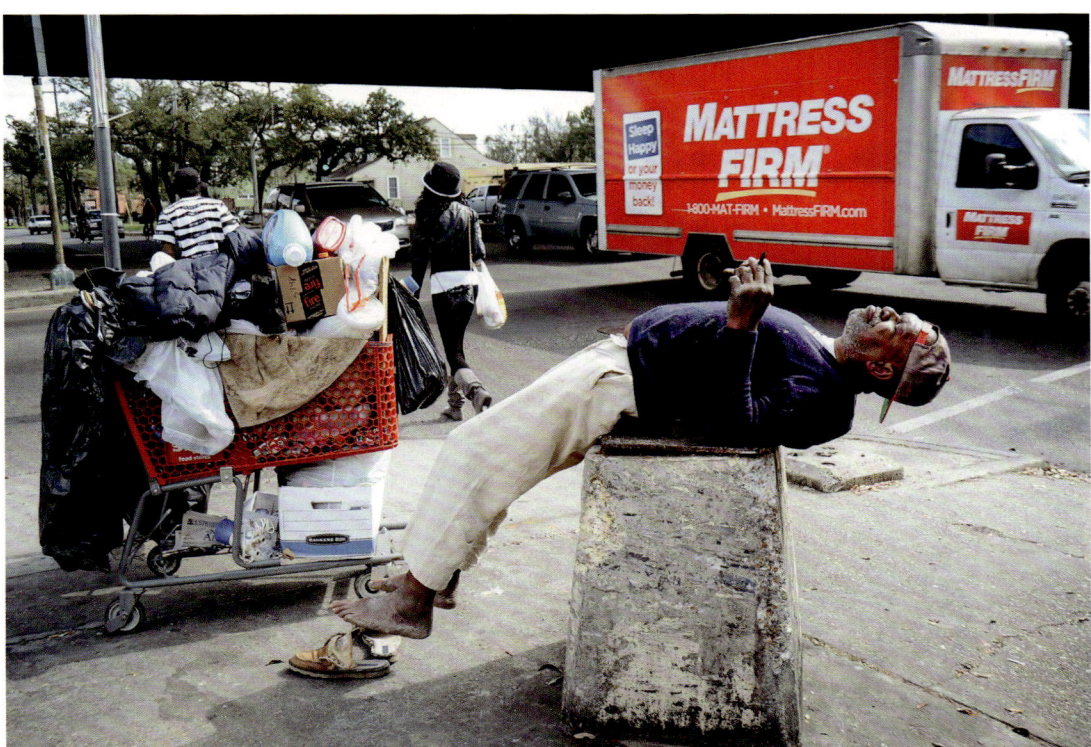

A man stretches his back on a concrete pillar on N. Claiborne Avenue as a bedding store truck rolls by, 2016.

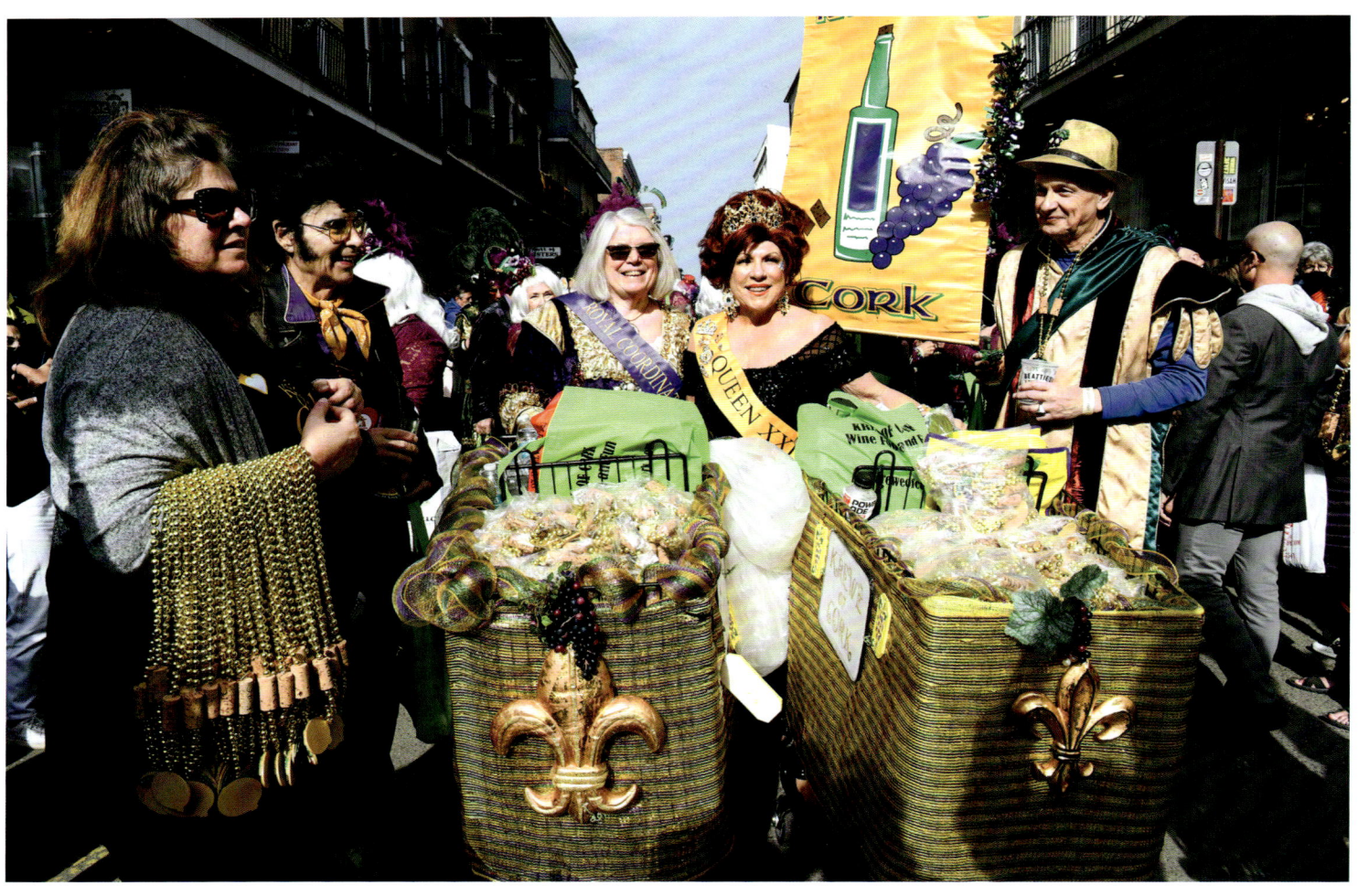

Two women in the Krewe of Cork parade carry their throws in decorated shopping carts in the French Quarter, 2022.

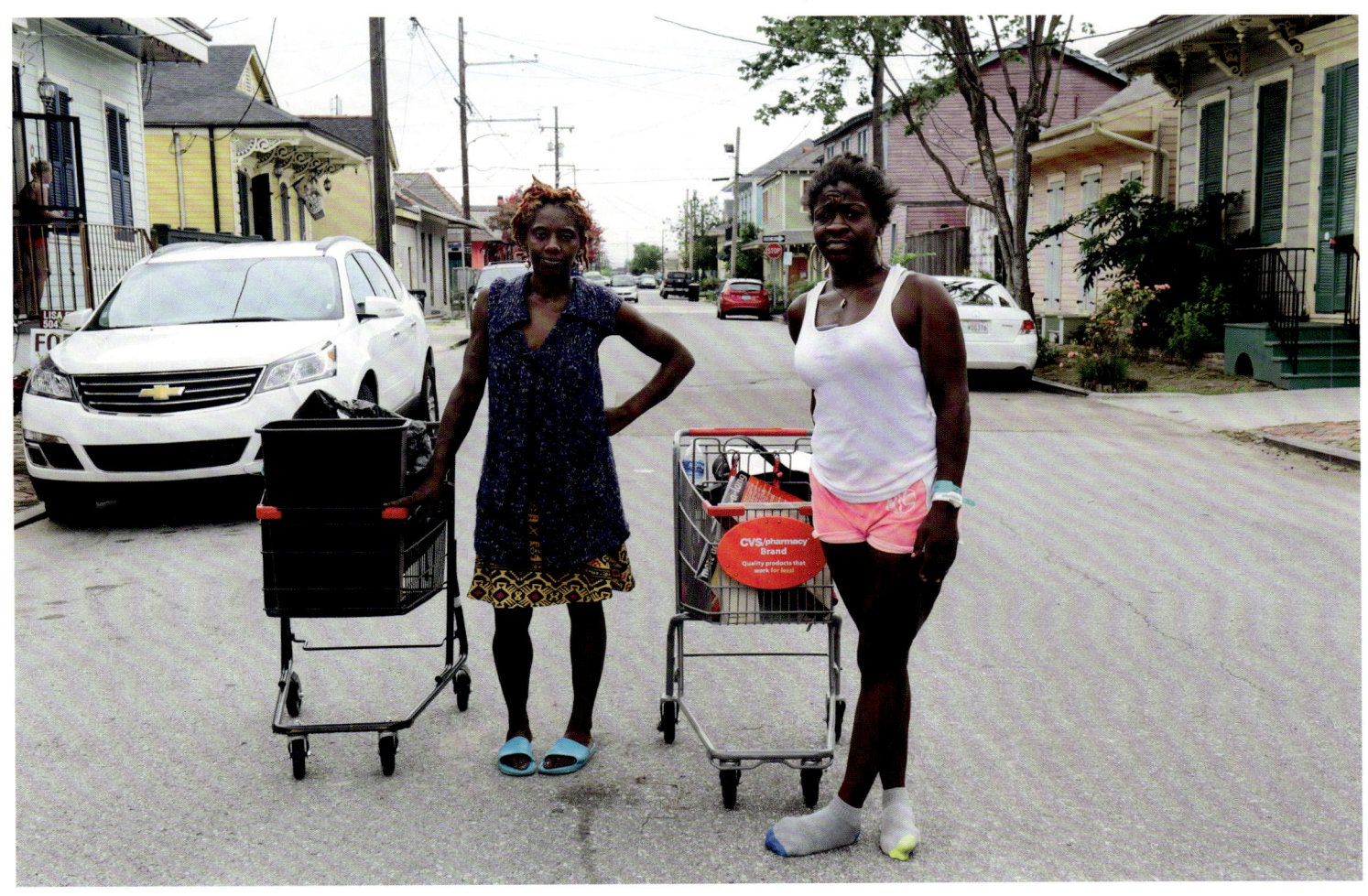

Two women carry their belongings in shopping carts through the Faubourg Marigny, 2017.

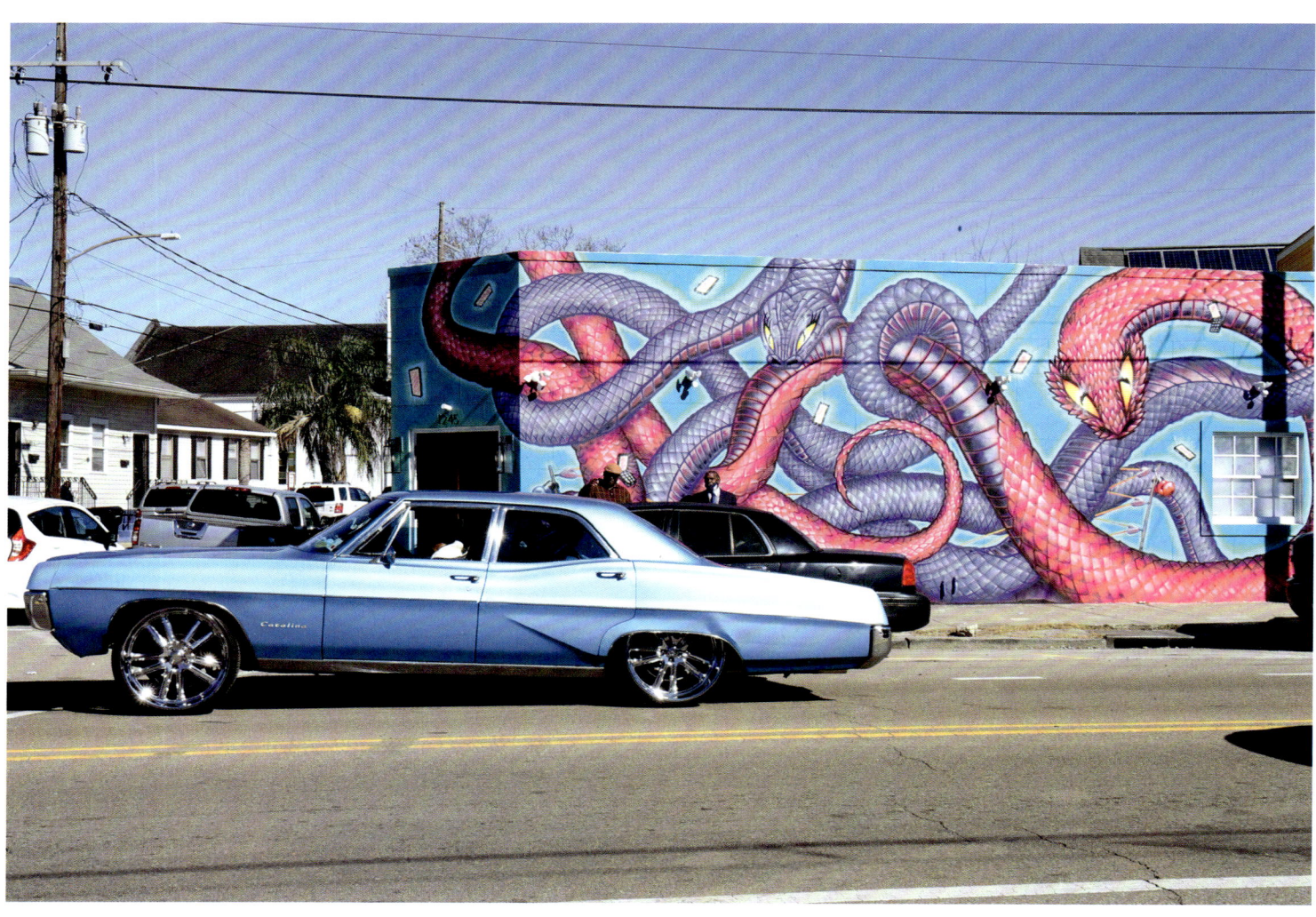

An antique car passes the mural titled *Two Girls Fighting* by graffiti artist Hugo Gyrl on St. Bernard Avenue, 2022. Hugo Gyrl is a Brooklyn-born queer graffiti artist based in New Orleans whose work reclaims public space for LGBTQ+ people and women, reminding viewers that "queerness has always been tied to rebellion and fighting for visibility."

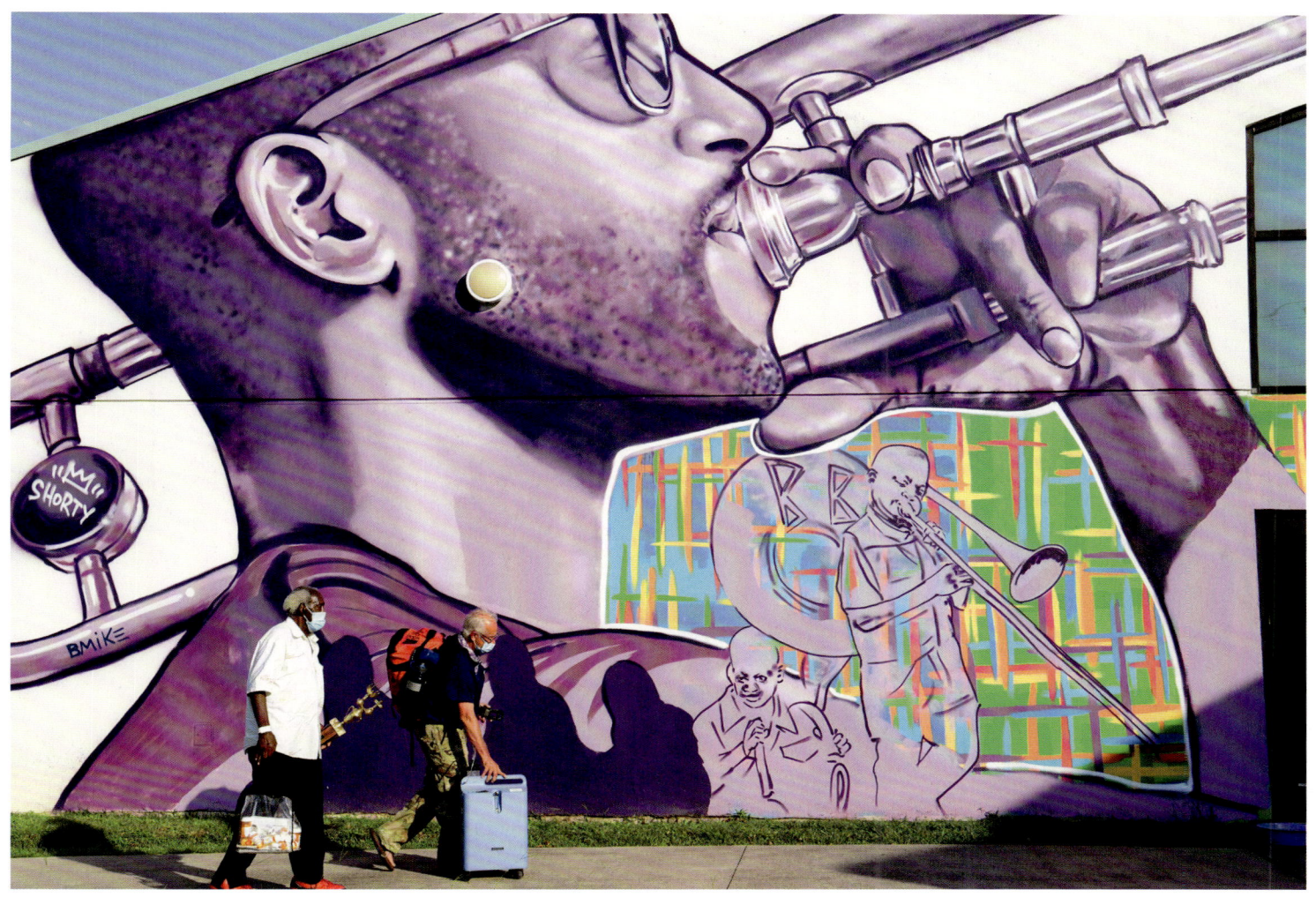

Residents seeking basic services walk by the Trombone Shorty mural created by Brandan "BMike" Odums on a wall of the Treme Community Center after Hurricane Ida knocked out power to the city, 2021. BMike is a muralist and multimedia artist renowned for graffiti and murals depicting African Americans. His landmark Studio Be is located in the Faubourg Marigny.

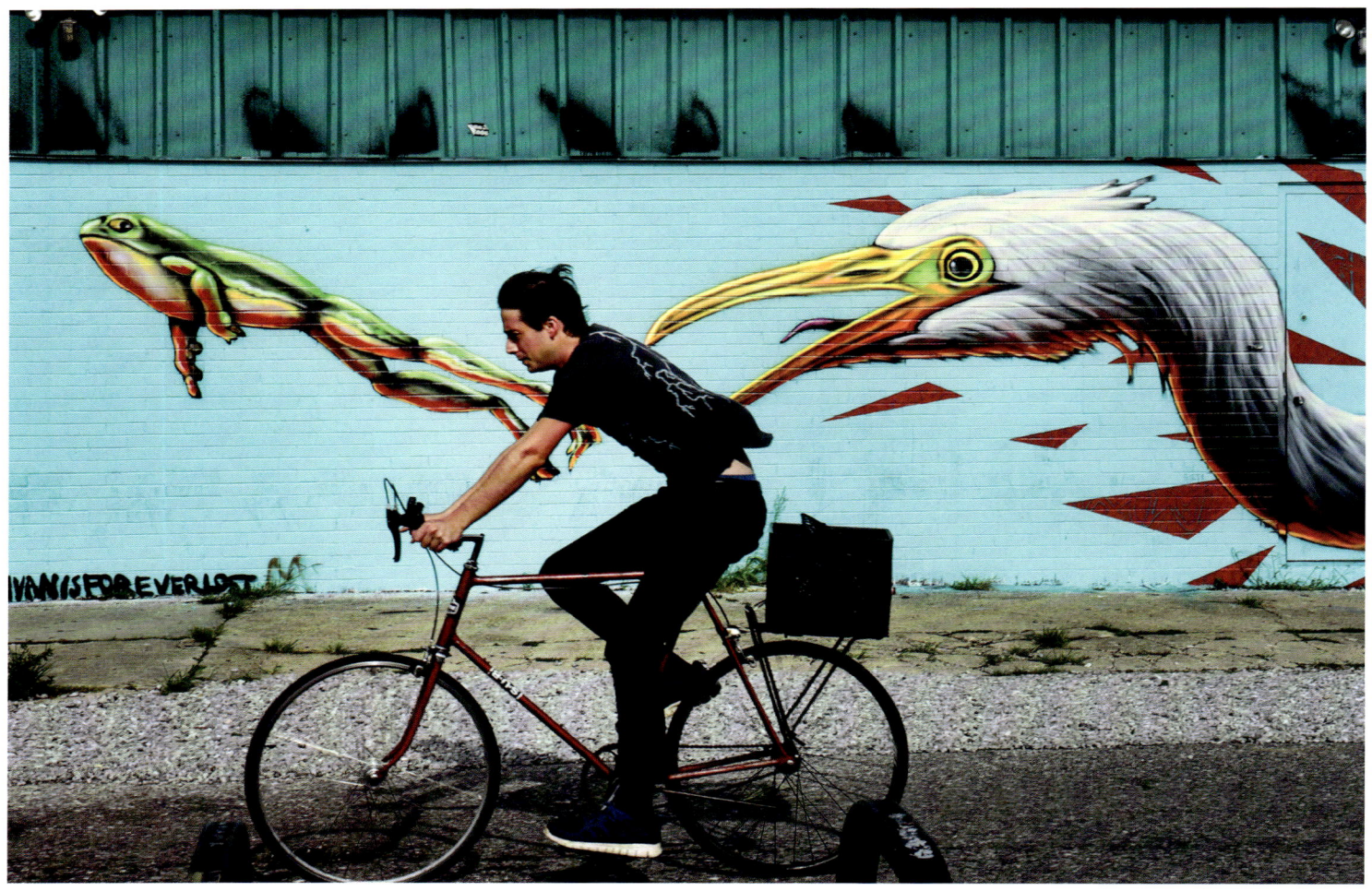

A man bikes by a mural created by international street artist Ivan Roque near St. Claude Avenue, 2017. Roque's work features concepts of birth, death, time, renewal, and social dynamics.

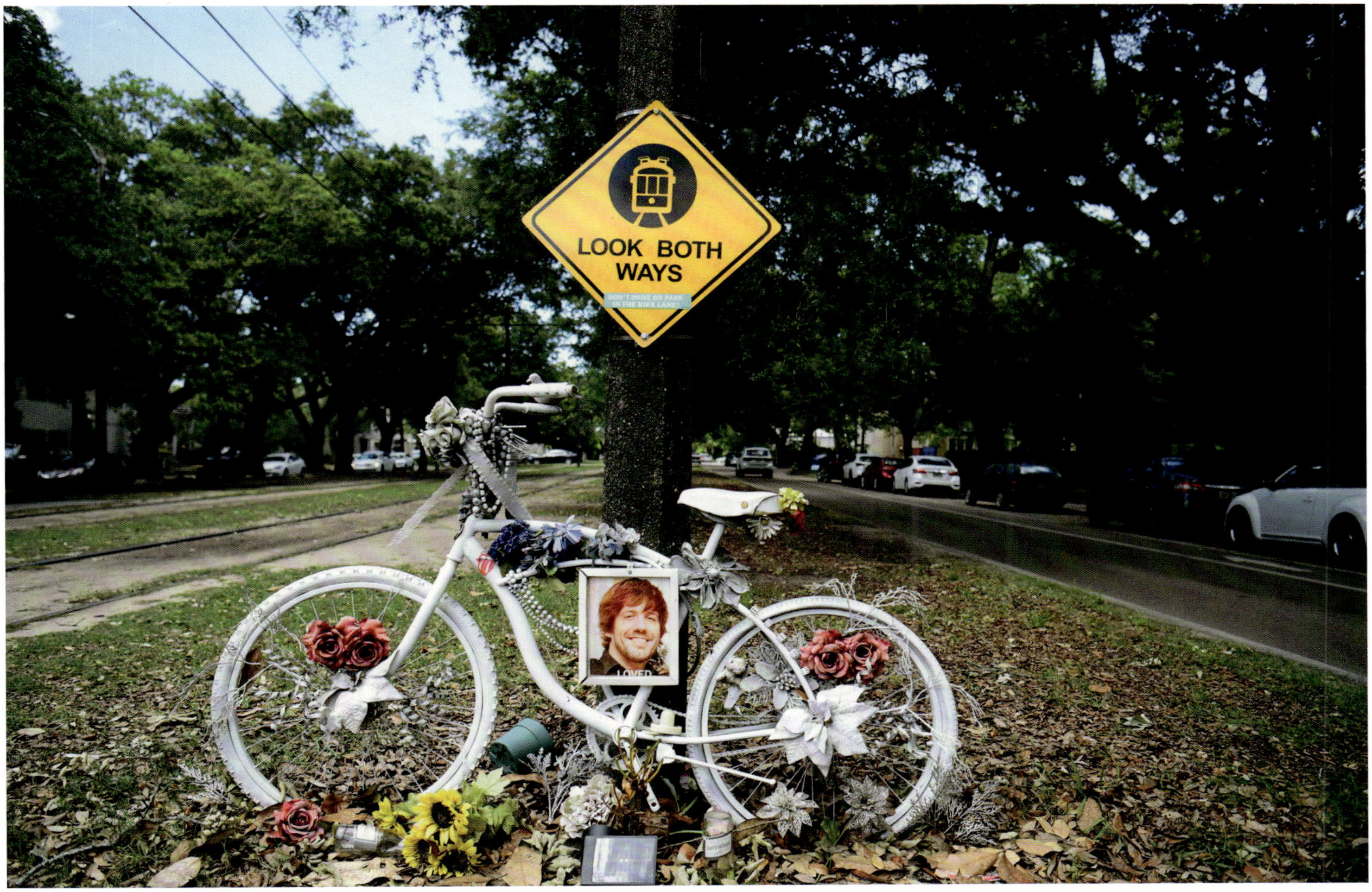

A Ghost Bike memorial for cyclist Frank Fisher, who was hit by a garbage truck in 2019, was erected on S. Carrollton Avenue's streetcar line. Ghost Bikes first appeared in New Orleans around 2015 to serve as roadside memorials for bicyclists killed or injured by a motor vehicle; they were also intended to remind drivers to share the road.

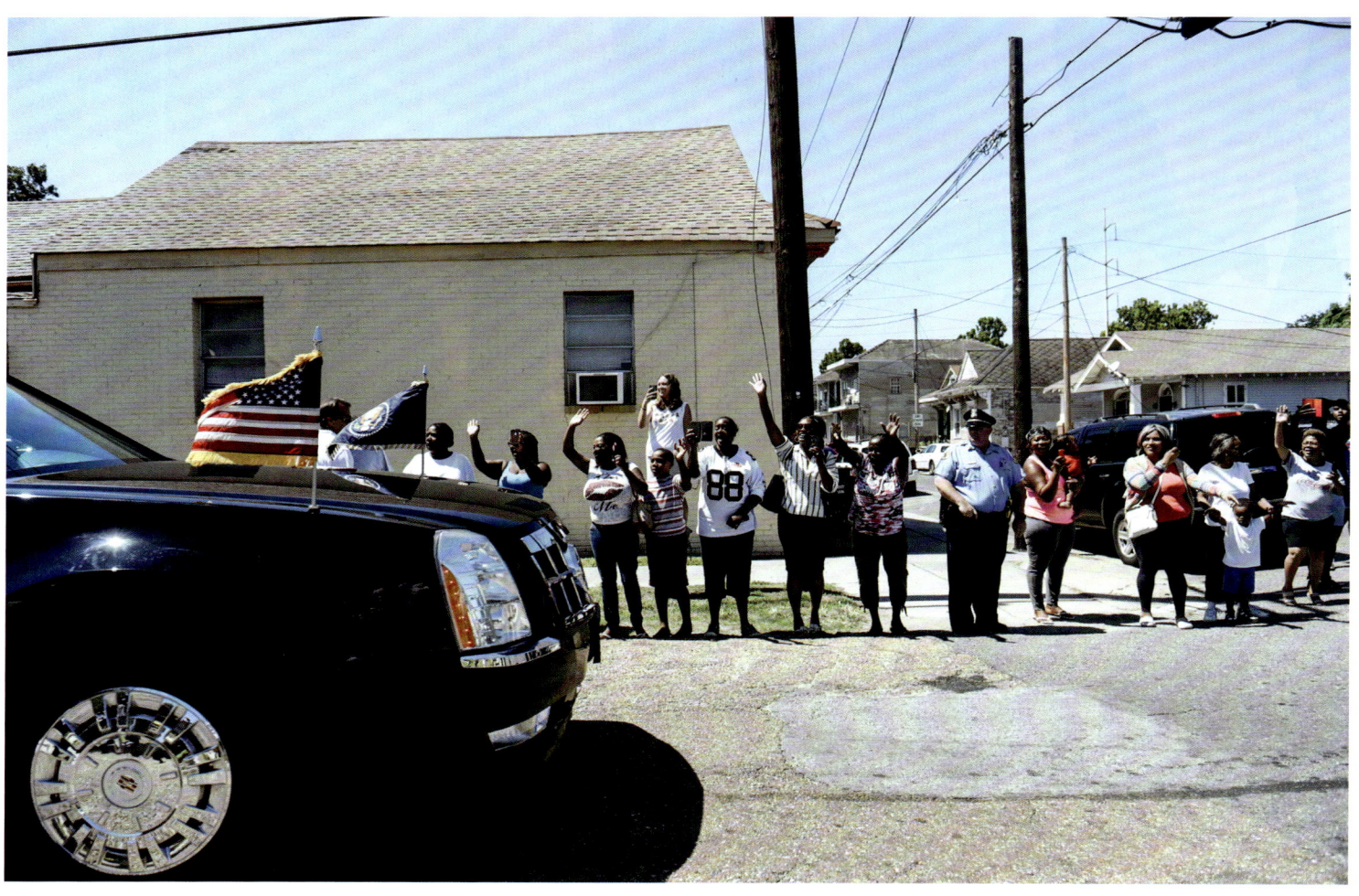

Residents wave to President Barack Obama as his motorcade rolls through Tremé
after lunch at Dooky Chase's during his visit to commemorate the tenth anniversary of
Hurricane Katrina, 2015.

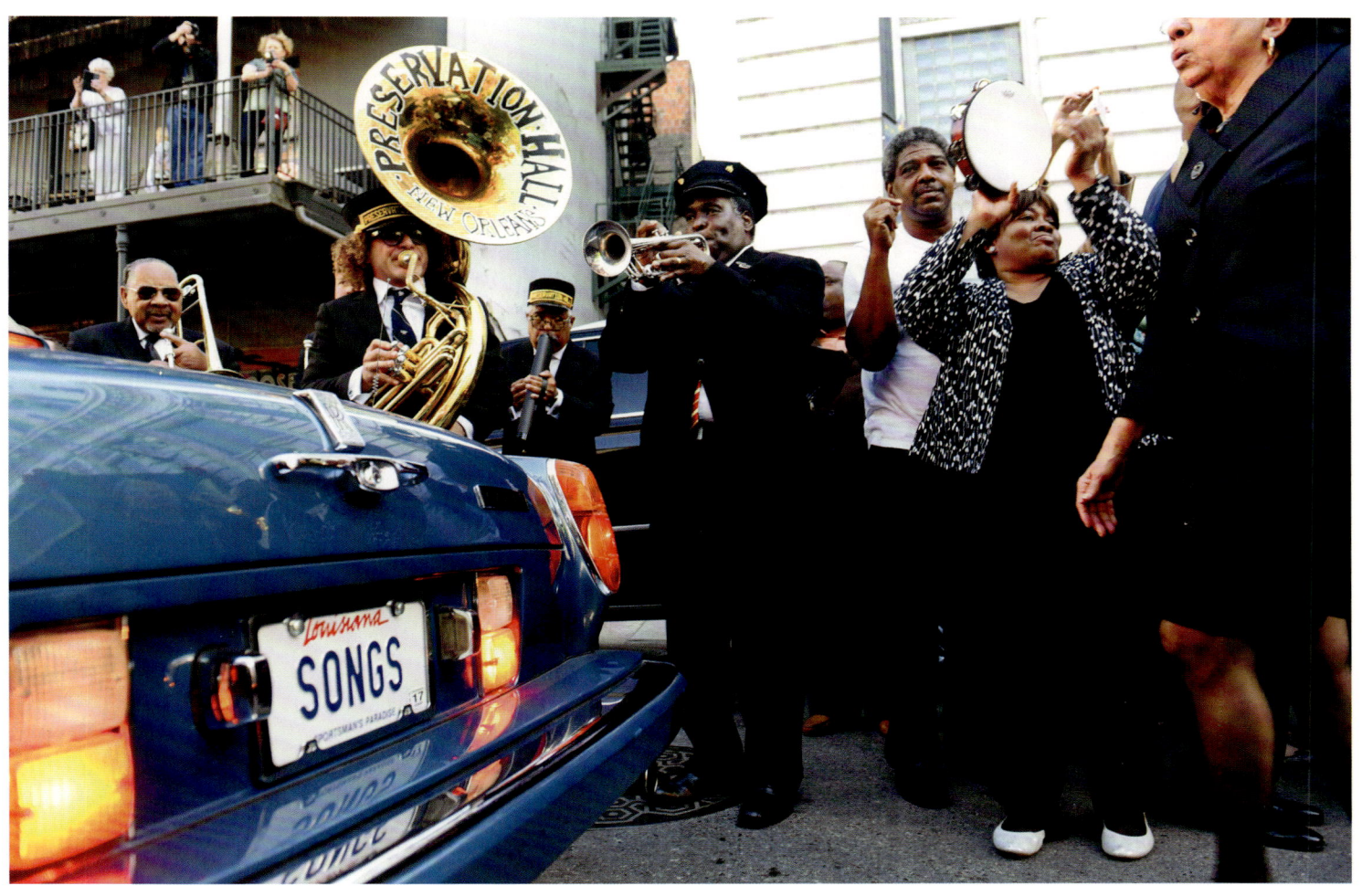

Songwriter Allen Toussaint's famed Rolls Royce, with a personalized license plate, leads his funeral procession from the Orpheum Theater, 2015.

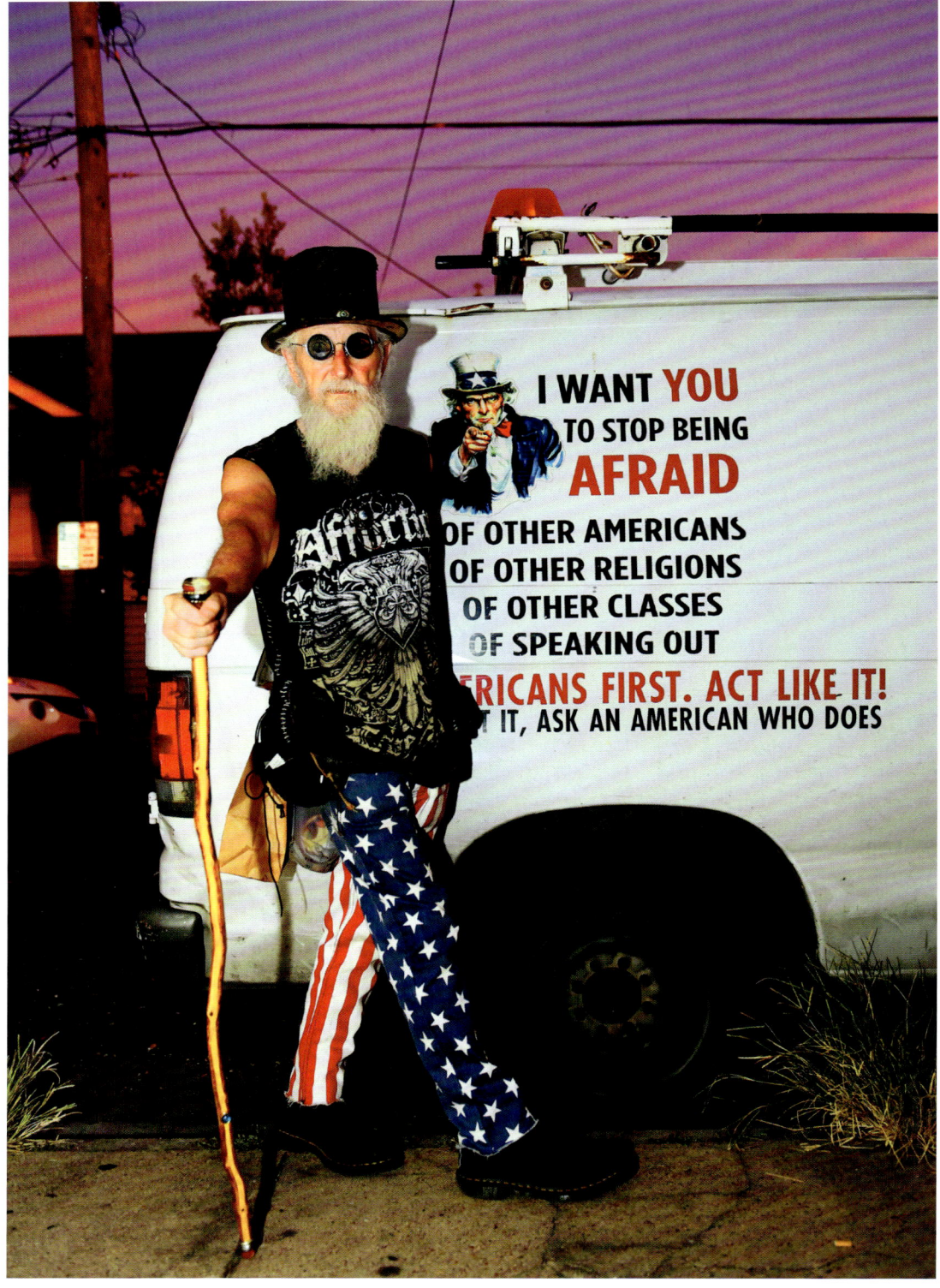

Amzie Adams poses next to a van with a patriotic message seen in the Faubourg Marigny, 2017. Born in 1944, Adams is a popular New Orleans multimedia artist who claims to have arrived in the city in the early 1970s as a "hippie"; at that time, he was frequently harassed by police. He now sells paintings for thousands of dollars and is featured in a mural on Frenchmen Street where he is a recognizable character.

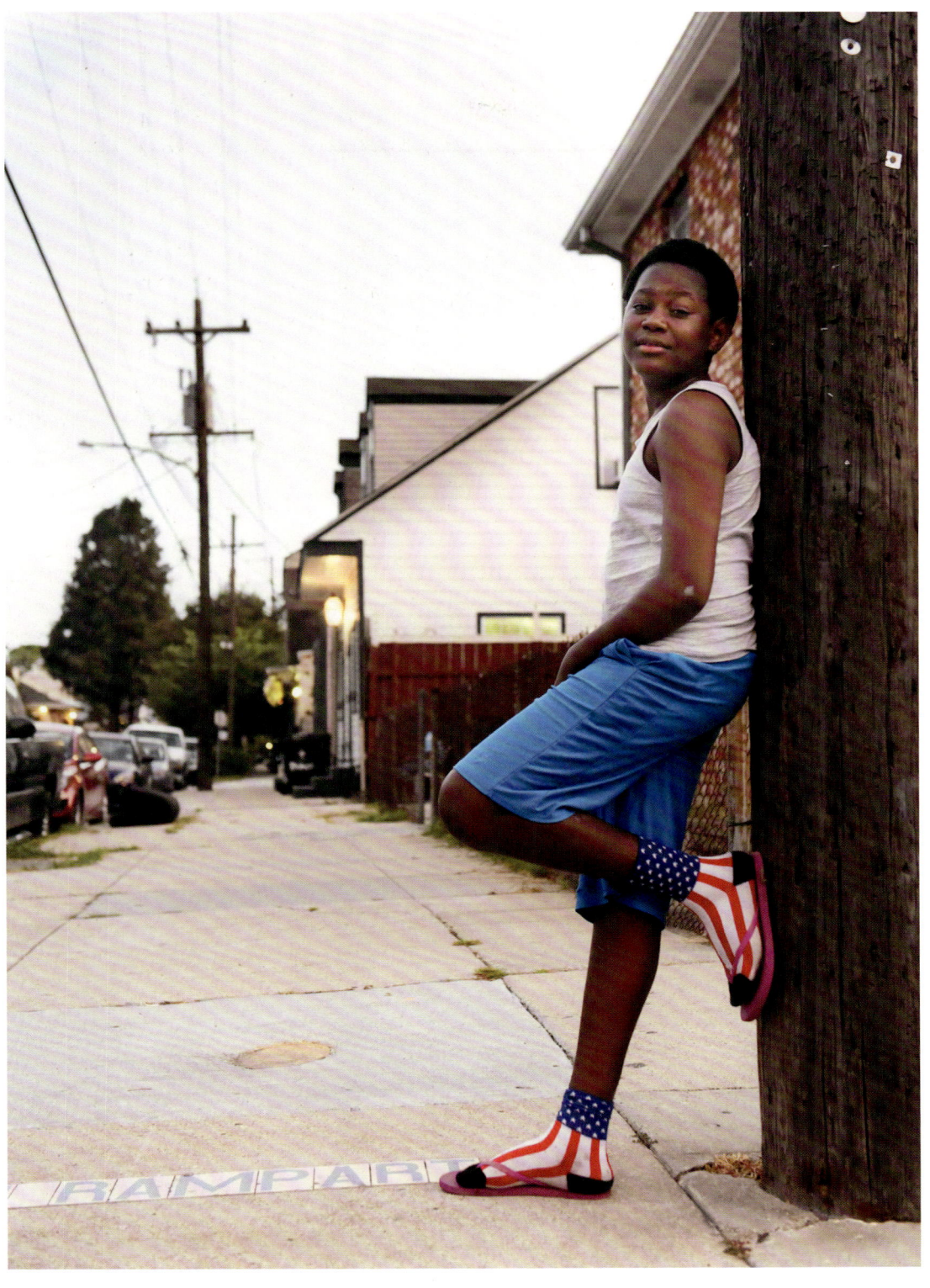

Daniel wears his American flag–decorated socks during his first month in New Orleans after emigrating from Honduras, 2015.

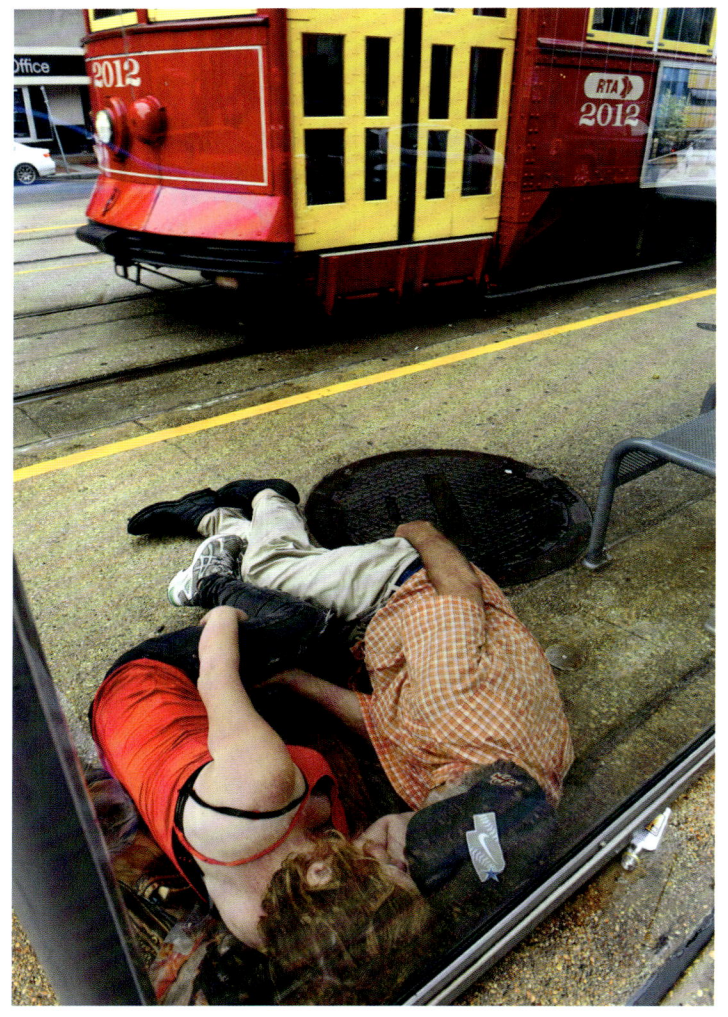

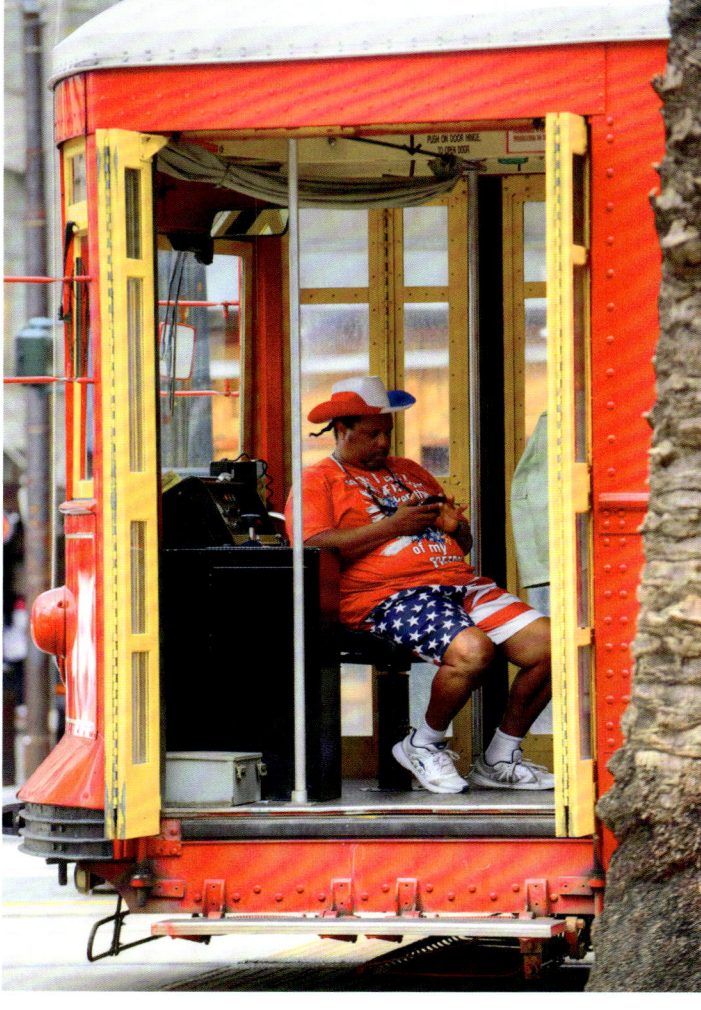

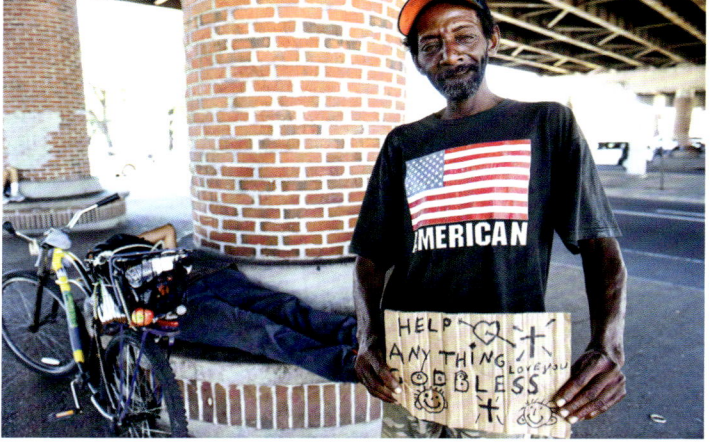

above left A couple sleeps on Canal Street as a streetcar passes, 2019.

above right A man is dressed in the colors of an American flag on a Canal Street streetcar, 2017.

left A man on N. Claiborne Avenue holds up a sign asking for help, 2015.

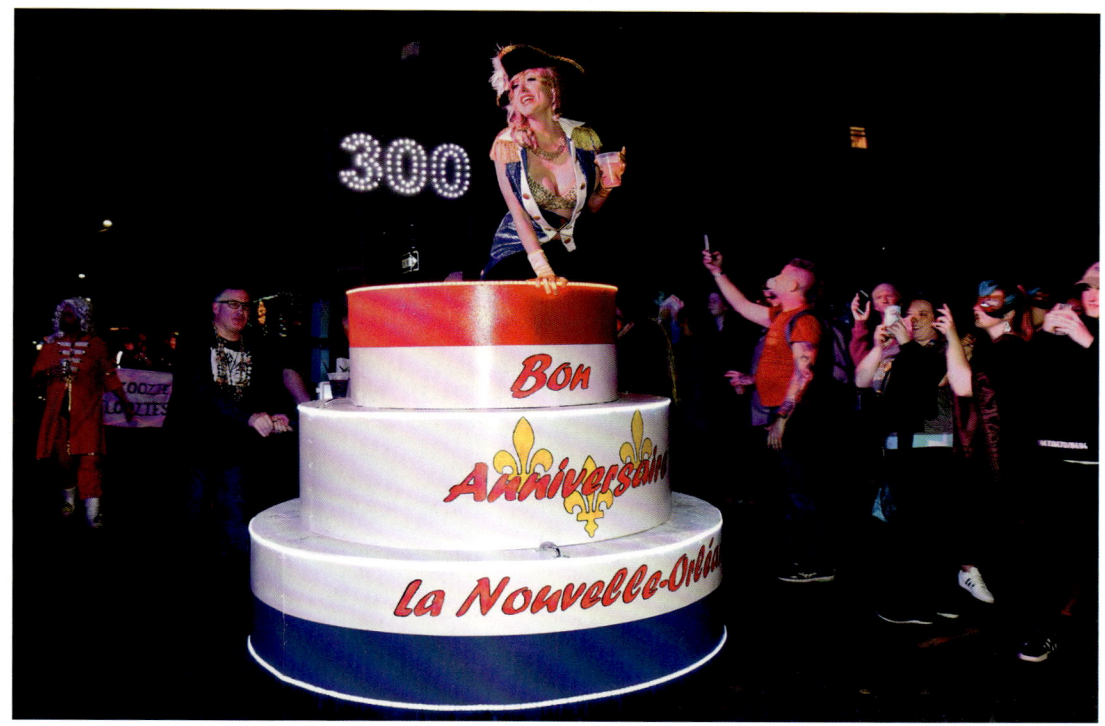

Burlesque artist and businesswoman Trixie Minx, born Alexis Graber, pops out of a cake celebrating the city's tricentennial during the Krewe du Vieux parade, 2018.

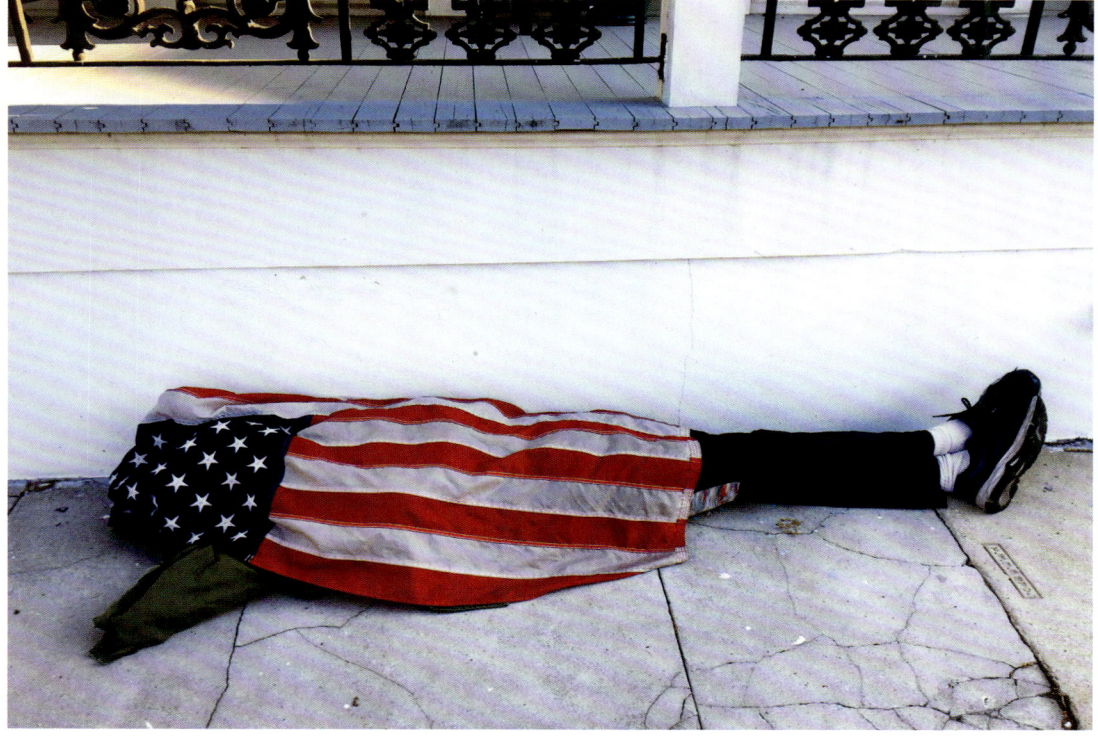

Covered in the American flag, a man sleeps on the sidewalk in the Faubourg Marigny, 2019.

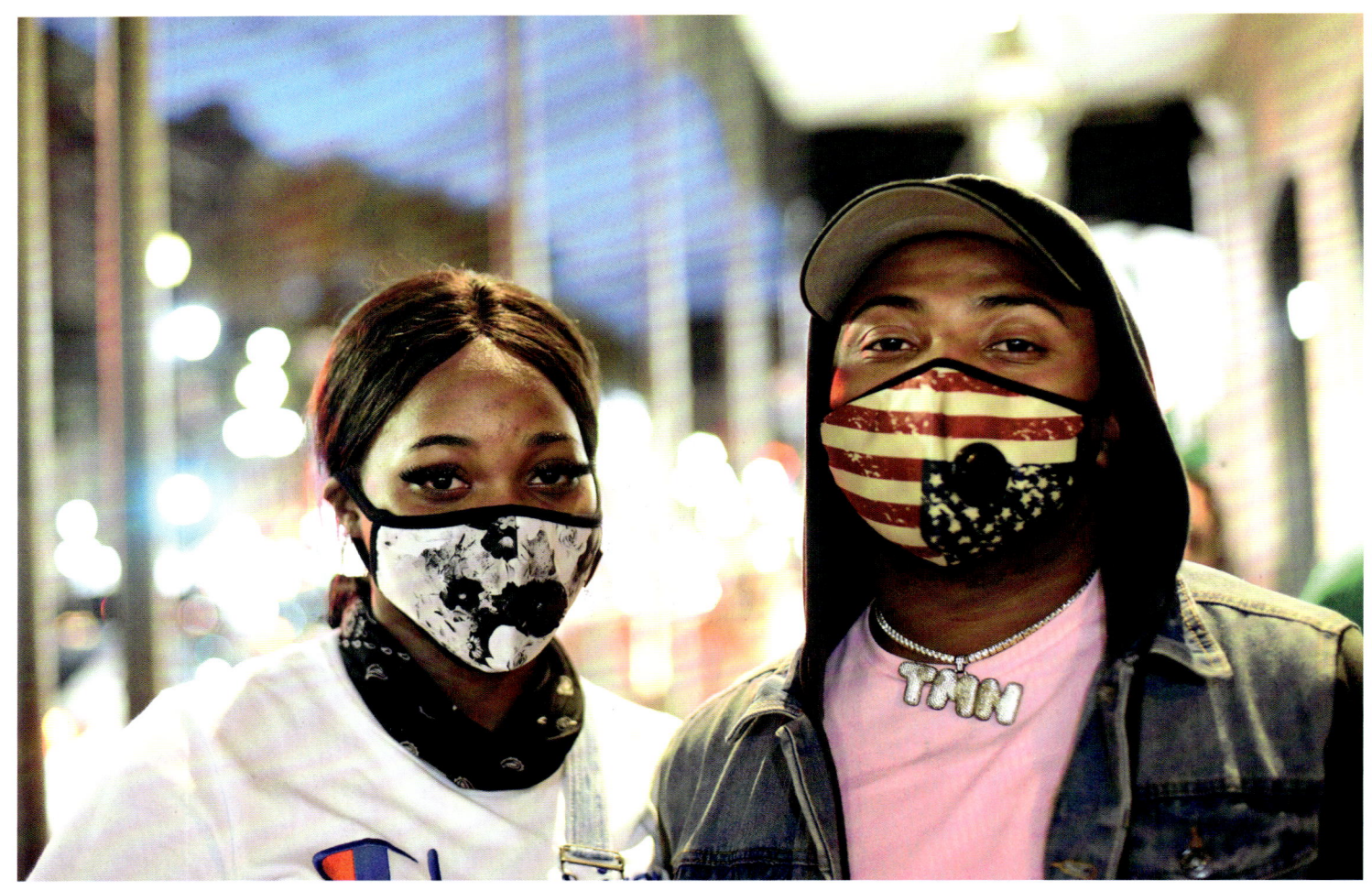

A couple on Canal Street dons masks during the COVID pandemic, 2020. According to the U.S. Flag Code, displaying the American flag upside down is only meant "as a signal of dire distress in instances of extreme danger to life or property." But lately, hanging the flag upside down is increasingly a symbol used by those on both sides of the political aisle.

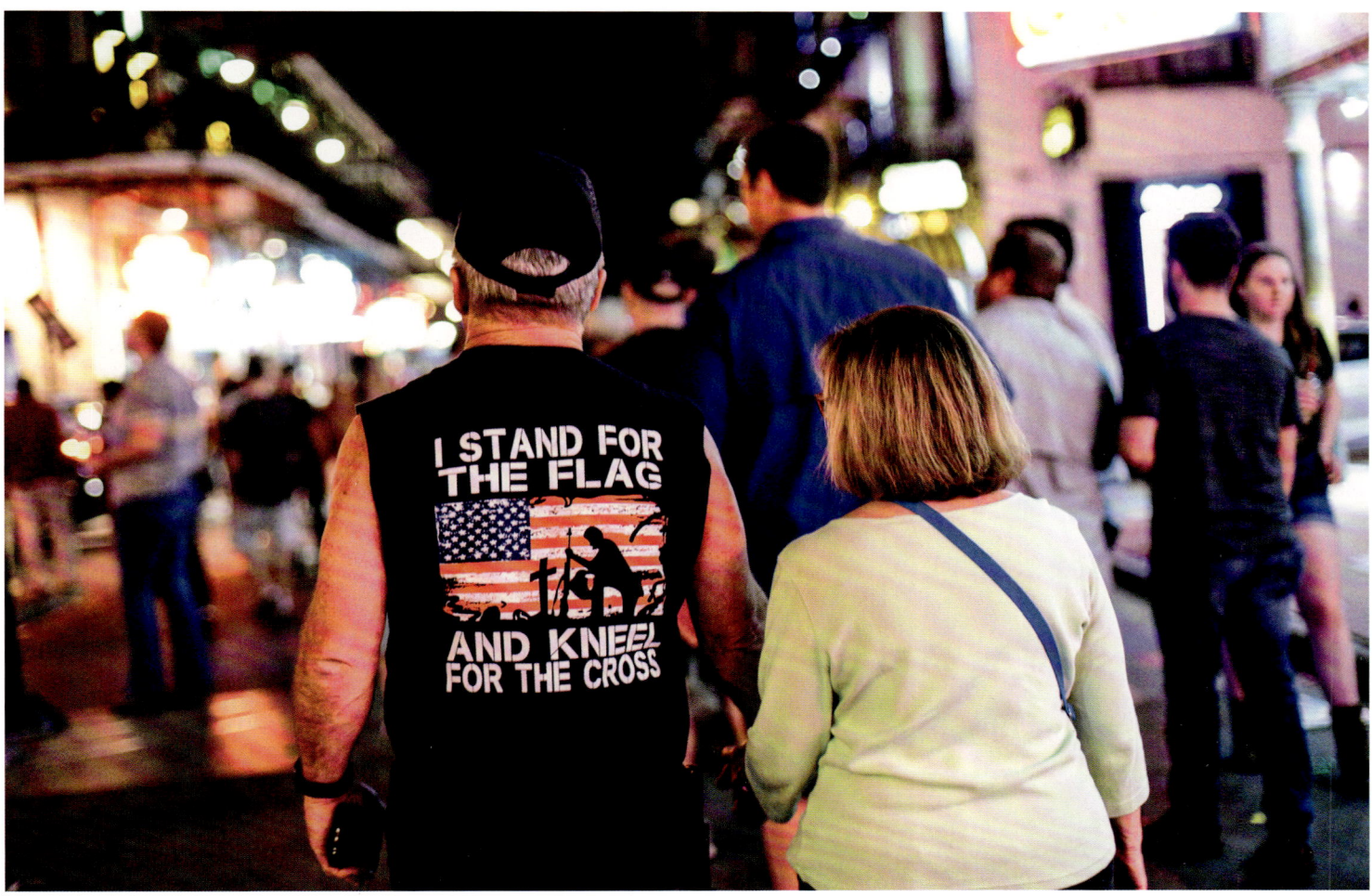

A couple walks on Bourbon Street, just hours before the pandemic lockdown in early 2020. The message on the man's T-shirt, "I Stand for the Flag and Kneel for the Cross," refers to the controversy sparked when NFL football player Colin Kaepernick kneeled in protest over police brutality against people of color; this action outraged many conservatives, who saw it as disrespect for the flag.

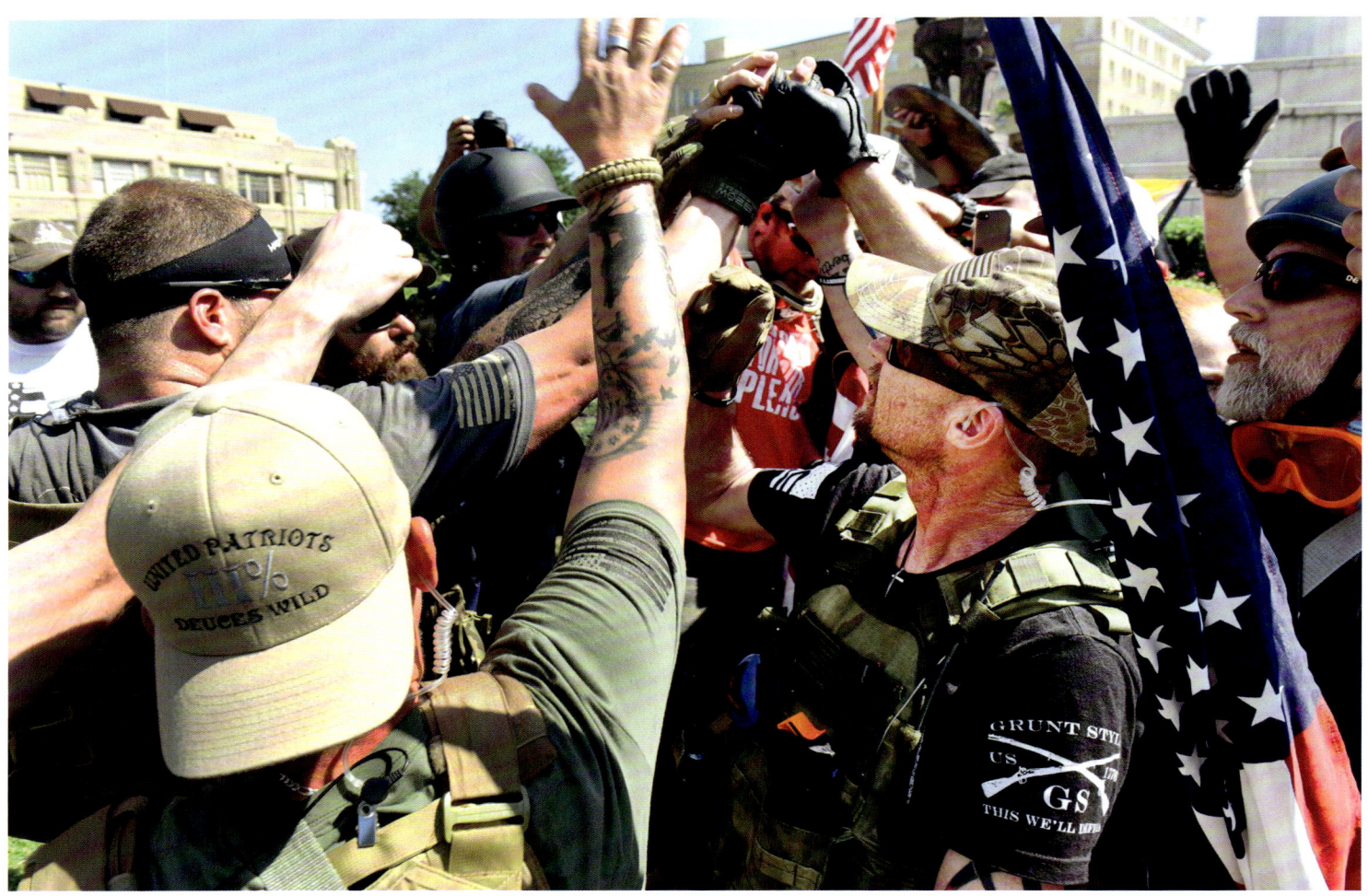

White supremacist groups unite at the foot of the Robert E. Lee monument, before it was removed in 2017. Groups such as the Ku Klux Klan and the Three Percenters descended on New Orleans when the city planned to remove four Confederate monuments, including the one of Robert E. Lee.

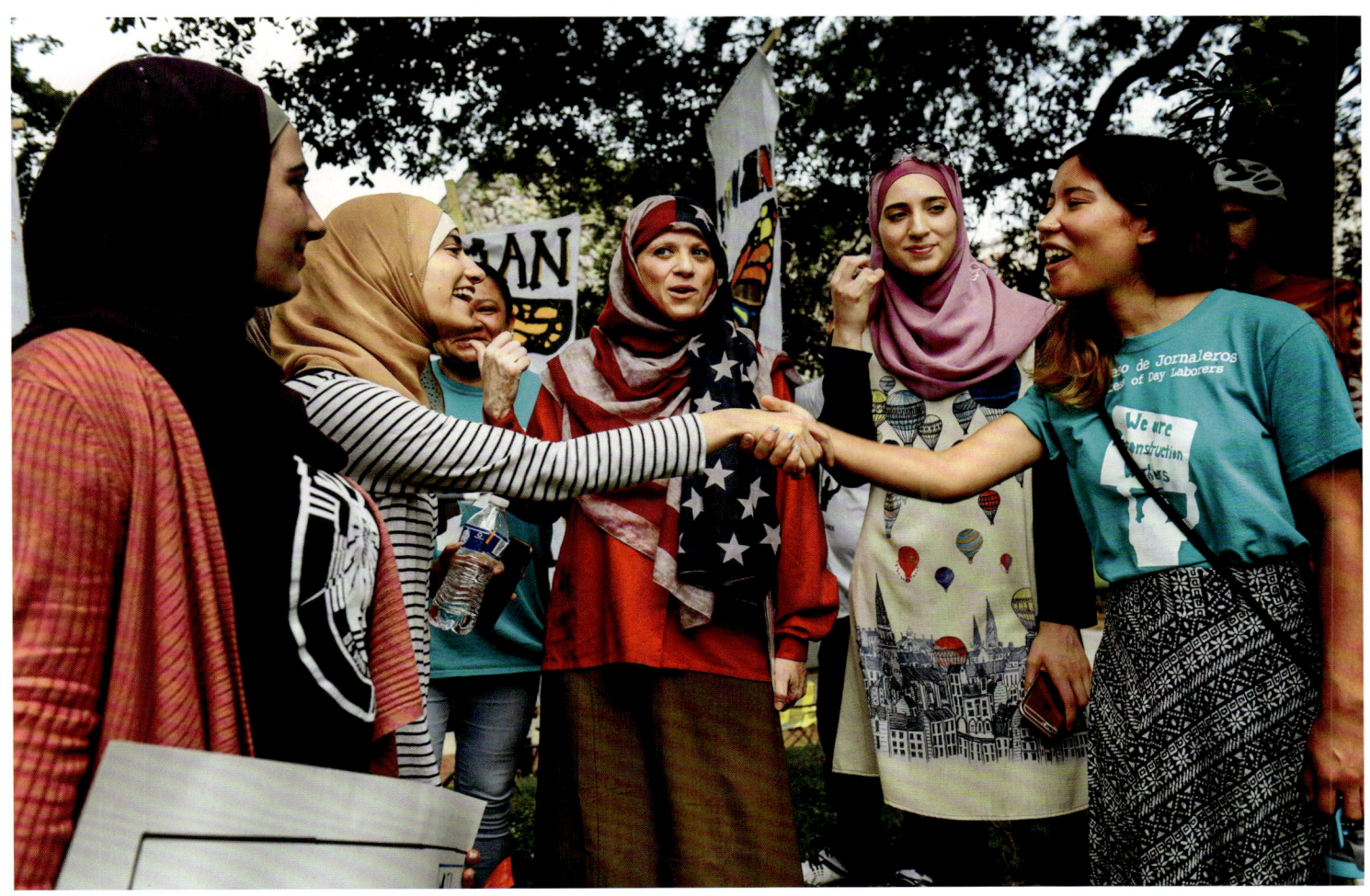

Muslim American activists unite with Hispanic American advocates during a protest of the Muslim travel ban implemented by executive order by then-president Donald Trump, 2017.

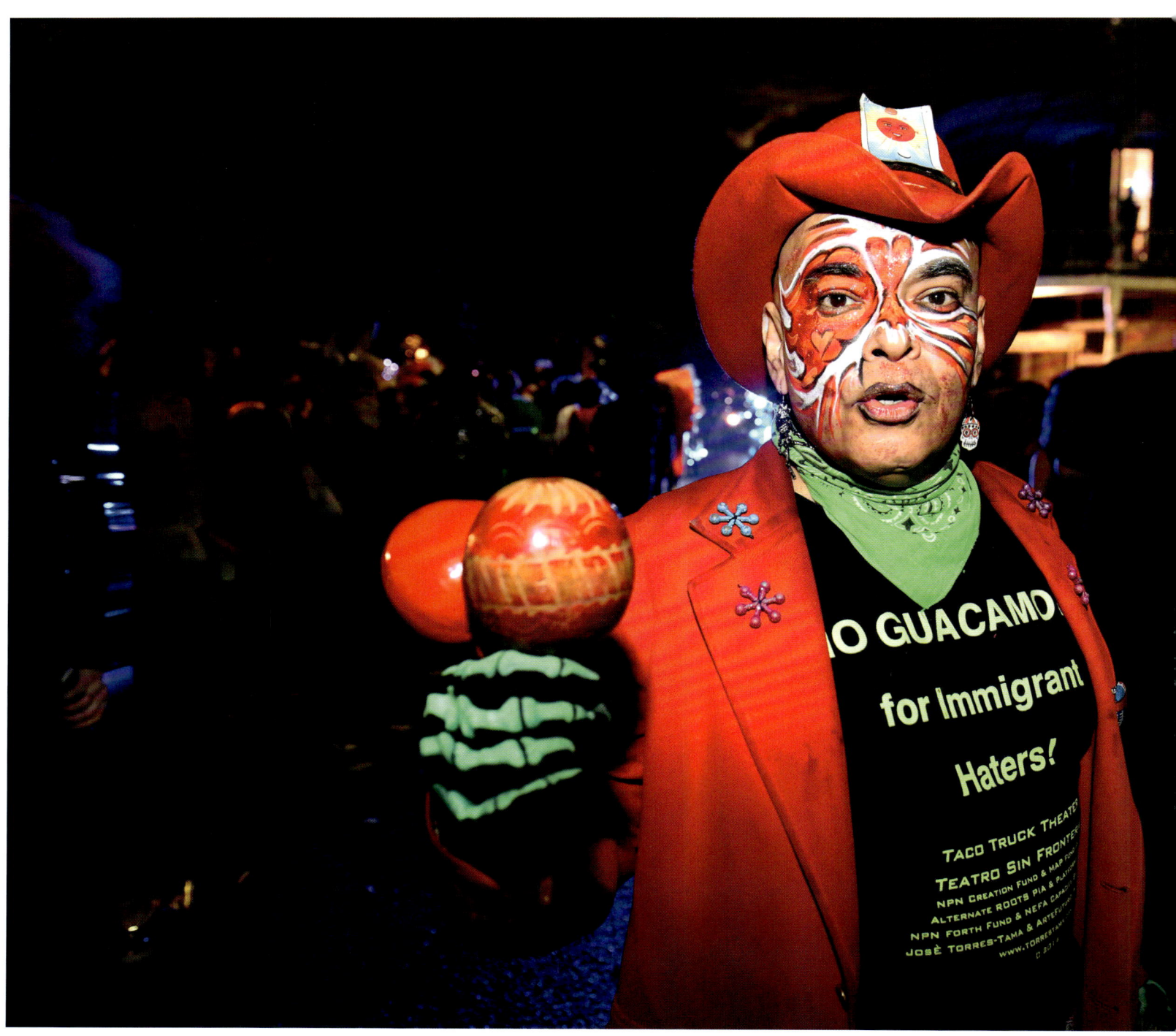

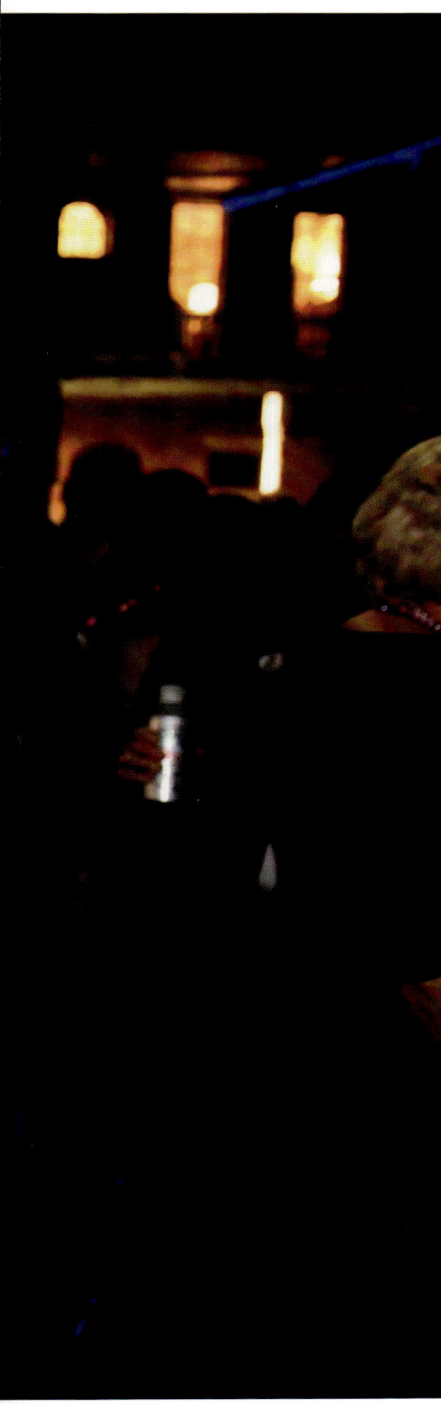

Journalist and performance and visual artist José Torres-Tama, who is dedicated to securing social justice for immigrants, wears his signature T-shirt "No Guacamole for Immigrant Haters!" during the Krewe du Vieux parade, 2017. Torres-Tama refers to himself as a "mestizo" of Quechua Indigenous heritage, and has lived in New Orleans for more than three decades, documenting the contributions of immigrants, particularly in the rebuilding after Hurricane Katrina.

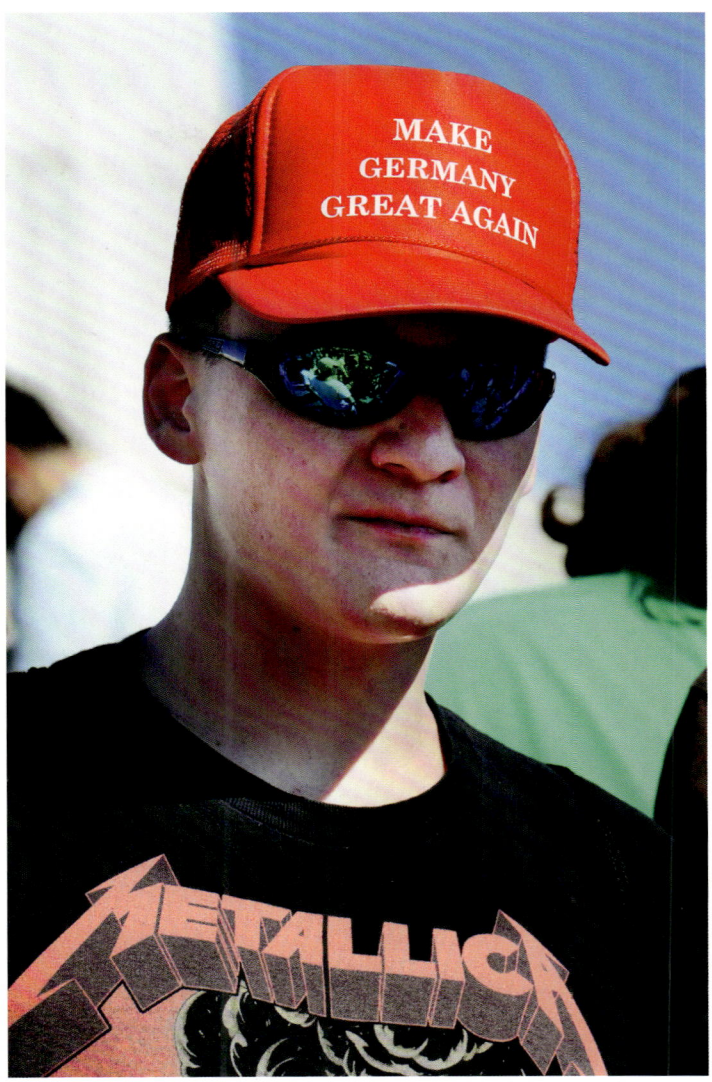

A white supremacist is seen at a protest against removing the Robert E. Lee monument at Lee Circle, 2017.

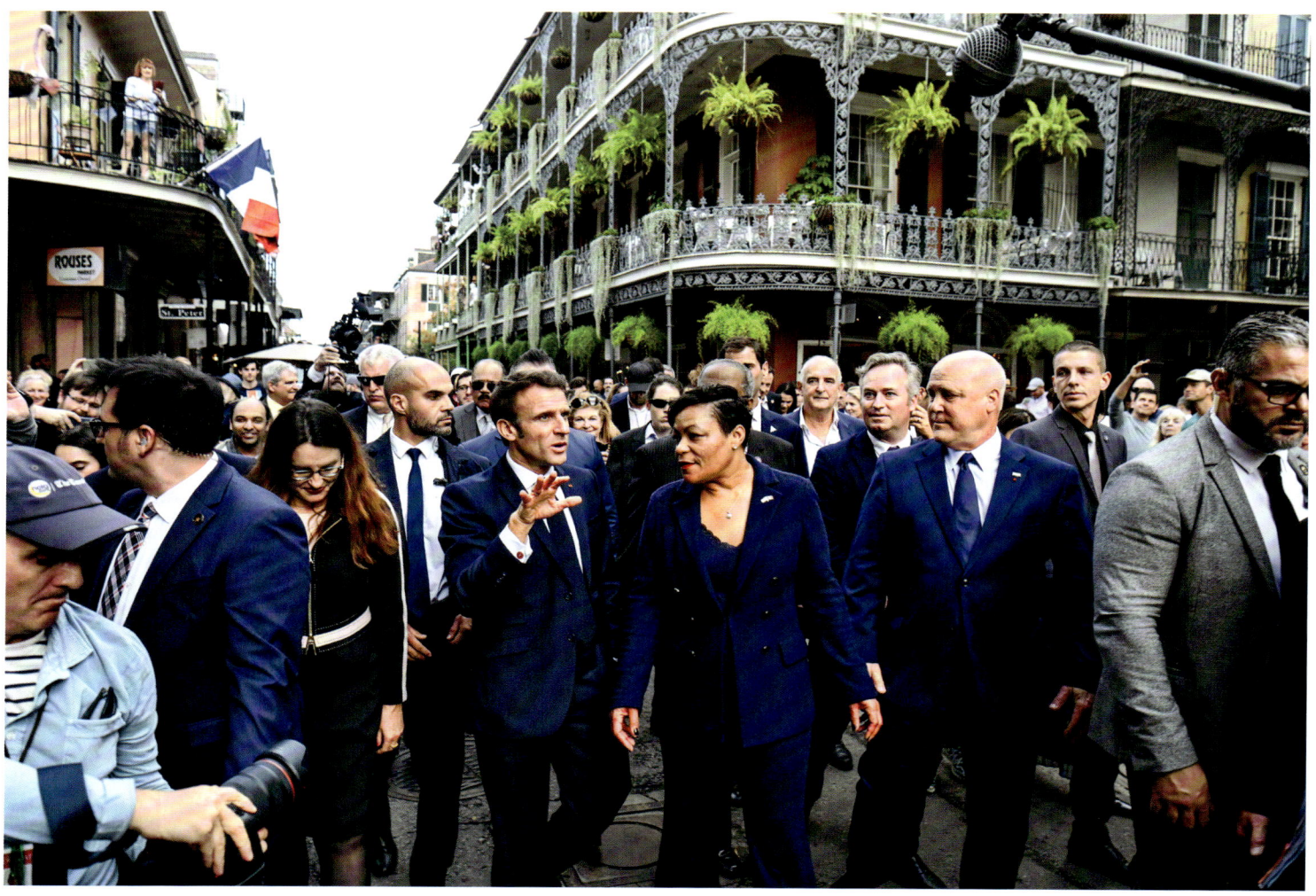

Francophiles and fans welcome French president Emmanuel Macron, seen here with New Orleans mayor LaToya Cantrell and former mayor Mitch Landrieu as they walk down Royal Street in the French Quarter during the leader's historic visit, December 2022. Macron was the first French president to visit the former French colony since Valèry Giscard d'Estaing, who came to New Orleans in 1976. Before that, President Charles de Gaulle visited in 1960.

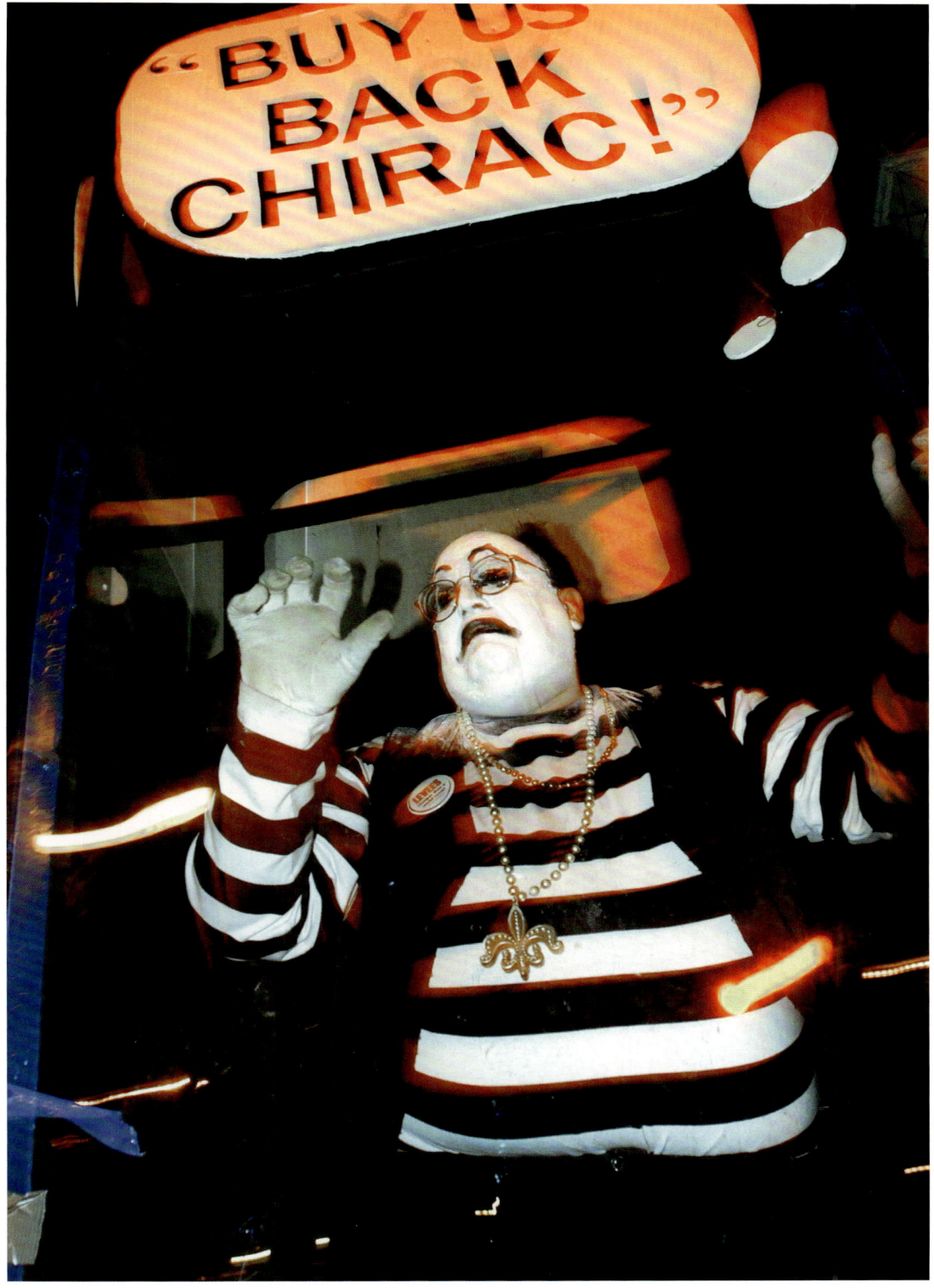

Ashley Morris channels Marcel Marceau, the French mime, in a plexiglass box float titled "Buy Us Back, Chirac!"—a humorous plea to then French president Jacques Chirac in the Krewe du Vieux parade, 2006. This parade was held just months after Hurricane Katrina devastated New Orleans. From 1953 to 1955 Chirac lived in New Orleans, where he worked as a cabbie and wrote his thesis on the Port of New Orleans. Morris, a popular blogger during the aftermath of Katrina, passed away in 2008.

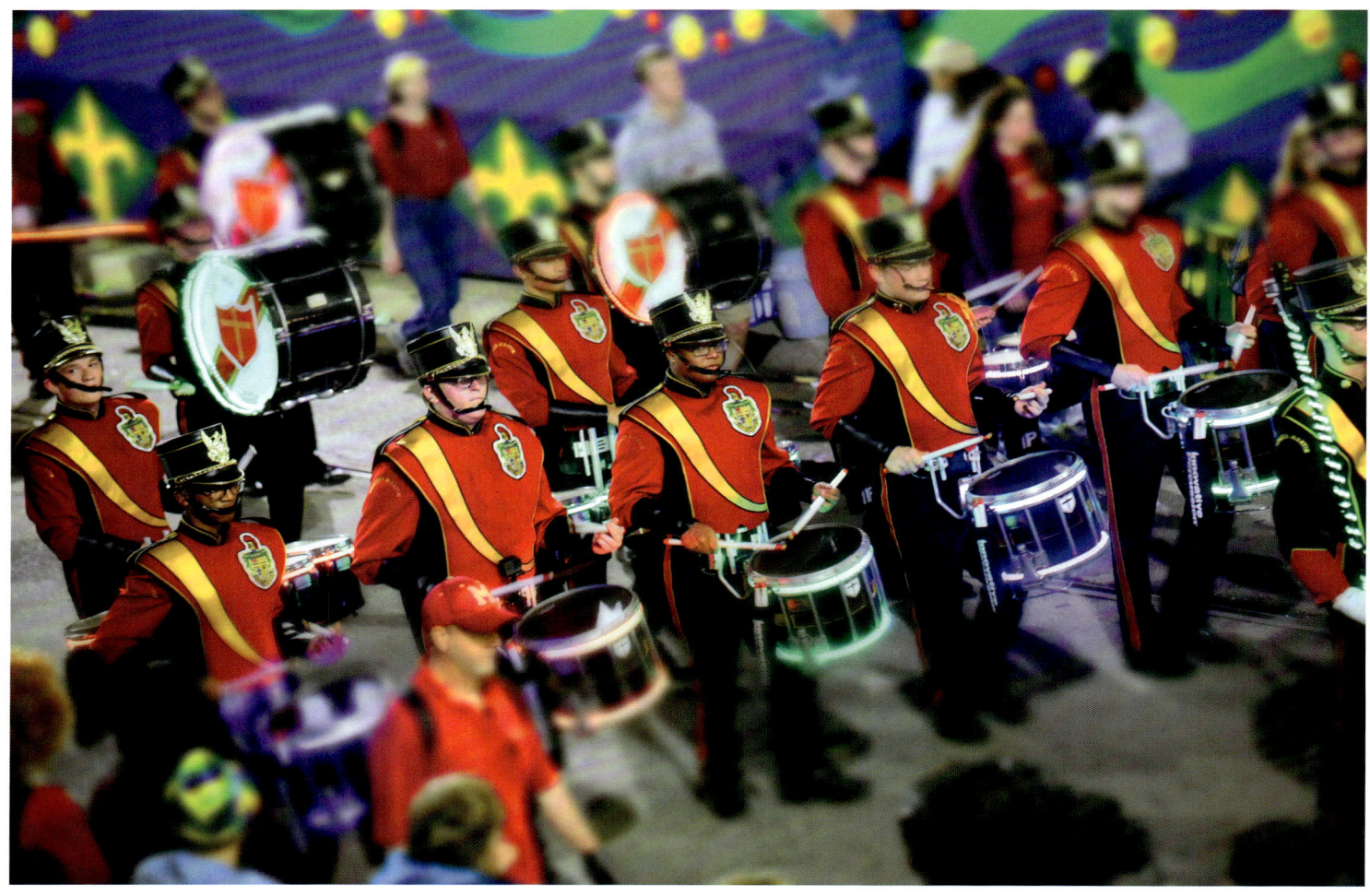

Brother Martin High School's Crusader Marching Band lights up their drums with LED lights during the Krewe d'Etat's night parade, 2019. The all-boys Catholic school's military-style band is known for its drumming excellence. In addition to performing in the Endymion and Krewe d'Etat parades, the band has performed for Pope John Paul II, for President Gerald Ford, for the Republican National Convention, in Disneyland, at the 1984 World's Fair, and at the Saints' first playoff game.

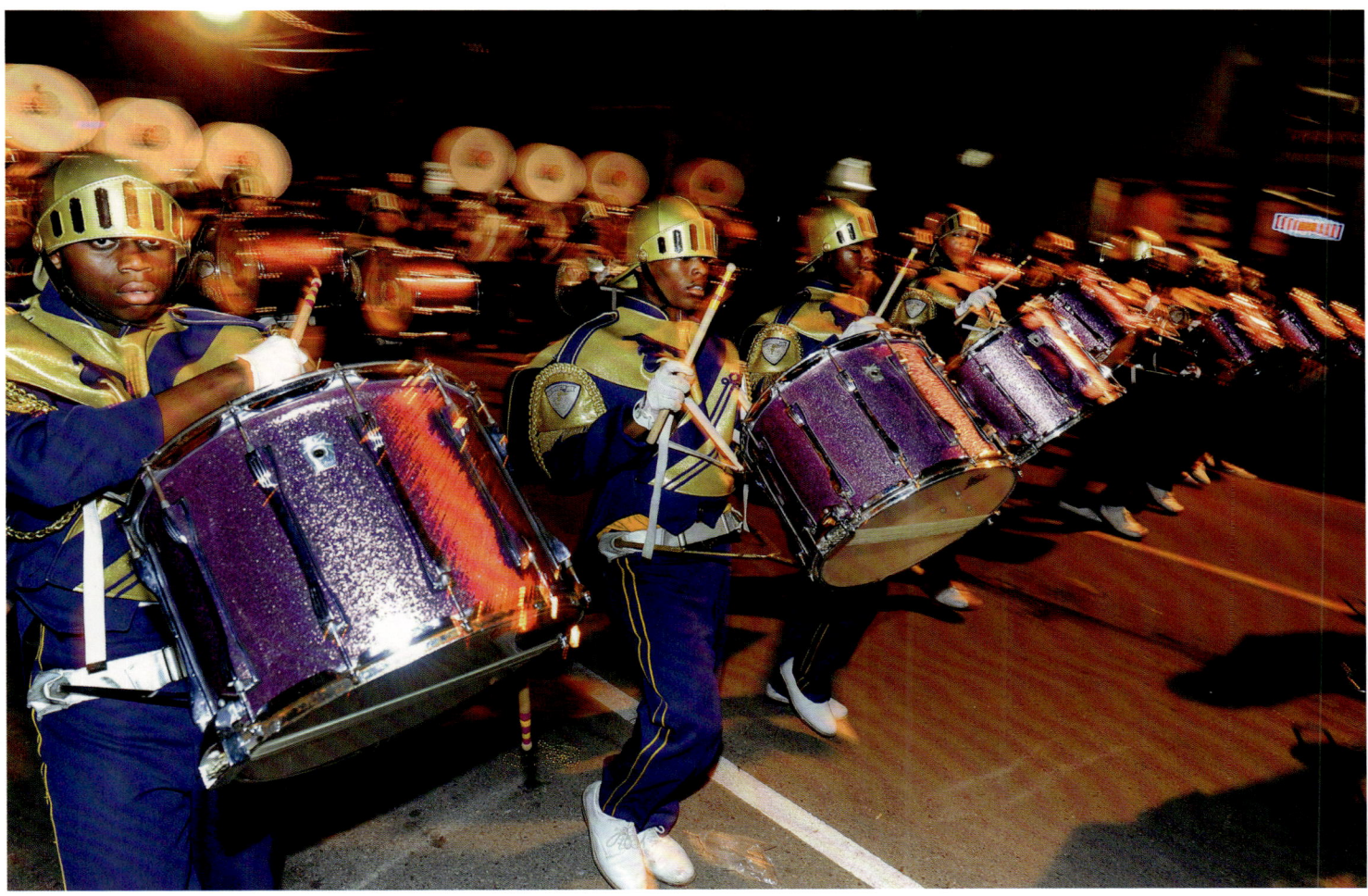

The famed St. Augustine Marching 100 marches during a night parade, 2014. The African American all-boys Catholic high school band has performed for Pope John Paul II, several U.S. presidents, five Super Bowls, and the Macy's Thanksgiving Day Parade. Most notably, the "best band in the land" is known for integrating Carnival when the Rex organization invited them to march in its parade on Mardi Gras Day 1967.

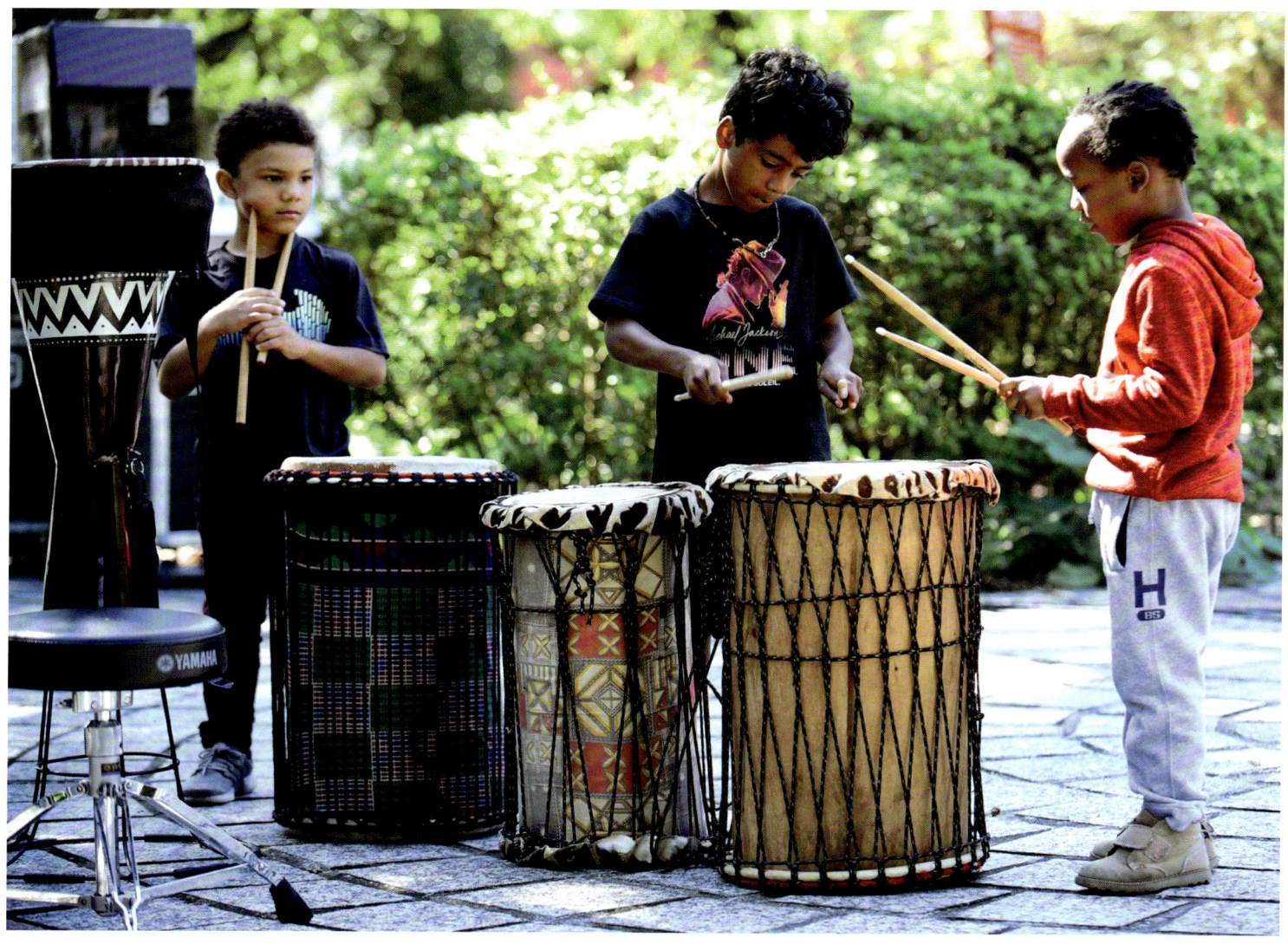

Kids participate in African drumming during the Blessing of the Drums in Congo Square, 2018. The tradition of Sunday afternoon gatherings with drum circles, singing, and dancing in historic Congo Square began when free and enslaved people of color gathered on Sundays, and continues today.

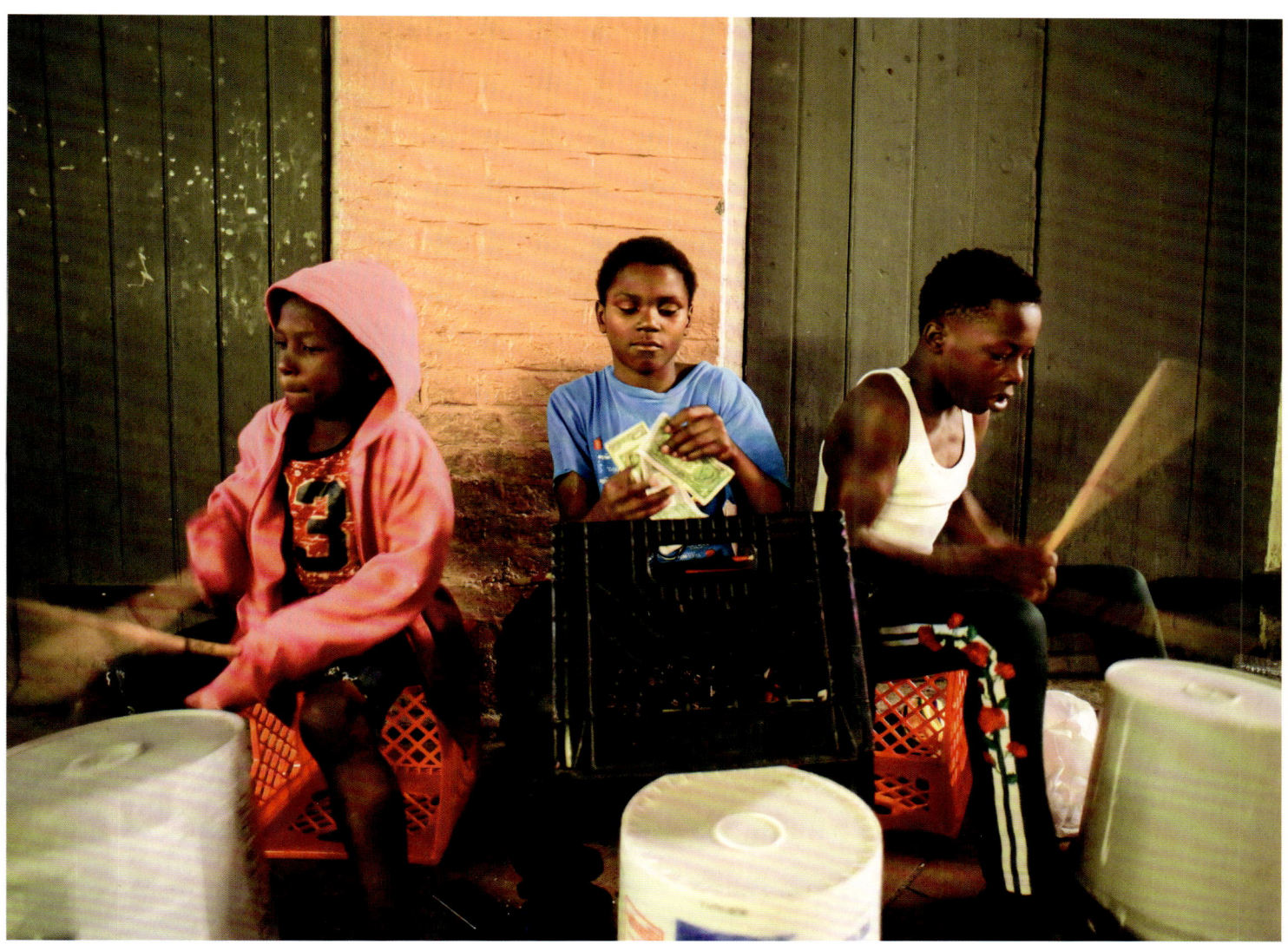

Bucket drummers perform on Bourbon Street, 2018. Though not unique to New Orleans, these young percussionists have exploded onto the scene, beating on plastic buckets for tips from tourists.

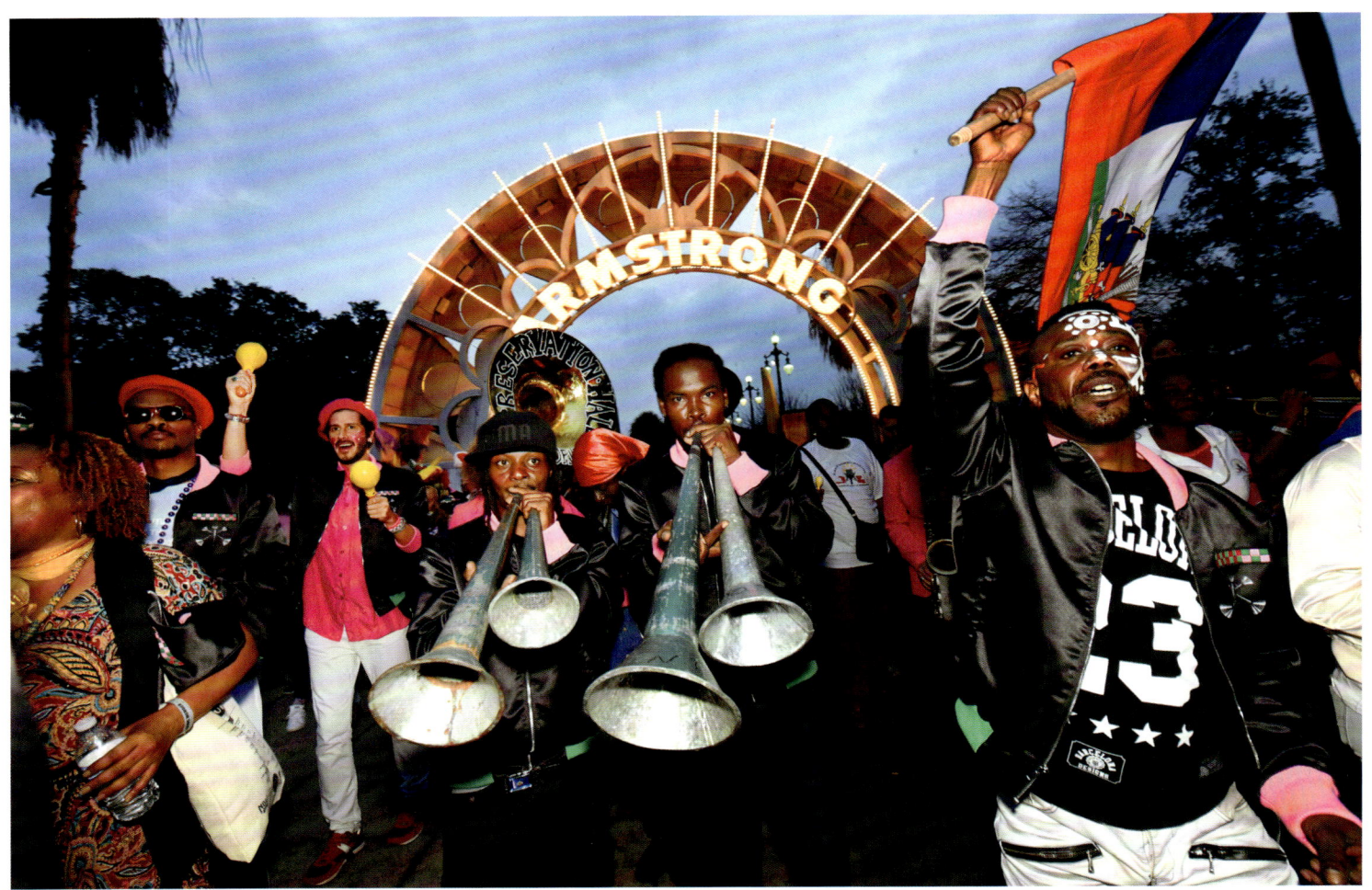

Haitian musicians join the Preservation Hall Jazz Band at Armstrong Park for the inaugural Krewe du Kanaval parade, 2018. Krewe du Kanaval was founded by Ben Jaffe, the creative director of Preservation Hall, and members of the Grammy Award–winning band Arcade Fire to celebrate cultural connections between Haiti and New Orleans.

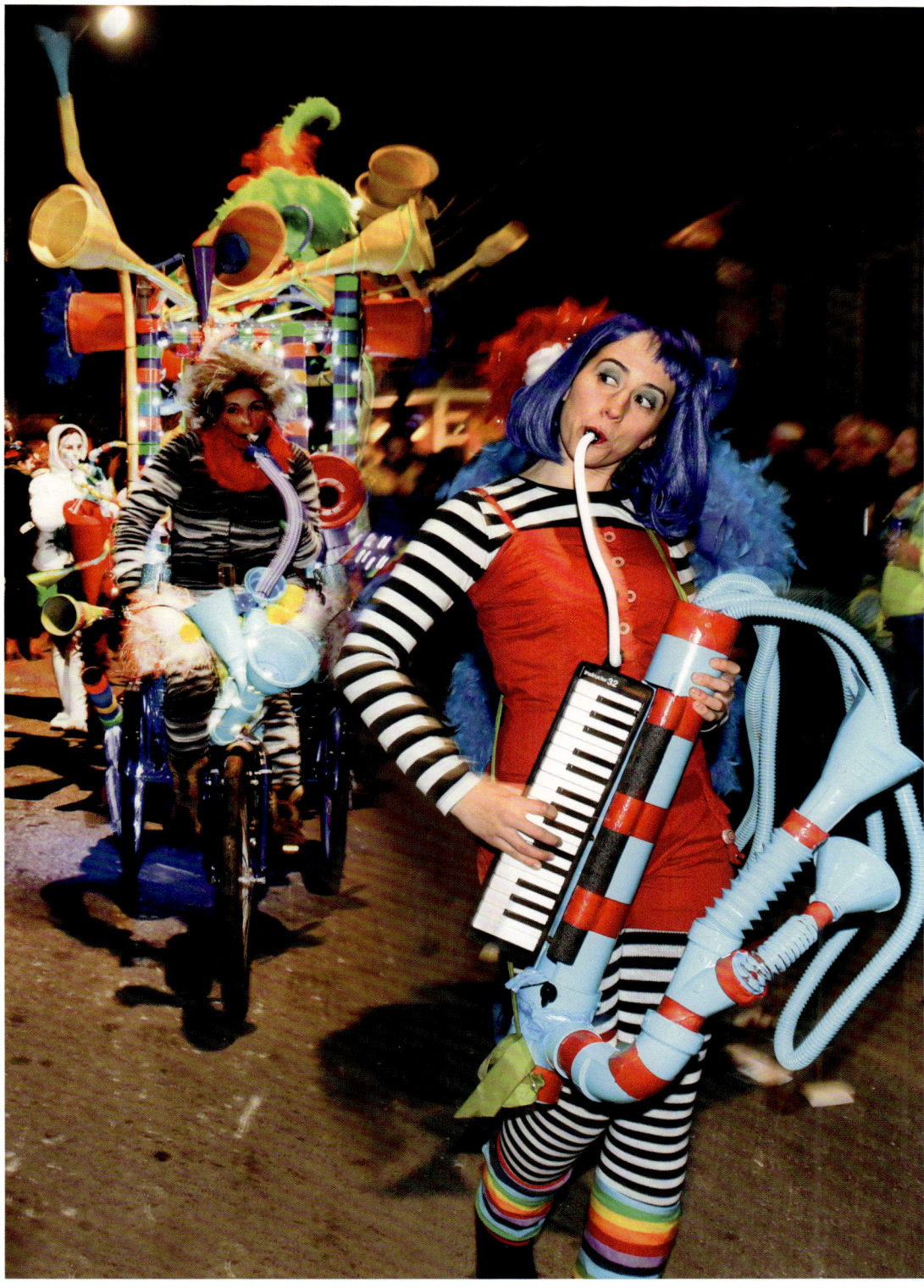

Members of Krewe de Seuss blow their home-made horns in the krewe*delusion* parade, 2016. Krewe de Seuss, founded in 2013 and "created by locals with a penchant for partying and ridiculousness," is inspired by the whimsical and impossible musical instruments imagined in the Dr. Seuss books.

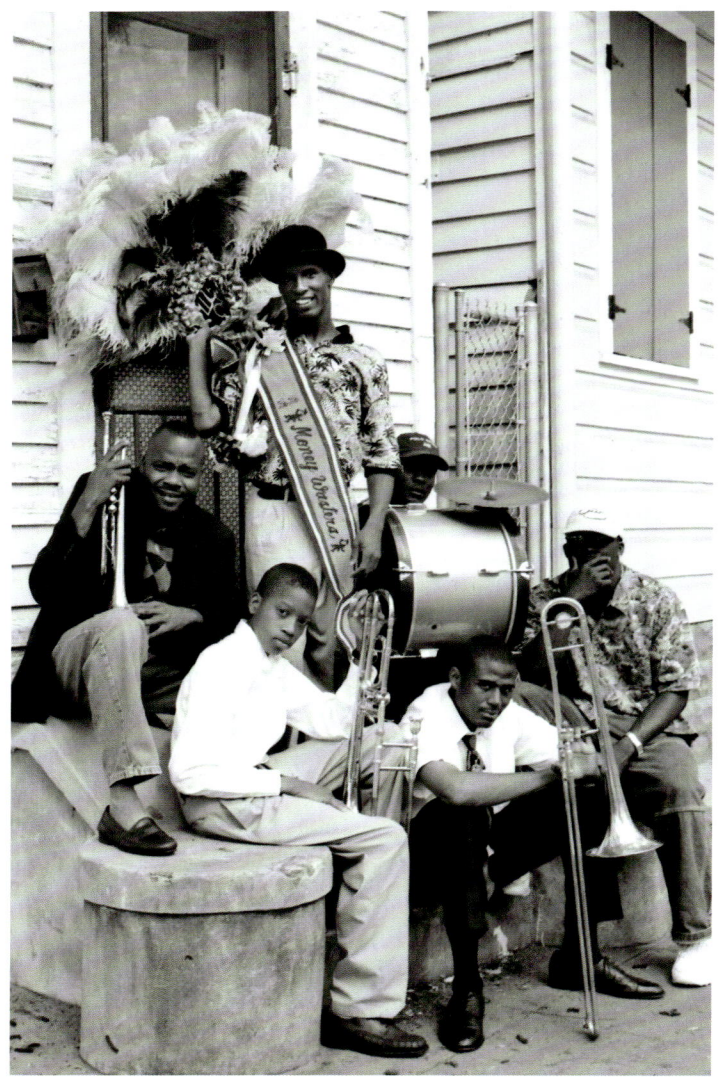

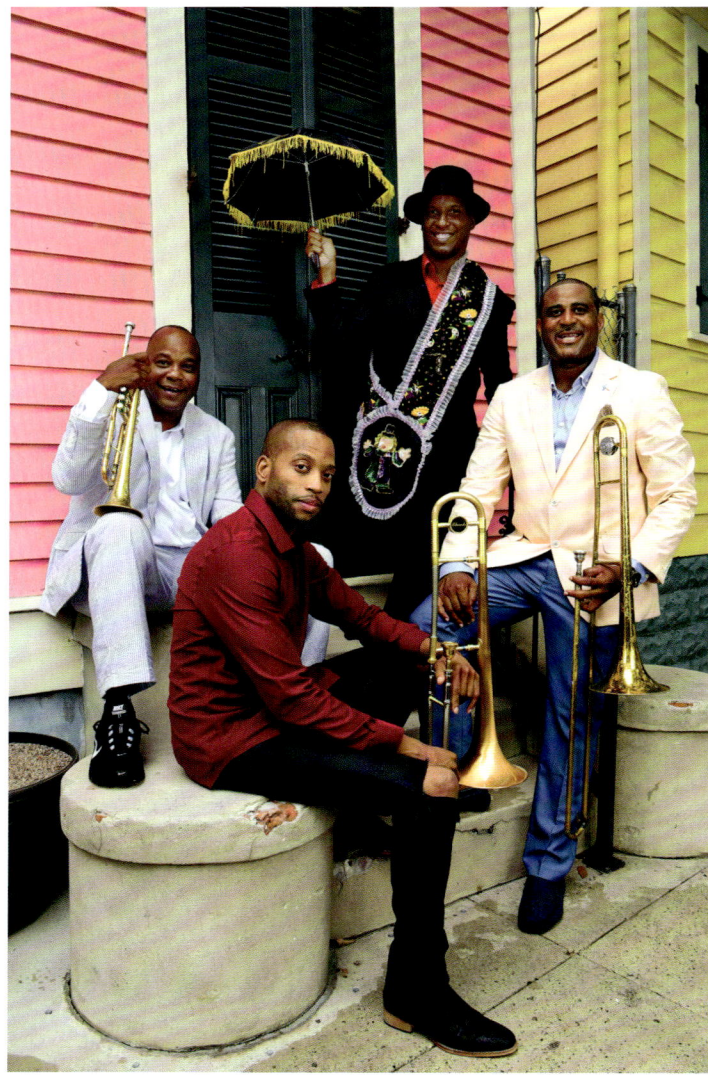

The musical Andrews family poses on a stoop in Tremé, before the neighborhood became gentrified, for a story in *Gambit*, a weekly alternative paper, about their family's musical legacy being carried on by the youngest member, Troy "Trombone Shorty" Andrews, 1998.

James, Troy, Bruce, and Glen David Andrews (*left to right*), the younger members of the Andrews family, pose on the same stoop, now a short-term rental, for an update in *Gambit*, 2018.

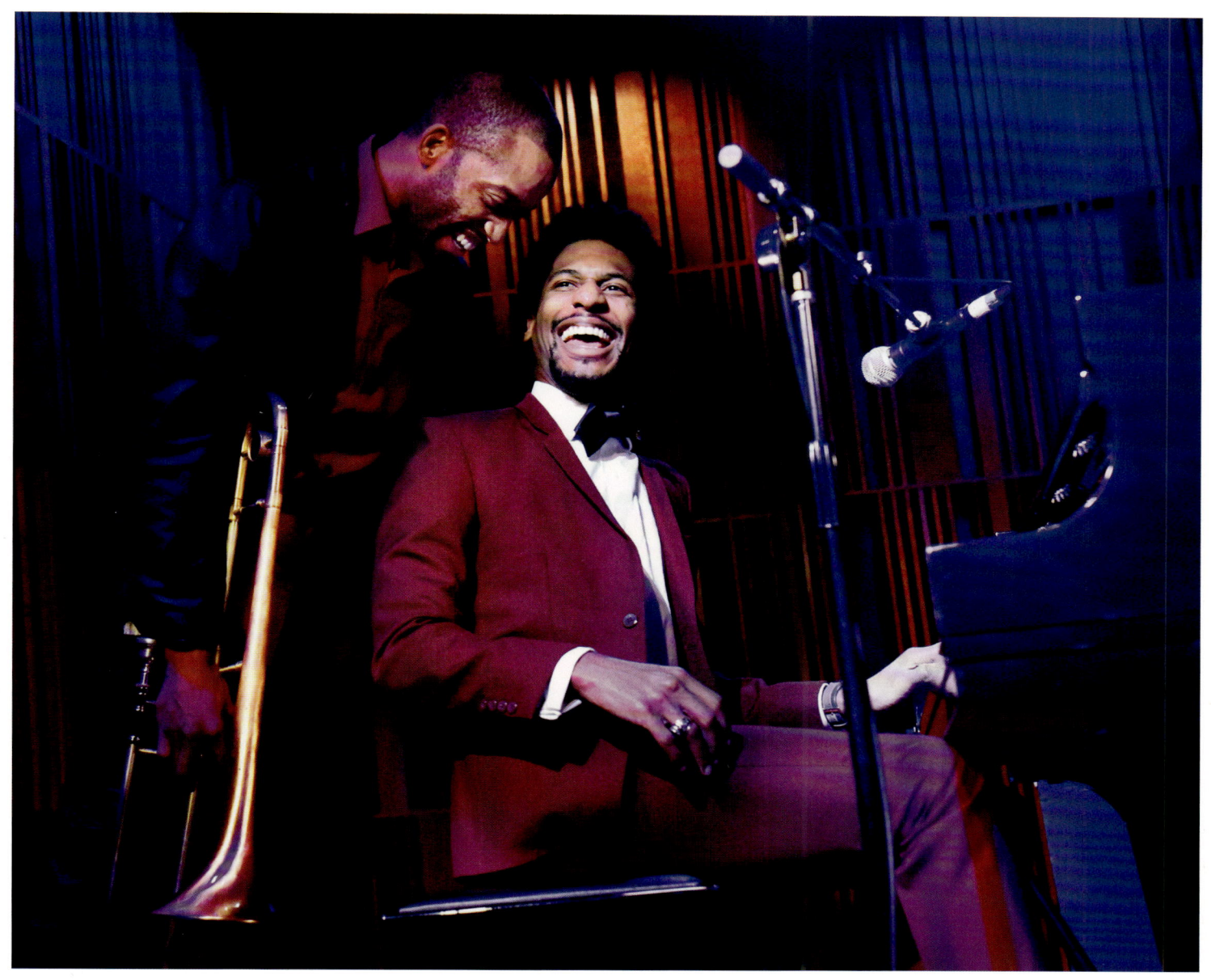

Grammy Award–winning musicians Troy "Trombone Shorty" Andrews and Jon Batiste perform together at the New Orleans Jazz Museum Gala, 2018. The beloved native sons, who met each other at jazz camp when they were just eleven and twelve years old, are now world renowned.

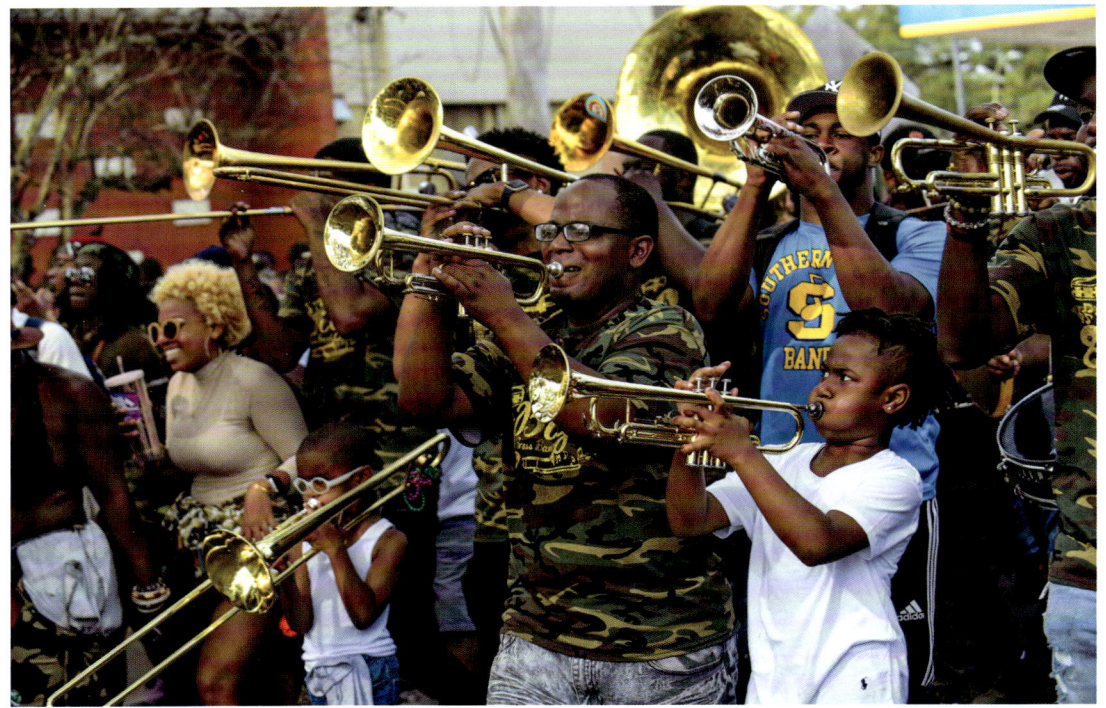

Trumpeter Eric Gordon Jr. (*center*) with the Big 6 Brass Band, a contemporary brass band founded in 2017, leads a second line parade while passing on the tradition to younger musicians, 2018.

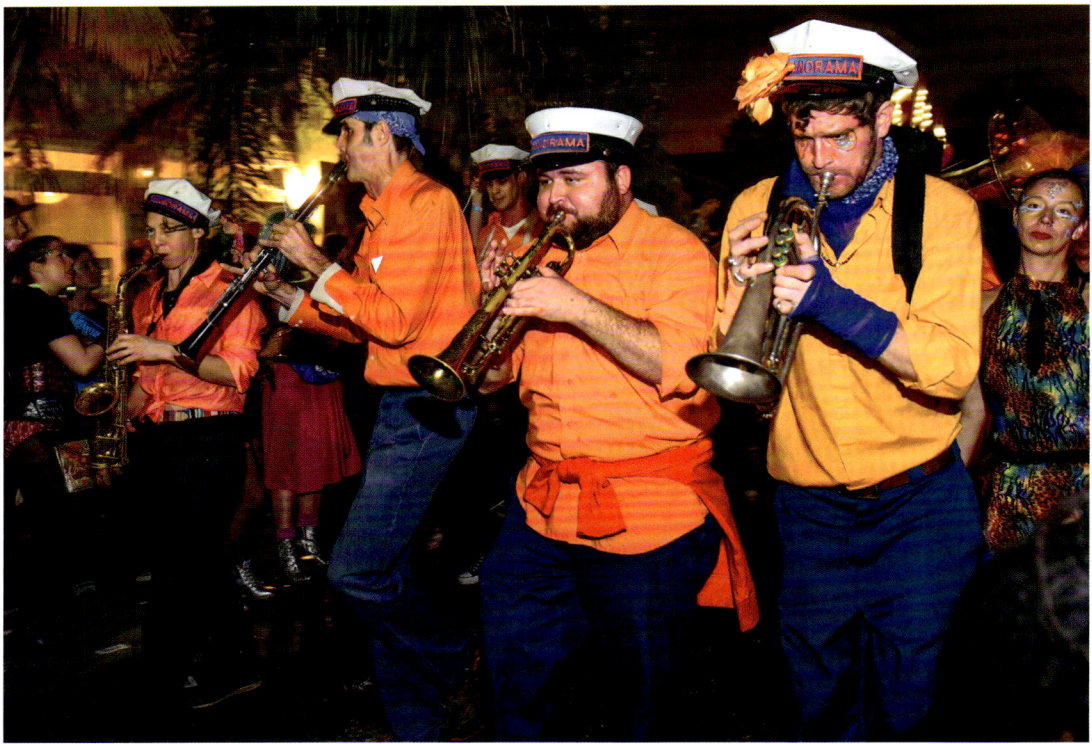

The Panorama Jazz Band, established in 1997 by clarinetist Ben Schenck (*second from left*), marches in the krewe*delusion* parade, 2017.

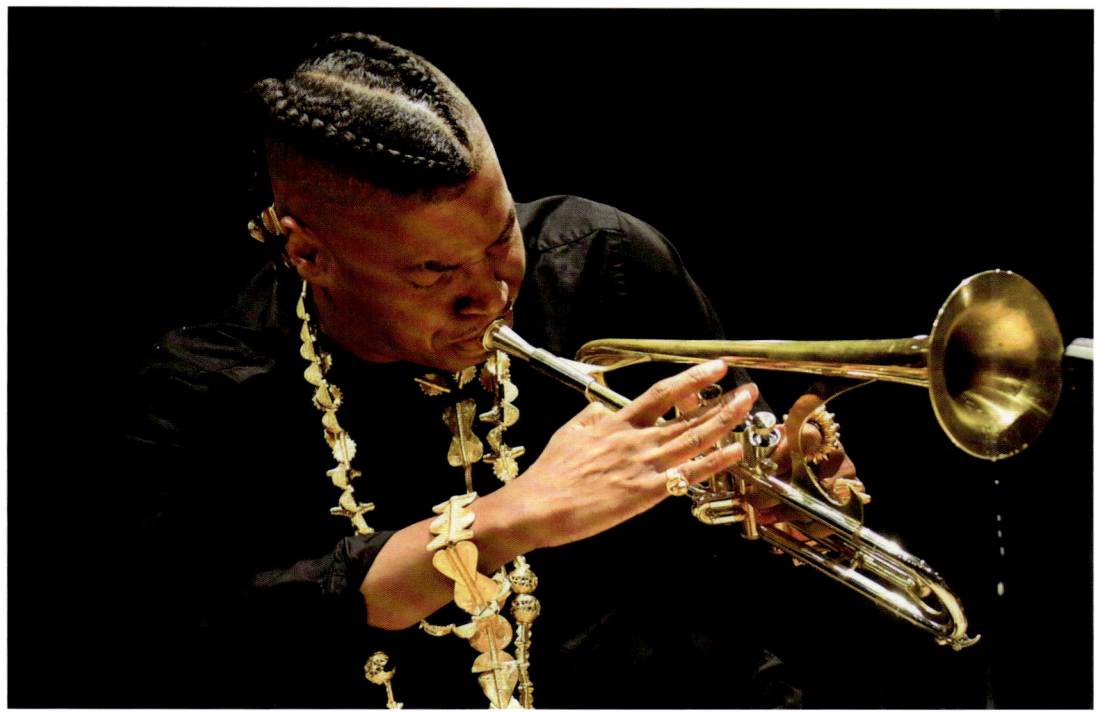

Award-winning and Grammy-nominated musician, composer, and producer Chief Xian aTunde Adjuah (formerly Christian Scott) performs at the New Orleans Jazz Market, 2017.

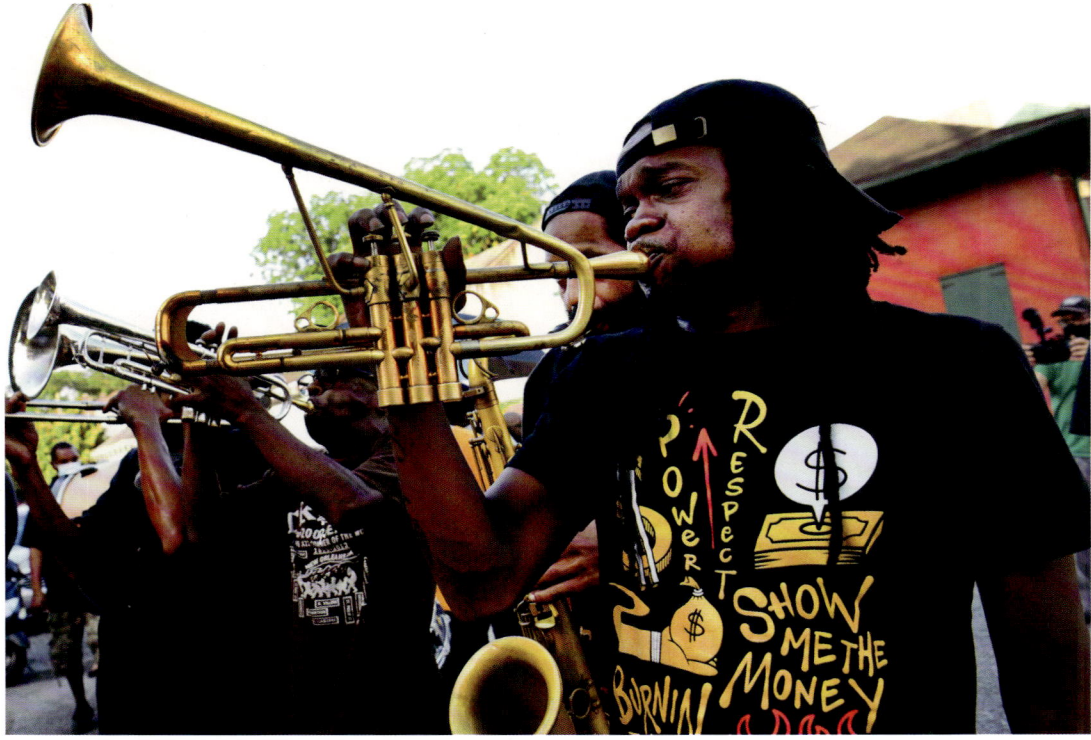

Sean Roberts (*foreground*) of the TBC (To Be Continued) Brass Band performs during a second line in Tremé, 2020.

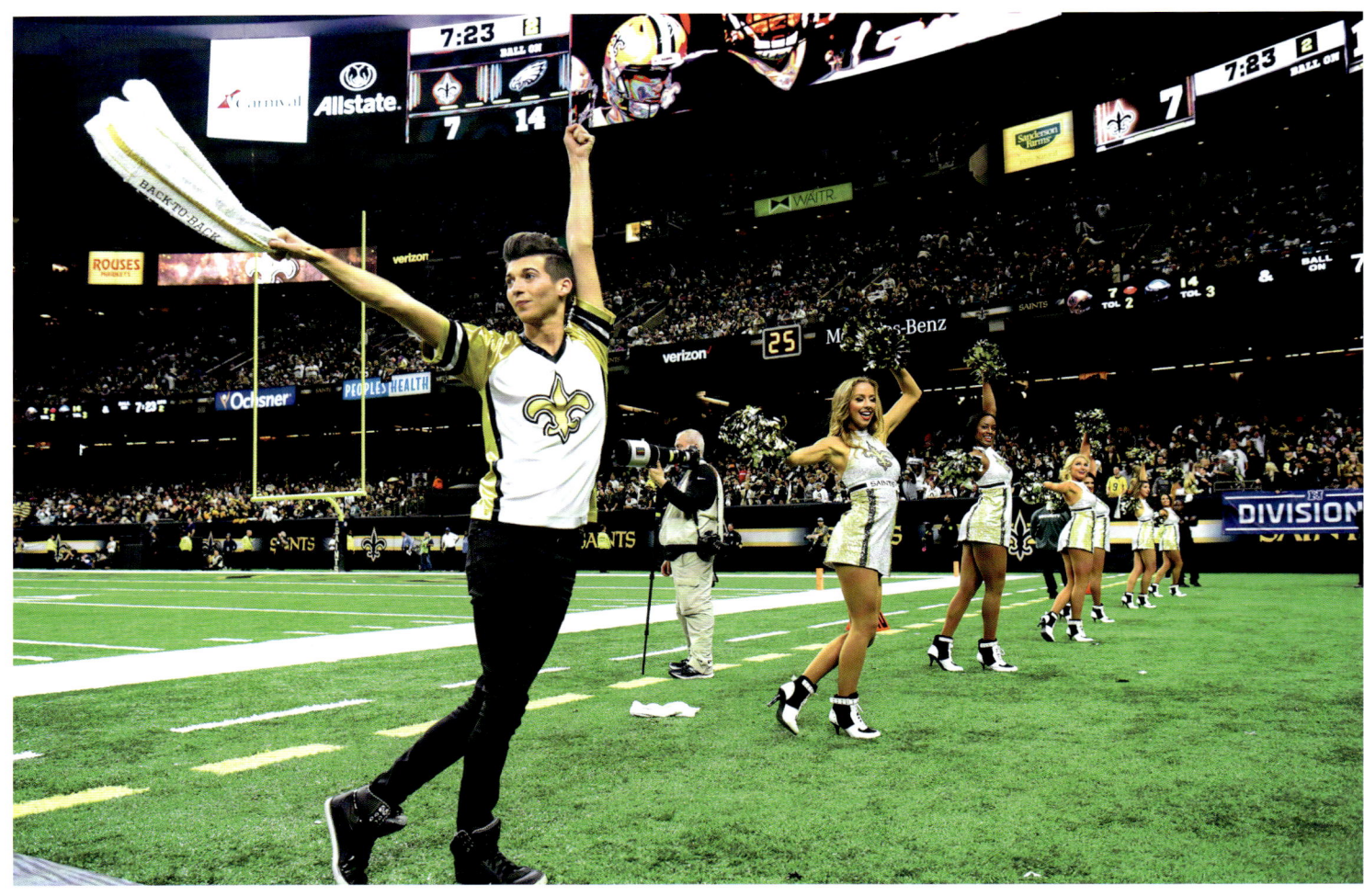

Jesse Hernandez hypes up the crowd in the Superdome in 2019. Hernandez became the first male member of the Saintsations, the cheerleading and dance squad for the New Orleans Saints, in 2018.

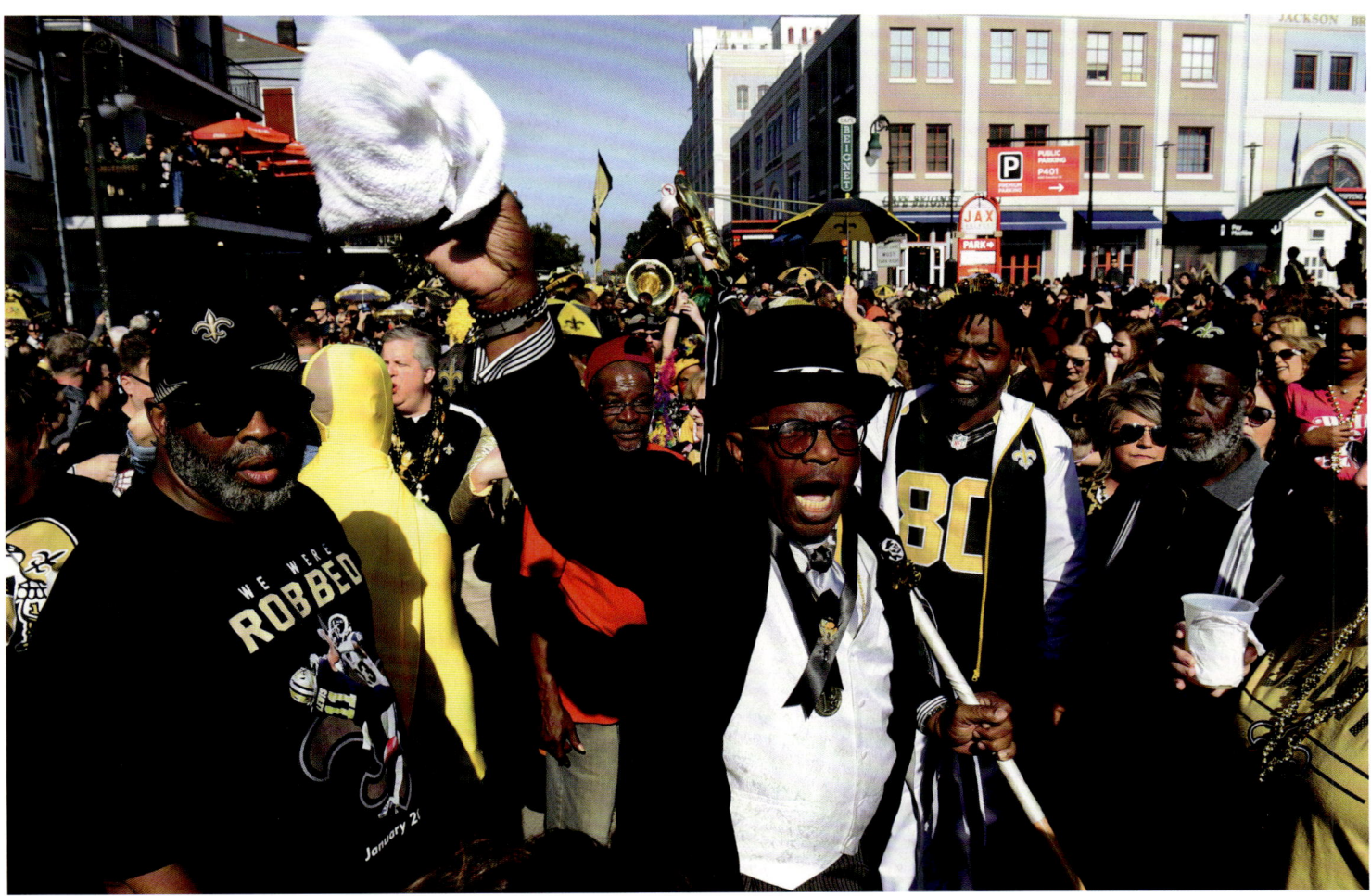

Clyde Adams (*center*), known to many as "Uncle Clyde," leads thousands of Saints fans through the French Quarter during the Boycott Super Bowl Parade in 2019. Fans boycotted the Super Bowl after the infamous "no-call" in the league championship game, when referees failed to throw any flags after a Rams defensive back leveled a Saints receiver with a helmet-to-helmet hit. This failure to call a penalty resulted in the Rams winning the game, robbing the Saints of what would have been their second trip to the Super Bowl.

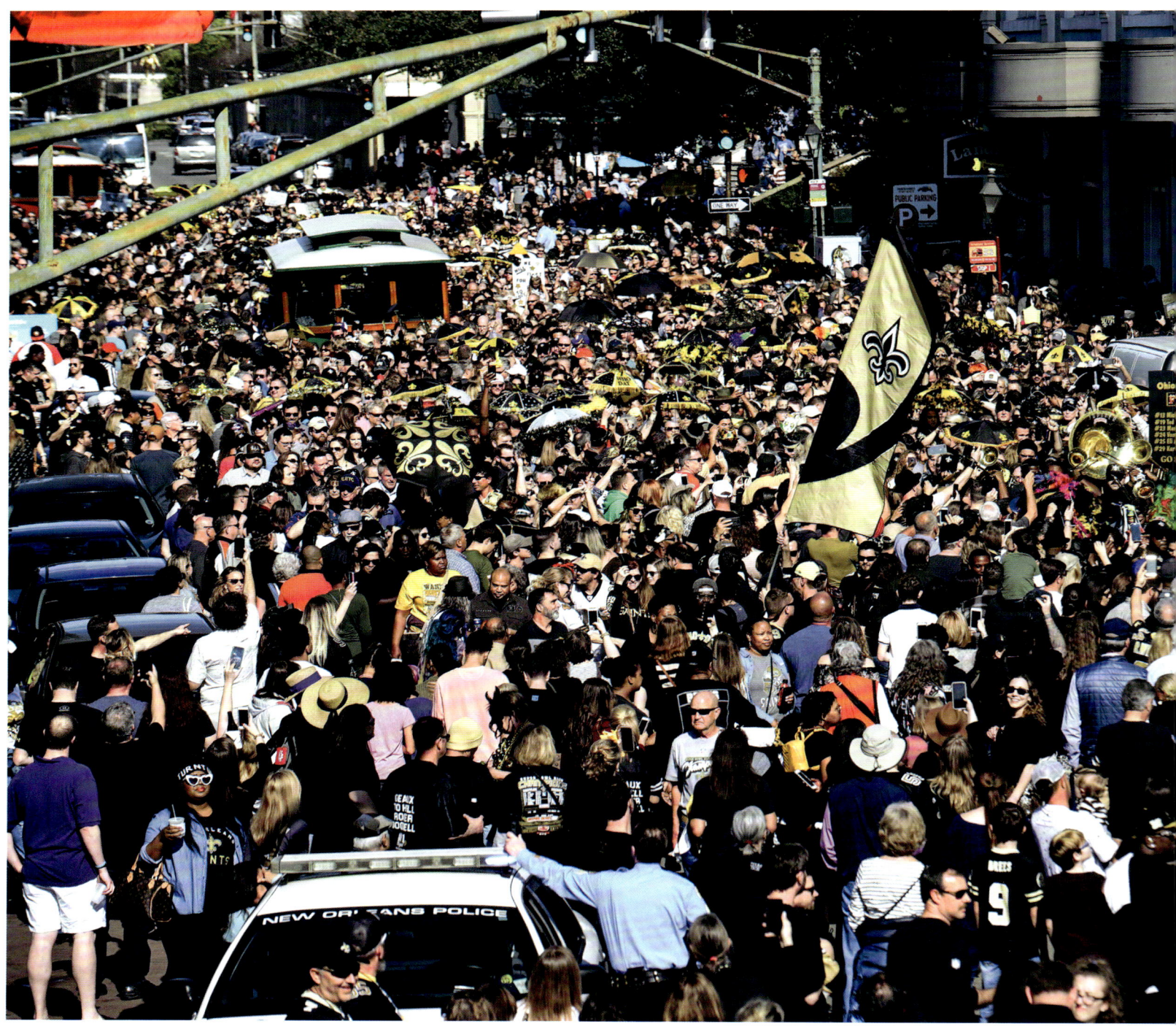

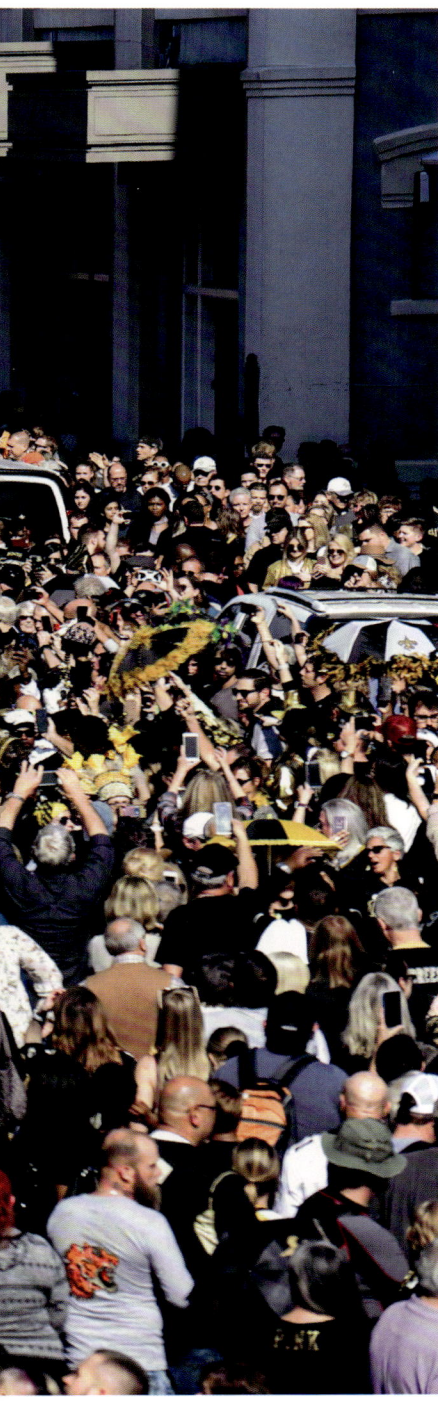

Saints fans fill the streets to protest the egregious no-call in the last minutes of the league championship game that cost the Saints a trip to the Super Bowl, 2019.

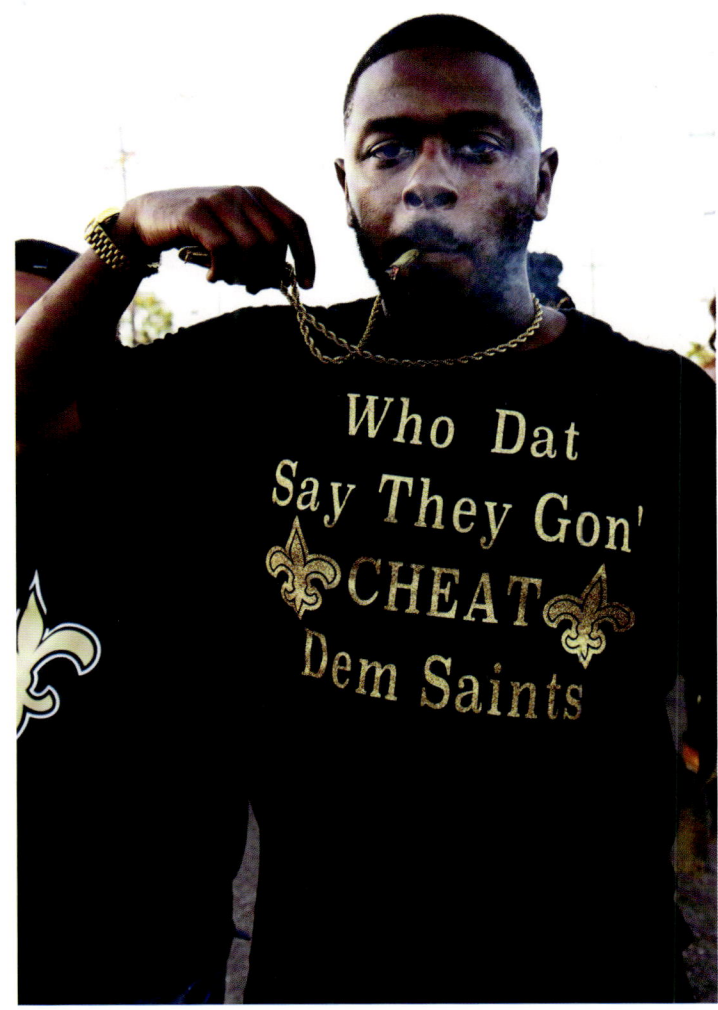

A disgruntled Saints fan, 2019.

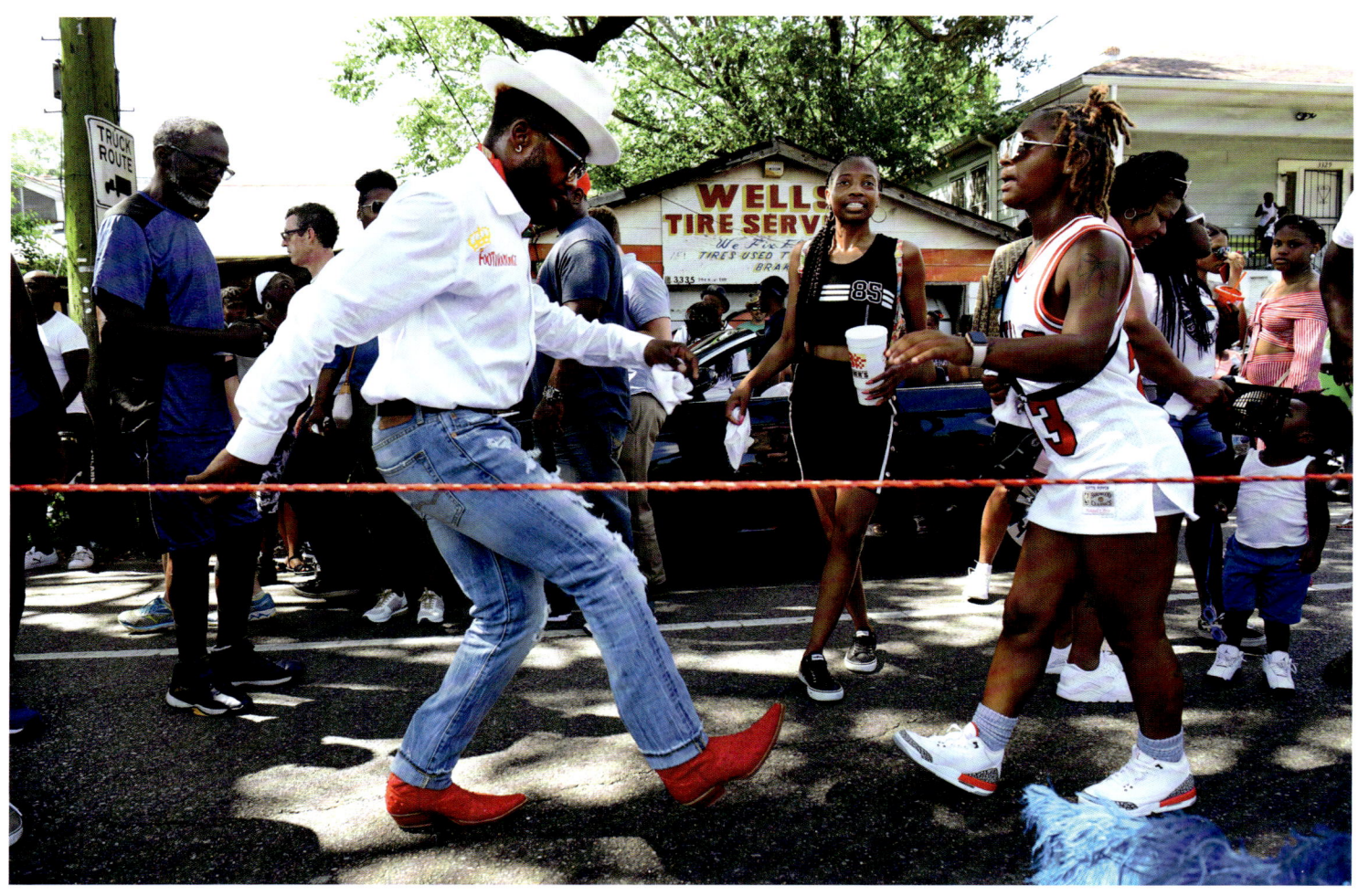

Dancers show off their fancy footwork outside the ropes, which are strung to separate club members from second-liners, 2018.

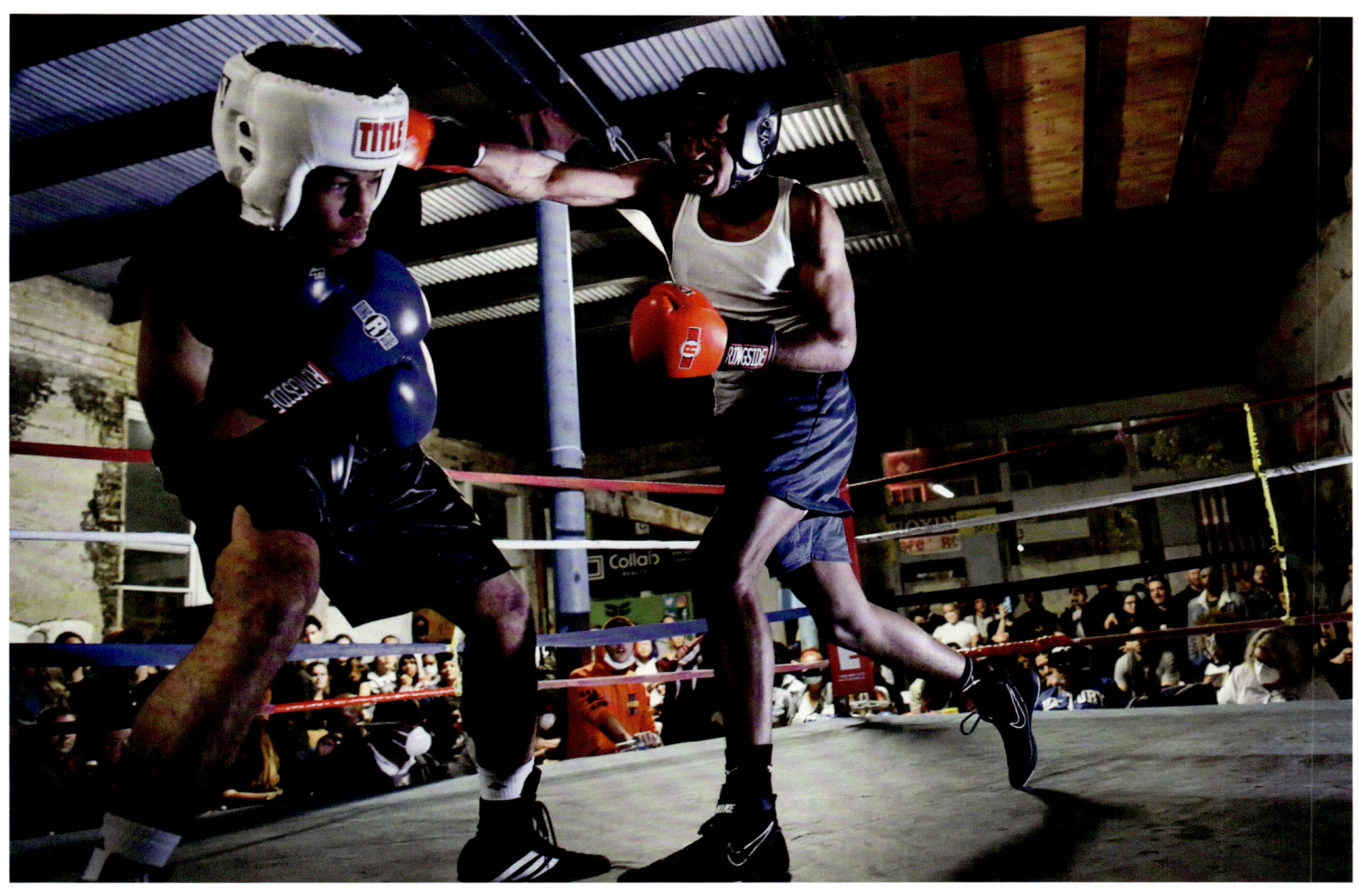

Amateur boxers show off their fancy footwork inside the ropes at Friday Night Fights, which had recently celebrated its fiftieth show, 2021.

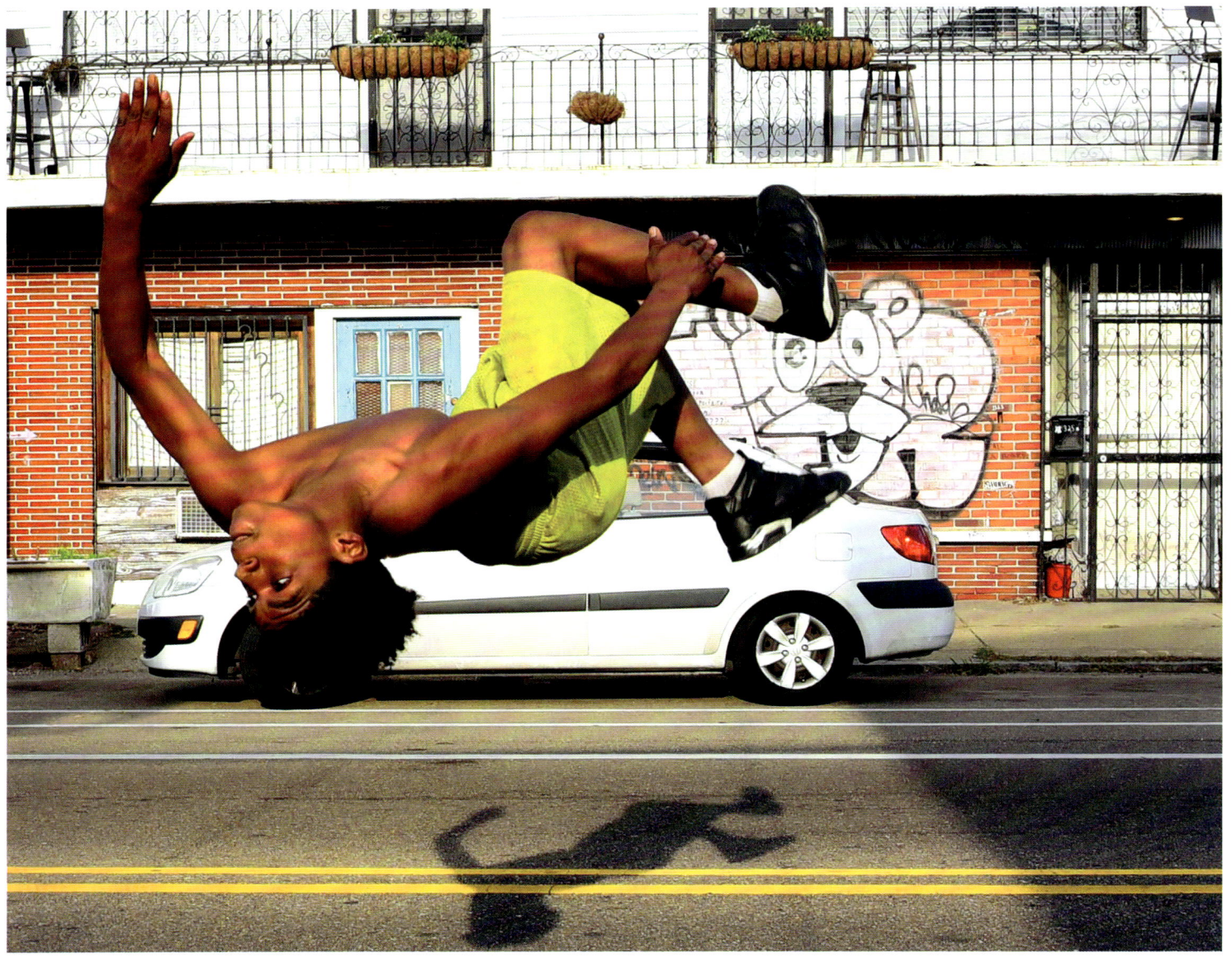

Reminiscent of the popular American gospel hymn "I'll Fly Away," a young man seems to defy gravity, hovering above his shadow on the yellow lines on St. Bernard Avenue, 2018.

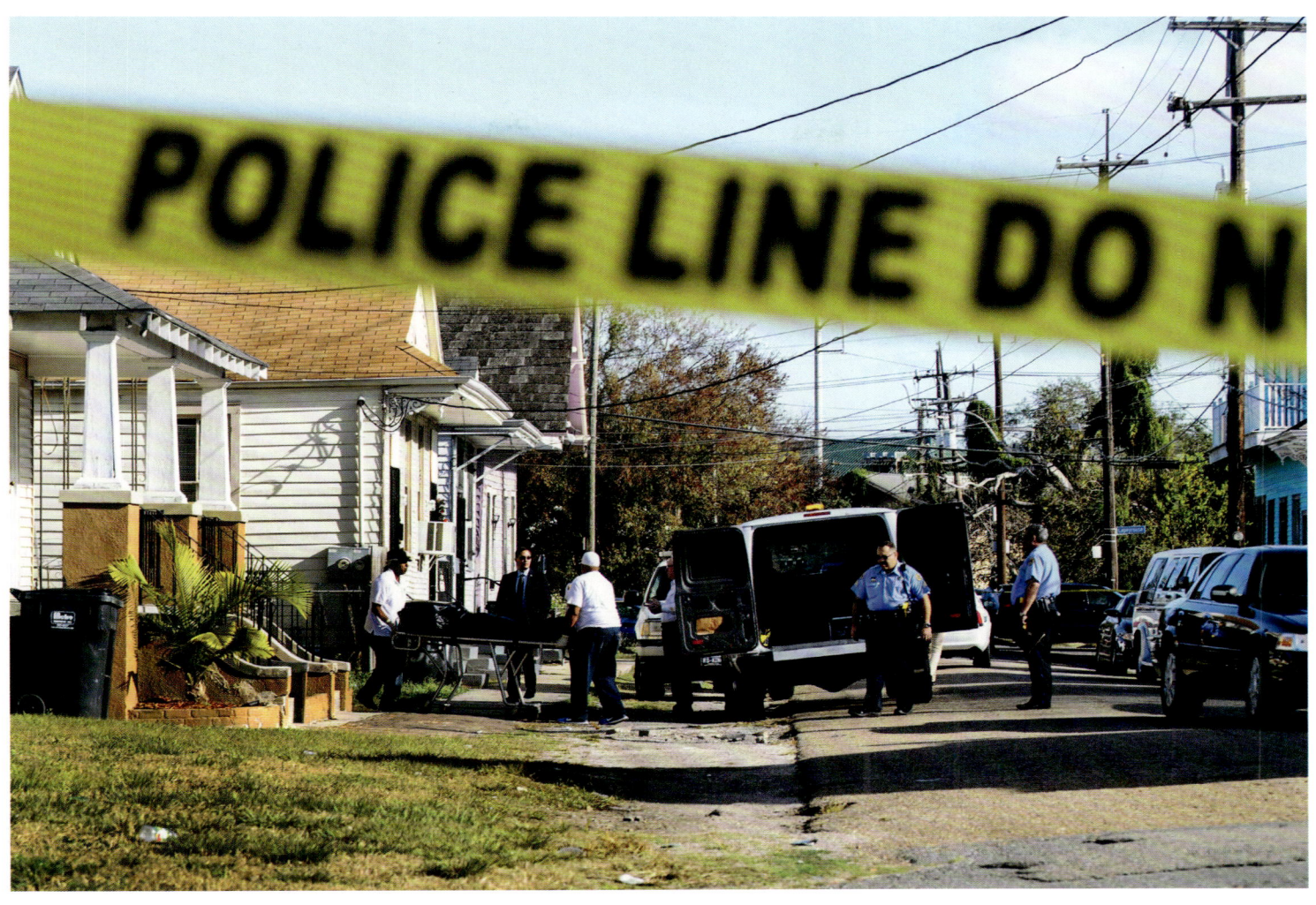

The Orleans Parish coroner's van arrives to transport a murder victim, seen below the yellow caution tape, in the Seventh Ward, 2015.

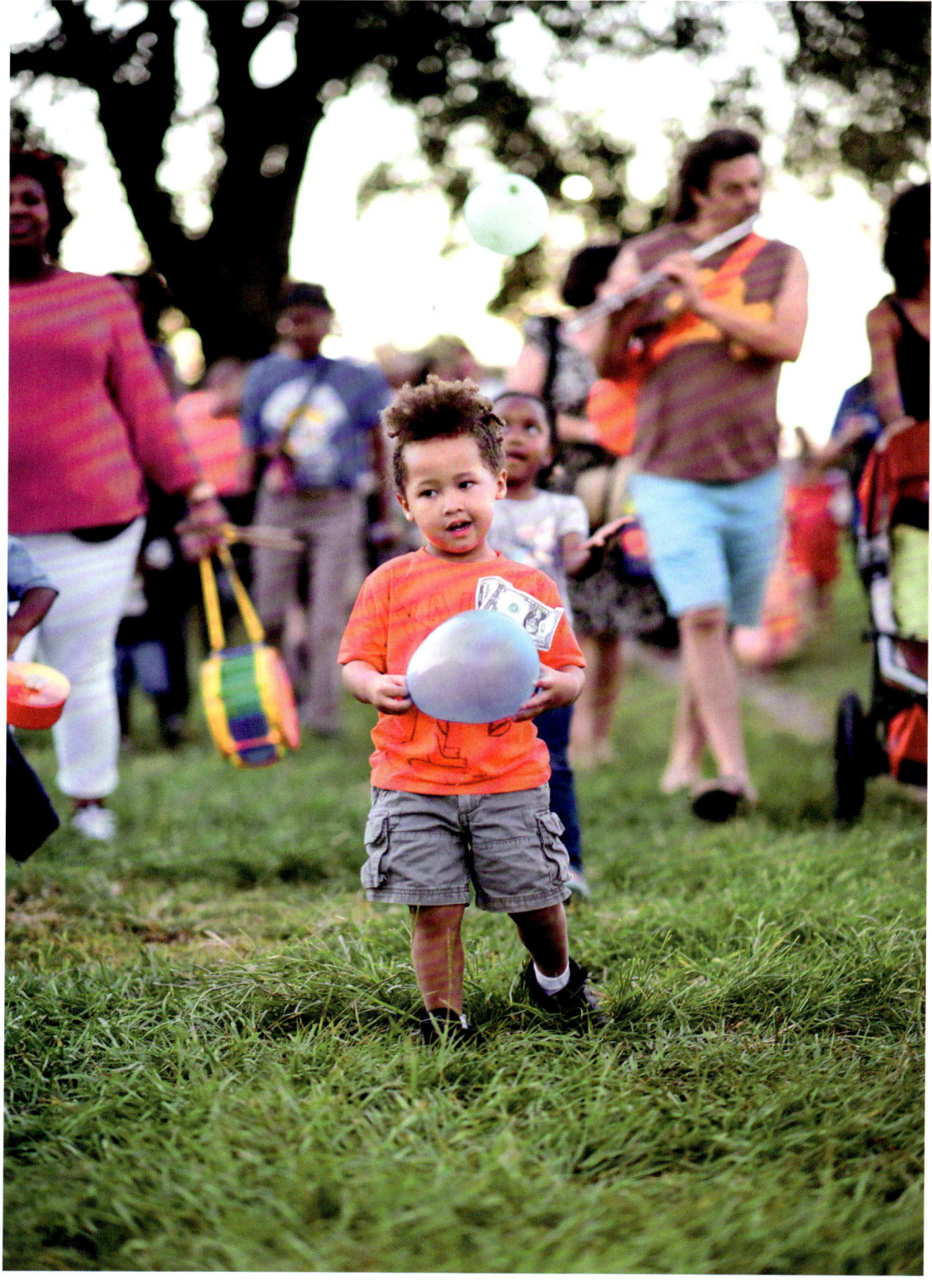

Kalim celebrates his third birthday with blue balloons and a second line on Bayou St. John, 2016.

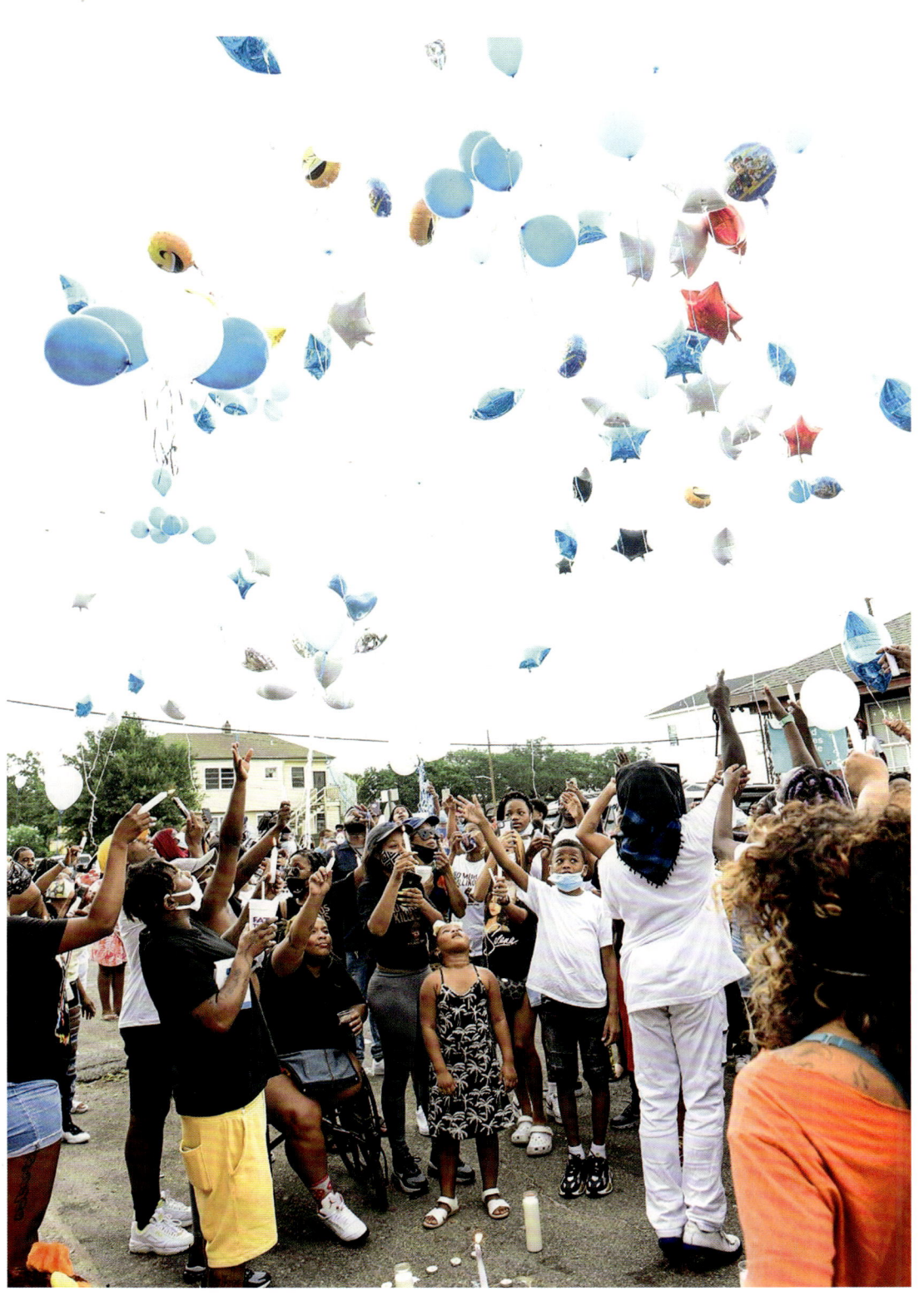

Mourners release blue balloons for nine-year-old Devante "D-Man" Bryant, who was fatally shot in the Seventh Ward, 2020. Bryant was one of ten juveniles murdered in the city in 2020. New Orleans led the country in murders per capita in 2022.

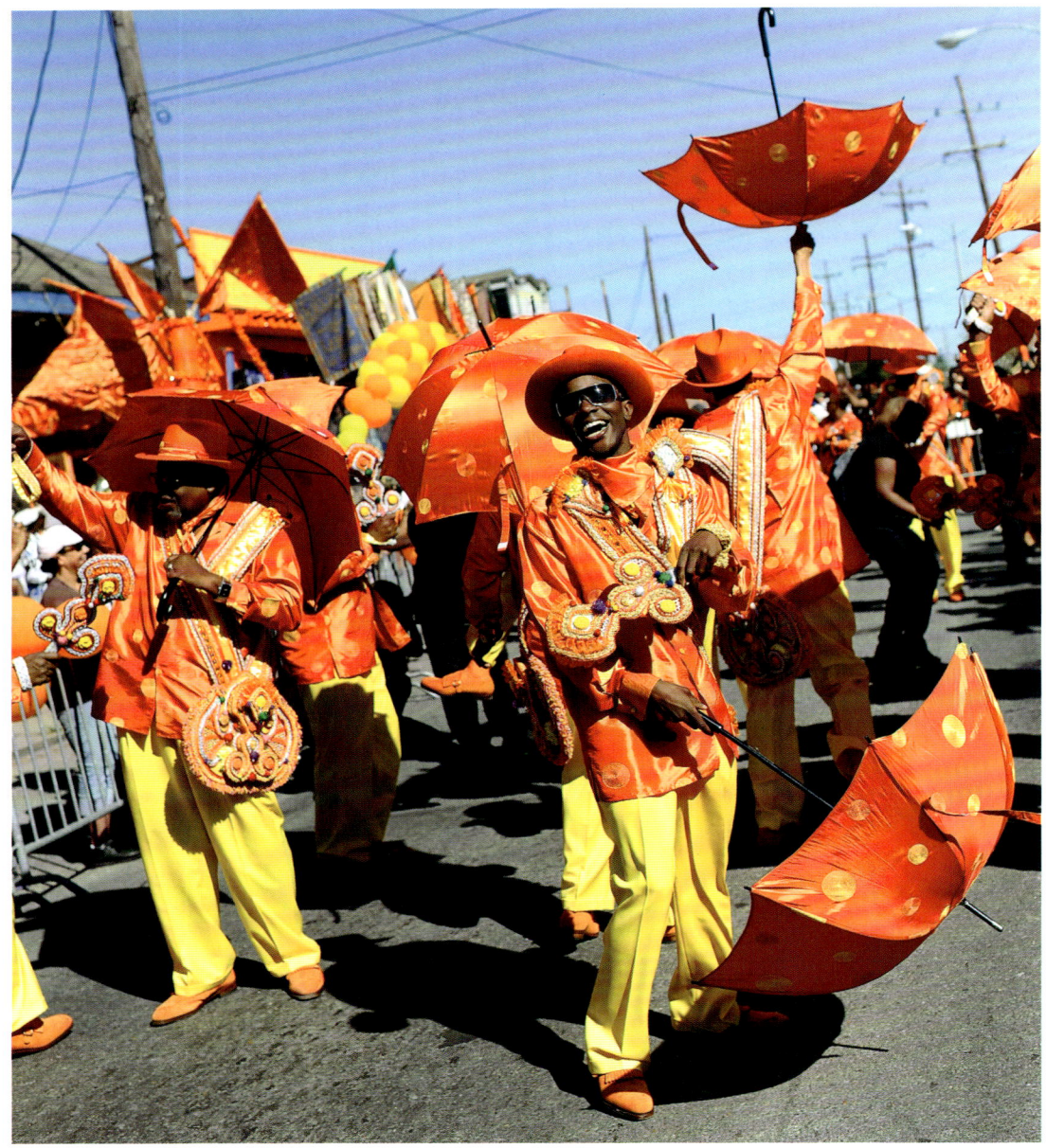

Members of the Black Men of Labor (BMOL) Social Aid and Pleasure Club dance during their annual second line, 2012. The club was formed in 1993 after the death of musician and mentor Danny Barker; he had introduced many young African American musicians to brass band music and the practice of playing a traditional funeral procession when he was a member of the Fairview Baptist Church. BMOL members pay homage to musicians, community activists, and working men.

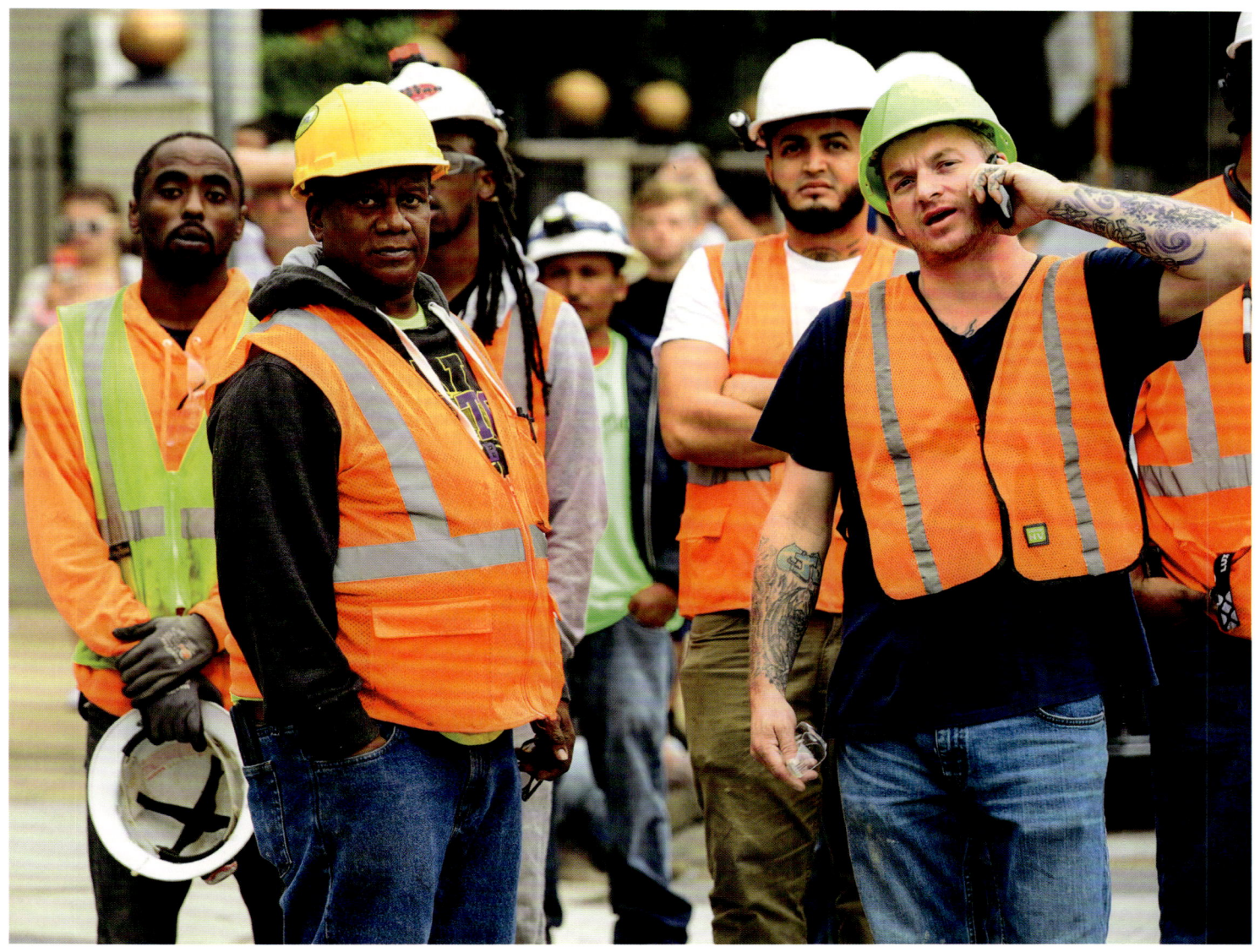

Construction workers look on in the moments after the 190-foot-tall Hard Rock Hotel construction project partially collapsed, killing three coworkers and injuring dozens of others, 2019. Two of the three bodies were removed from the site ten months later. Still under investigation, the tragic collapse is thought to have been caused by the construction company's poor engineering and safety practices and the city's failure to adequately inspect the construction process.

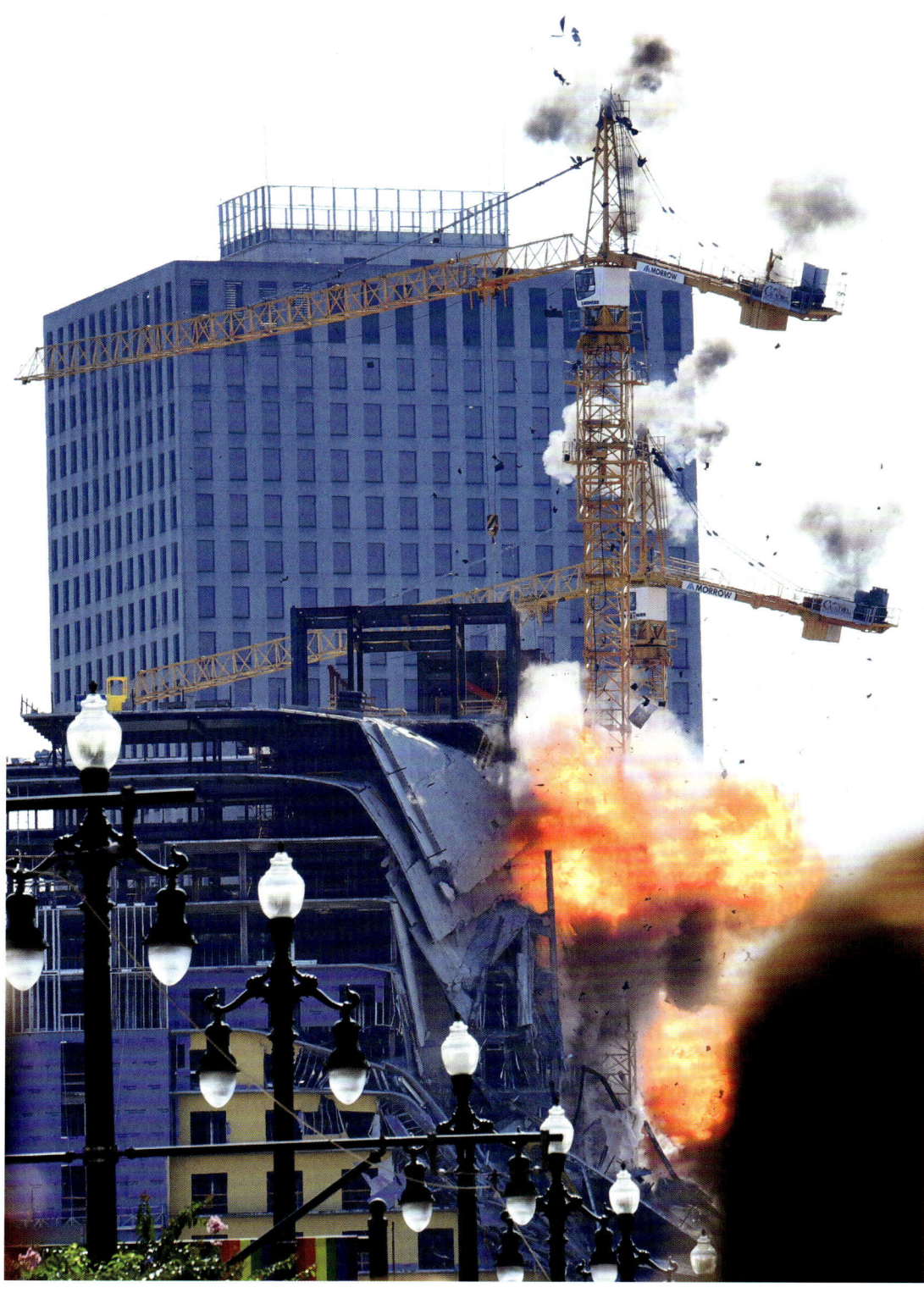

A dynamite-controlled demolition takes down two construction cranes that were hovering precariously for more than a week at the site of the partially collapsed Hard Rock Hotel, 2019.

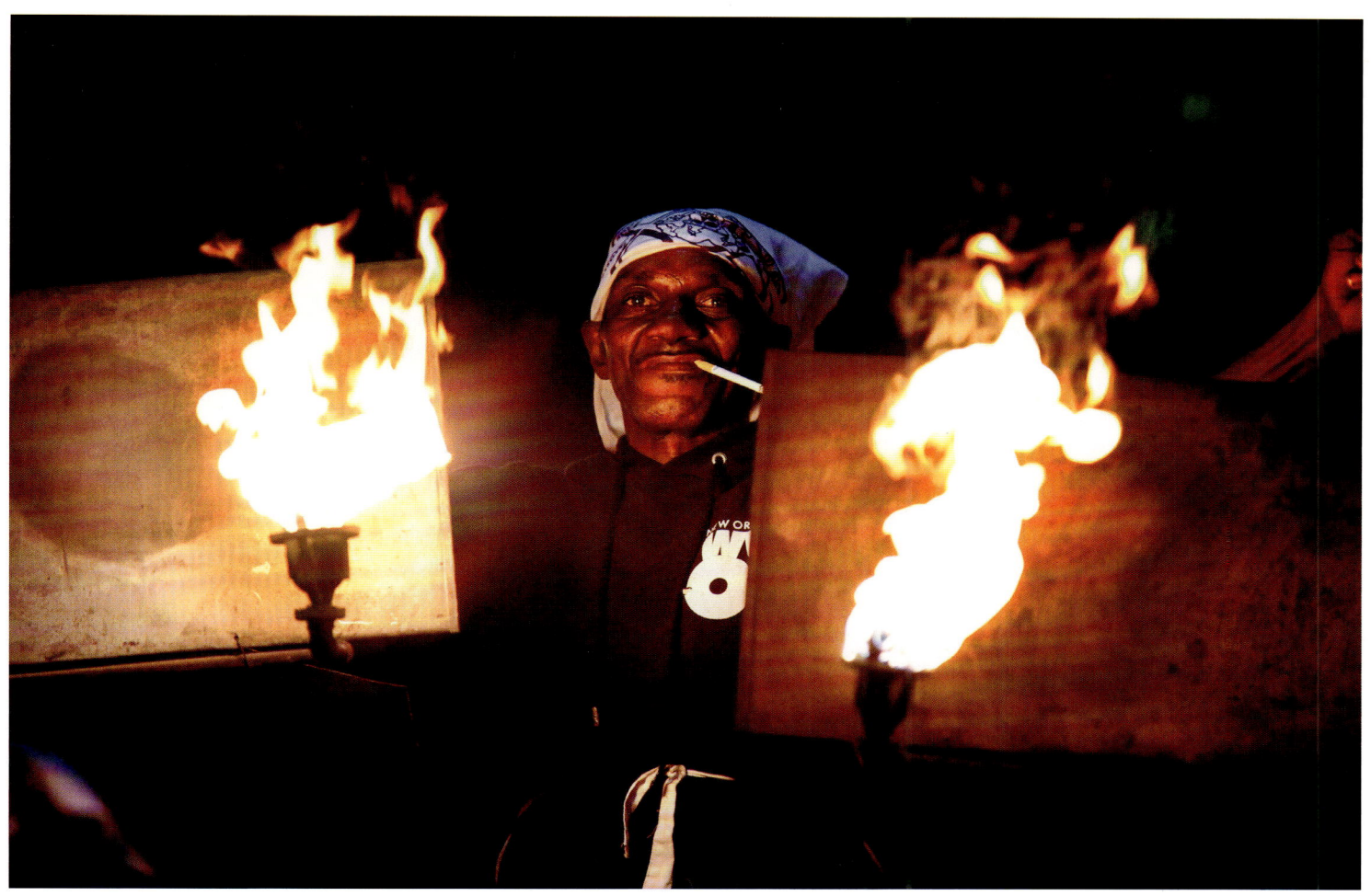

A flambeaux carrier lights the way for a night parade, 2019. Historically, flambeaux carriers served as beacons, lighting up the parade route so parade goers could enjoy the spectacle of night festivities. The first flambeaux carriers were enslaved people. Today, flambeaux is seen as a kind of performance art, and viewers often throw money toward the carriers.

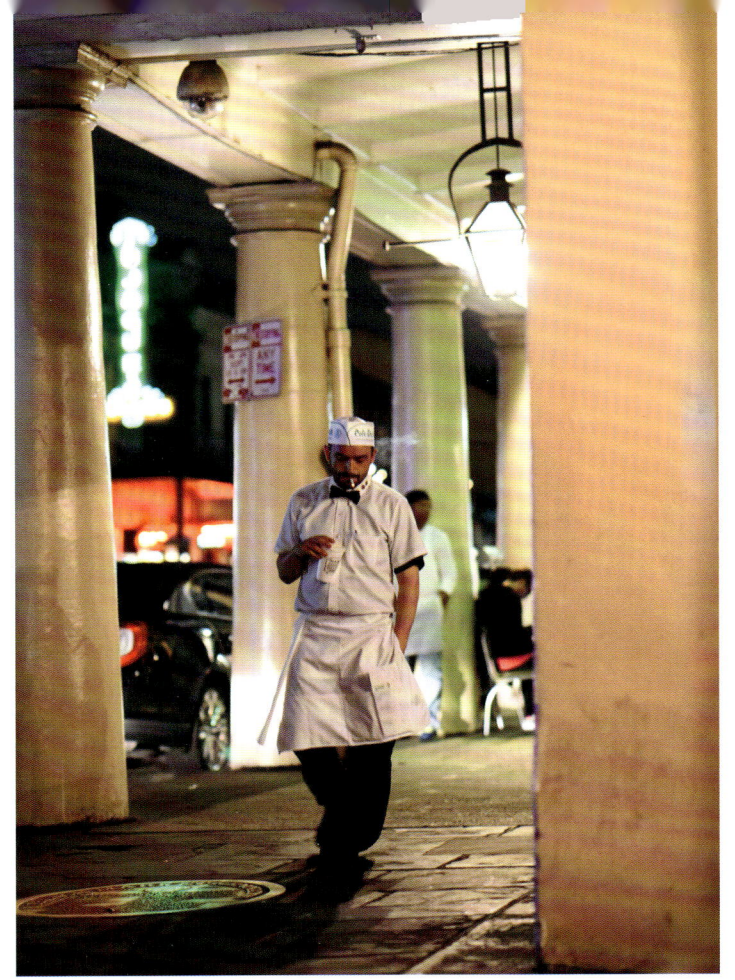

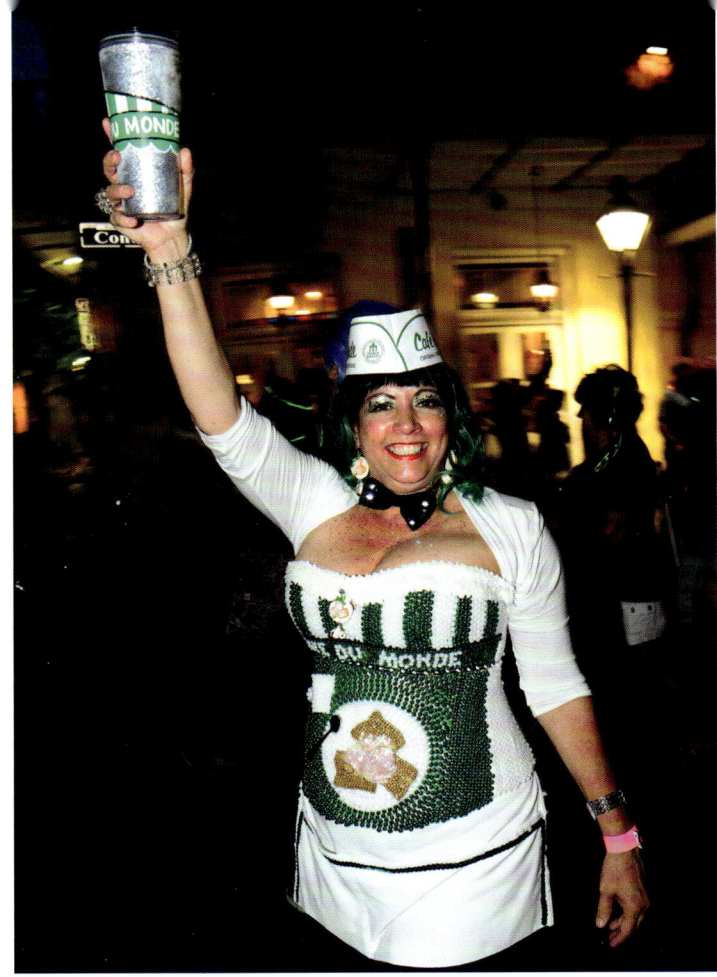

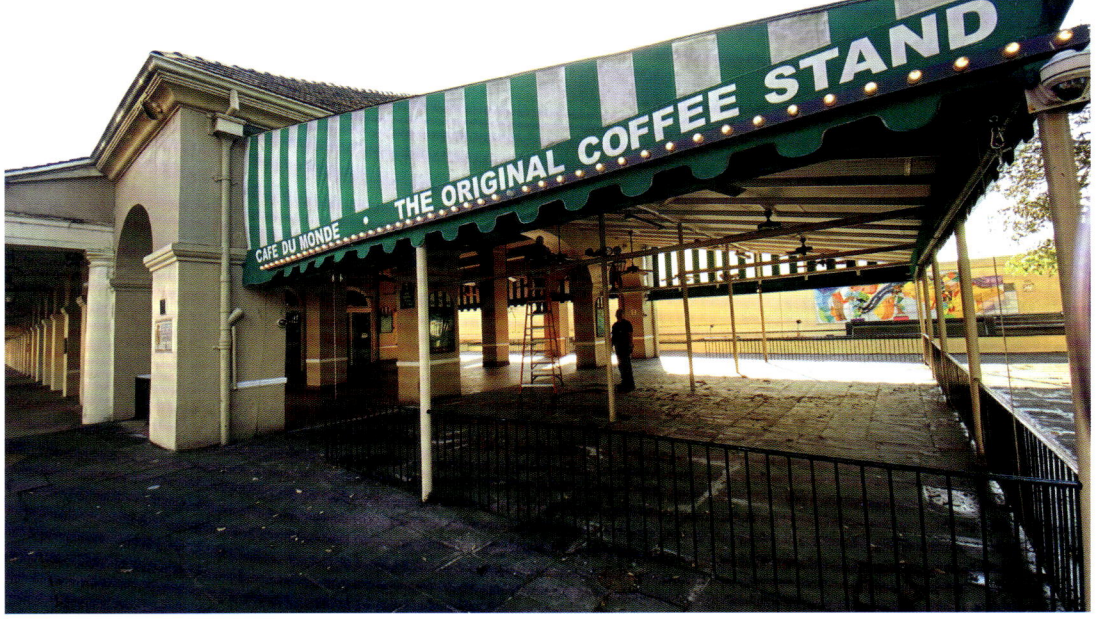

above left A Café du Monde server takes a smoke break, 2016.

above right Karen Molinario of the Crescent City Dames, a krewe known for creating and wearing beaded corsets, pays homage to the iconic coffee stand at the annual FestiGals parade, 2018.

left Café du Monde is eerily empty during the pandemic, 2020.

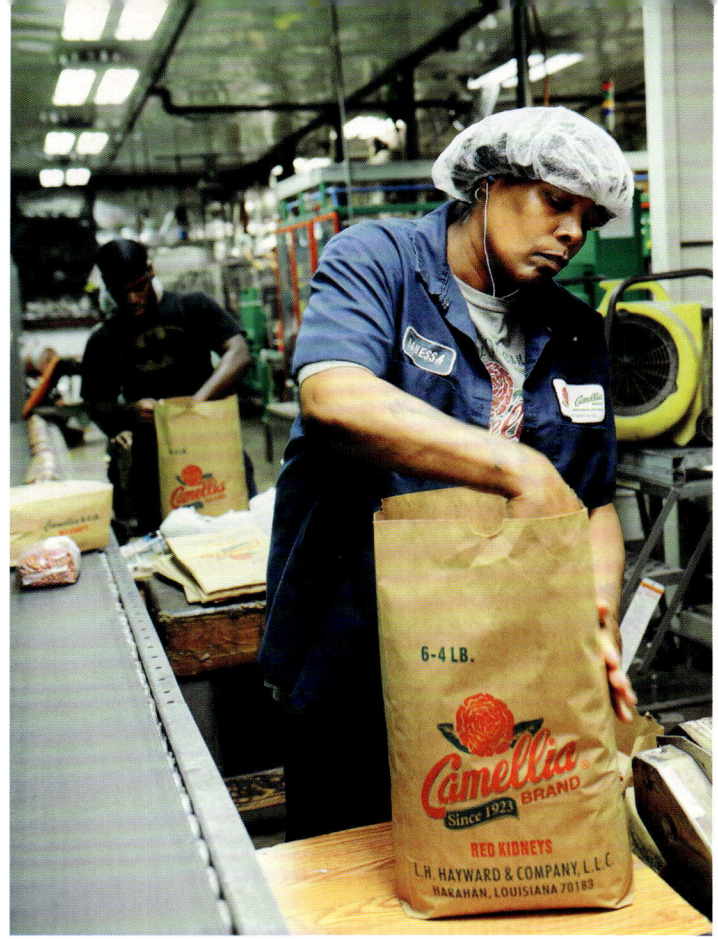

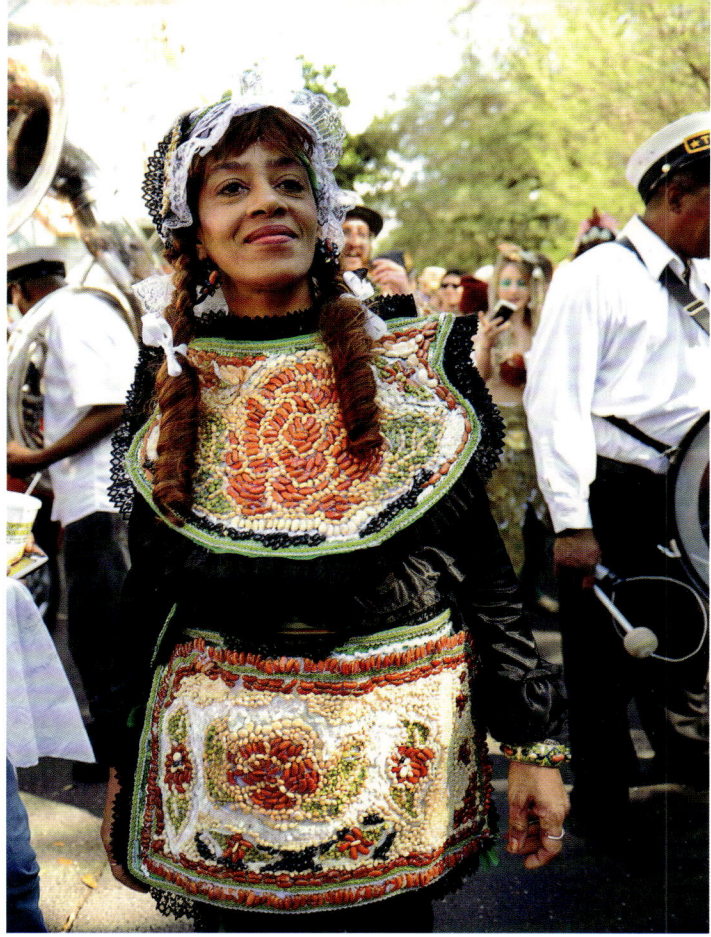

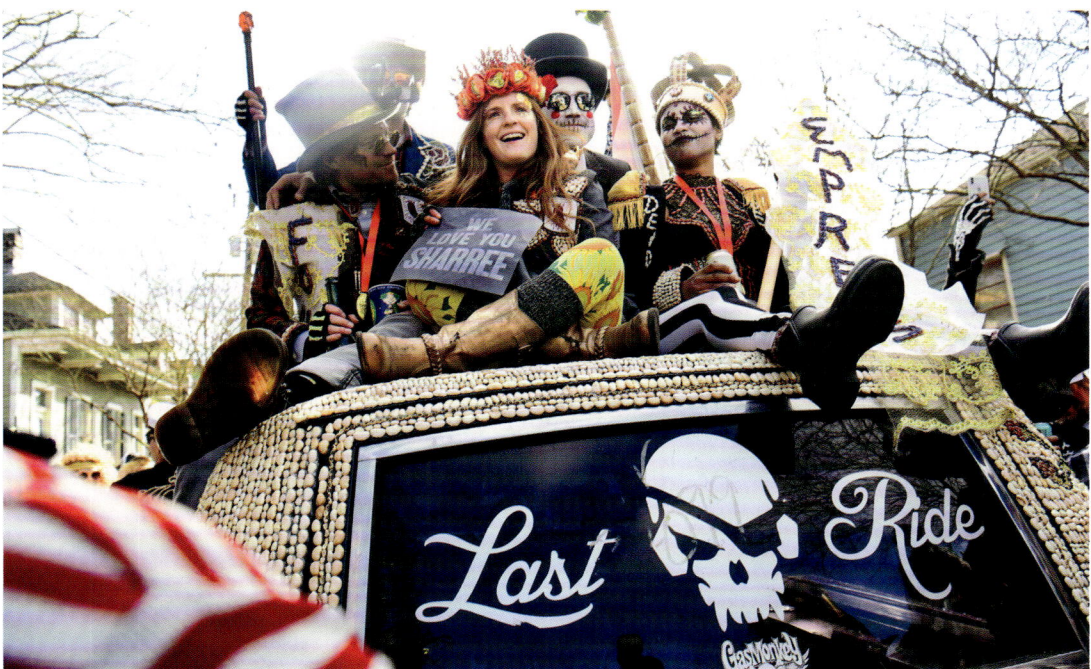

above left Vanessa Smith works at the Camellia Beans packaging facility, 2014.

above right Resa "Cinnamon Black" Bazile pays tribute to the iconic Camellia red bean at the Red Beans parade, 2018.

left Krewe of Dead Beans members commemorate the "Last Ride" of Sharree Walls, a bicyclist killed by a drunk driver in 2019.

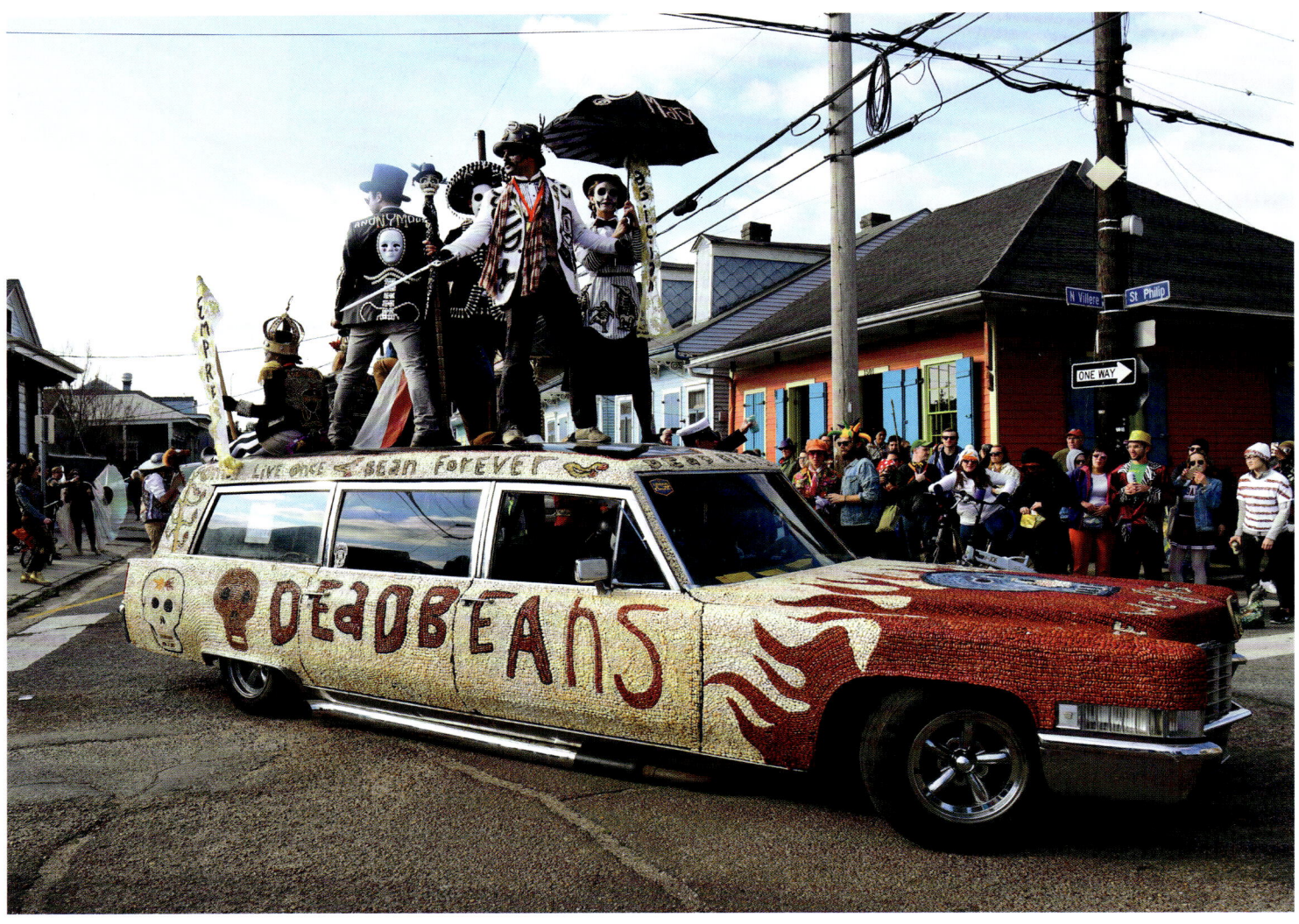

Members of the Krewe of Dead Beans ride atop a hearse decorated with red beans during its annual parade, 2018. The Krewe of Dead Beans, formed in 2018 as a spinoff of the Red Beans krewe, displays themes of death. Its parade starts in Bayou St. John and meets up with the Red Beans marchers in Tremé on the Monday before Mardi Gras, known as Lundi Gras.

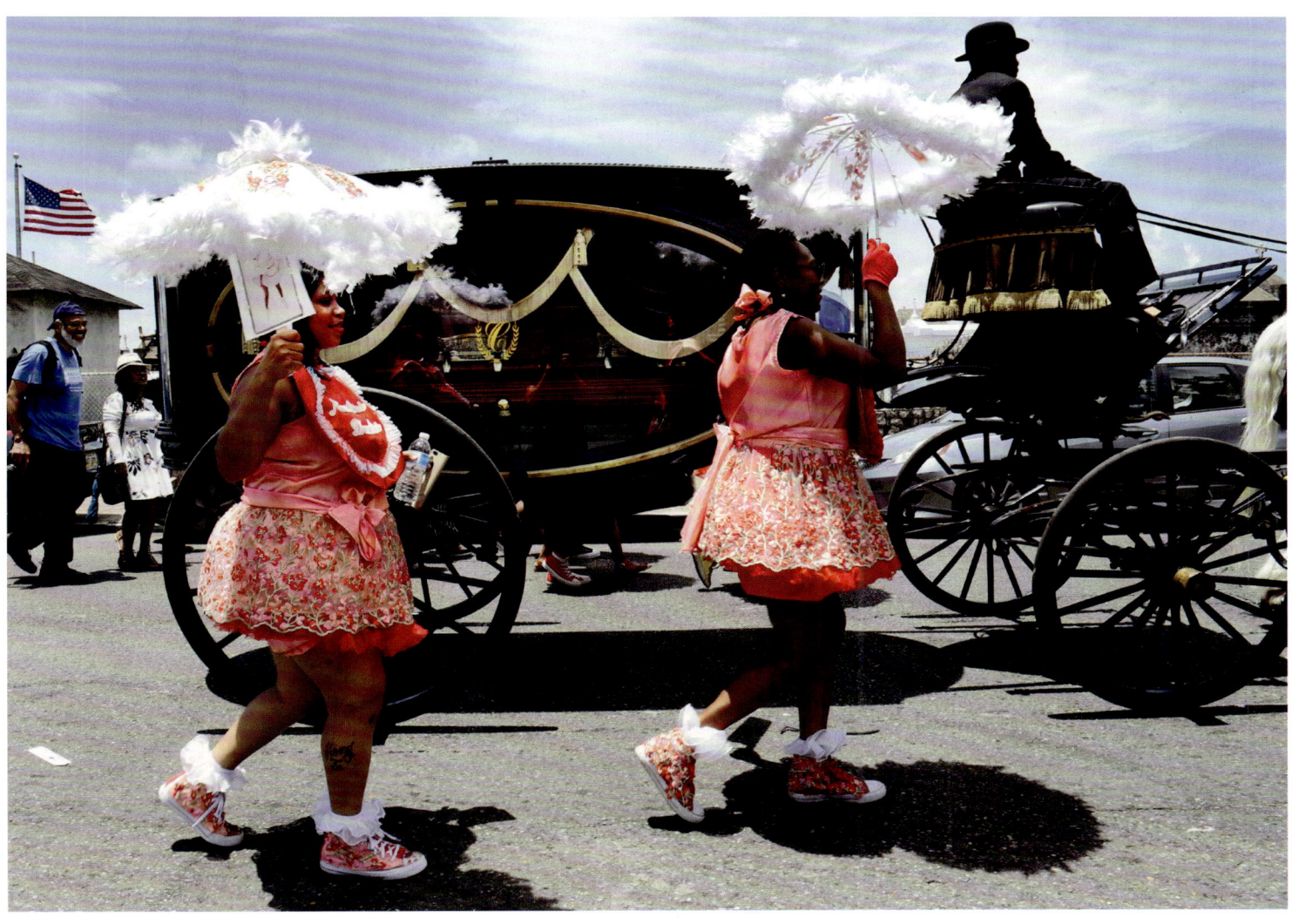

Baby Dolls escort a horse-drawn hearse during a funeral for Eva "Tee Eva" Perry, 2018. Perry, who died at the age of eighty-three, was also known as the "Praline and Pie Lady" for her praline business and participated in the Carnival Black Masking tradition of the Baby Dolls.

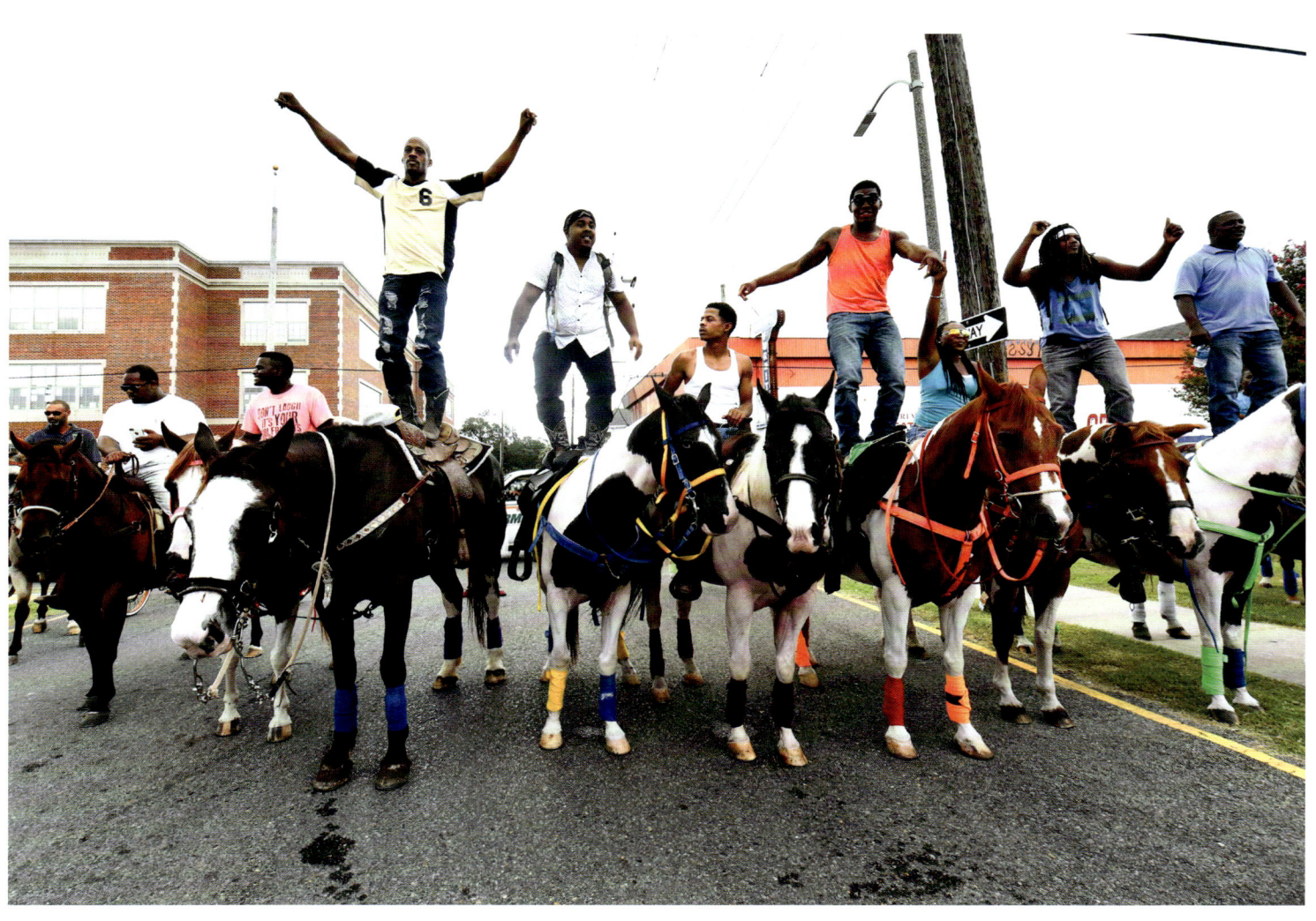

The "urban cowboys" of the Deep South Riding Club celebrate during a second line commemorating the tenth anniversary of Hurricane Katrina on St. Claude Avenue, 2015.

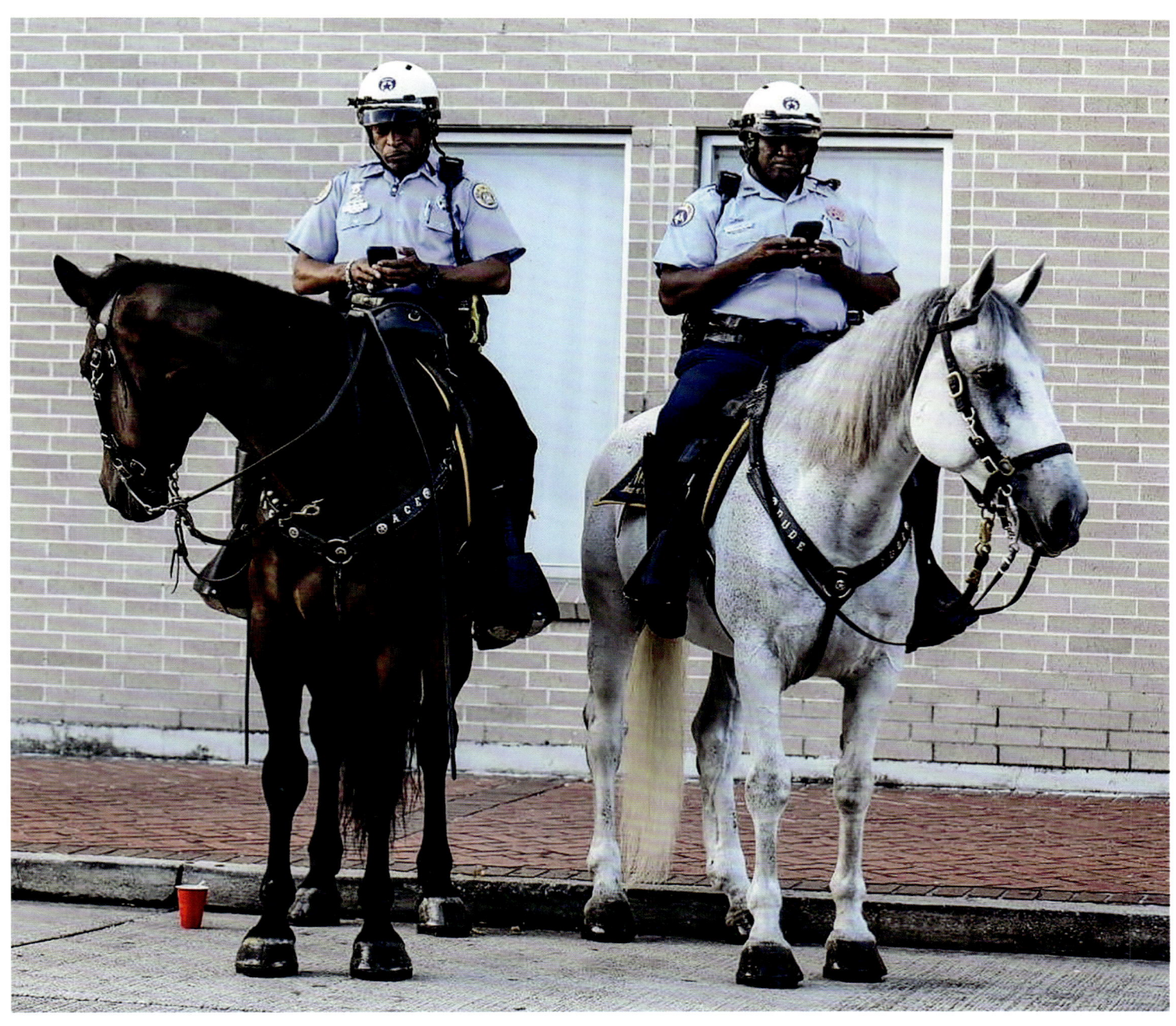

NOPD police officers look at their cellphones during the "Night Out Against Crime" event, 2018. The annual event started in the 1990s as a community-wide gathering to raise crime awareness, reduce crime, and increase support of law enforcement.

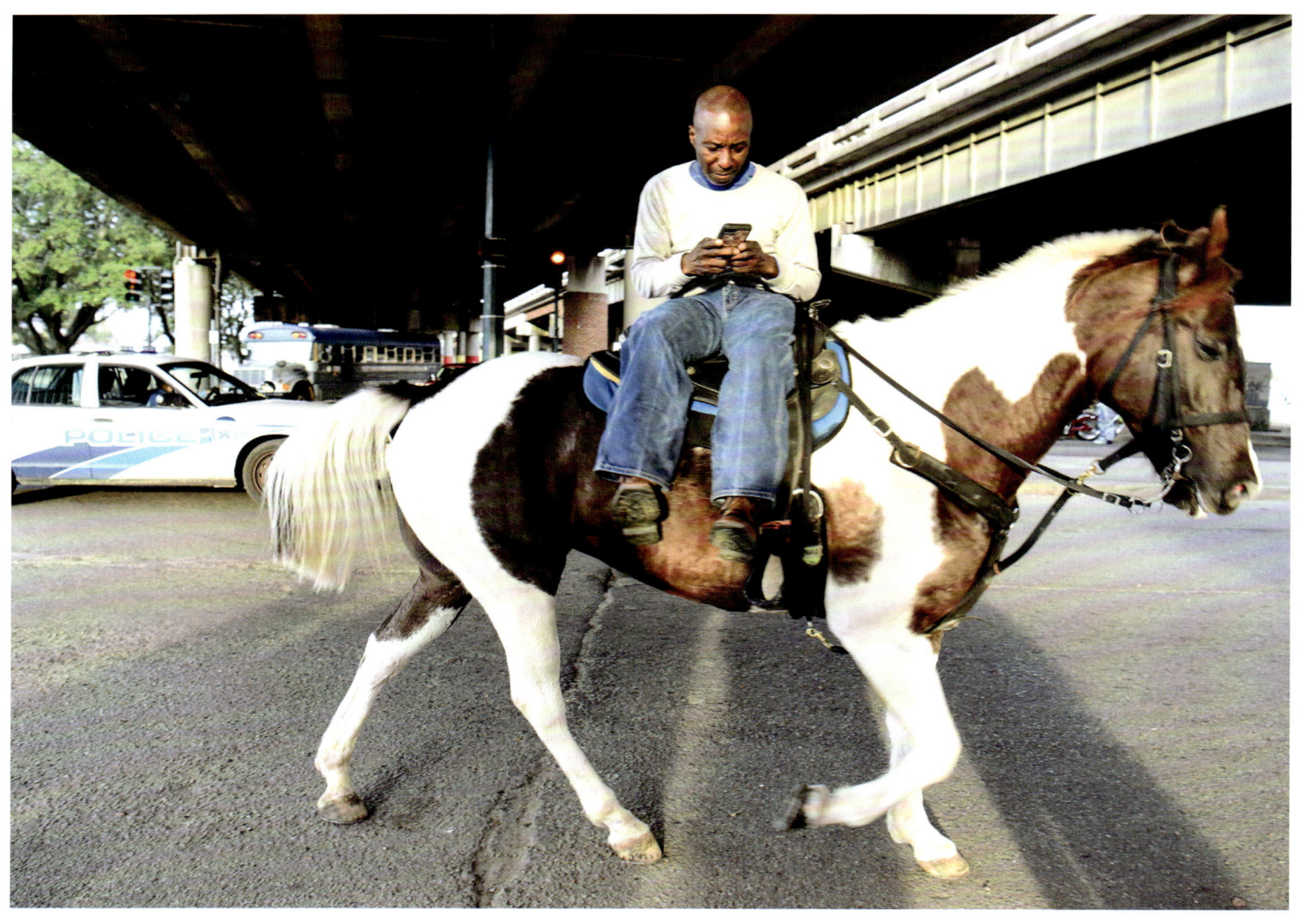

"Uncle" Lee Shezbie rides his horse Sunshine on St. Bernard Avenue, 2018.

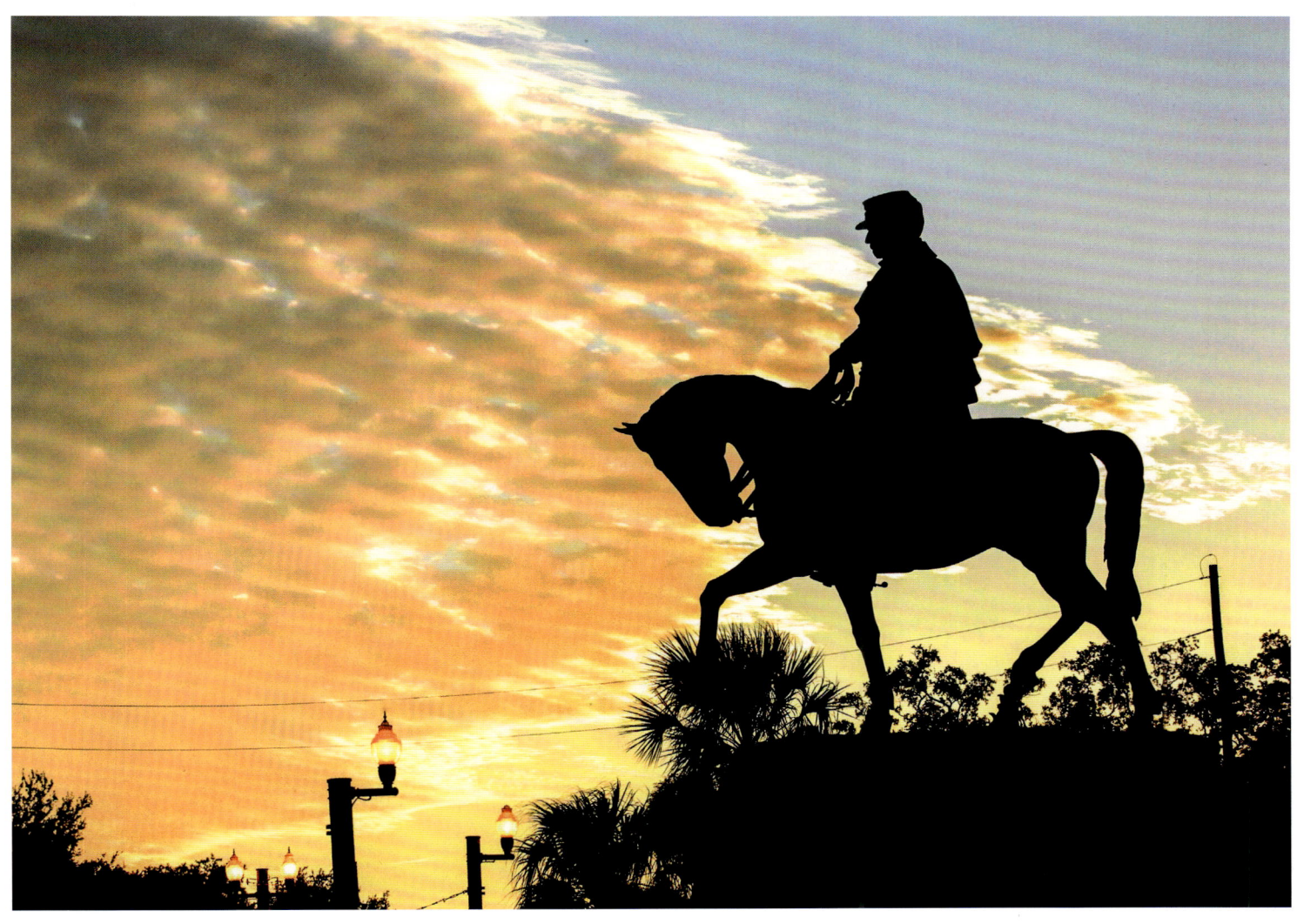

The sun sets behind the monument of Confederate general P. G. T. Beauregard before it was removed from its pedestal at the entrance to City Park in 2017.

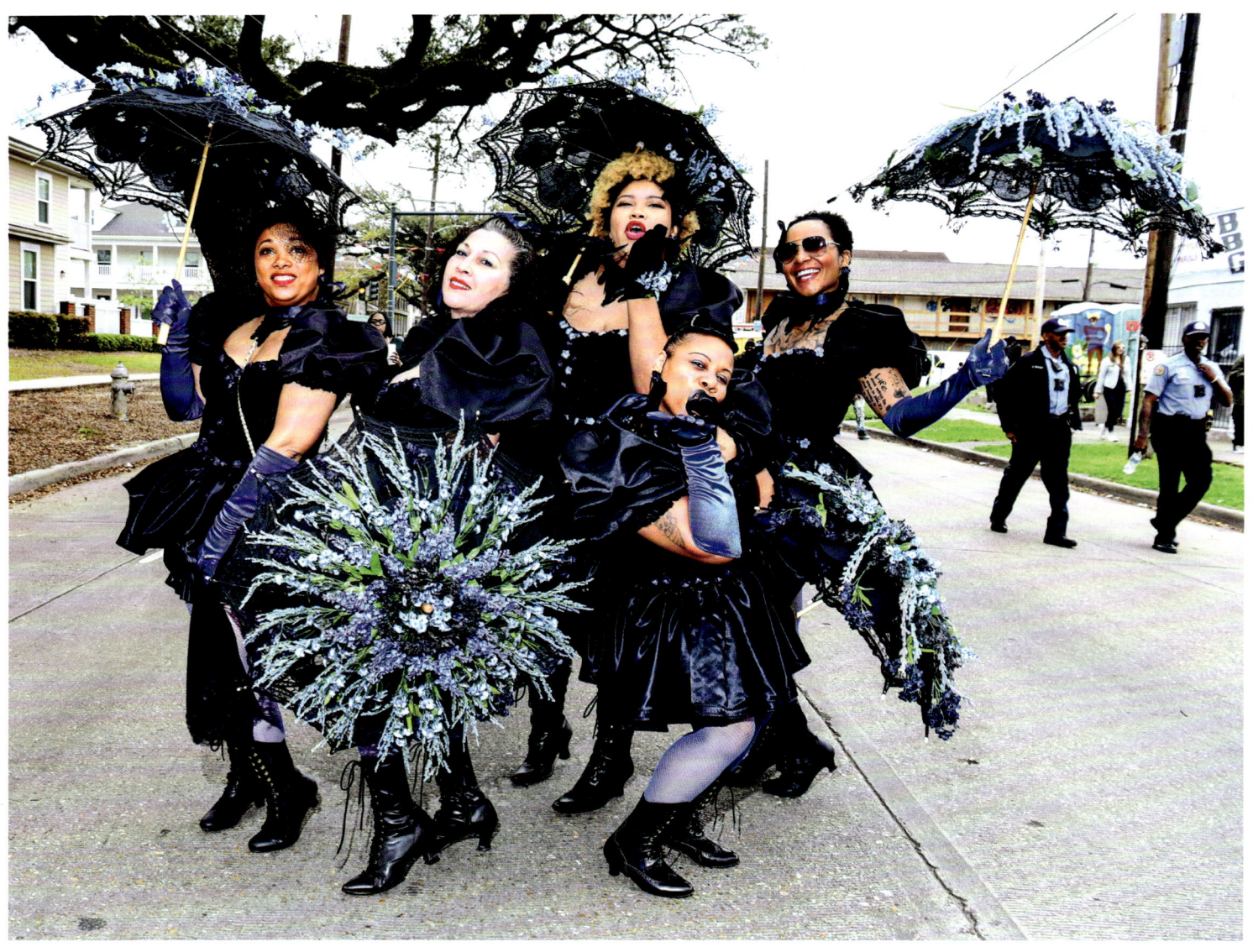

The Mahogany Blue Baby Dolls parade in black and blue satin during Super Sunday, 2019. They are a family-centric ensemble of professional women led by Anita Oubre, who carry on the Black Masking tradition into the modern era.

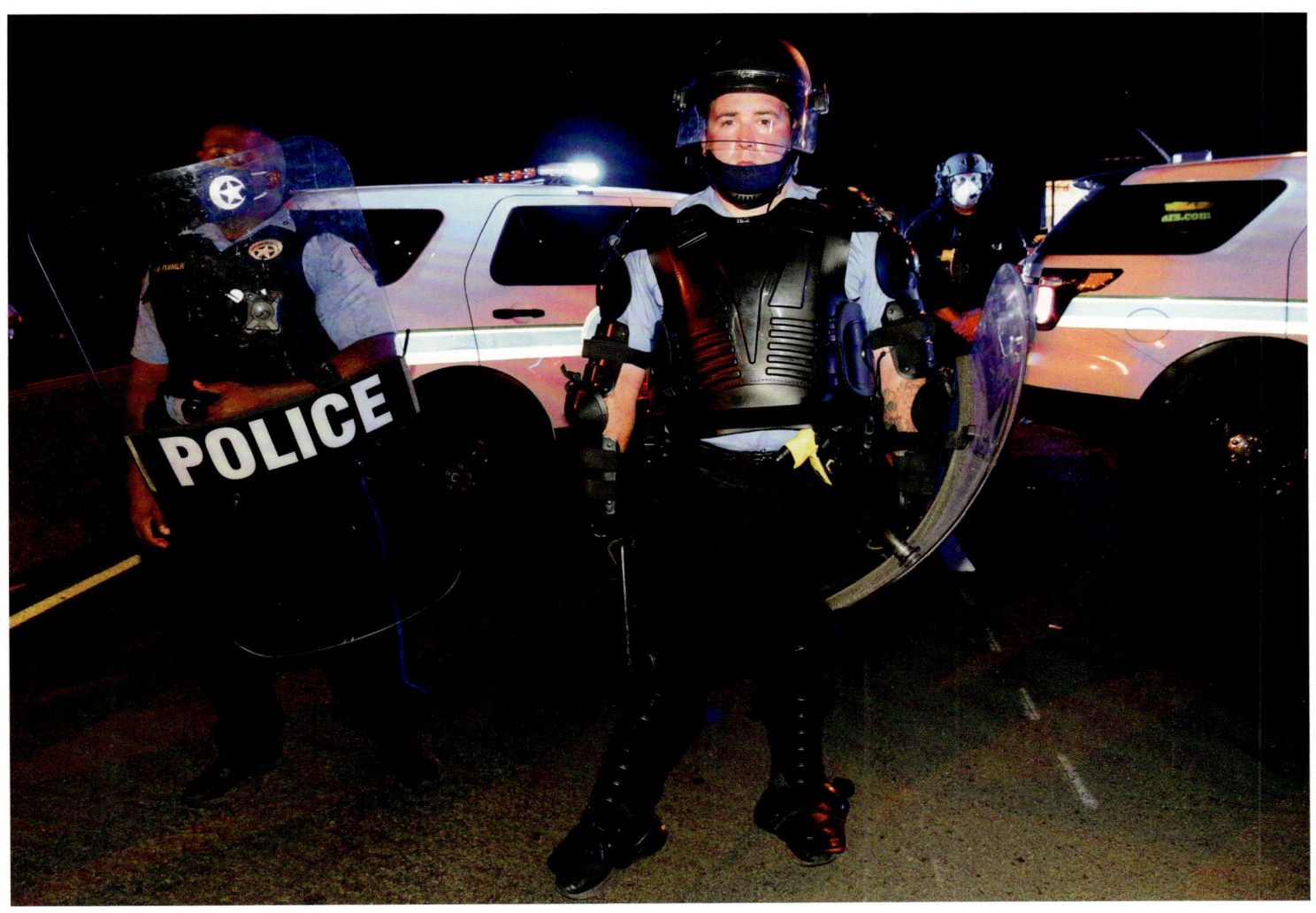

Police officers wield protective shields and combat gear on the Interstate 610 flyover during a protest that erupted after the murder of George Floyd by police officer Derek Chauvin in Minneapolis, 2020.

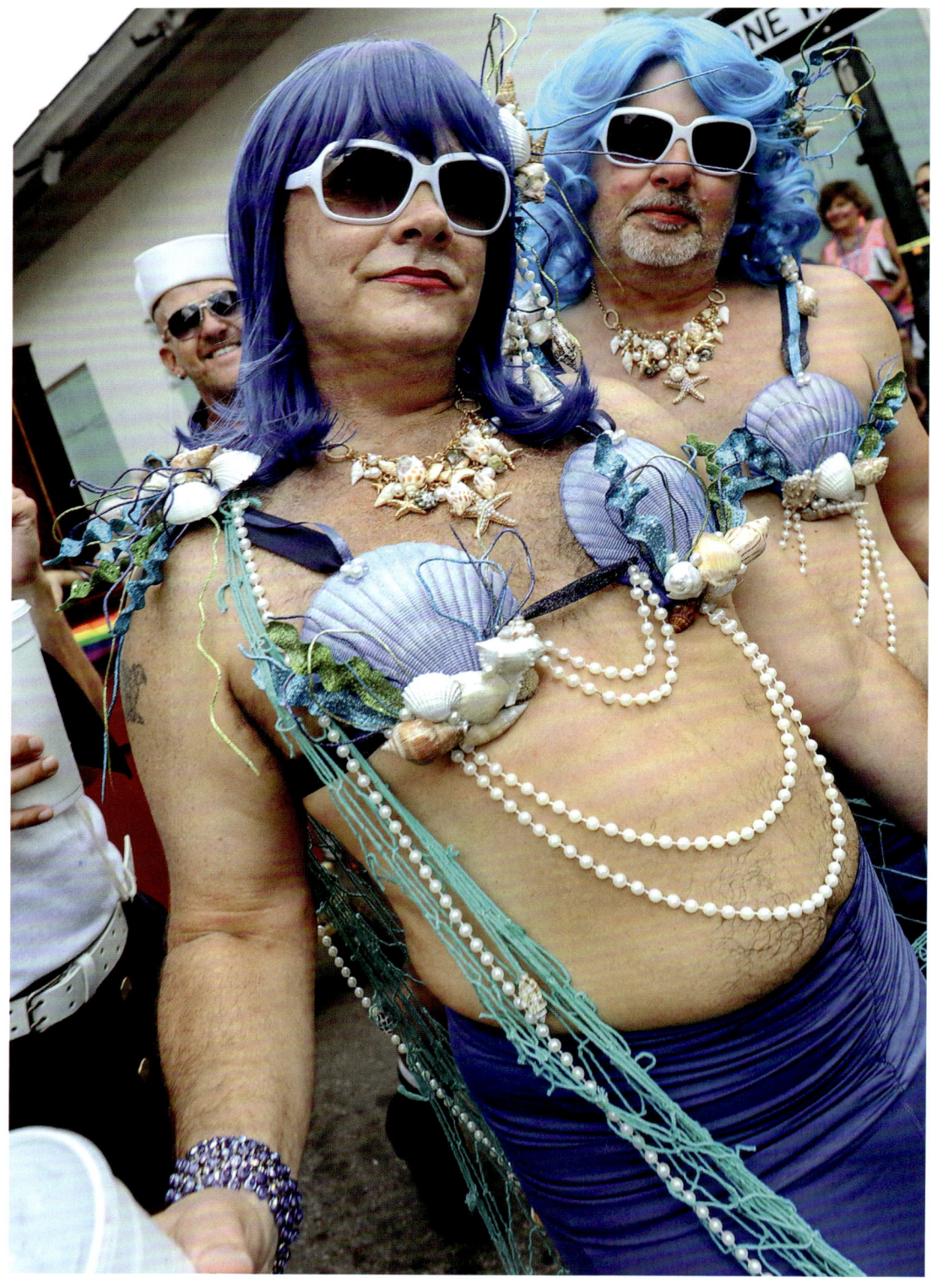

Southern Decadence revelers cover up in blue shells, 2013.

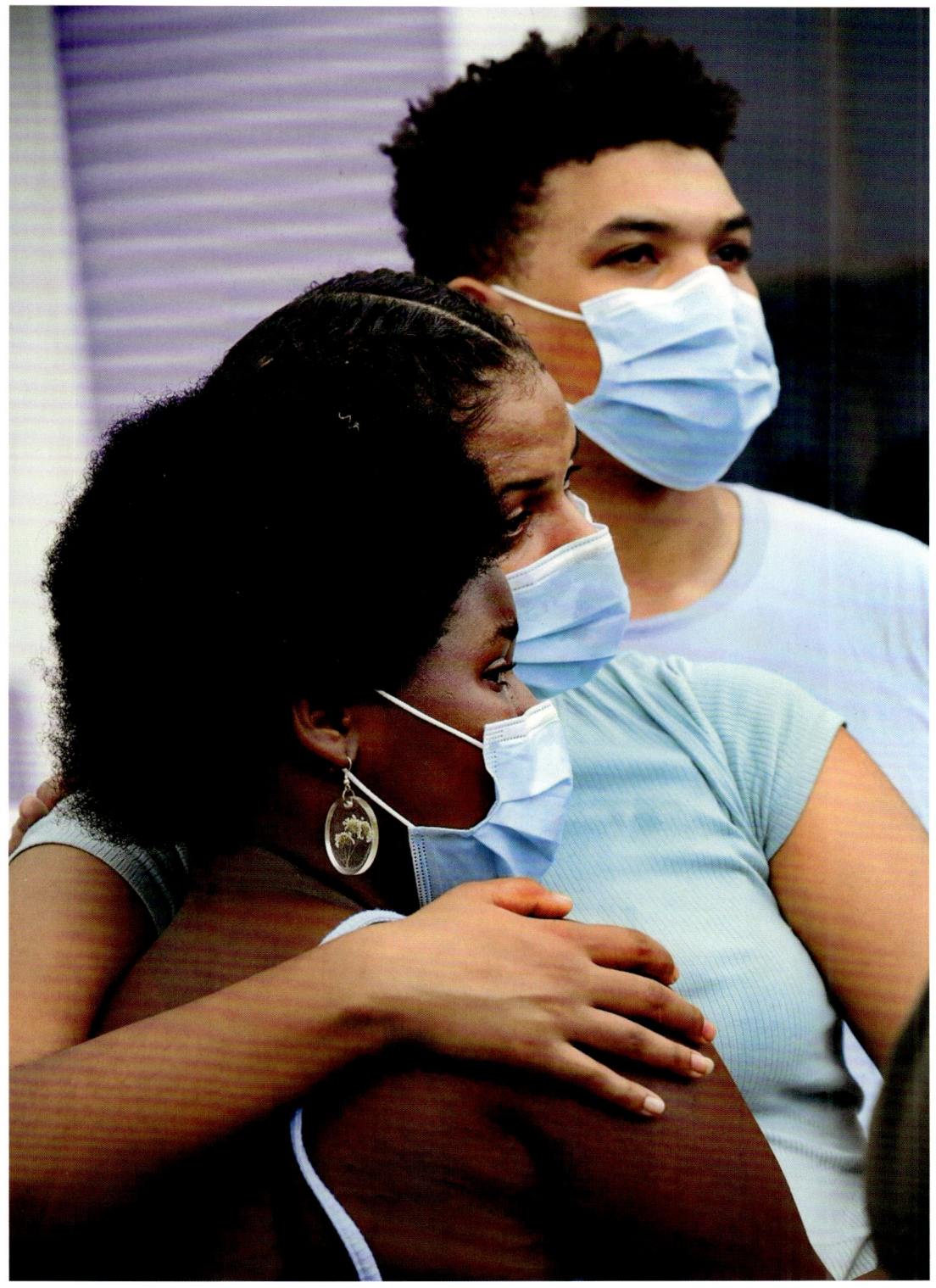

Mourners wearing blue pandemic masks console each other at a vigil for nine-year-old Devante Bryant, who was fatally shot in the Seventh Ward, 2020.

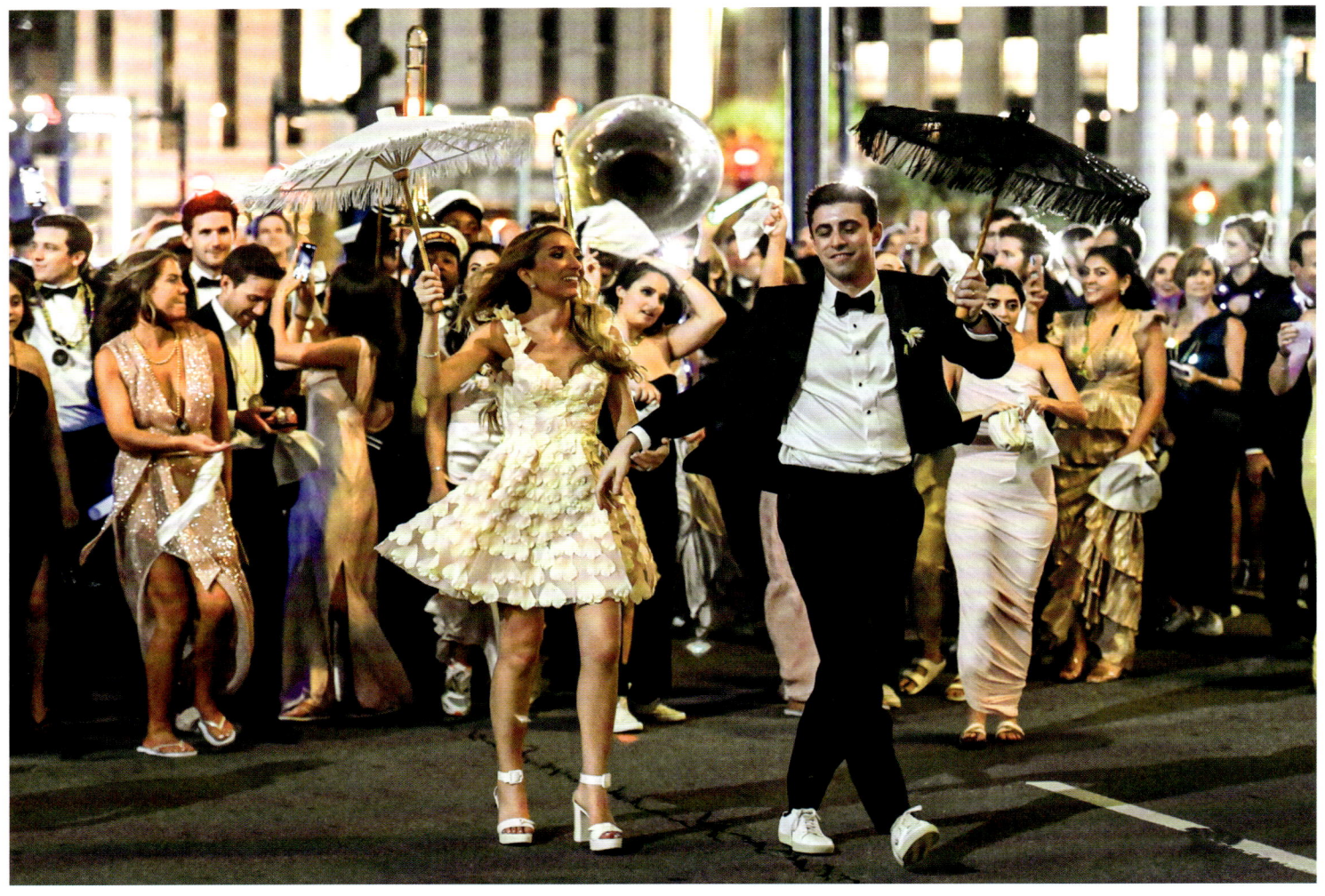

A couple celebrates their wedding with a midnight second line parade down Canal Street, 2022.

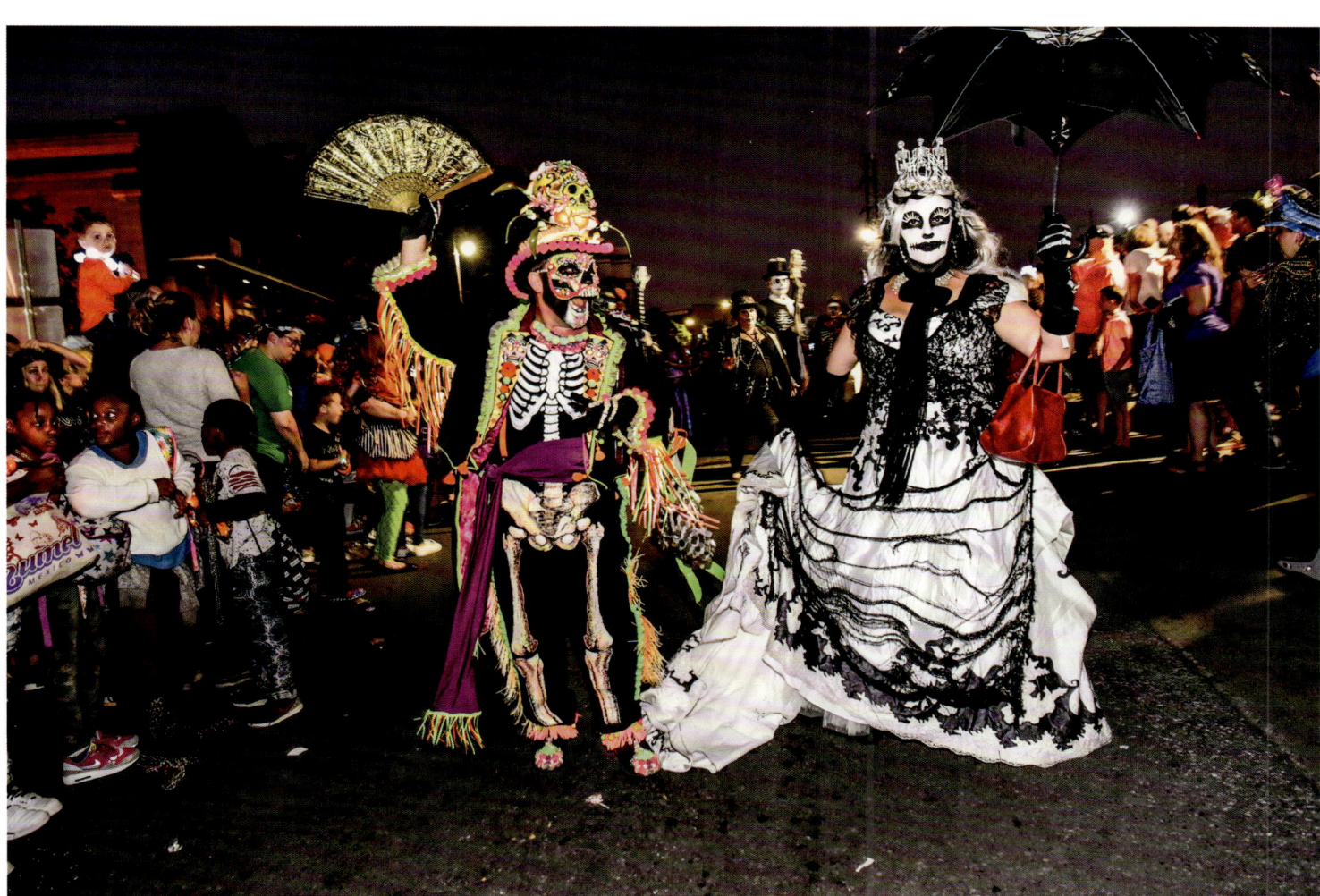

A couple costumes as bride and groom in the Krewe of Boo's Halloween parade in the French Quarter, 2019. The Krewe of Boo was founded in 2007 by Blaine Kern Sr. as a fundraiser for Hurricane Katrina relief. After several years passed with no parades, it was "revived from the dead" in 2013, becoming New Orleans's official annual Halloween parade under the reins of Blaine's son Brian.

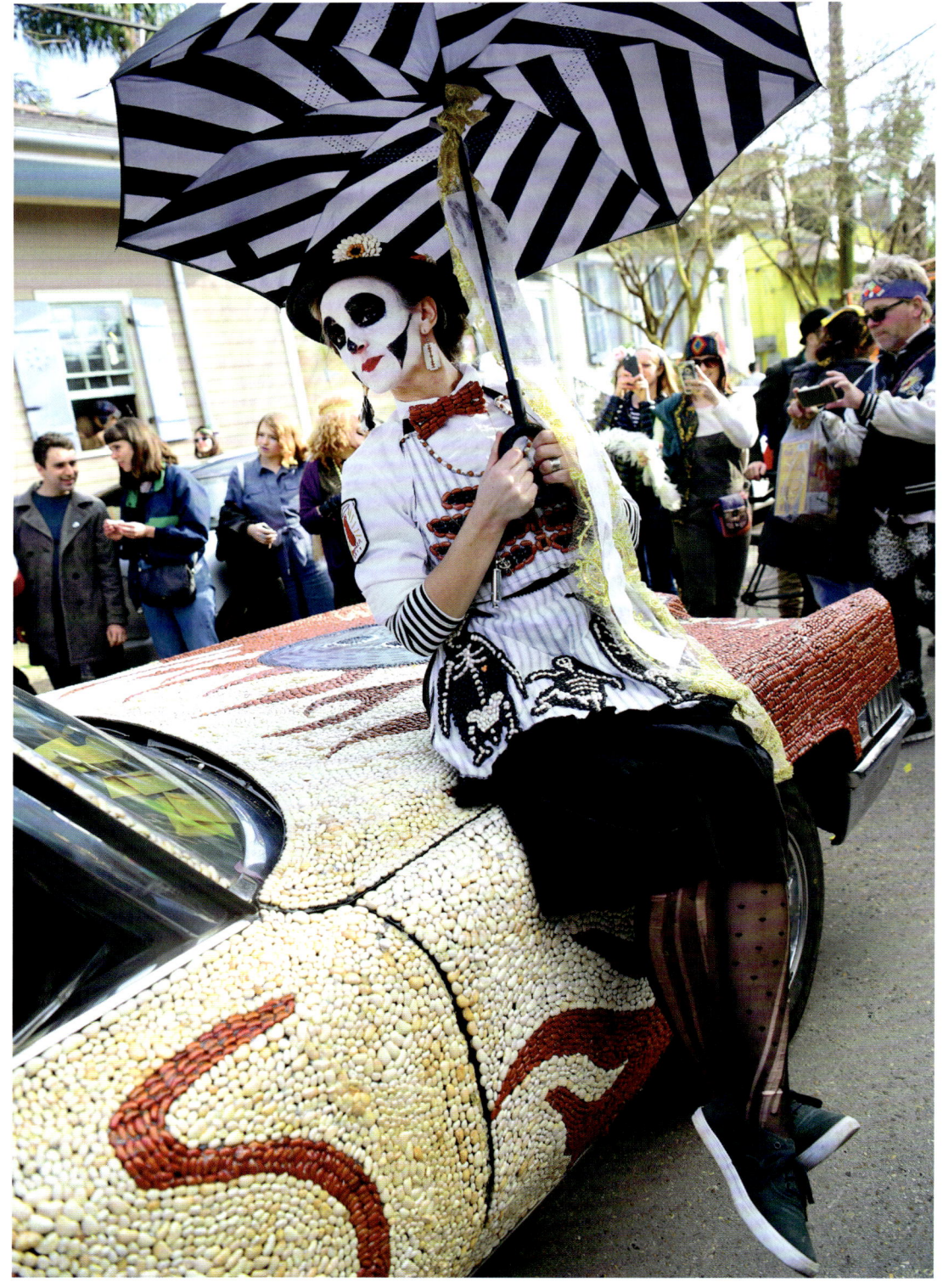

A Krewe of Dead Beans costumer carries an umbrella in its annual Lundi Gras parade in Tremé, 2019.

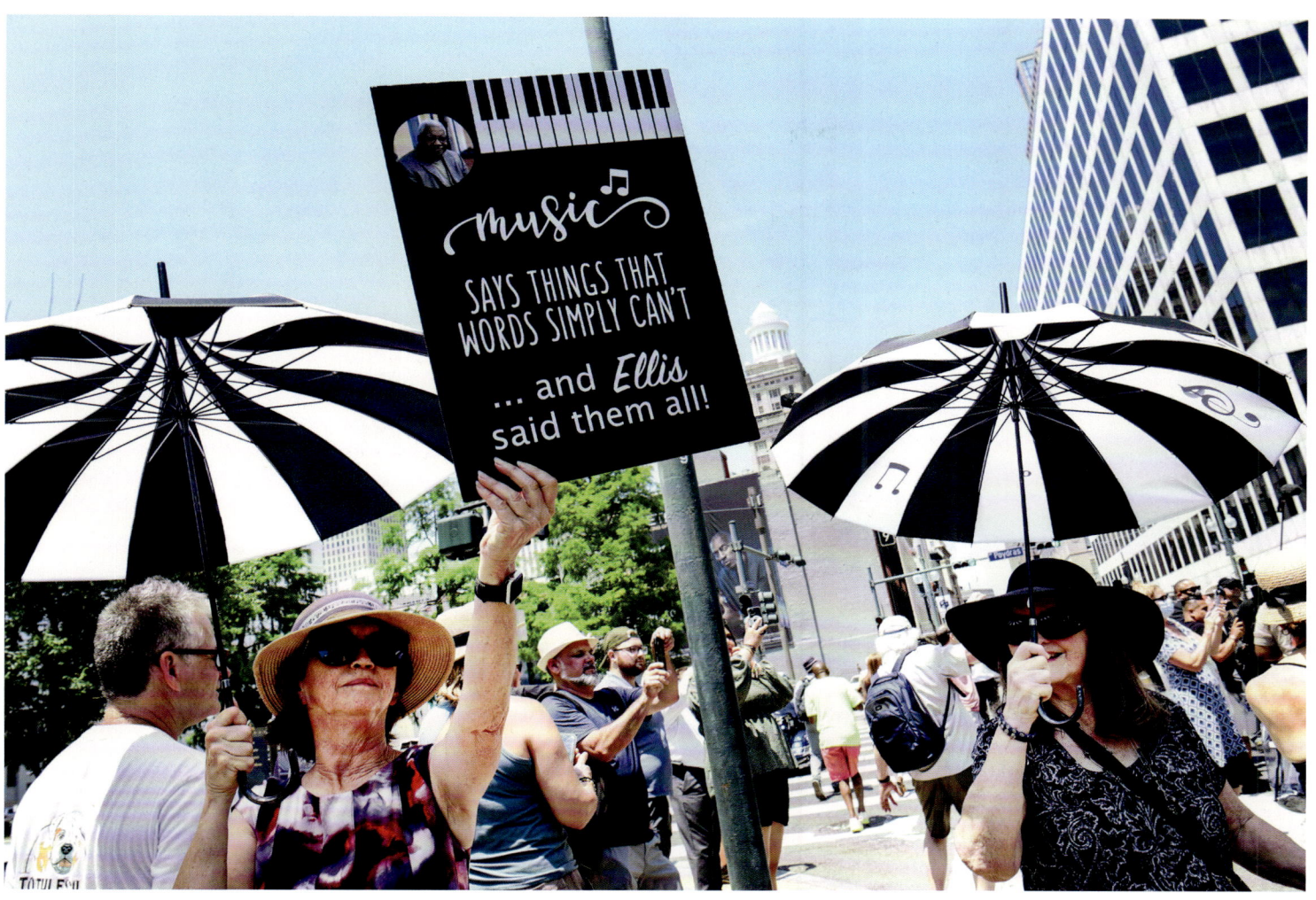

Fans of Ellis Marsalis Jr. twirl umbrellas and hold up a sign during the musician's funeral procession, 2022. Marsalis (1934–2020), a piano master considered the patriarch of New Orleans jazz, passed away early in the pandemic due to complications from COVID. His funeral procession was held two years later after pandemic mandates were lifted.

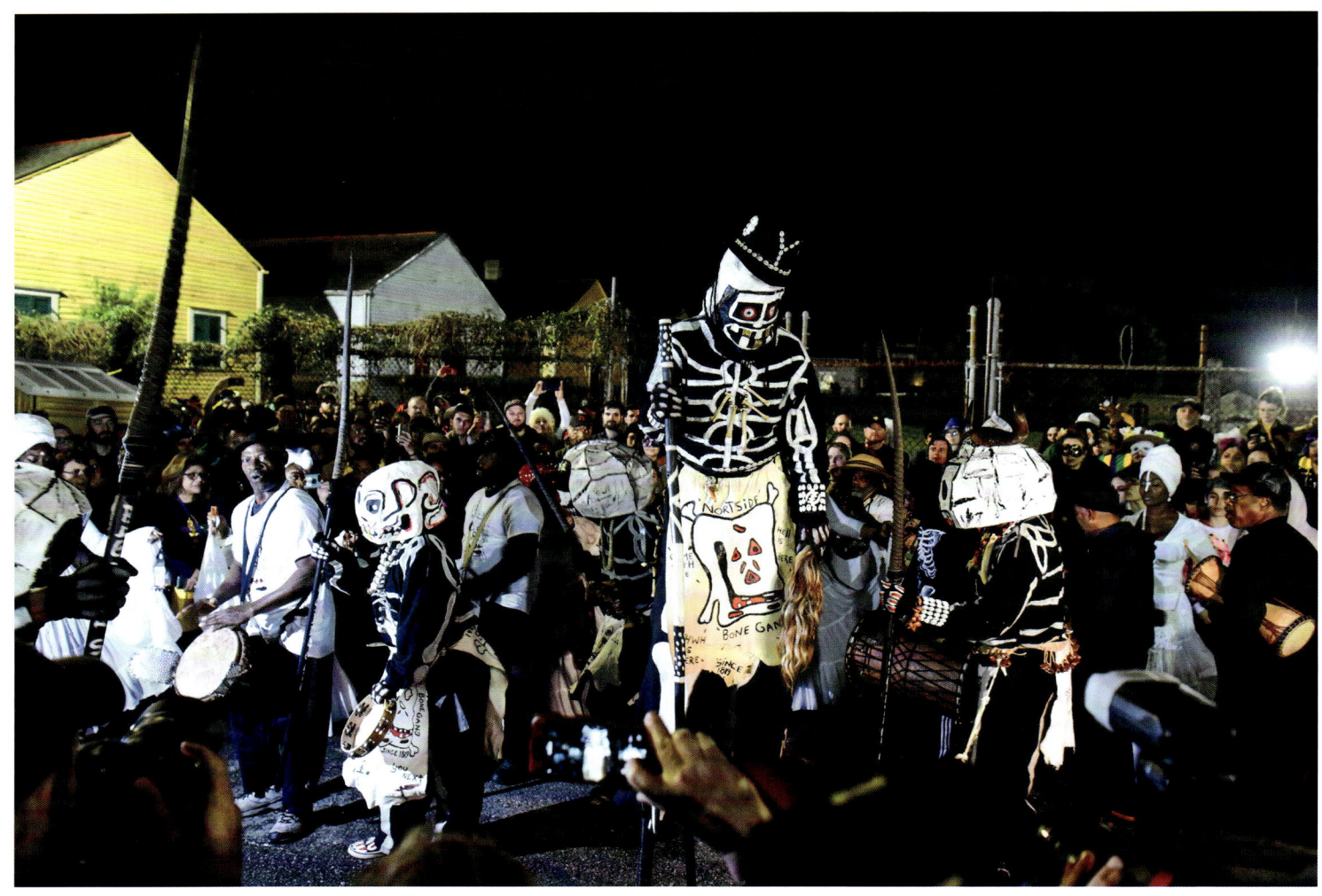

The North Side Skull and Bone Gang meets before dawn on Mardi Gras in the Sixth Ward, 2020, less than three weeks before the city-wide shutdown in response to the global pandemic. The 200-year-old predawn tradition of Black Masking kicks off Mardi Gras in the Tremé neighborhood as members costume as skeletons wearing oversized papier-mâché heads, going door to door to wake residents with a message that life is fleeting, so get your life straight before you die.

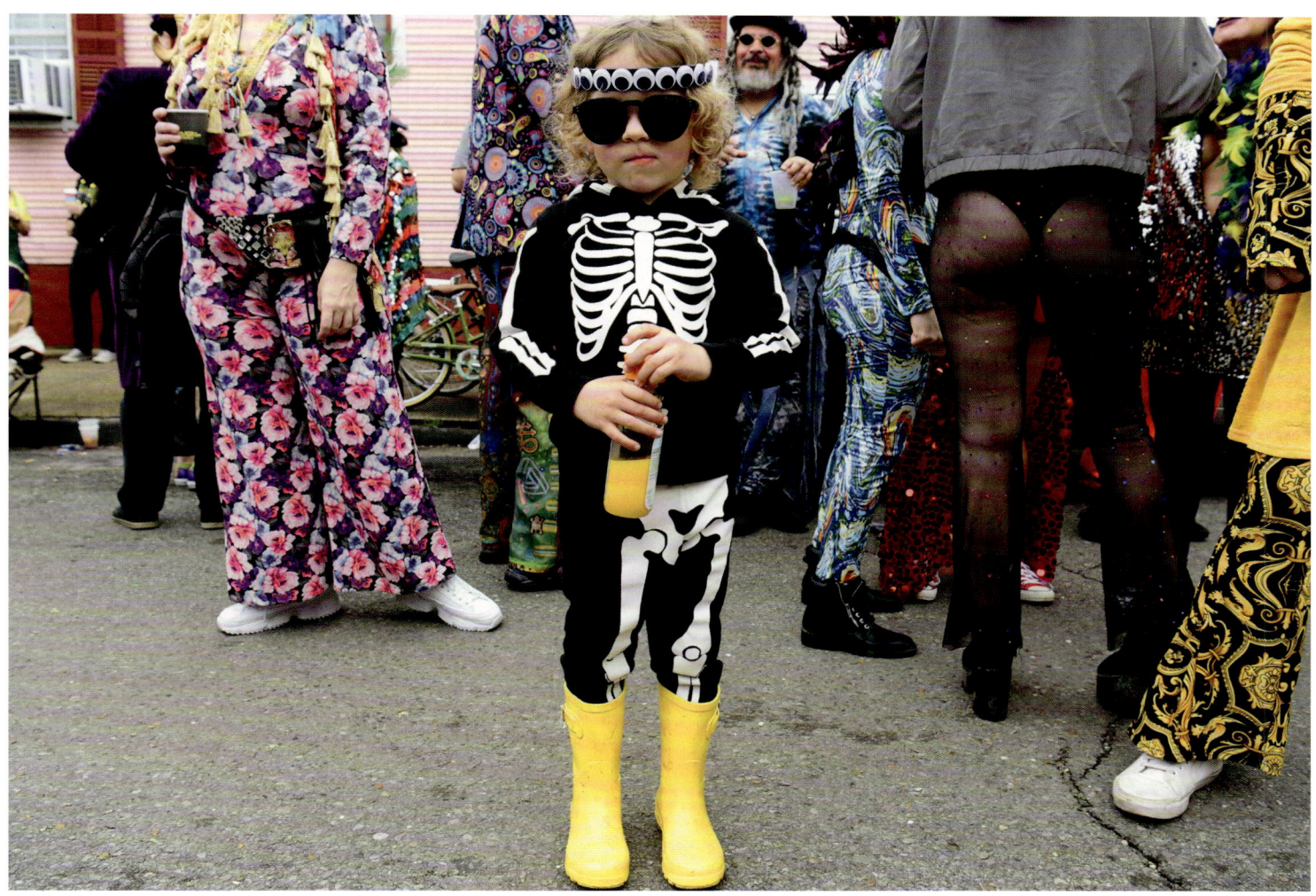

Five-year-old Clovis Lewis costumes as "Skin and Bones" on Mardi Gras Day in the Faubourg Marigny, 2020. Three weeks later, Lewis's public school, where he was attending kindergarten, shut down for in-person learning because of the pandemic, forcing many children to attend school online, on and off, for nearly two years.

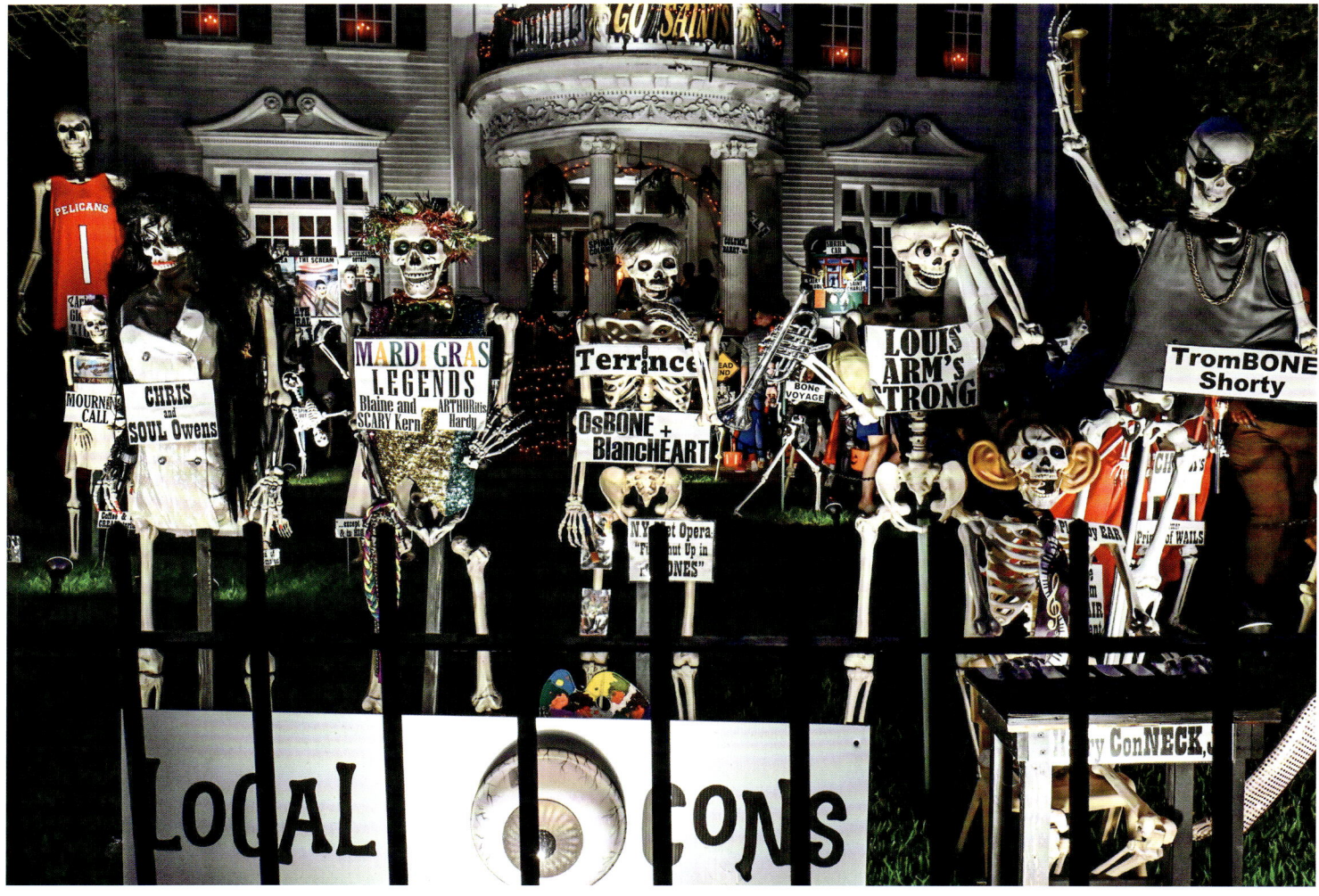

The Skeleton House at the Uptown home of Darryl and Louellen Berger celebrates its twentieth Halloween by tickling onlookers' funny bones with punny skeletons that celebrate the city's "Local EYE-cons," 2022.

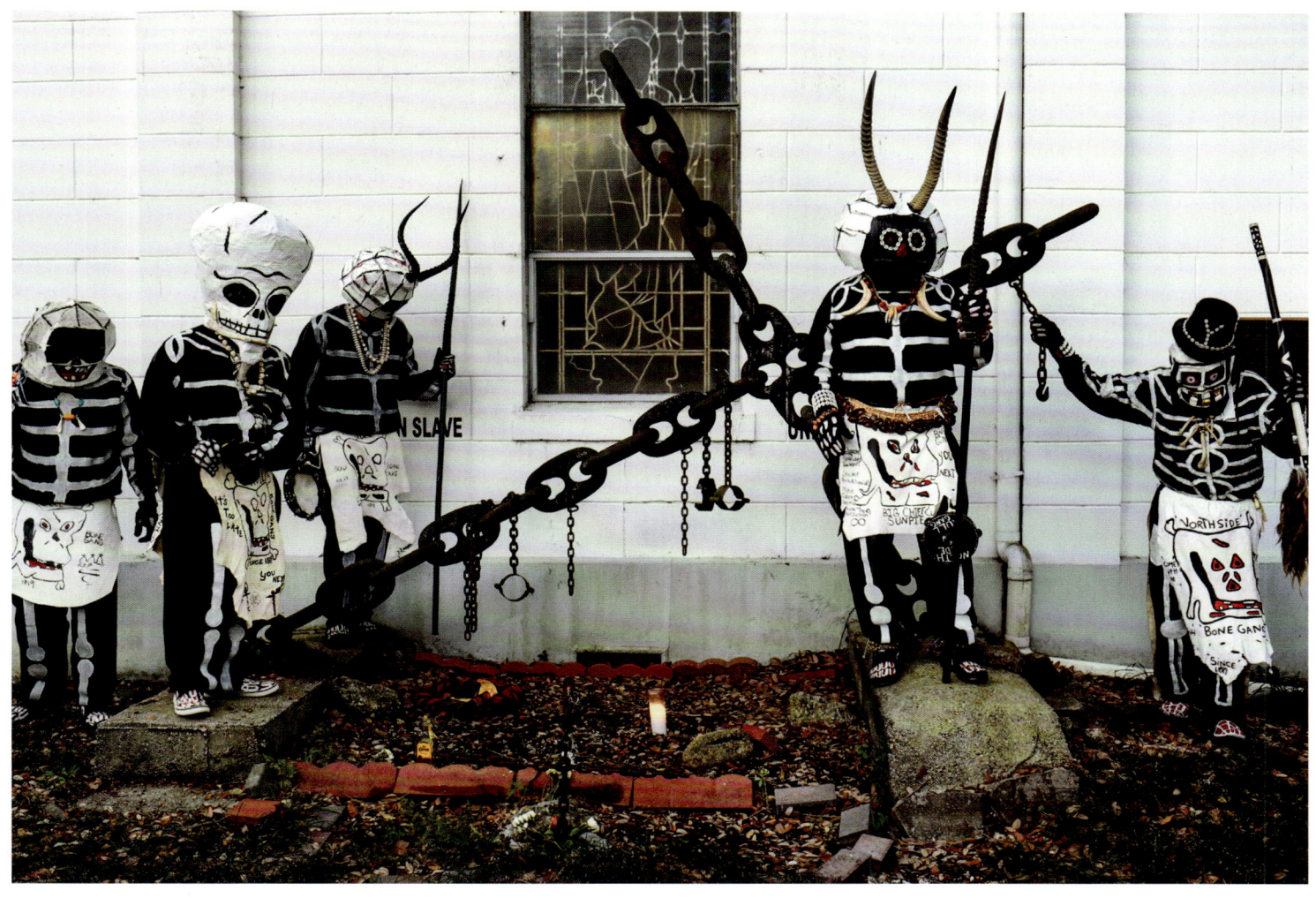

The North Side Skull and Bone Gang gathers at the Tomb of the Unknown Slave outside
St. Augustine Church in Tremé on Mardi Gras morning, 2022.

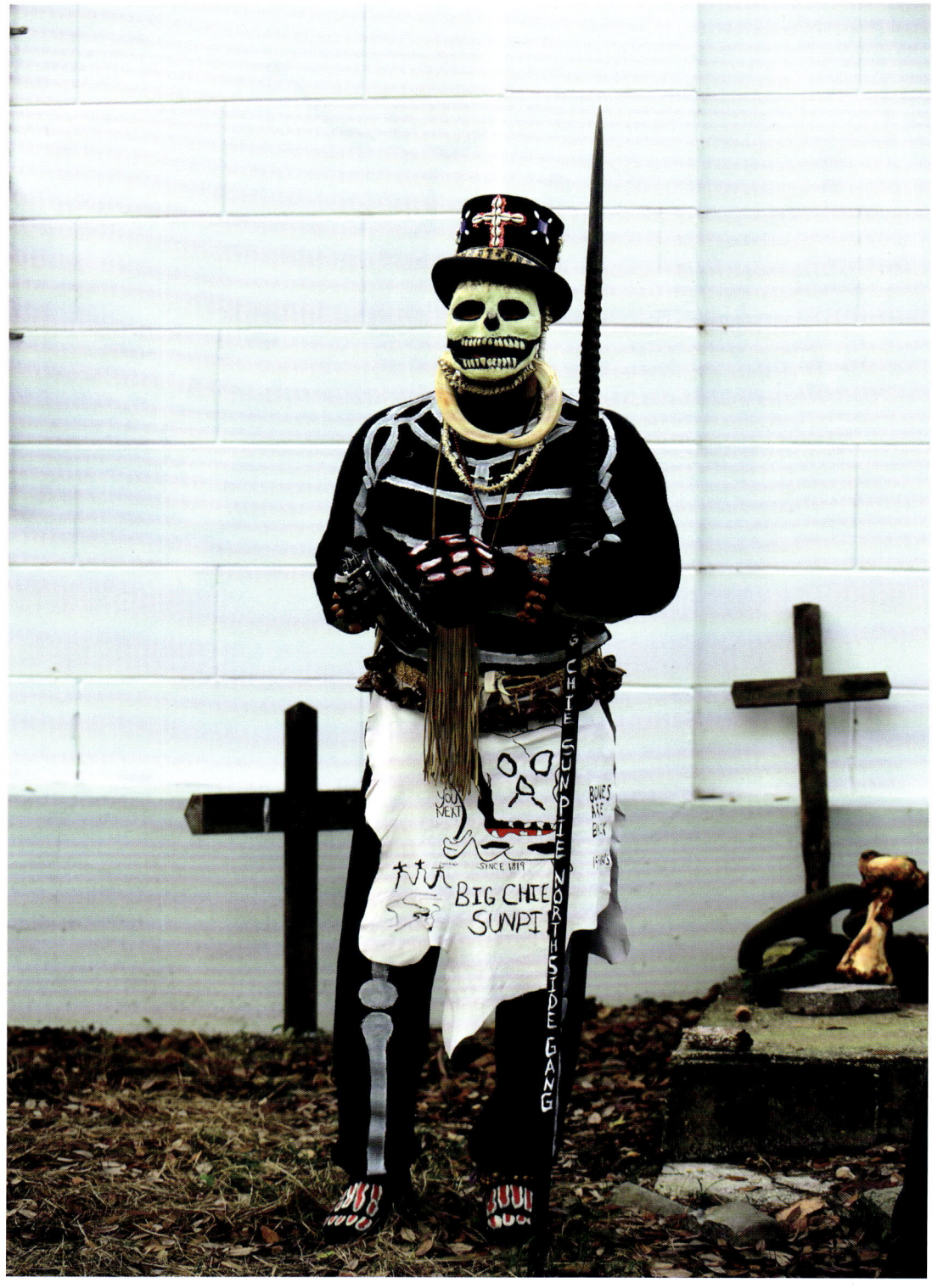

Bruce "Sunpie" Barnes, who heads the current North Side Skull and Bone Gang, sings at St. Augustine Church at the Tomb of the Unknown Slave, 2018. "Get your life together, (because) next time you see us, it's too late to cry."

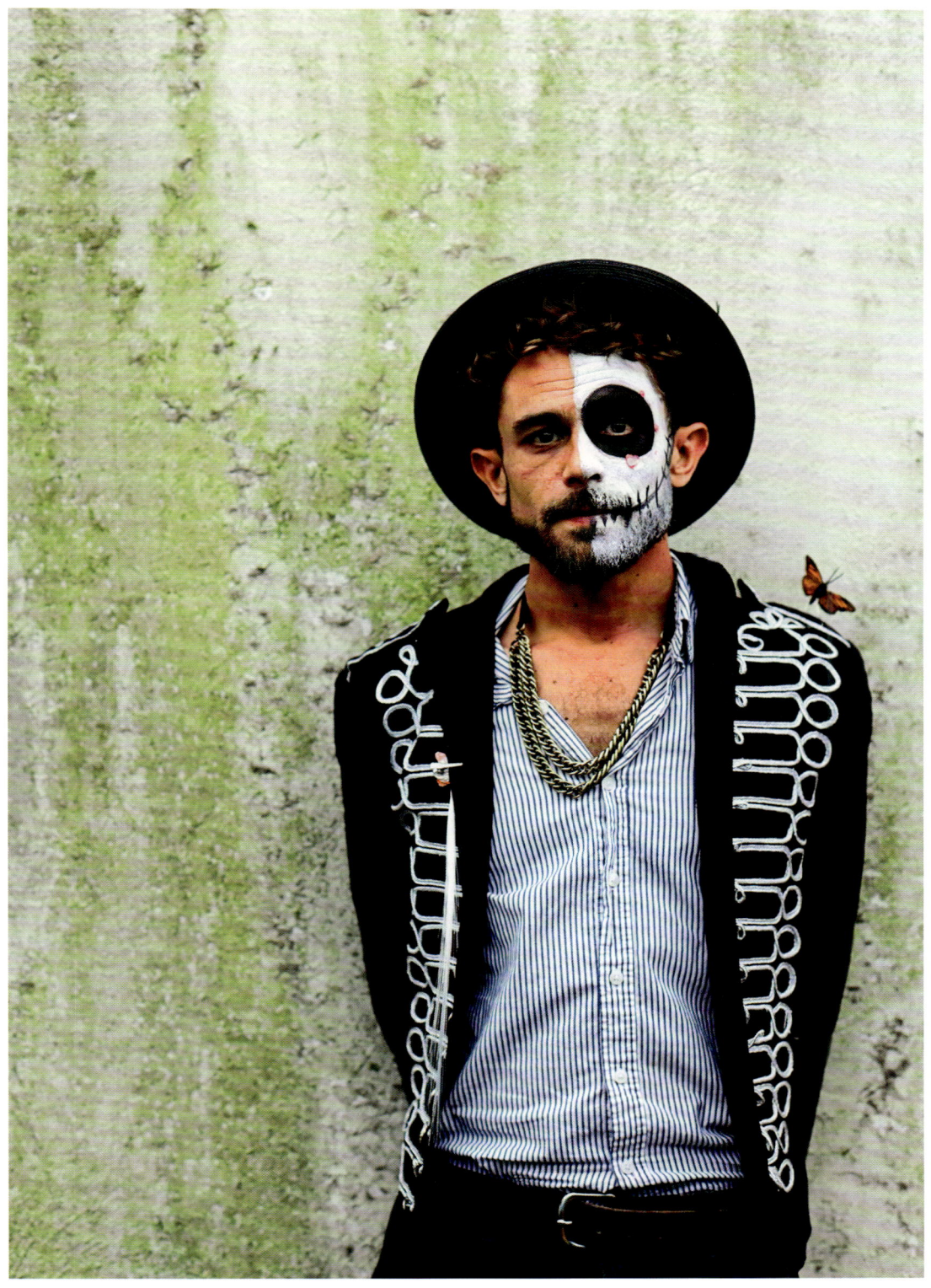

Austin Feldbaum participates in the Krewe de Mayahuel's *Día de los Muertos* (Day of the Dead) parade, a Mexican-style carnivalesque procession to honor the dead, 2022. The monarch butterfly on his shoulder is believed to hold the spirits of the departed in Mexican Day of the Dead culture.

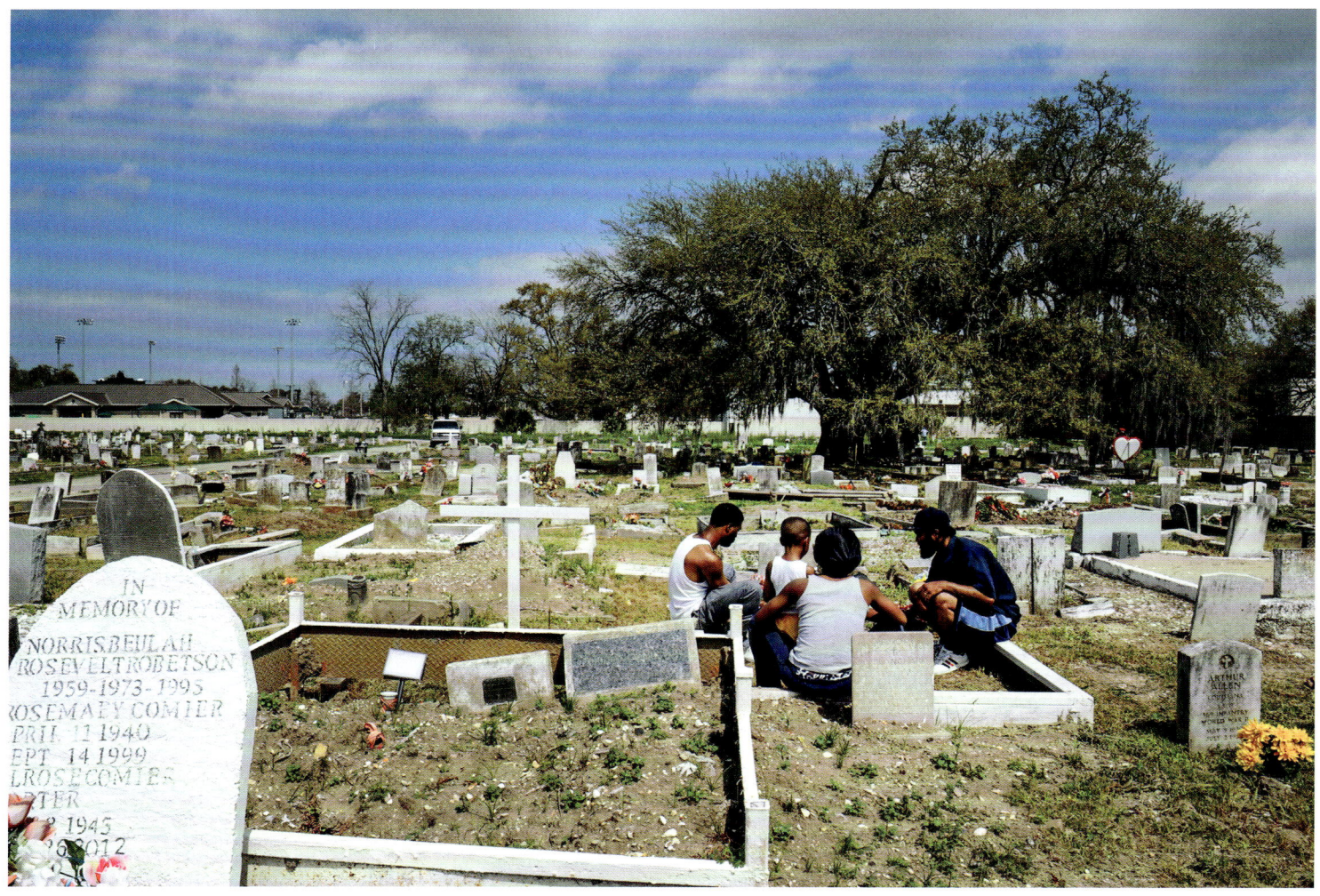

A family gathers at a grave site in Holt Cemetery on All Saints' Day, 2014. Holt Cemetery is a potter's field that was established in 1879 to inter the bodies of the poor and those without families.

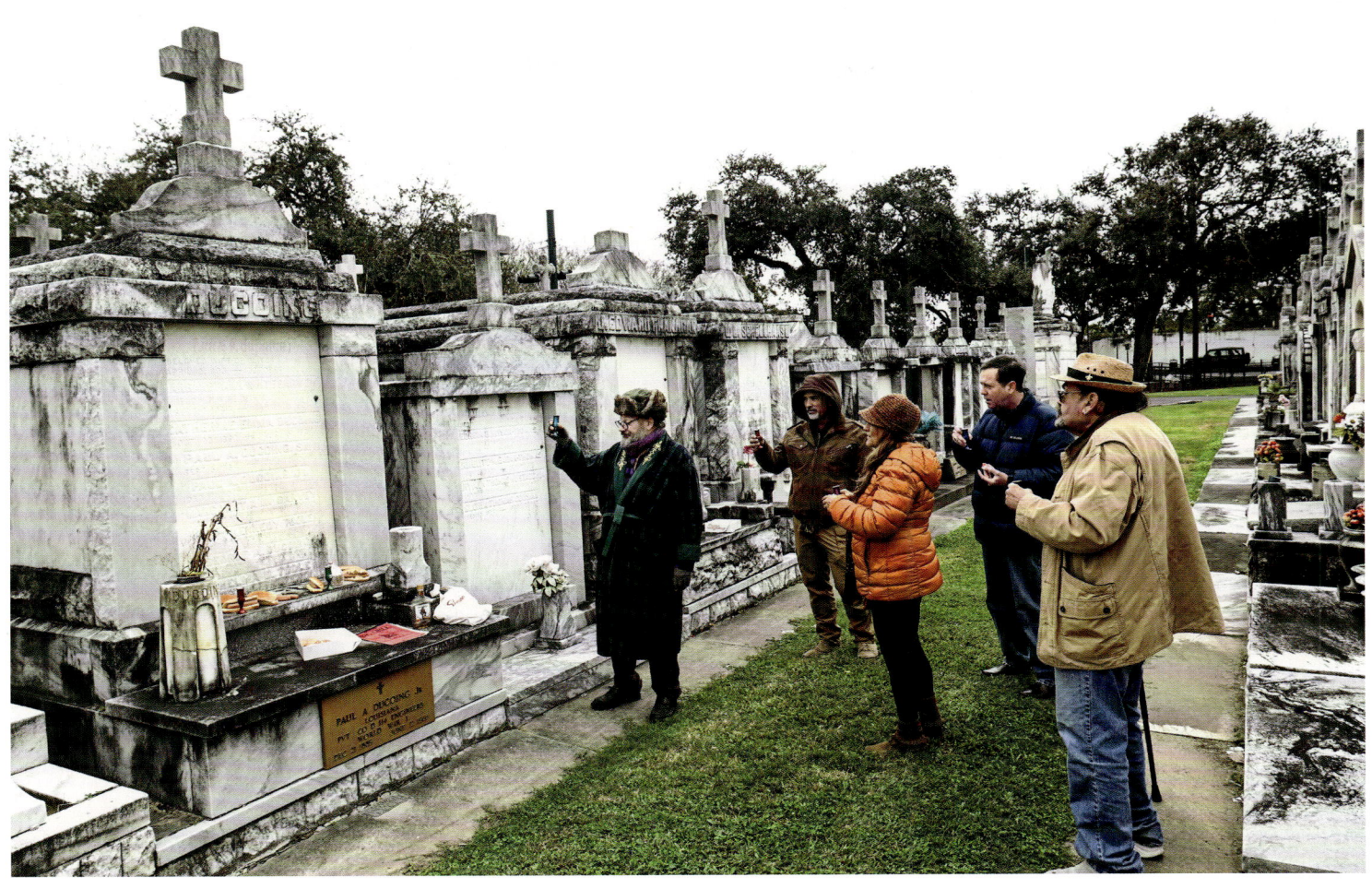

David Roe and friends raise a toast and leave offerings at the tomb of author John Kennedy Toole on his birthday in December 2022. Toole would have been eighty-five years old. He died by suicide years before his posthumously published book *A Confederacy of Dunces,* a cult classic widely considered a canonical work of modern literature, won the Pulitzer Prize for fiction in 1981. Toole is interred at Greenwood Cemetery with his mother, Thelma Toole.

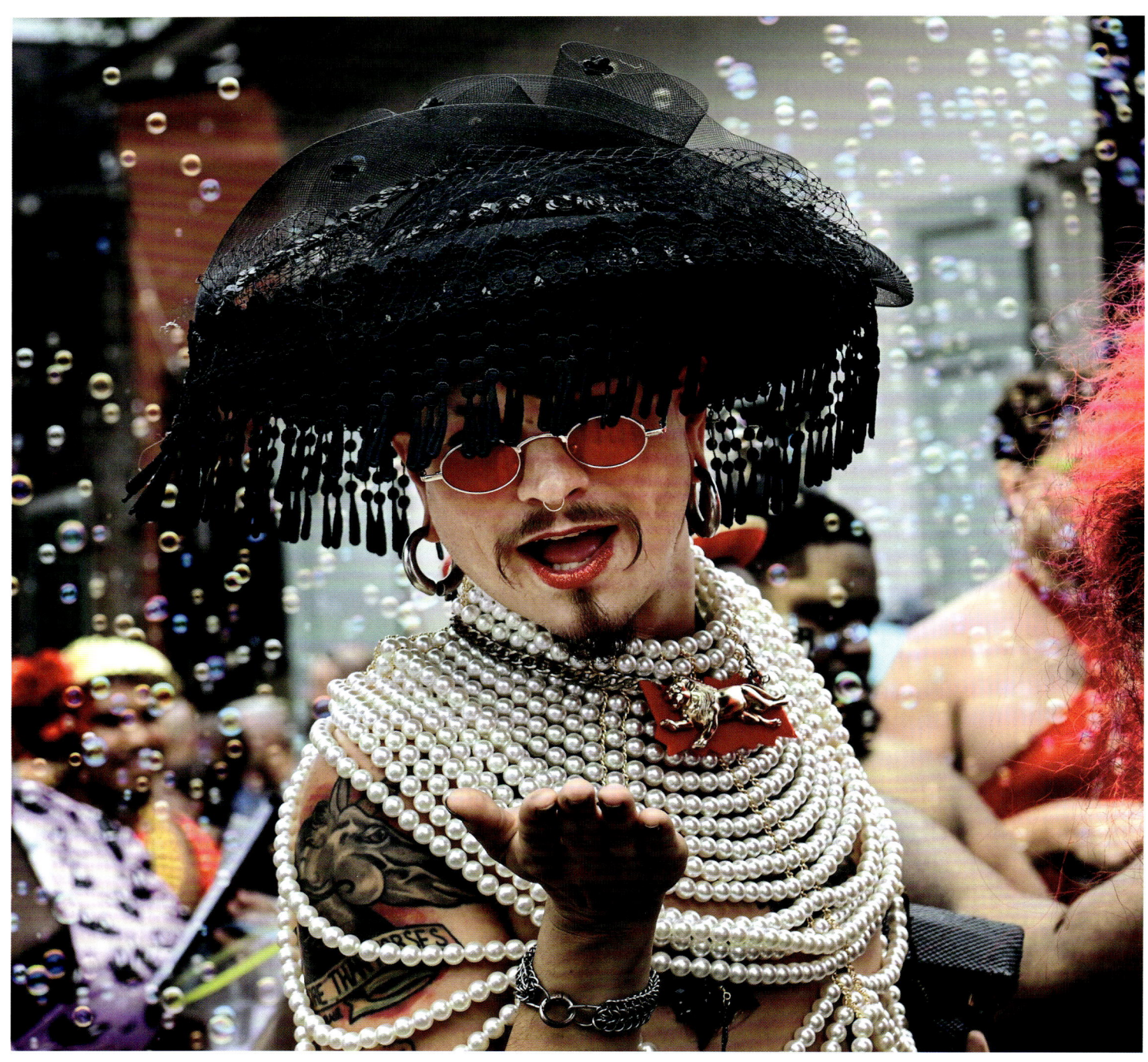

Aaron Yeager blows a kiss in Southern Decadence's fiftieth anniversary parade, 2022.

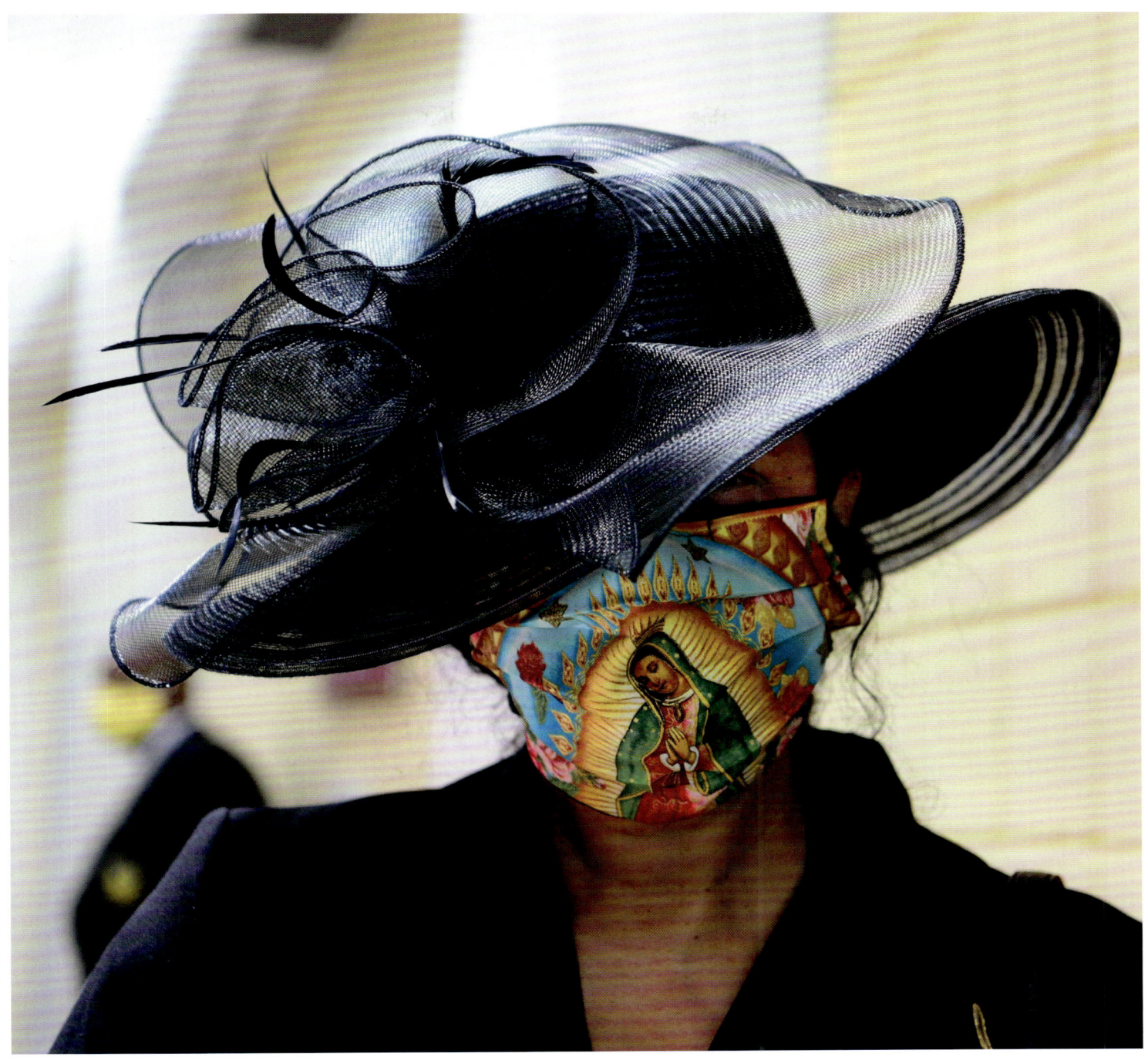

Dianne Honoré attends the funeral for Kim Boutte, Big Queen of the Spirit of Fi Yi Yi and the Mandingo Warriors, who was killed in a double shooting in 2020.

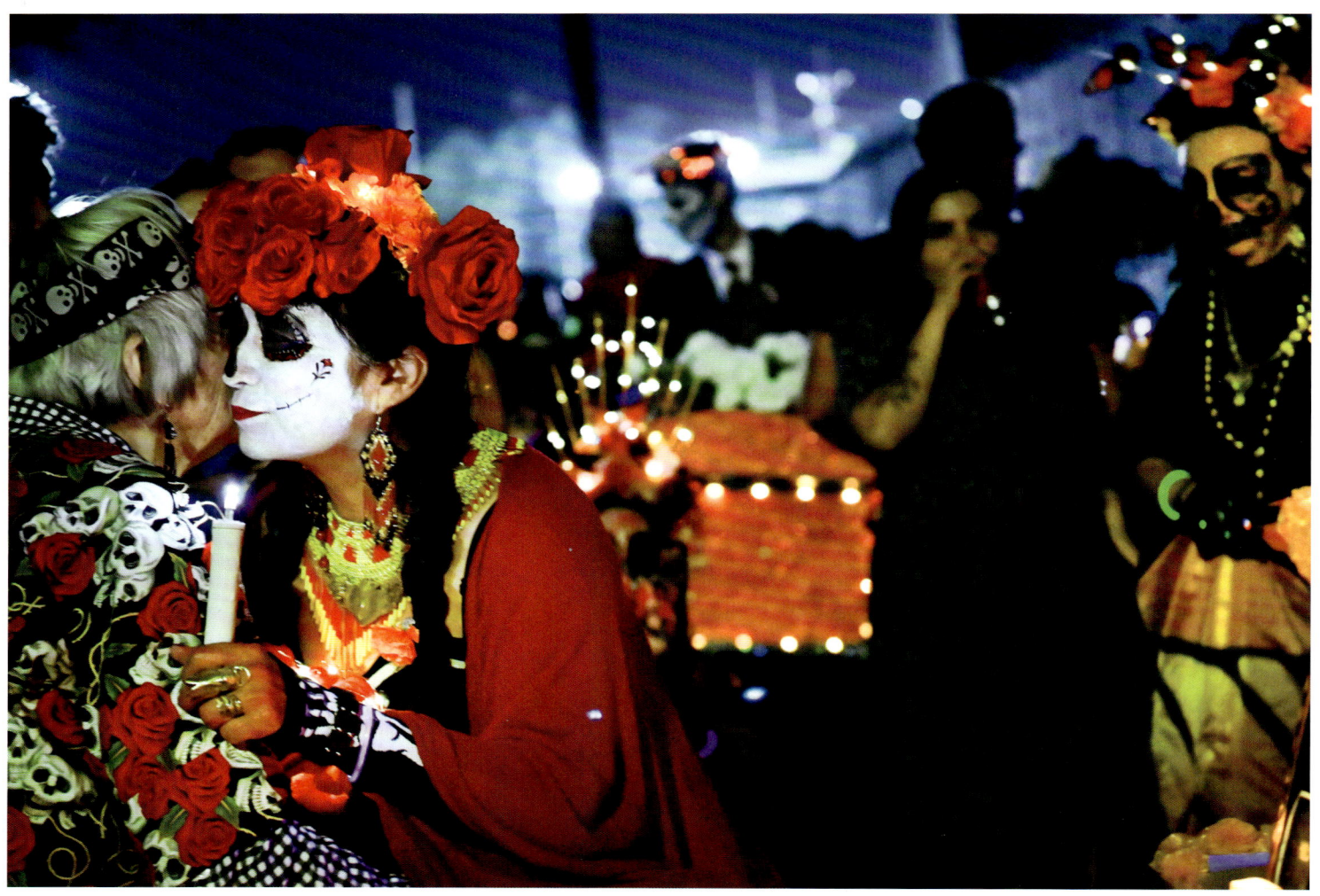

Nancy Ochsenschlager and Rachel Ornelas embrace during a candlelight ceremony honoring the dead at the Krewe de Mayahuel's Día de los Muertos celebration at St. Roch Cemetery, 2022. Mayahuel, which takes its name from the Aztec goddess of fertility and agave, honors the dead with a rolling altar float in the shape of a pyramid, on which participants can place photos and belongings of loved ones who have died.

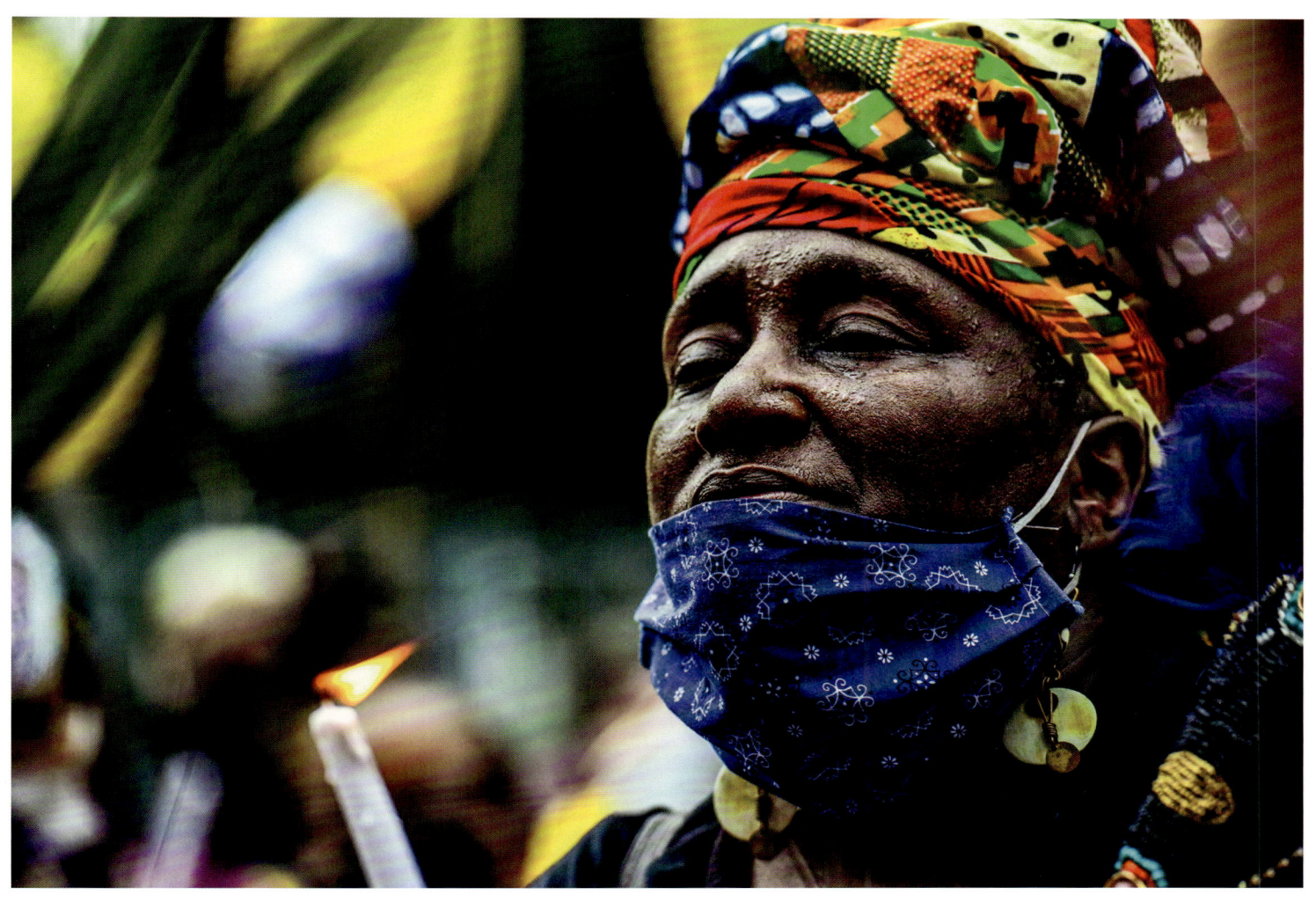

Ausettua Amor Amenkum mourns the passing of Kim Boutte at a candlelight vigil, 2020.

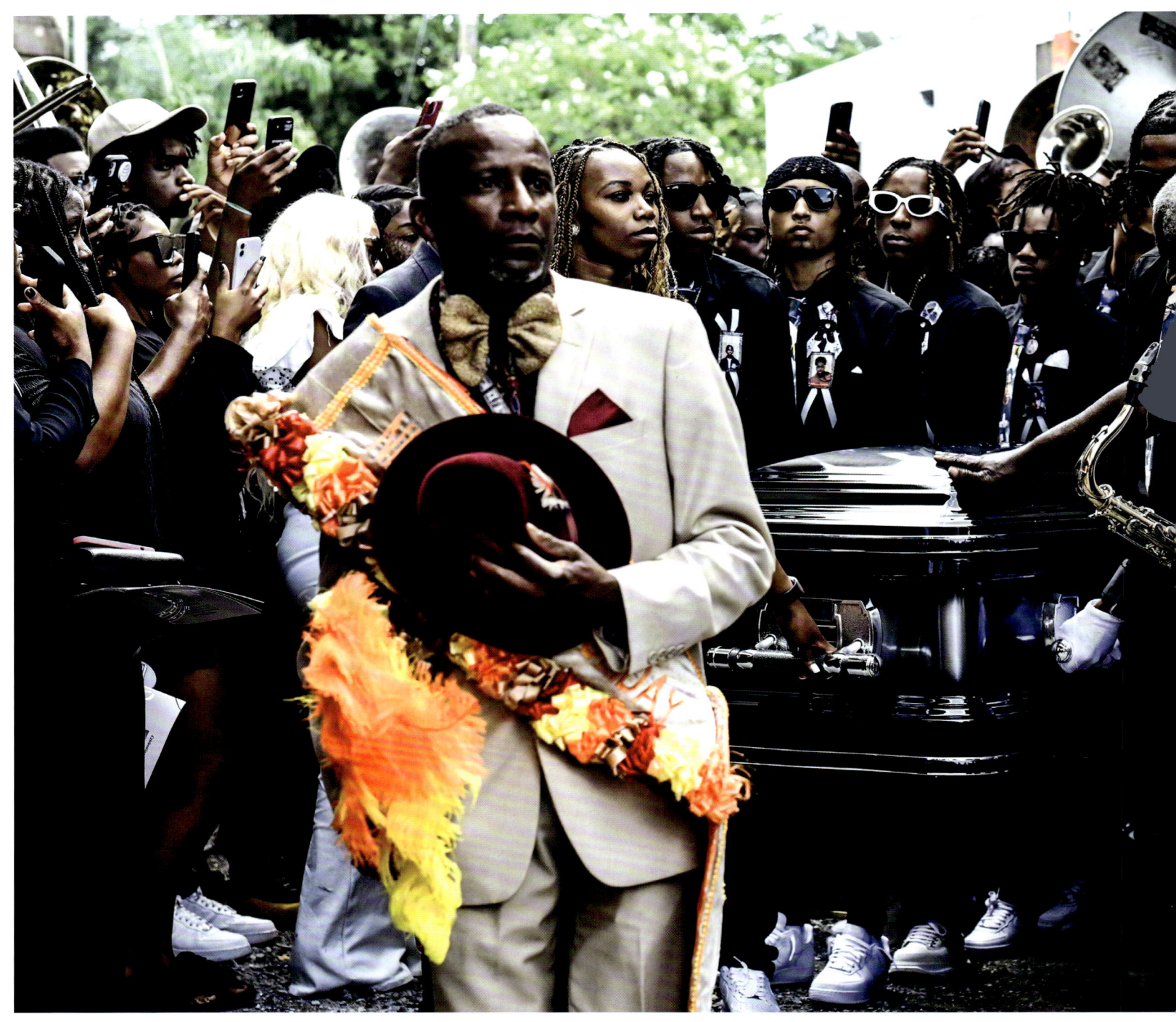

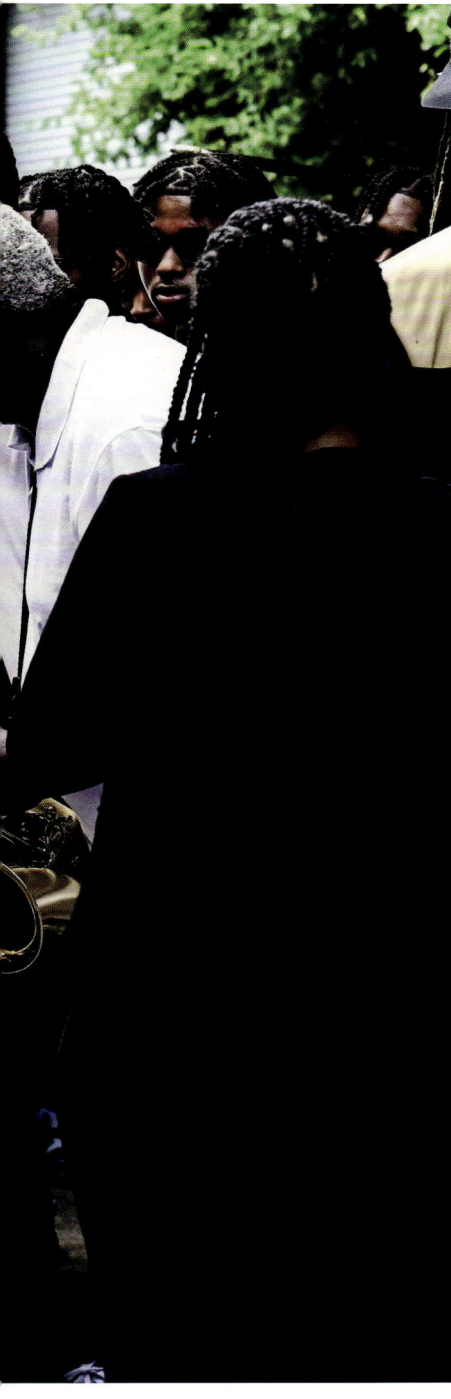

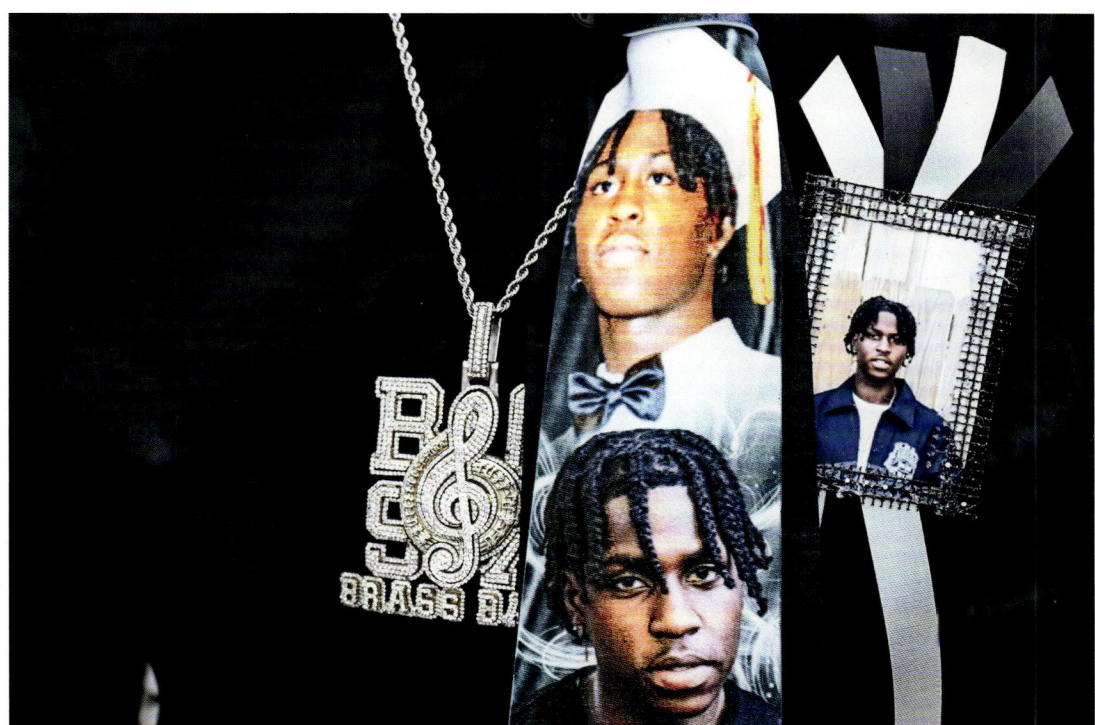

Teenagers carry the casket of their friend Revell Dewan "Velly Vell" Andrews, who was fatally shot after attending summer theater camp by a 14-year-old he didn't know. An up-and-coming musician and straight A student who had recently graduated from McDonogh 35 Senior High School, Andrews planned to attend Southern University in Baton Rouge starting in the fall. "He was one of the best children to ever be a child," wrote reporter Katy Reckdahl, who was described at the funeral as Revell's "honorary mom." Andrews became the city's 120th murder victim halfway through the year, 2023.

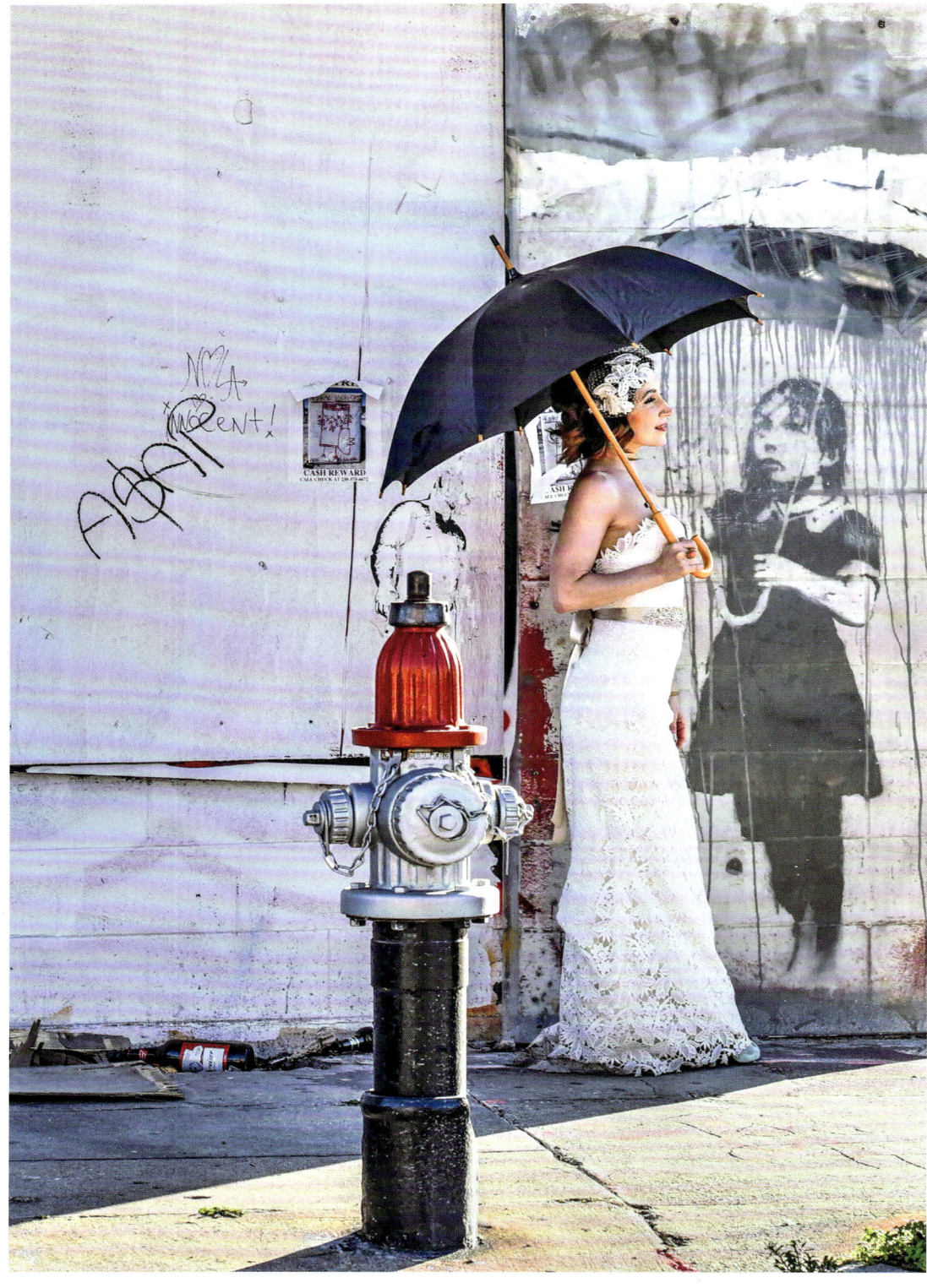

A bride poses near Banksy's *Rain Girl* on St. Claude Avenue, 2016. Banksy is a graffiti artist rumored to be from England, who is known for his anti-authoritarian art that is often made in public spaces. He created several works in New Orleans in the aftermath of Hurricane Katrina, though only a couple have survived. A Los Angeles art dealer was identified as the person who attempted to steal *Rain Girl* by drilling the valuable mural out of the wall in 2014.

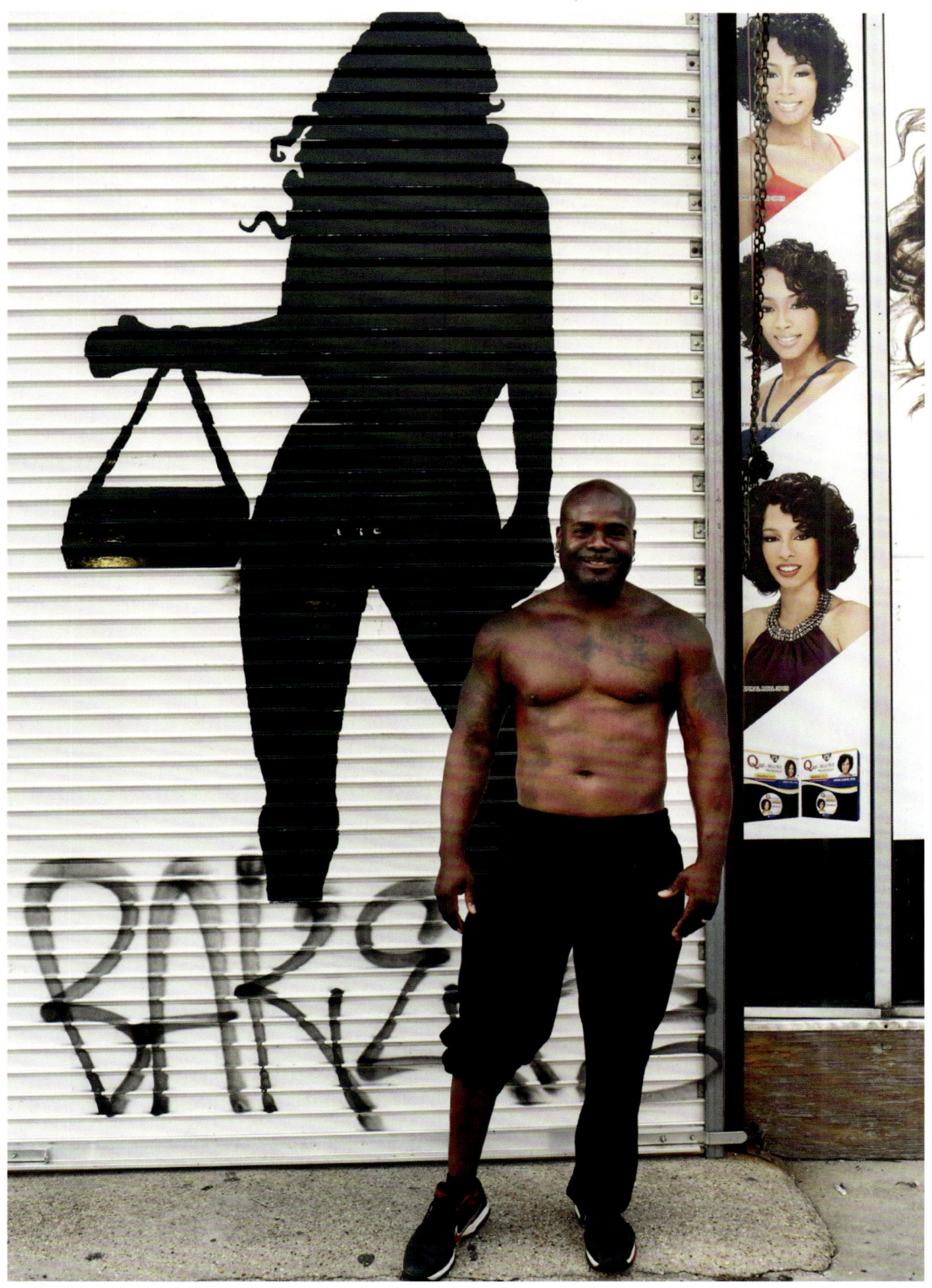

A shirtless man poses near High Maintenance Beauty Supply store on St. Claude Avenue, 2017.

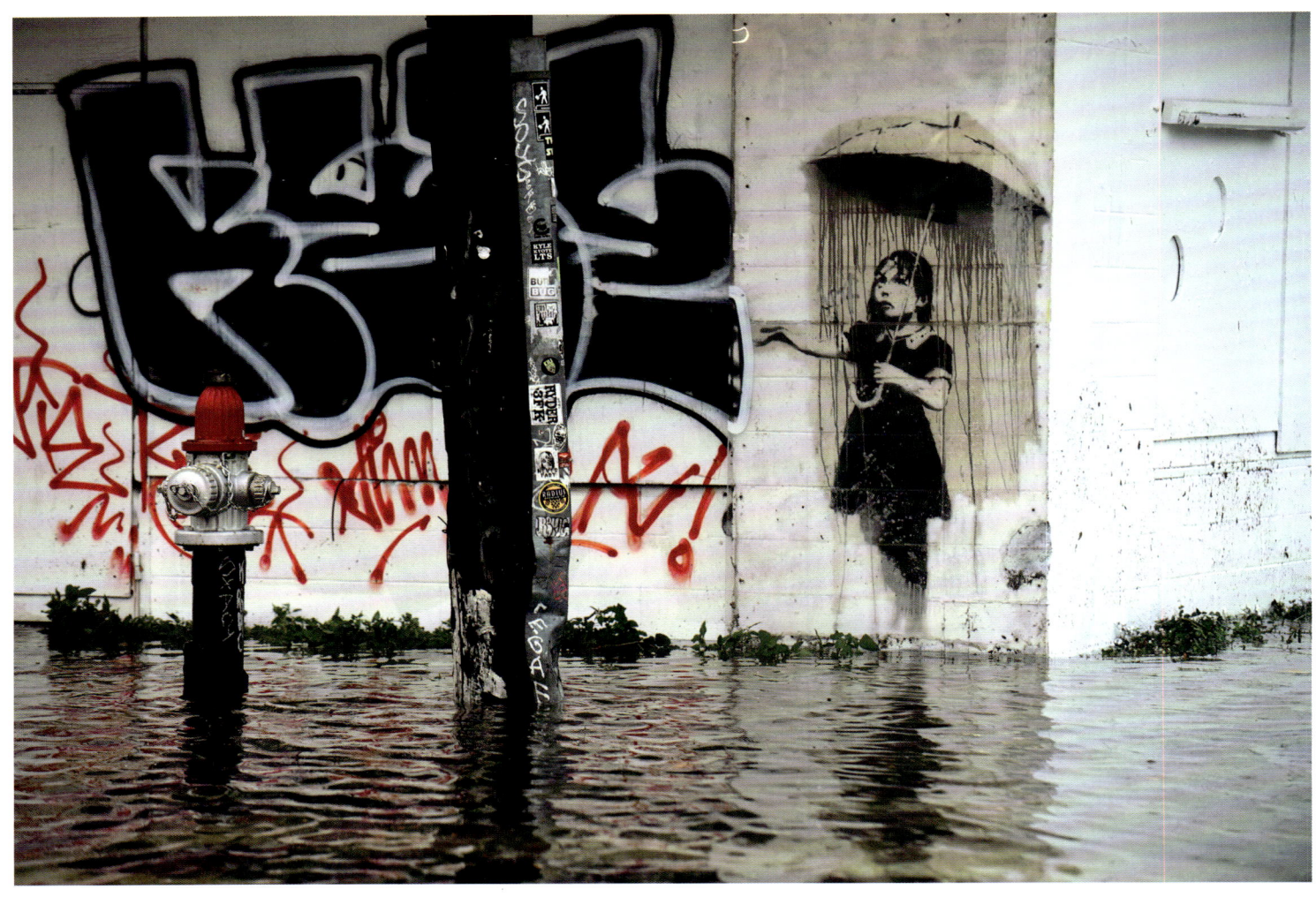

Banksy's iconic *Rain Girl* is surrounded by street flooding after a rainstorm, 2019.

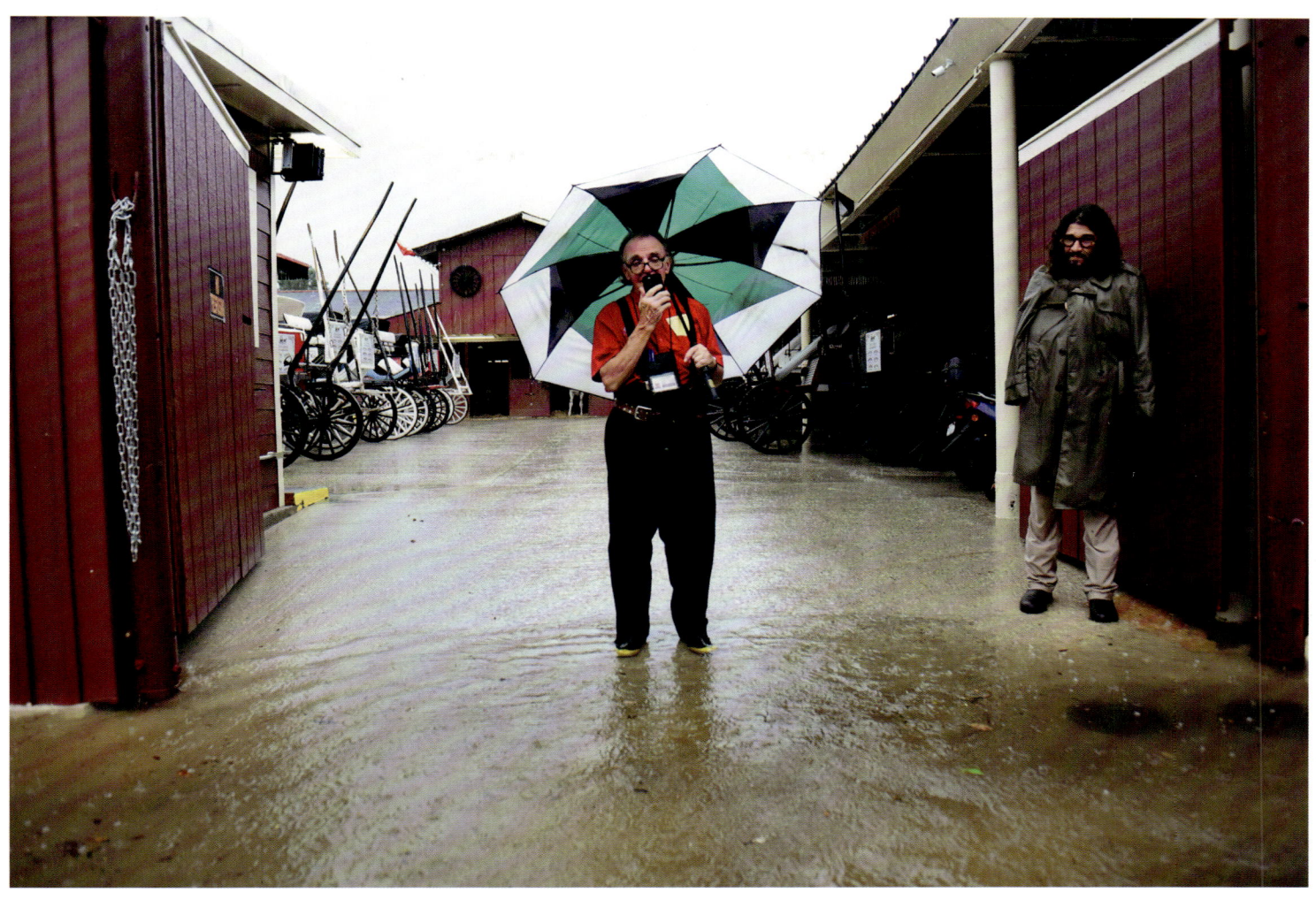

The Royal Carriages mule barn begins to flood during torrential rainstorms in Faubourg Marigny, 2017.

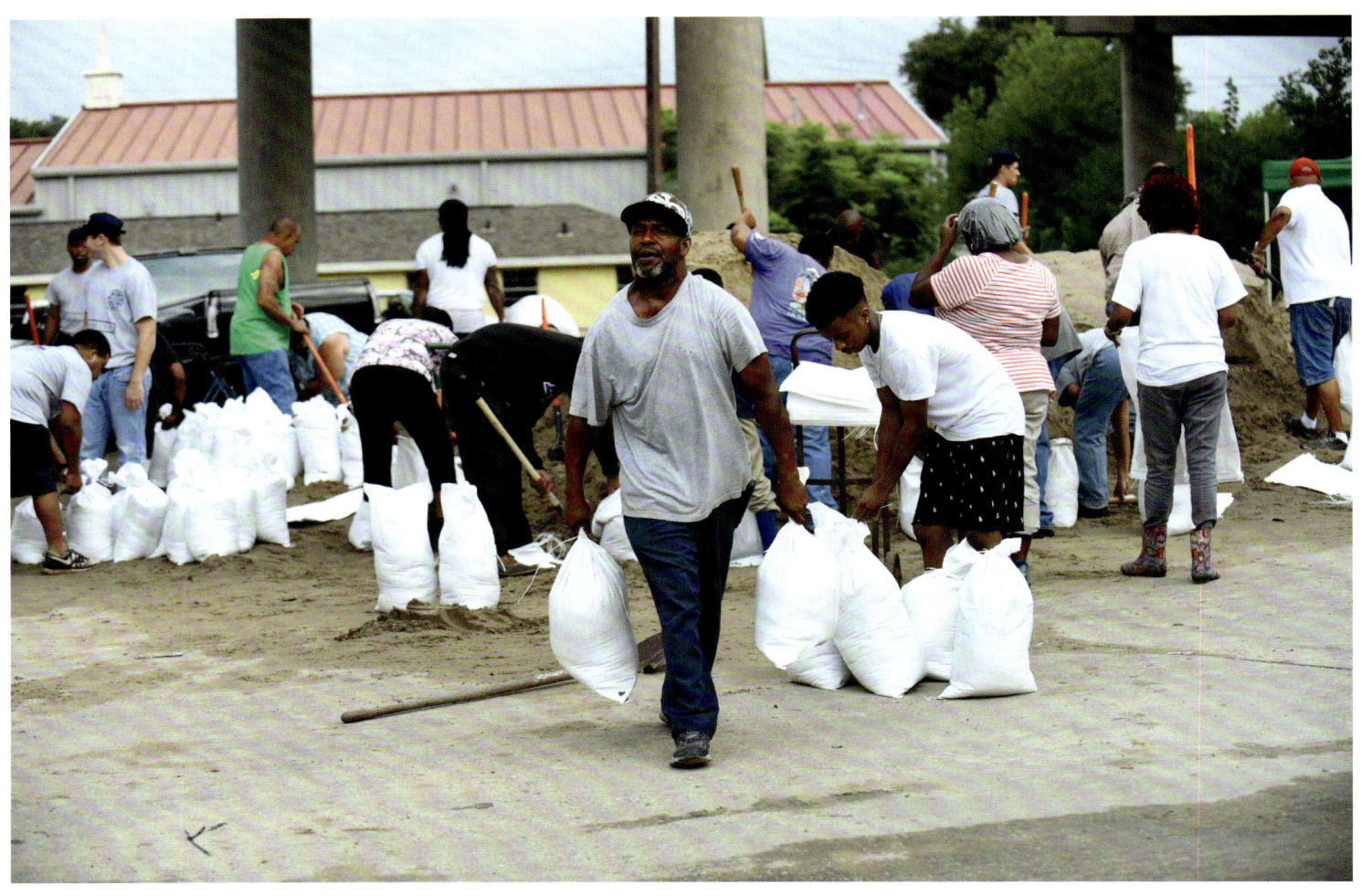

Residents pick up sandbags in preparation for Hurricane Harvey, 2017. Although New Orleans was spared, Harvey caused widespread catastrophic flooding in Texas.

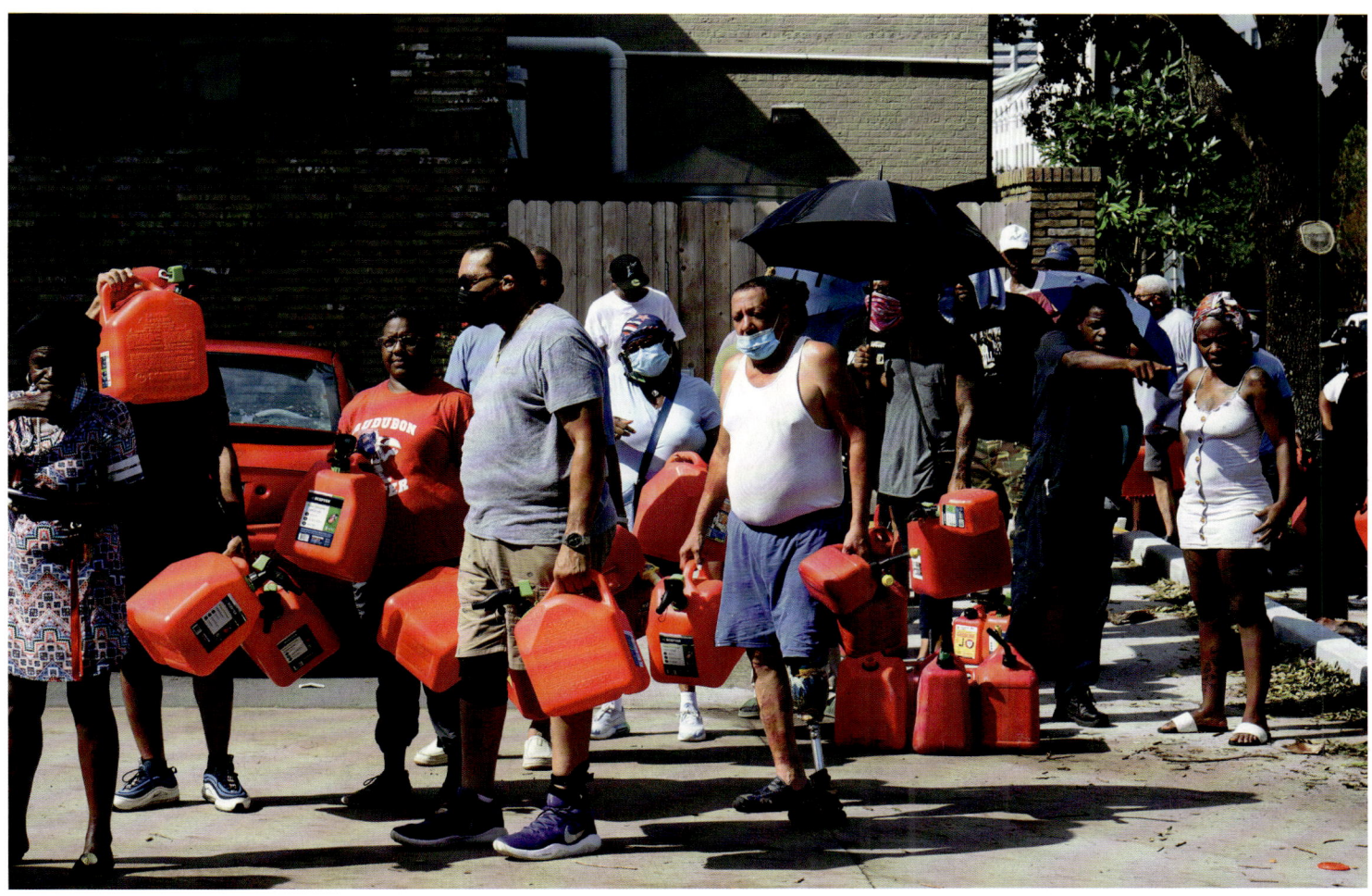

Residents wait in long lines for gasoline after Hurricane Ida, 2021. New Orleans was spared a direct hit, but the hurricane left citizens without electricity and other city services for weeks. The Category 4 storm killed more than fifty people and left many communities to the west of New Orleans devastated. Their recovery continues today.

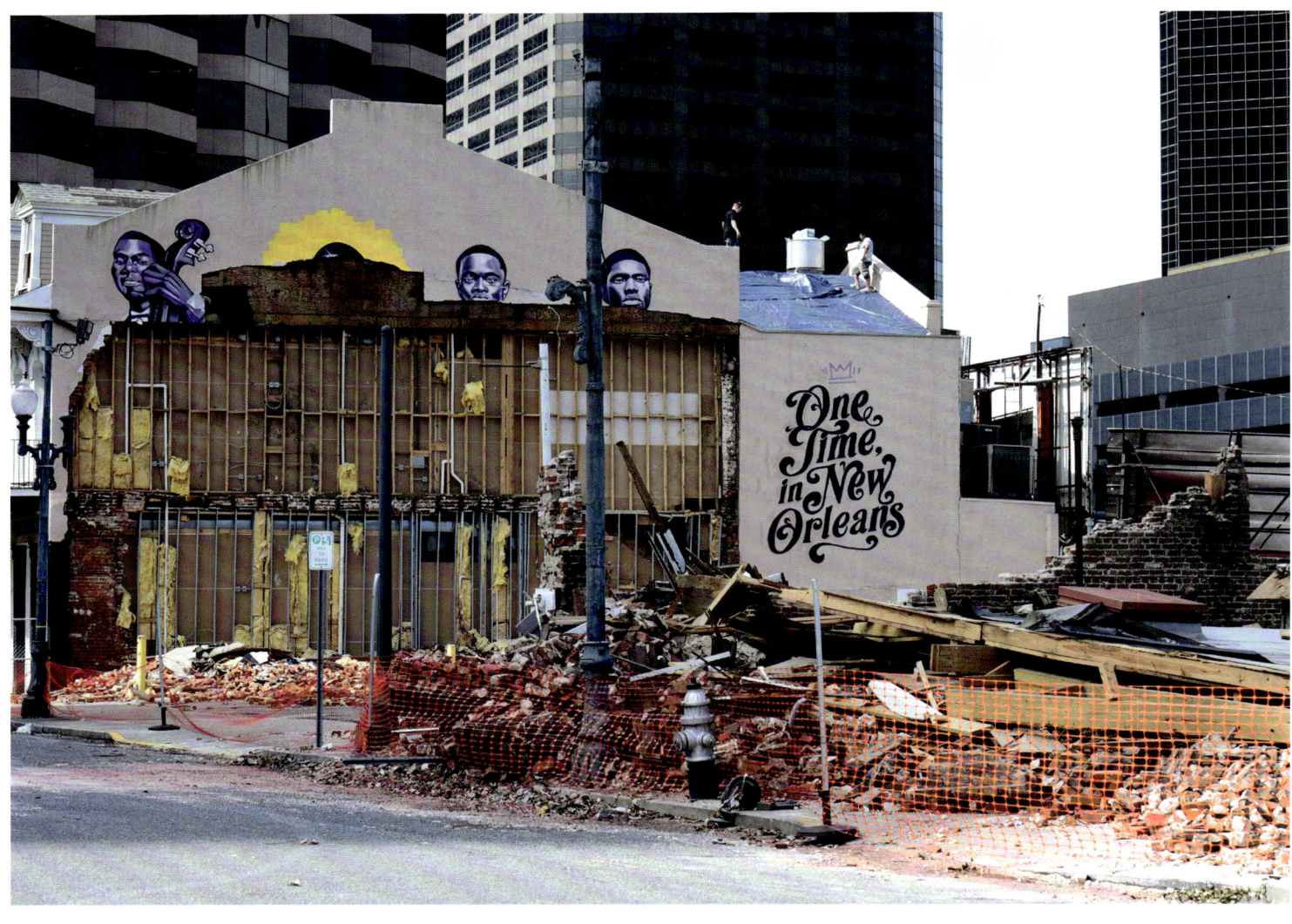

The wall on which Brandan "BMike" Odums's *One Time in New Orleans* mural was painted collapsed during Hurricane Ida, 2021.

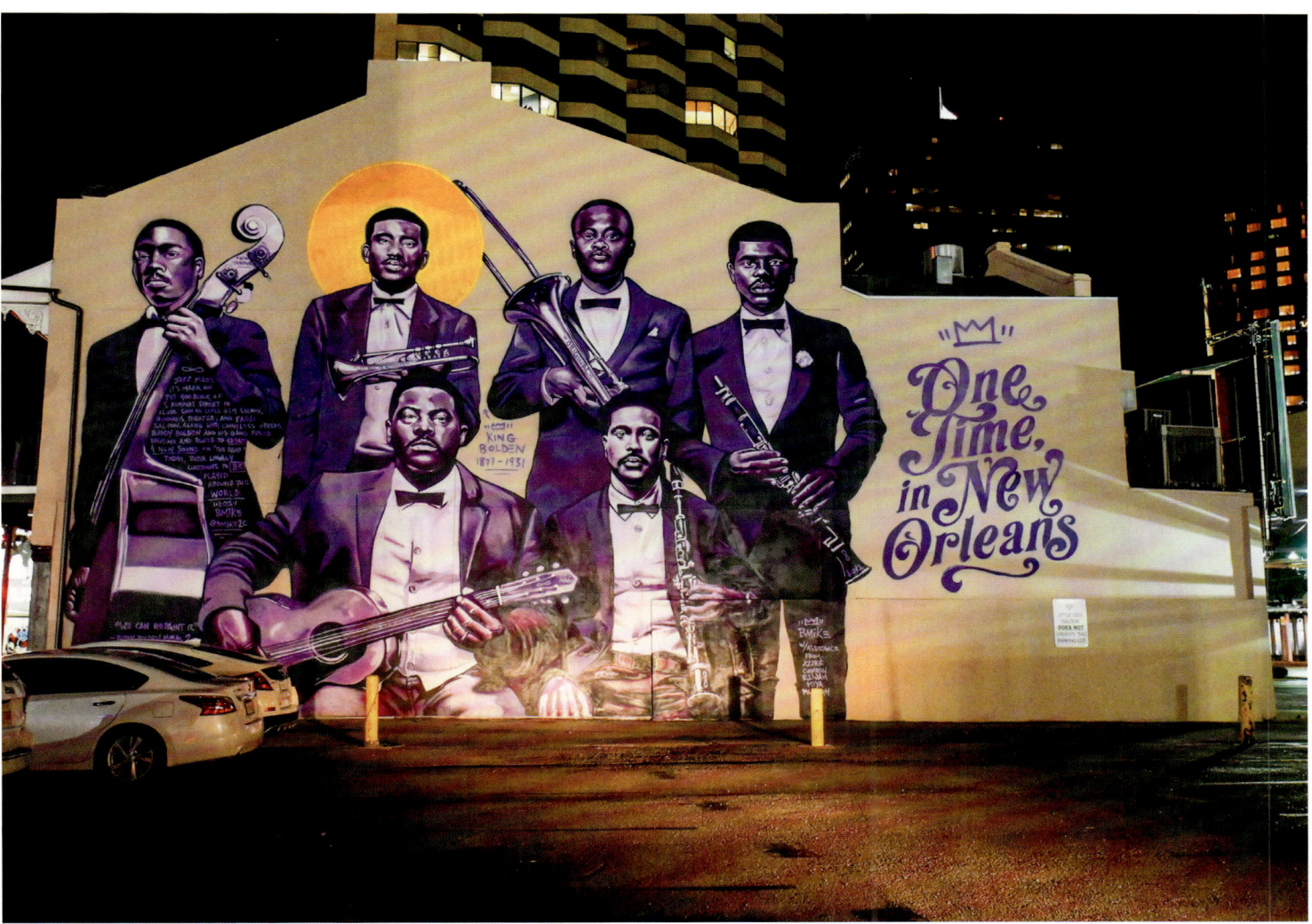

The *One Time in New Orleans* mural by Brandan "BMike" Odums is restored and dedicated to musician Buddy Bolden, 2022. Bolden (1877–1931) was a cornetist who was regarded by his contemporaries as a key figure in the development of New Orleans–style "jass," later called jazz.

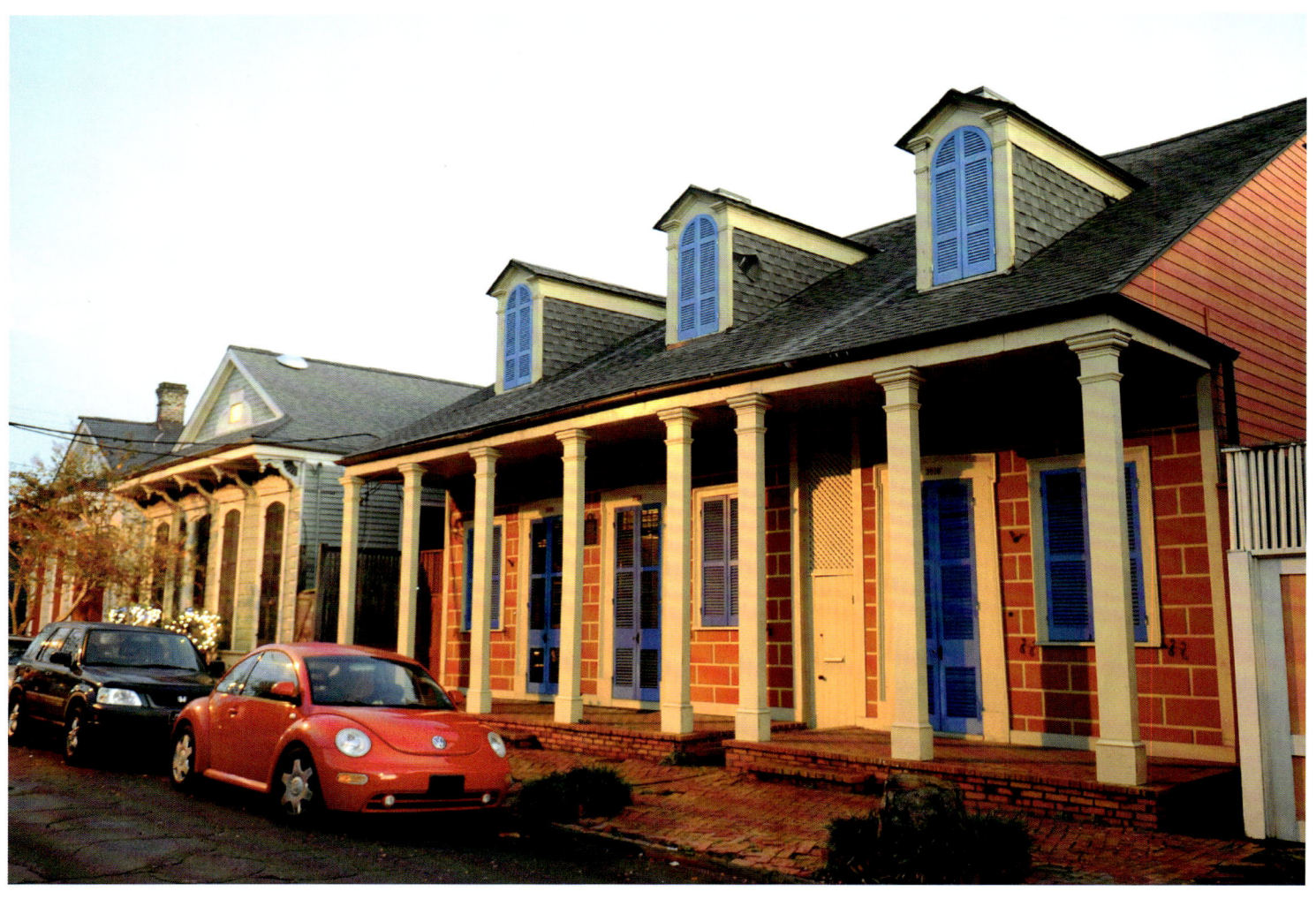

Colorful Creole cottages line Burgundy Street in the Faubourg Marigny, 2015. These cottages—the main urban house type during the early nineteenth century—were built by those of French descent or free people of color, some of whom had emigrated from Haiti. They are seen today mostly in the Faubourg Marigny and French Quarter.

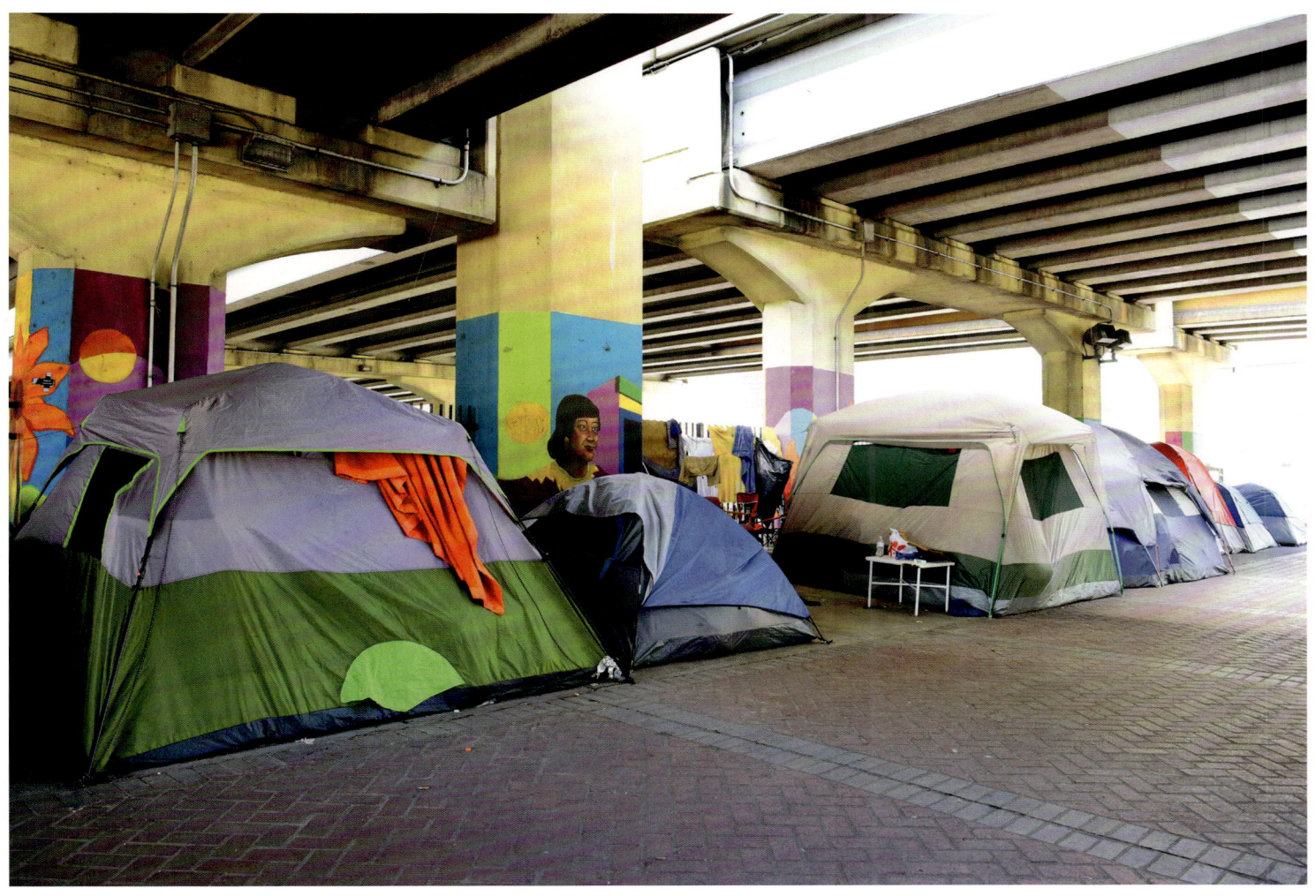

Tents line Calliope Street under the overpass, 2020. The exponential growth of homeless encampments has become part of New Orleans's twenty-first-century landscape.

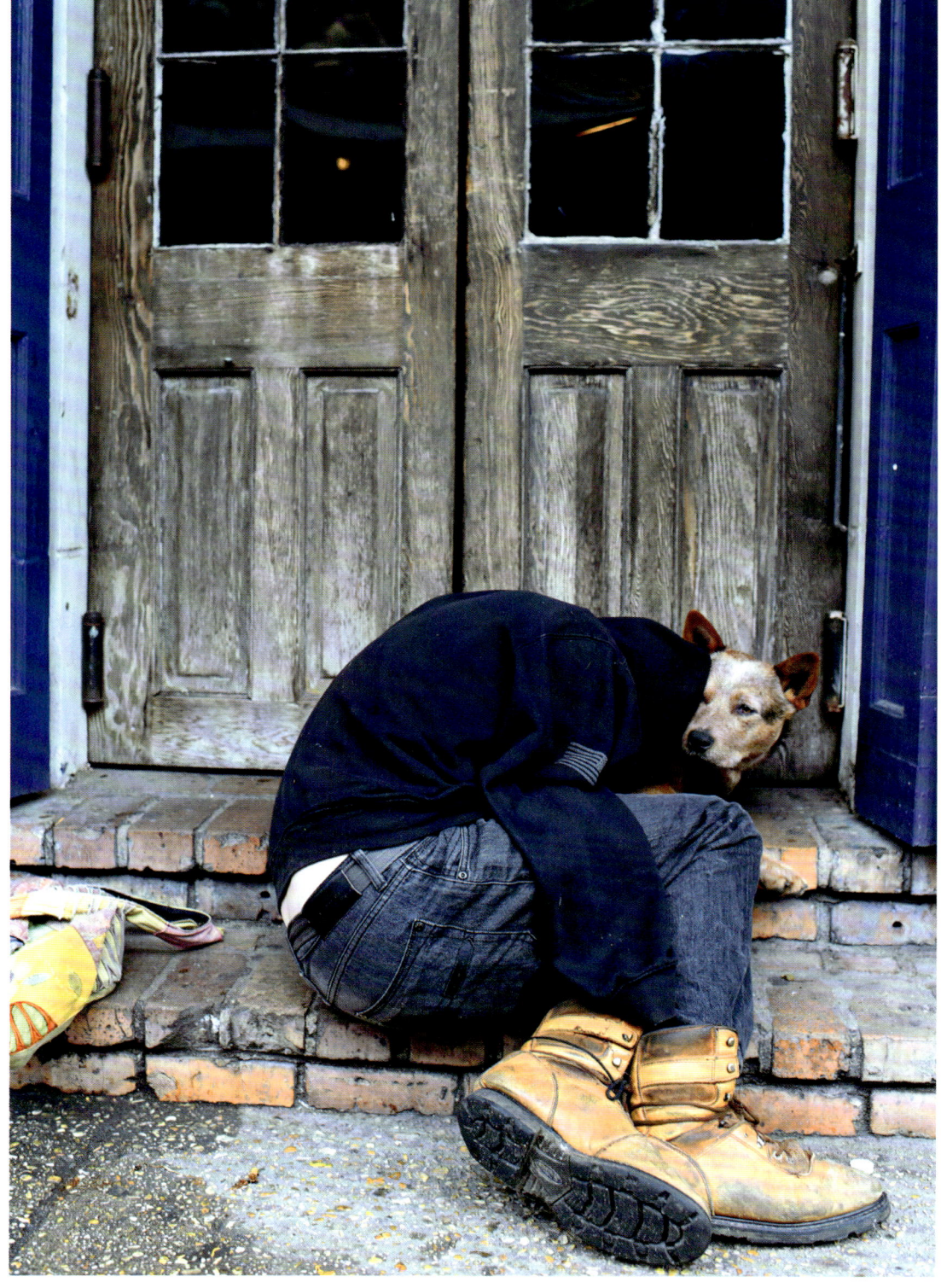

Bourbon Street, 2016.

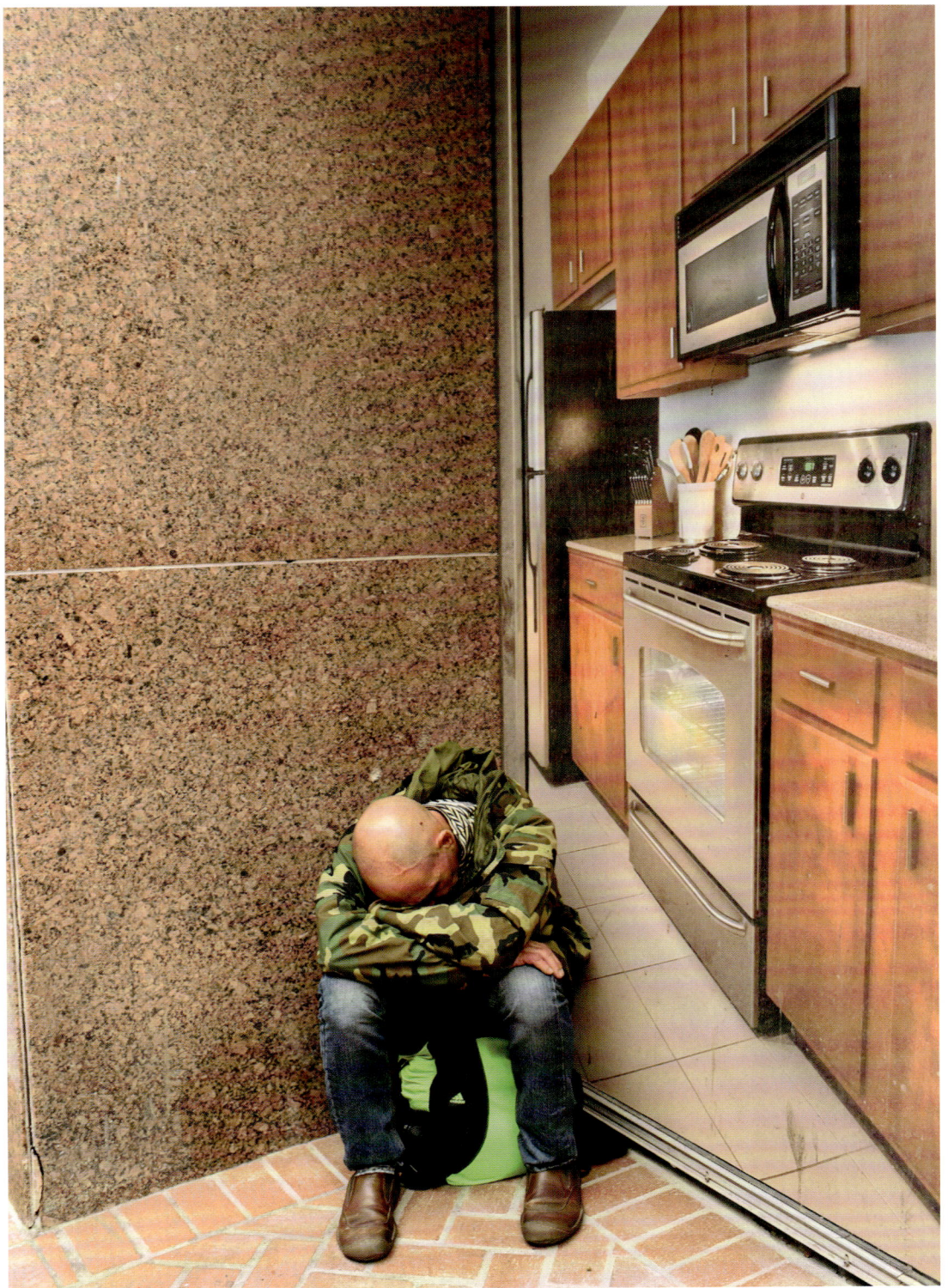

Central Business District, 2016.

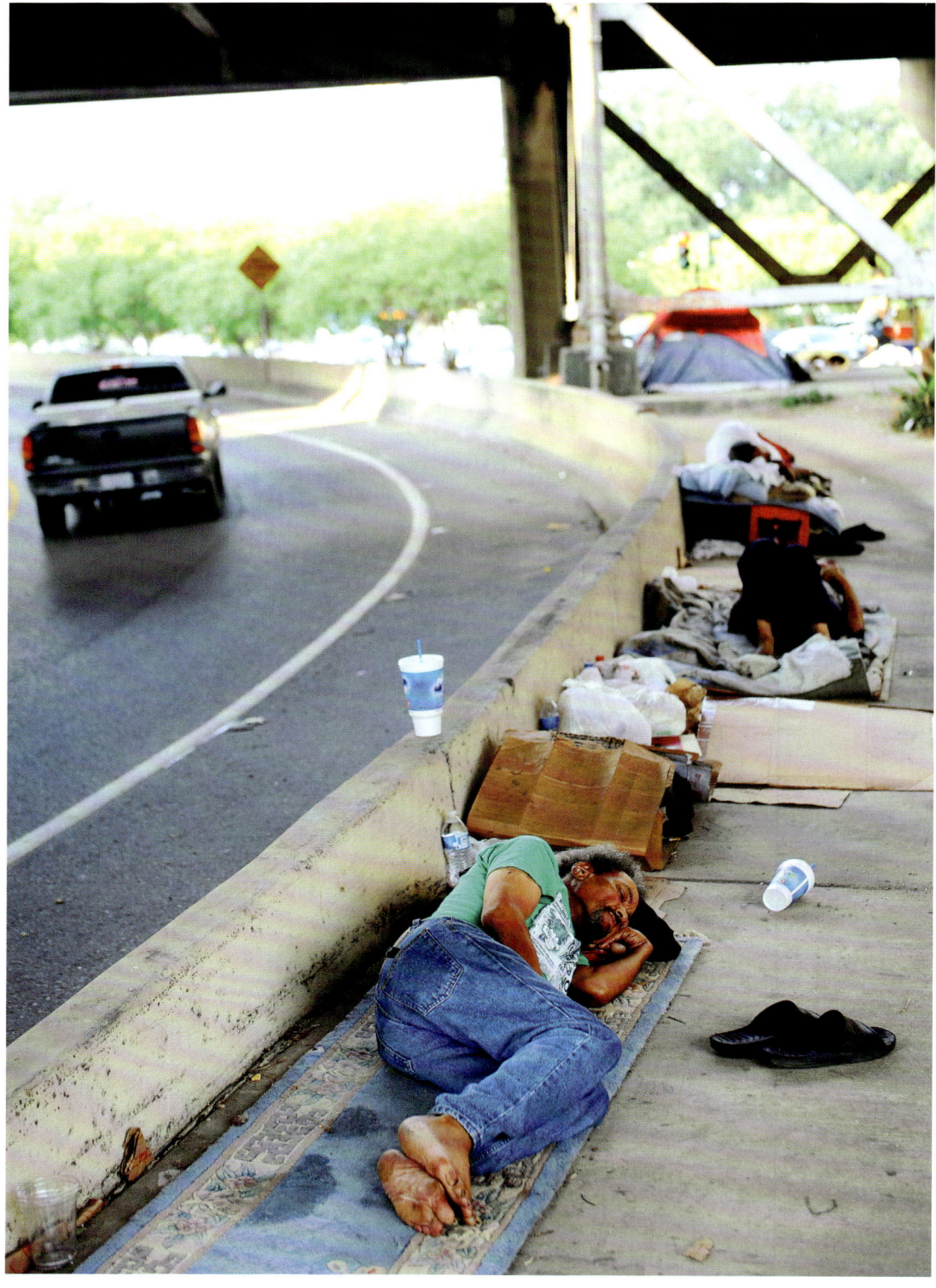

Unhoused people sleep close to the I-10 ramp near the Convention Center, 2018.

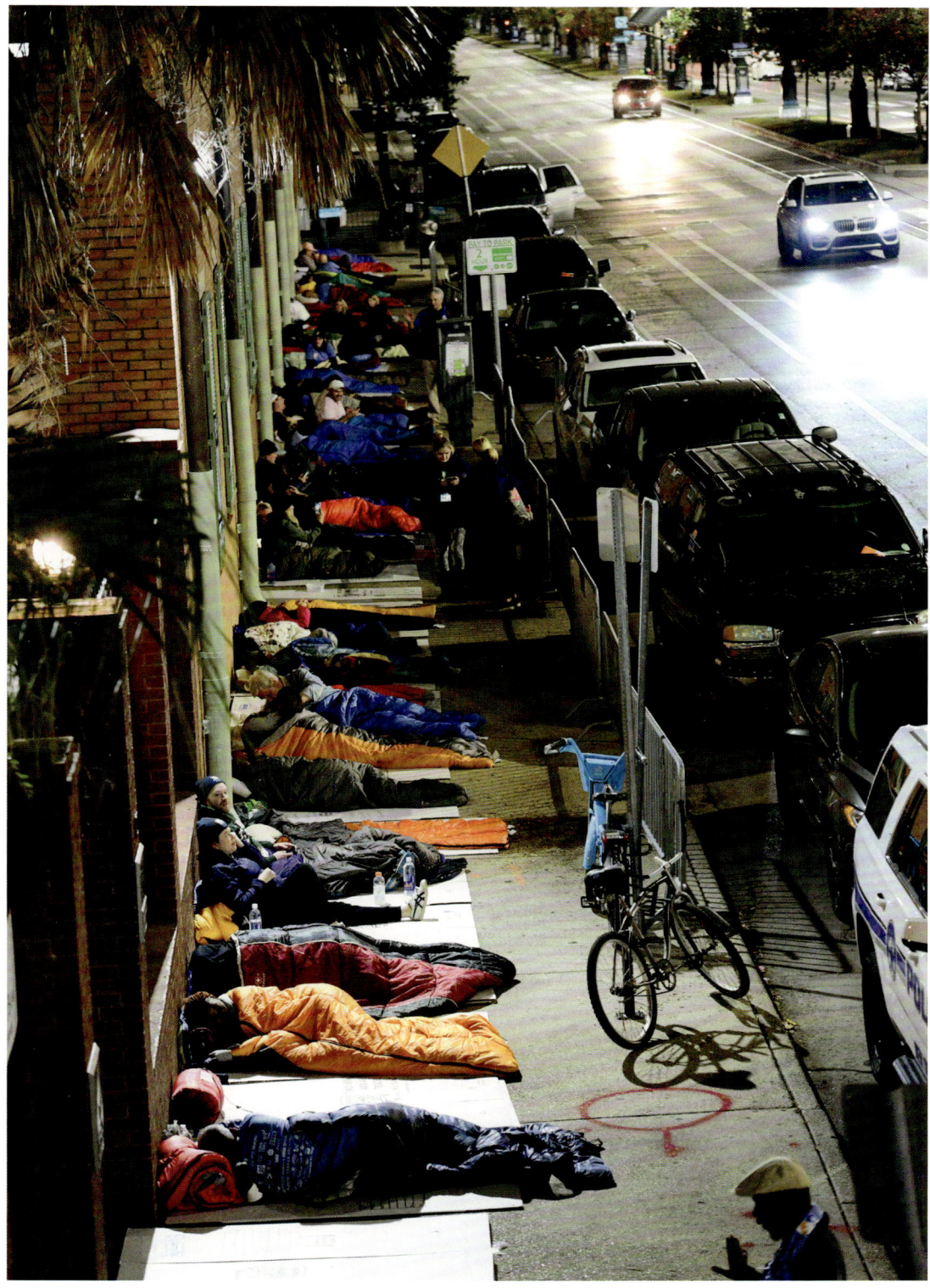

Volunteers sleep on the sidewalk during the annual Covenant House Sleep Out, 2021. The Covenant House Sleep Out raises money and awareness about homelessness; it benefits the youths that Covenant House has served since 1987.

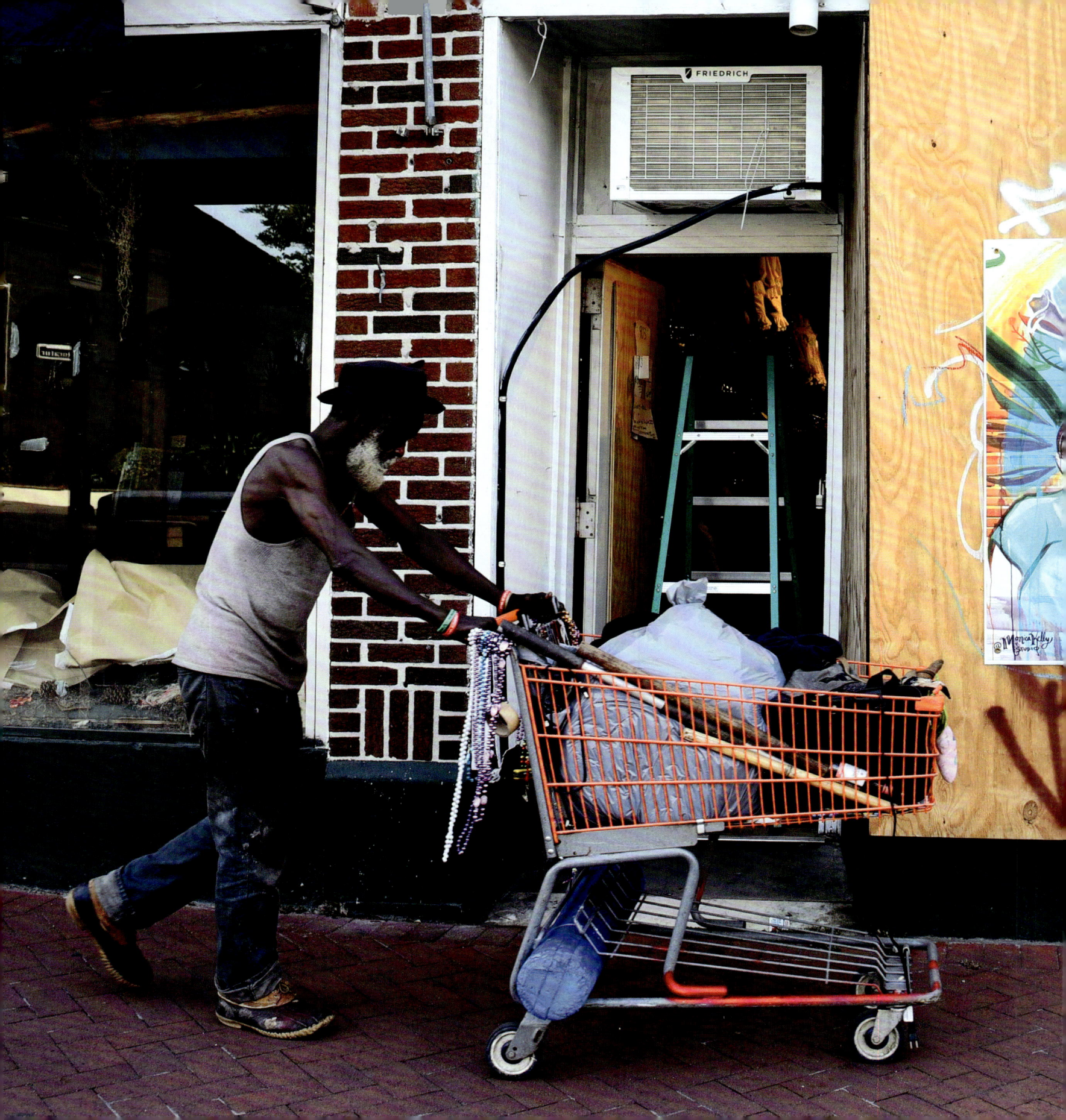

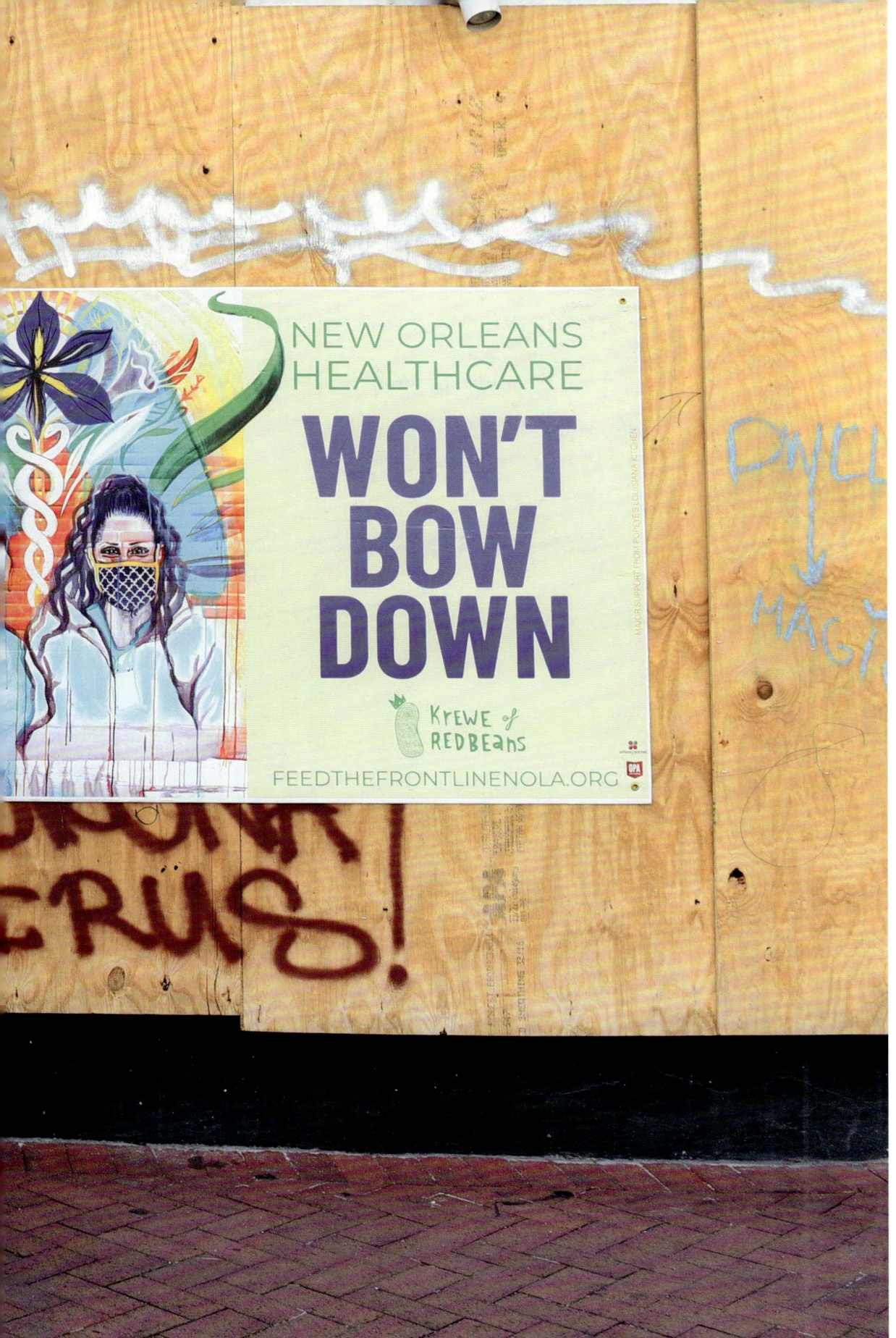

A man pushes his cart down Decatur Street during the pandemic, 2020.

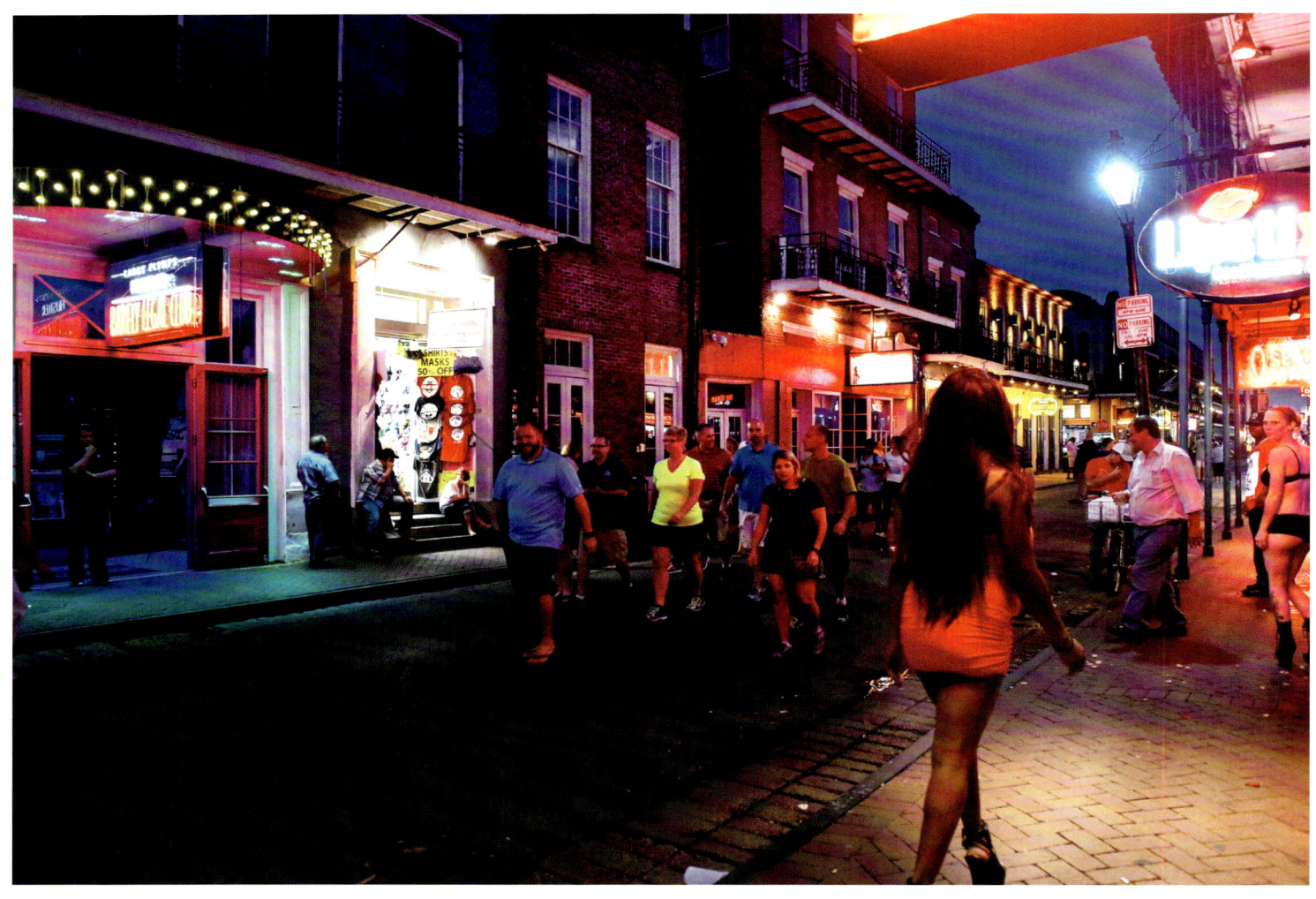

Strip clubs on Bourbon Street, 2015.

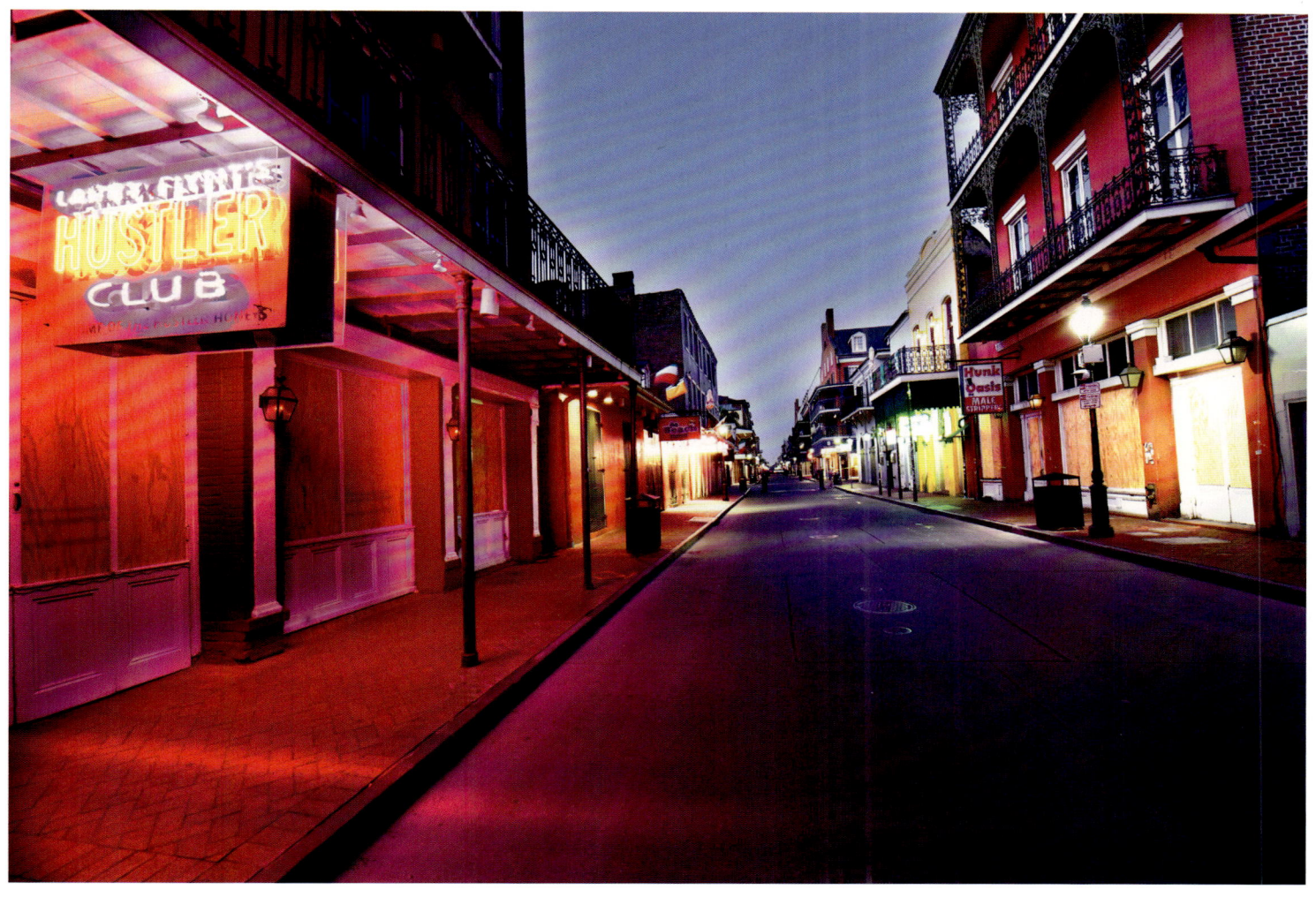

Bourbon Street during the pandemic lockdown, 2020.

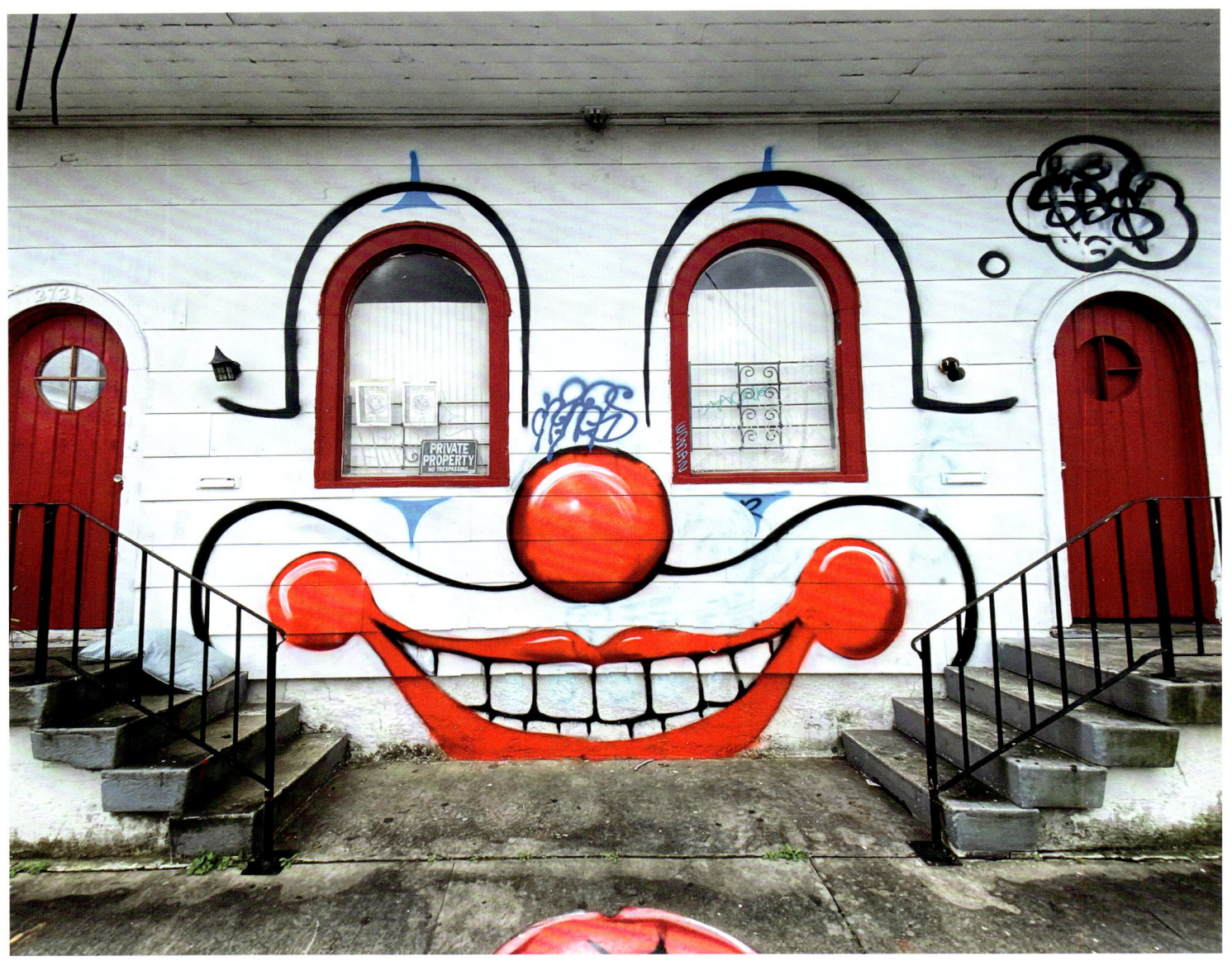

A house painted as a clown on St. Claude Avenue, 2021.

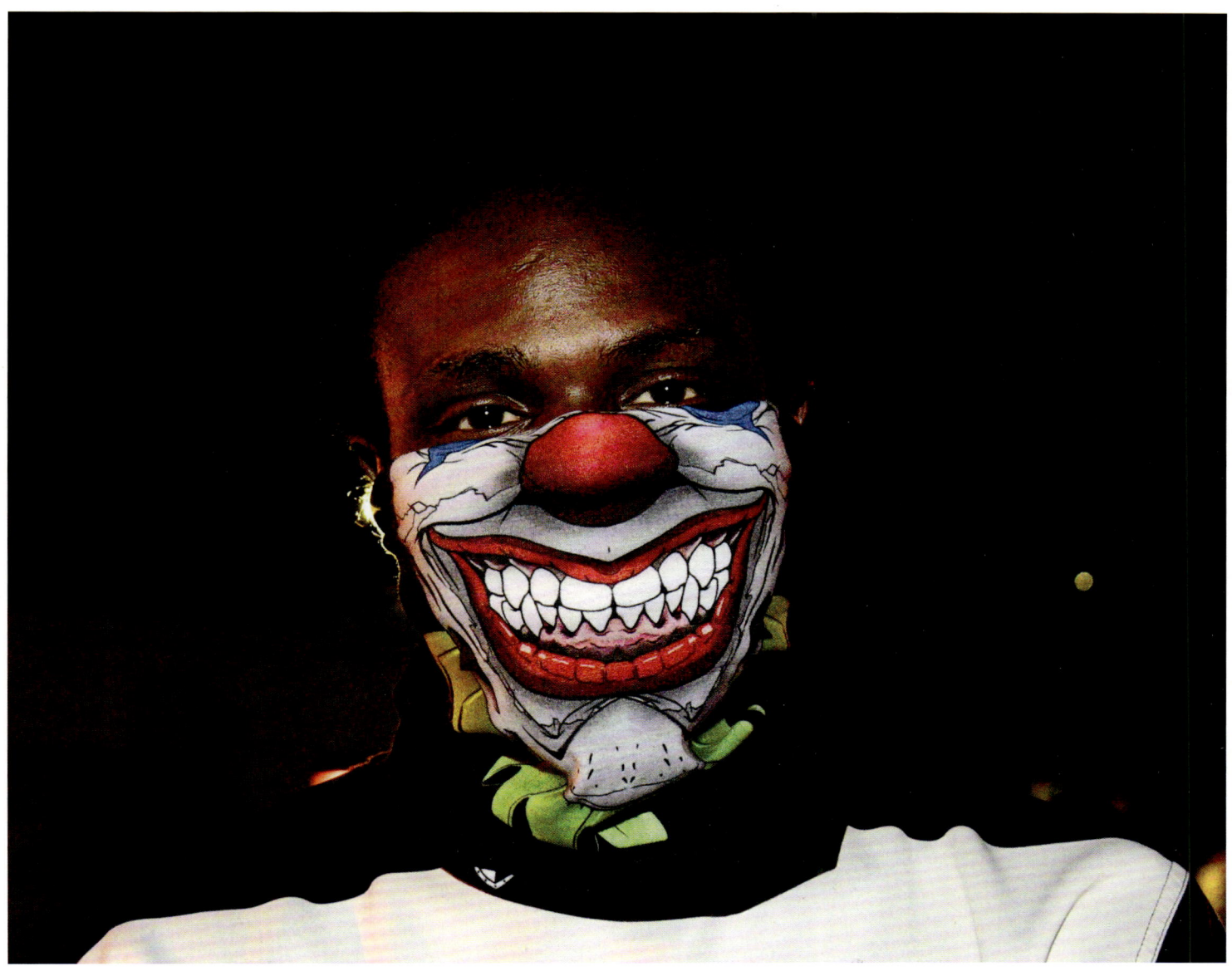

A man wears a clown COVID mask to a Black Lives Matter protest after the murder of George Floyd by a white police officer, 2020.

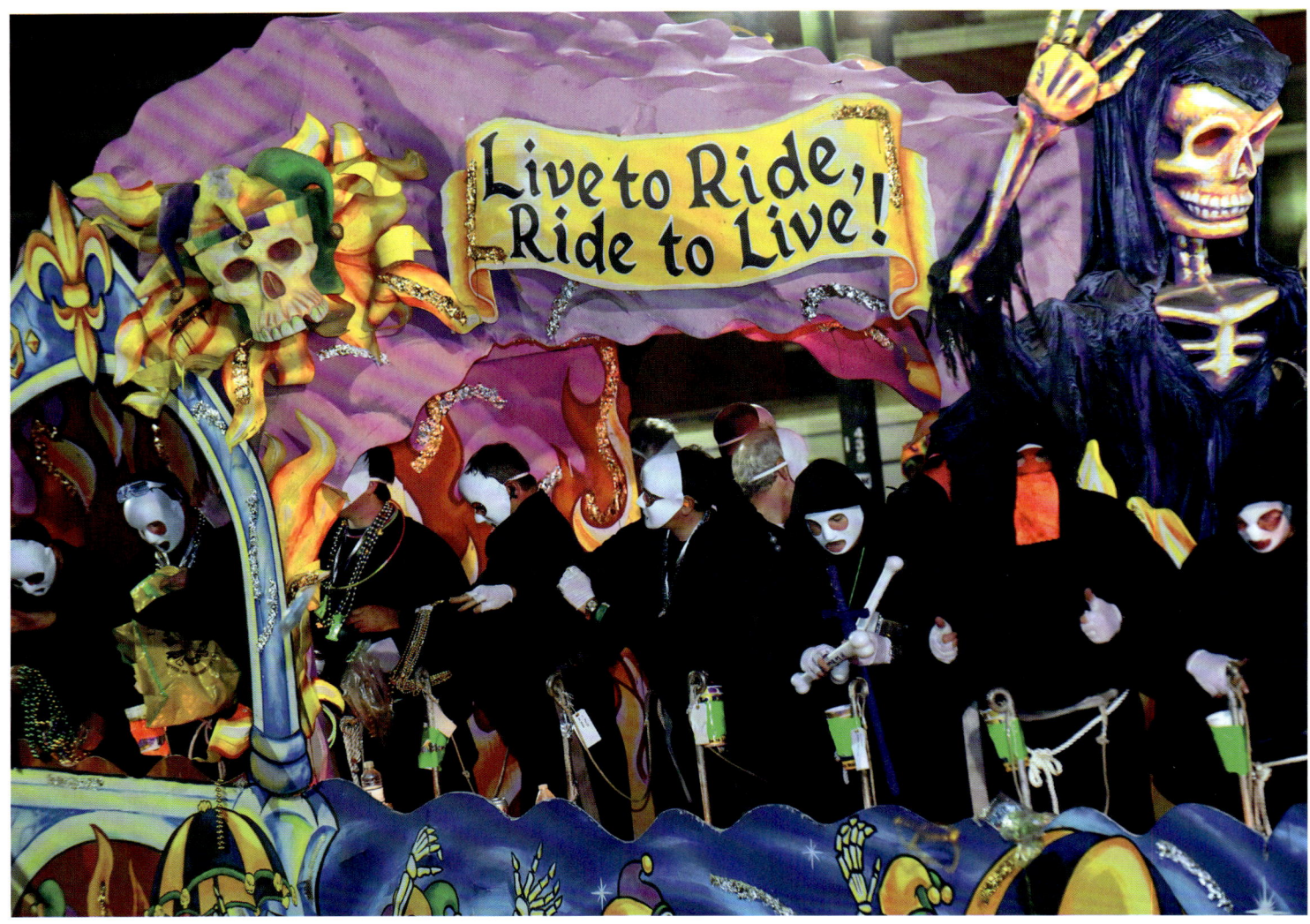

Krewe d'Etat's "Live to Ride, Ride to Live" float during its parade, 2018. Krewe d'Etat is a Carnival krewe known for its satirical themes and floats. Its inaugural parade rolled in 1998.

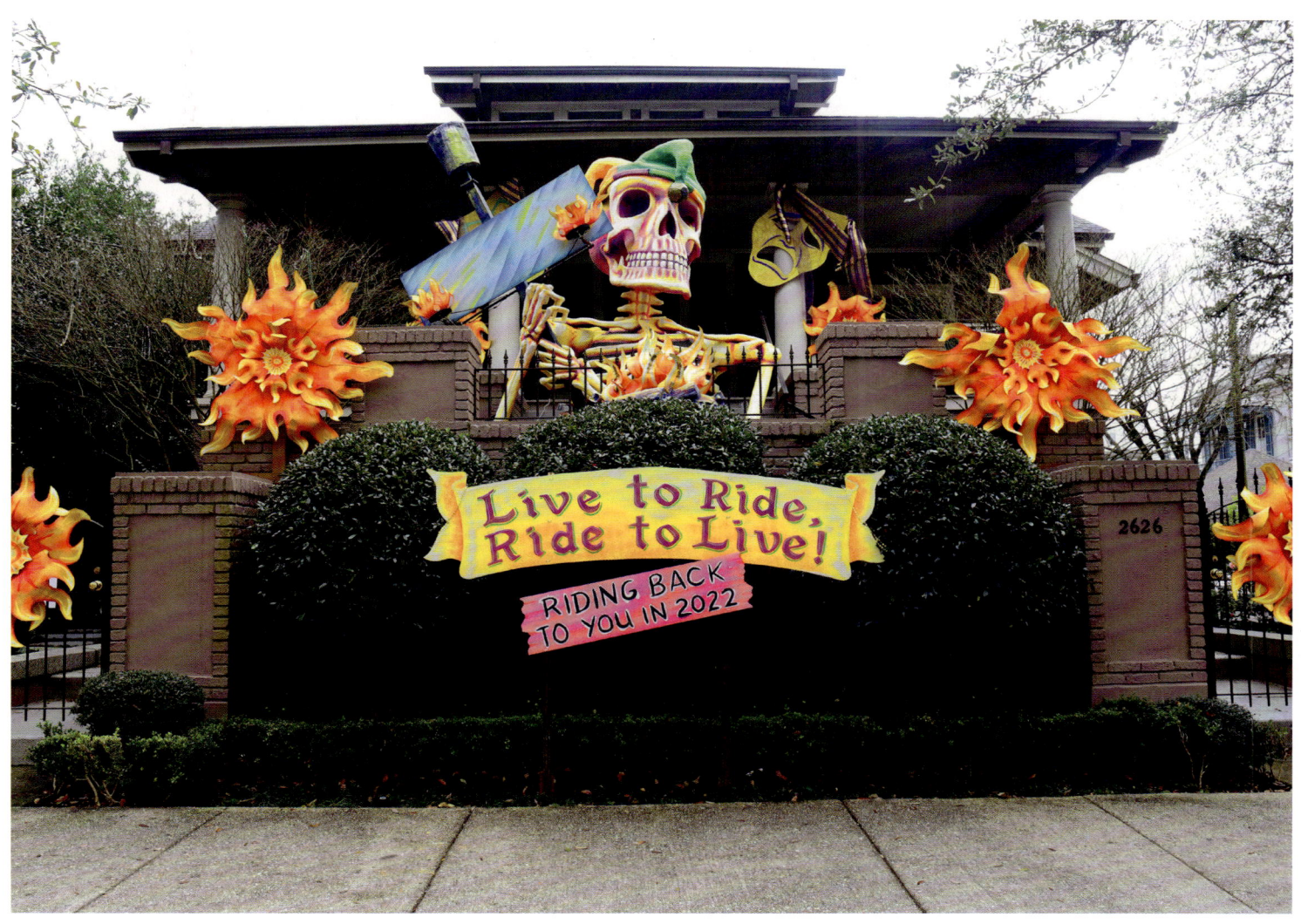

In one of the Krewe of House Floats, Royal Artists decorated an Uptown home to pay homage to the iconic Krewe d'Etat signature float, 2021. The Krewe of House Floats, the brainchild of Megan Boudreaux, decorated homes in every corner of the city when the pandemic shut down Mardi Gras.

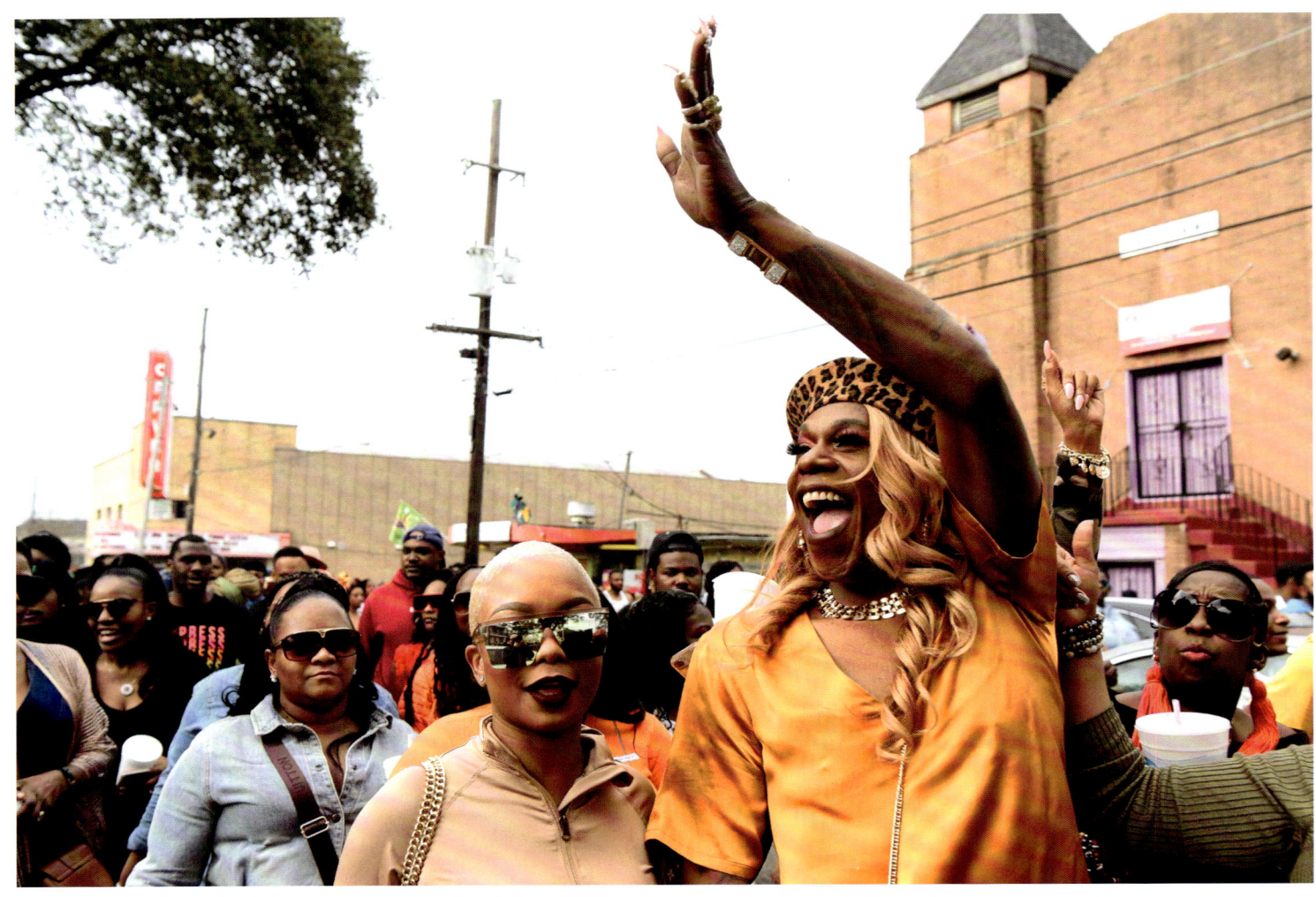

Big Freedia, also known as the "Queen of Bounce," waves to fans during a Sunday second line, 2020. Big Freedia, born in 1978 as Freddie Ross Jr., is an American rapper, author, and TV personality known for bounce music. Big Freedia's work can be heard on some of Beyoncé's recent recordings.

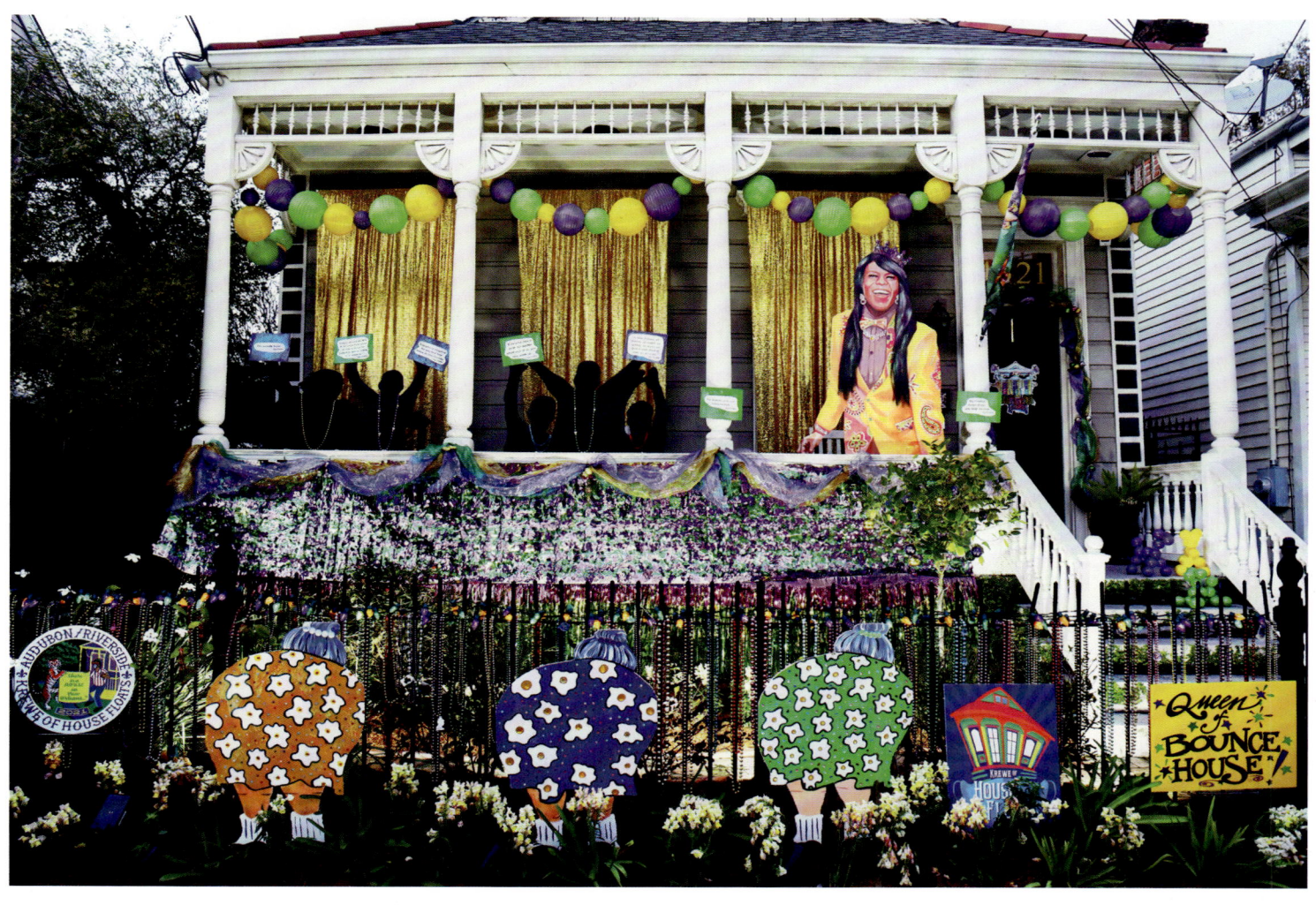

Homeowner Sarena Teng decorated her Uptown home as the "Queen of Bounce" house float, 2021.

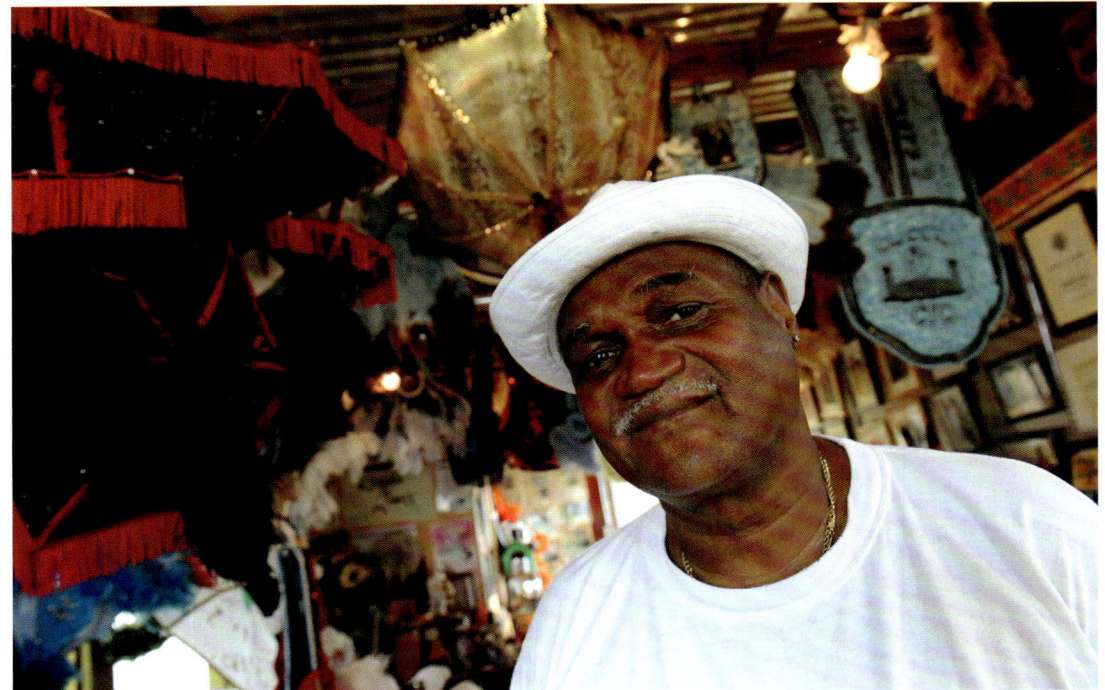

Ronald Lewis at his museum, House of Dance and Feathers, 2011.

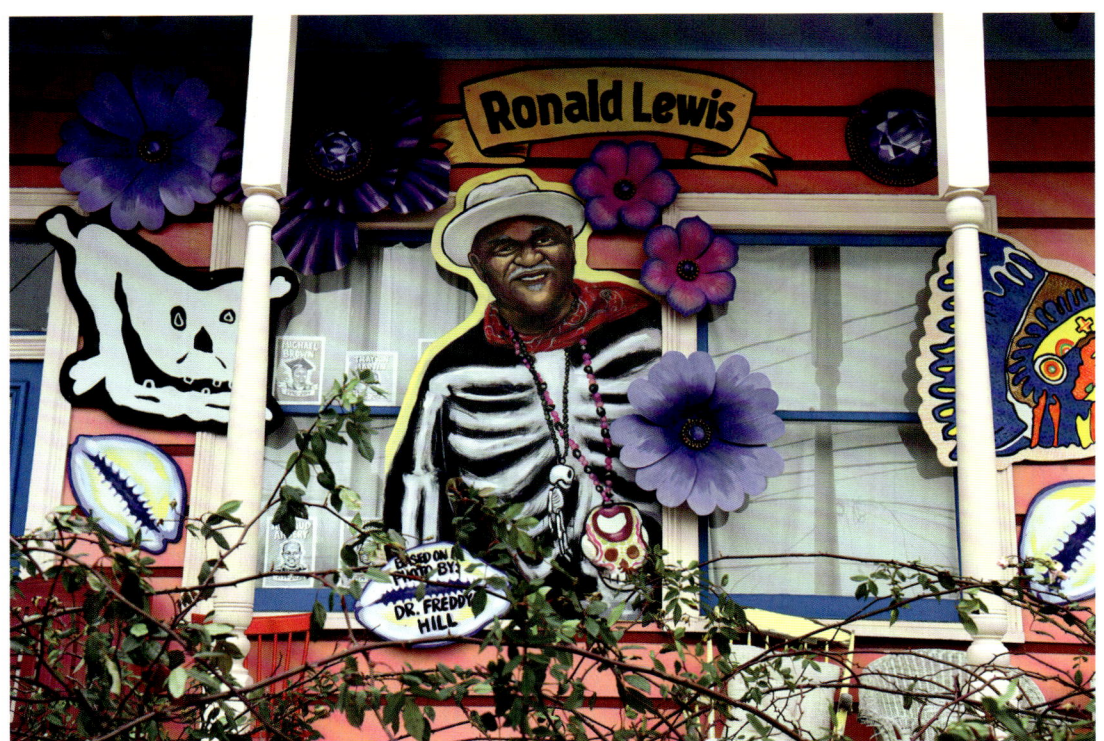

The Ronald Lewis house float in the Seventh Ward, 2020. Ronald Lewis (1951–2020) died early in the COVID pandemic. He was the first resident to move back to the Lower Ninth Ward after Hurricane Katrina and, with the help of volunteers, built the House of Dance and Feathers in his backyard, a museum that preserved performance traditions and street culture of the city. The colorful museum was named after the book he wrote about Black culture in 2009.

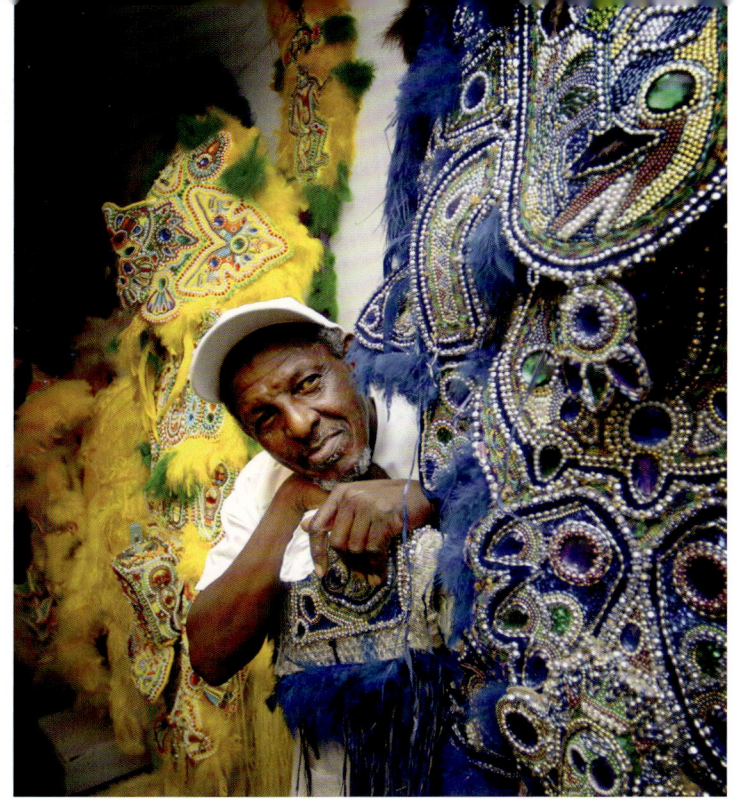

Sylvester "Hawk" Francis at the Backstreet Cultural Museum, 2008. Francis (1946–2020) was the beloved photographer and documentarian who preserved Black culture in the Backstreet Cultural Museum, which he founded in 1999; it was considered the heart of the Tremé neighborhood because it hosted many cultural traditions. He died during the COVID pandemic, and the museum was later severely damaged by Hurricane Ida in 2021.

The Sylvester "Hawk" Francis house float, 2020.

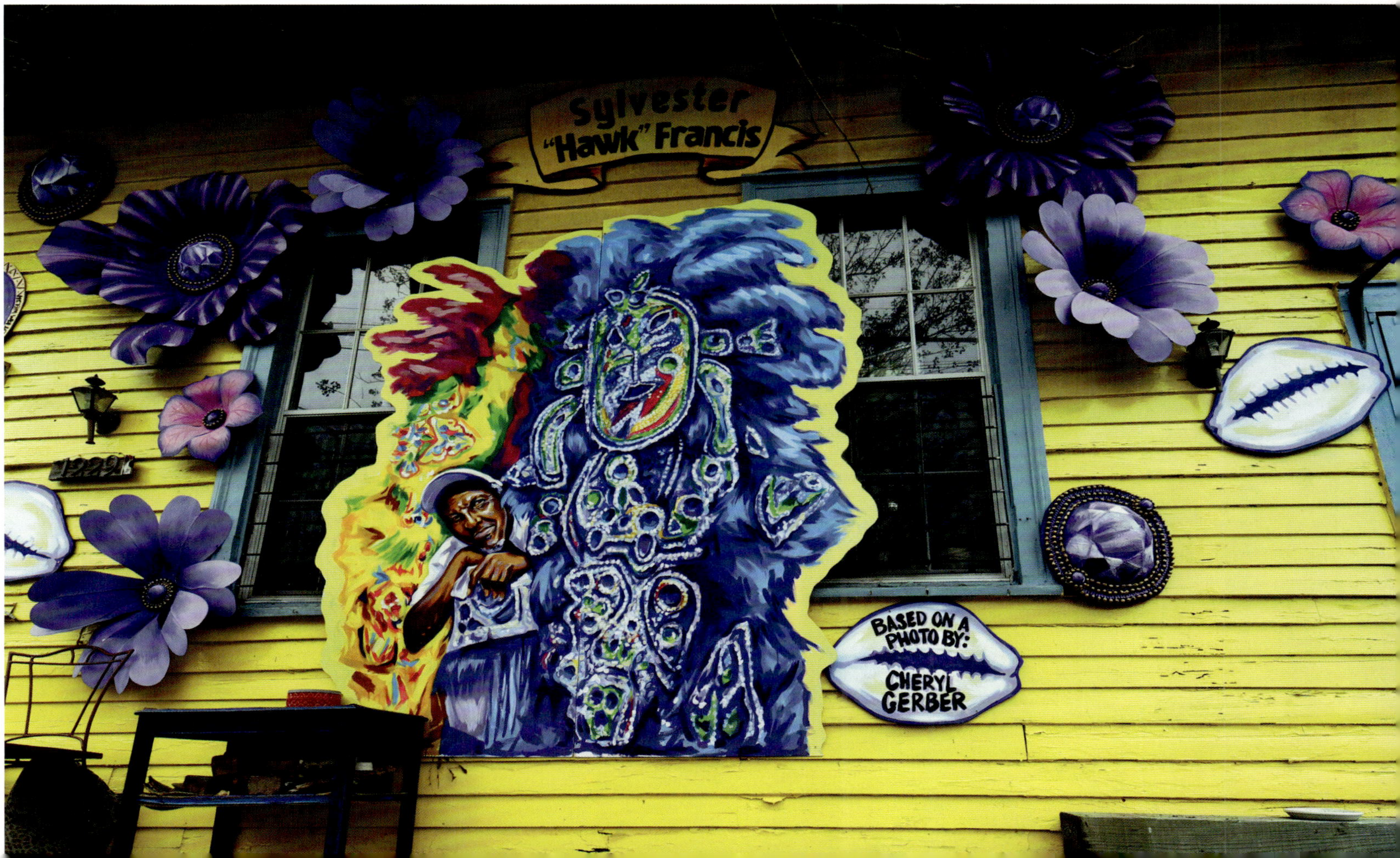

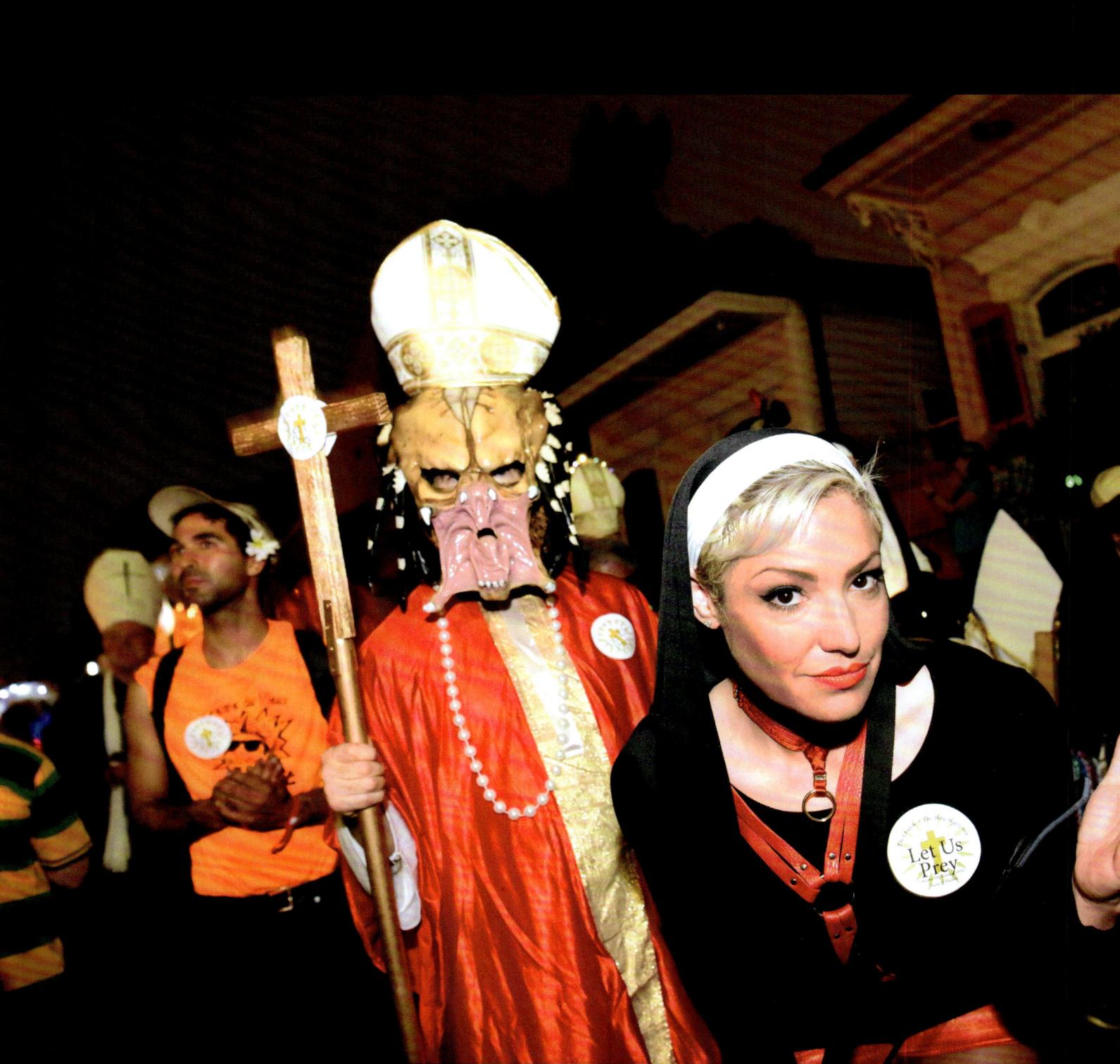

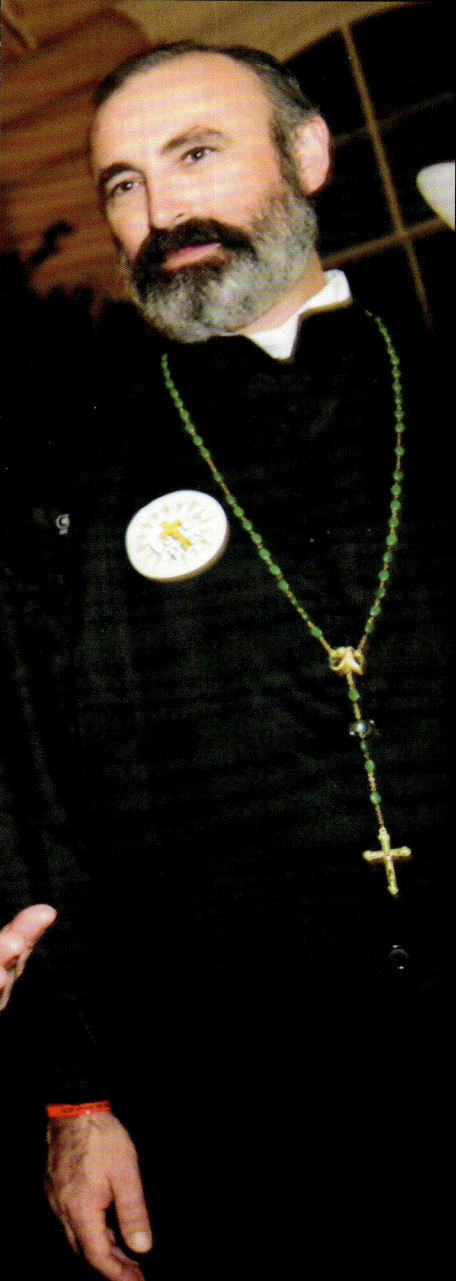

PART II

Saints and Sinners

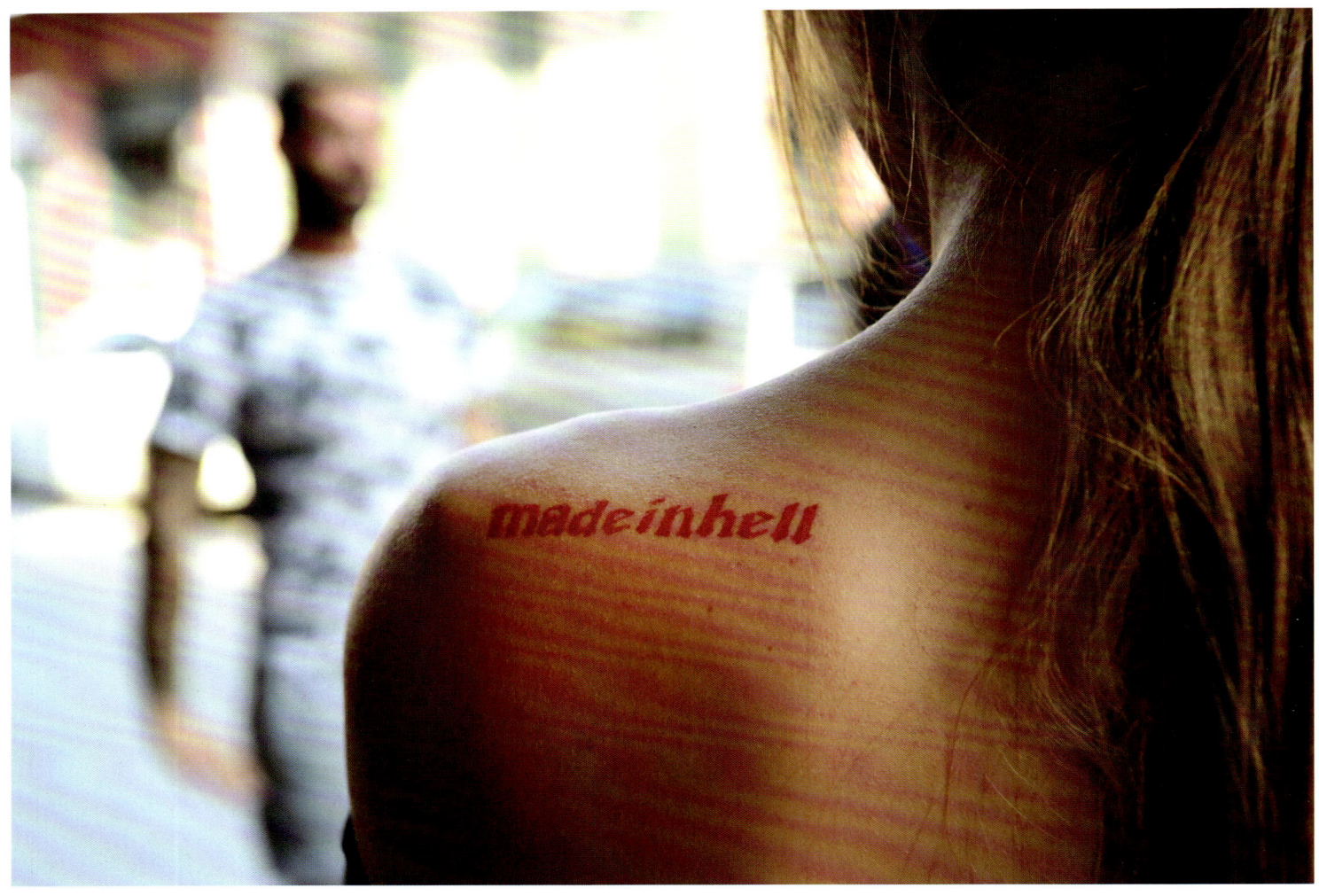

A "Made in Hell" tattoo is seen on the shoulder of a woman strolling on Bourbon Street while social distancing during the pandemic, 2021.

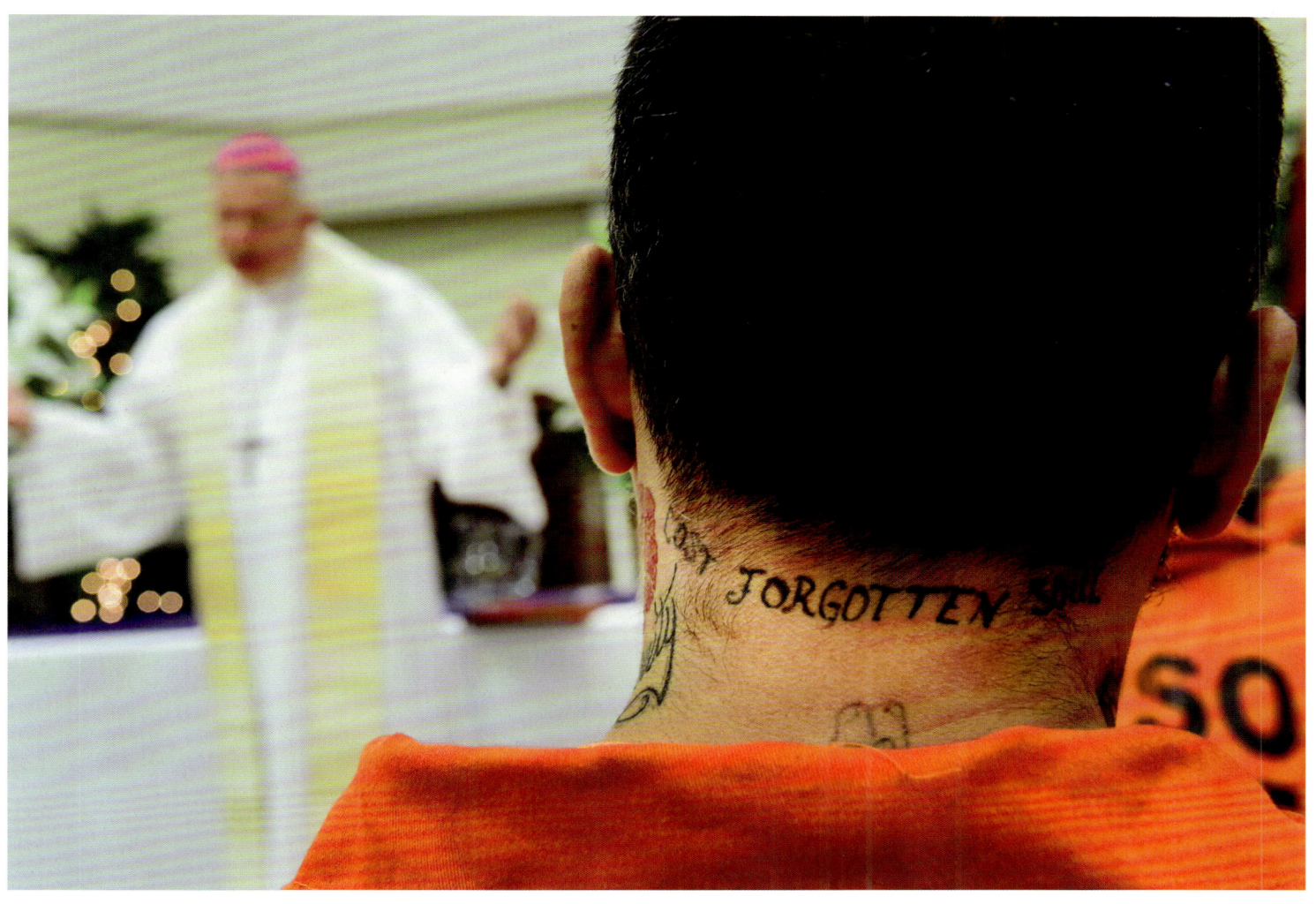

A "Lost Forgotten Soul" tattoo is seen on the neck of a prisoner participating in a religious ceremony at Orleans Parish Prison, 2018.

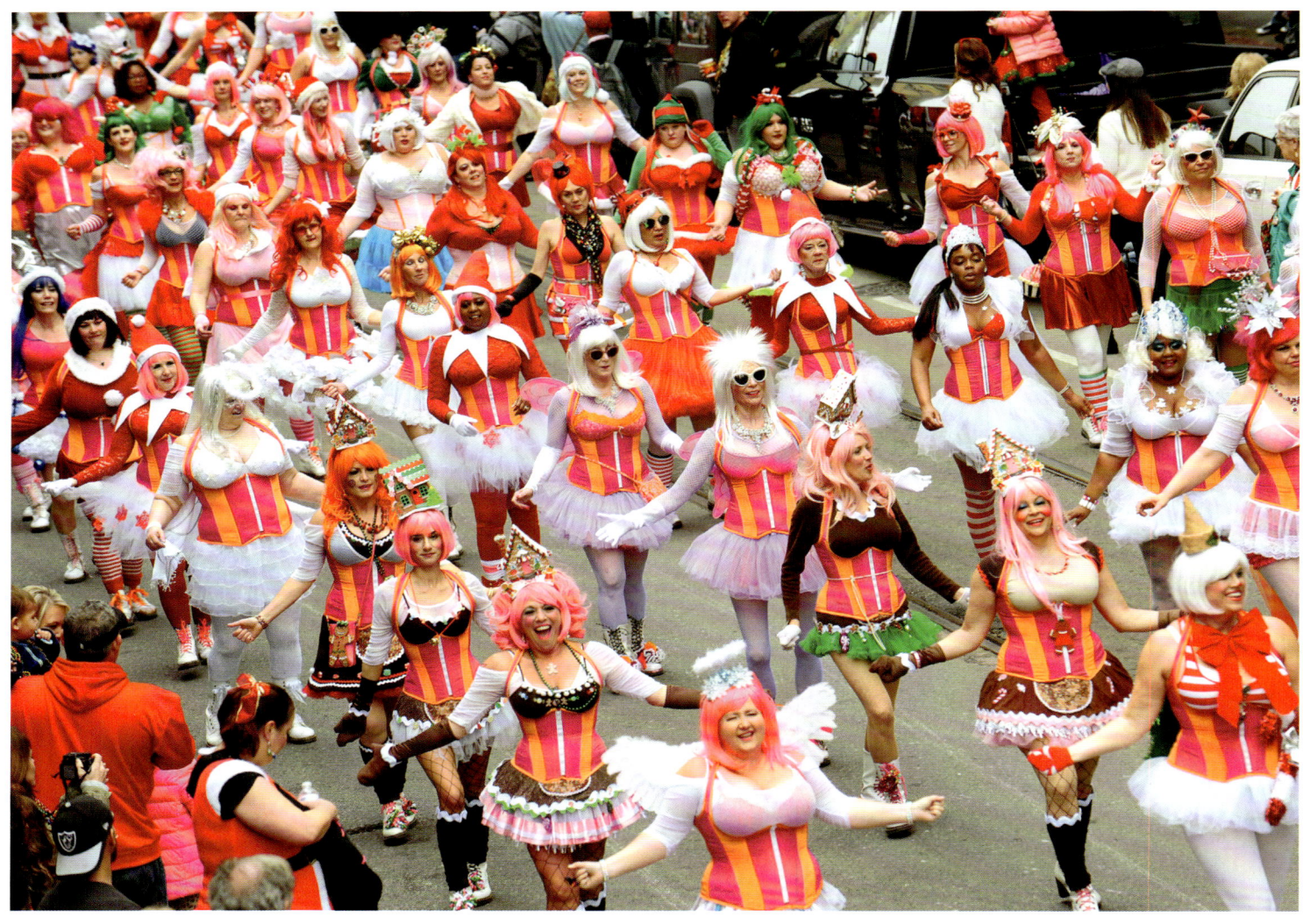

The Pussyfooters, the all-female marching club founded in 2002, dance as angels and elves in the Krewe of Jingle Christmas parade, 2016.

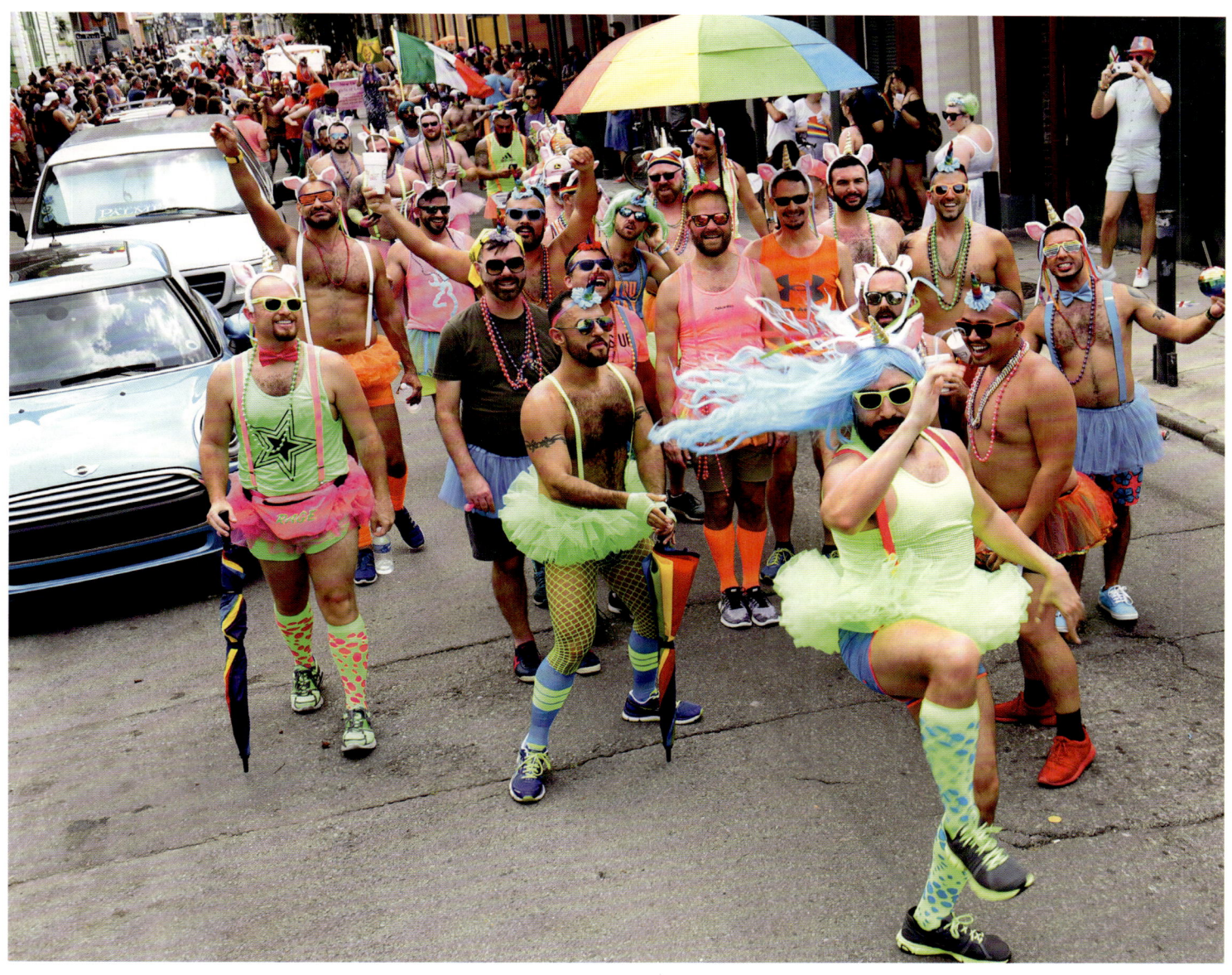

The Unicorns marching krewe dance in neon colors in the Southern Decadence parade themed "Electrified," 2017.

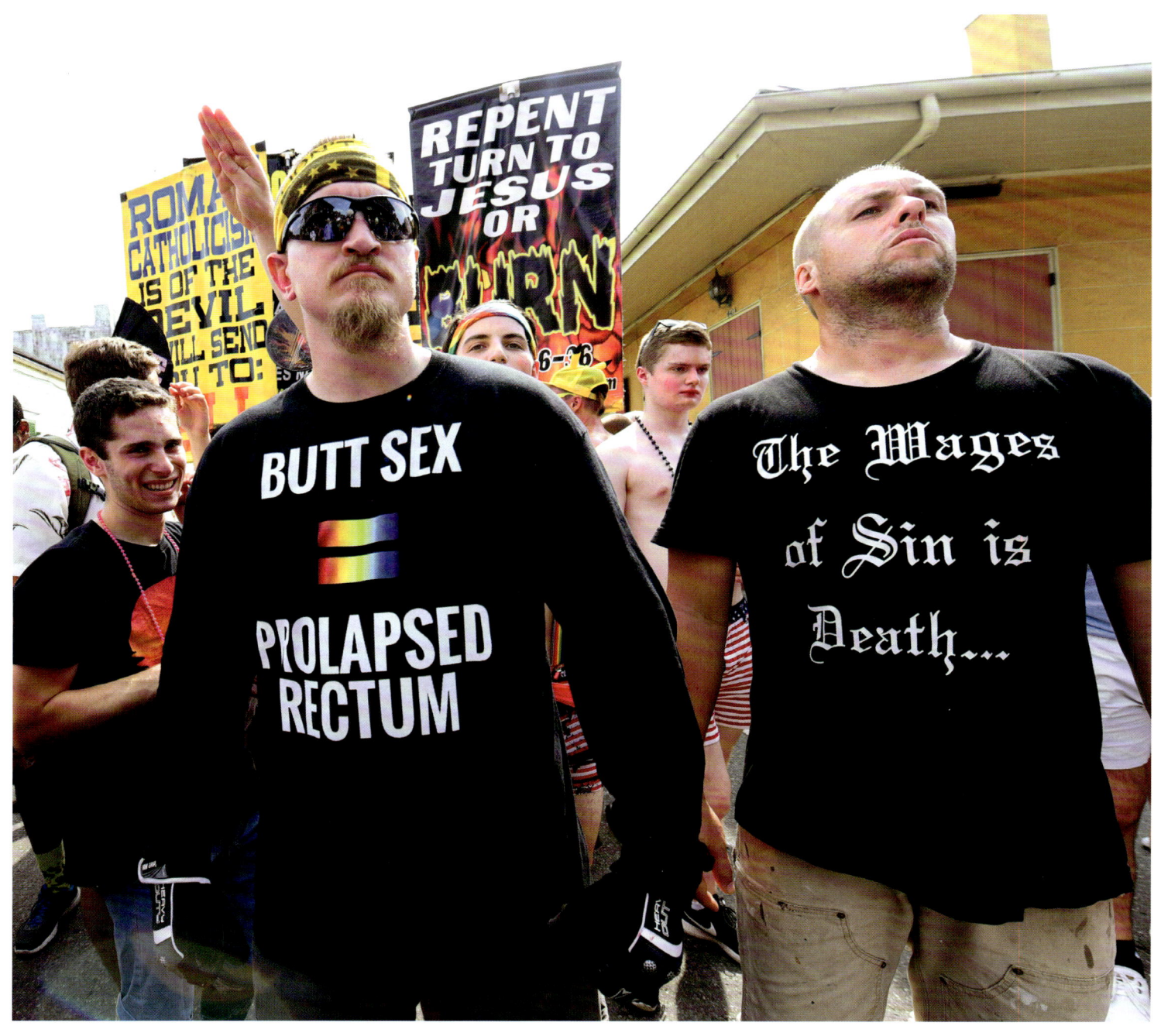

Protesters wear black T-shirts with anti-LGBTQ+ messages during the Southern Decadence parade, 2017.

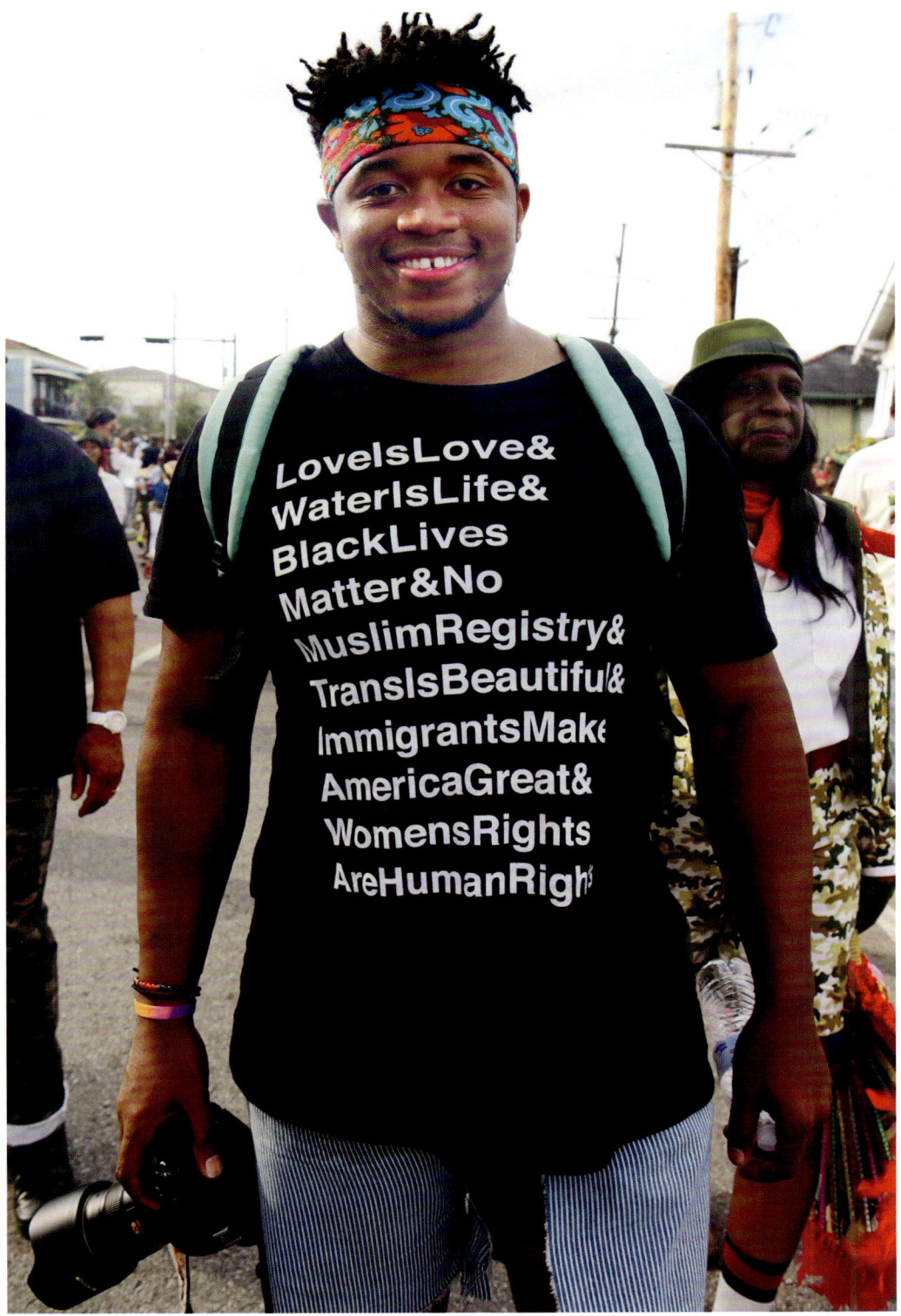

Photographer Kewon Hunter wears a black T-shirt expressing love for marginalized communities at a second line, 2018.

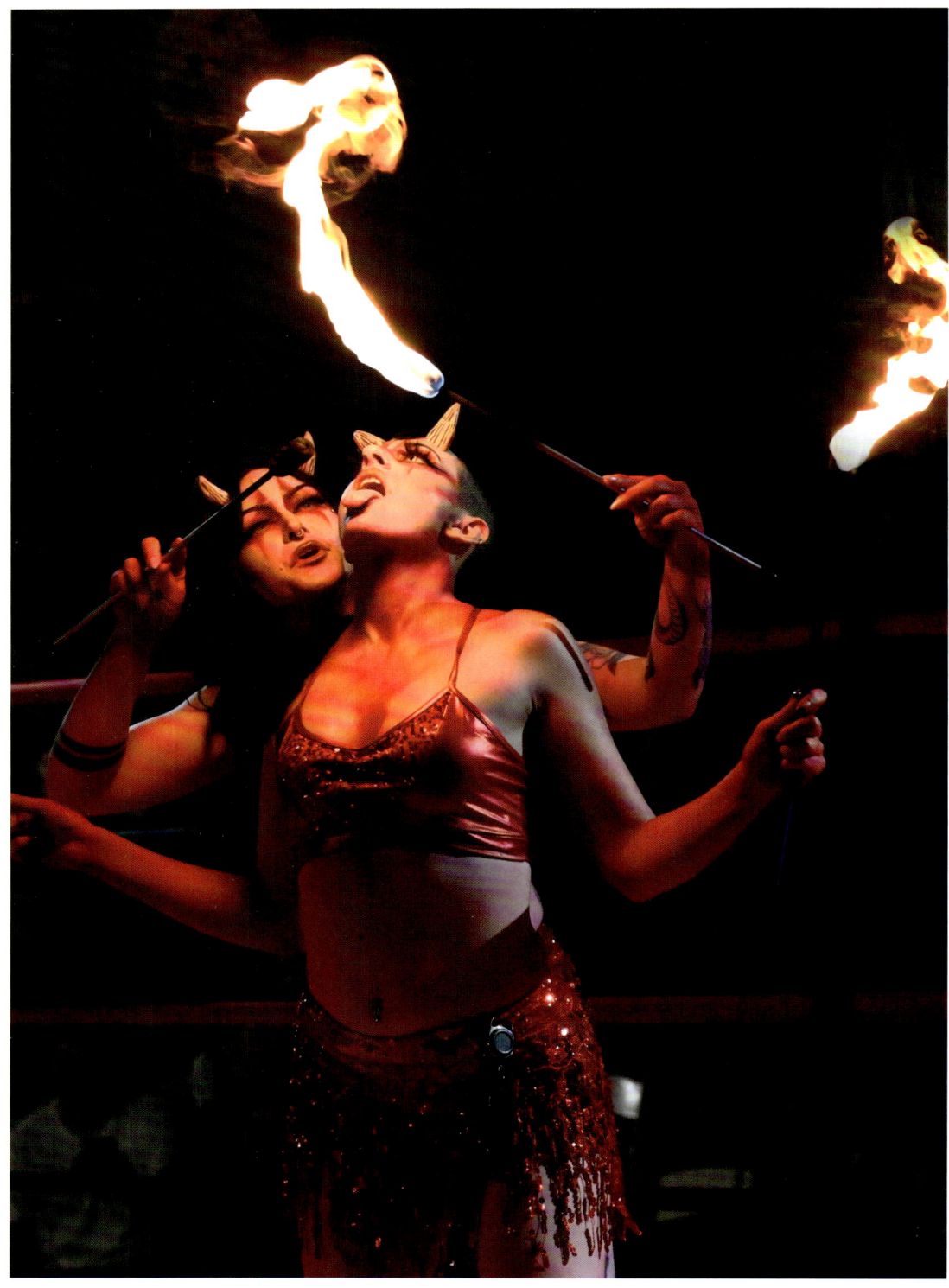

Cassidy and Juju perform a fire-breathing act between boxing matches at Friday Night Fights in Central City, 2022.

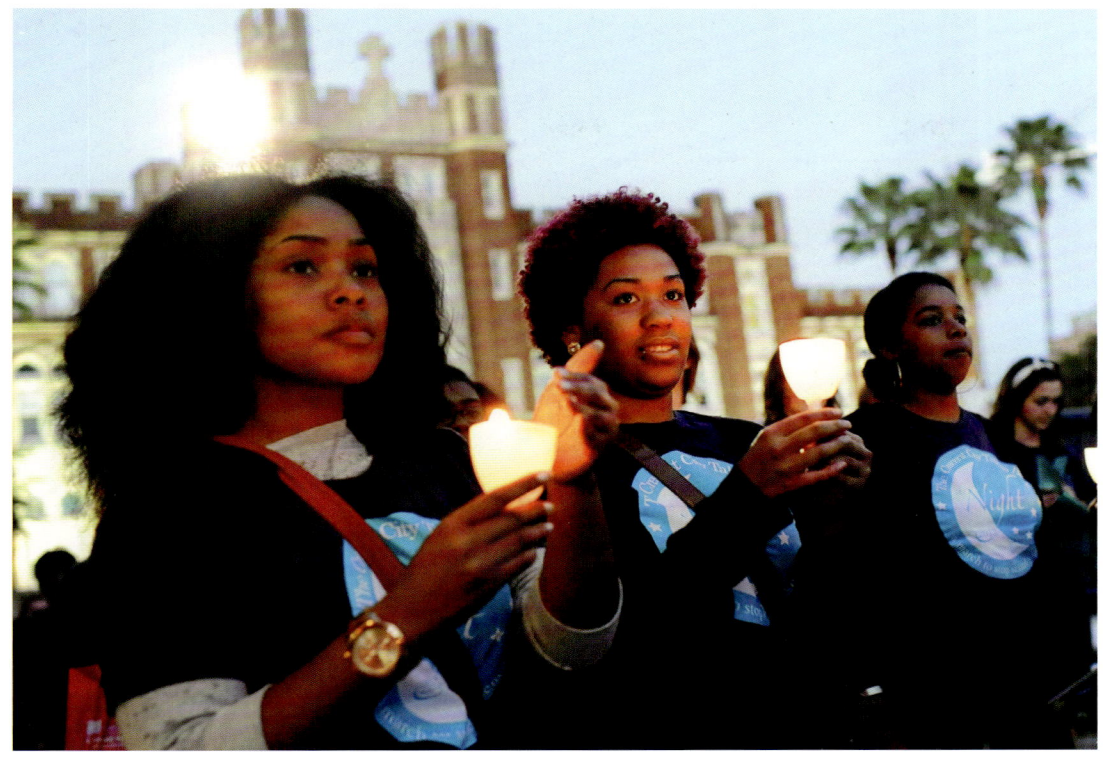

Students from area universities participate in the Crescent City's annual "Take Back the Night" candlelight event and march, bringing awareness to sexual assault and domestic abuse, held at Loyola University, 2013.

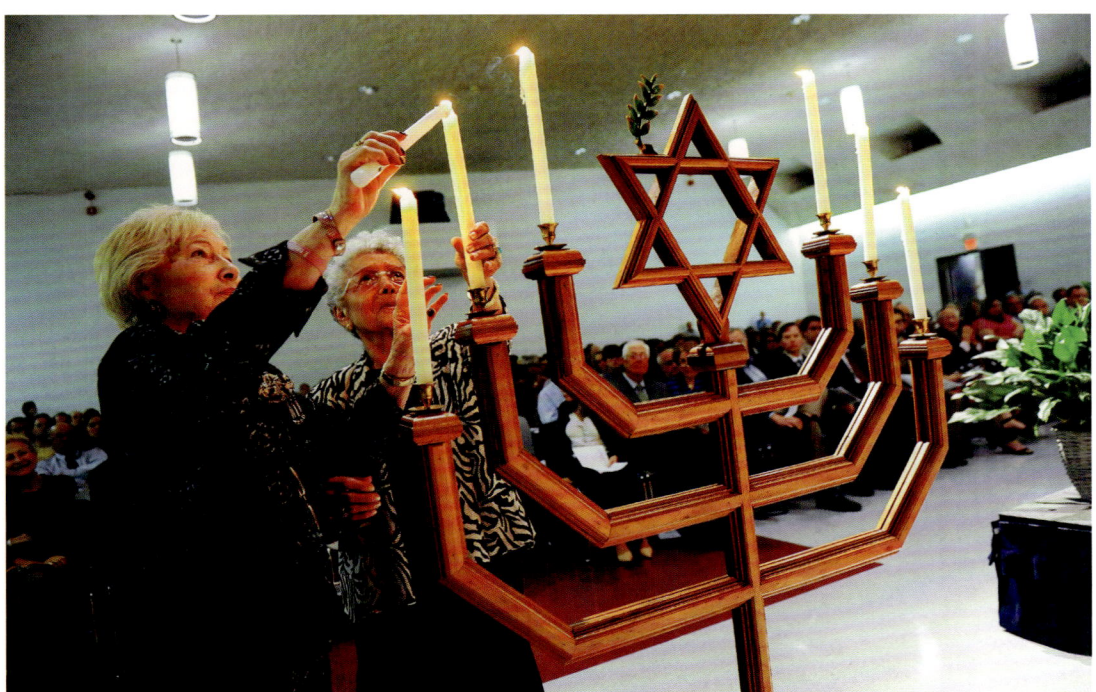

Two women light a menorah during Yom HaShoah, a memorial program to remember and honor New Orleans survivors of the Holocaust, at the Uptown Jewish Community Center, 2014.

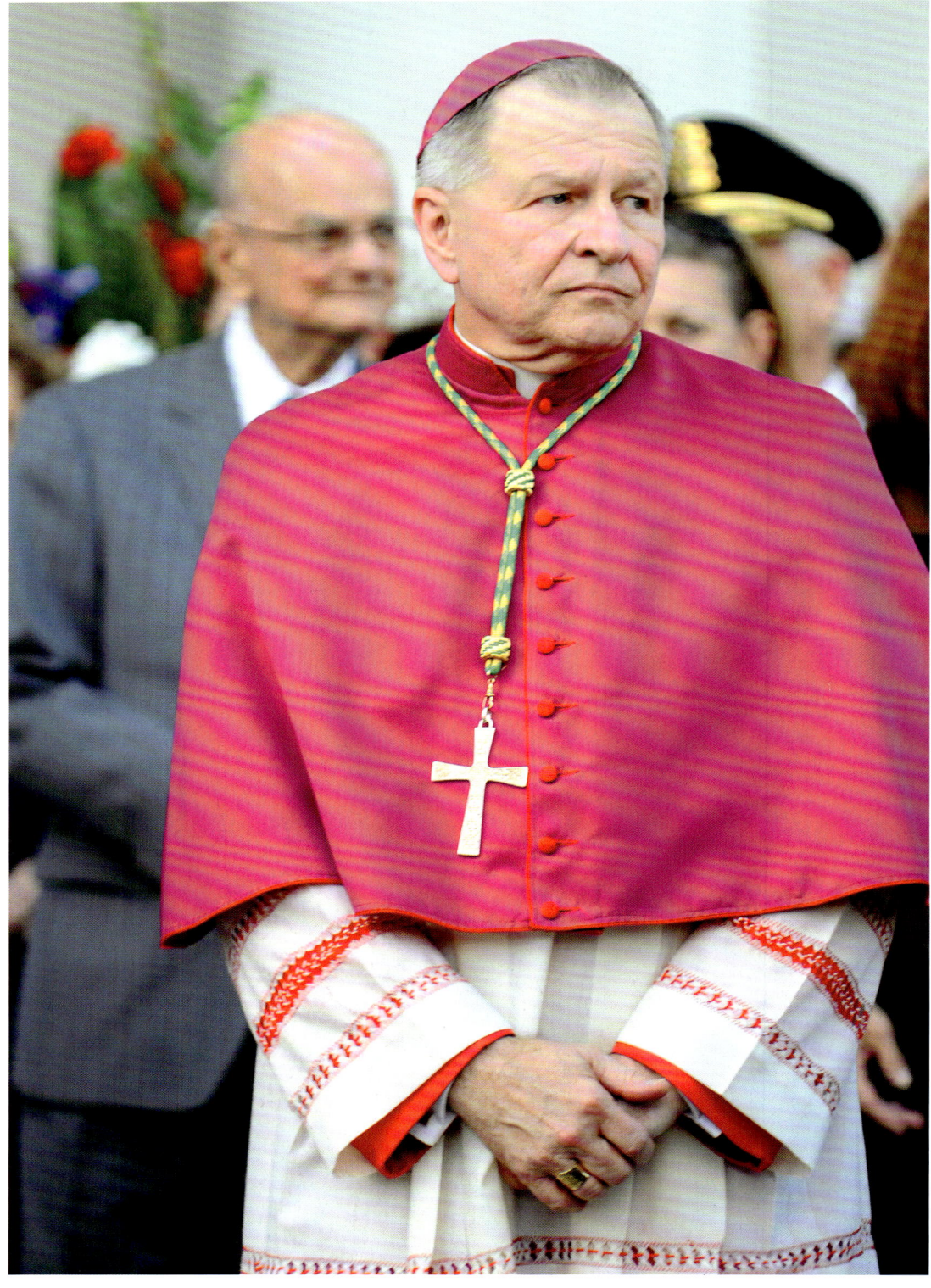

Archbishop Gregory Aymond at St. Louis Cathedral for the funeral of Archbishop Philip Hannan, 2011. Aymond became the fourteenth archbishop of New Orleans in 2009. He is the first native New Orleanian to serve as archbishop in the 230-year history of the Archdiocese of New Orleans.

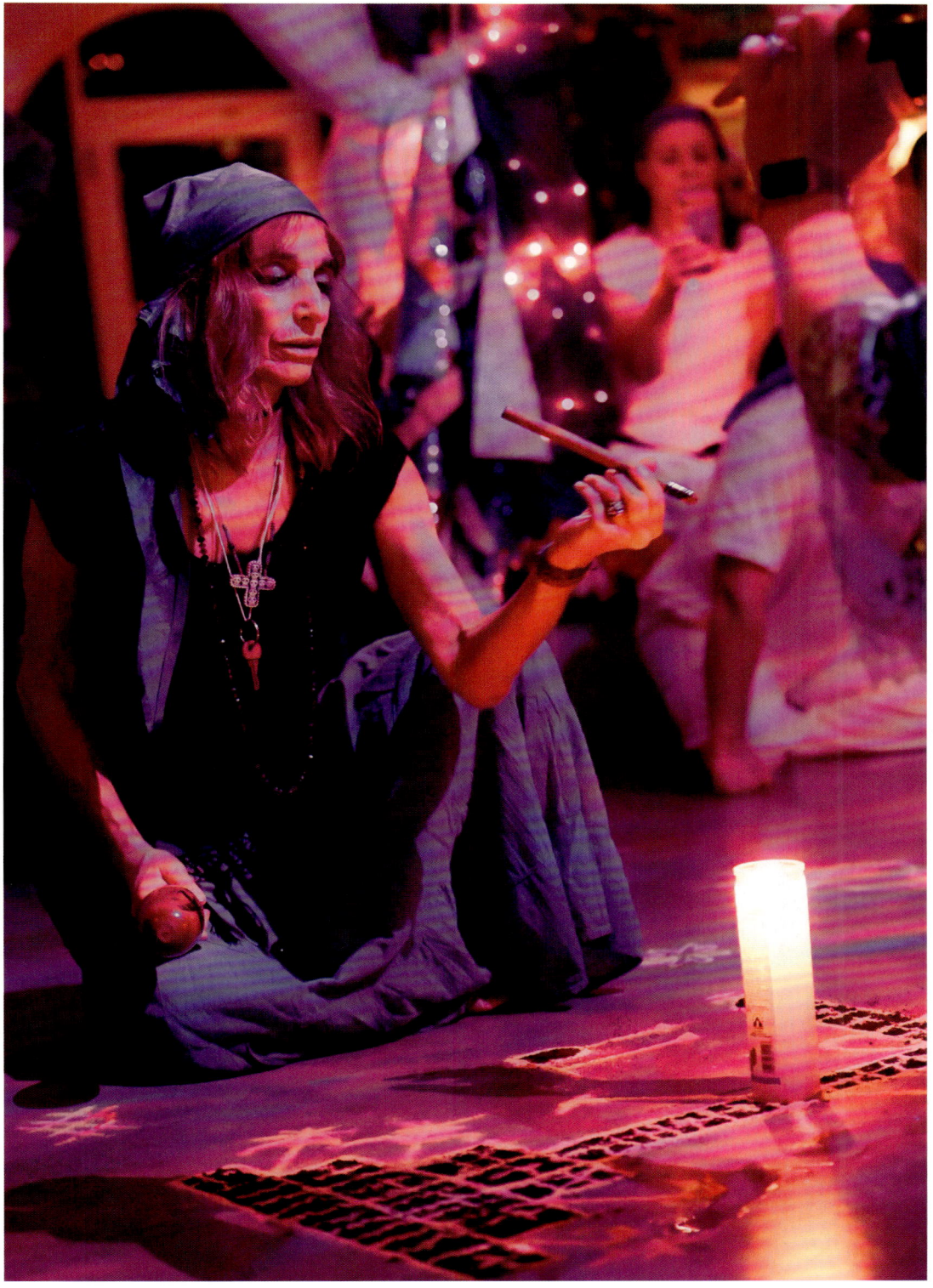

Voodoo Priestess Sallie Ann Glassman performs an All Souls' Day ceremony at the Healing Center, 2022. Glassman, a self-described Ukrainian Jew from Maine, has been practicing Voodoo in New Orleans since 1977; in 1995, she became one of the few white Americans to be ordained by the traditional Haitian initiation.

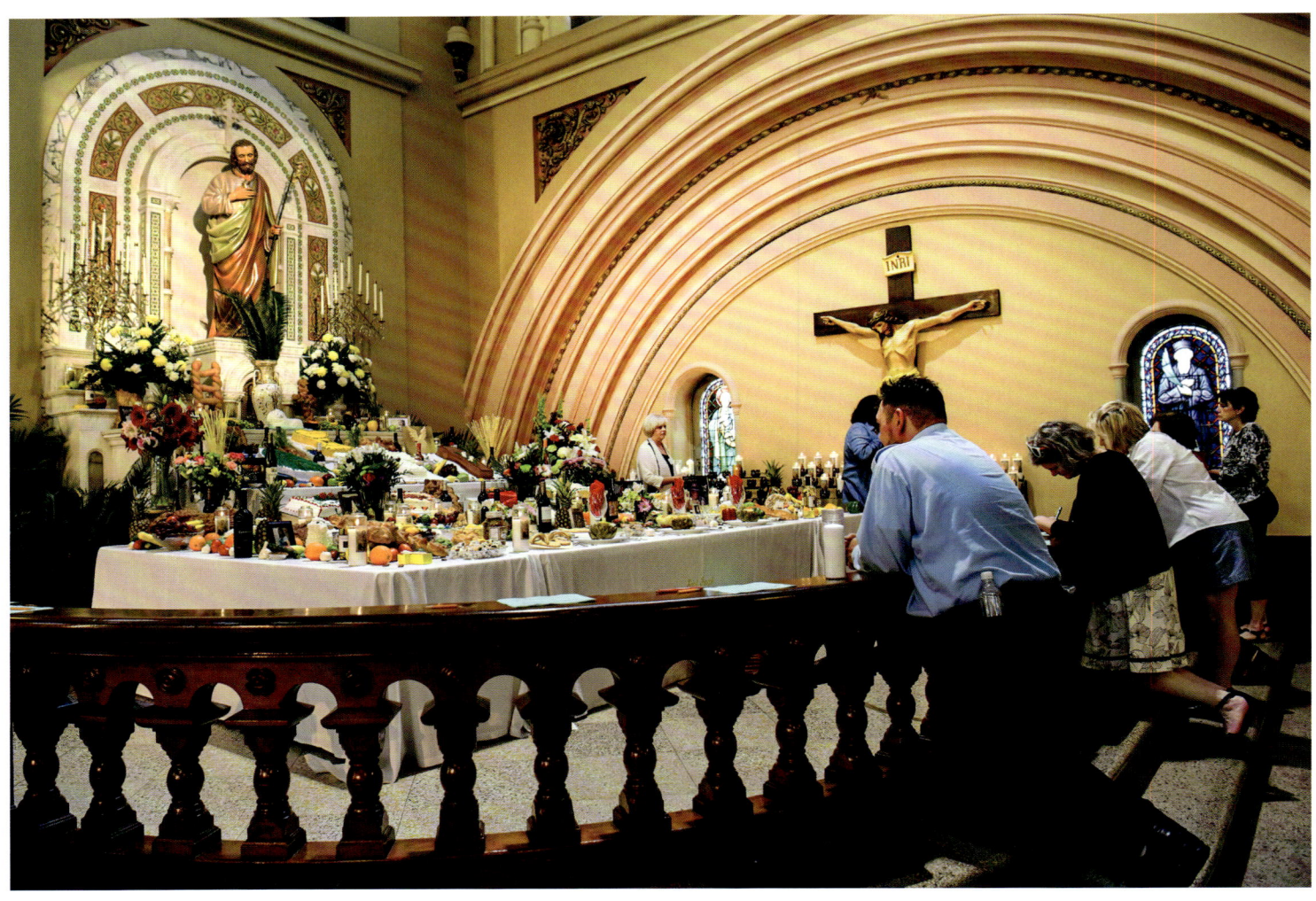

Churchgoers kneel at a St. Joseph's Day Altar at St. Joseph Catholic Church, 2018. St. Joseph's Day is a citywide event held every March 19; it features public and private altars of food and drink commemorating the relief that St. Joseph provided during the famine in Sicily. The tradition began in the late nineteenth century when Sicilian immigrants settled in New Orleans.

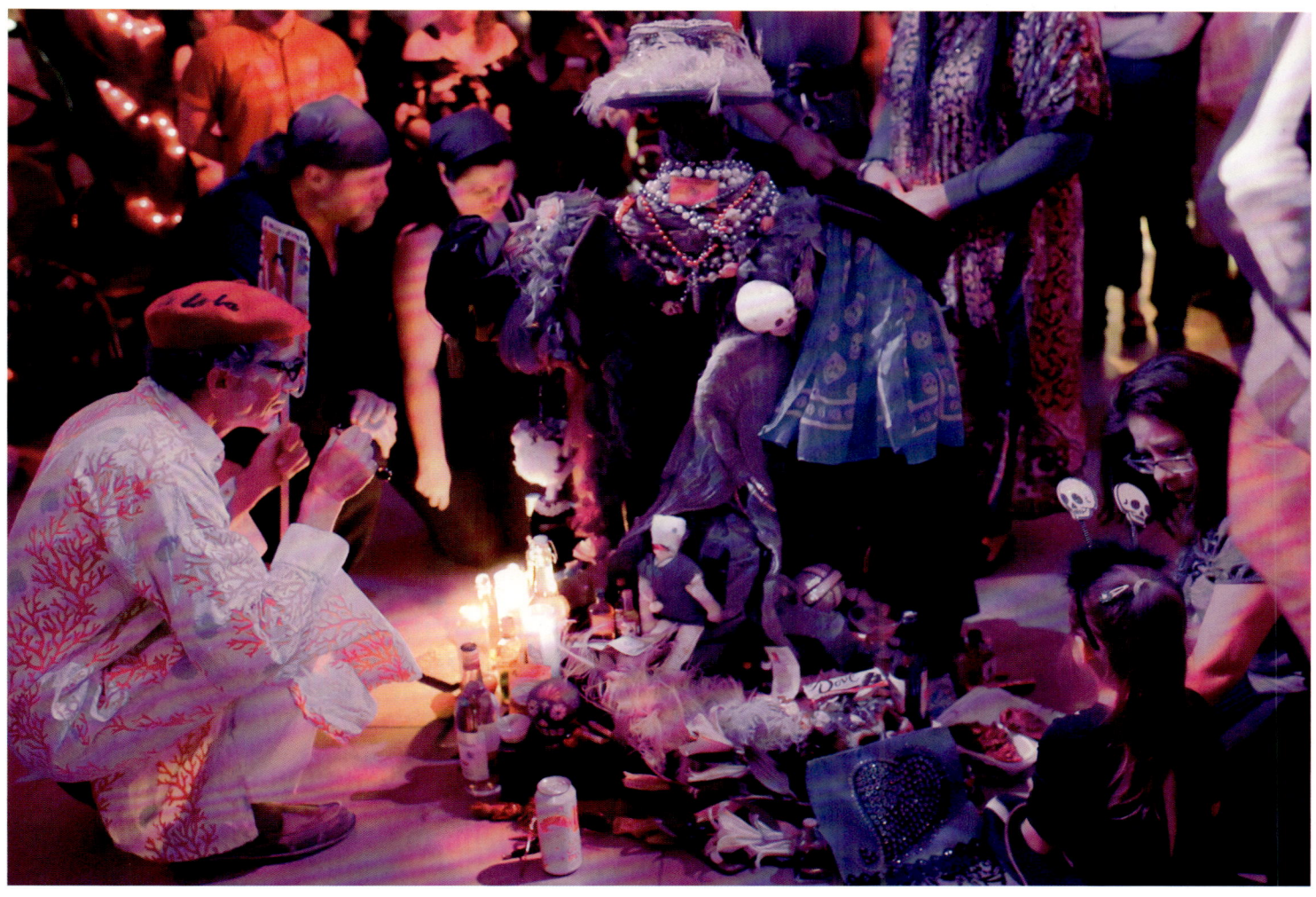

Steve Lohman, during an All Souls' Day Voodoo ceremony, places a candle near an altar for his father Maury, who died three days earlier at the age of 103, 2022.

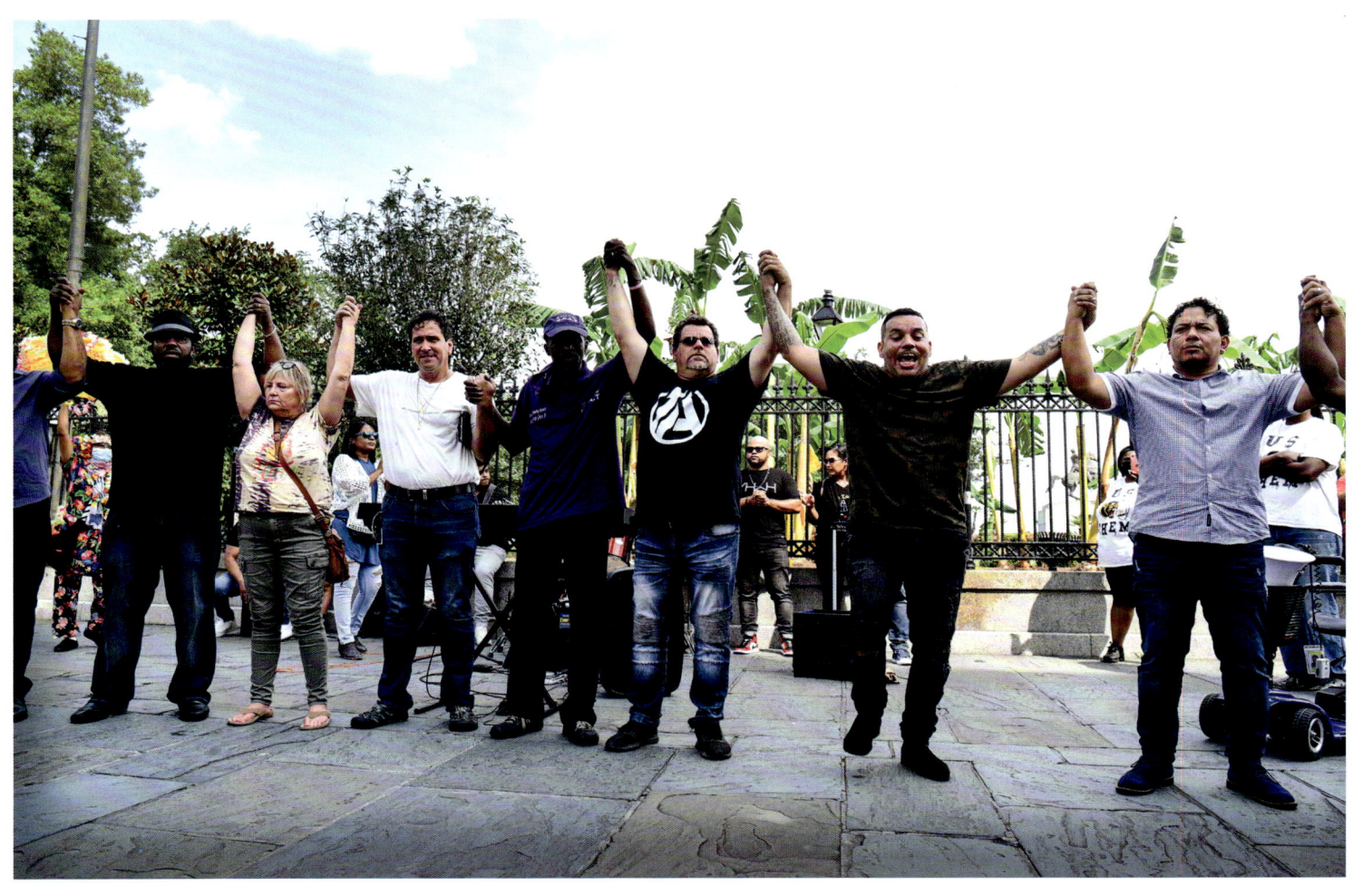

Faith leaders from across the city come together for a vigil in Jackson Square in response to the pandemic and racial unrest, 2020.

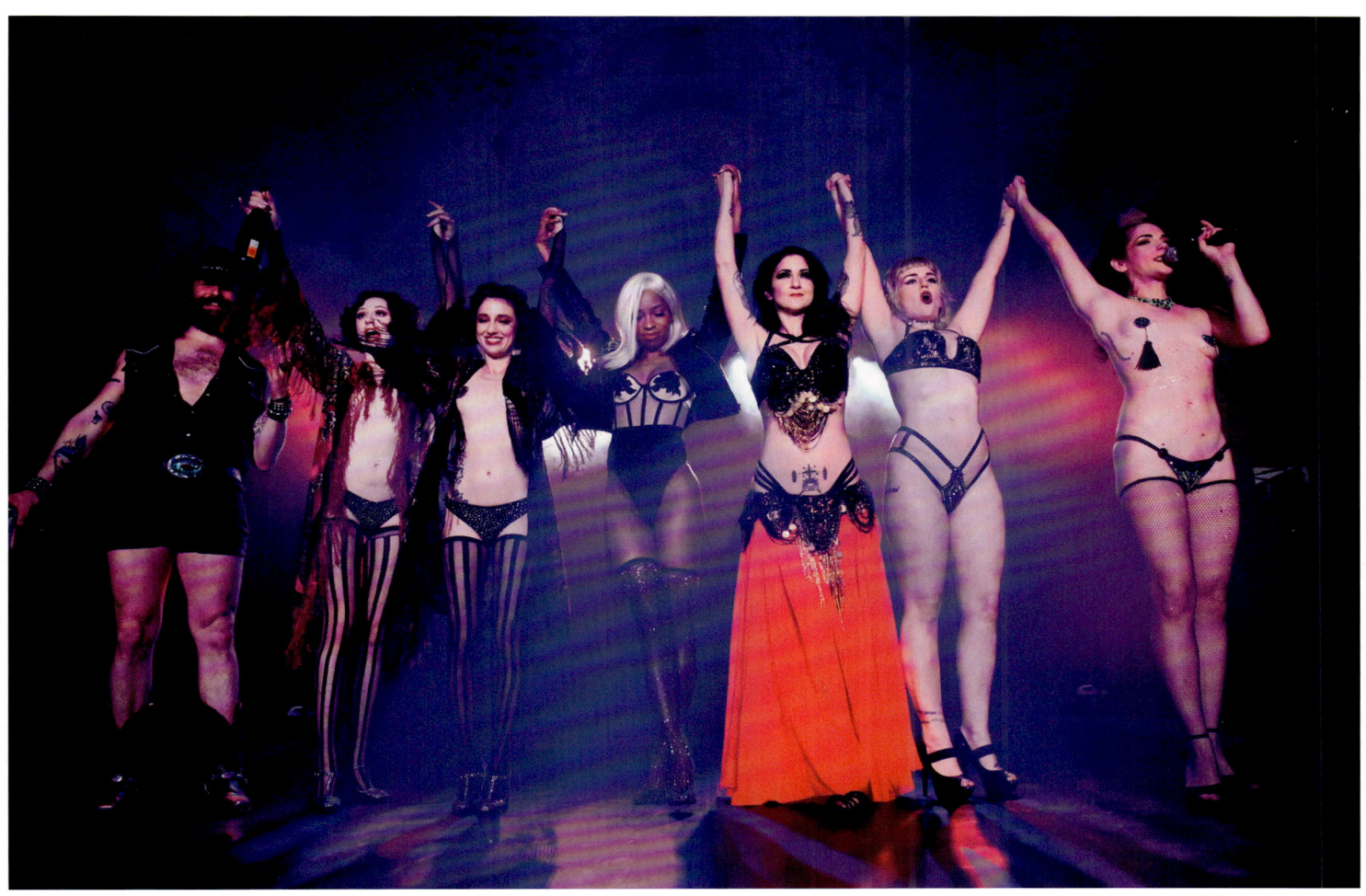

The Bad Girls of Burlesque take a curtain call after a performance at the Foundation Room in the House of Blues, 2018. This troupe celebrates "the wicked, the wayward, and the wanton," and their performances are produced by Rick Delaup, the owner and producer of New Orleans Burlesque.

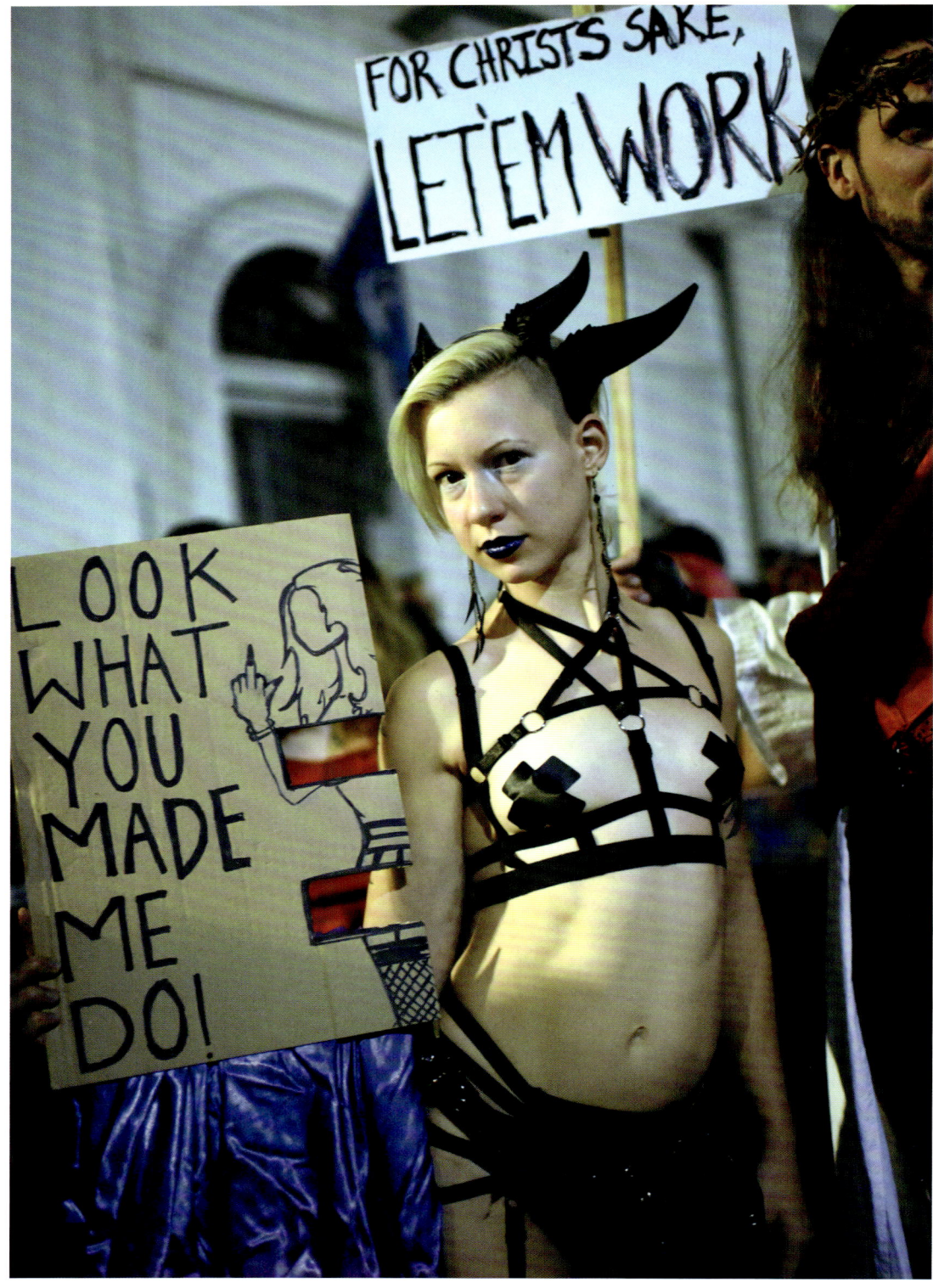

Bex Crow protests during the Strippers' March, more formally known as the Unemployment March, 2018. Strippers and other employees protested the closure of several strip clubs in the French Quarter after ATF agents issued violations for prostitution and drug use. Many of the women saw the closure as motivated by a conservative agenda.

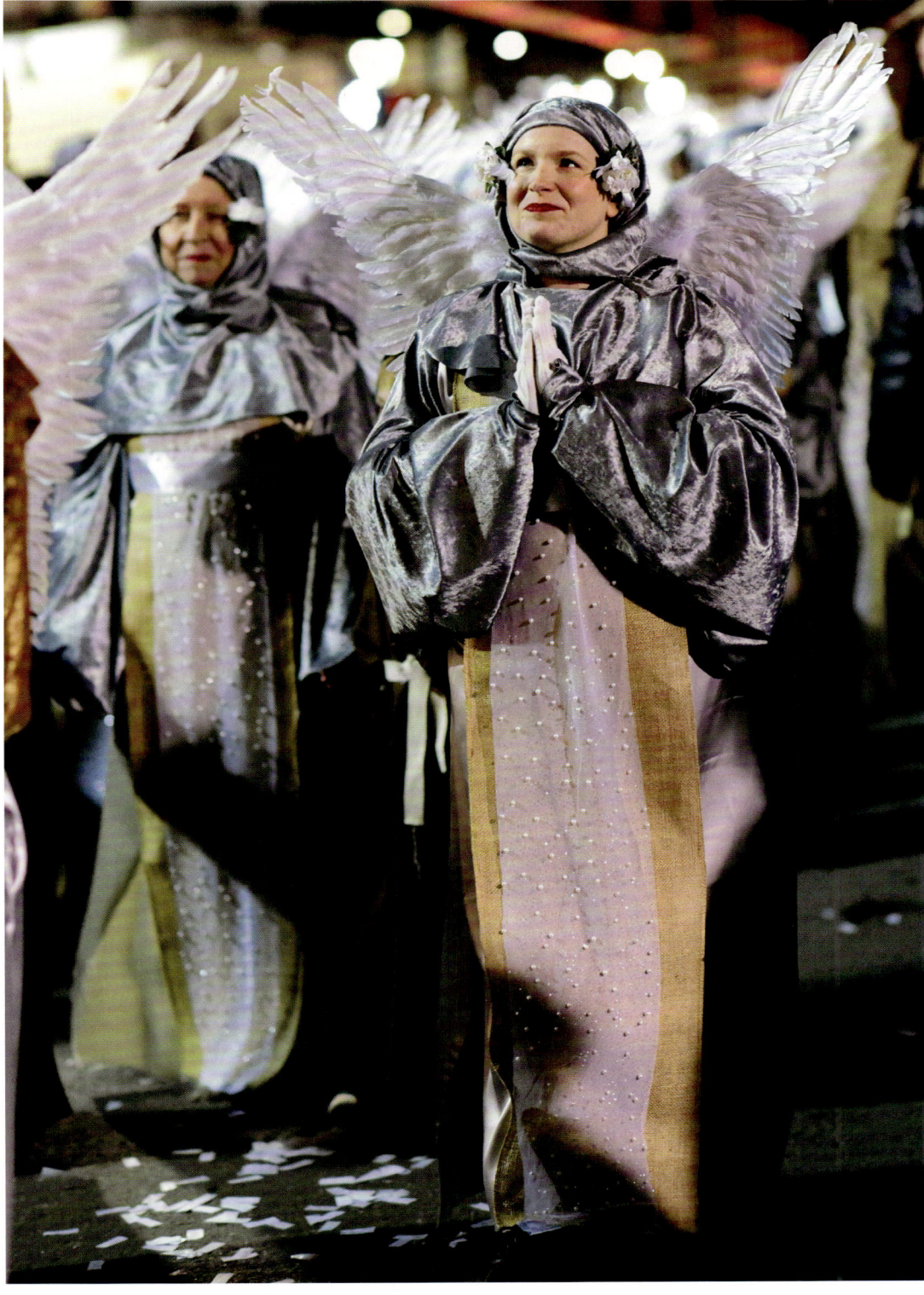

The Krewe de Jeanne d'Arc Mardi Gras walking parade's "Chorus of Angels," 2016. The parade held annually on January 6 was founded in 2008 to honor St. Joan of Arc, the patron saint of France and the unofficial patron saint of New Orleans, while promoting the city's French cultural heritage.

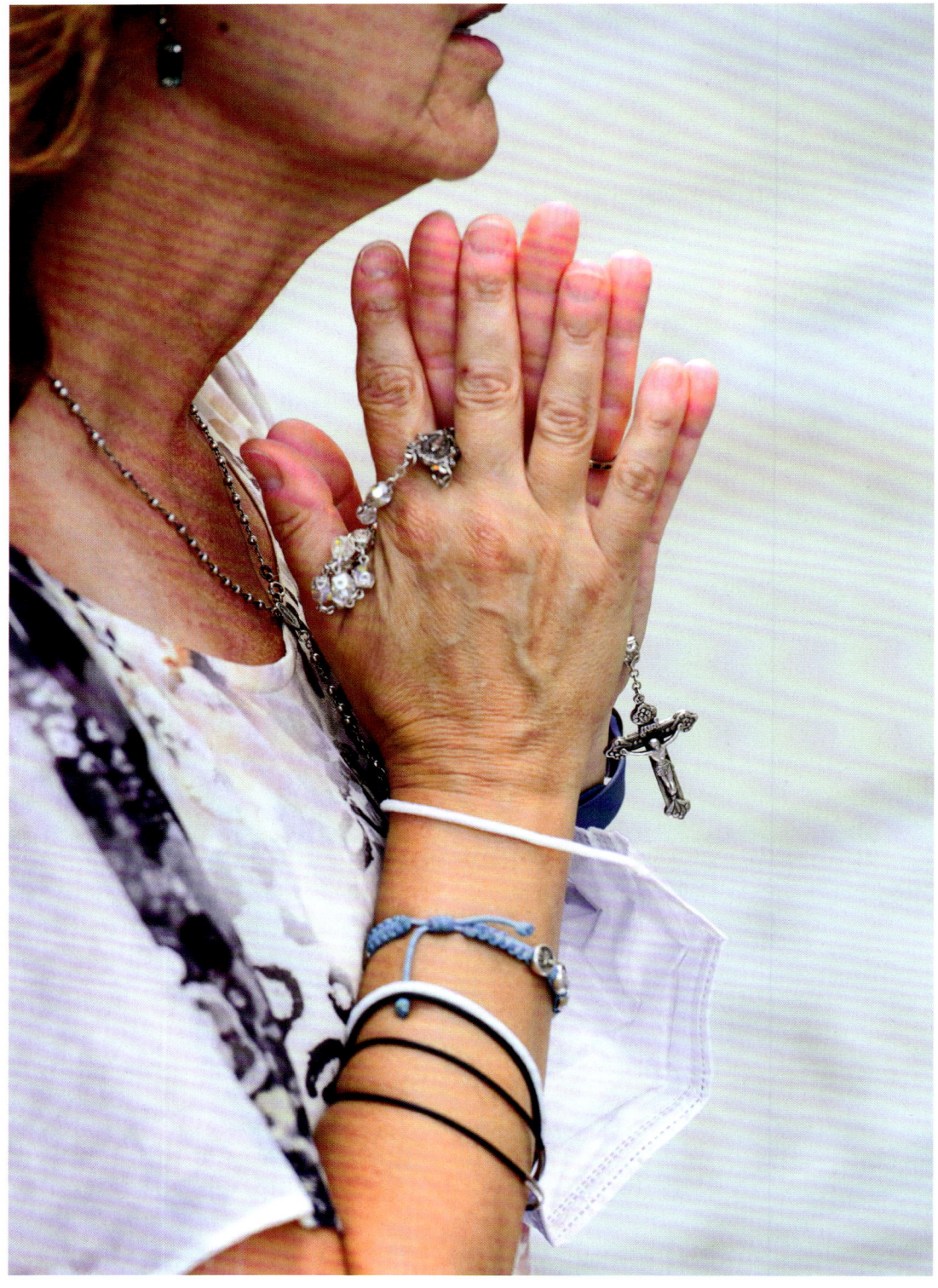

A woman prays for healing during the pandemic at St. Louis Cathedral, 2020.

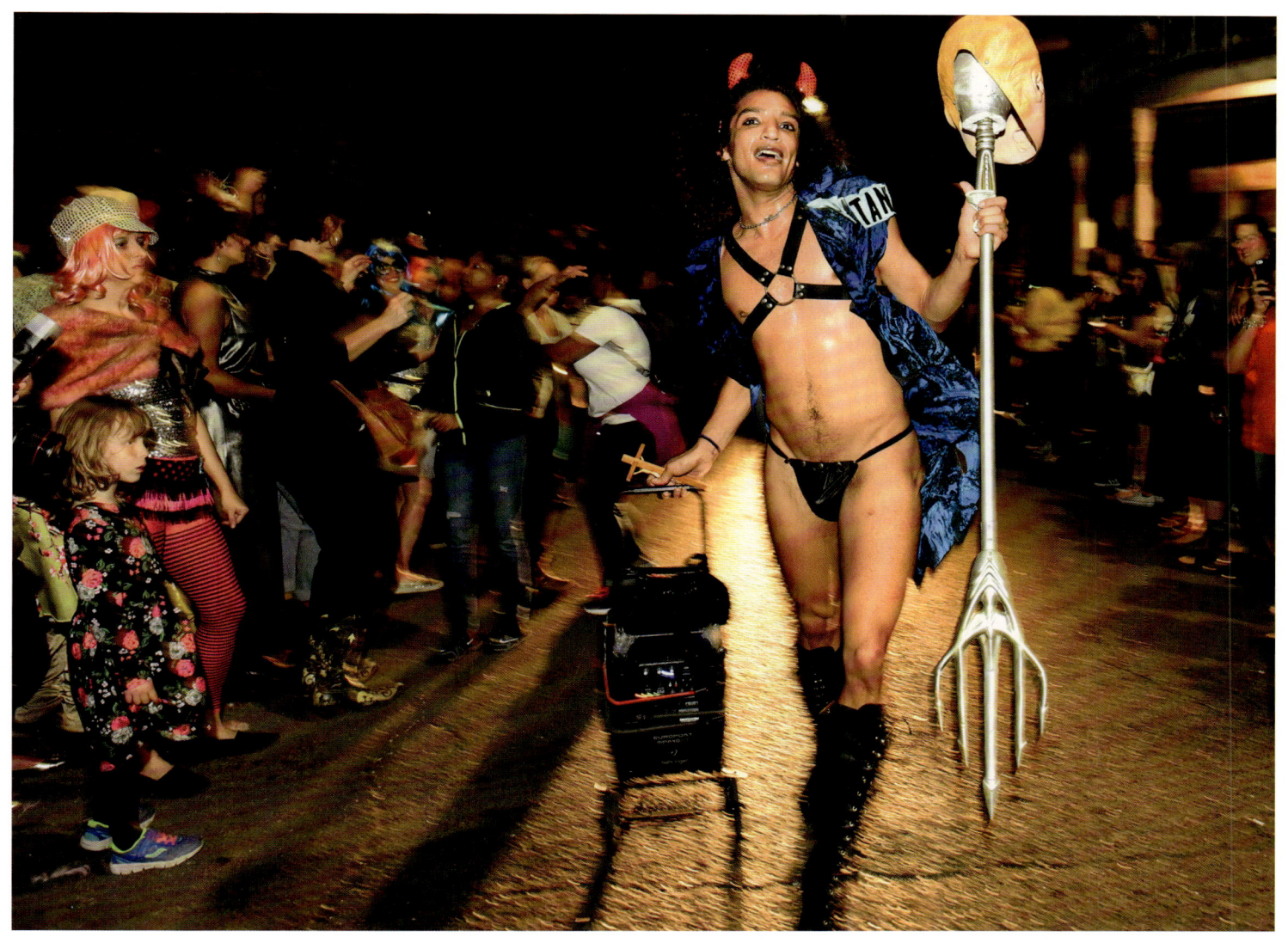

A reveler masks as Satan during the Krewe du Vieux parade in the Faubourg Marigny, 2017.

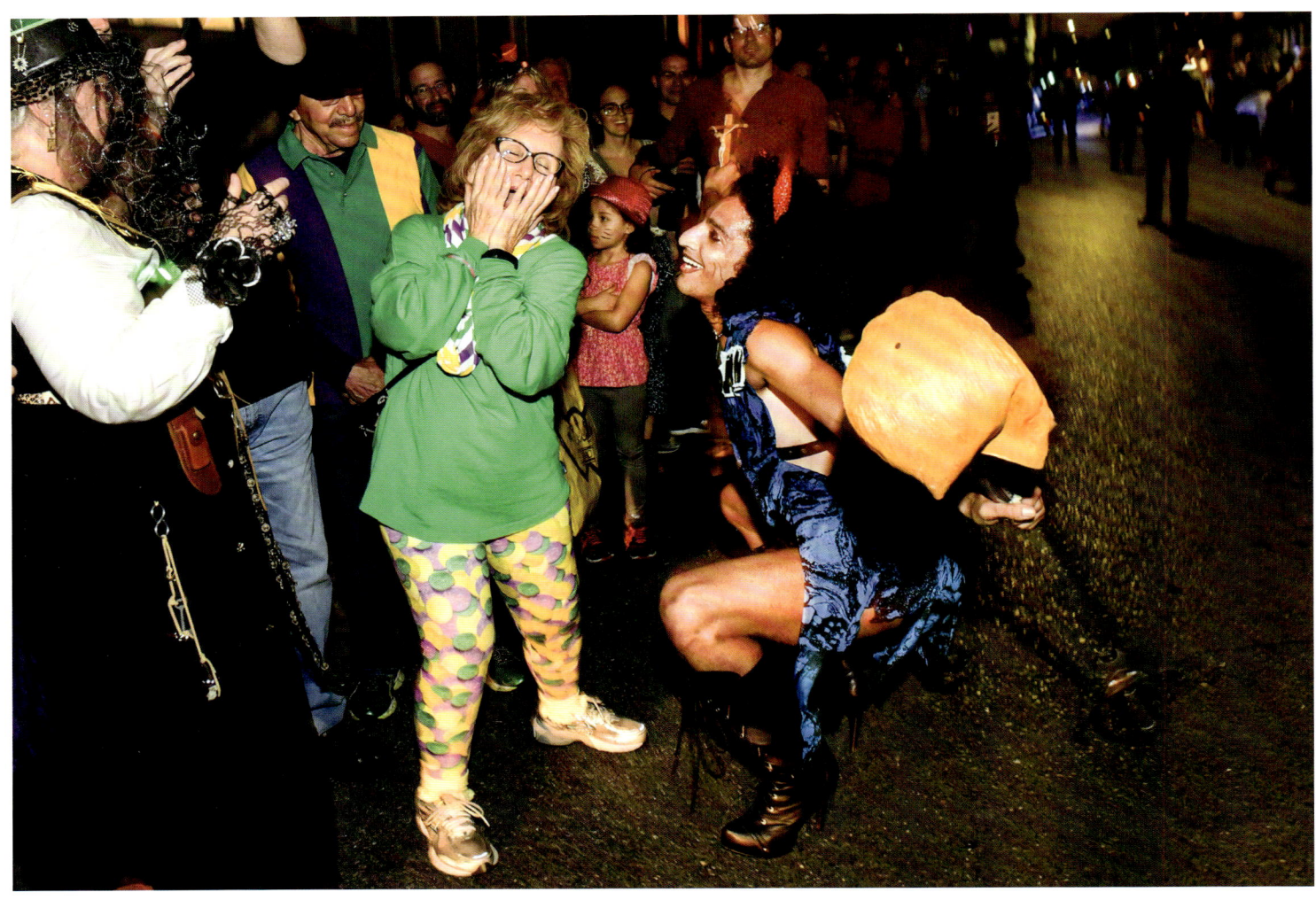

A woman reacts to the "Devil Made Me Do It" reveler masking as Satan in the Krewe du Vieux parade, 2017.

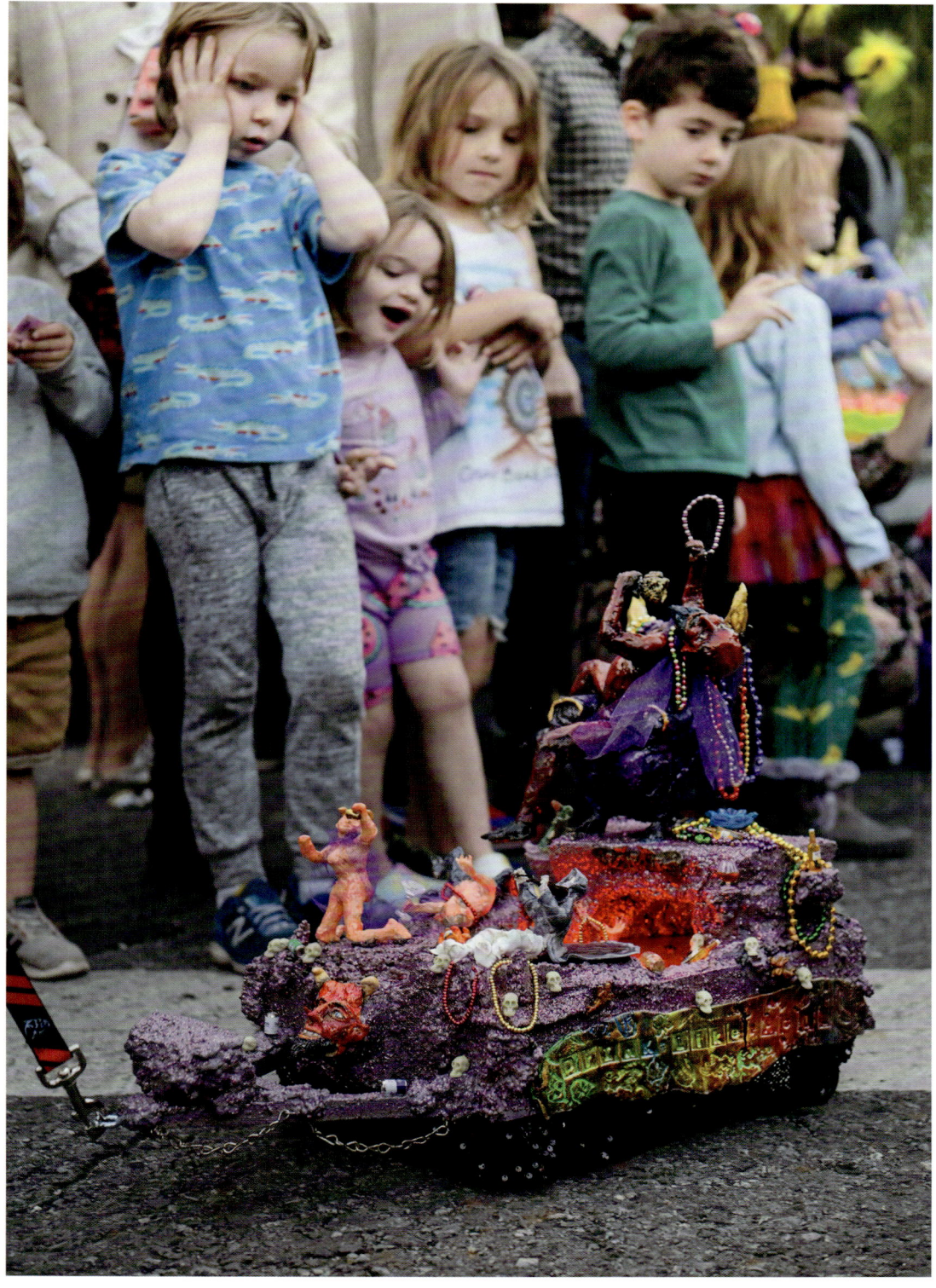

Children Loen Krejci, Adelyn Krejci, and Arlo Lawson react to the "Drink Like Hell" float in the 'tit Rəx parade in the Faubourg Marigny, 2023.

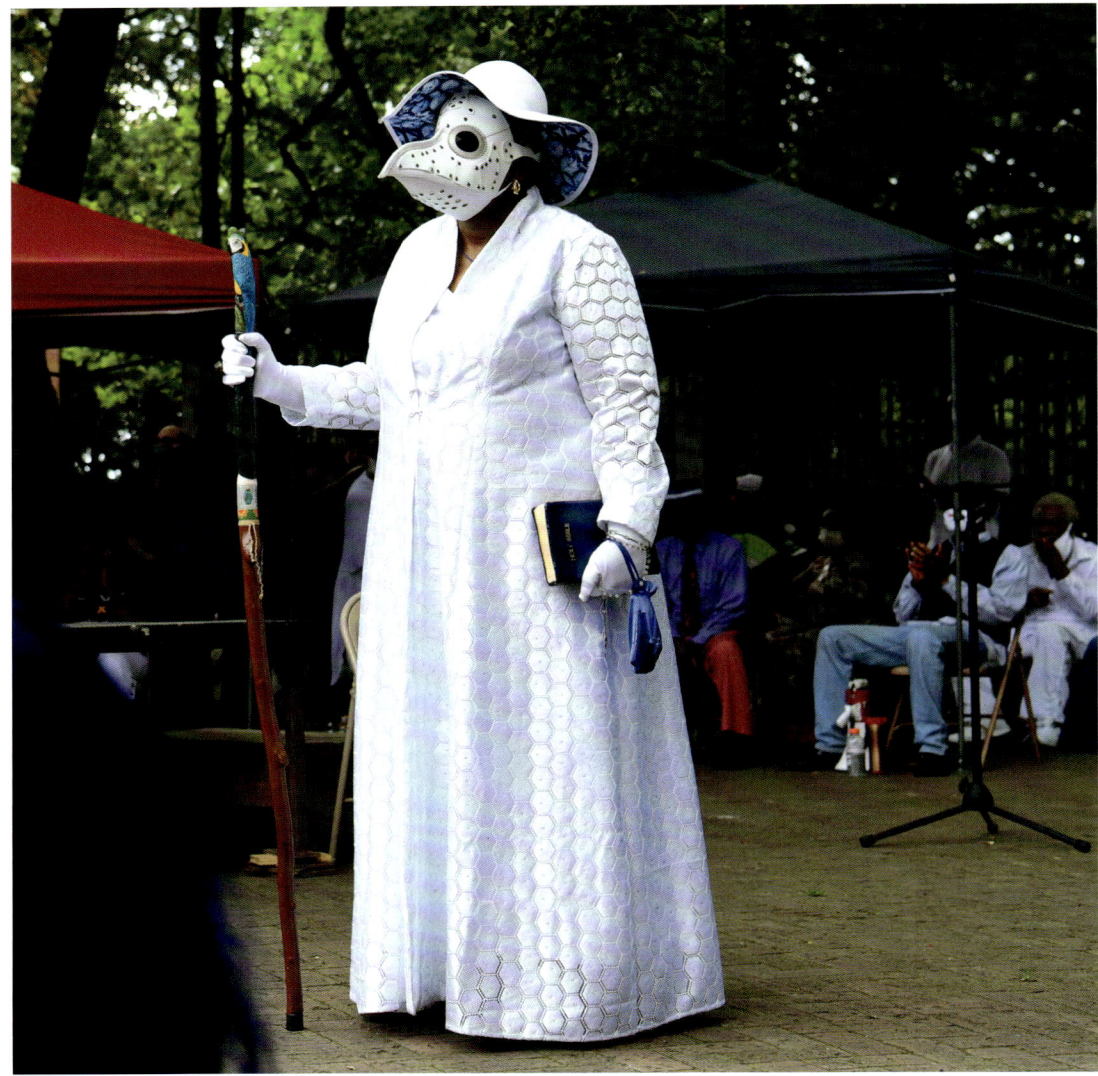

Cherice Harrison-Nelson debuts the "Plague Doctor" figure during a prayer vigil held outside Congo Square for the Black Lives Matter movement and the COVID pandemic, 2020. Harris, a former New Orleans public-school teacher, is the cofounder of the Mardi Gras Indian Hall of Fame and Queen of the Guardians of the Flame Maroon Society. She performs and presents African history and her personal experience in New Orleans to the rest of the country and abroad.

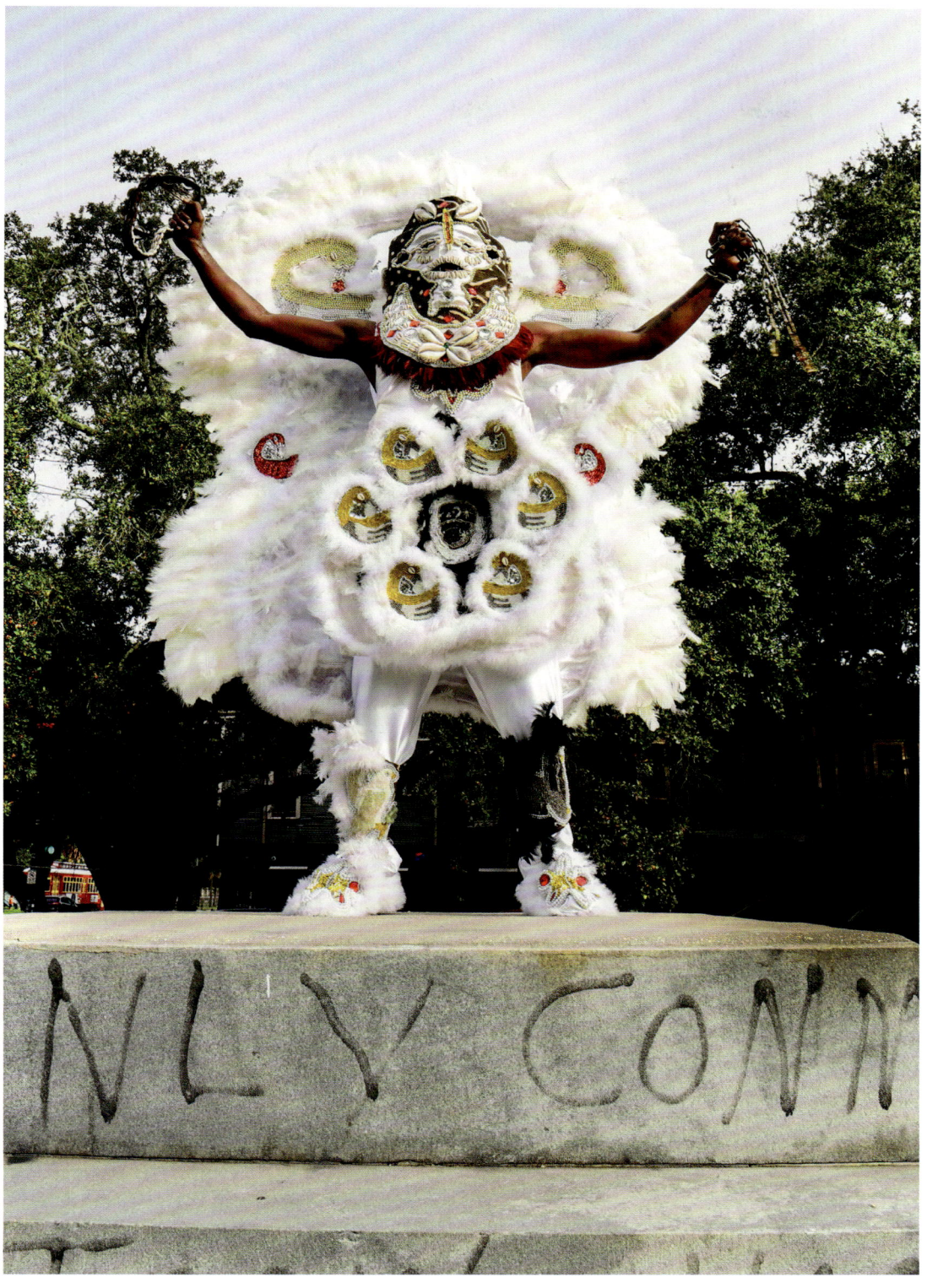

Trail Chief Peteh Muhammad Haroon of the Golden Feather Hunters poses atop the pedestal where the Confederate monument to Jefferson Davis once stood, 2020. Haroon is a poet and educator. The primary motif of his suit is the Ghanaian Sankofa symbol that honors the past while guiding the future.

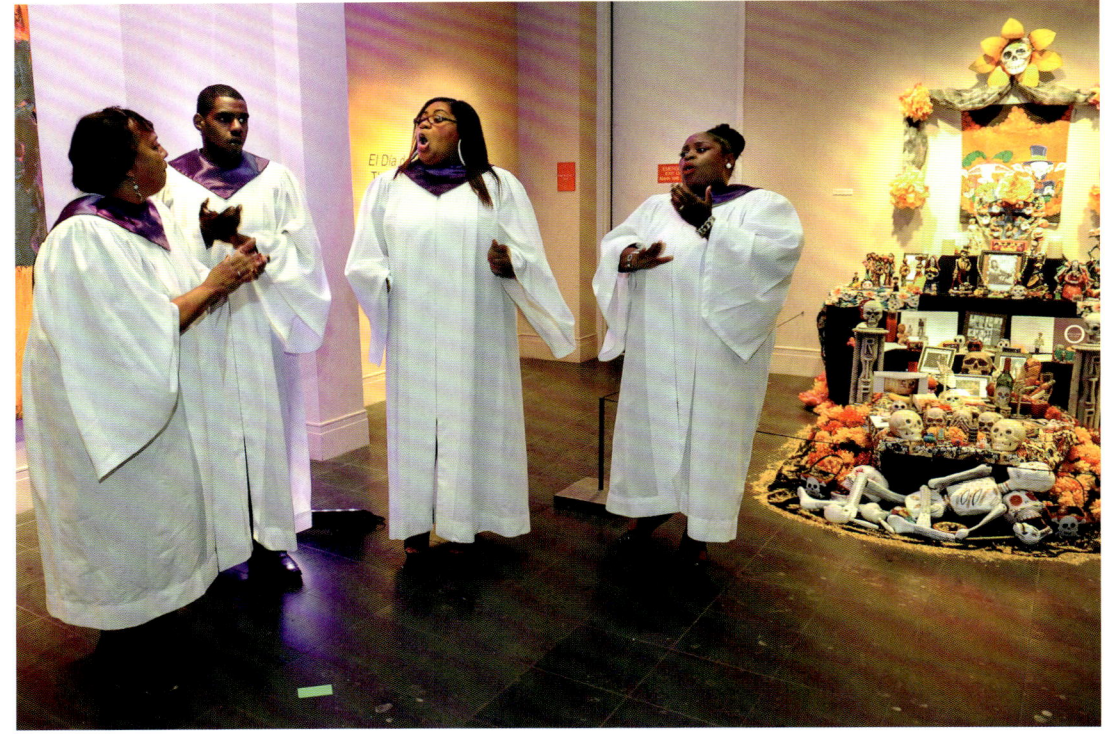

Betty Winn & One A-Chord Gospel Singers at the Ogden Museum's "O What a Night!" annual fundraiser, 2014.

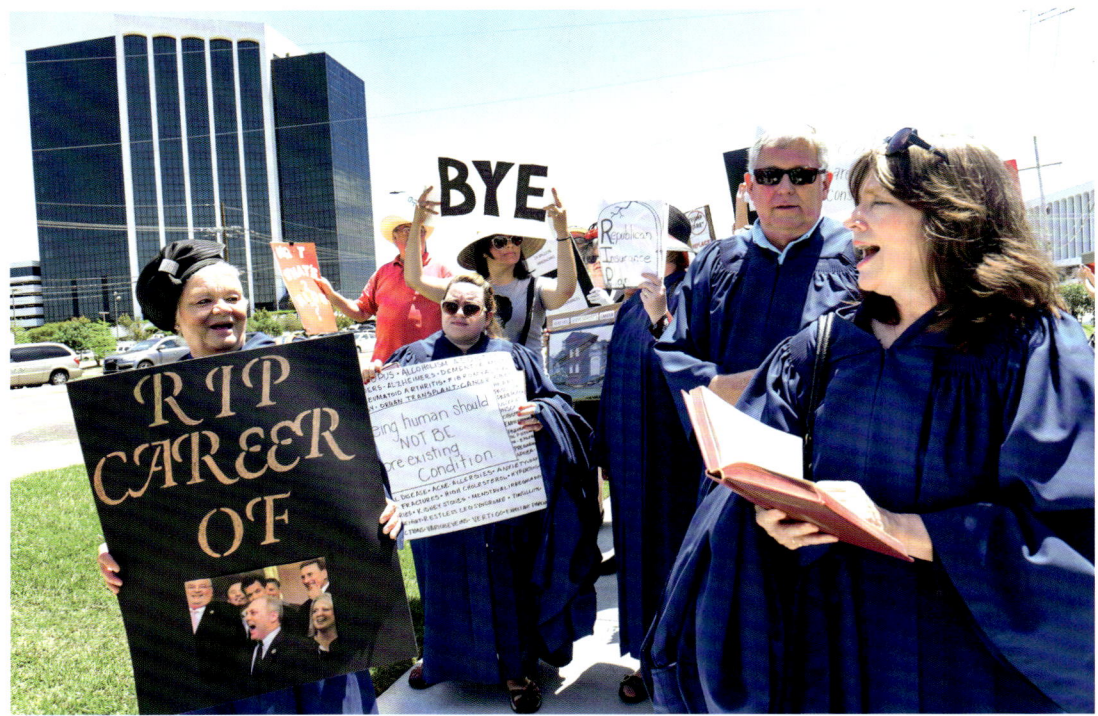

Protesters stage a gospel choir and funeral procession for Congressman Steve Scalise's career after he voted to repeal the Affordable Care Act, 2017.

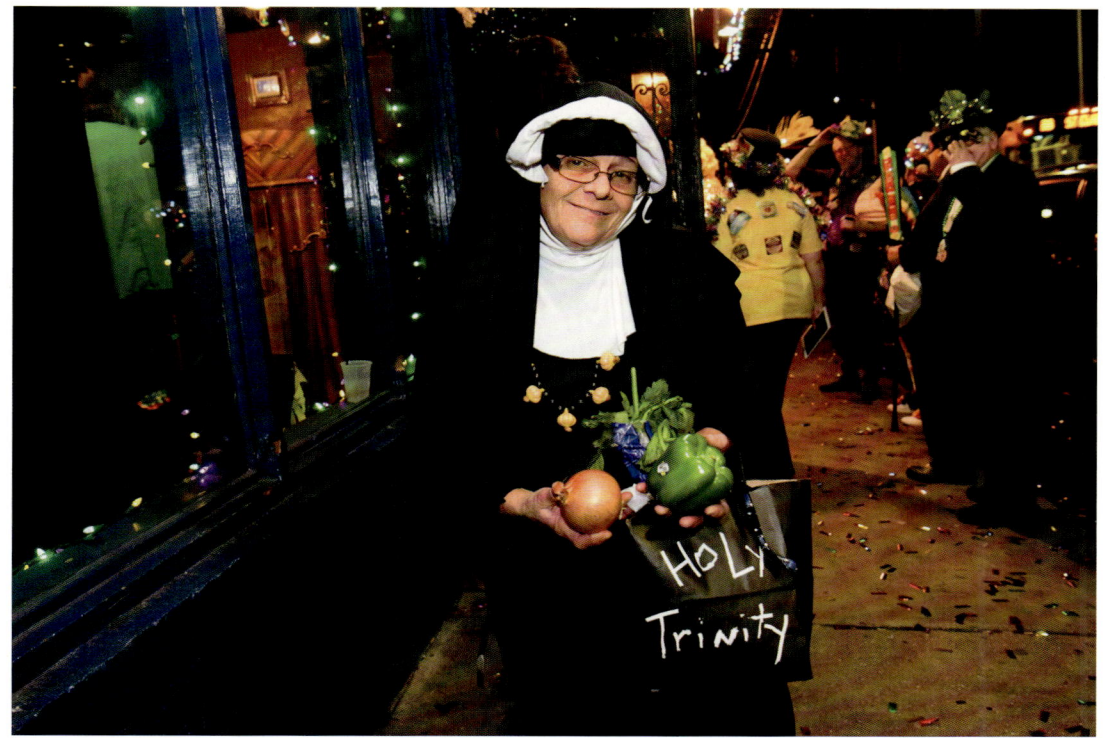

A woman costumes as the "Holy Trinity" during the Société des Champs Elysée Ball, 2019. The "holy trinity" in Cajun and Creole cuisine refers to onions, bell peppers, and celery.

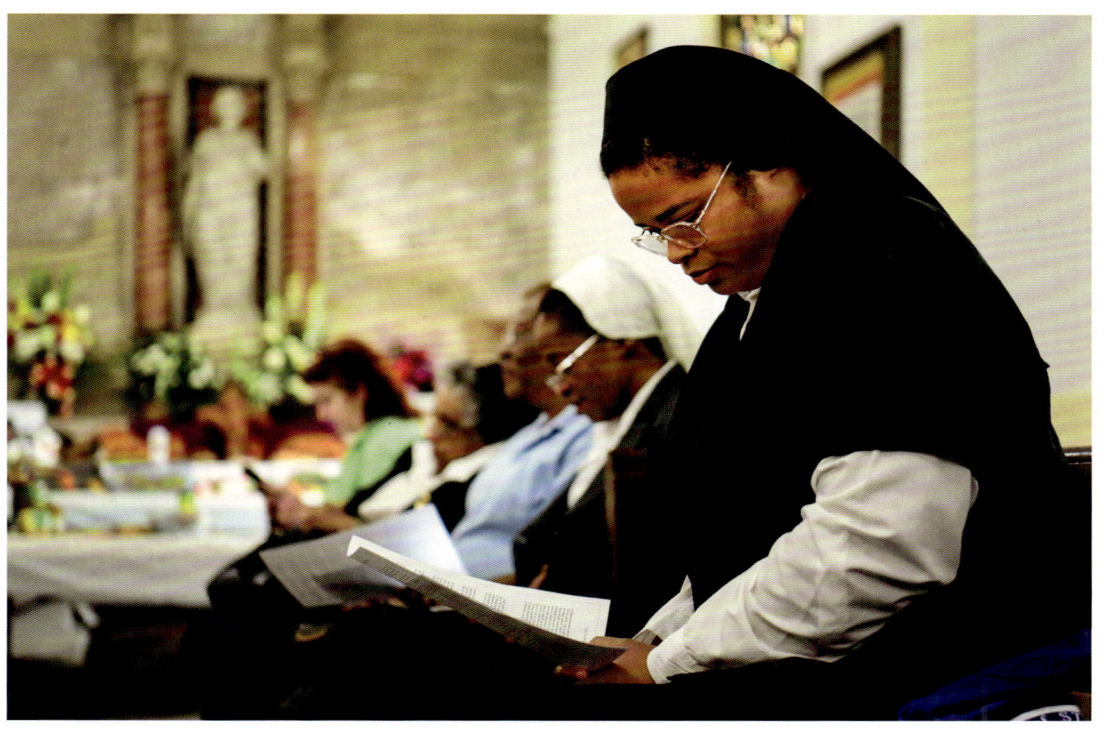

Sisters of the Holy Family pray at St. Augustine Church in Tremé at the St. Joseph's Day Altar, 2018. The Sisters of the Holy Family, founded in 1837 by Henriette DeLille, is a Catholic order of African American nuns whose mission is to minister to the poor and promote justice.

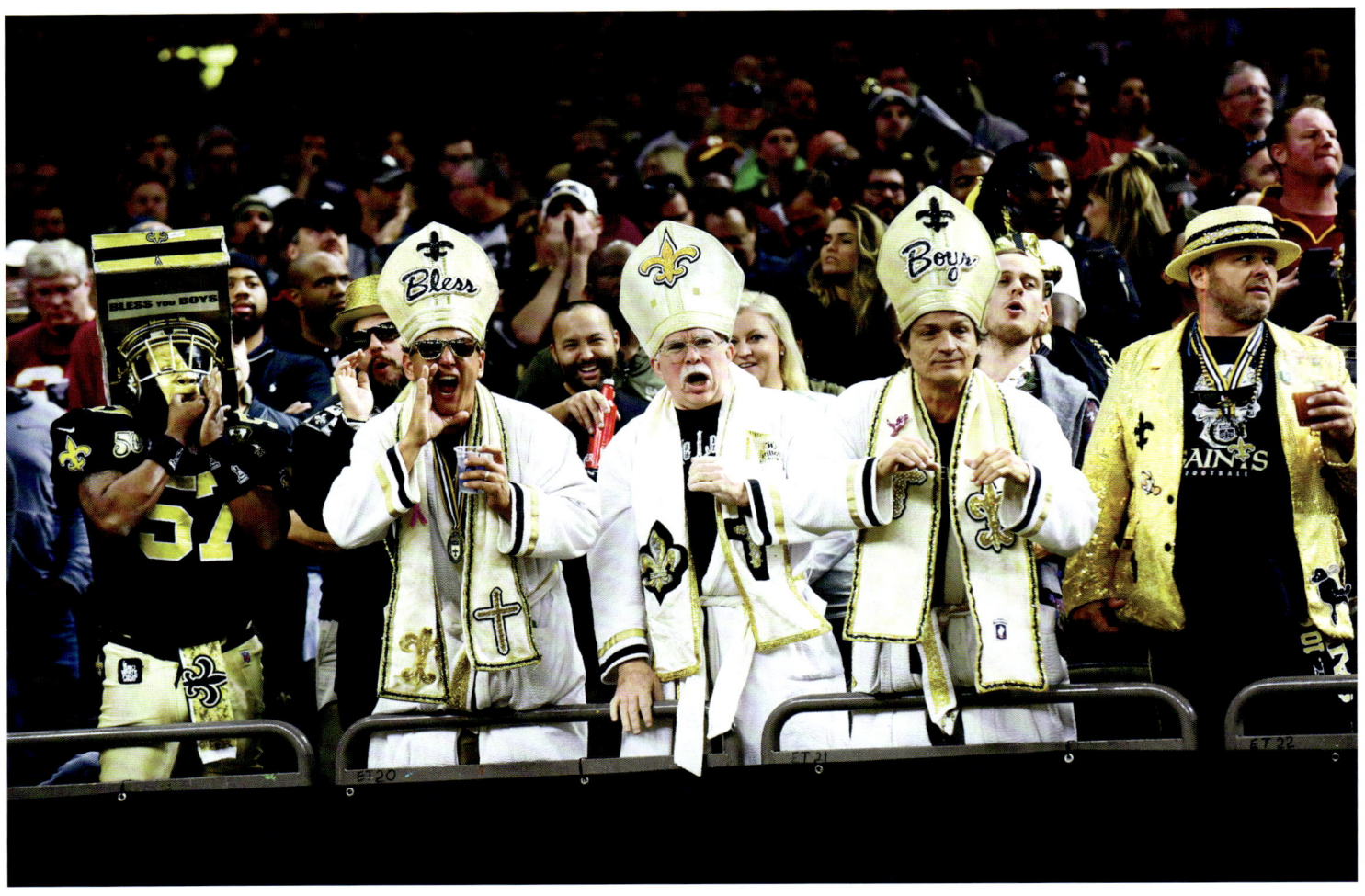

"Superfans" cheer on their beloved Saints in the Superdome, 2019.

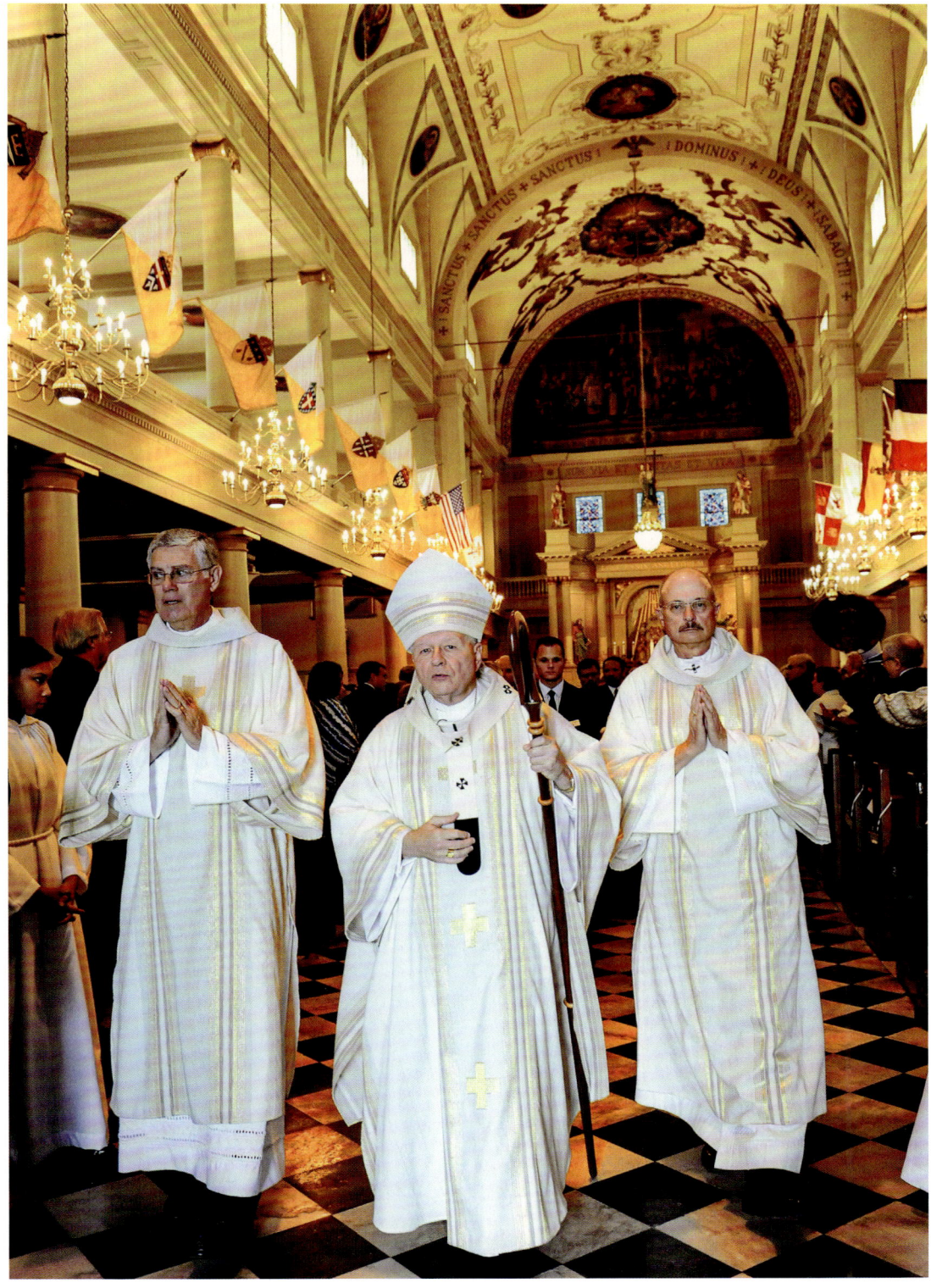

Archbishop Gregory Aymond (*center*) and clergy exit St. Louis Cathedral after the funeral of Congresswoman Lindy Boggs, 2013. Marie Corinne Morrison Claiborne "Lindy" Boggs (1916–2013) served as a member of the U.S. House of Representatives and later as U.S. Ambassador to the Holy See. She was the first woman elected to Congress from Louisiana.

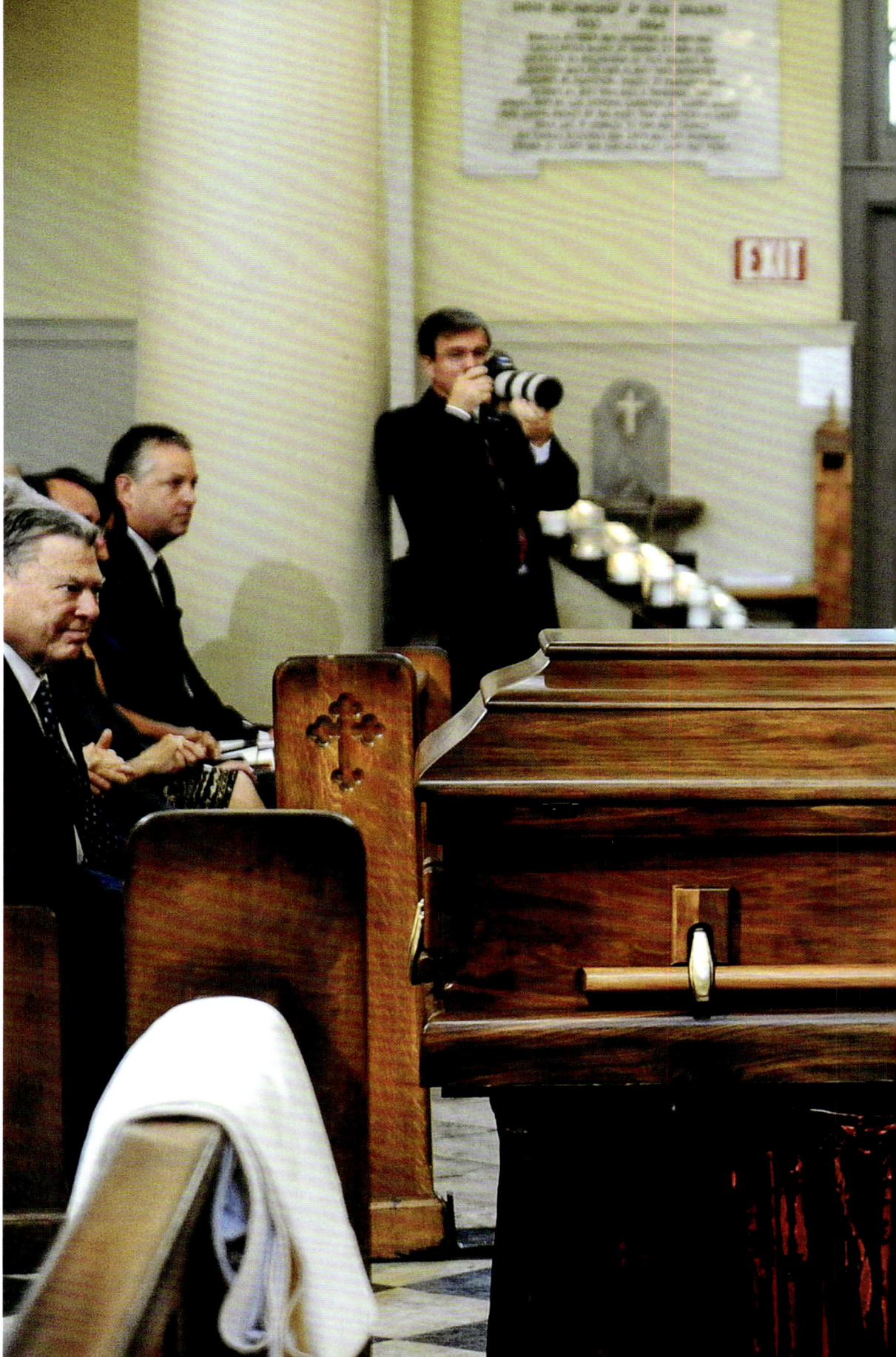

Civil rights leader and congressman John Lewis pays respects to Lindy Boggs at St. Louis Cathedral, 2013. Lewis passed away in 2020.

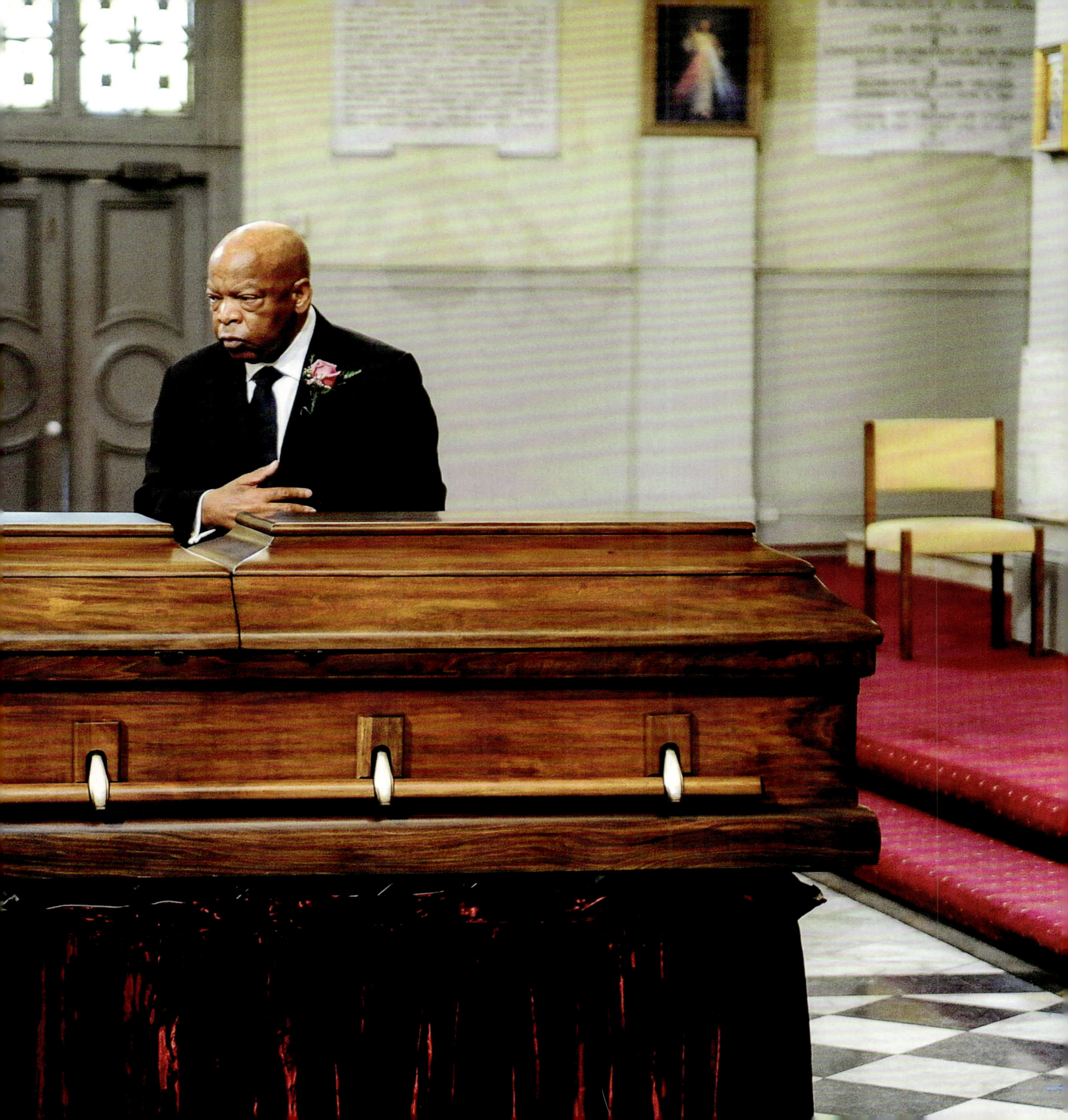

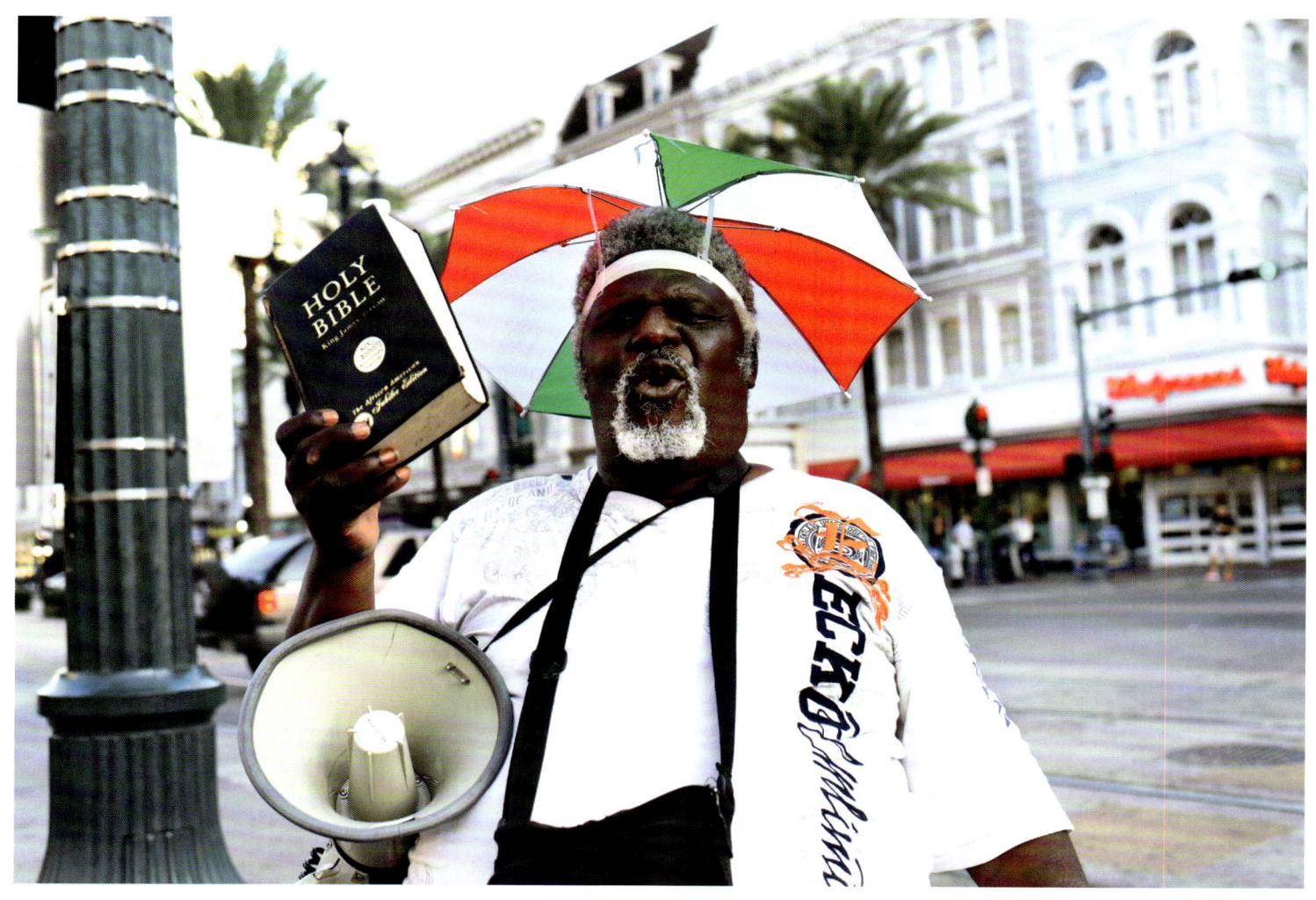

Reverend Keith "Umbrella Man" Sam has preached on Canal Street for more than forty years, 2016.

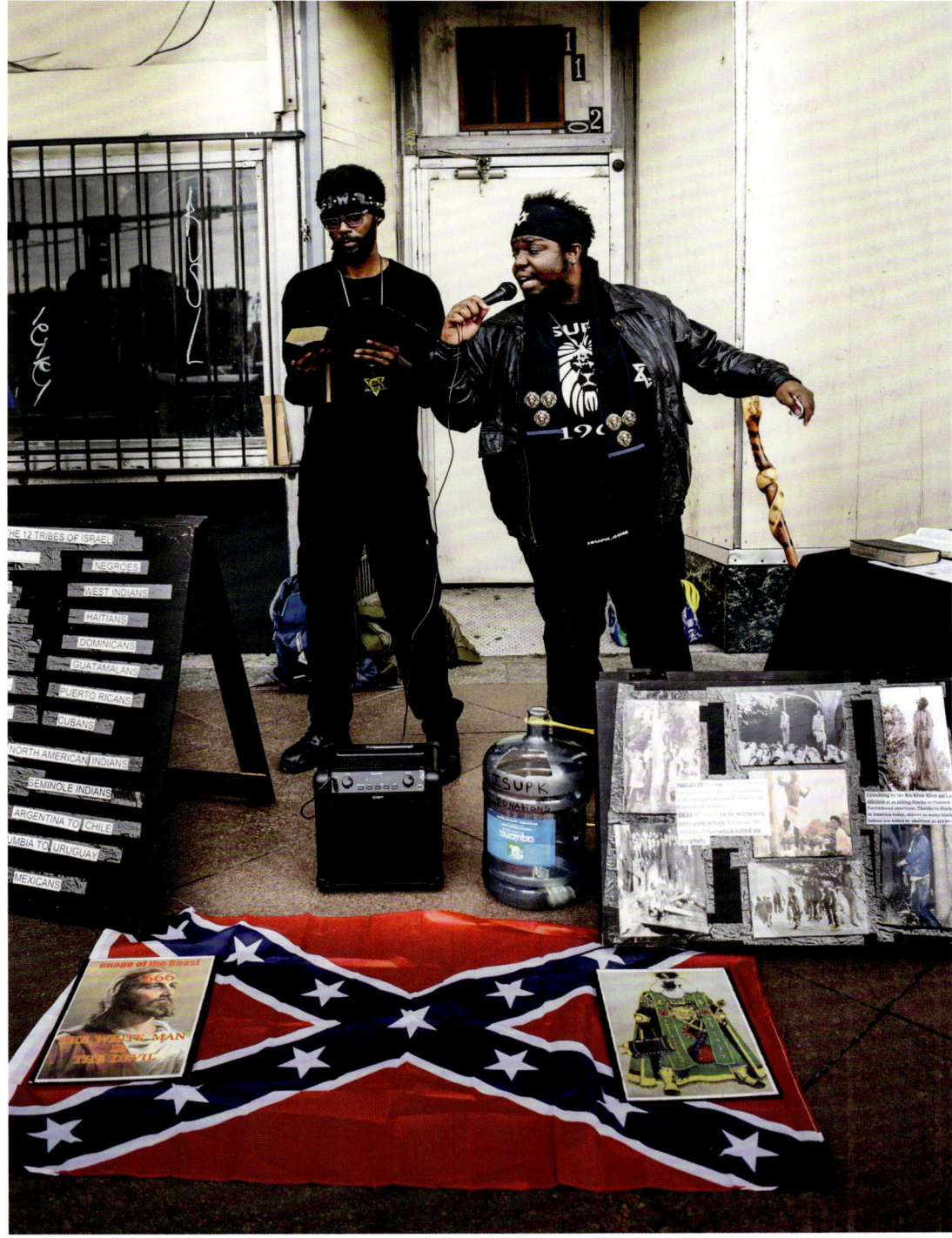

Members of the Israelite School of Universal Practical Knowledge (ISUPK) Louisiana preach on Canal Street, 2018. ISUPK is a nonprofit organization and Black supremacist extremist religious sect, considered a hate group by the Southern Poverty Law Center.

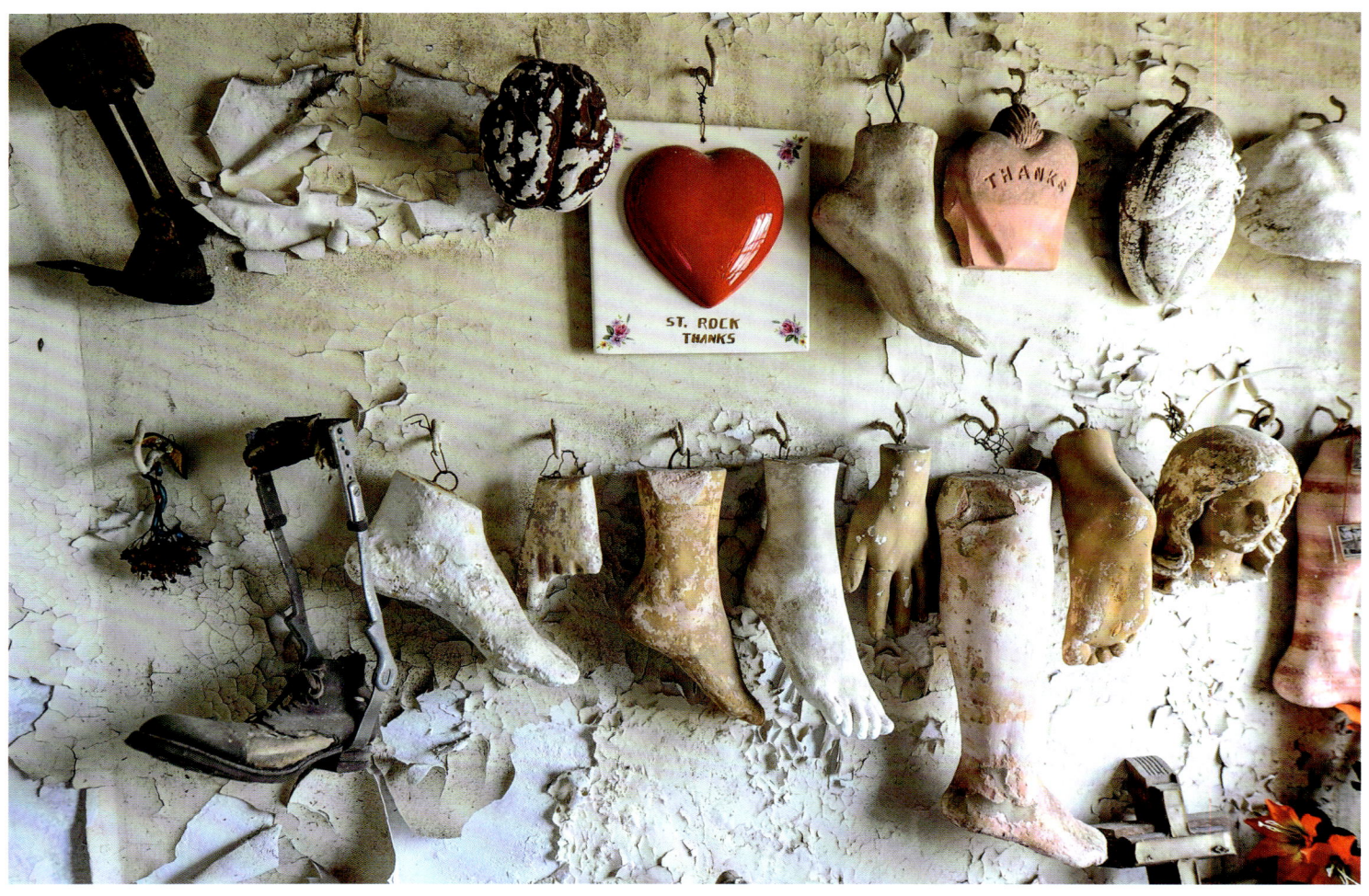

Replicas of feet, limbs, and internal organs hang from the walls of a room in the St. Roch Cemetery chapel, offerings from people who wanted to be healed, 2013.

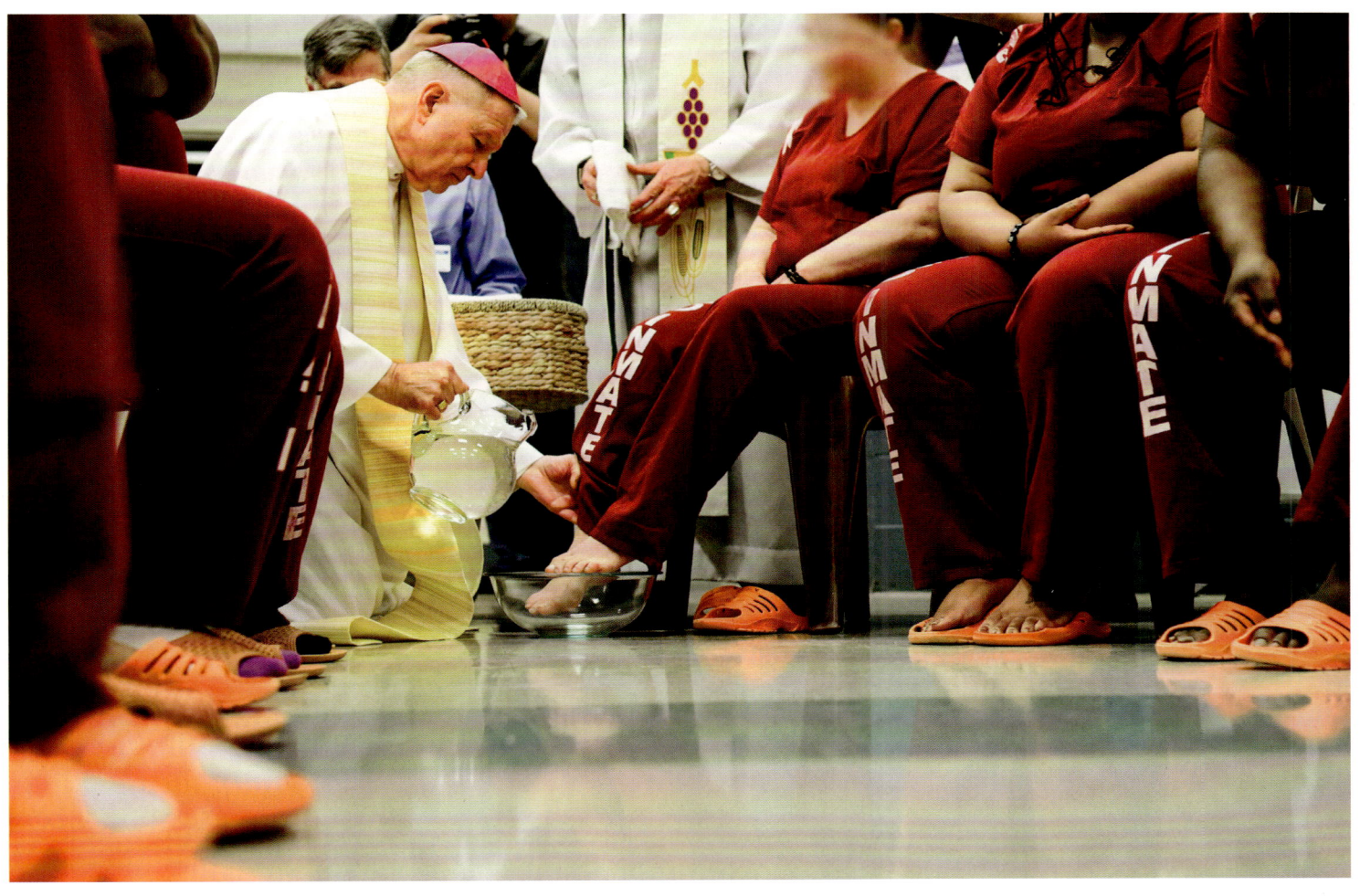

Archbishop Gregory Aymond washes the feet of female inmates during Holy Week at Orleans Parish Prison, 2018.

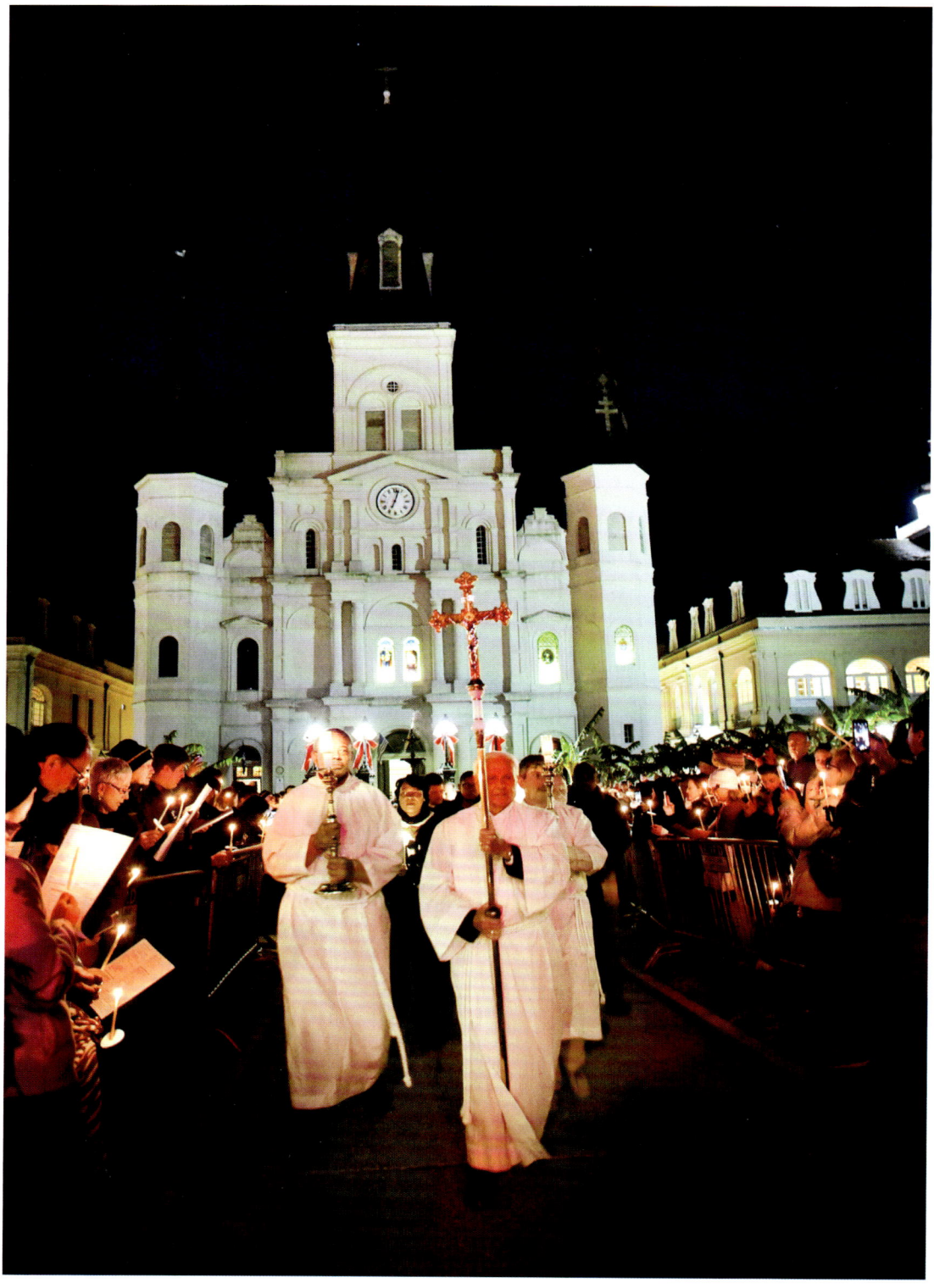

Catholic clergy from St. Louis Cathedral lead a procession to Jackson Square for Christmas caroling, 2018. The free candlelight event has been an annual holiday tradition since 1946.

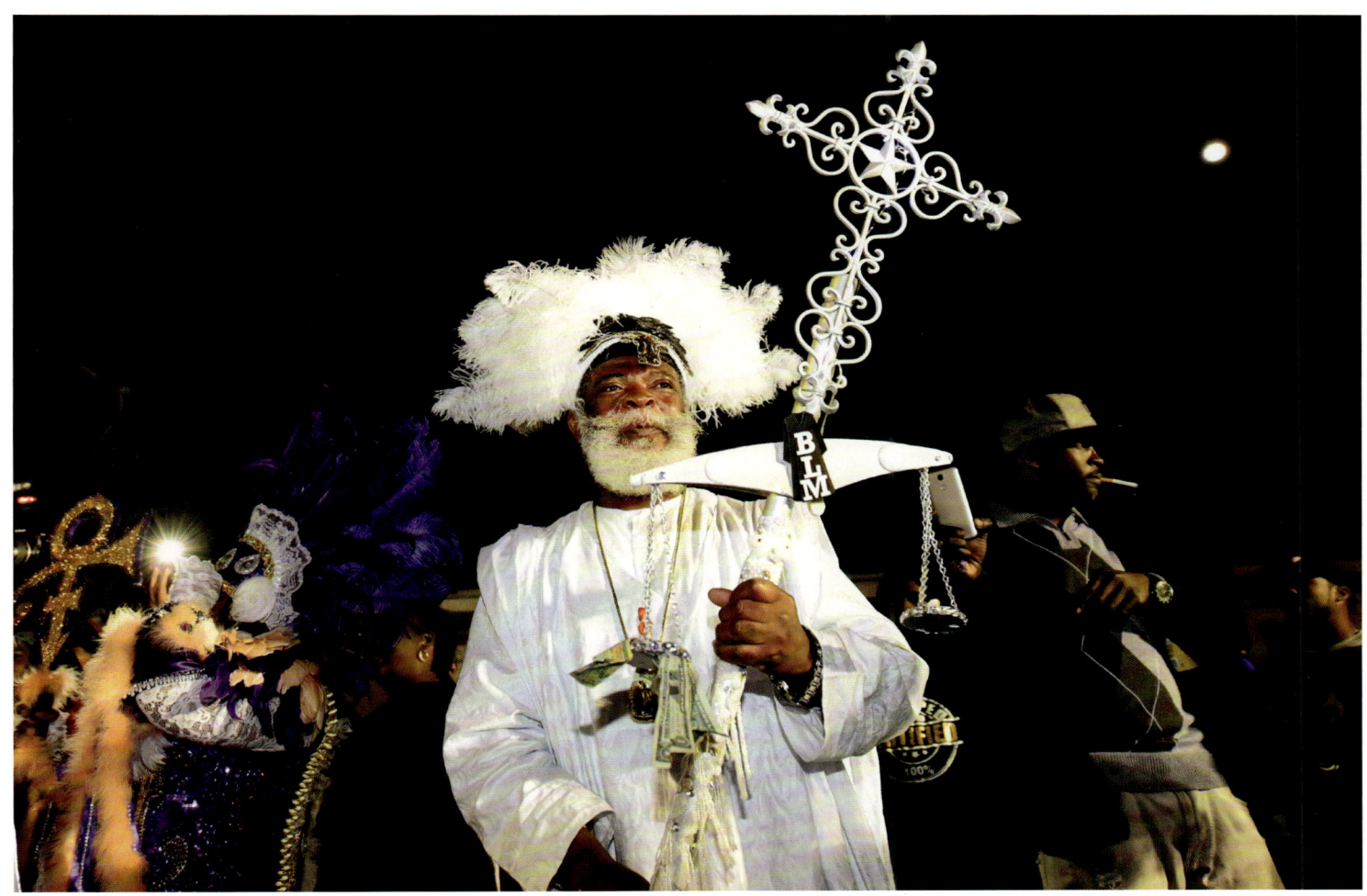

Andrew Wiseman carries a cross honoring the Black Lives Matter movement on St. Joseph's Night in Central City, 2018. The cross, which features unbalanced scales of justice, was created by Cherice Harrison-Nelson.

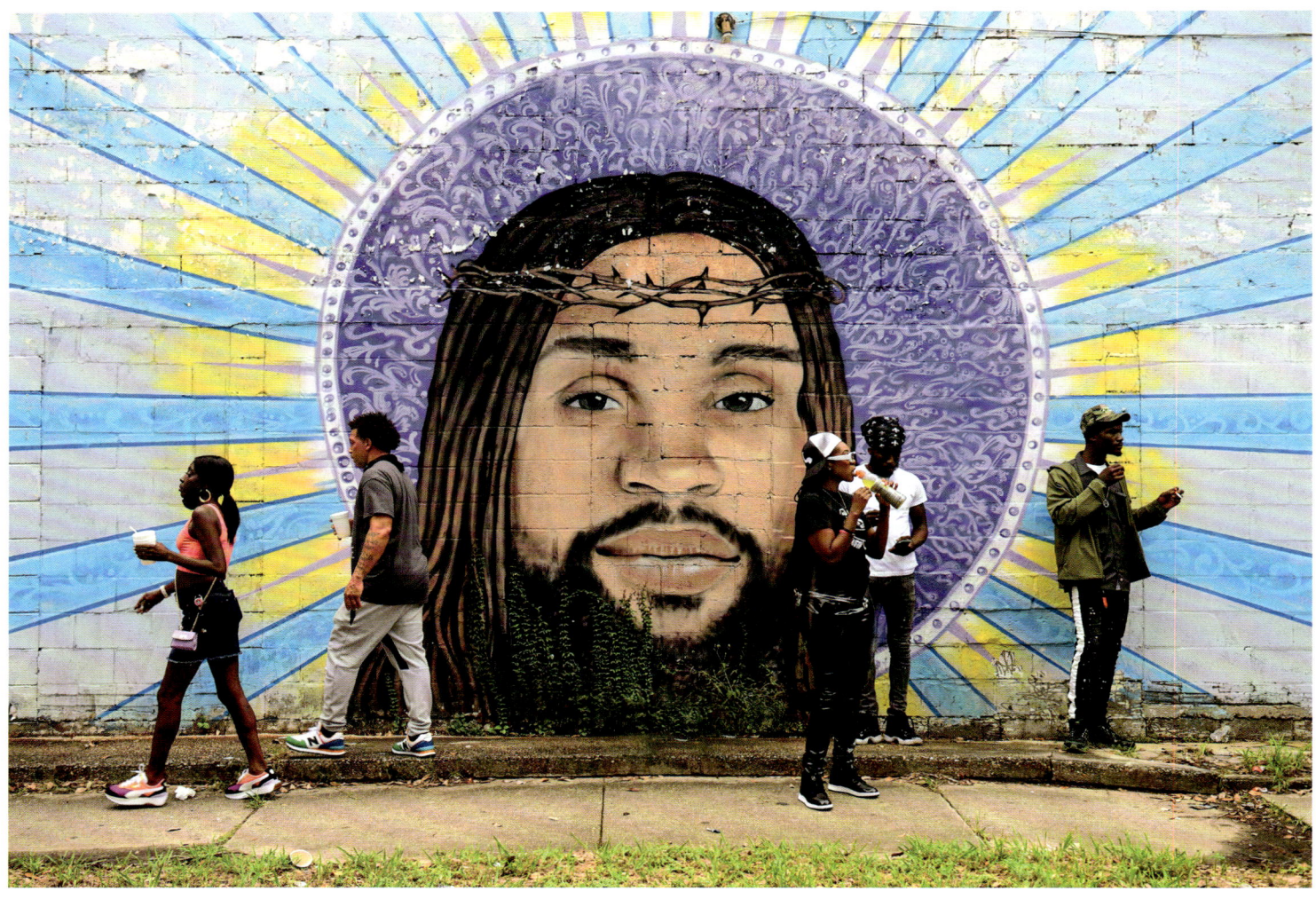

Black Jesus mural in Central City, 2021.

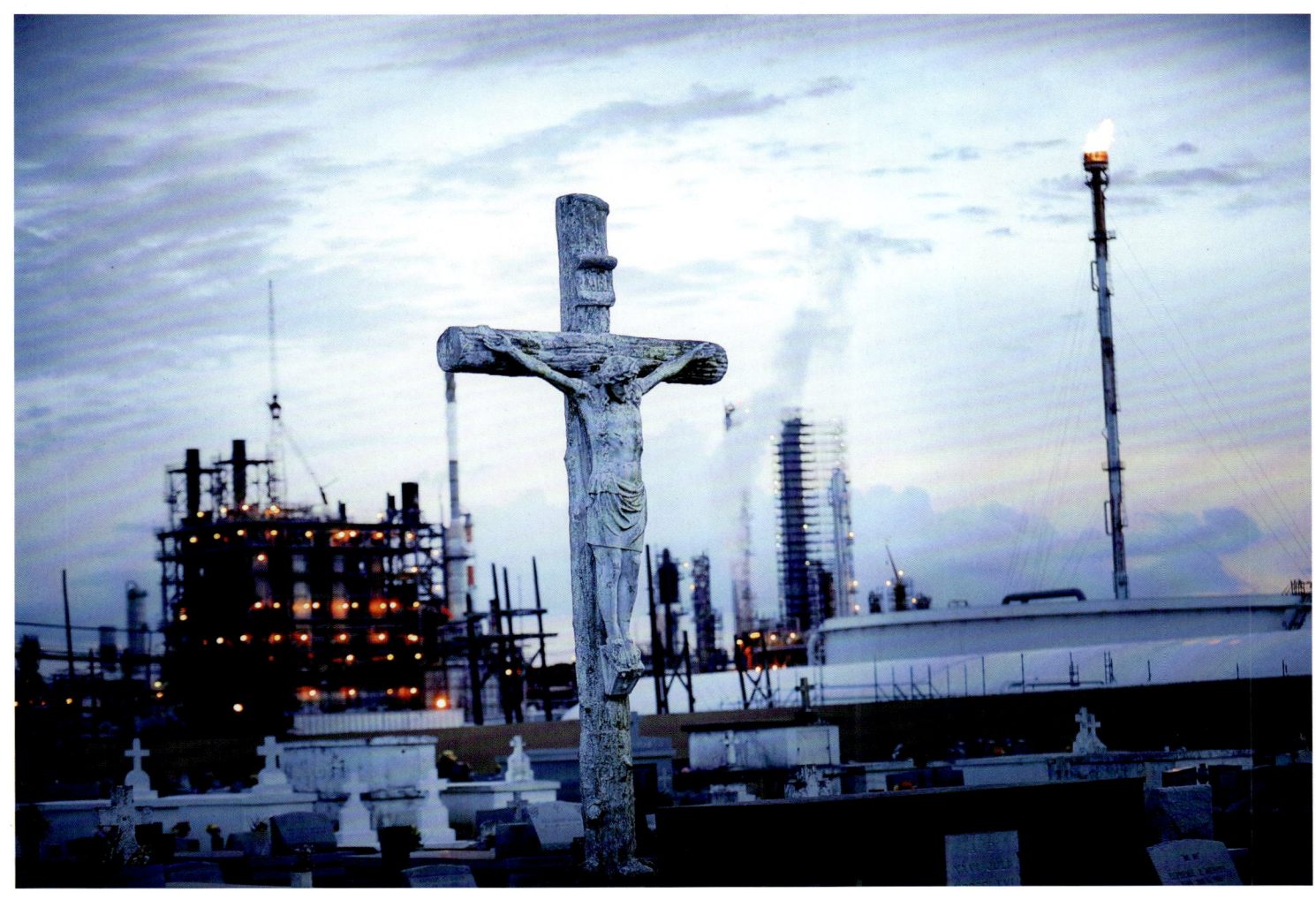

A statue of Jesus hovers over the Holy Rosary cemetery in "Cancer Alley," the regional nickname given to an eighty-five-mile stretch of land along the Mississippi River between Baton Rouge and New Orleans, which contains more than 150 petrochemical plants and refineries, 2016.

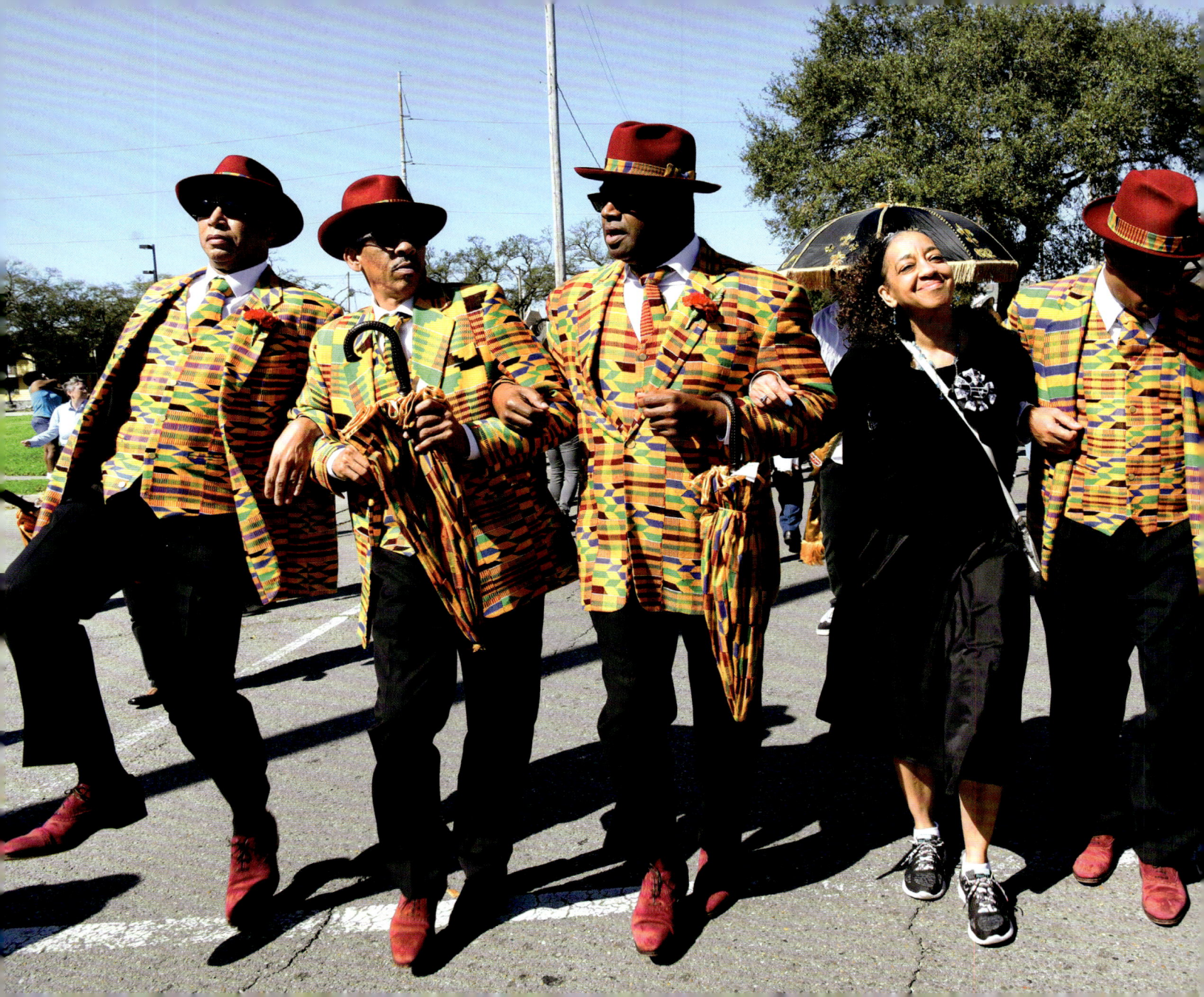

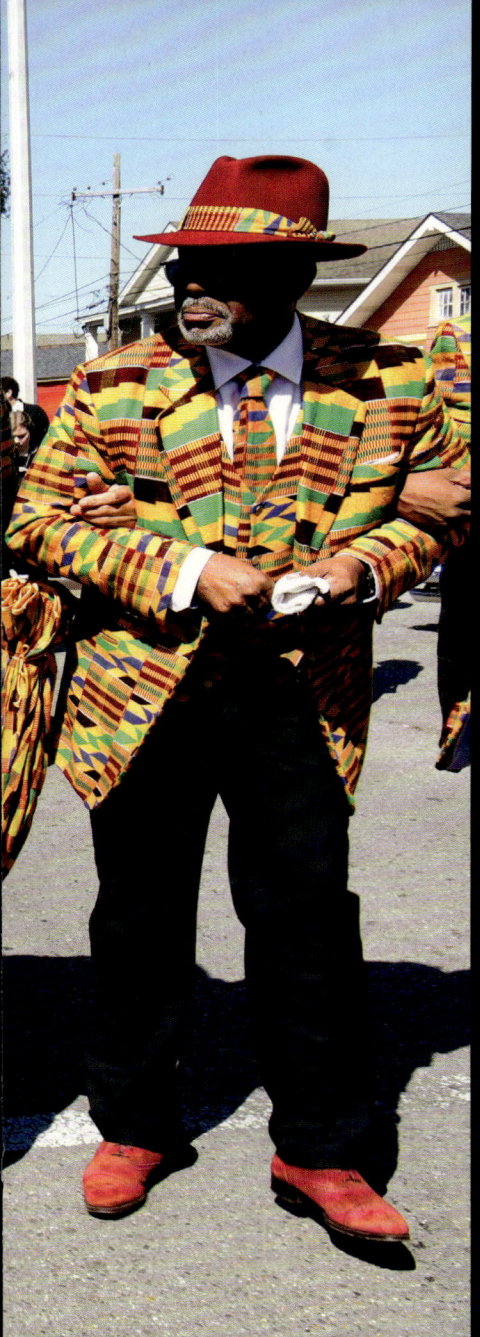

PART II

When the Saints Go Marching

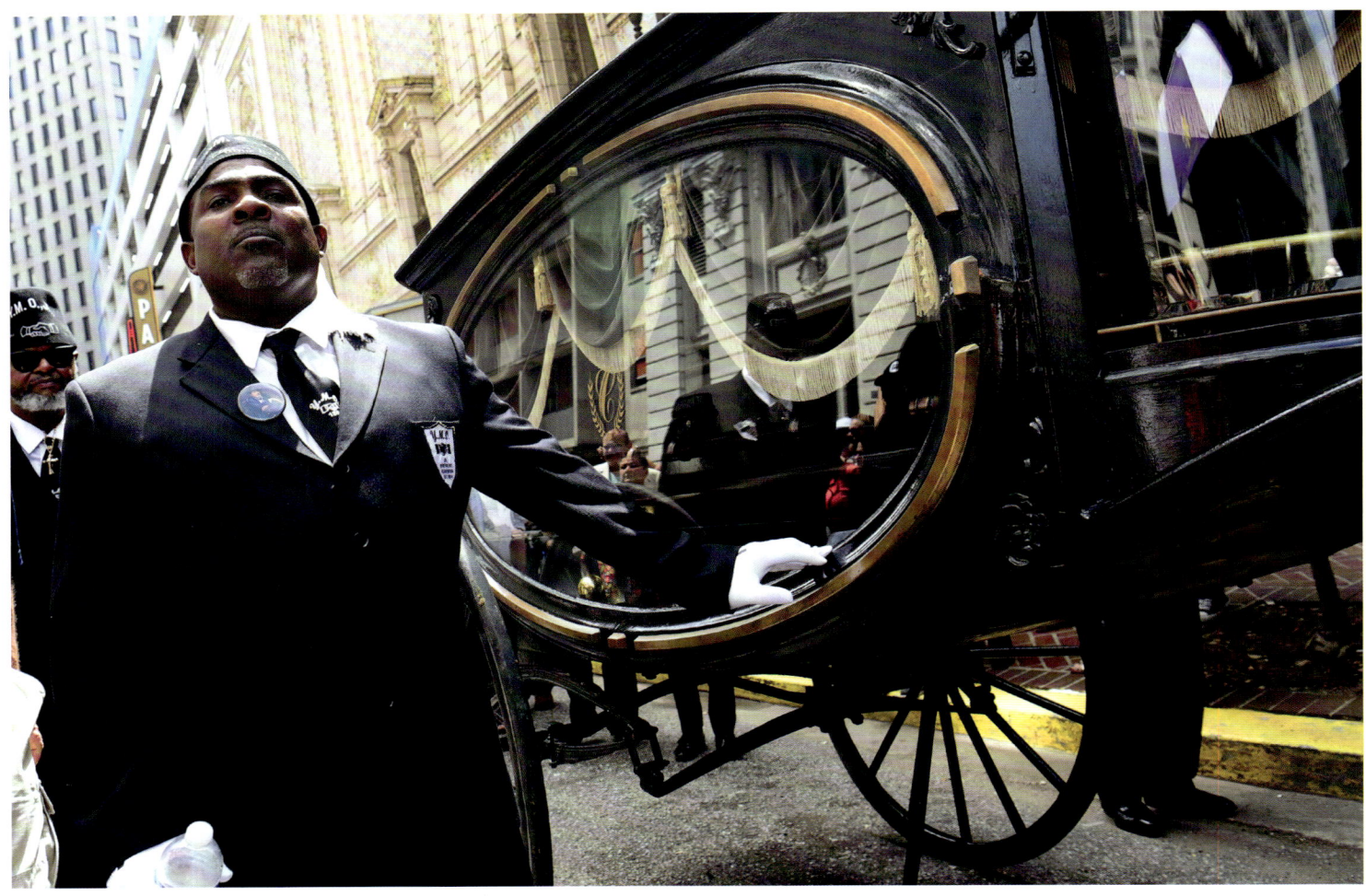

Members of the Young Men Olympians Benevolent Society (YMOBS) escort Dr. John's funeral hearse, 2019. YMOBS, considered the oldest active benevolent association in the state and celebrating 140 years of service, is not a social aid and pleasure club, but is strictly a benevolent society—pooling money for funerals, feeding the homeless, and other community initiatives.

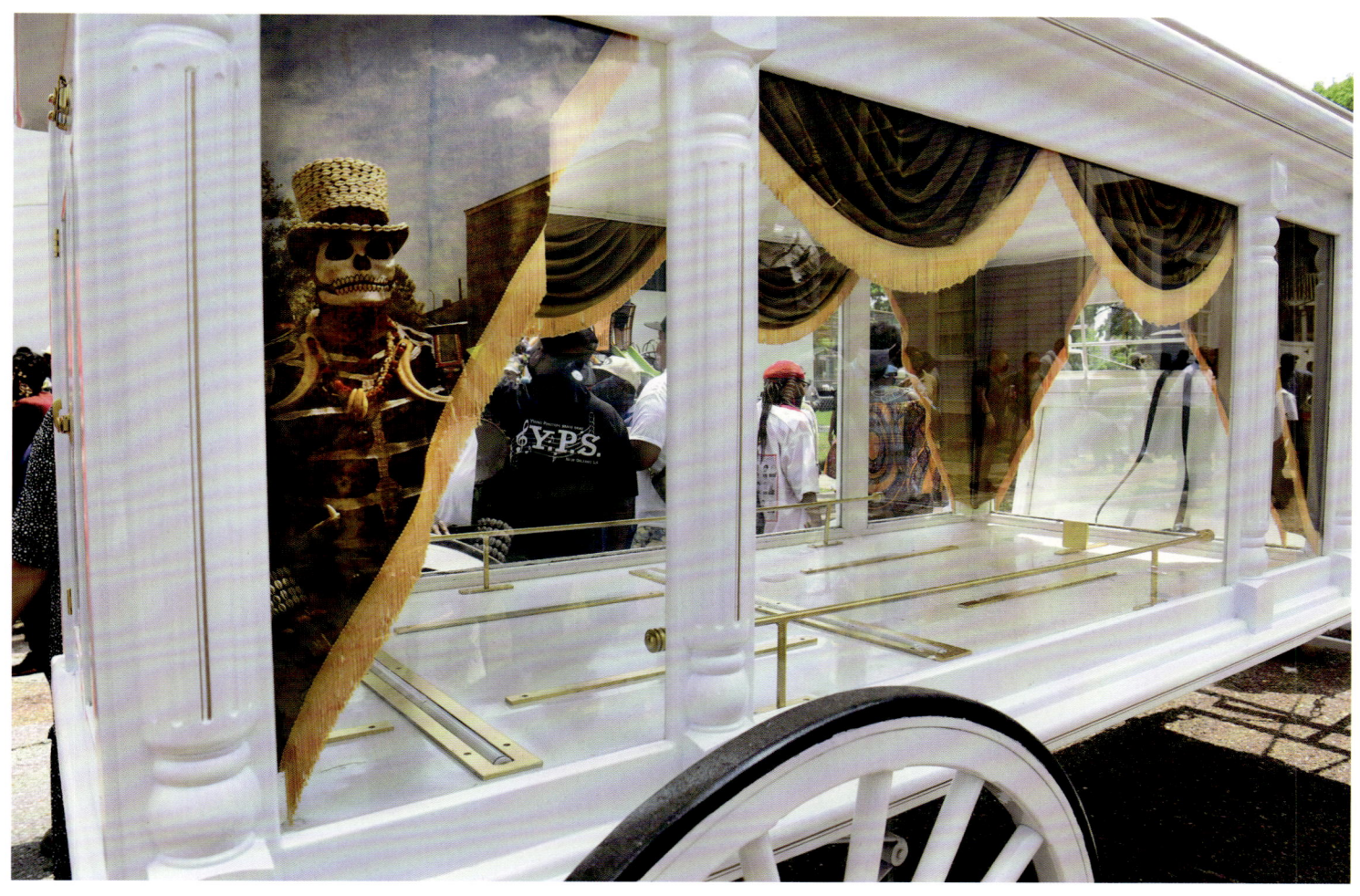

Bruce "Sunpie" Barnes, dressed in his skeleton suit, is seen in a reflection in the hearse awaiting the coffin at Big Chief Keelian "Dump" Boyd's funeral, 2021.

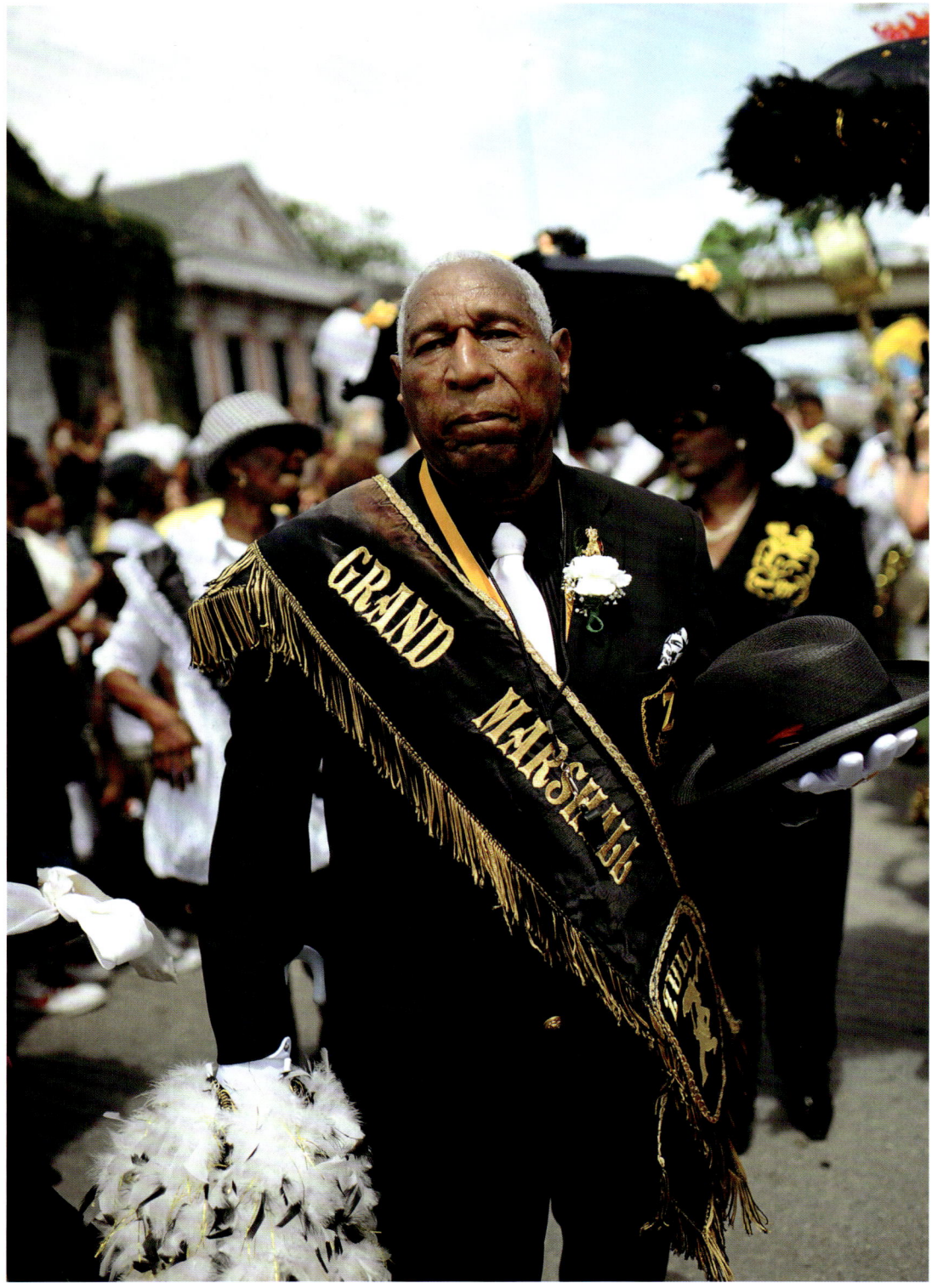

Zulu Grand Marshal Norman Thomas leads the funeral procession for musician "Uncle" Lionel Batiste, 2012. Batiste was the longtime bass drummer and vocalist with the Treme Brass Band.

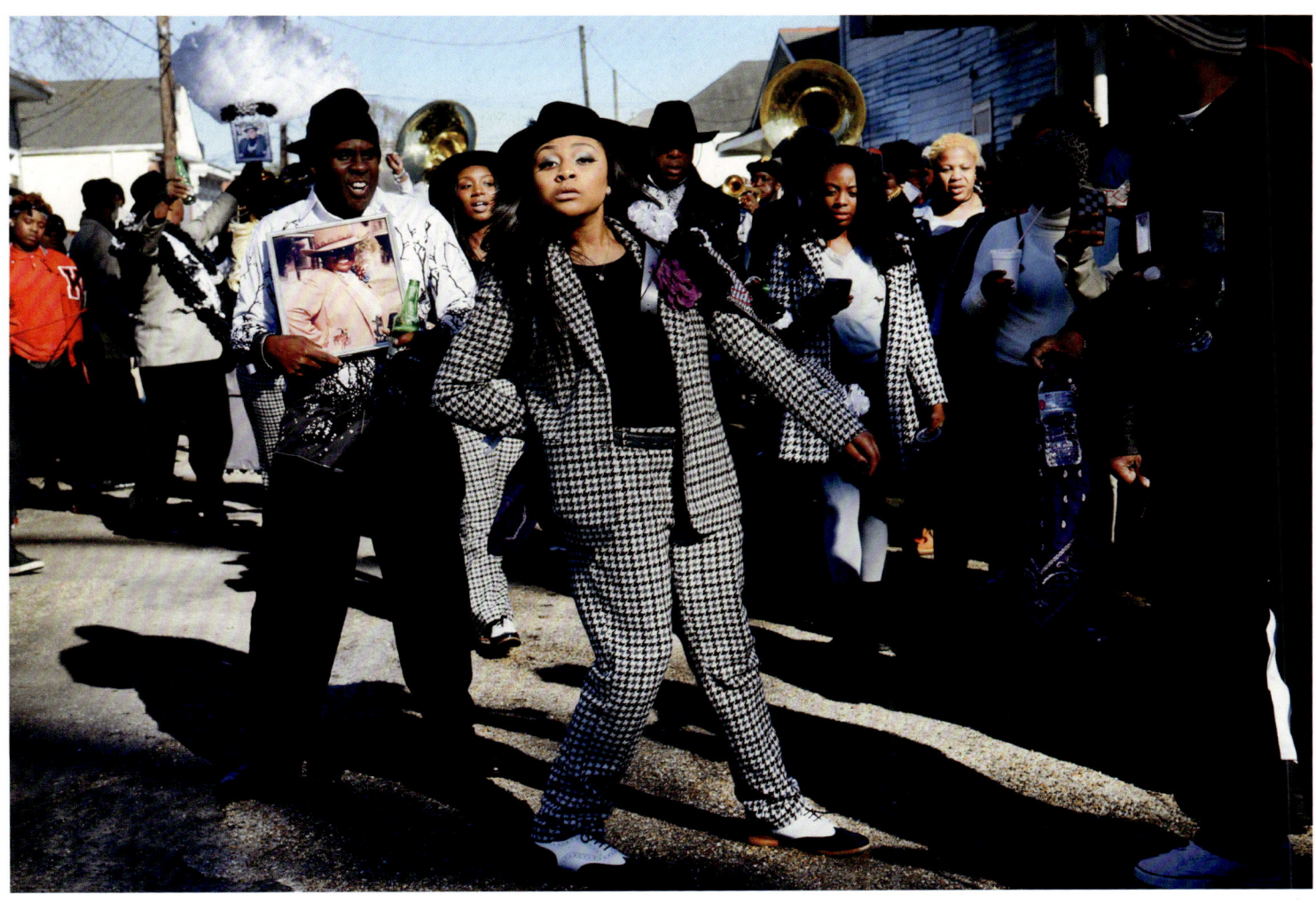

Diamon Raymond leads the Lady Jetsetters memorial second line honoring Naomi "Shorty" Gibson, the club's founder, Uptown, 2018.

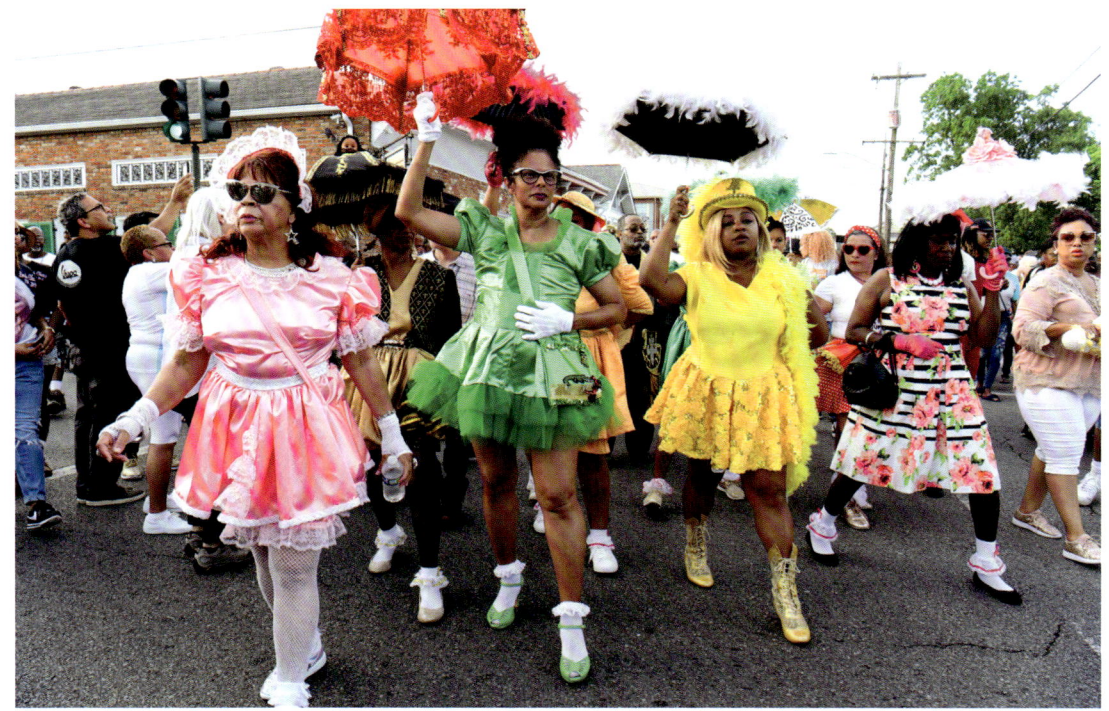

Baby Dolls walk during a dirge at Chef Leah Chase's memorial second line, 2019.

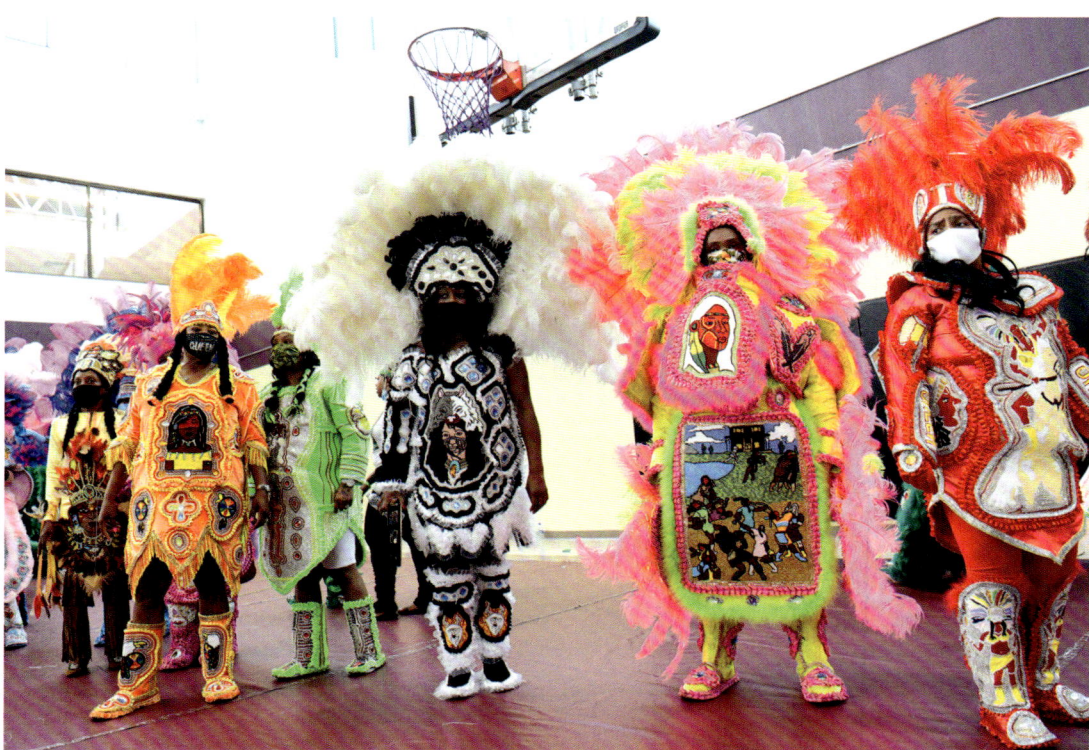

Black Masking Indian queens pay respects at Big Queen Kim Boutte's funeral, 2020.

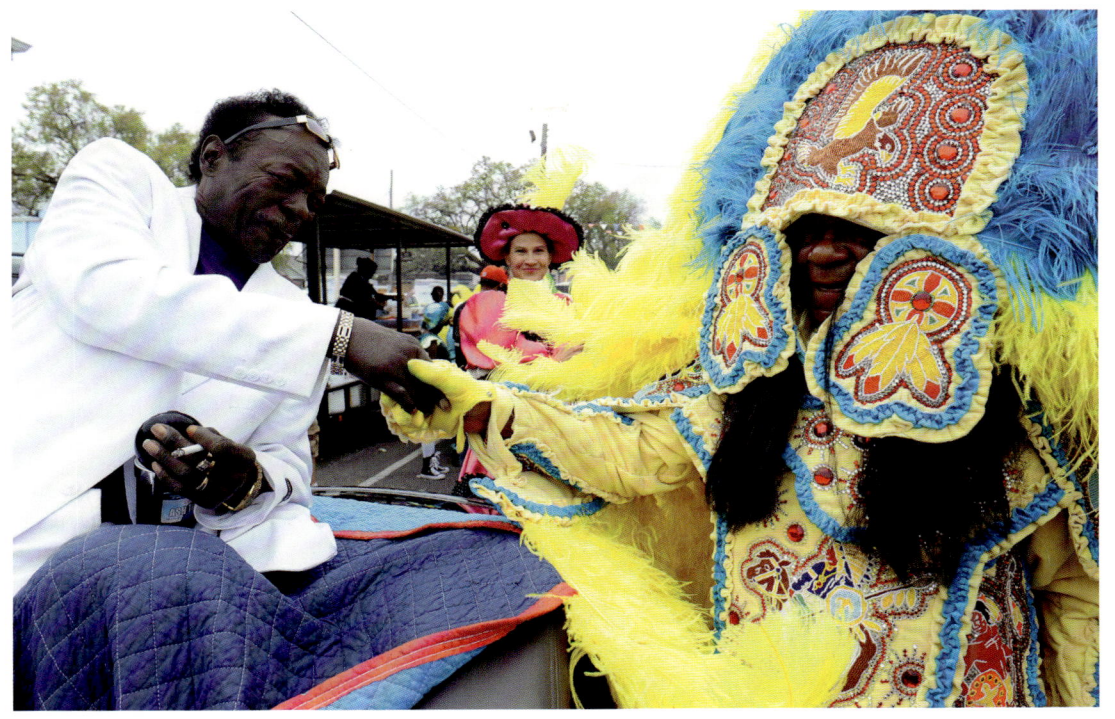

Bo Dollis (*left*) greets Monk Boudreaux, his longtime friend and musical collaborator, on Super Sunday, Uptown, 2013.

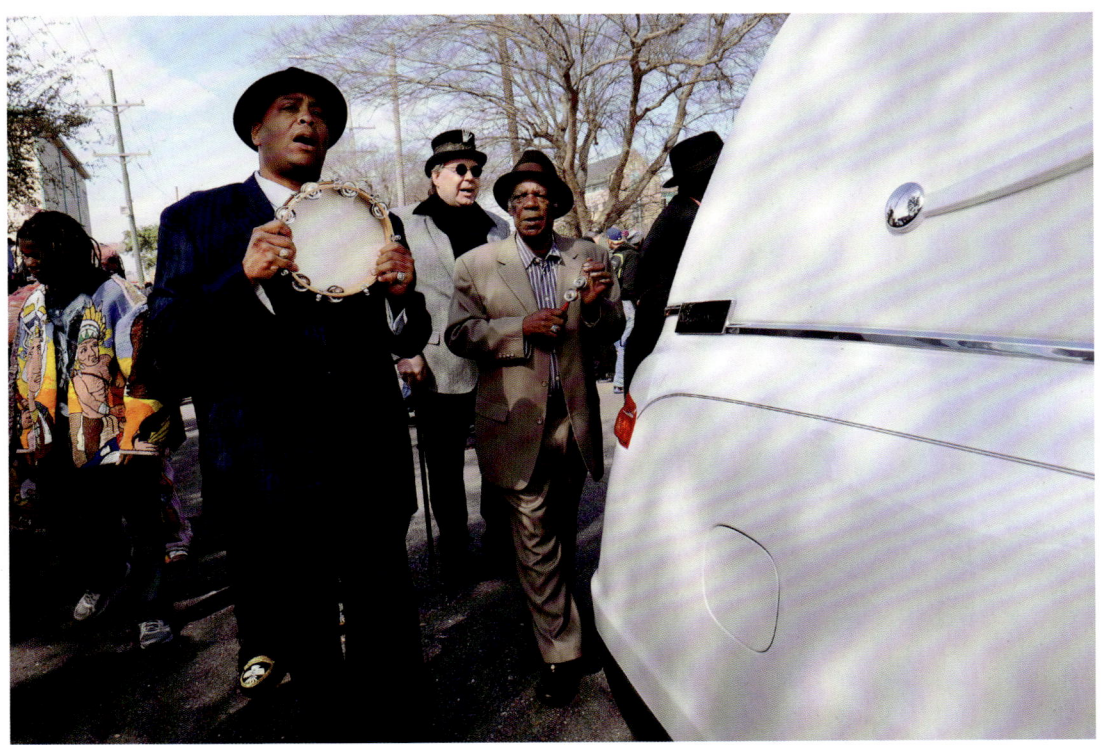

Big Chief Monk Boudreaux (*center*) follows the hearse at Bo Dollis's funeral, 2015. Dollis (1944–2015), born as Theodore Emile Dollis, was the longtime Big Chief of the Wild Magnolias Black Masking Indians and an acclaimed recording artist. Boudreaux, born in 1941 as Joseph Pierre Boudreaux, is an African American singer and musician and Big Chief of the Golden Eagles Black Masking Indian tribe.

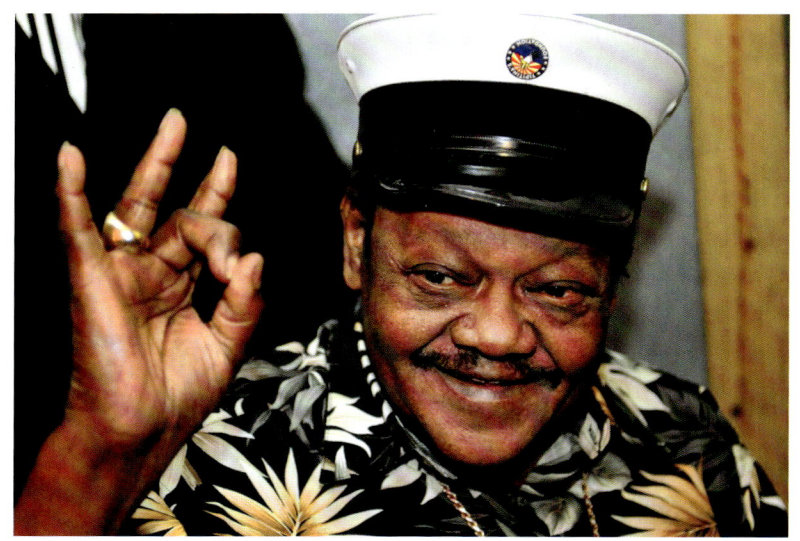

Fats Domino signals to fans at Tipitina's music club, 2008.

Fans cross the Industrial Canal bridge during Fats Domino's funeral procession as they second line to his home in the Lower Ninth Ward, 2017. Domino, born Antoine Dominique Domino Jr. (1928–2017), was one of the pioneers of rock and roll who sky-rocketed to national fame in the 1950s, securing his place in the Rock & Roll Hall of Fame.

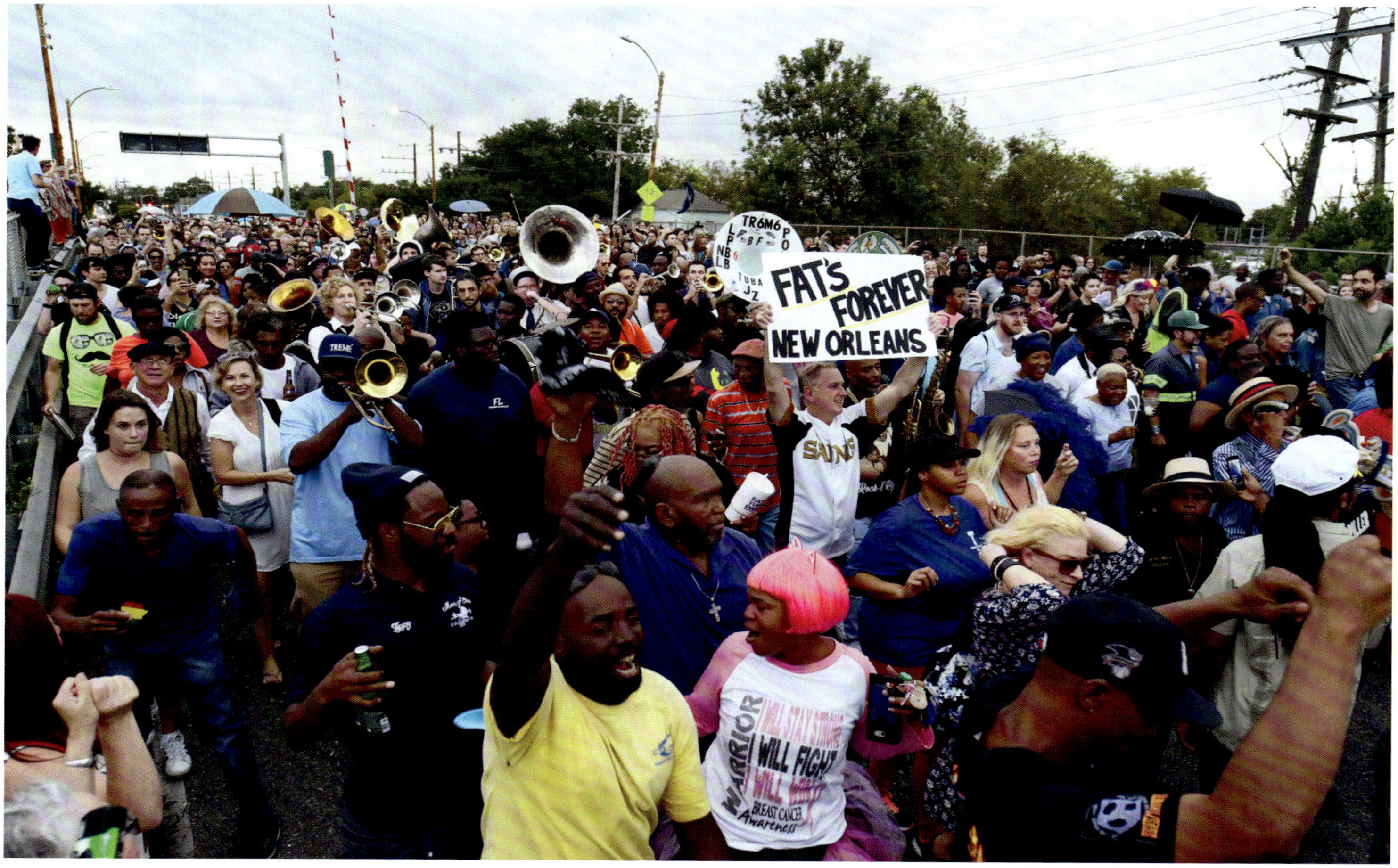

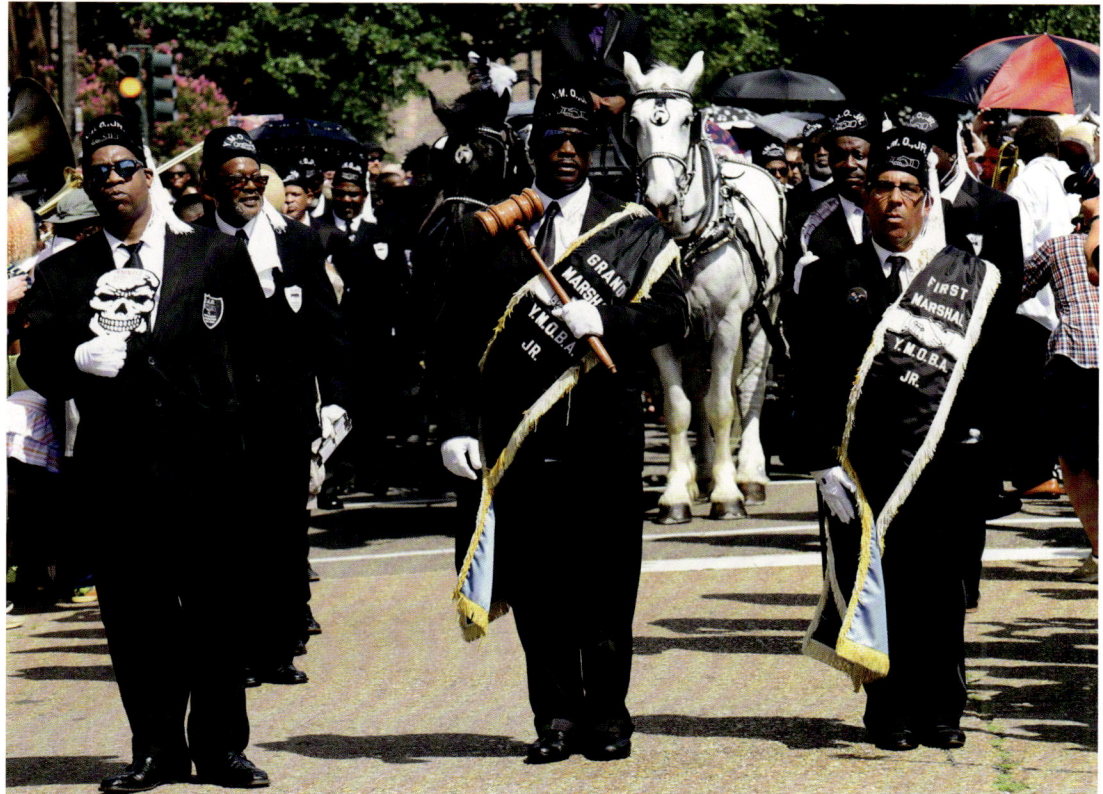

Members of the Young Men Olympians Benevolent Society pay their respects at Dr. John's funeral, 2019.

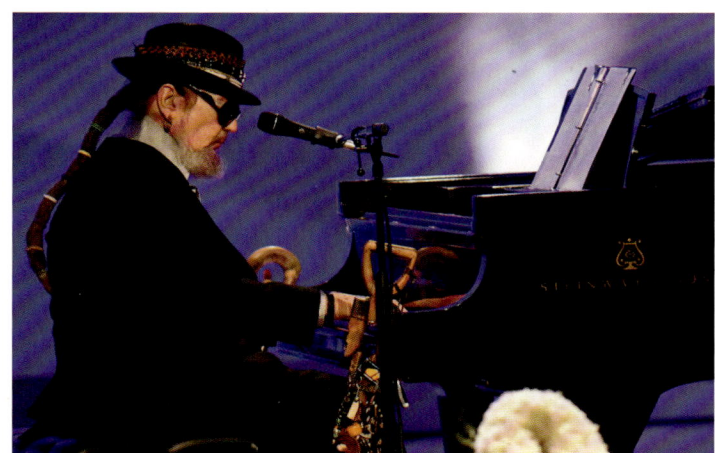

Dr. John performs at Allen Toussaint's funeral, 2015.

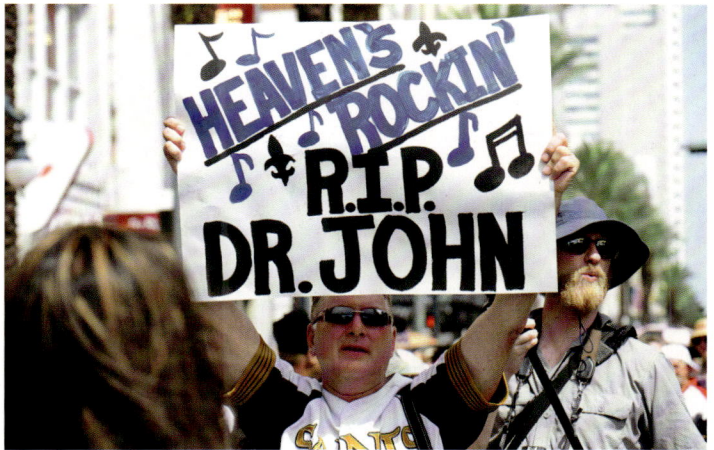

Larry "Sign Man" Rolling at Dr. John's funeral procession, 2019.

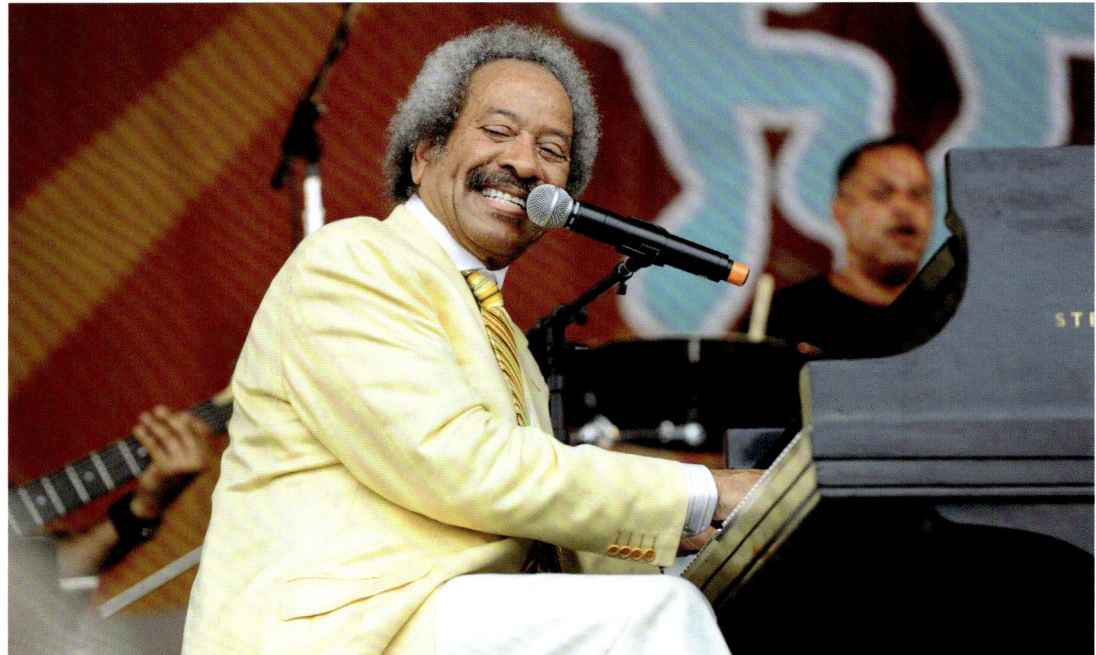

Allen Toussaint performs at Jazz Fest, 2009.

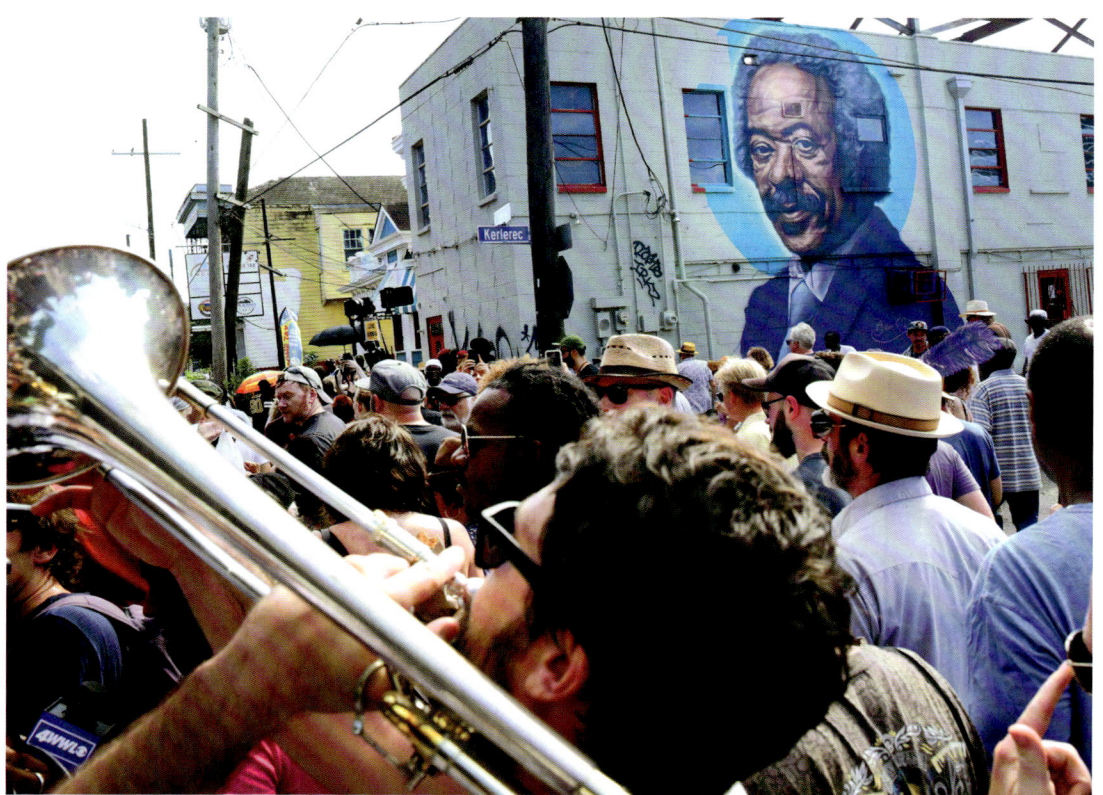

A memorial second line for Dr. John passes the Toussaint mural, by Brendon Palmer-Angell, in Tremé, 2020. Toussaint (1938–2015) was an American musician, songwriter, arranger, and record producer, who was an influential figure in New Orleans rhythm and blues from the 1950s to the end of the century. He was described as "one of popular music's great backroom figures" and is most famous for his song "Southern Nights," made popular in 1977 by country music singer Glen Campbell.

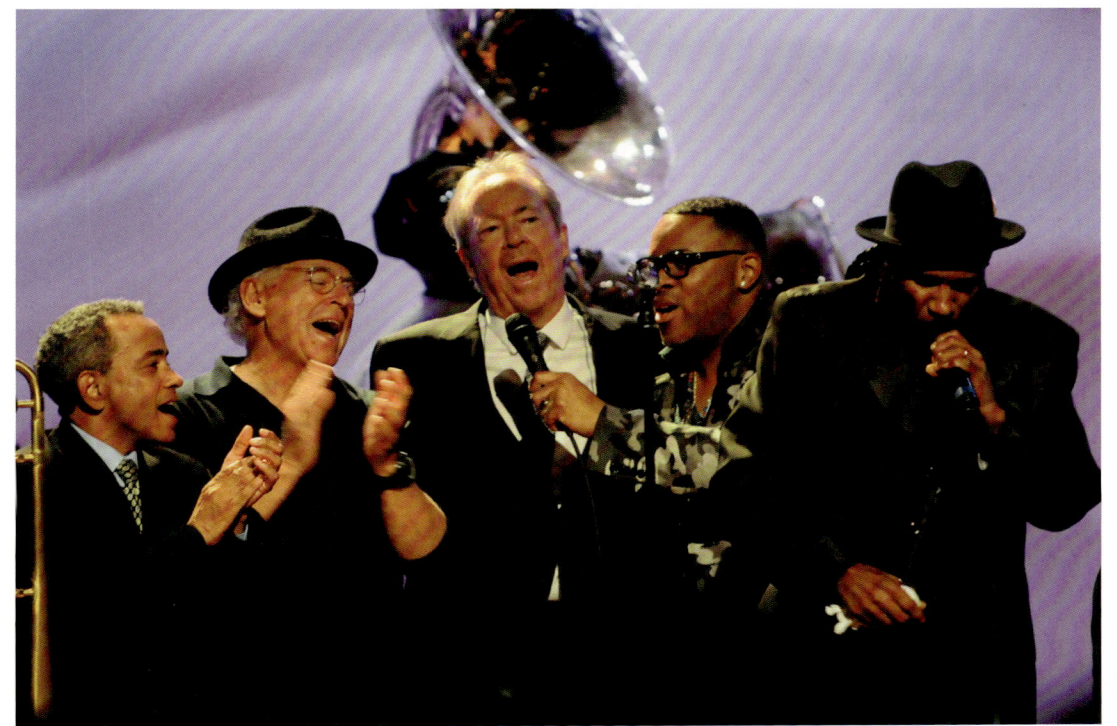

John Boutte, Jimmy Buffett, Boz Scaggs, Davell Crawford, and Cyril Neville (*left to right*) sing in tribute to Toussaint at the Orpheum Theater, 2015.

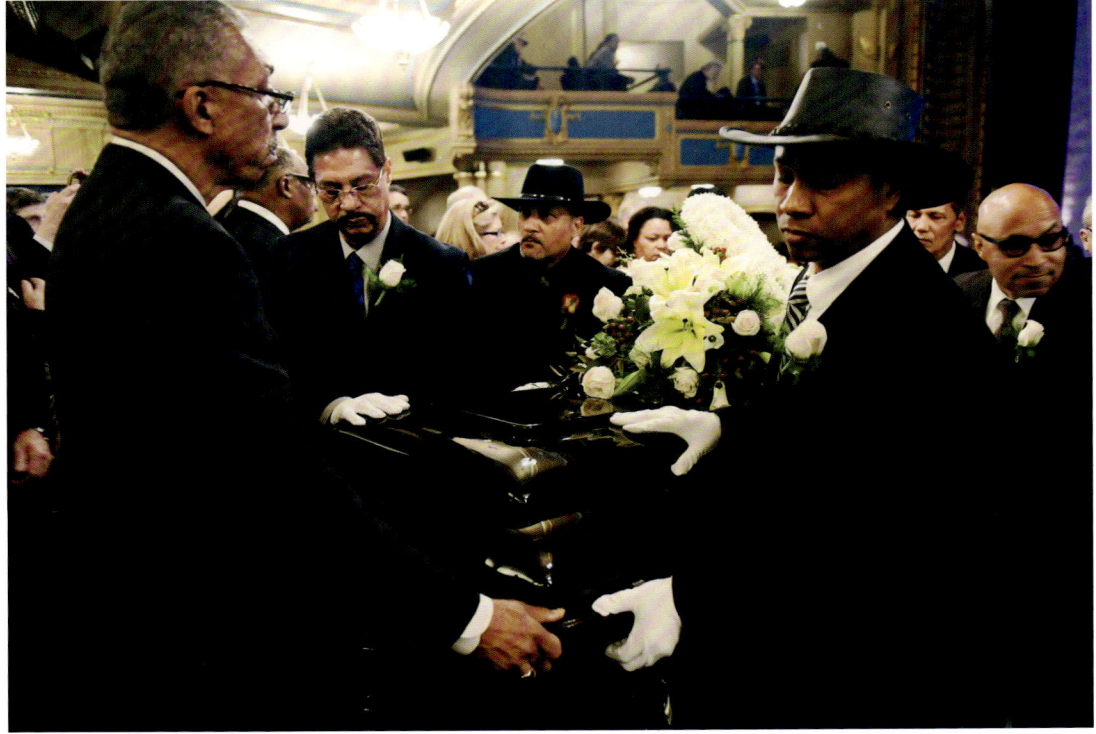

Pallbearers carry Toussaint's coffin, 2015.

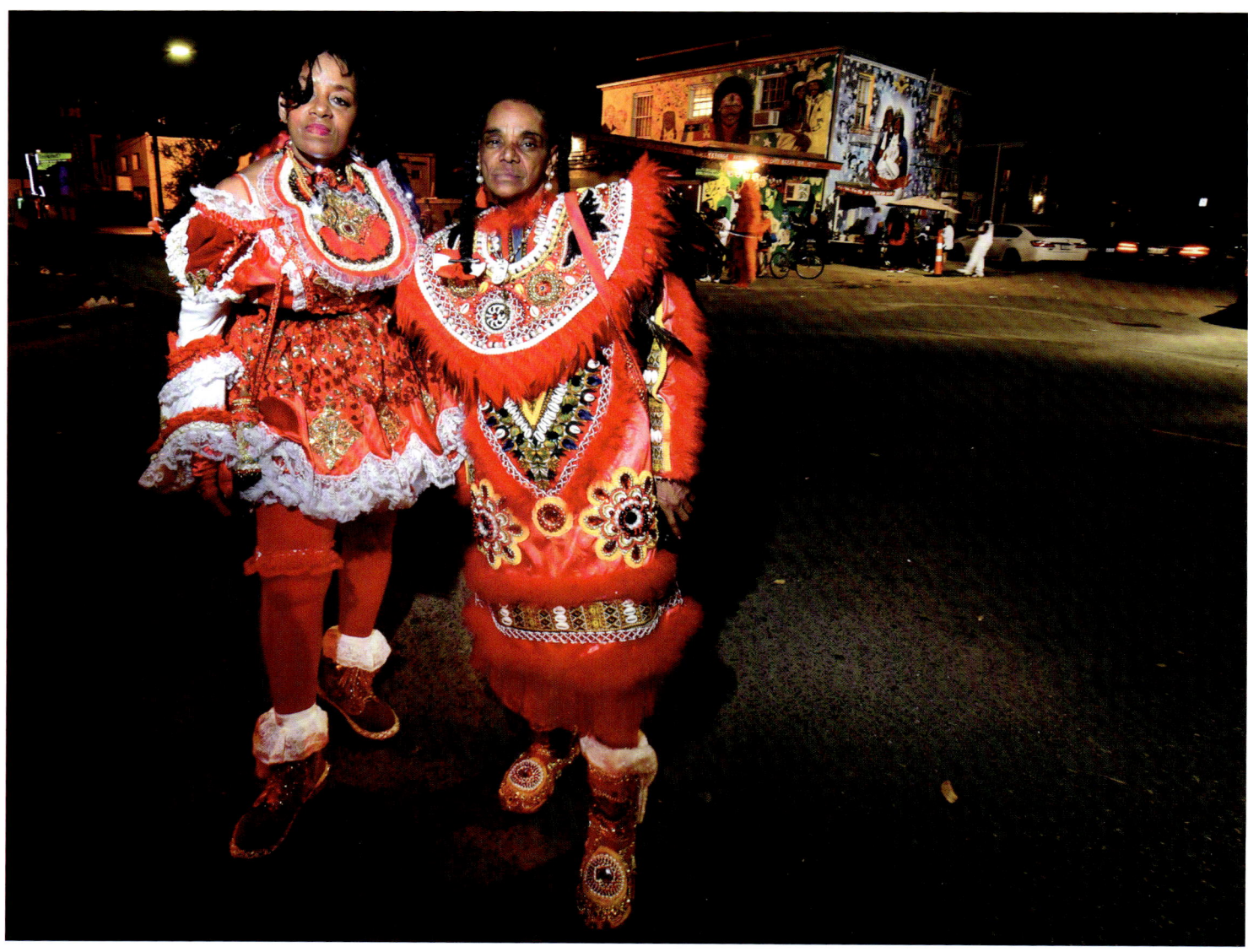

Cinnamon Black poses with Kim Boutte outside the Mother-in-Law Lounge on St. Joseph's Night in the Seventh Ward, 2018. Resa "Cinnamon Black" Bazile is a Baby Doll, Voodoo priestess, and Black Masking Indian queen, considered one of the city's most important culture bearers. Kim Boutte (1964–2020), beloved Big Queen of the Spirit of Fi Yi Yi and the Mandingo Warriors, was killed in a double shooting in 2020, sending shock waves throughout the cultural community.

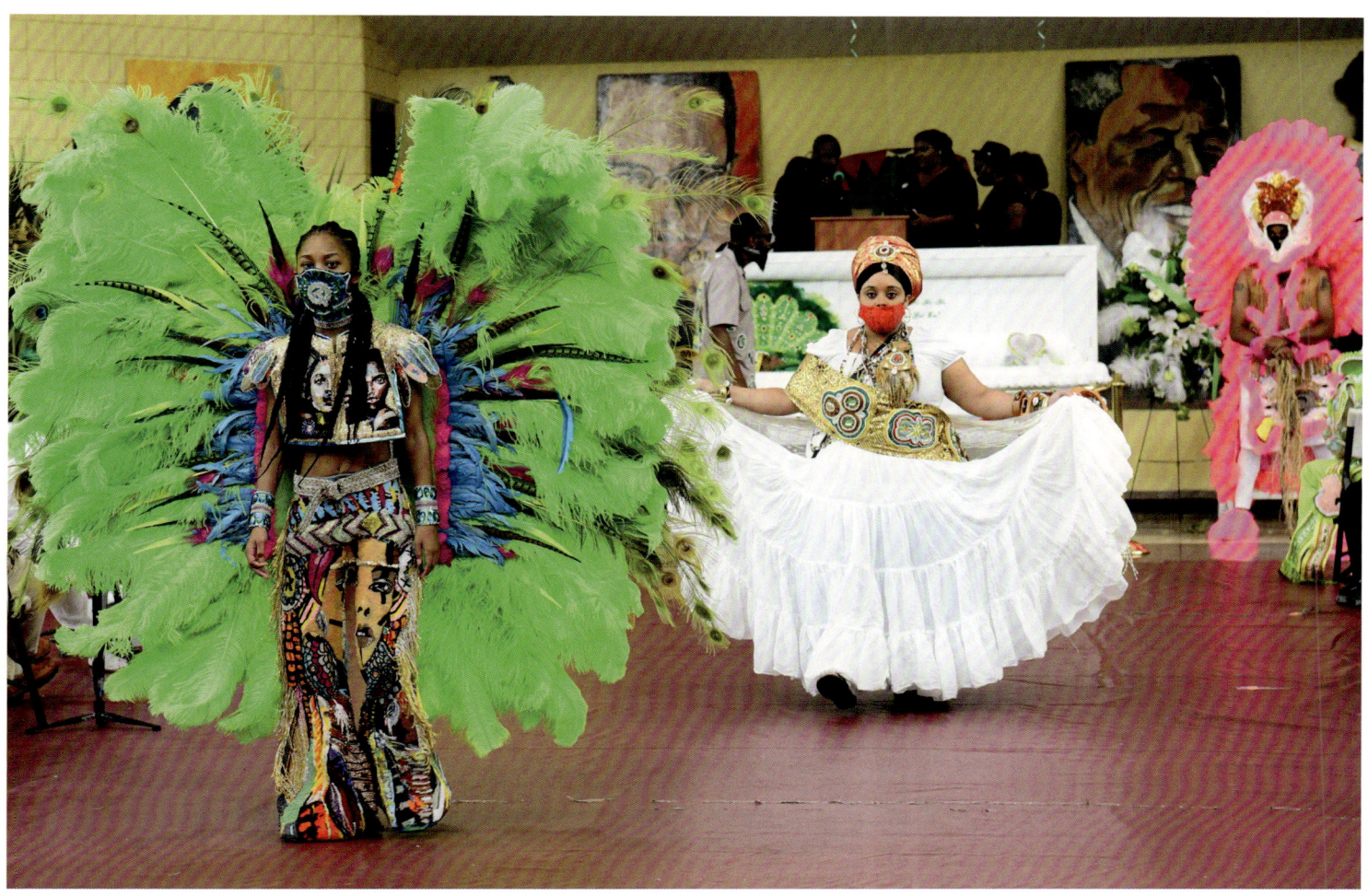

Queen Tahj Williams and Voodoo Queen Kalindah Laveaux pay their respects at Big Queen Kim Boutte's funeral, 2020. Williams, a Black Masking Indian with the Golden Eagles and a recent Tulane graduate, has been featured in national magazines, as well as in Jon Batiste's video for his Grammy-winning song "Freedom." Laveaux, a singer and Voodoo priestess, is dedicated to honoring New Orleanians during their middle passage and Africans who have been enslaved around the world.

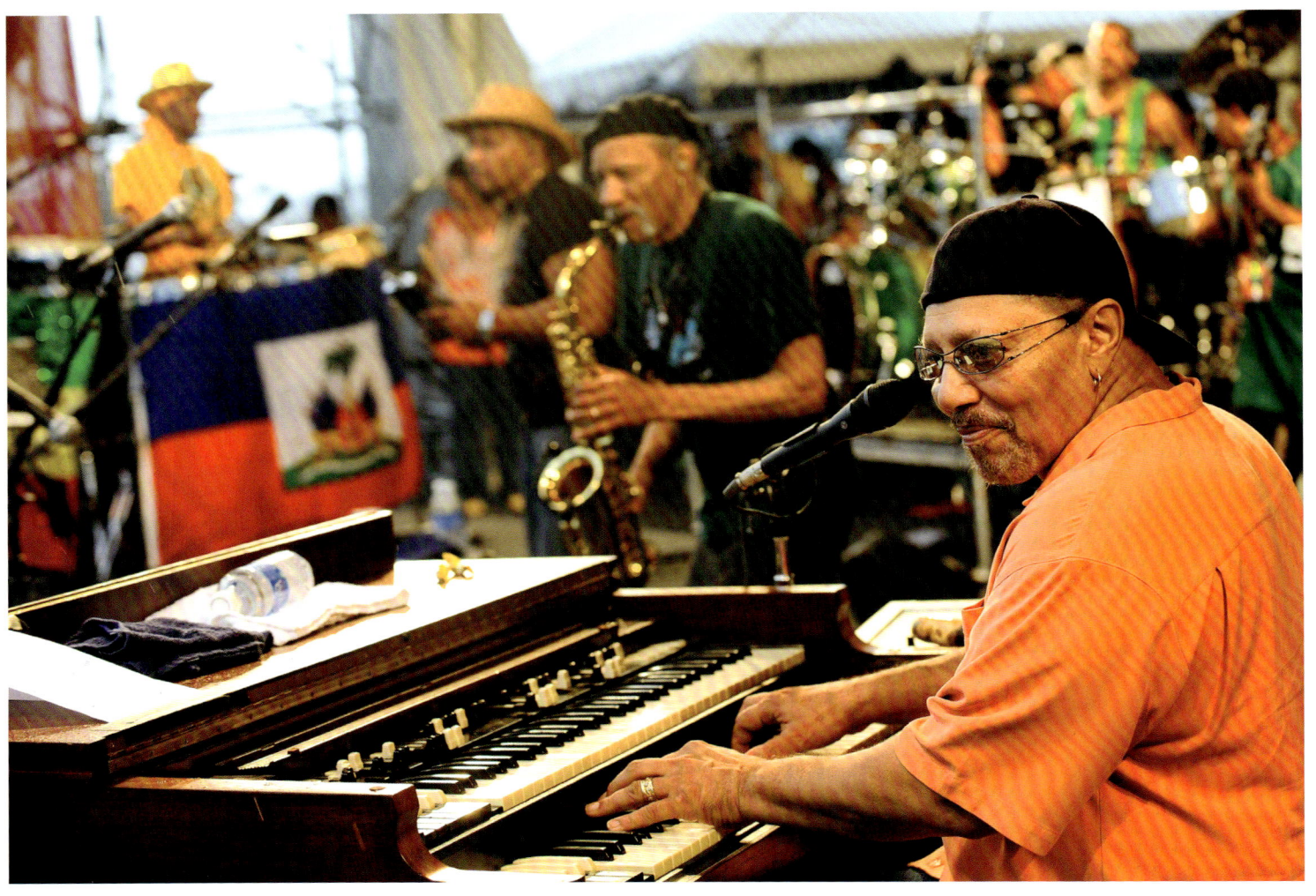

Art Neville performs with the Neville Brothers (Cyril, Aaron, and Charles Neville) at Jazz Fest, 2017. Neville (1937–2019) was a singer, songwriter, and keyboardist with his brothers, who were a staple of the New Orleans music scene for decades.

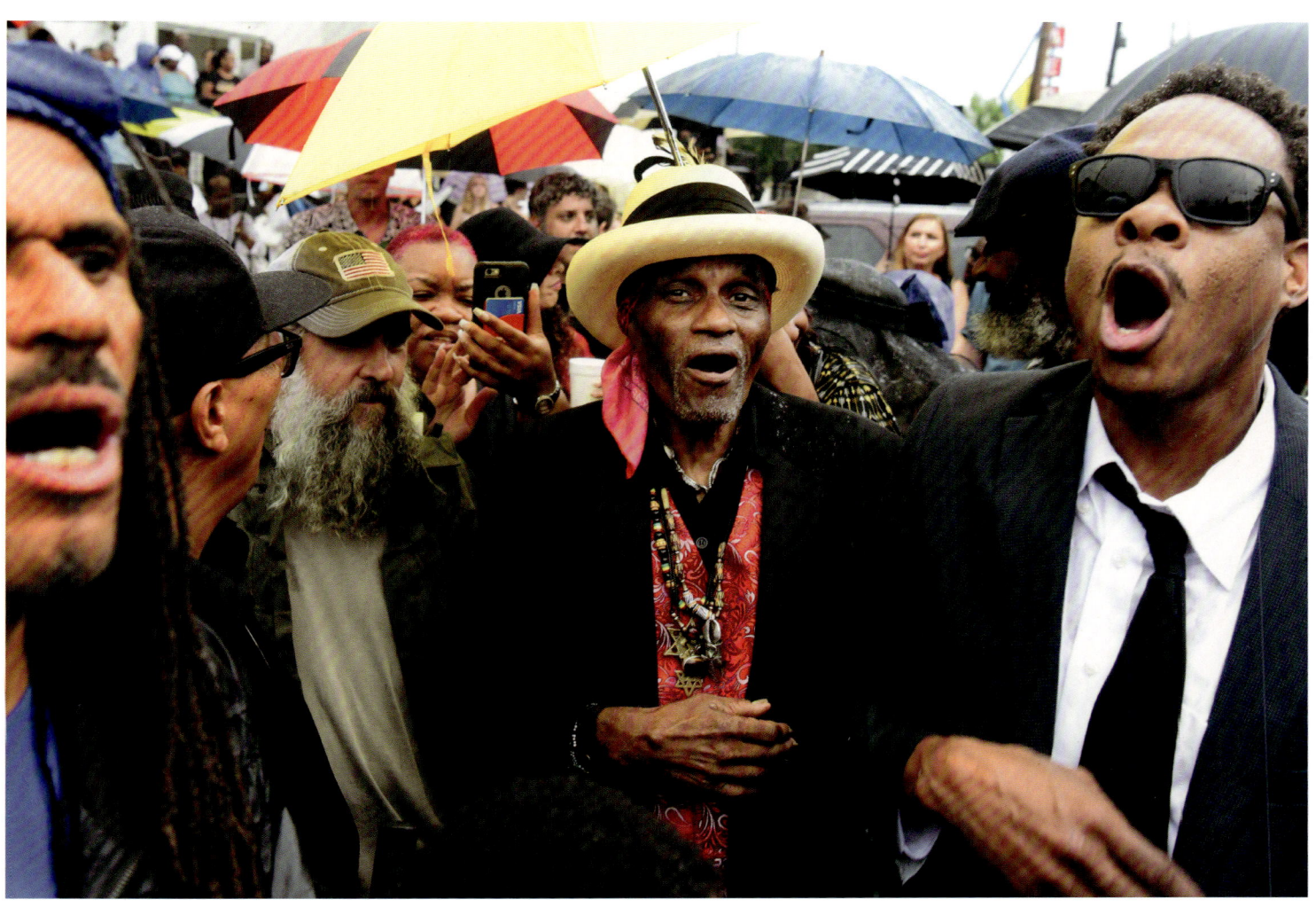

Cyril Neville (*center*) and trombonist Corey Henry (*left*) sing at Art Neville's funeral, 2019.

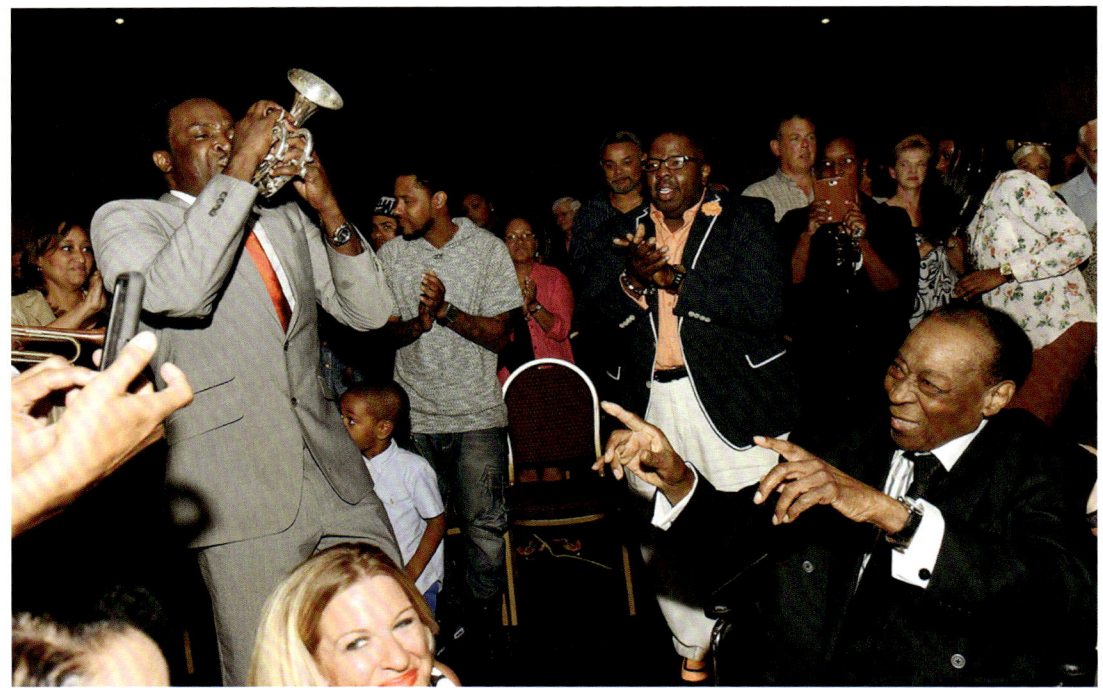

Trumpeter Shamarr Allen serenades Dave Bartholomew at the historic Carver Theater during a tribute to the collaboration between Bartholomew and Fats Domino, 2015.

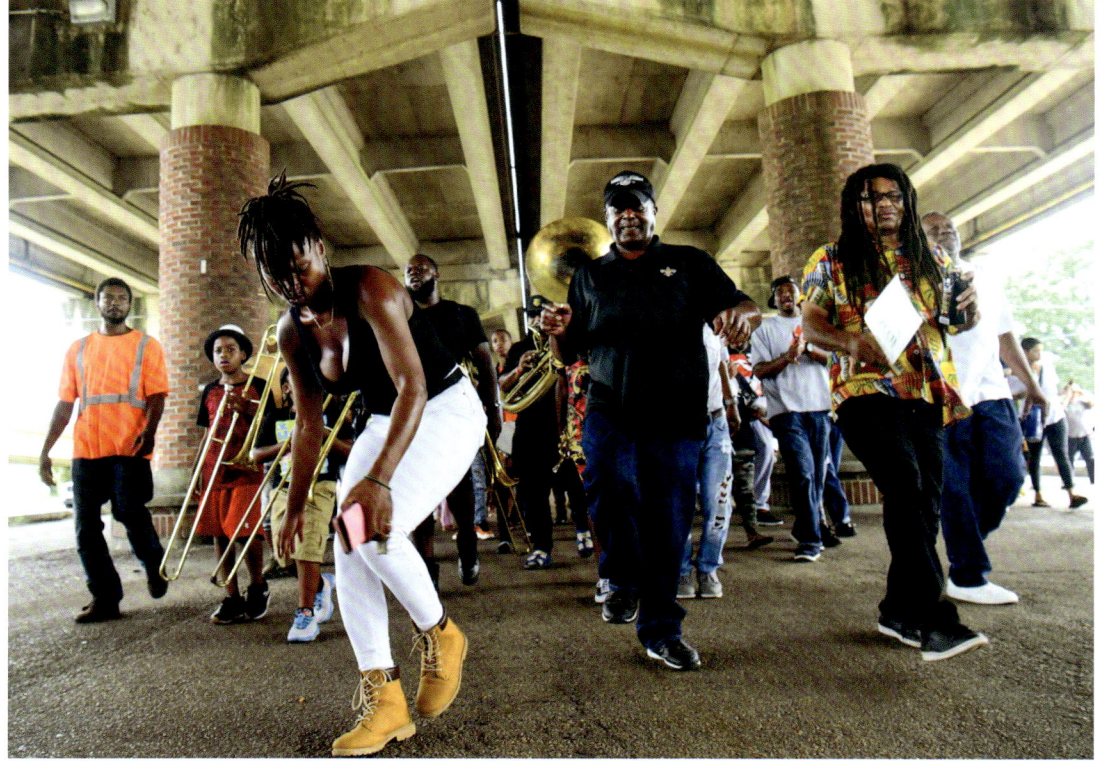

Under the overpass in the Seventh Ward, mourners form an impromptu memorial second line for Dave Bartholomew hours after hearing news of his passing, 2019. Bartholomew (1918–2019) was an influential musician, trumpeter, bandleader, composer, arranger, and record producer, responsible for a slew of number-one hits and the successful careers of many New Orleans musicians.

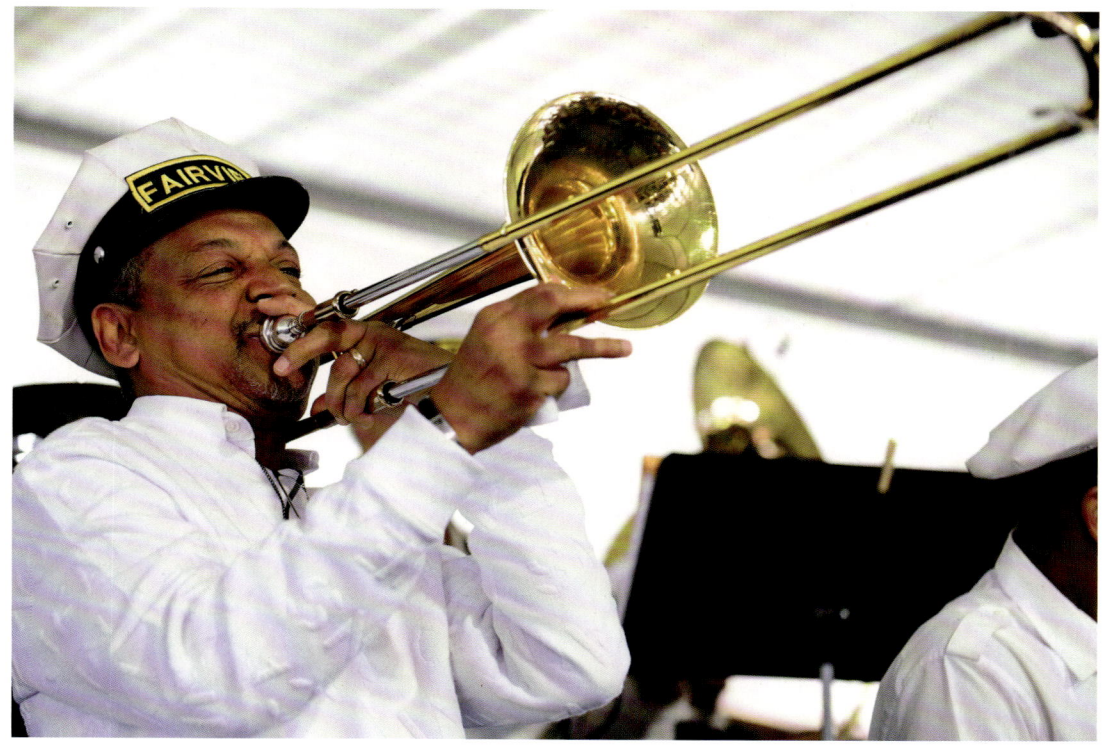

Lucien Barbarin performs in the Economy Hall jazz tent at Jazz Fest, 2019.

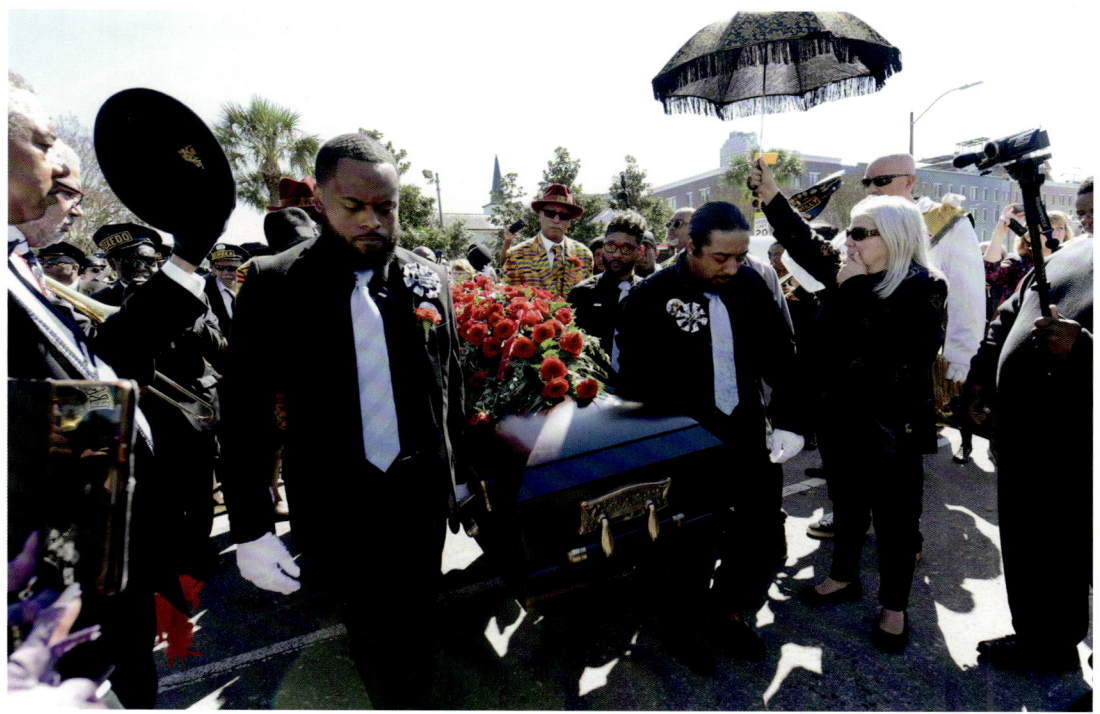

Funeral for Lucien Barbarin, 2020. Barbarin (1956–2020) was a celebrated trombonist who toured internationally with the Preservation Hall Jazz Band and with Harry Connick Jr.

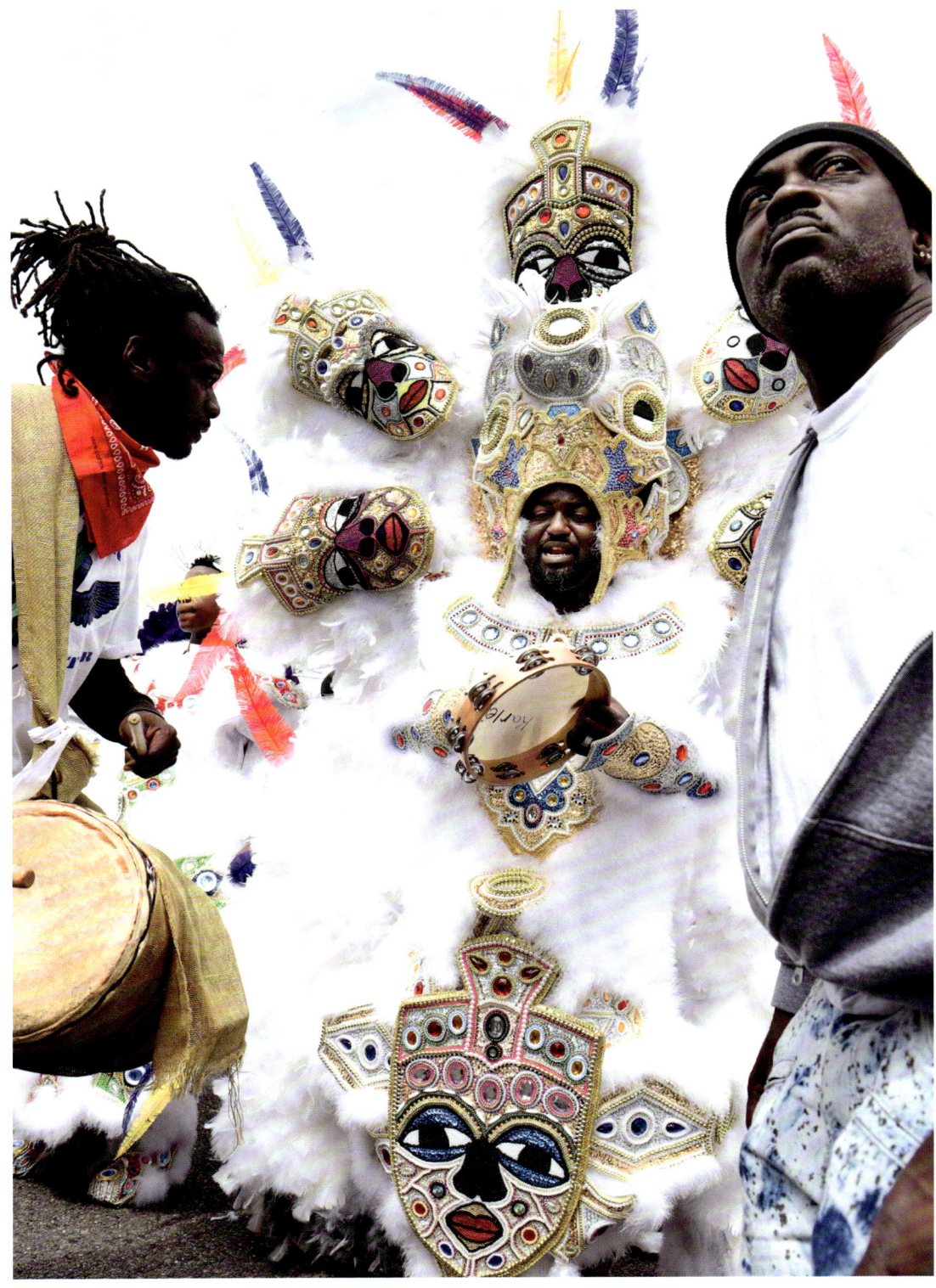

Big Chief Keelian "Dump" Boyd chants on Super Sunday in Central City, 2019. Boyd (1984–2021) was an artist and Big Chief of the Young Maasai Hunters Black Masking Indian tribe he founded in 2018.

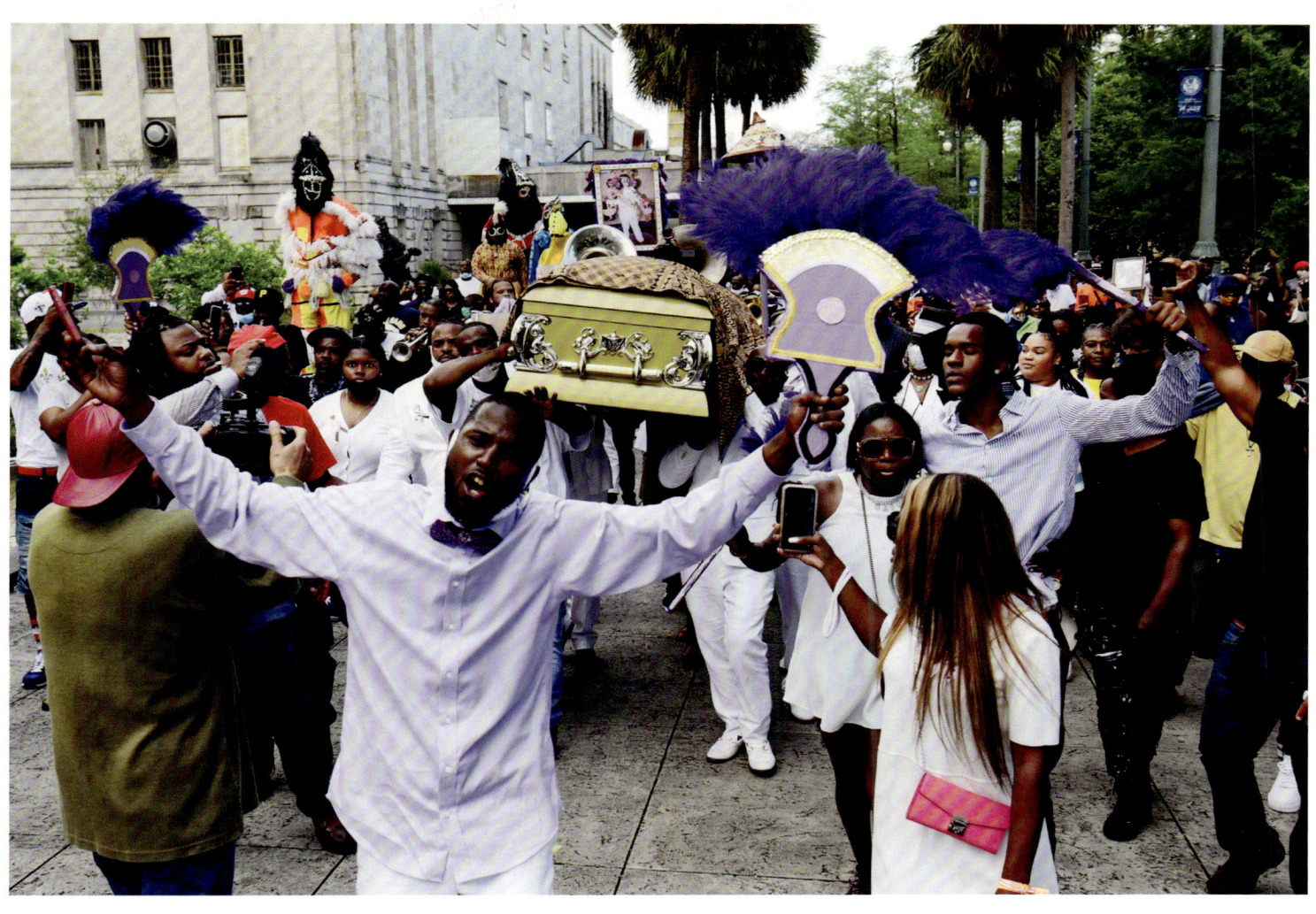

Big Chief Dump's funeral proceeds past Congo Square in Armstrong Park in Tremé, 2021.

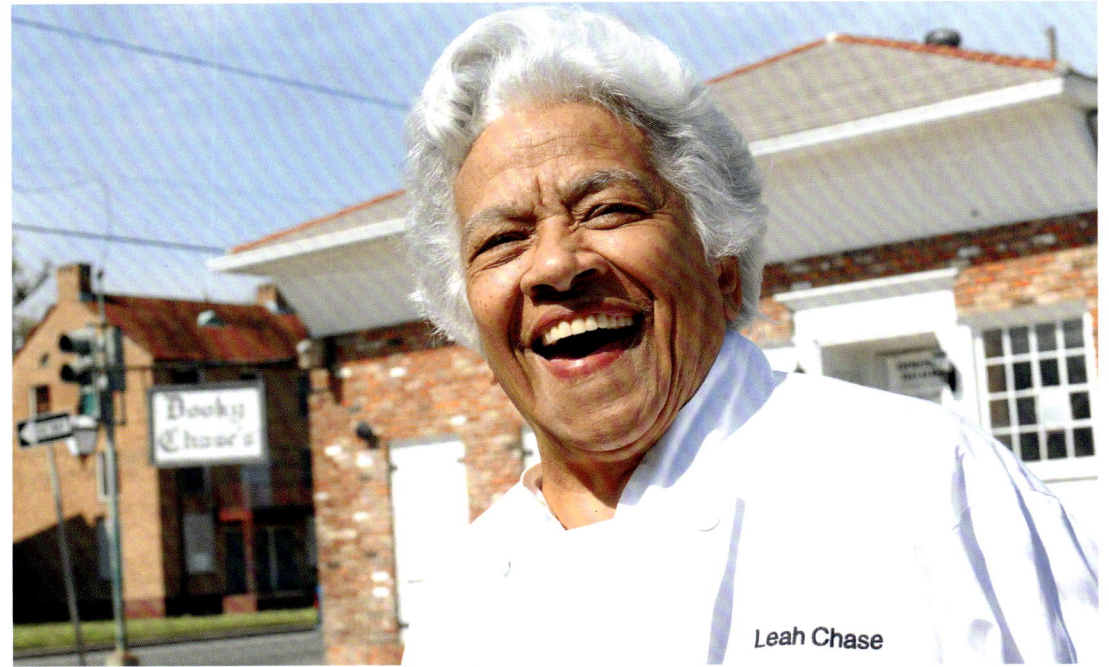

Chef Leah Chase stands outside her family's Dooky Chase's restaurant in Tremé, 2007.

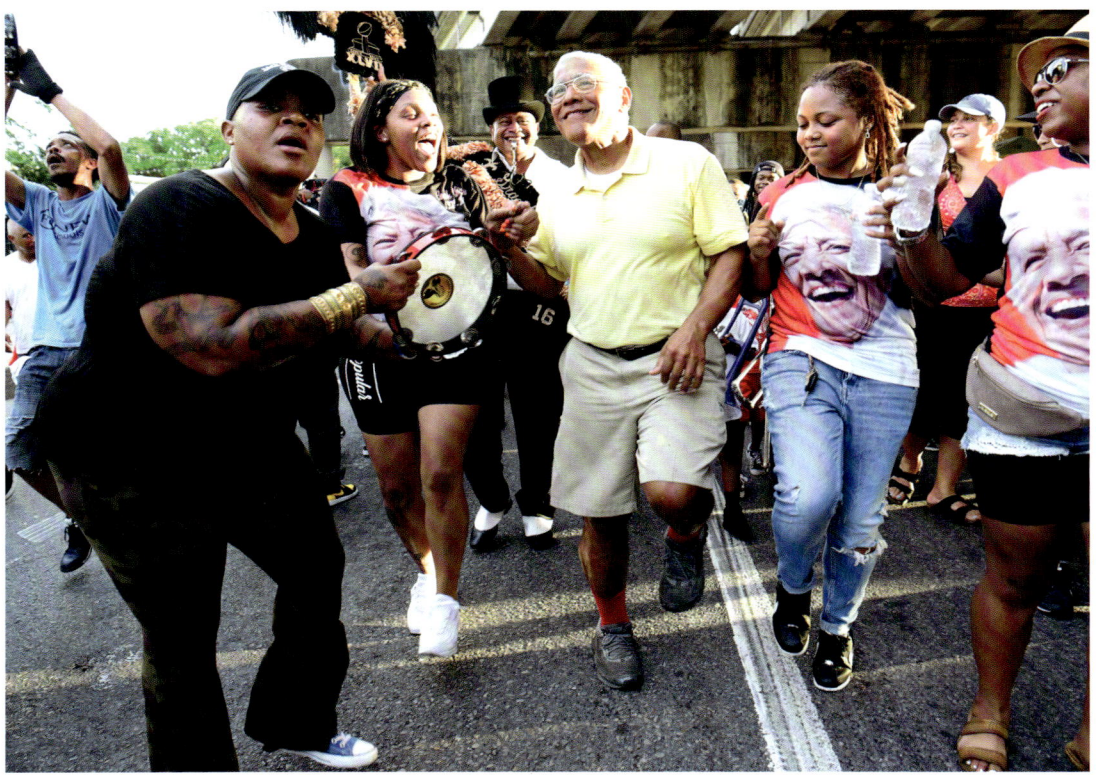

Dooky Chase Jr. and family members dance at a memorial second line for Leah Chase, 2019. Chase (1923–2019), the longtime chef at Dooky Chase's, was considered the "Queen of Creole Cuisine." She was an author, television personality, restaurateur, art collector, and activist, known for feeding activists and organizers during the civil rights movement. Her restaurant, one of the first integrated eating places in New Orleans, became a meeting place for white and Black musicians.

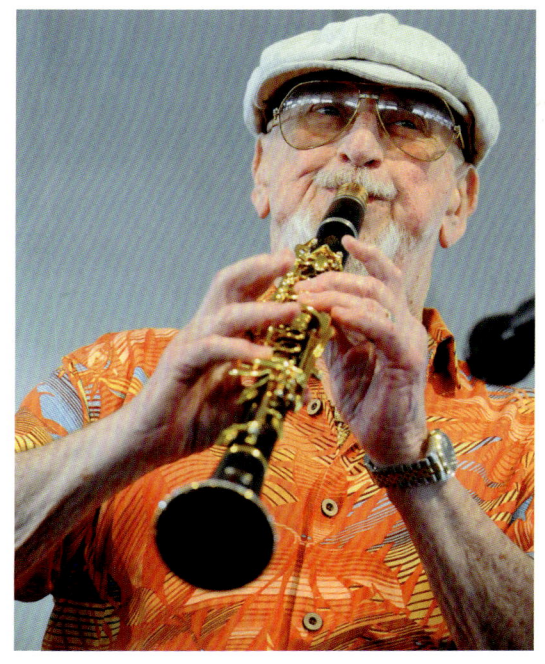

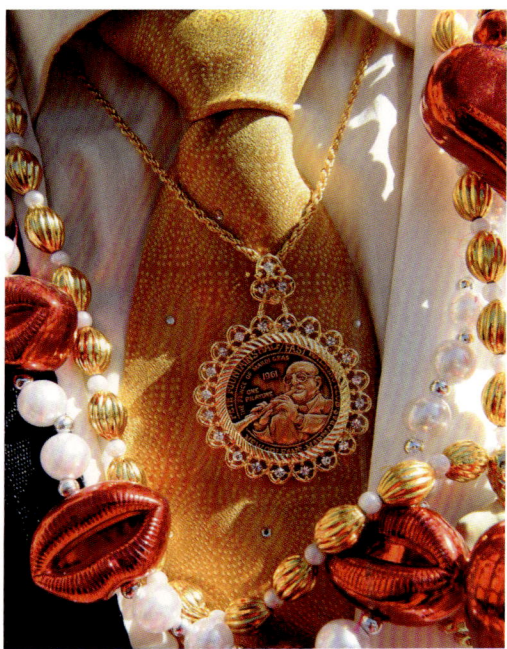

left Pete Fountain performs in the Economy Hall jazz tent at Jazz Fest, 2009.

right A doubloon necklace commemorates Pete Fountain's Half Fast Walking Club, 2015.

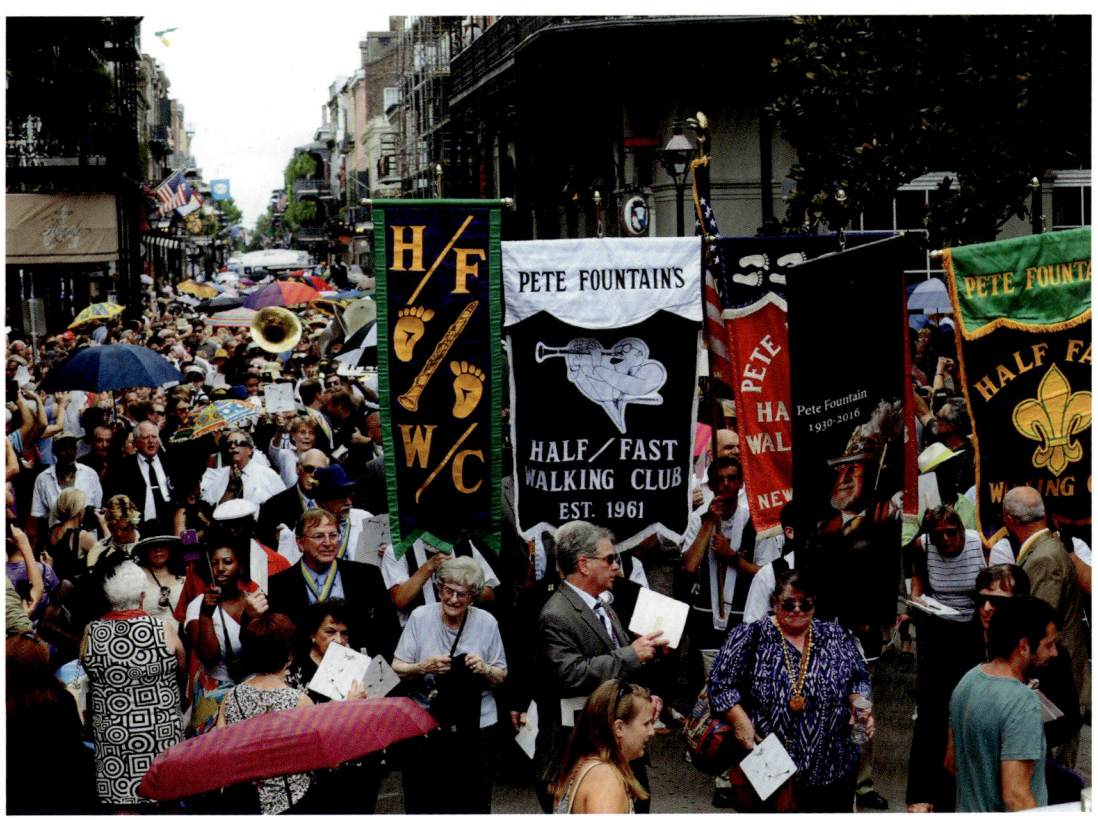

The funeral for Pete Fountain proceeds through the French Quarter, 2016. Fountain (1930–2016), born Pierre Dewey LaFountaine Jr., was an internationally known jazz clarinetist who gained fame as a featured performer with the Lawrence Welk Orchestra and show before moving back to New Orleans; there he opened his own club and led the Half Fast Walking Club on Mardi Gras Day for decades.

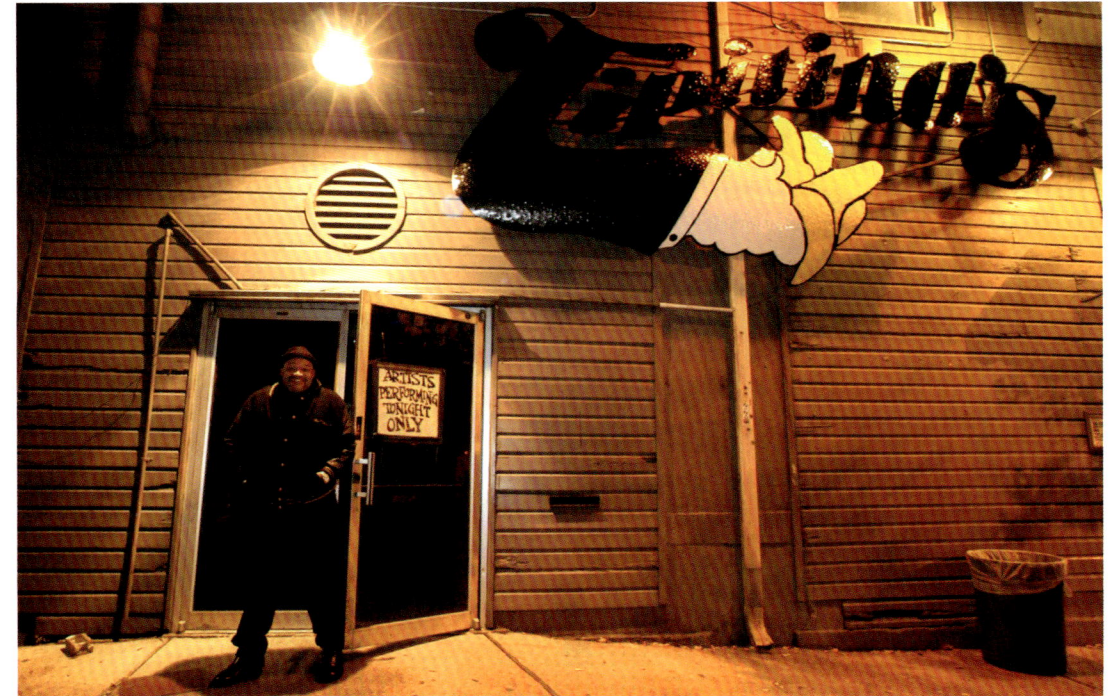

Jo "Cool" Davis stands guard at the backstage entrance of Tipitina's, 2003.

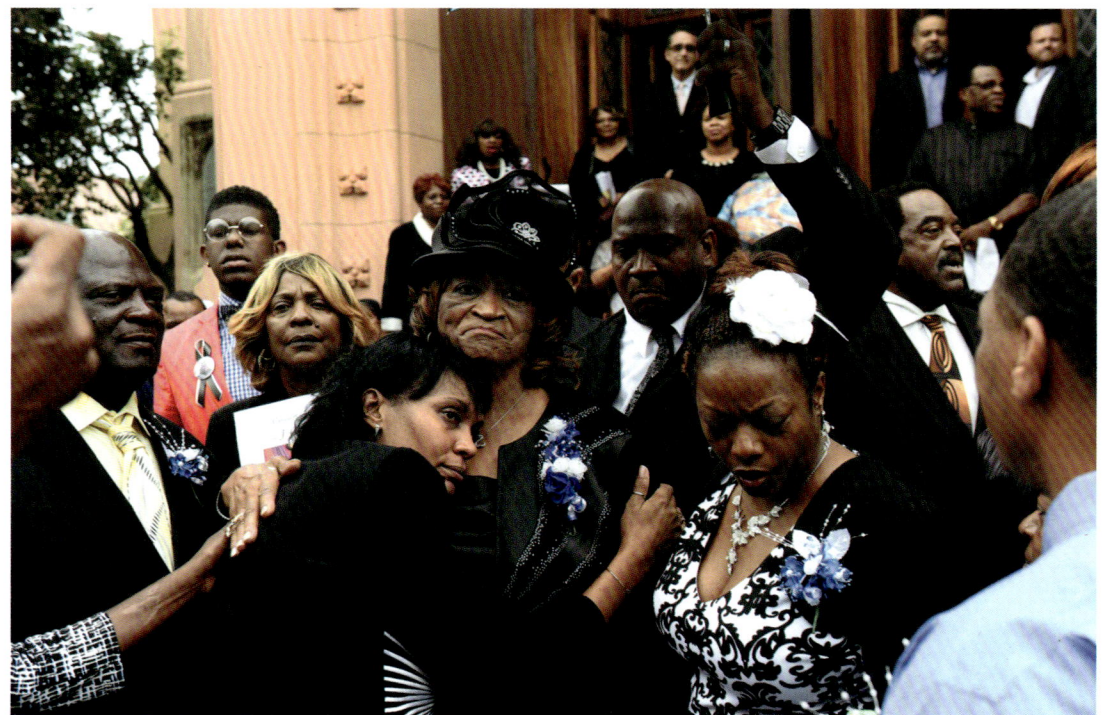

Widow Evelyn Davis at Jo Cool's funeral at Trinity Church, 2016. Davis (1953–2016) was a charismatic gospel singer, former boxer, longtime doorman, and master of ceremonies at the famed Tipitina's live music club.

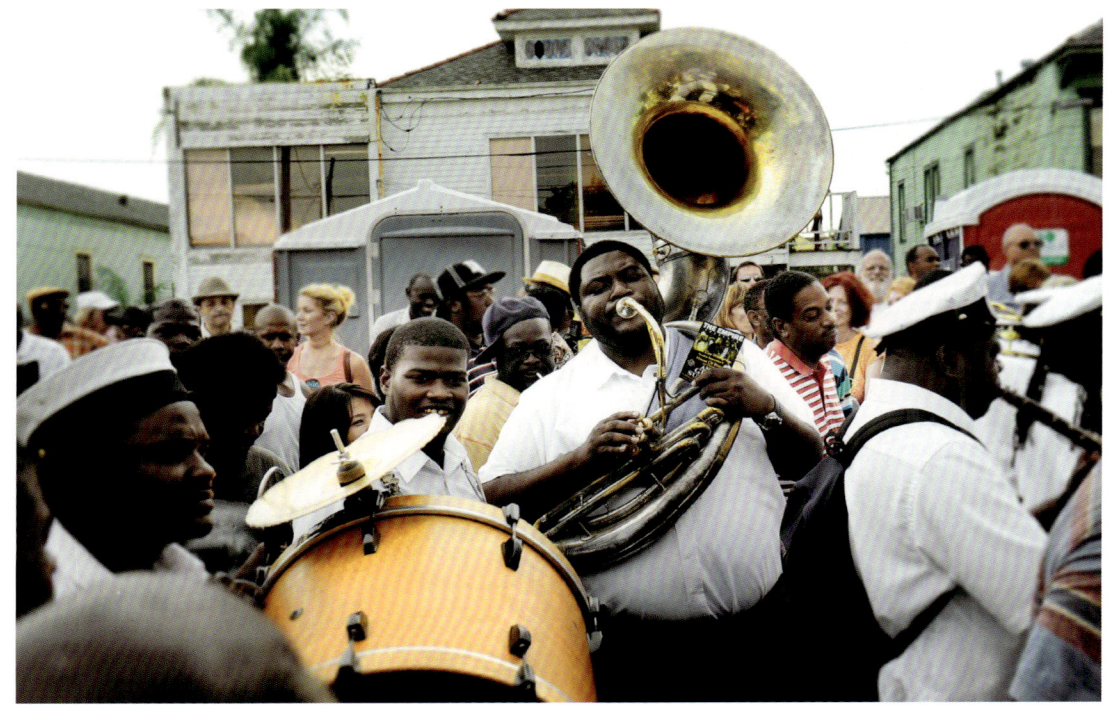

Hot 8 Brass Band sousaphonist Bennie Pete, 2009.

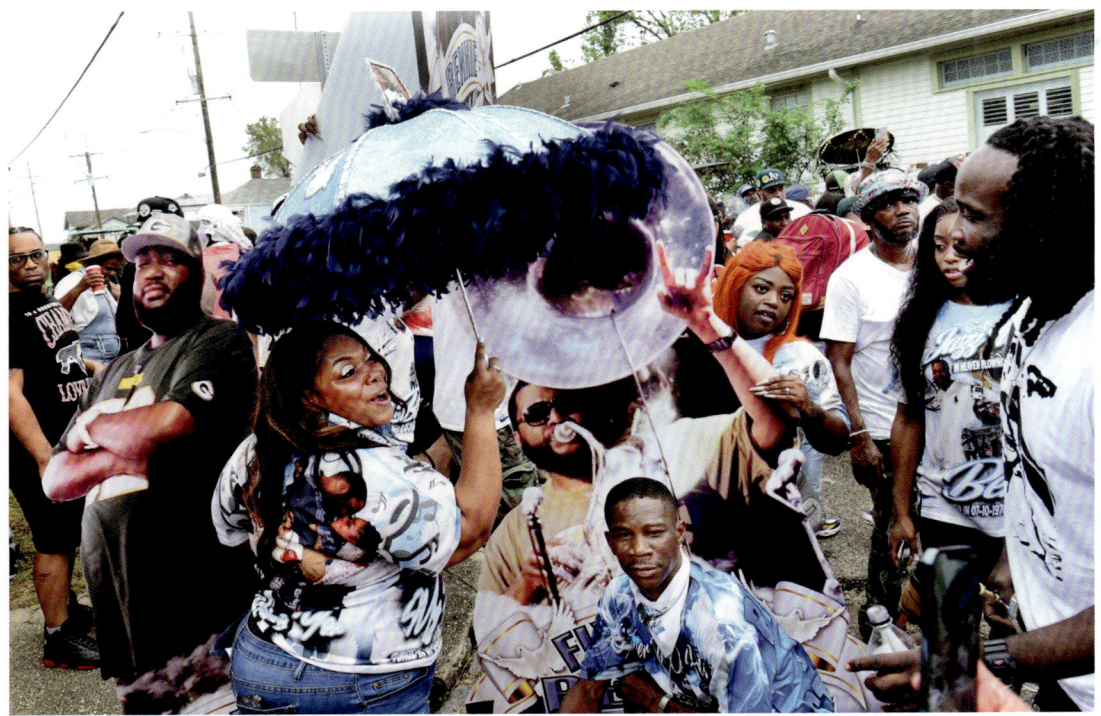

Lameka Segura-Pete, Pete's widow, celebrates his life during a second line after his funeral, 2021. Pete (1976–2021), who died of complications from COVID, was a co-founder and leader of the Hot 8 Brass Band, who dedicated himself to preserving the musical traditions of New Orleans.

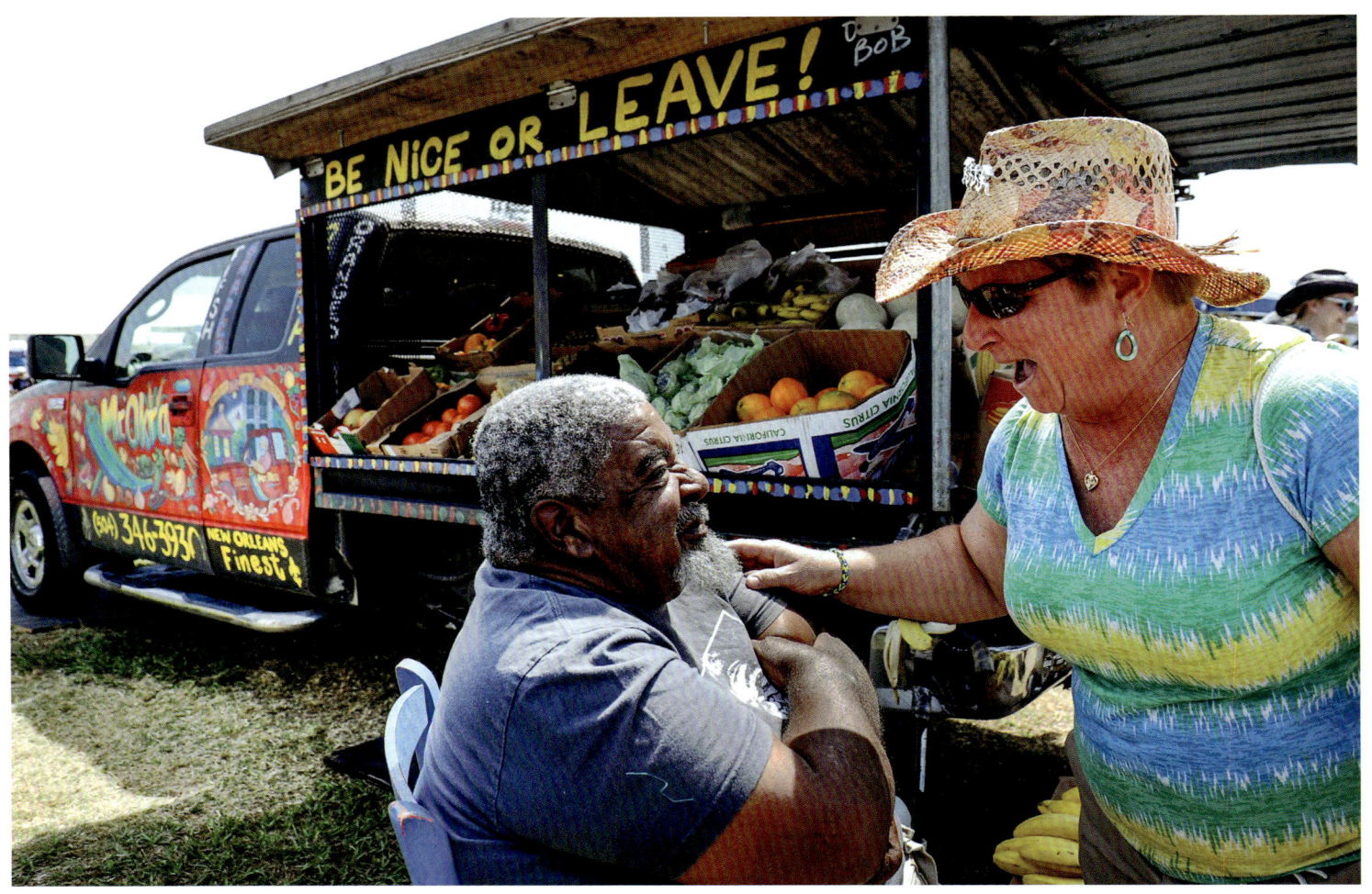

Mr. Okra is greeted by a fan on the grounds of Jazz Fest, 2014. Mr. Okra (1943–2018), whose real name was Arthur Robinson, was a roving produce vendor who became a local celebrity in his final years for his deep bellowing voice amplified through a megaphone. It could be heard throughout the neighborhoods, calling out, "I've got strawberries and bananas, sweeeet peaches and broccoli."

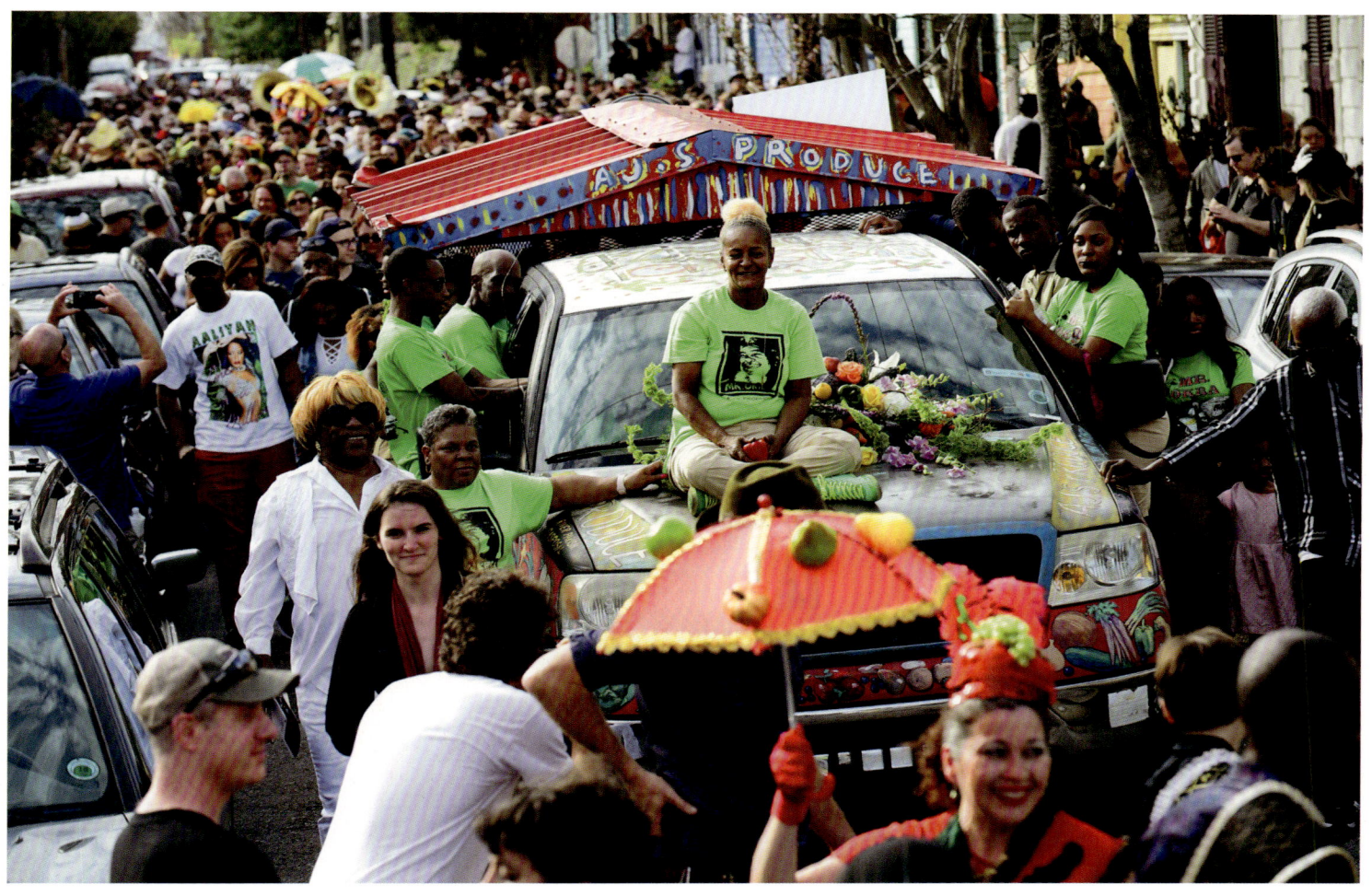

Sergio Robinson, now known as Ms. Okra, rides atop her father's famous truck at his funeral, 2018.

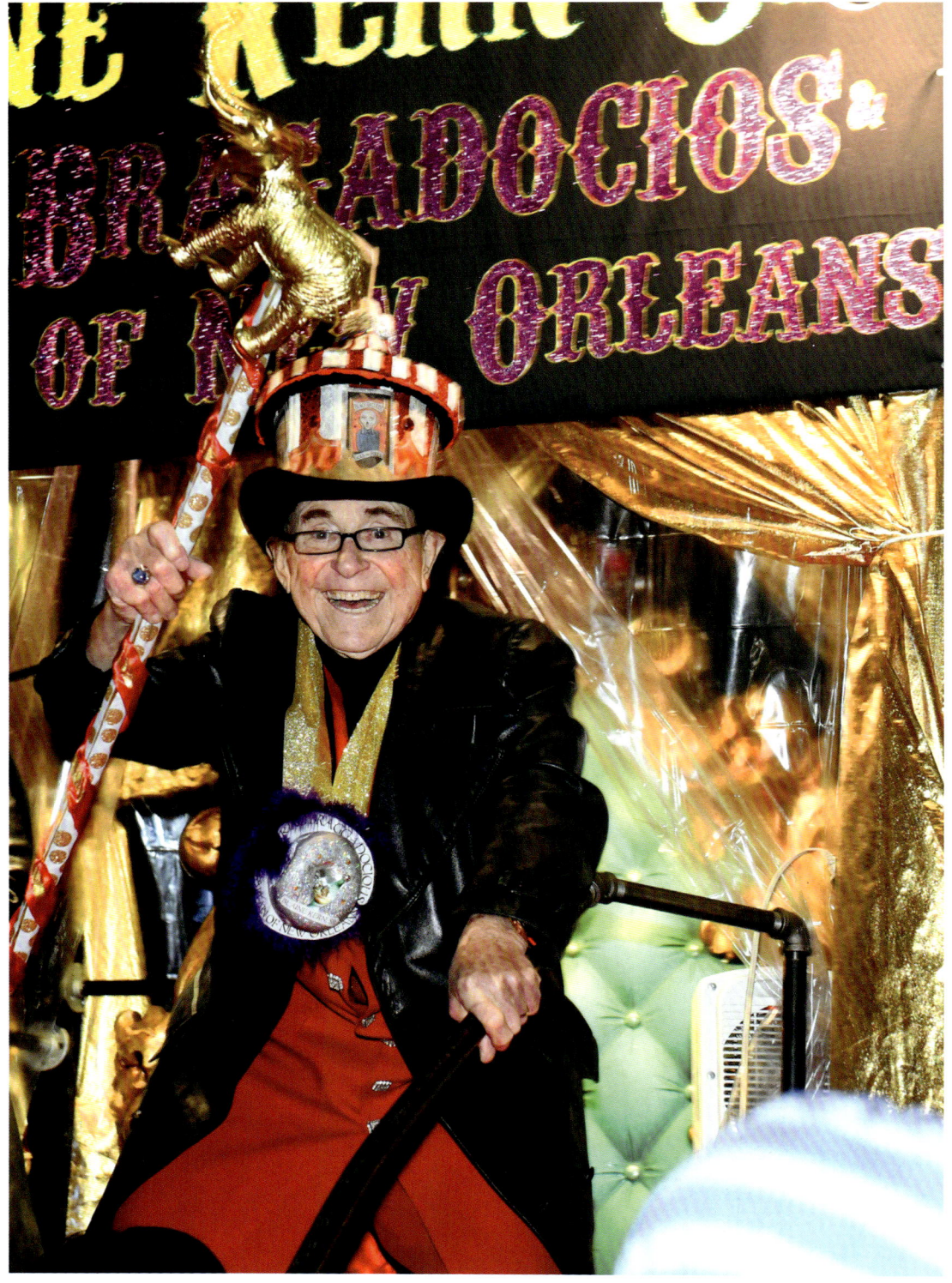

Blaine Kern Sr. reigns as "King Bragadocious and Captain of New Orleans" in krewe*delusion*, 2016. Kern (1927–2020), known as Mr. Mardi Gras, was credited for turning Mardi Gras into a huge global event by building innovative and spectacular parade floats.

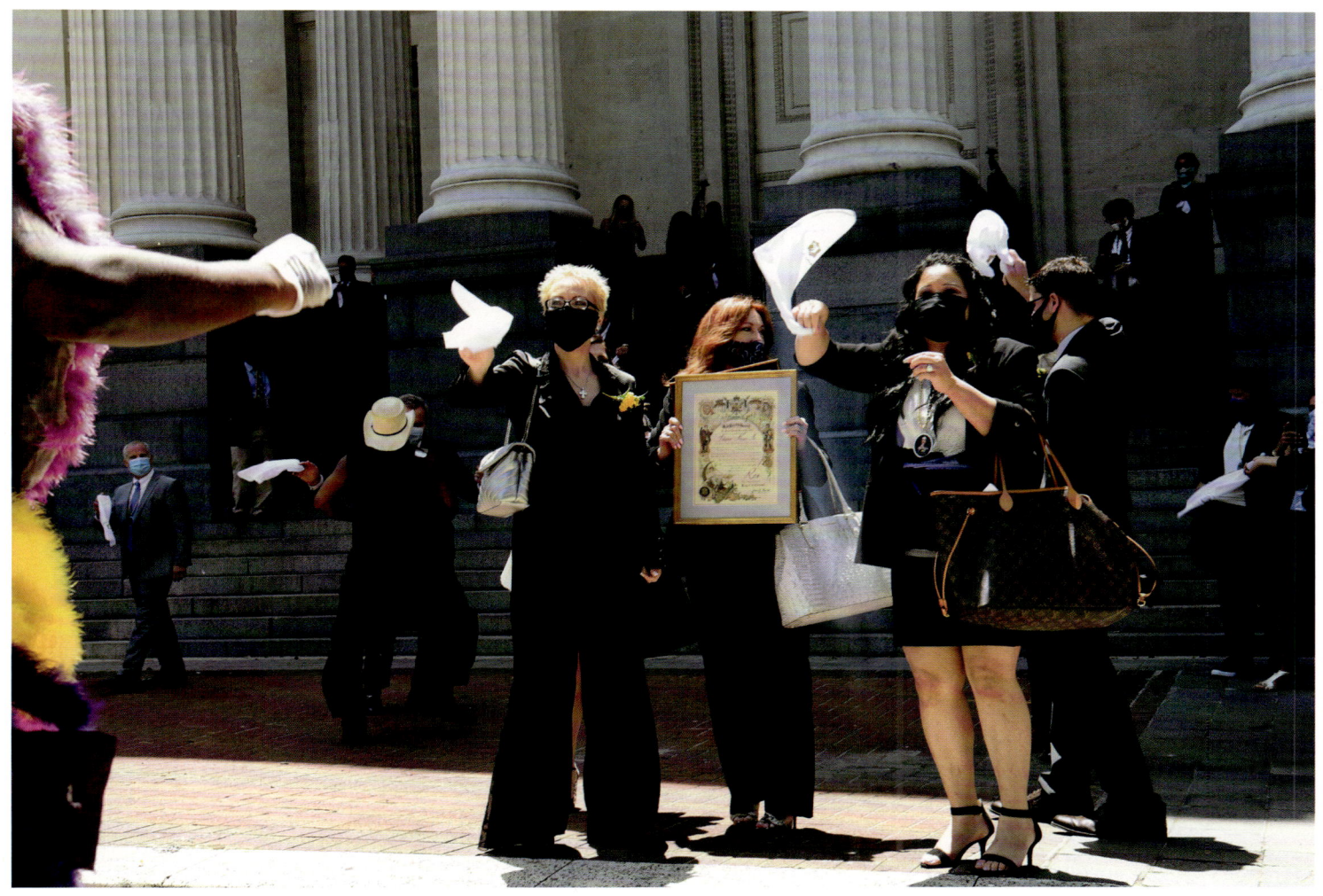

Blaine Kern's family waves white handkerchiefs during his funeral at Gallier Hall held during the pandemic, 2021. The custom of white handkerchiefs at traditional funeral processions goes back to the times when men and women carried white handkerchiefs and would wave them to join in the celebration of the lives of the recently departed.

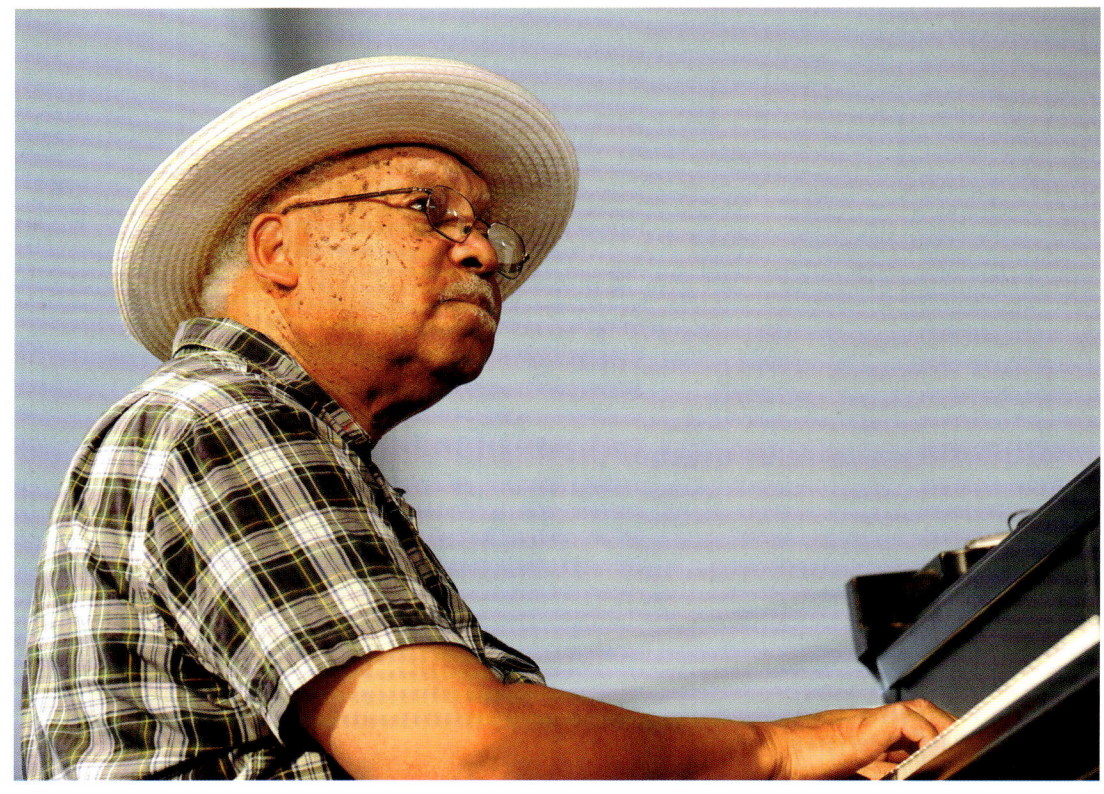

Ellis Marsalis Jr. performs at Jazz Fest, 2009.

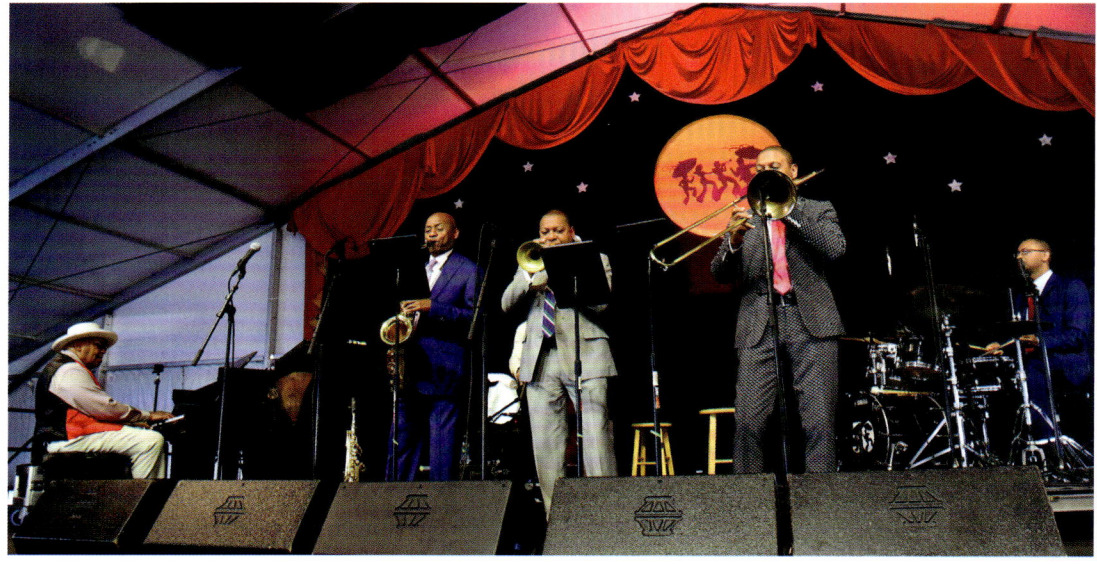

Ellis performs with sons Branford, Wynton, Delfayo, and Jason Marsalis at Jazz Fest, 2019.

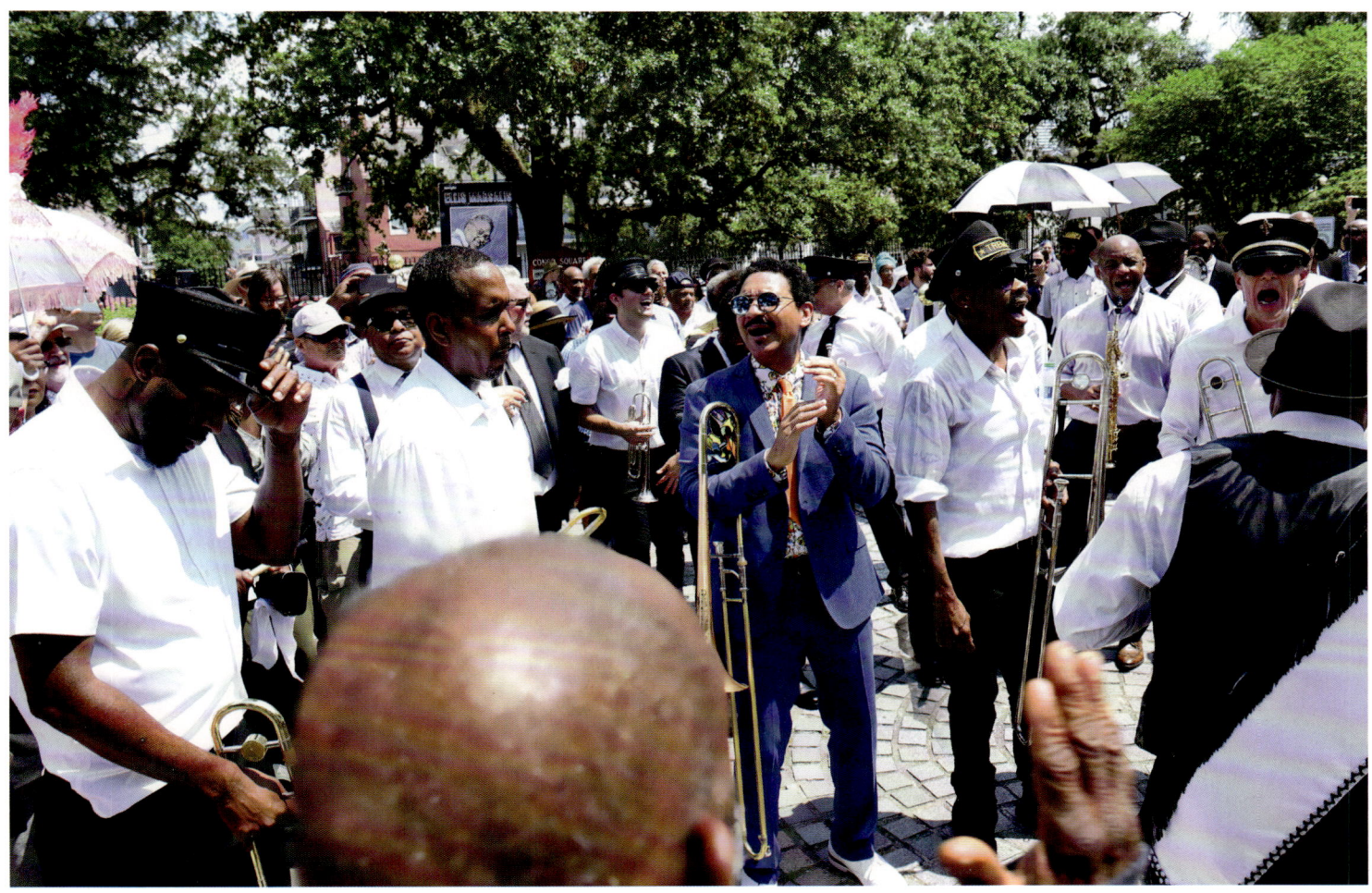

Wynton, Delfayo, and Branford Marsalis were among the dozens of musicians at their father Ellis Marsalis's memorial second line at Congo Square, 2022. Ellis passed away from COVID in 2020 but his funeral was delayed due to pandemic restrictions.

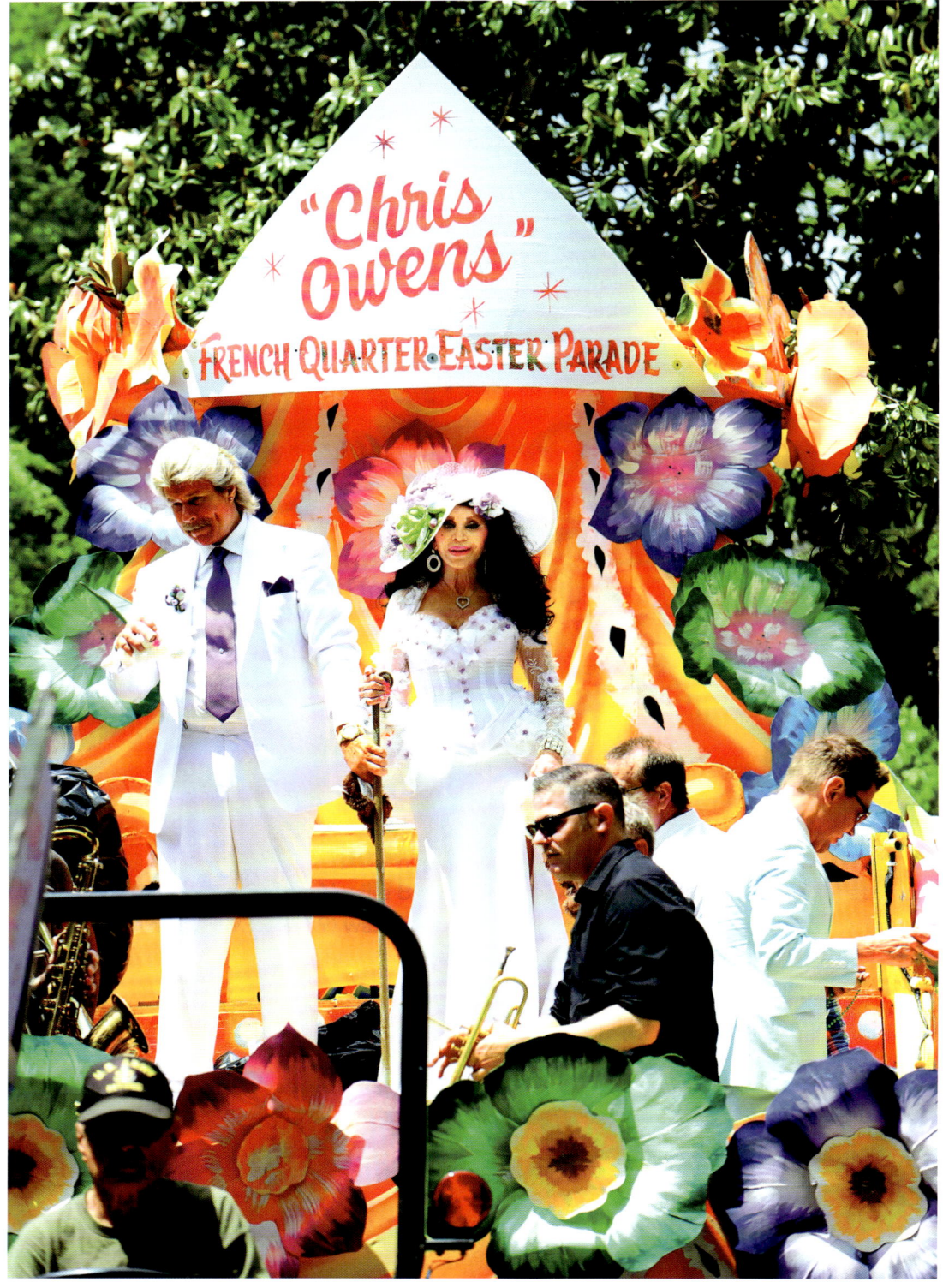

Chris Owens with her longtime companion Mark Davison, leading her annual Easter parade, 2017. Owens (1932–2022) was a cabaret dancer, Bourbon Street club owner, and entrepreneur known for her flashy clothes, generosity, and youthful appearance. Davison died in 2018.

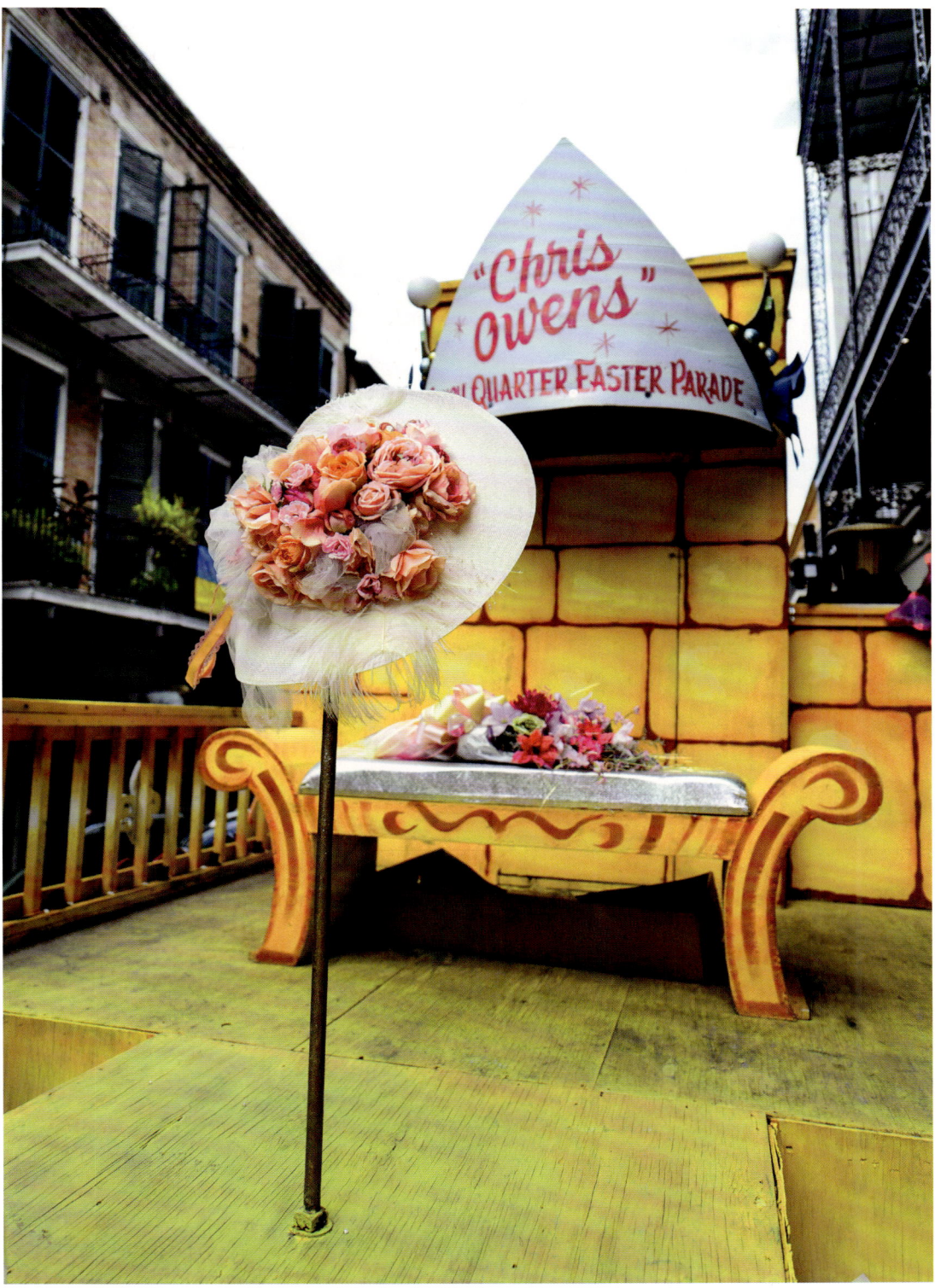

The "Chris Owens" French Quarter Easter Parade goes on days after her passing with flowers and her Easter bonnet displayed in her place, 2022.

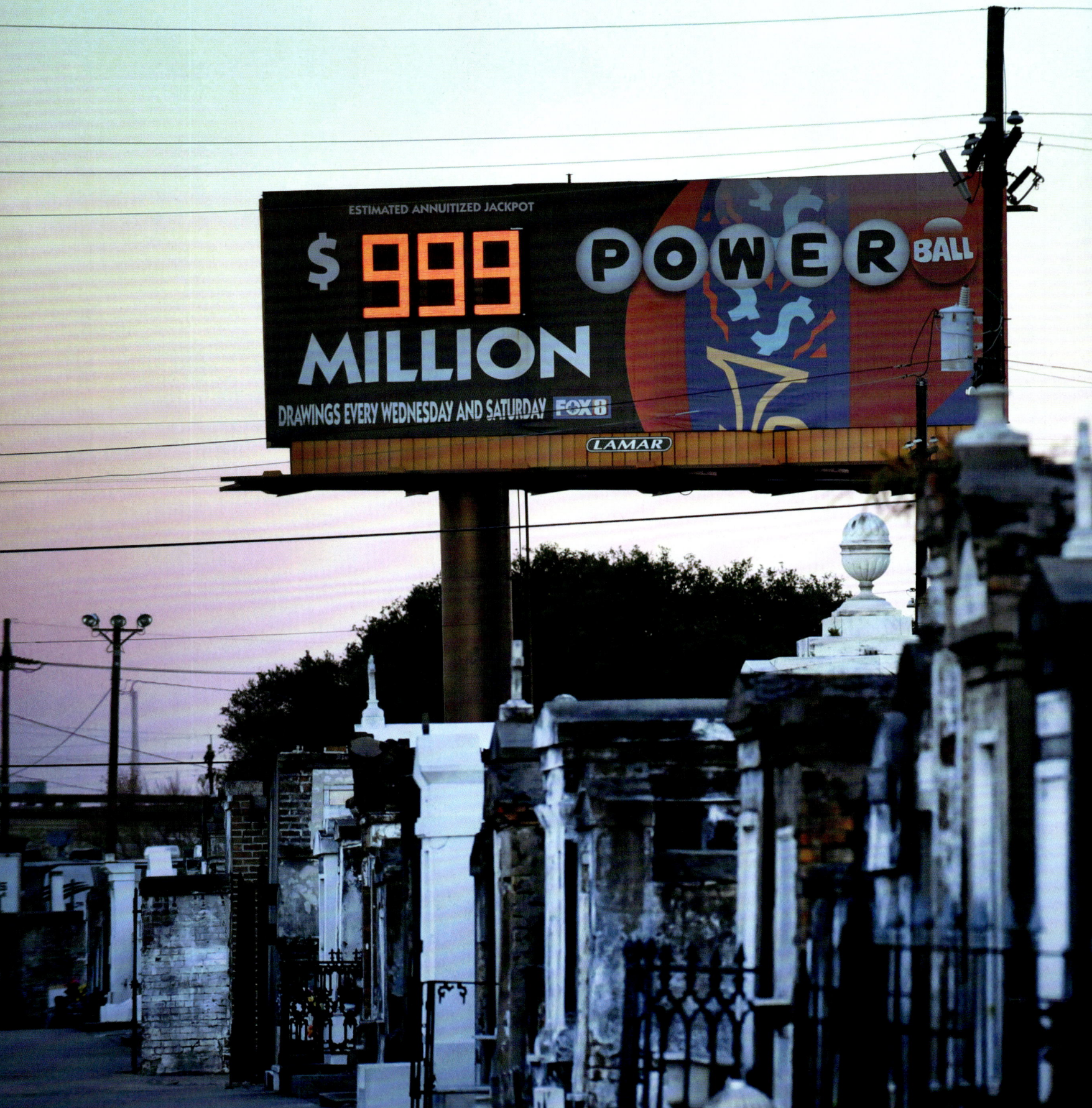

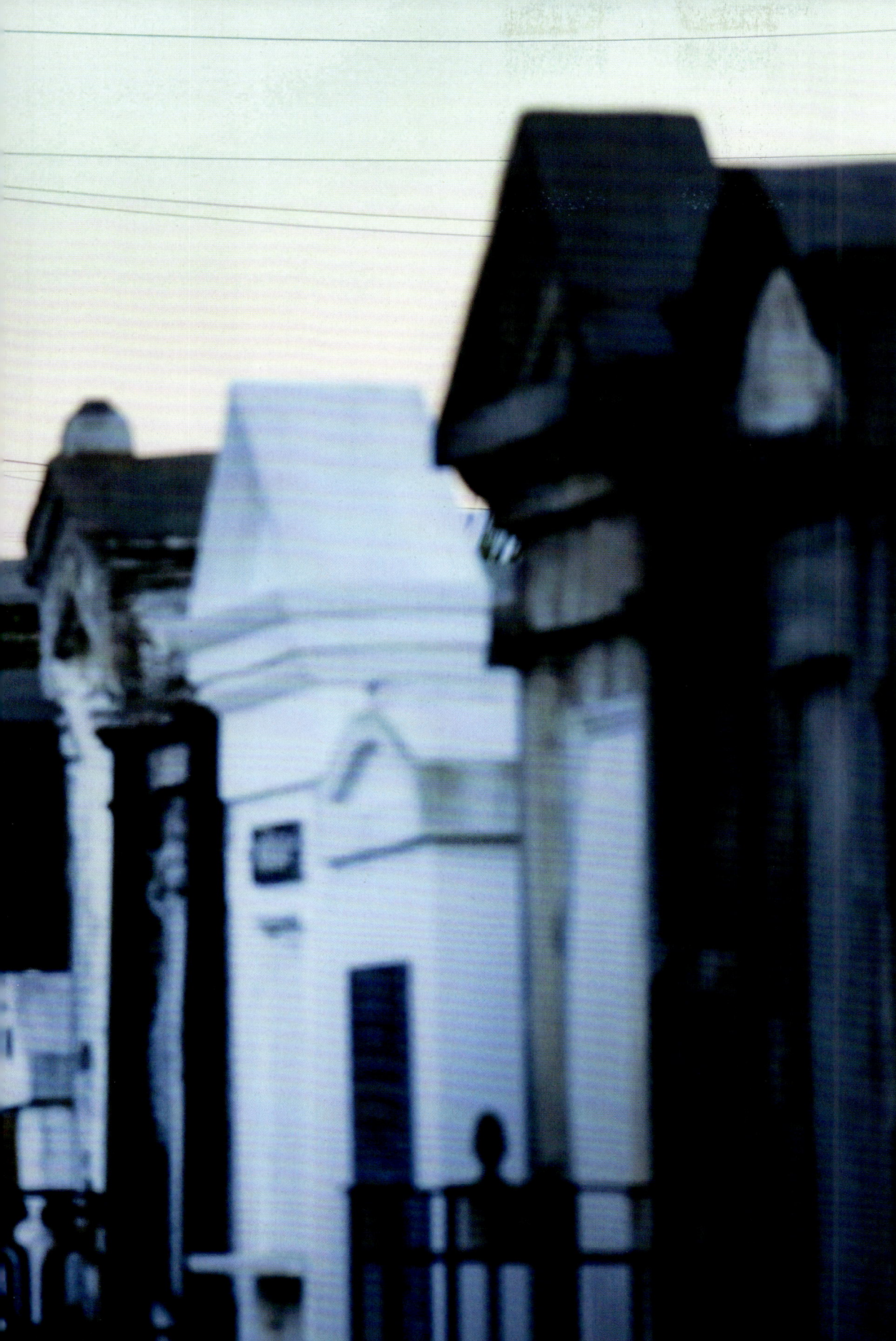

"Can't Take It with You"
at St. Louis Cemetery
No. 2, 2016.

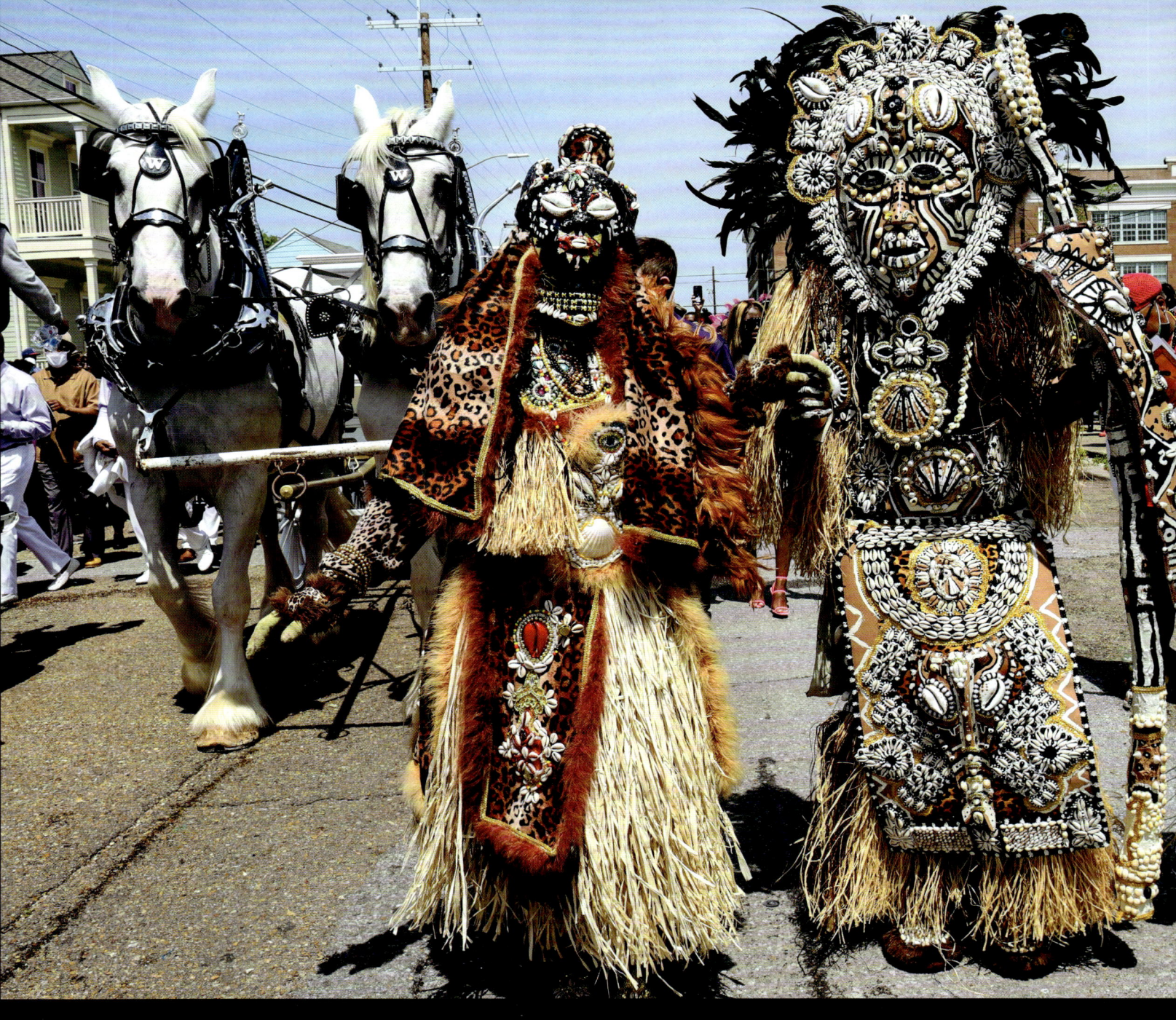

Big Chief Victor Harris's Spirit of Fi Yi Yi and the Mandingo Warriors, 2021.

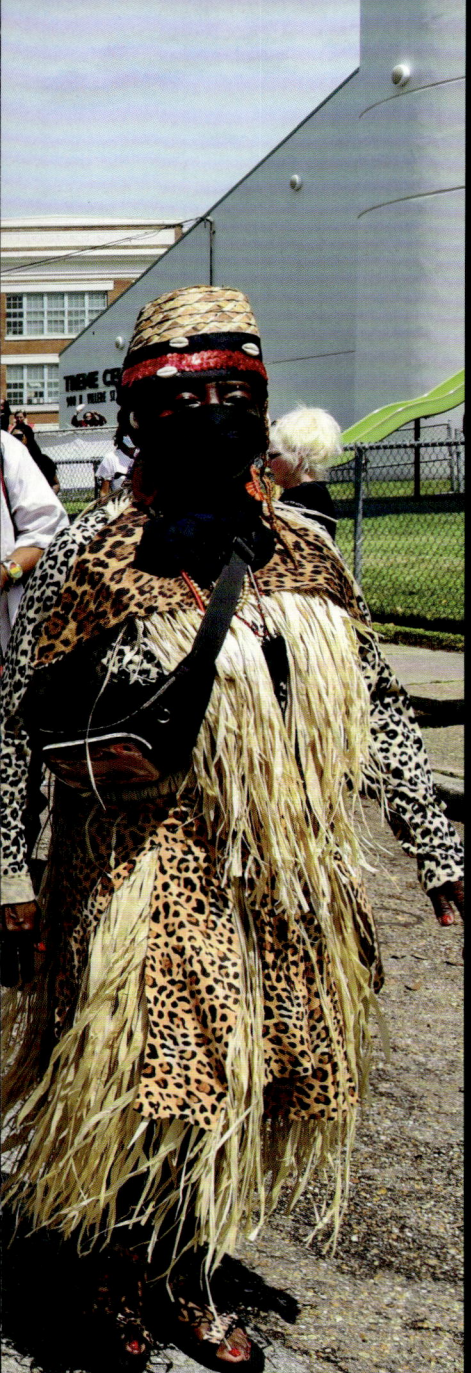

Part IV

We Won't Bow Down

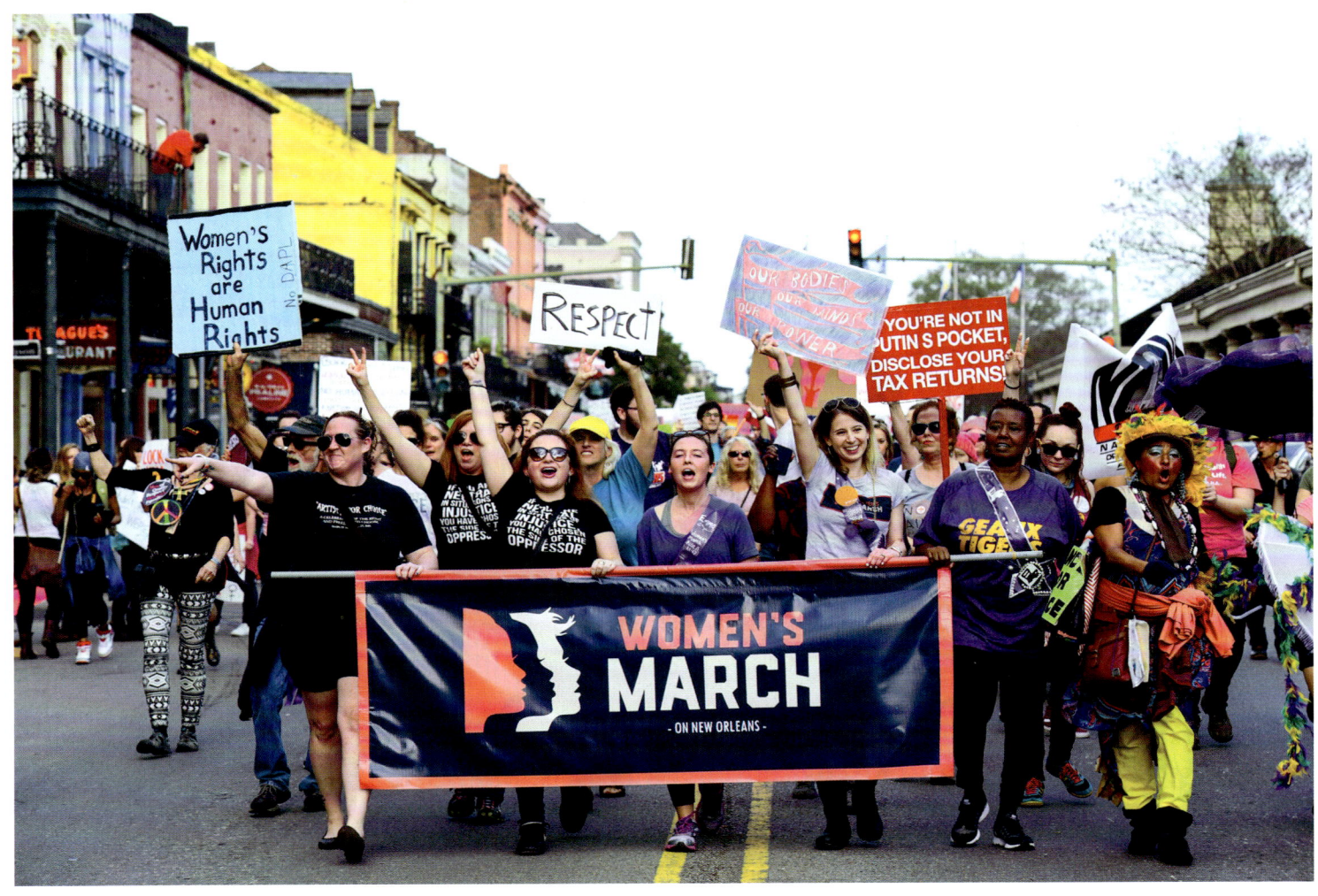

New Orleans women participate in the Women's March, a worldwide protest demanding rights for women, held the day after the inauguration of Donald J. Trump as president, 2017.

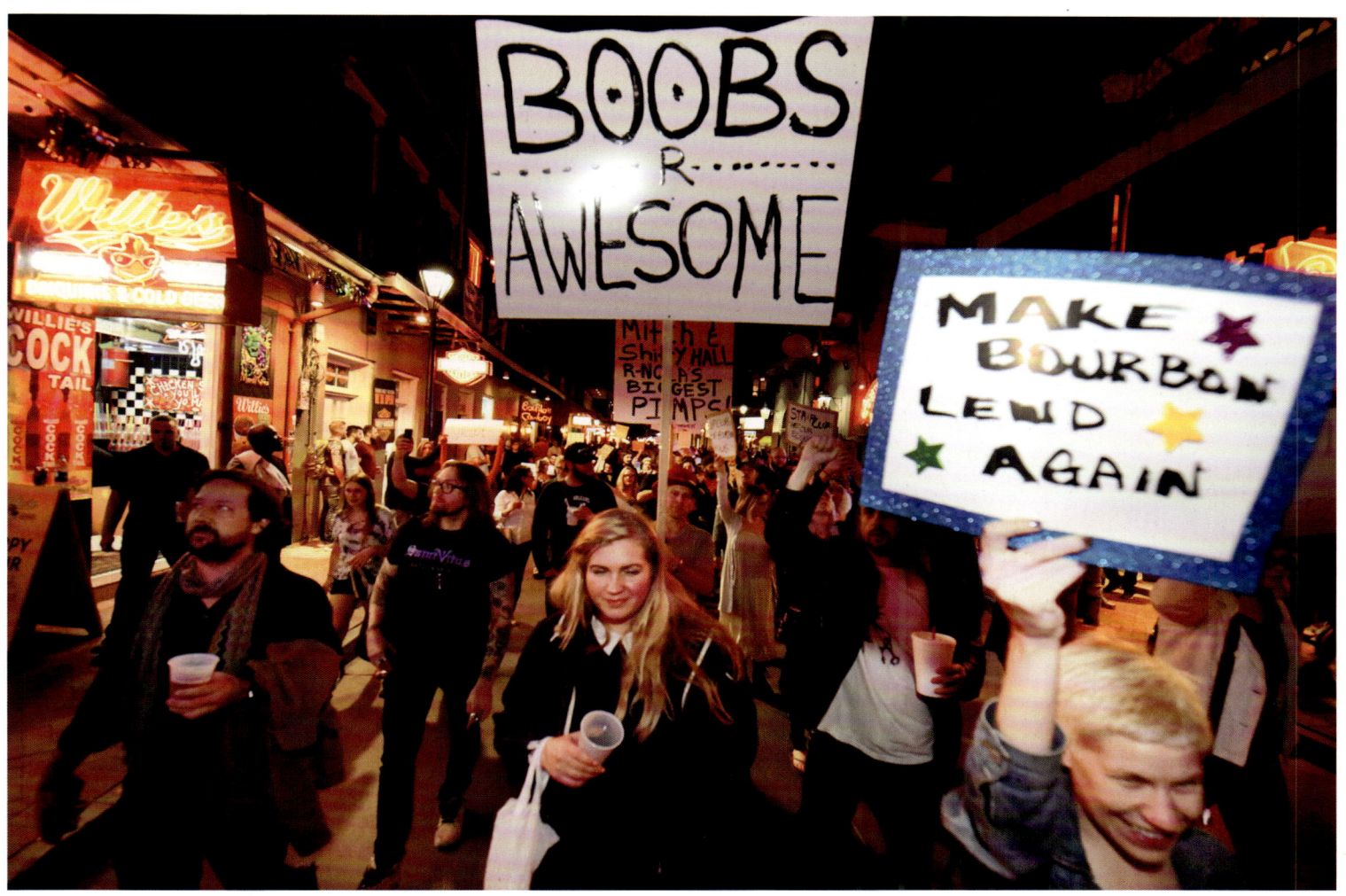

Strippers and club employees participate in the Strippers' March, formally known as the Unemployment March, after the closure of several strip clubs in the French Quarter by ATF agents who cited them for prostitution and drug violations, 2017.

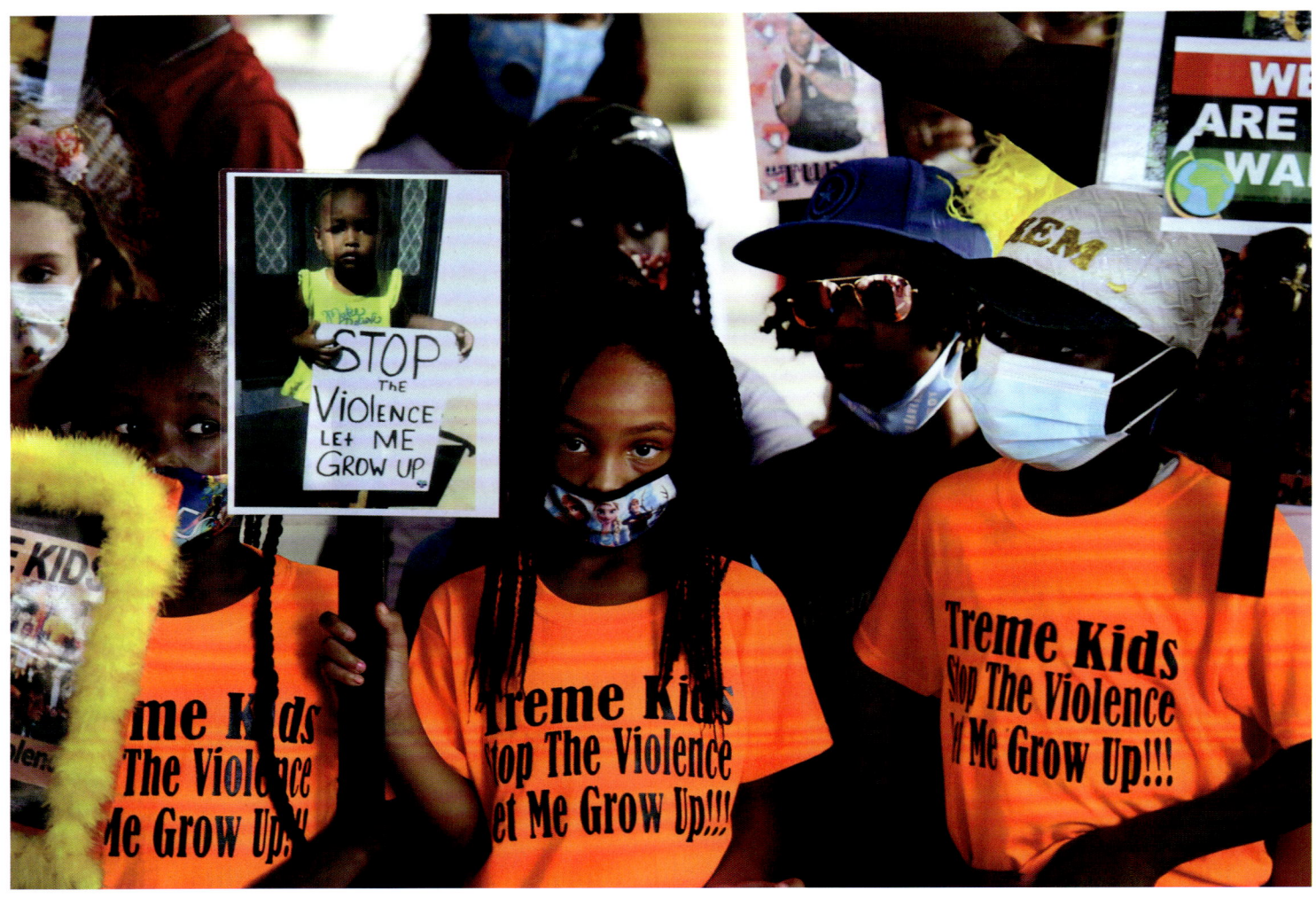

Children participate in the Treme Kids Stop the Violence March, an annual children-led protest organized by Janice Kimble, 2020.

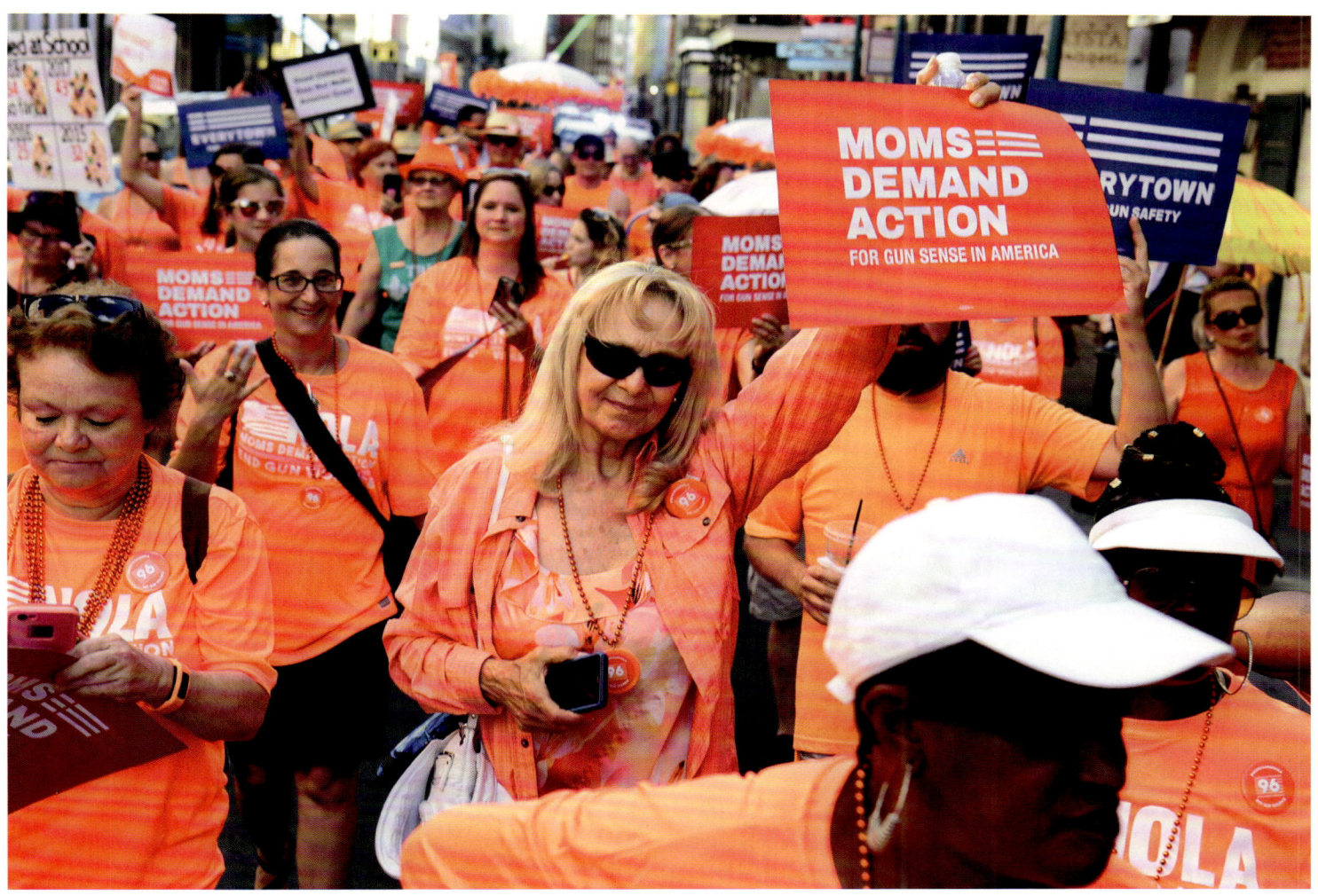

New Orleans women march with Moms Demand Action, a nonpartisan movement demanding solutions to the nation's gun violence crisis, 2018.

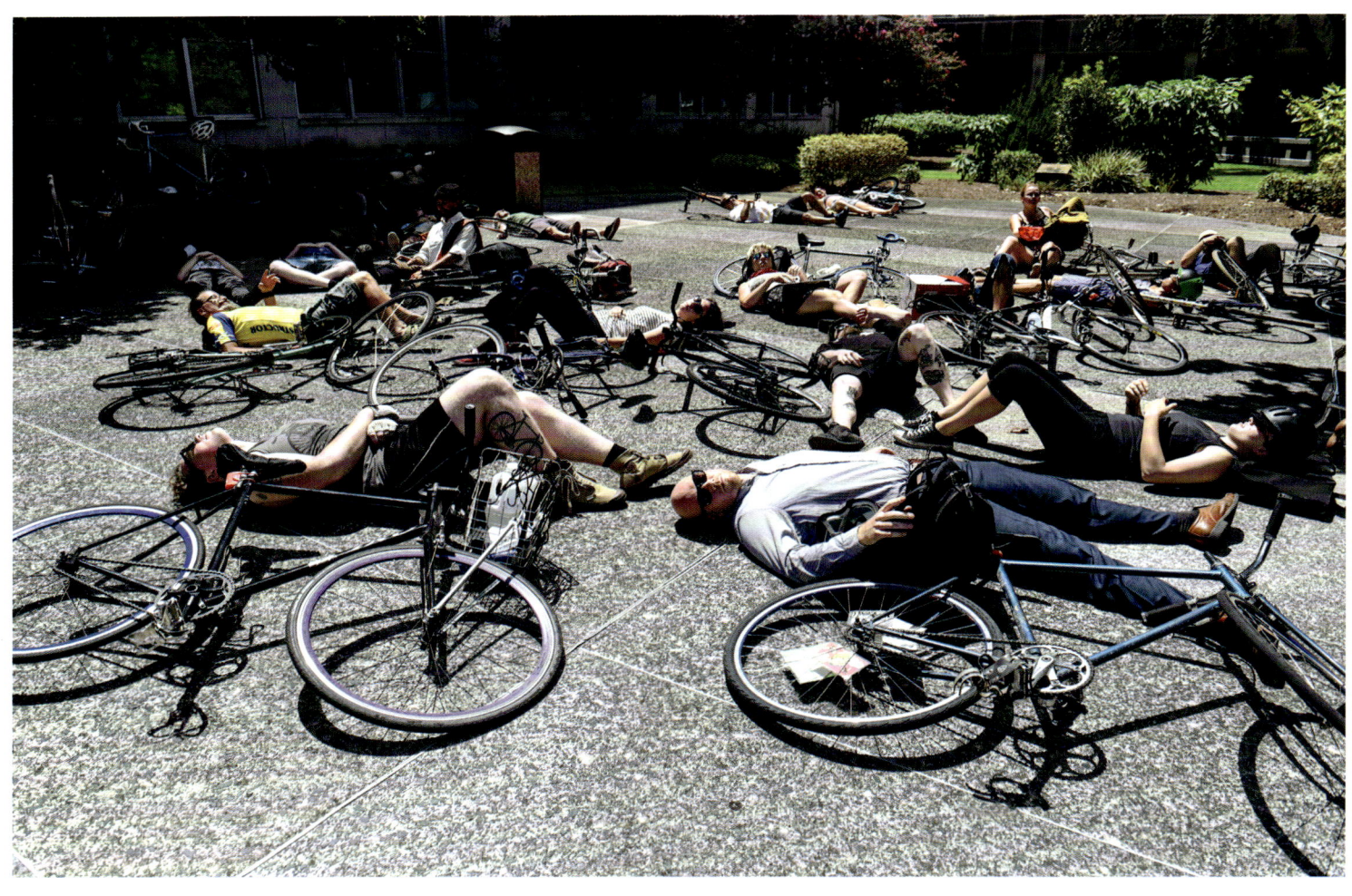

Cyclists stage a "bike die-in" protest at City Hall to highlight the dangers of cycling after six cyclists were killed in crashes, 2015.

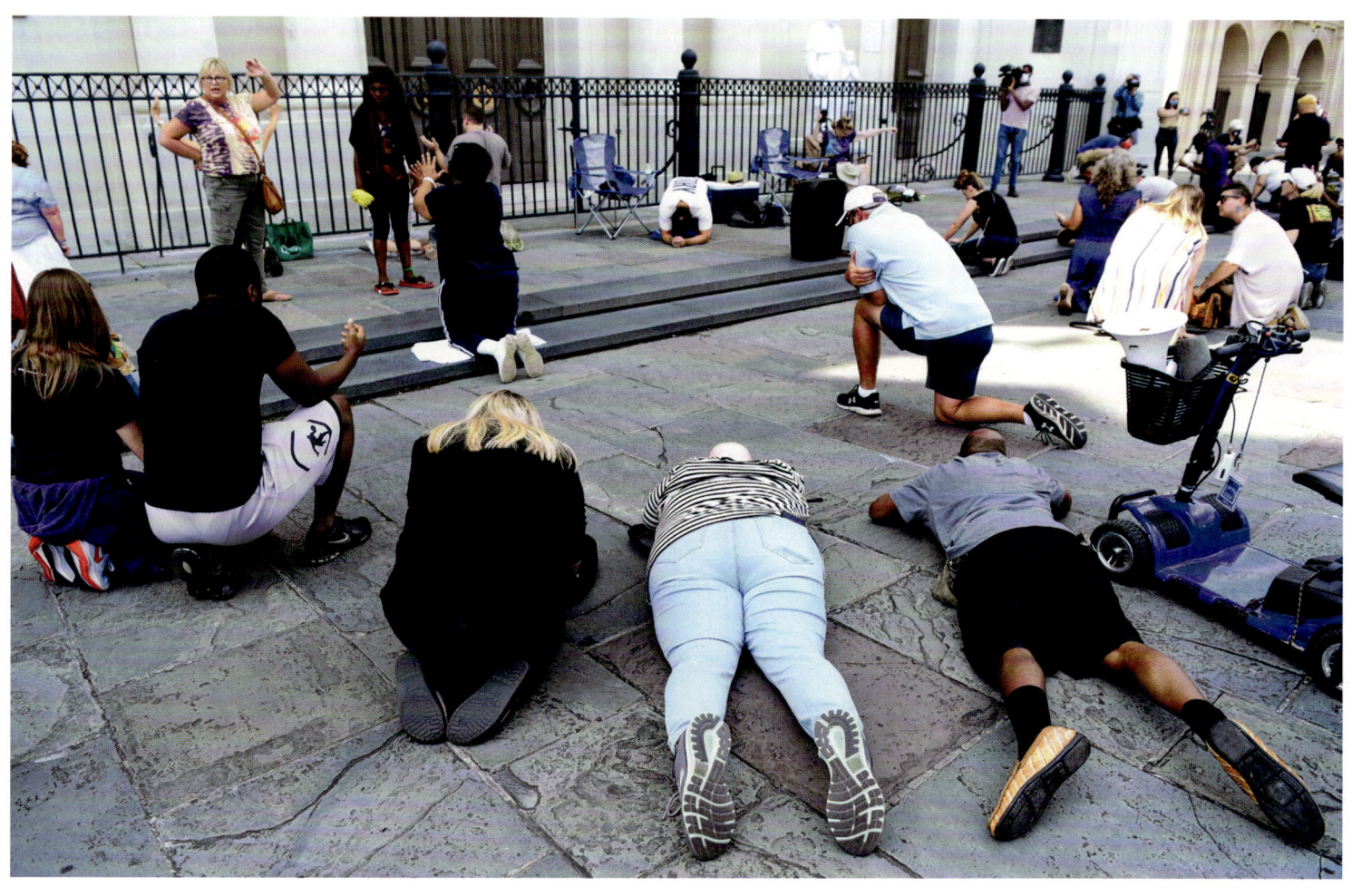

Christians gather to pray in front of St. Louis Cathedral for healing from racism and the COVID pandemic, 2020.

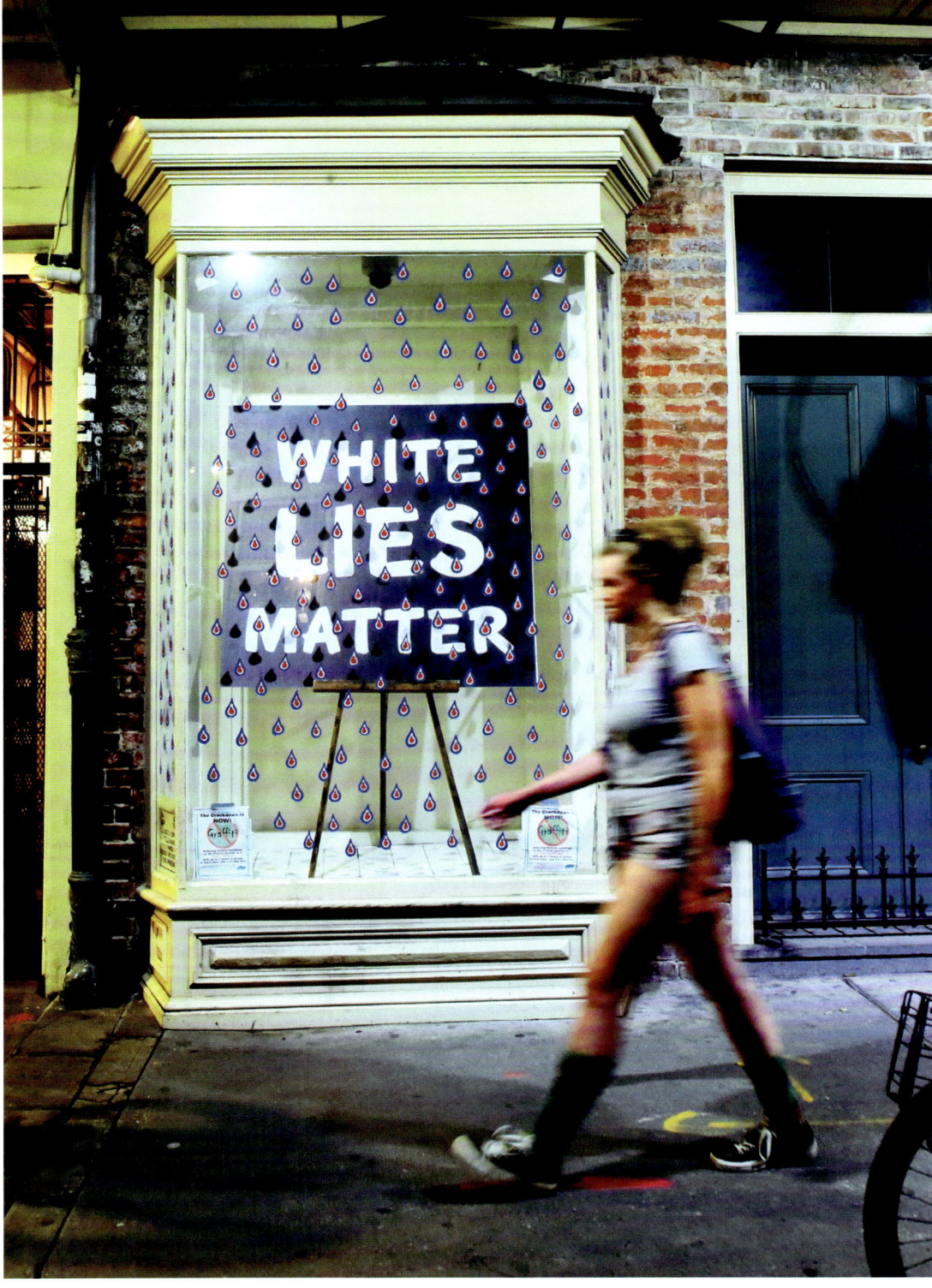

White Lies Matter sign on Decatur Street, 2017.

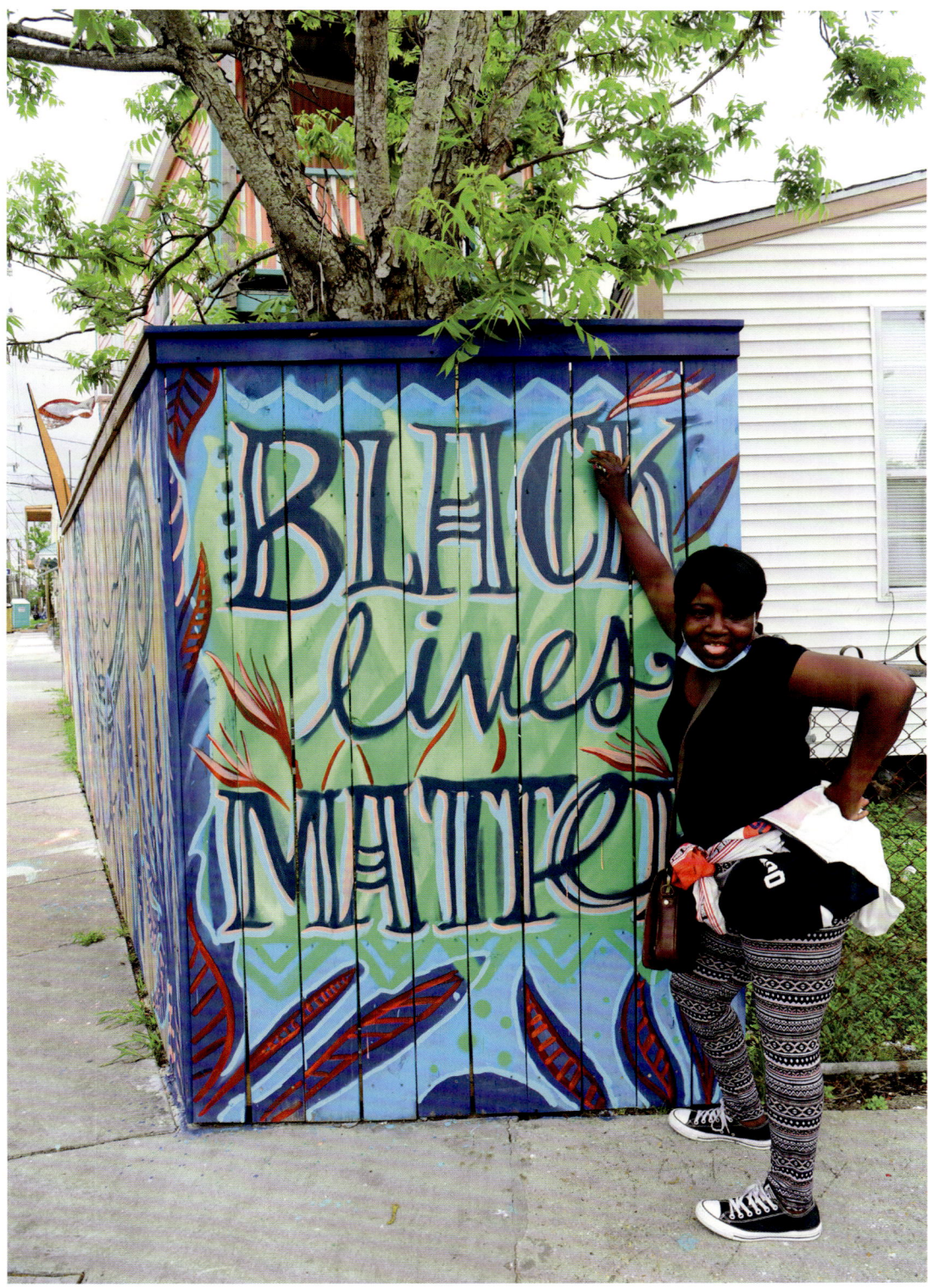

Black Lives Matter art on
St. Bernard Avenue, 2020.

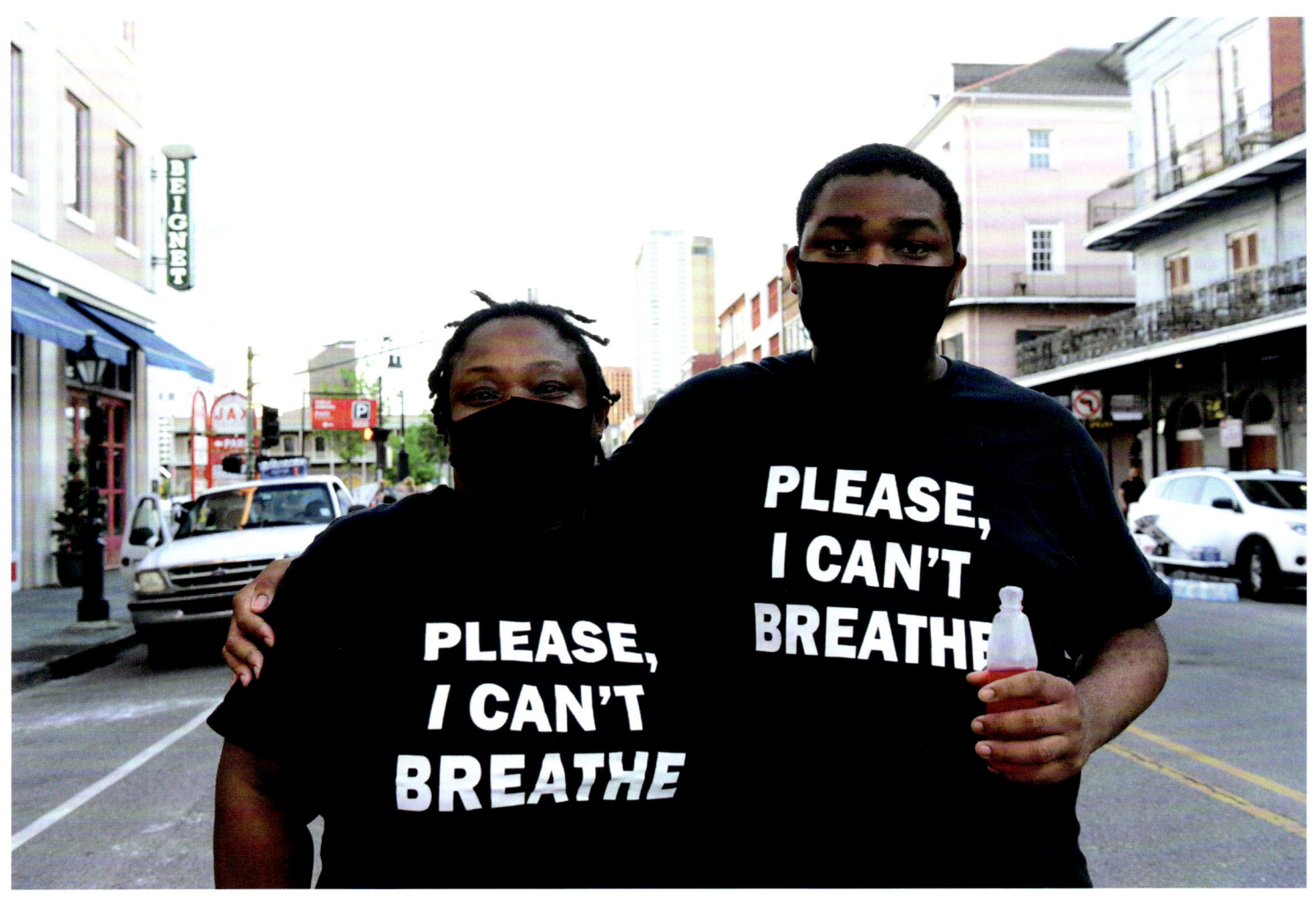

Black Lives Matter protesters take to the streets after the killing of George Floyd but practice social distancing during the pandemic, 2020.

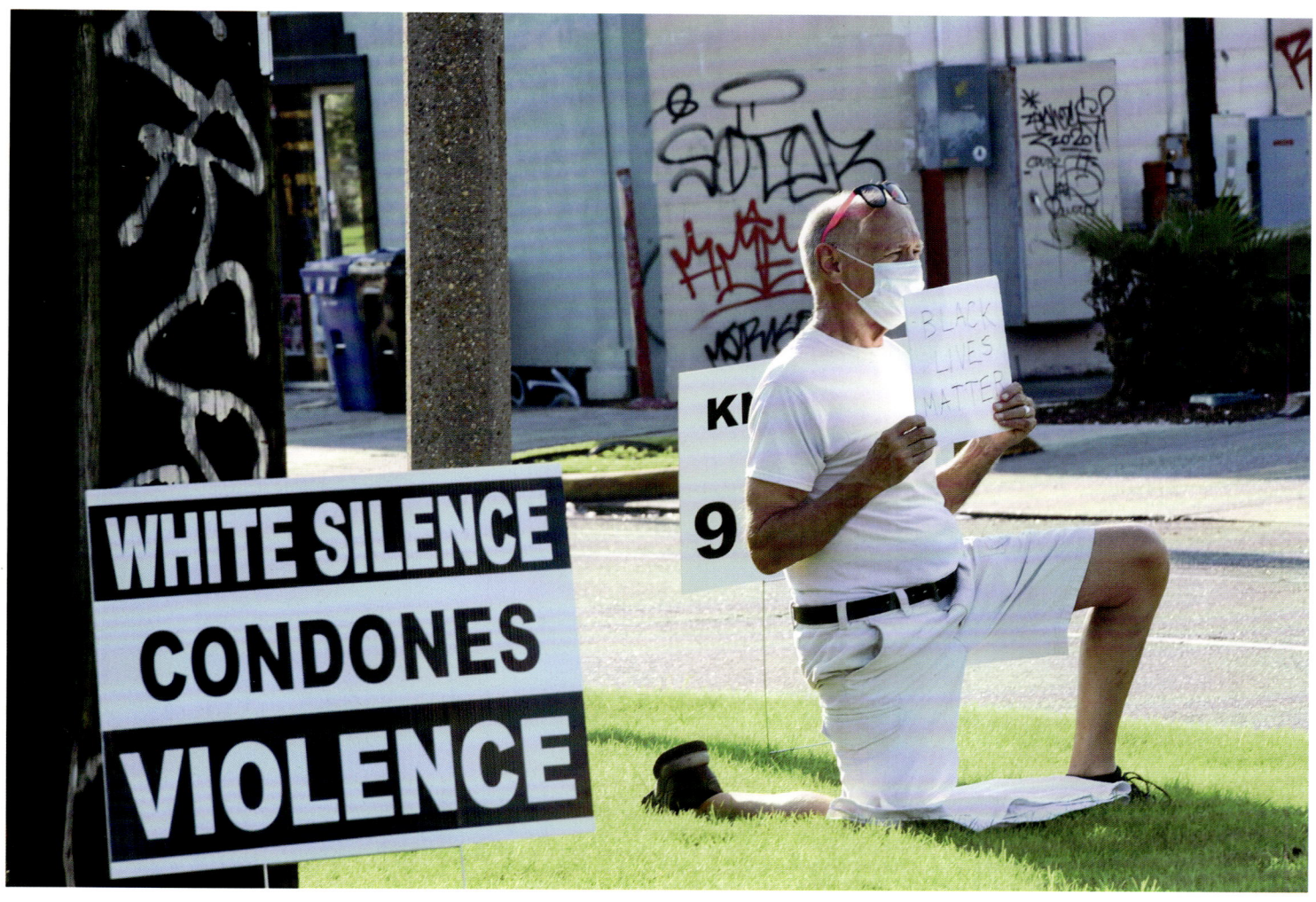

Linton Carney silently protests on St. Claude Avenue for several days in mid-June, going down on one knee for nine minutes, the number of minutes a police officer kneeled on George Floyd's neck, 2020.

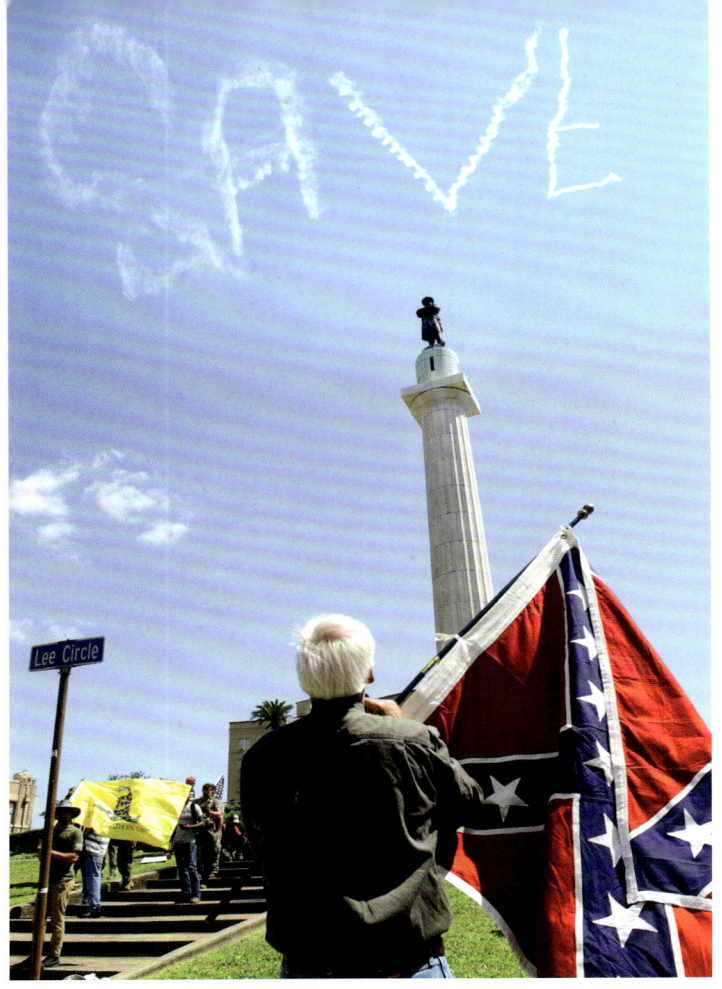

Save Our Monuments, a group dedicated to saving the city's Confederate monuments, commissions a skywriter to display "SAVE" above the statue of Gen. Robert E. Lee, 2017.

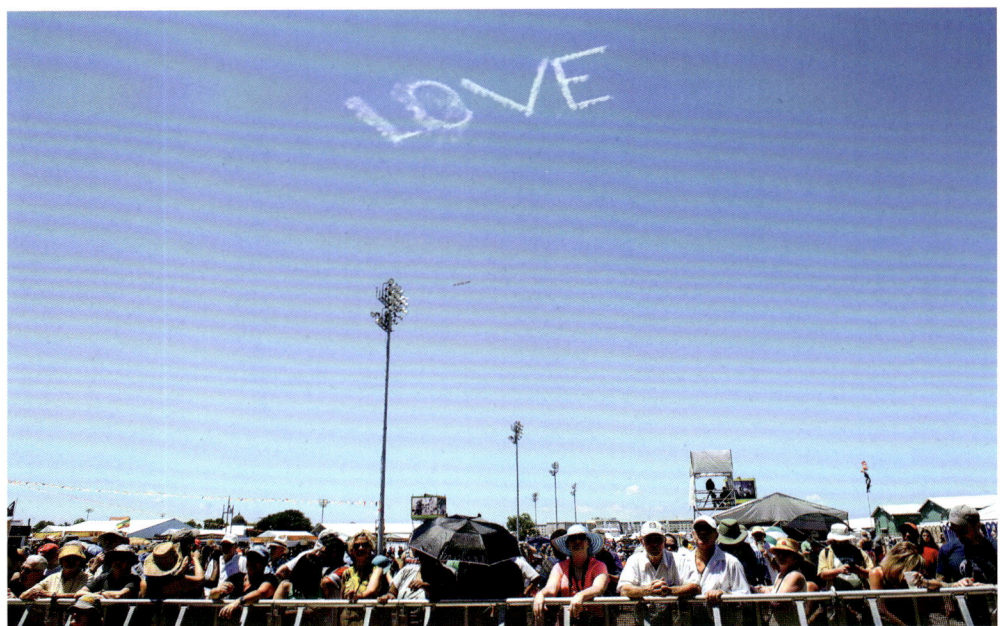

A skywriter creates "LOVE" over Jazz Fest, 2016.

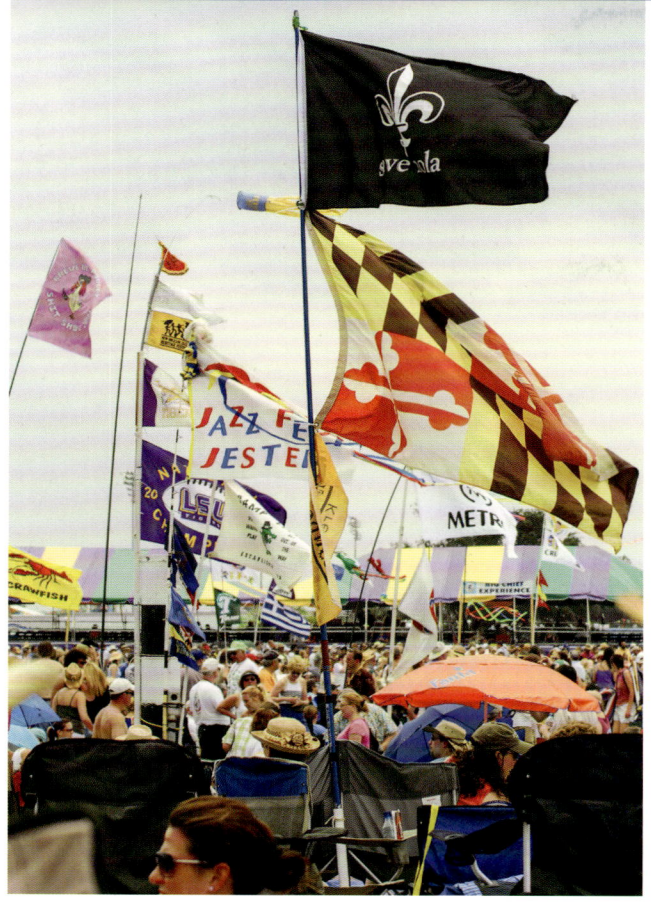

Music lovers fly flags at Jazz Fest, 2016.

Confederate and various flags fly near the Beauregard monument during its removal, 2017.

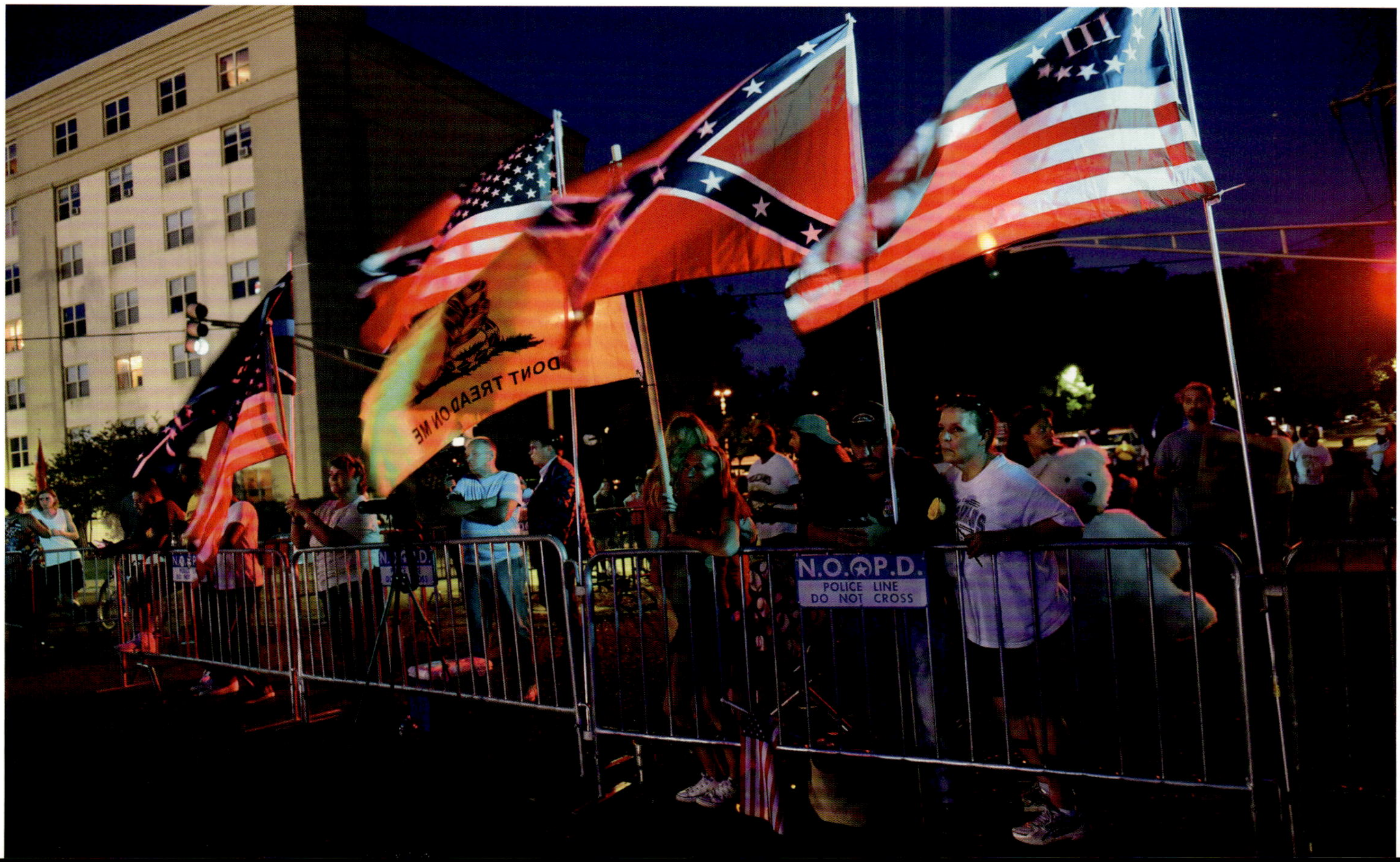

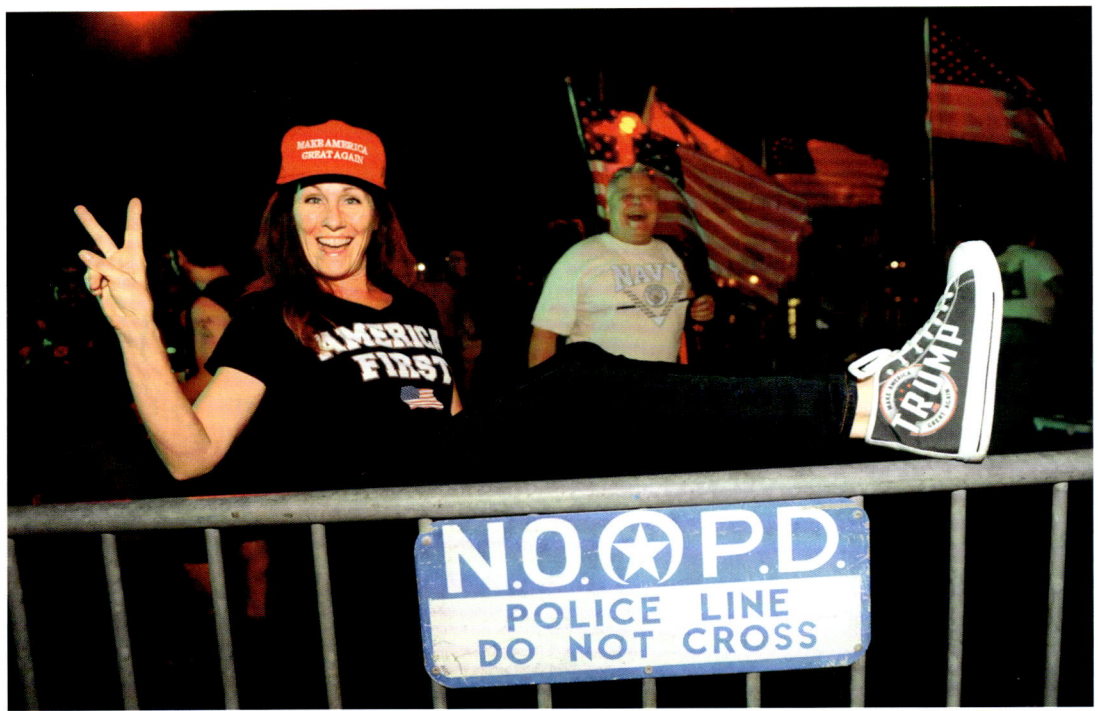

A Trump supporter shows off her pride while protesting the removal of the monument of Gen. Beauregard, 2017.

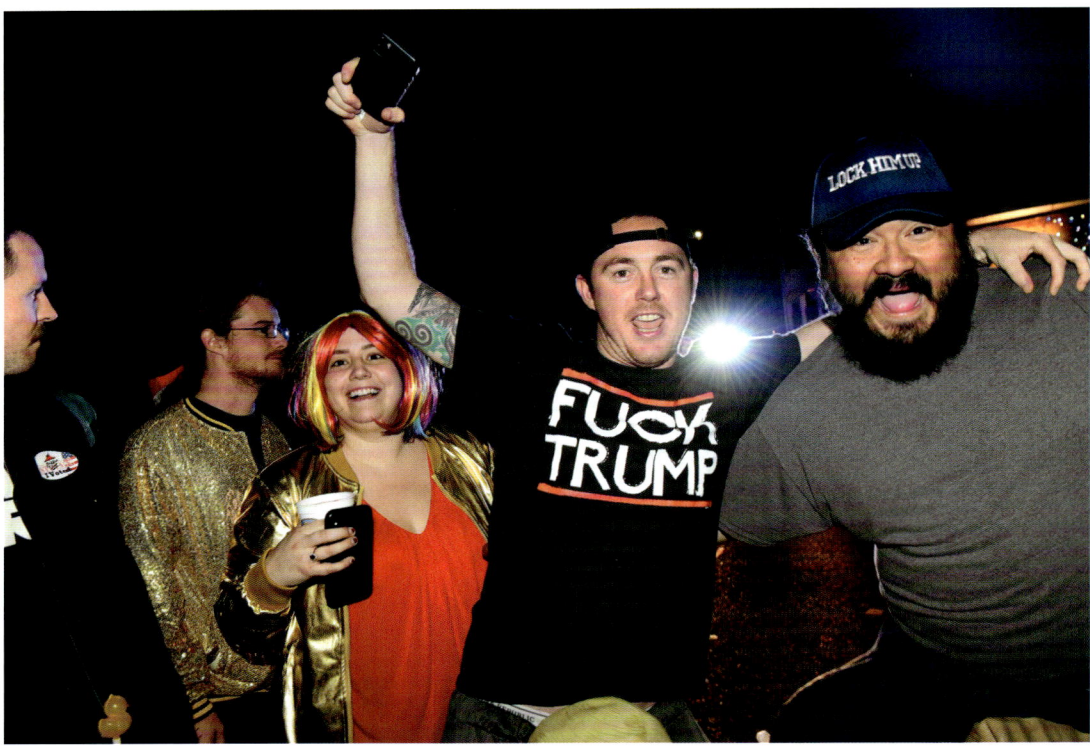

Trump opponents parade with Krewe du Vieux, which was themed "Erection 2020," 2020.

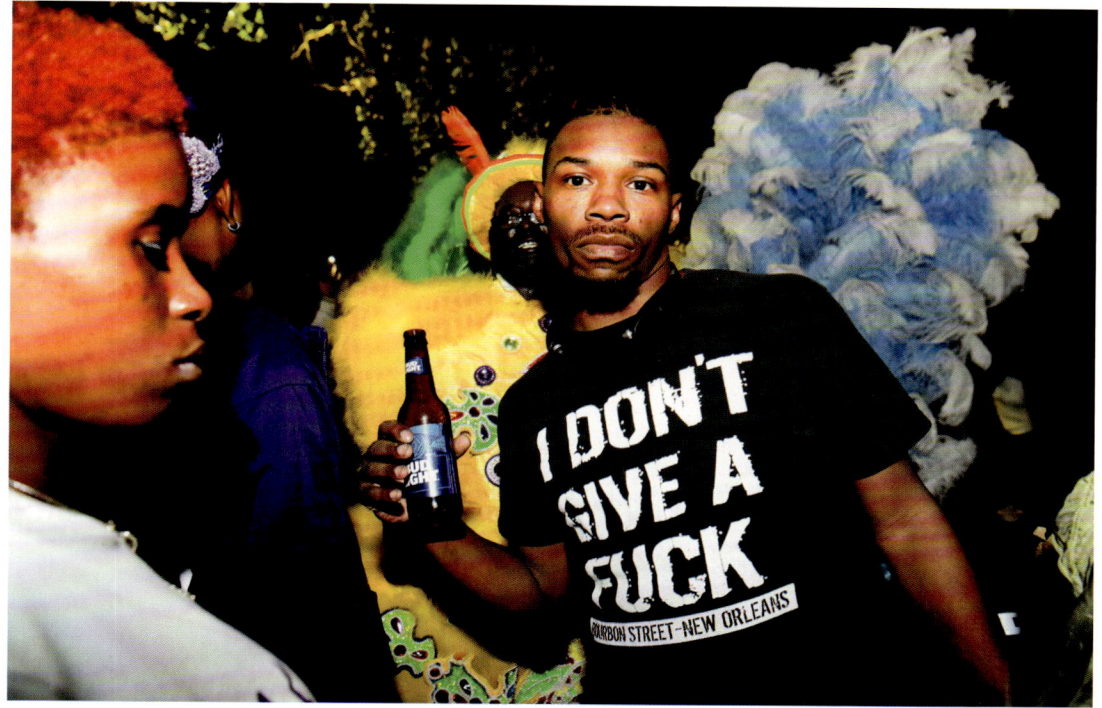

As seen on St. Joseph's Night in Central City, 2019. A man wears a T-shirt to describe his feelings.

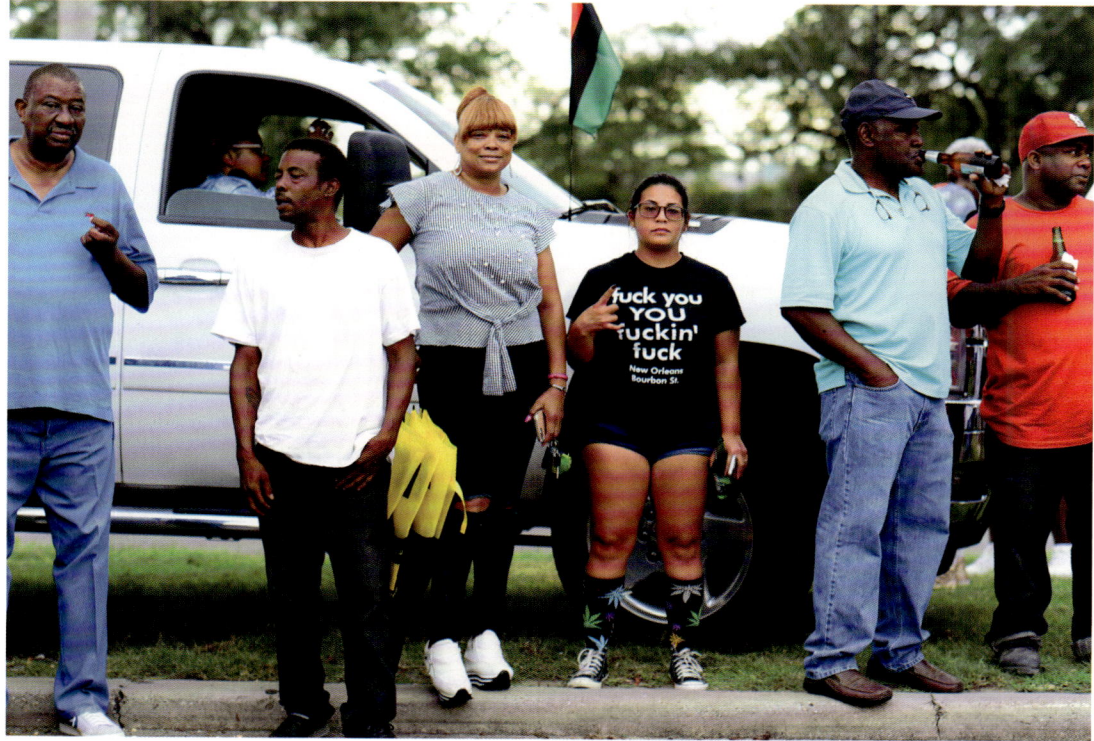

As seen at a second line in the Seventh Ward, 2018. A woman wears a T-shirt emblazoned with the words made famous by blogger Ashley Morris in a rant to outsiders who questioned whether New Orleans should be rebuilt after Hurricane Katrina.

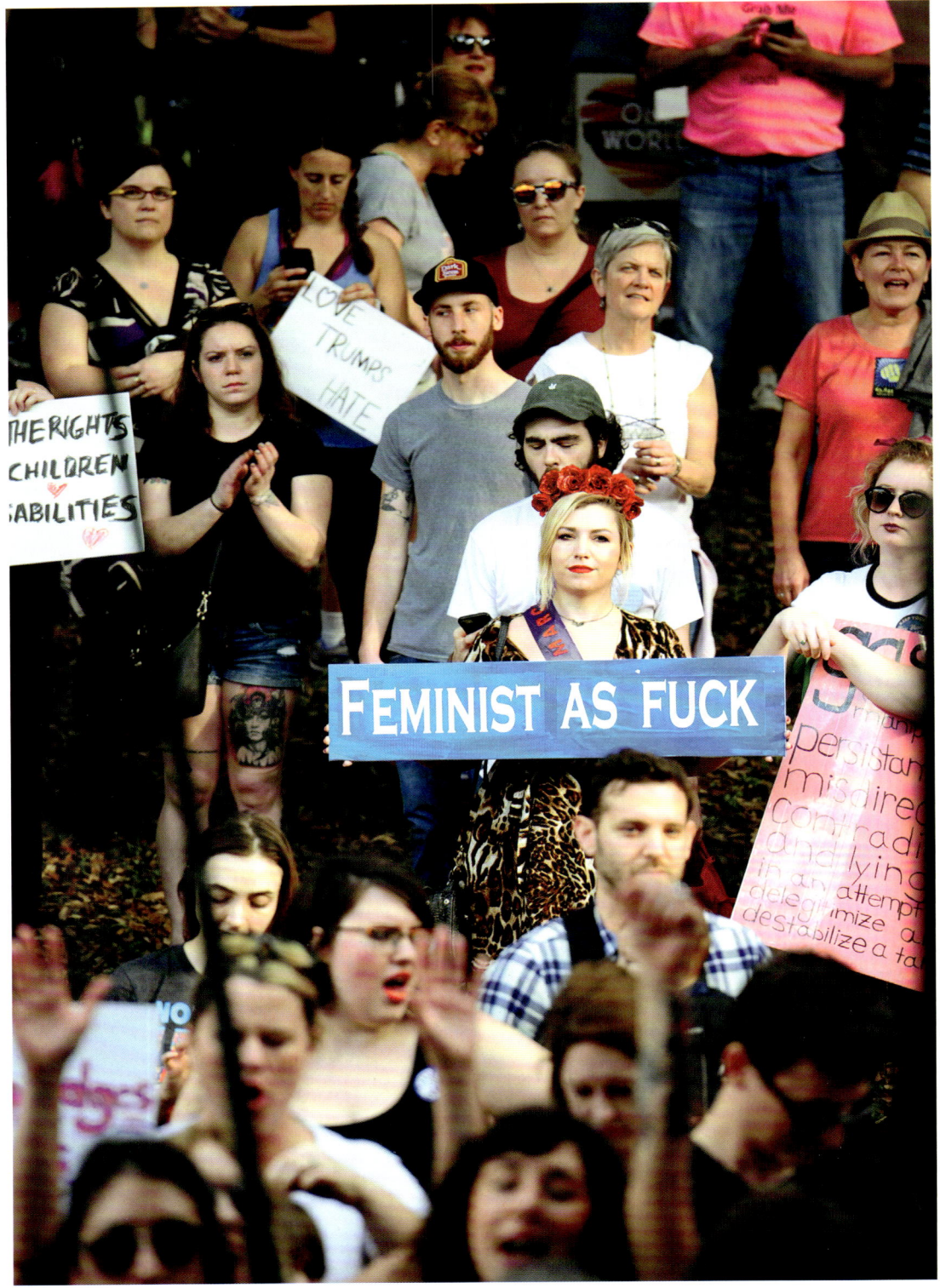

A woman holds up a sign at a protest, prompted by the anti-women policy positions and rhetoric of the recently inaugurated Donald J. Trump, 2017.

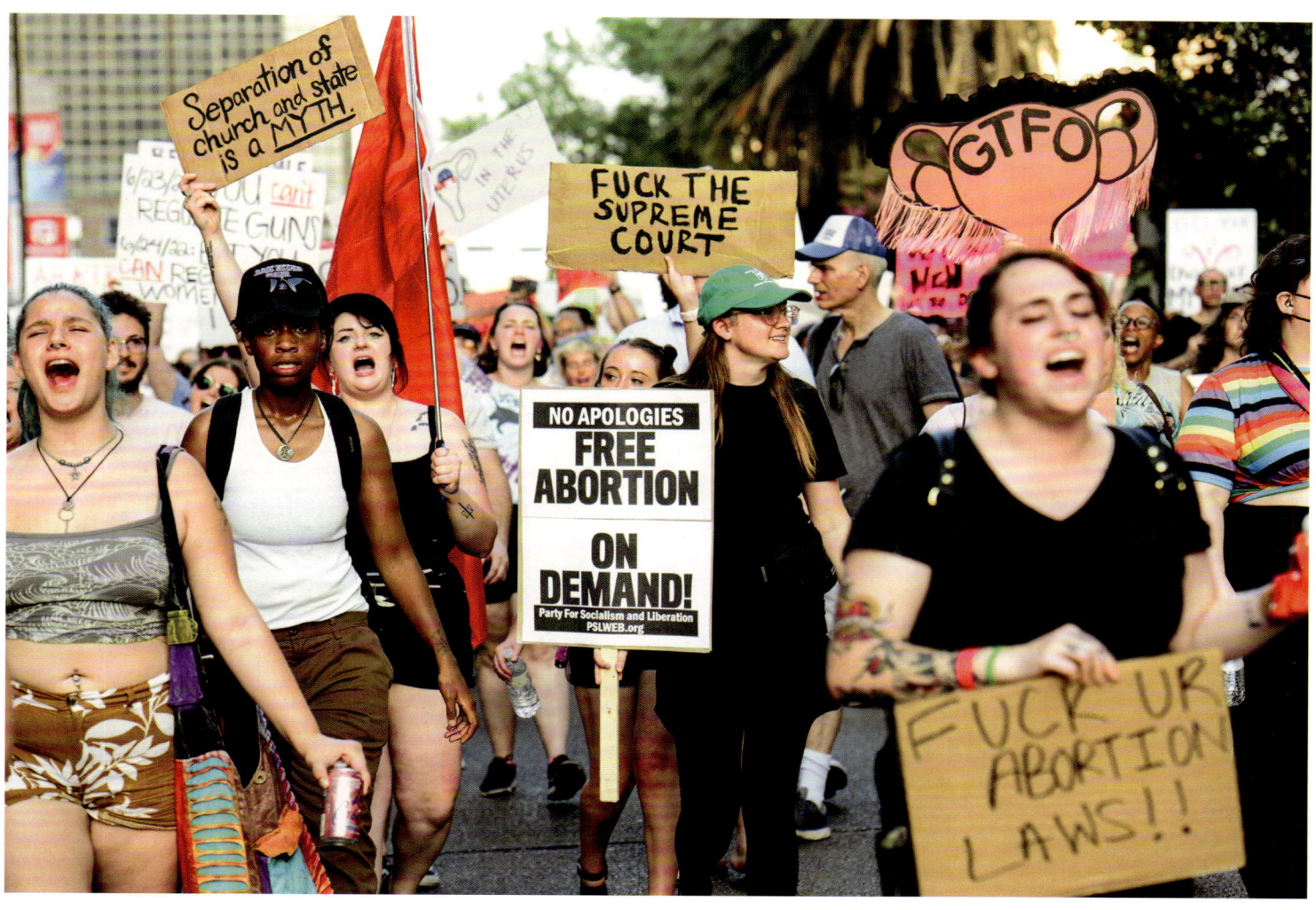

Pro-choice supporters march in a large protest after the Supreme Court's decision to overturn *Roe v. Wade,* 2022.

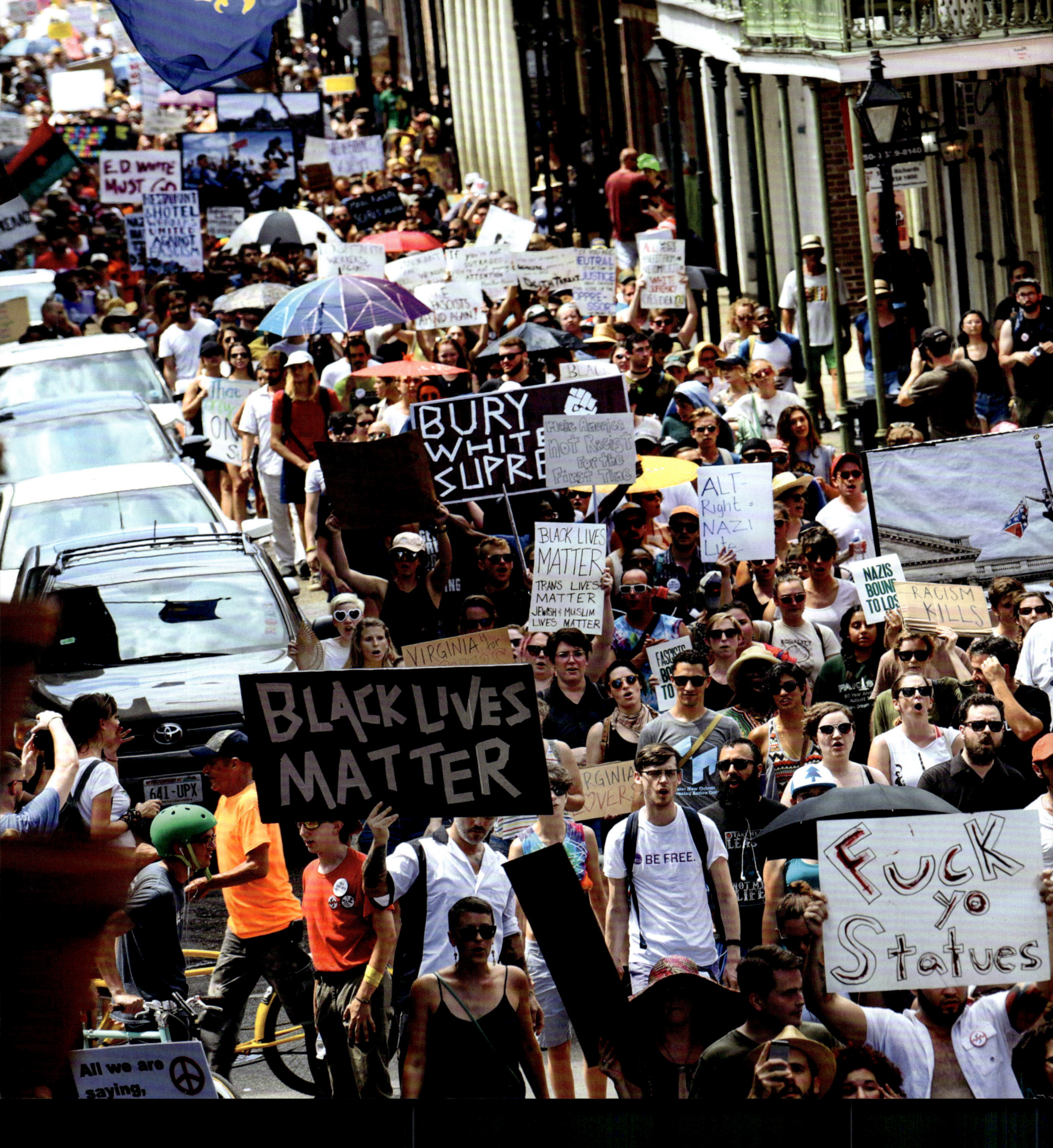

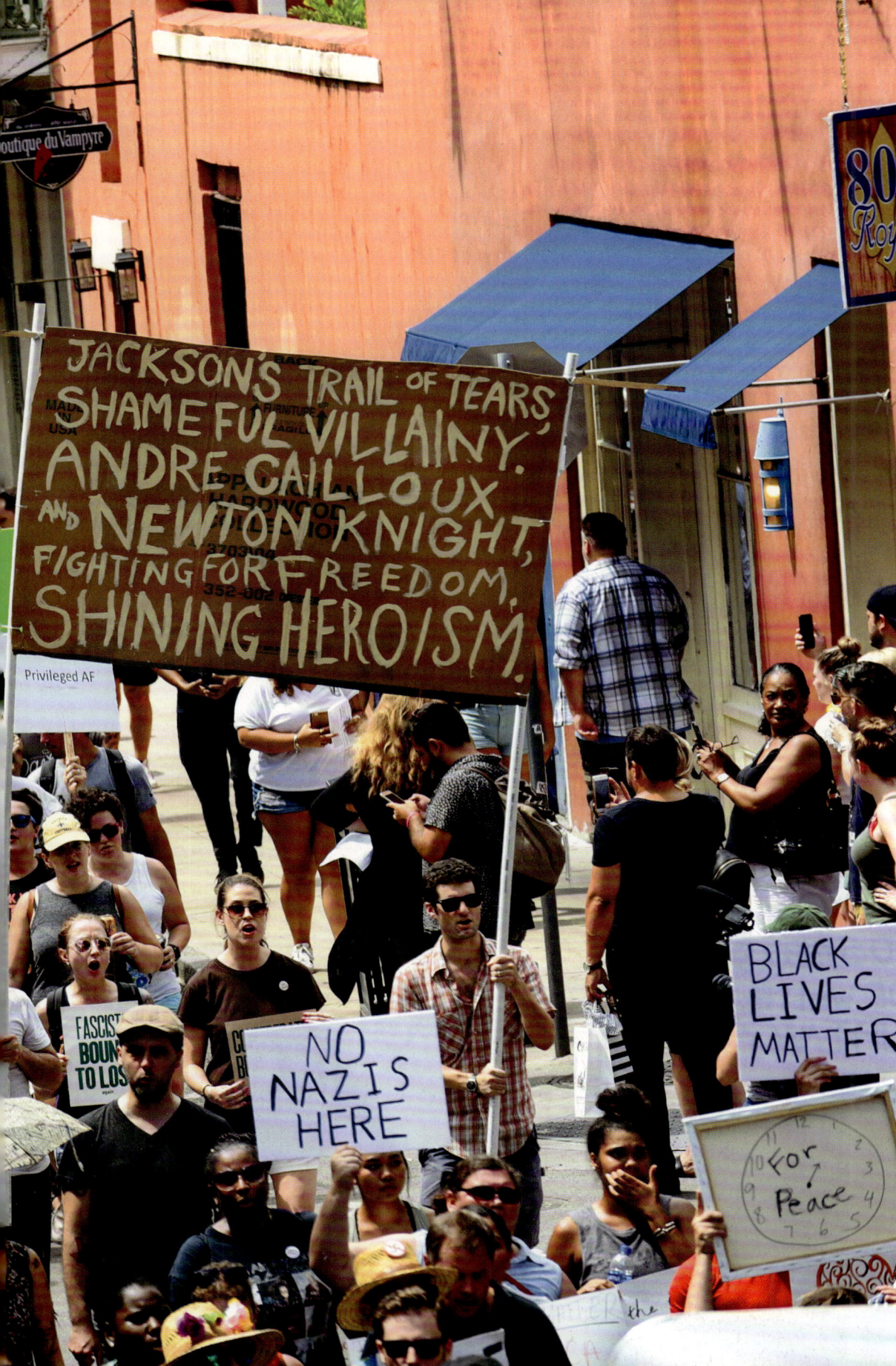

The Take 'Em Down NOLA protest winds through the French Quarter, 2017. Take 'Em Down NOLA is the grassroots activist group formed with the mission of taking down all Confederate monuments and symbols of white supremacy in the city.

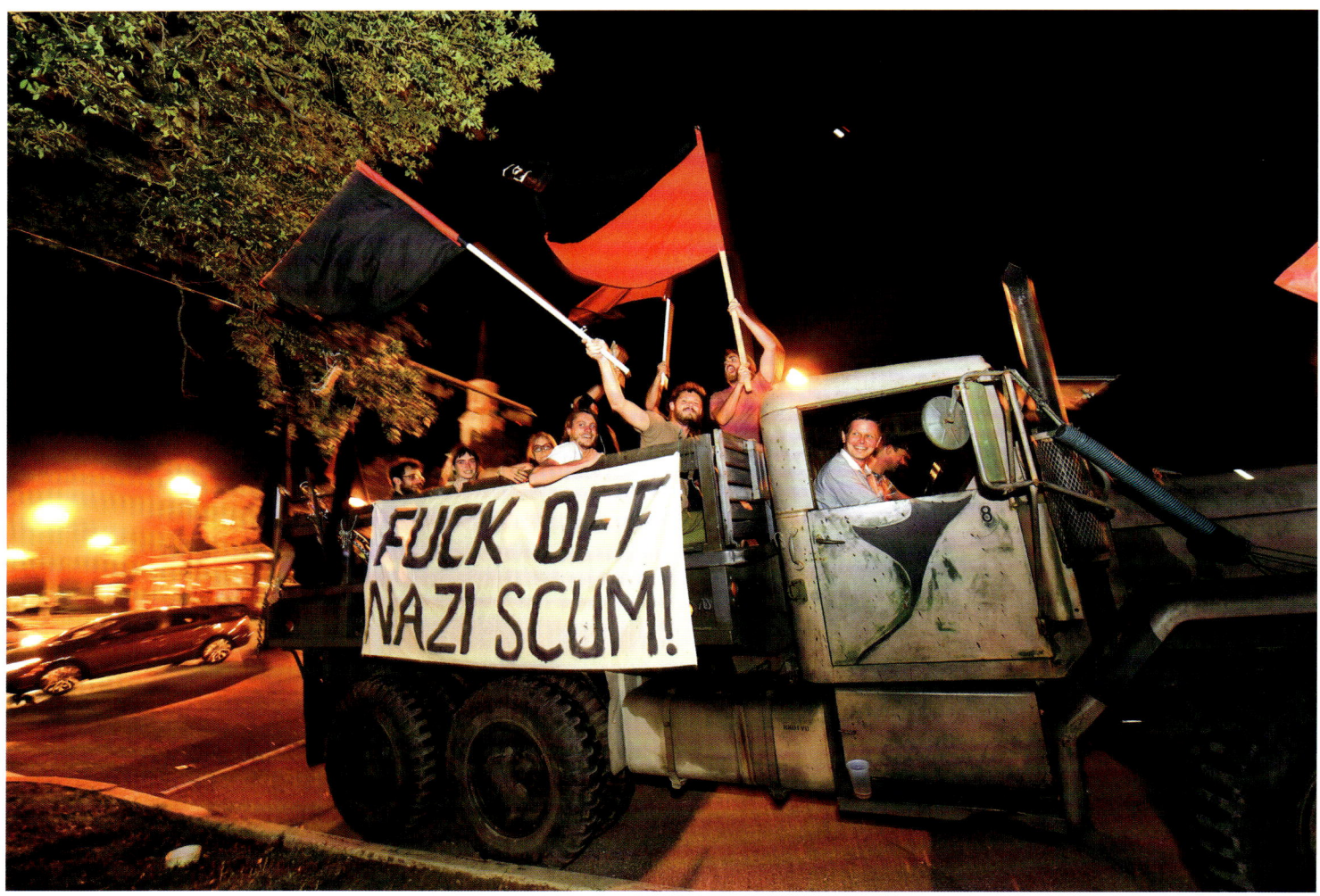

Counterprotesters arrive at the Jefferson Davis monument to confront protesters fighting the statue's removal, 2017. Davis was the president of the Confederate States from 1861–1865; his statue had stood on Jefferson Davis Parkway for 105 years. In 2020, the city renamed the street Norman C. Francis Parkway, after the longtime president of Xavier University, a historically Black university, which is located near the southwestern end of the parkway.

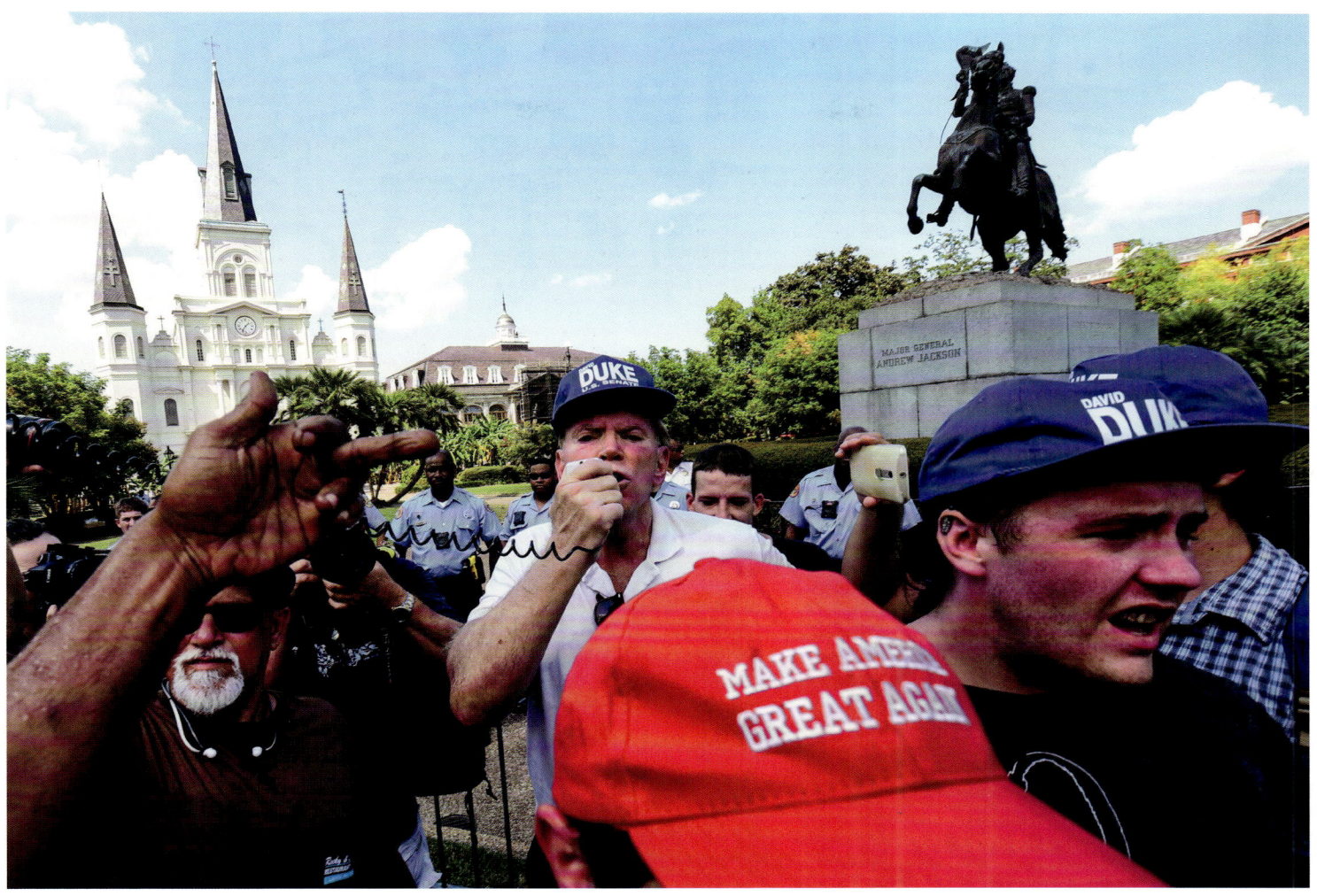

Take 'Em Down and Black Lives Matter protesters confront David Duke, who crashed their demonstration in Jackson Square, 2016. Duke, born in 1950, is a white supremacist, antisemitic conspiracy theorist, far-right politician, convicted felon, and former Grand Wizard of the Ku Klux Klan.

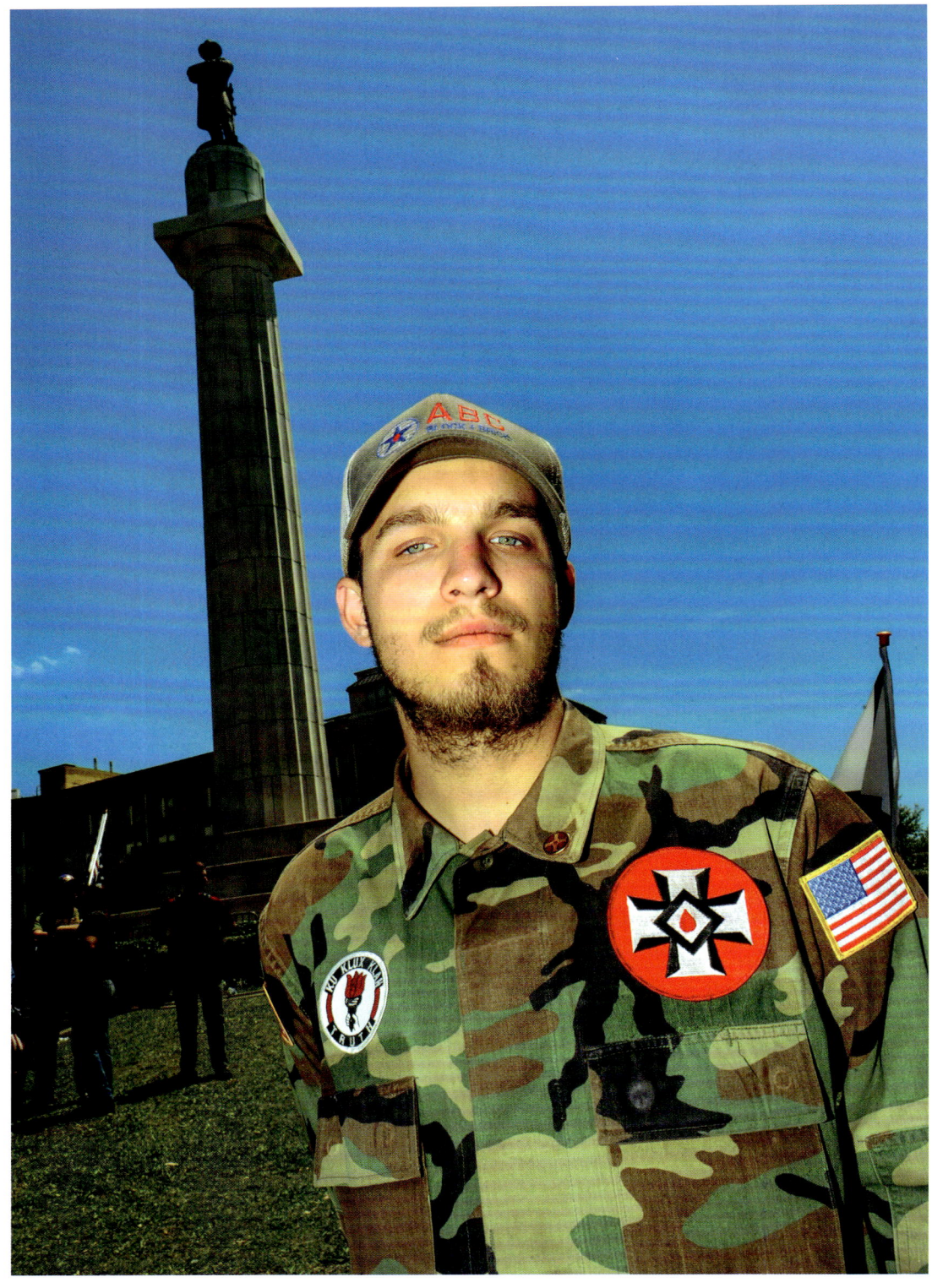

A Ku Klux Klan member poses in front of the Gen. Robert E. Lee monument, 2017.

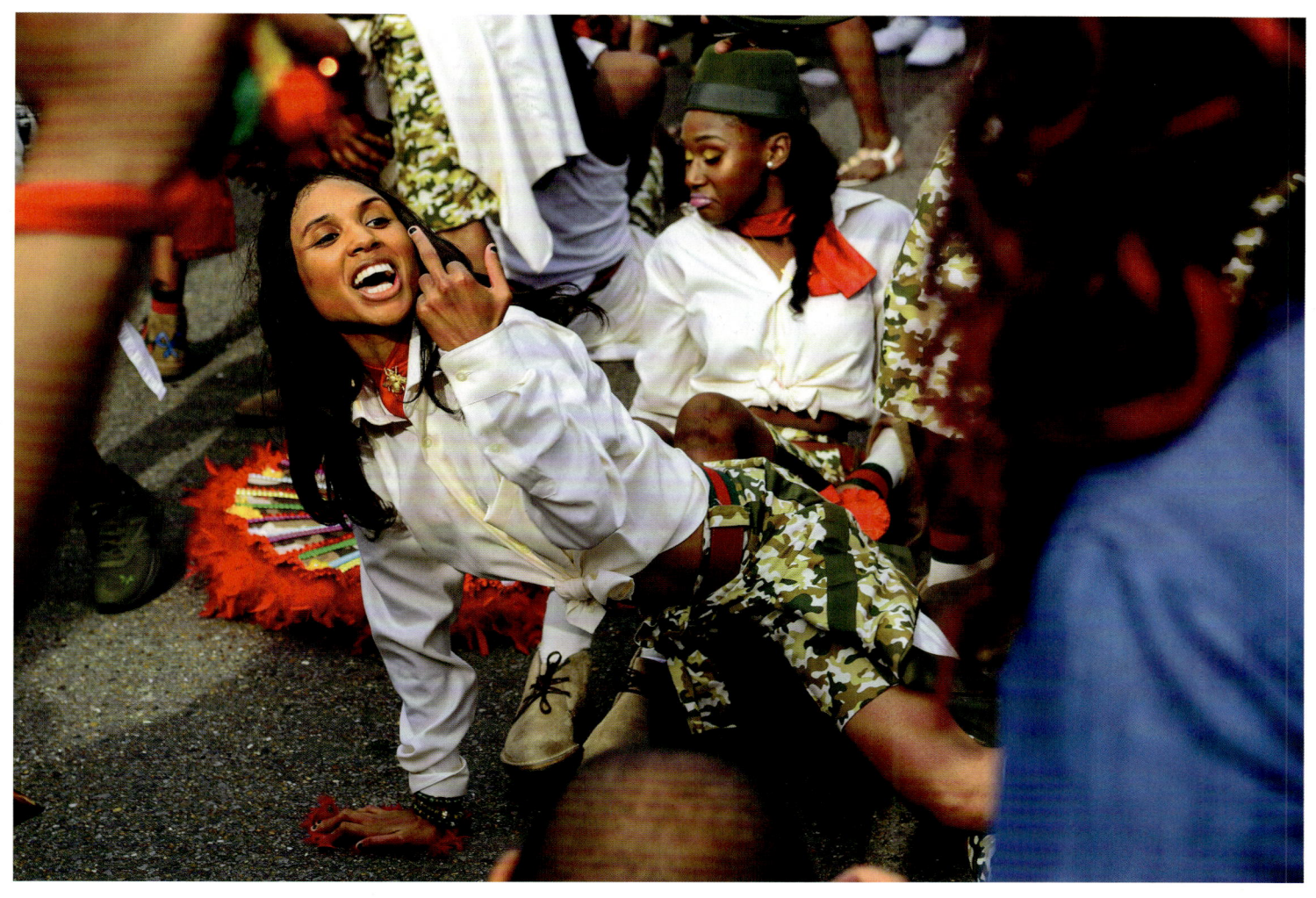

Shanté Savanto dances on the ground during the Treme Sidewalk Steppers' second line, 2018.

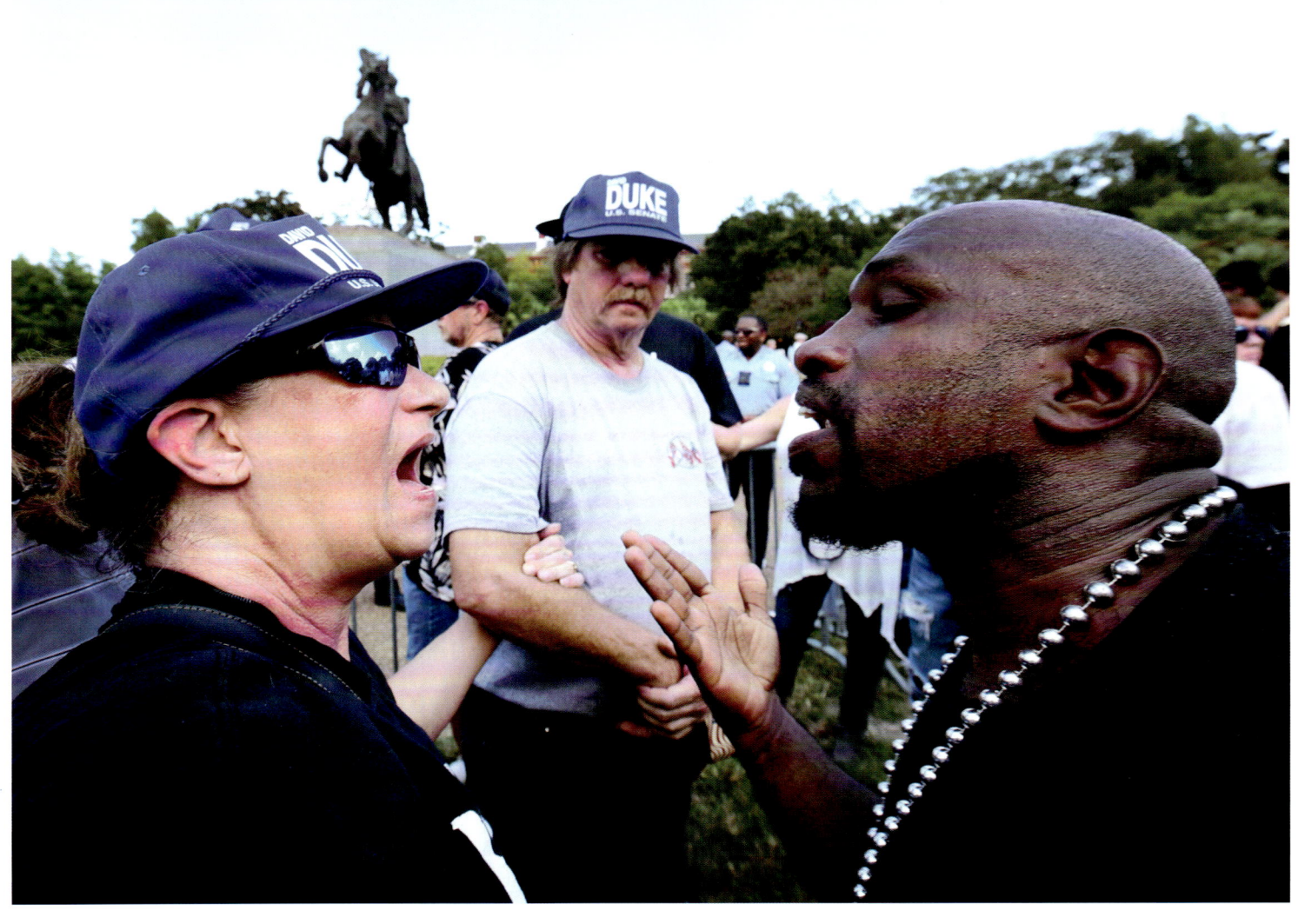

David Duke supporters argue with a Take 'Em Down protester in Jackson Square, where activists tried but failed to remove the statue of Andrew Jackson, 2016.

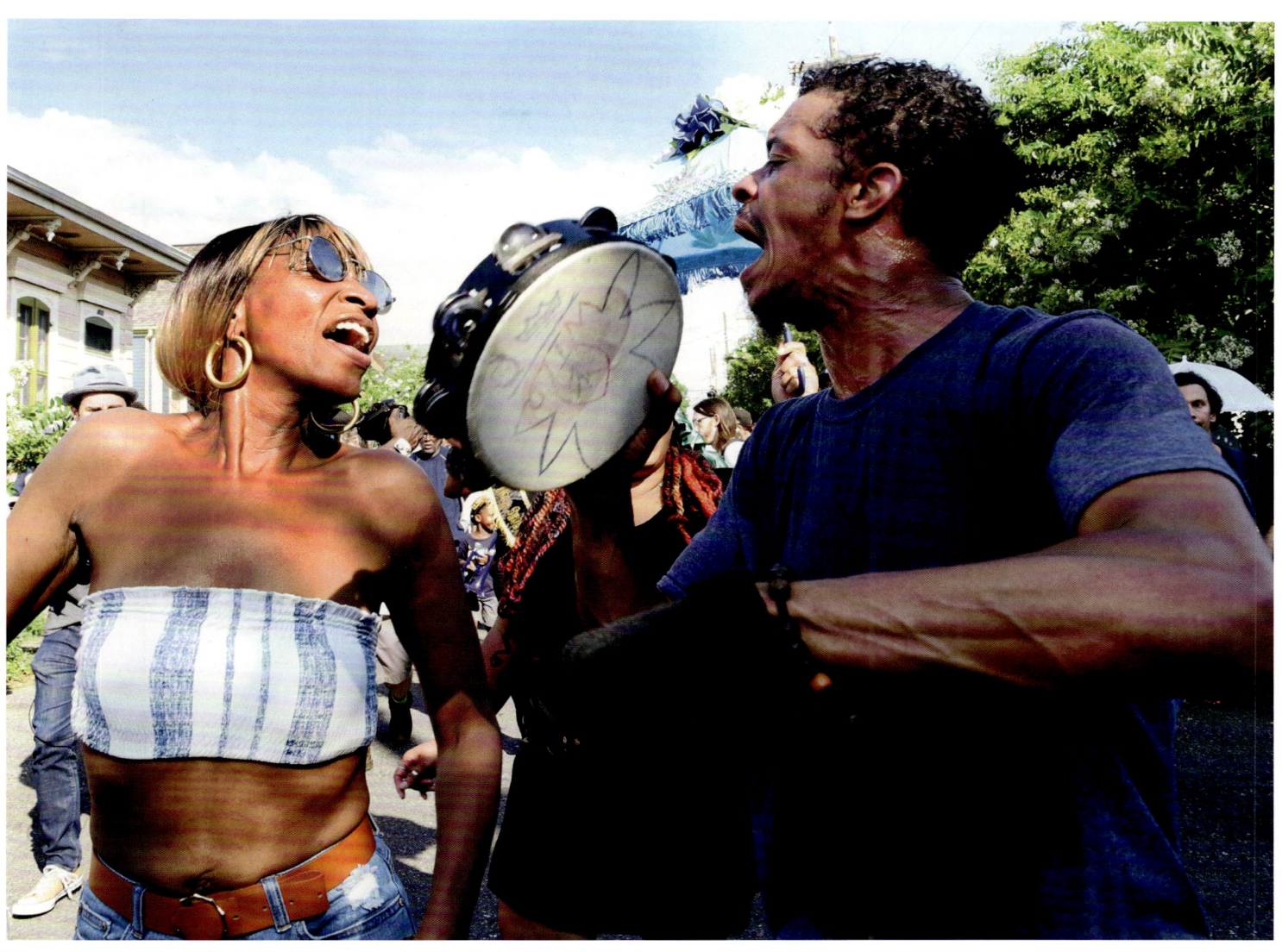

Judy "Oohpoopahdoo" Hill and her nephew sing during the memorial second line for musician Dr. John in Tremé, 2019.

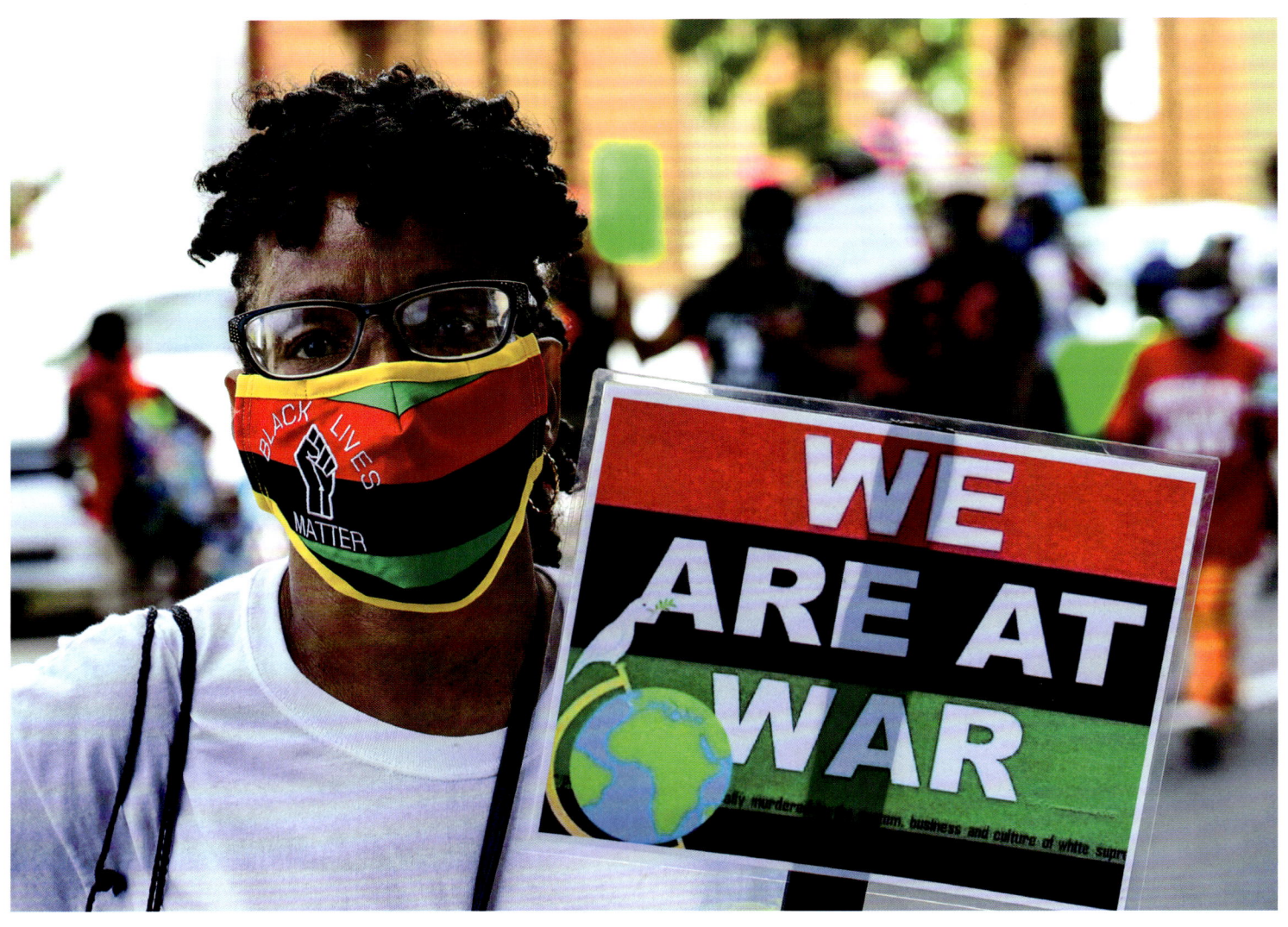

Janice Kimble, organizer of Treme Kids Stop the Violence March, 2020.

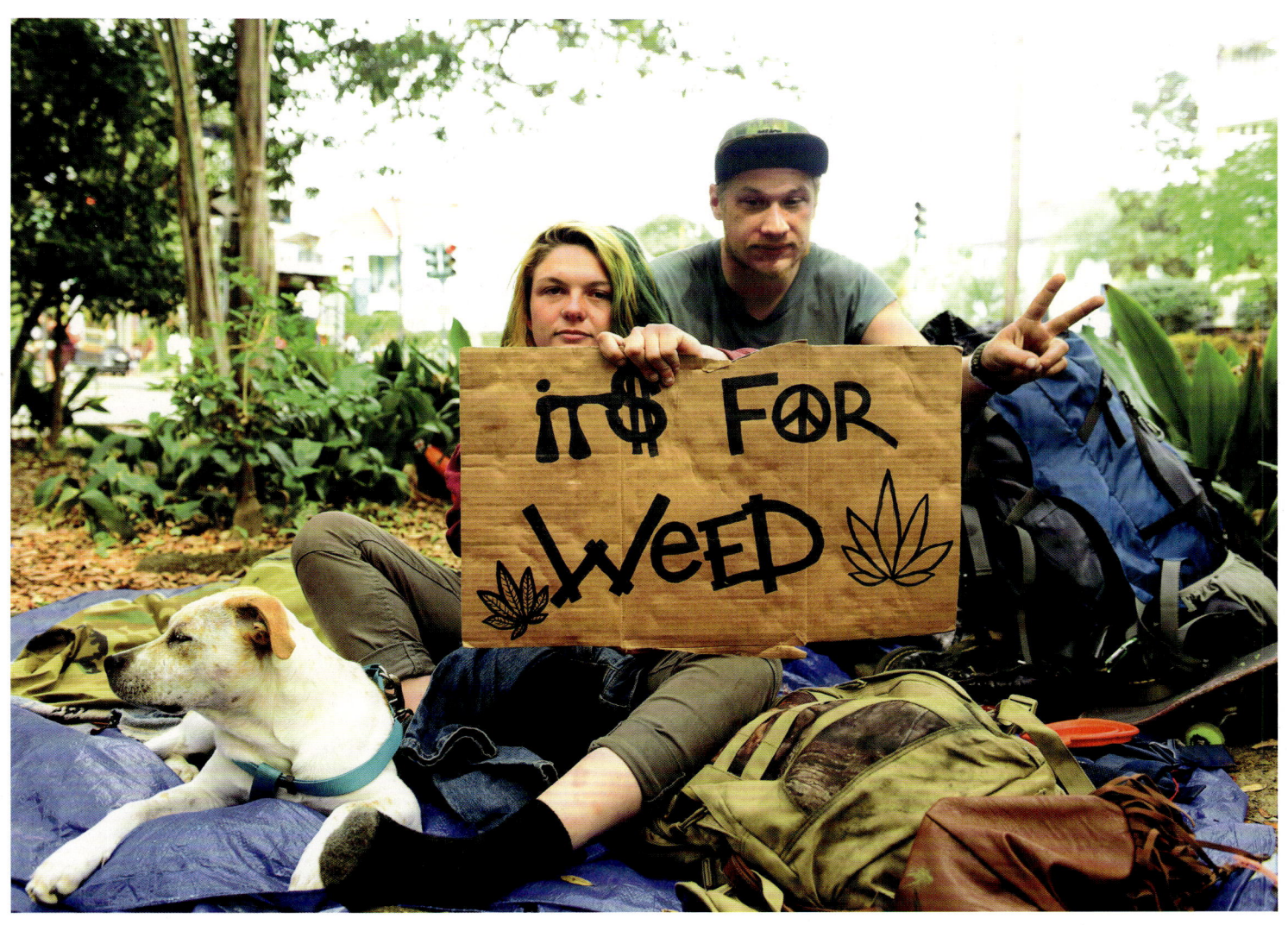

"Travelers," who hop trains and travel to New Orleans every fall, flash peace signs and hold up money-for-weed posters, 2017.

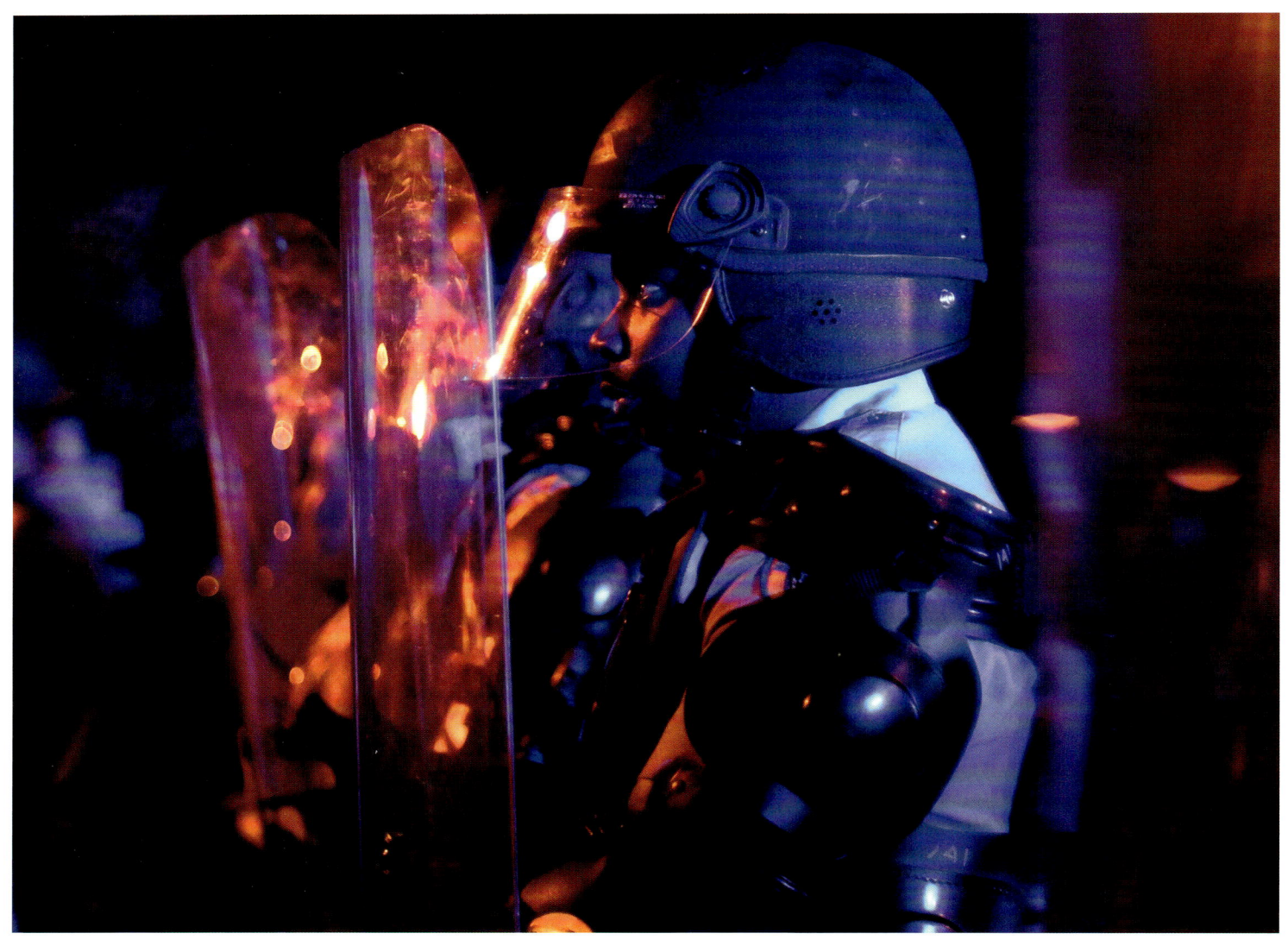

Policemen on the I-610 flyover gear up to confront Black Lives Matter protesters after the murder of George Floyd, 2020.

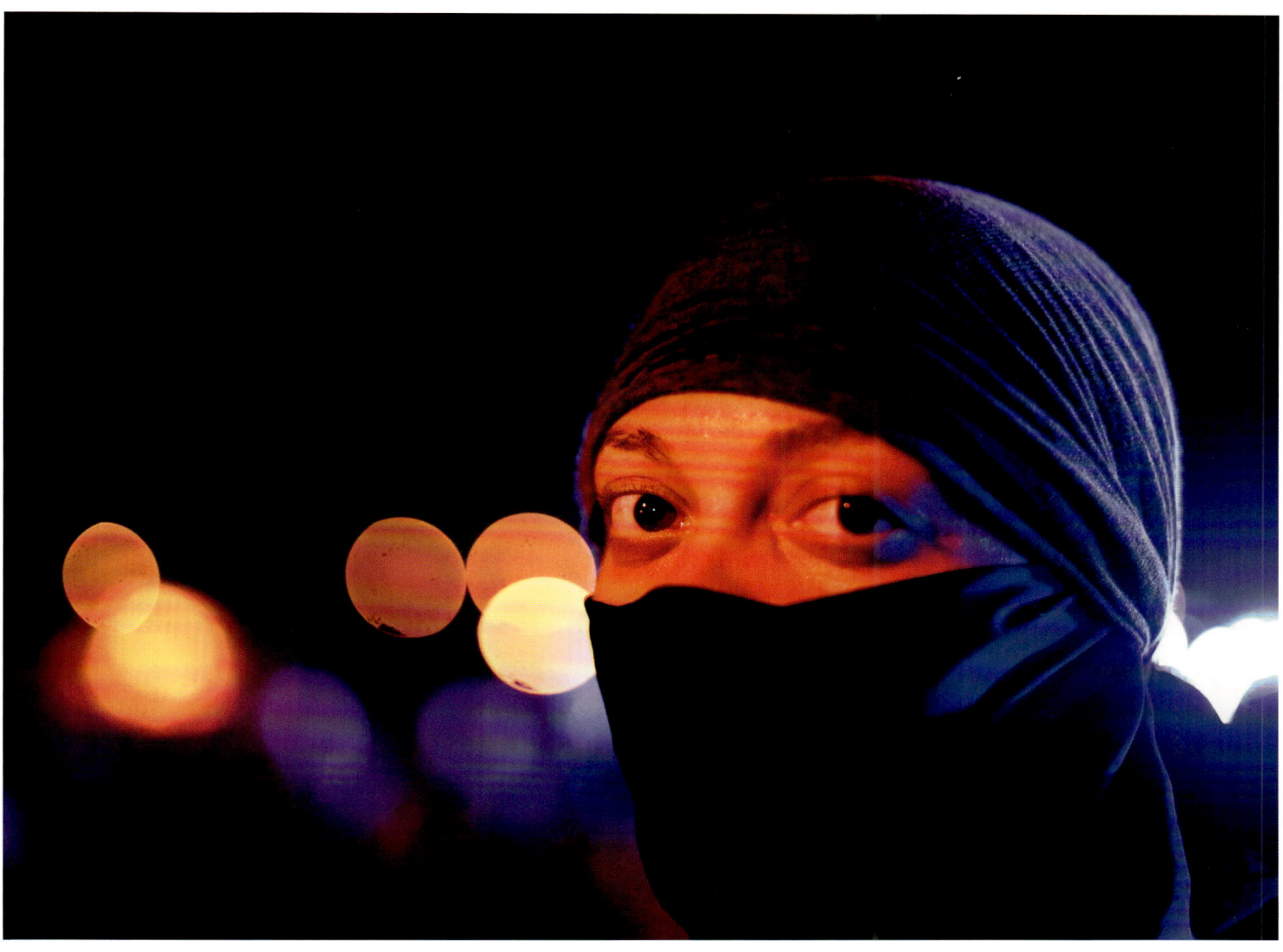

A protester at a Black Lives Matter march on the I-610 flyover held after the murder of George Floyd, 2020.

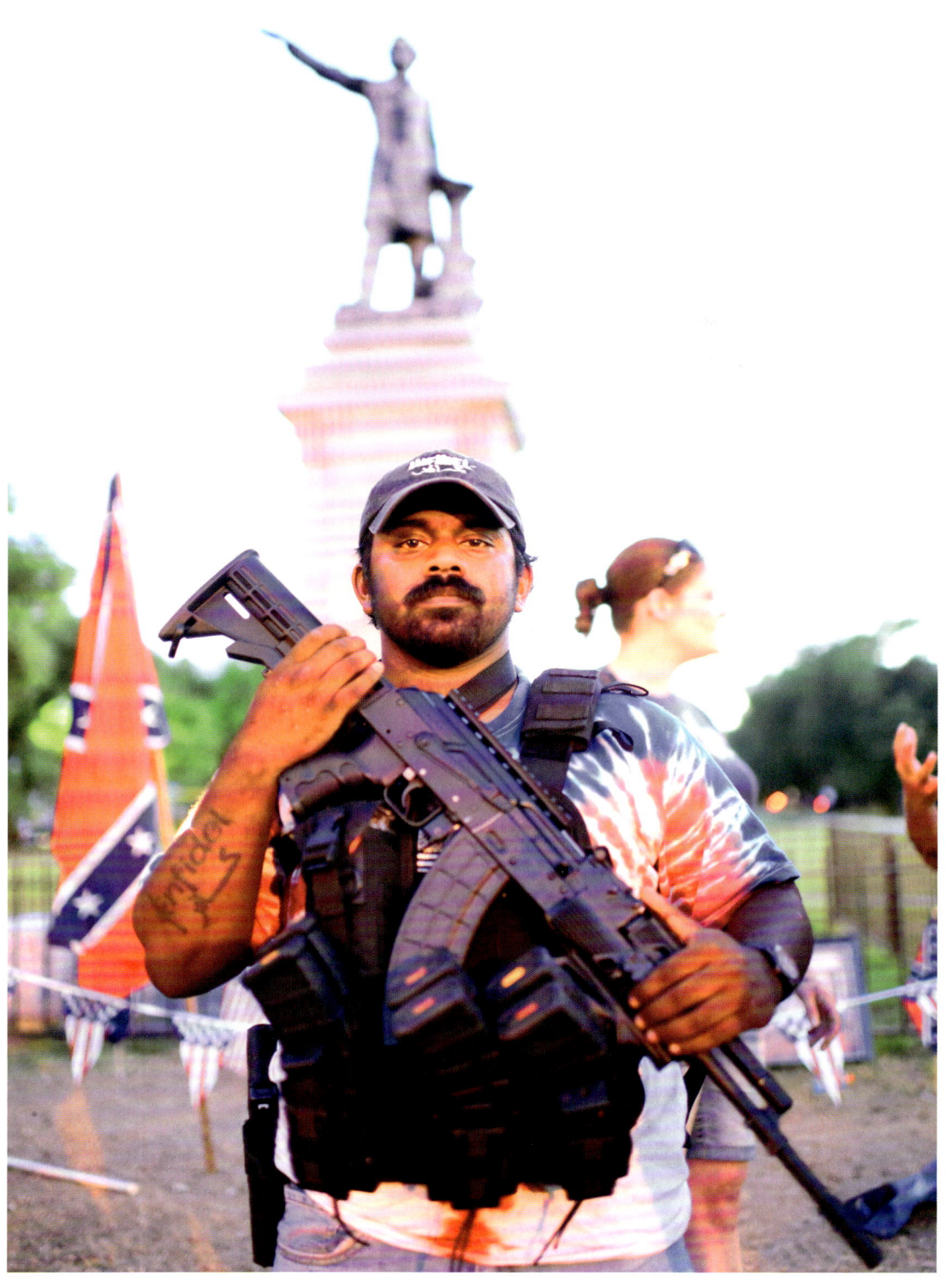

Kanjaksha Katta arms himself with a long rifle while he protests the removal of the monument of Confederate president Jefferson Davis, 2017.

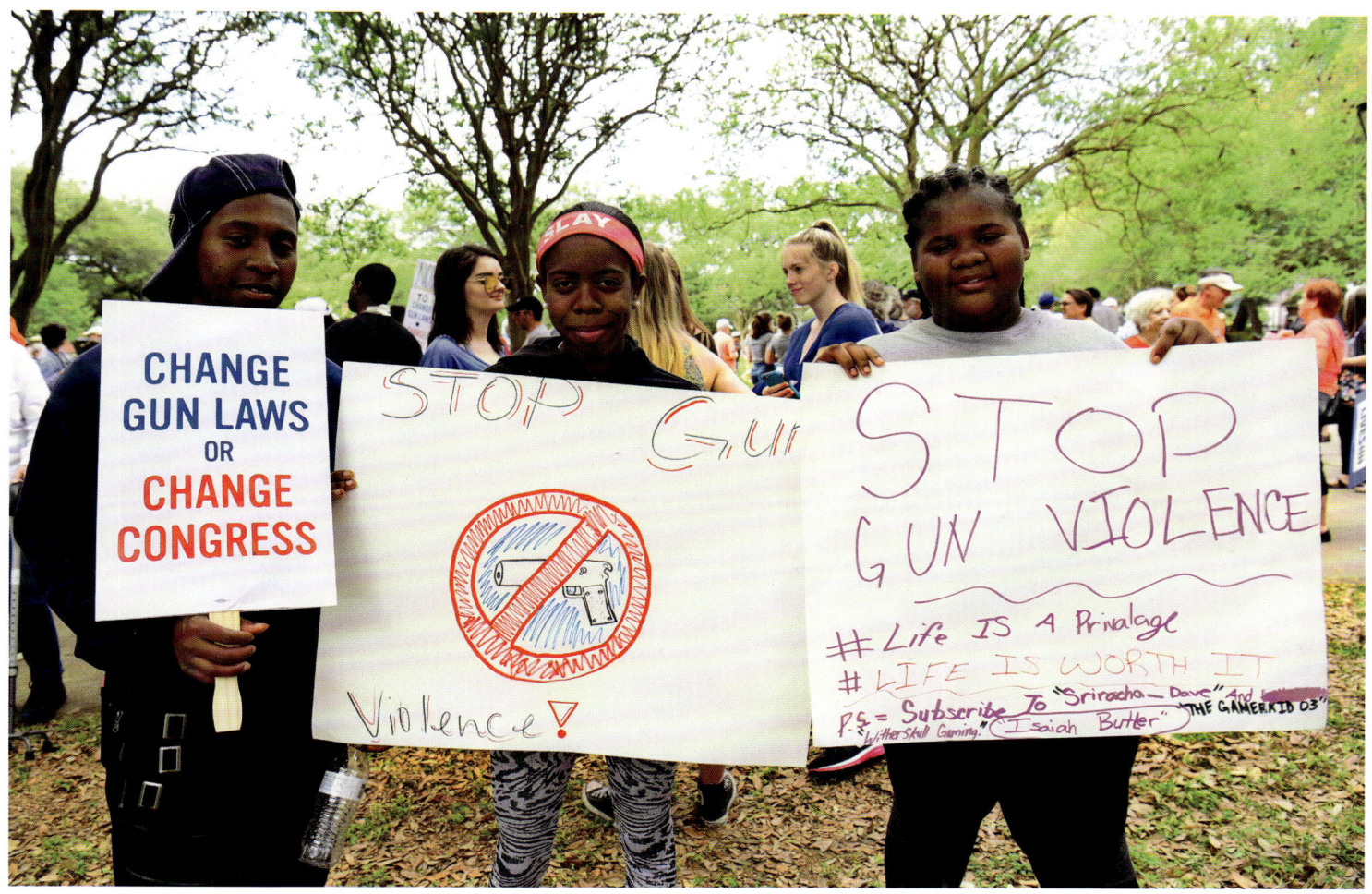

Young people participate in the March for Our Lives protest, 2018. March for Our Lives, born out of a tragic school shooting, is a youth-led movement dedicated to promoting civic engagement and action to end gun violence.

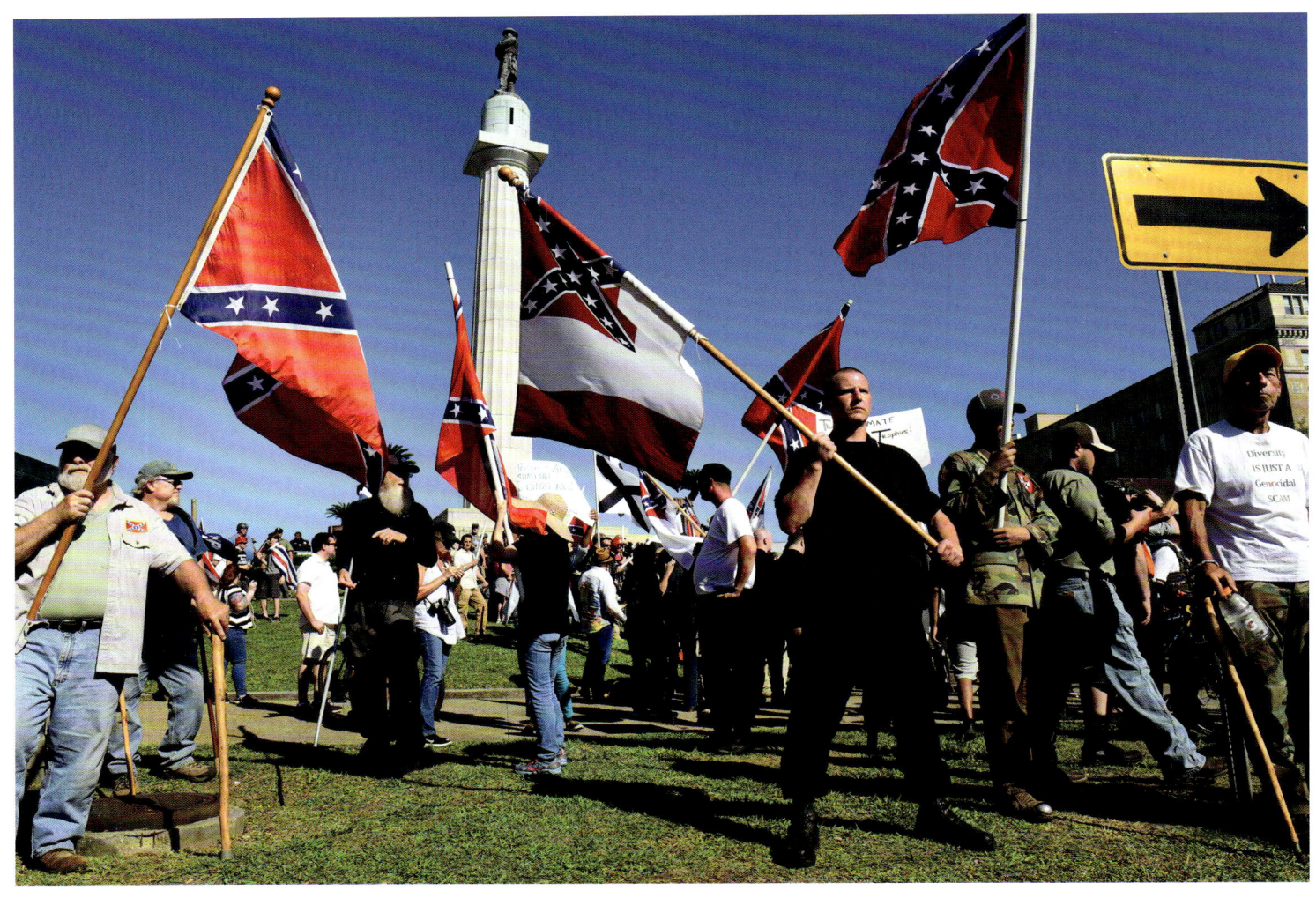

White supremacists wave Confederate flags near the Robert E. Lee Confederate monument, 2017.

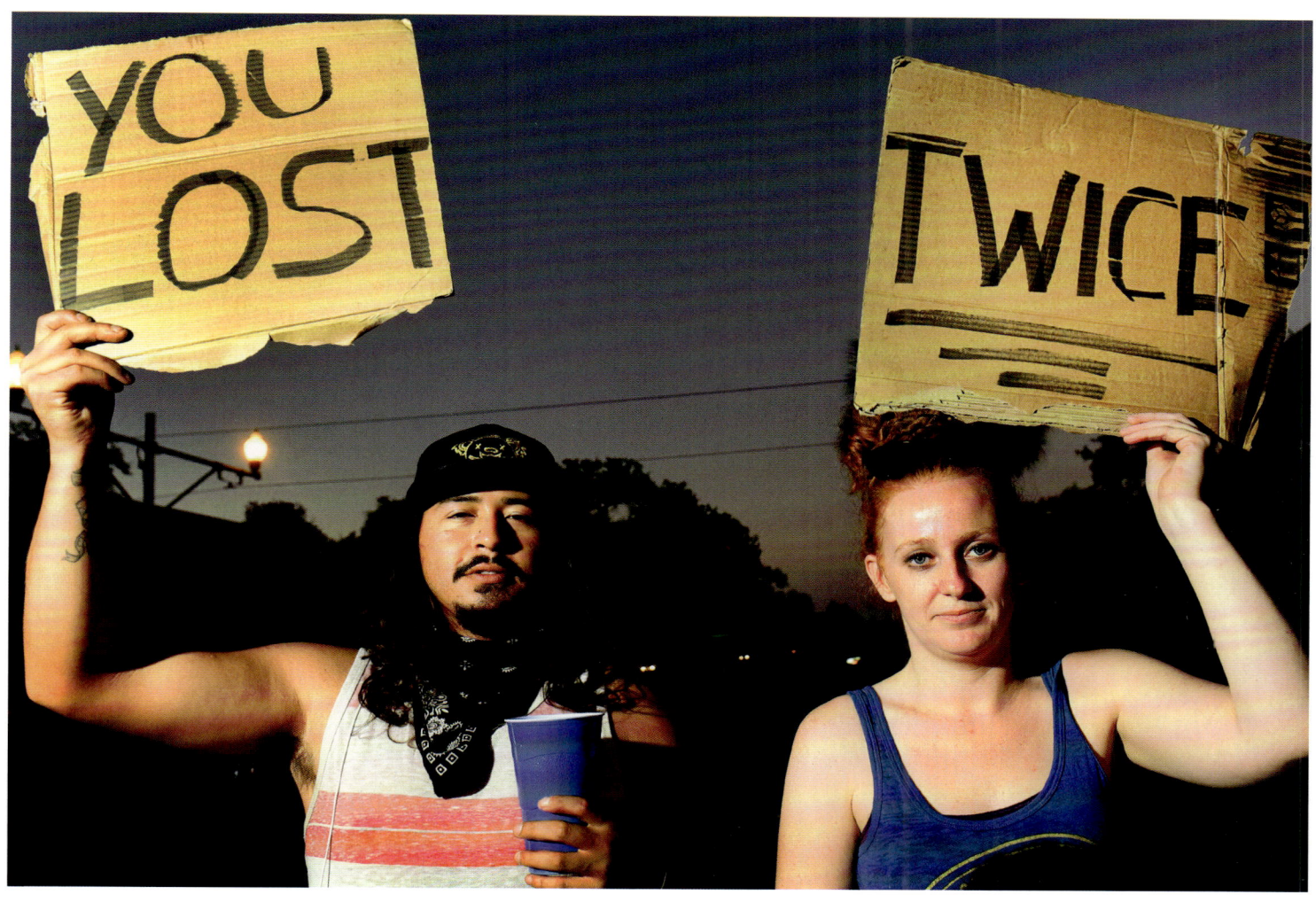

Counterprotesters hold signs at the site of the Jefferson Davis Confederate monument before it was removed, 2017.

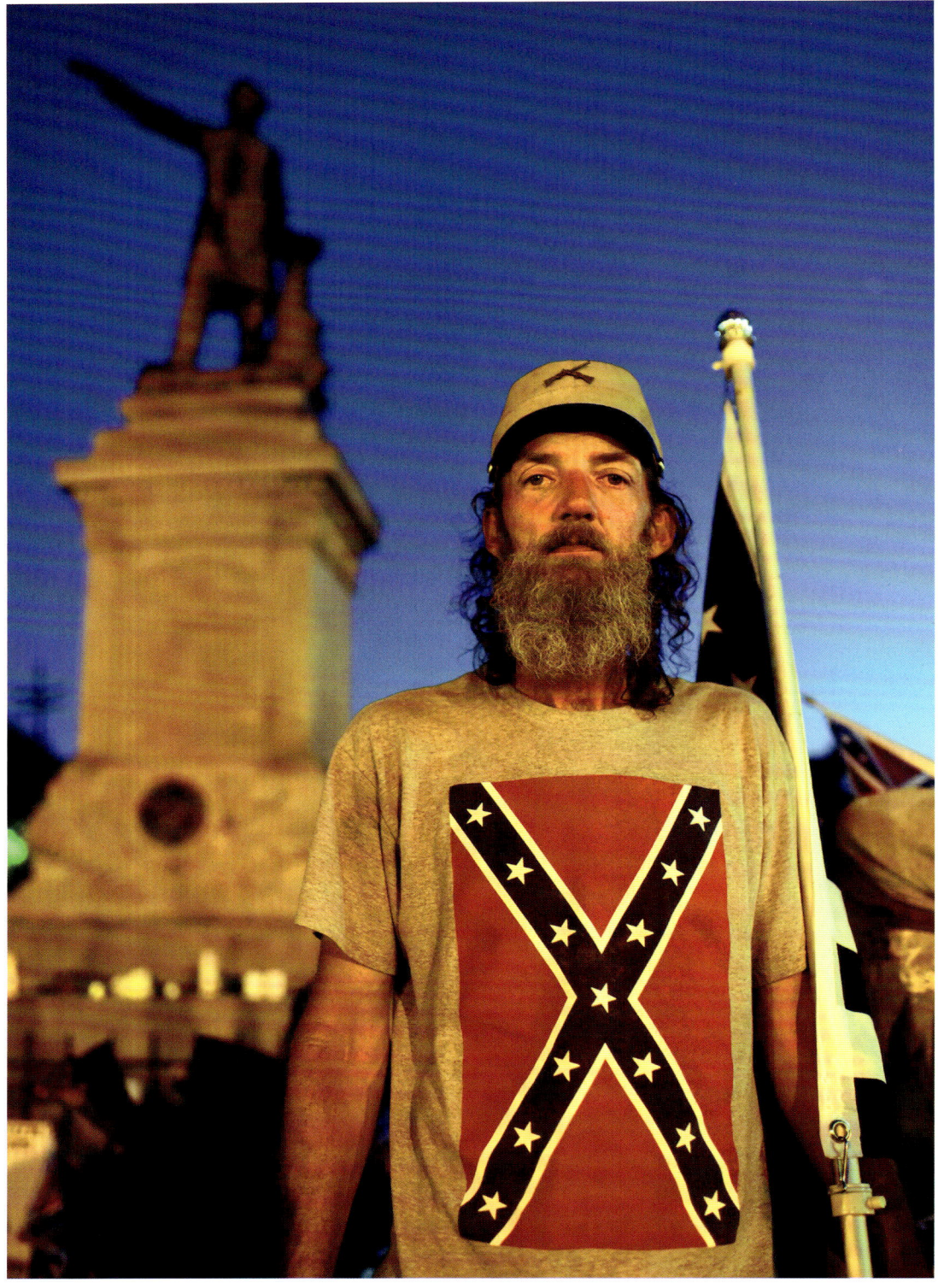

James del Brock protests the removal of the Jefferson Davis statue, 2017.

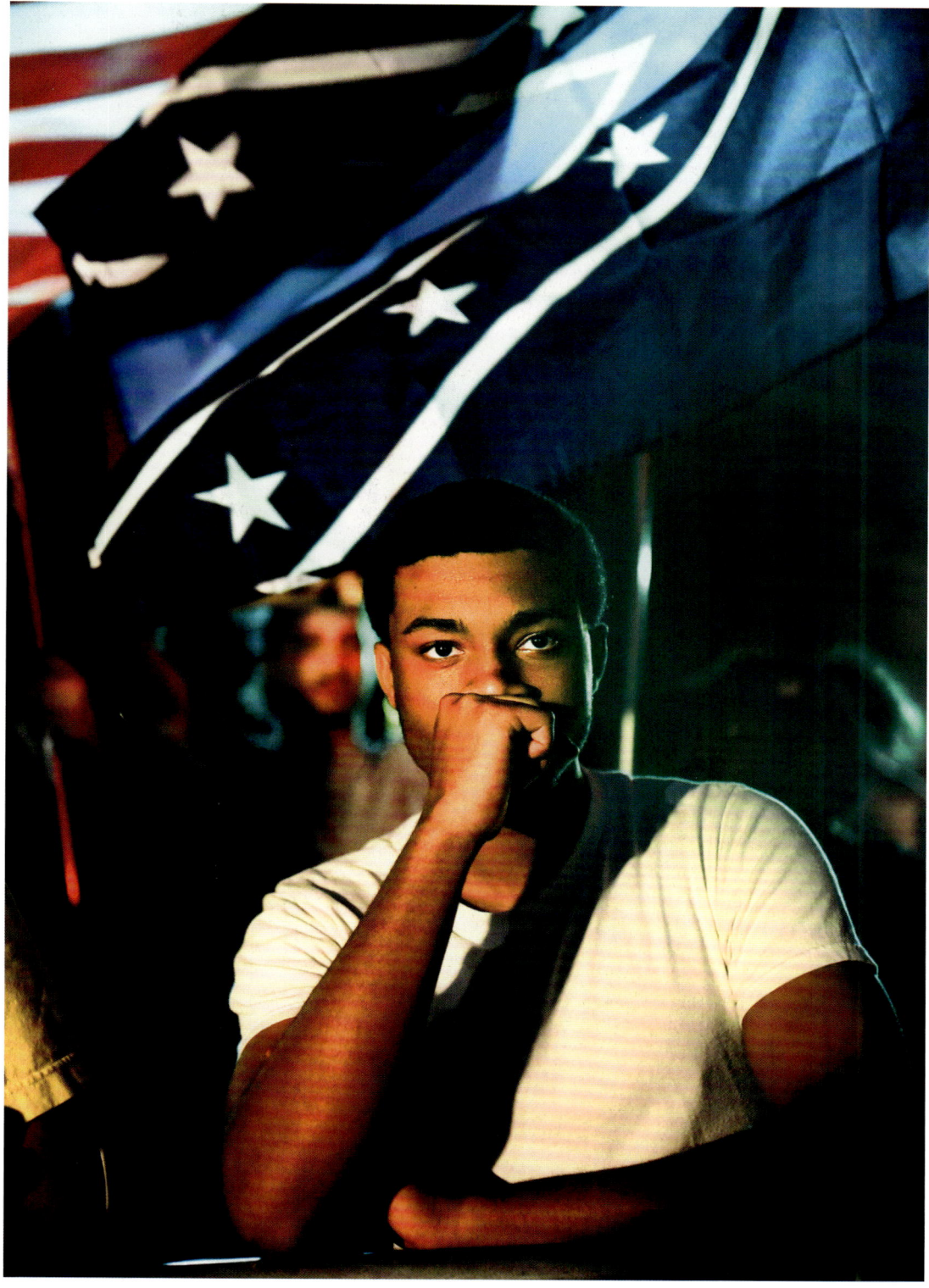

Matthew Moore witnesses the removal of the statue of Beauregard, the Confederate general, 2017.

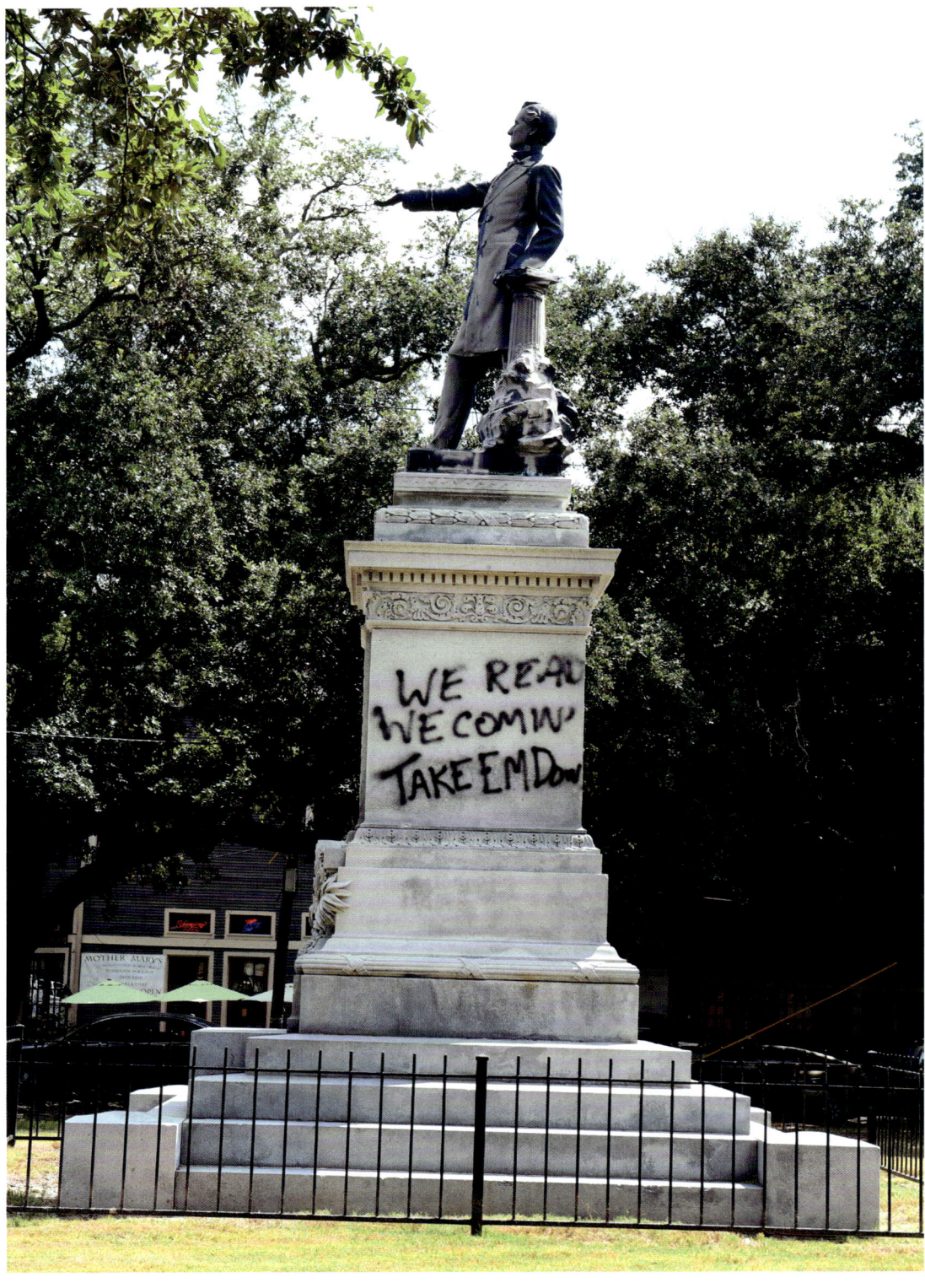

Graffiti is seen on the Jefferson Davis monument, 2016.

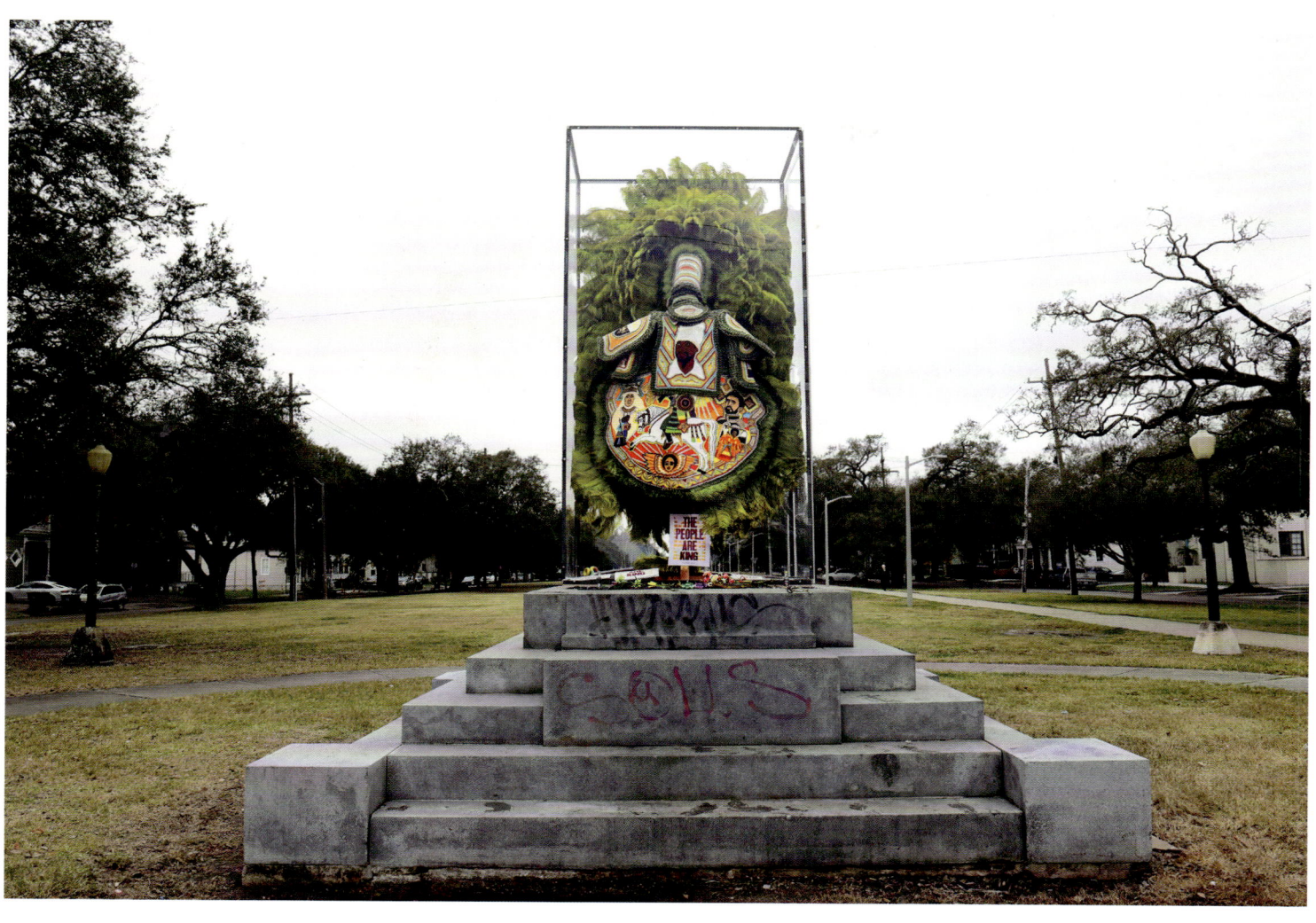

Young Seminole Hunters Big Chief Demond Melancon's Indian suit is displayed on Mardi Gras Day where Jefferson Davis once stood, 2020.

Robert E. Lee monument, 2015.

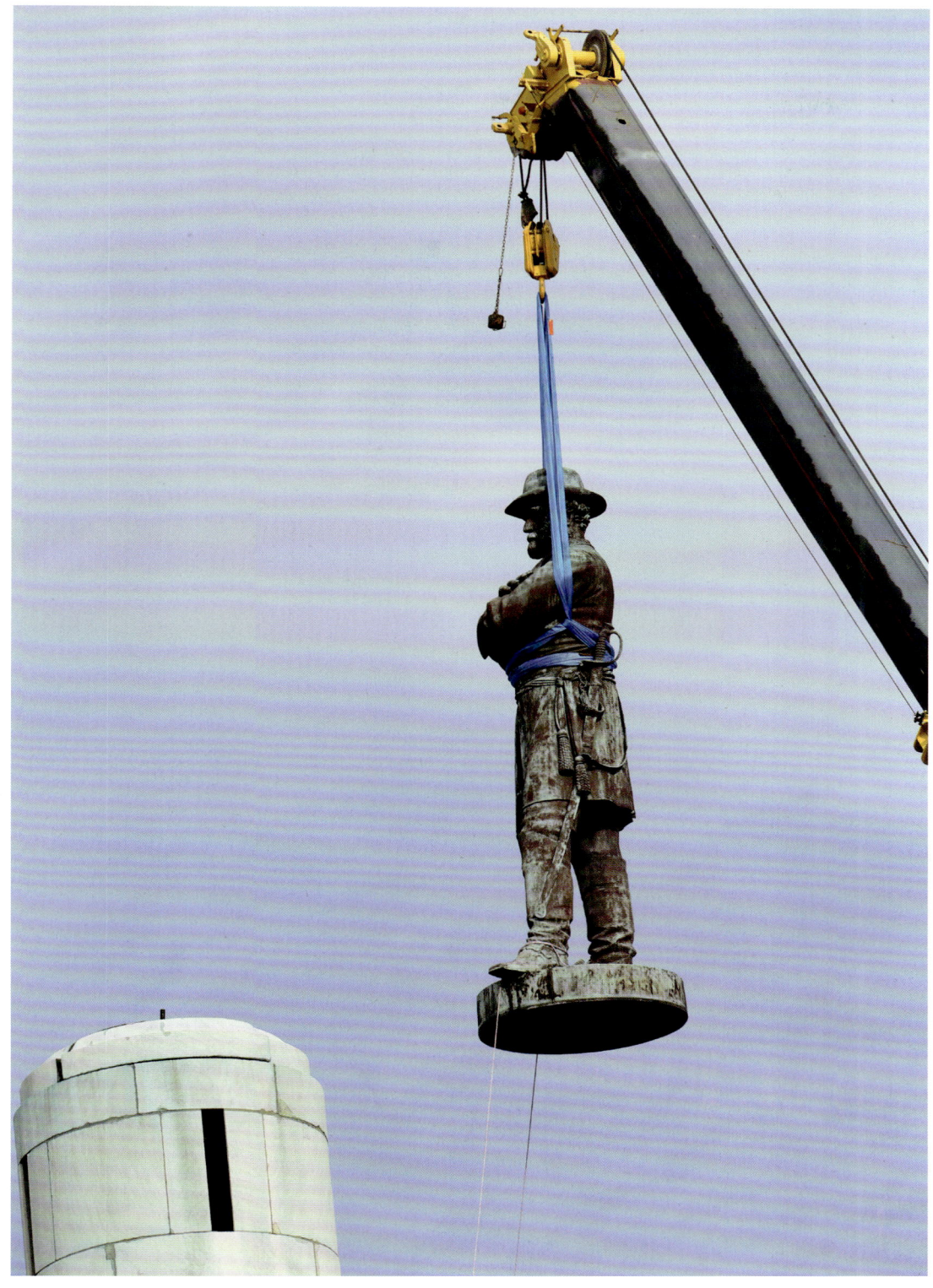

Removal of the
Robert E. Lee statue,
2017.

Celebration erupts after the Robert E. Lee monument is removed, 2017.

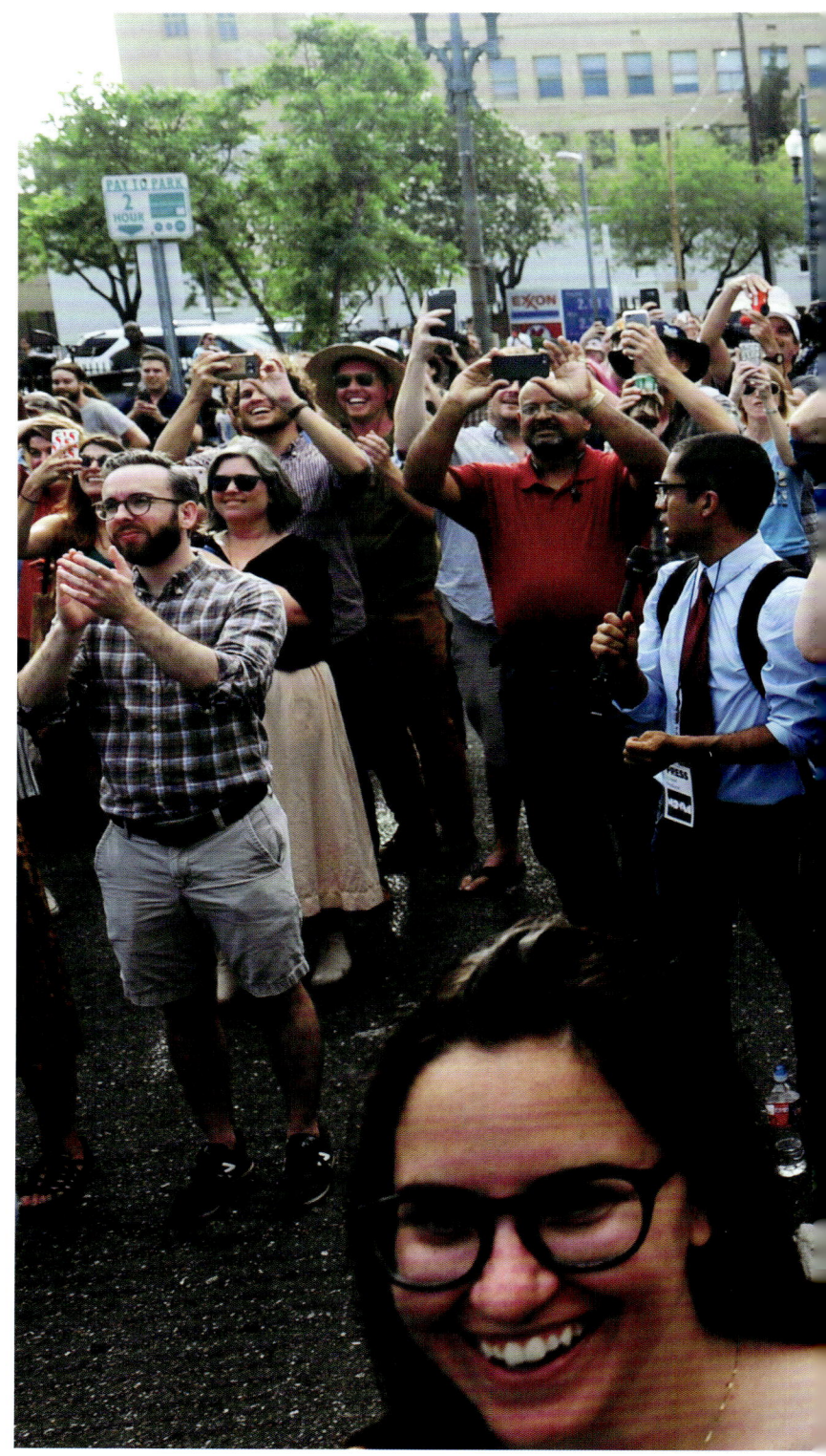

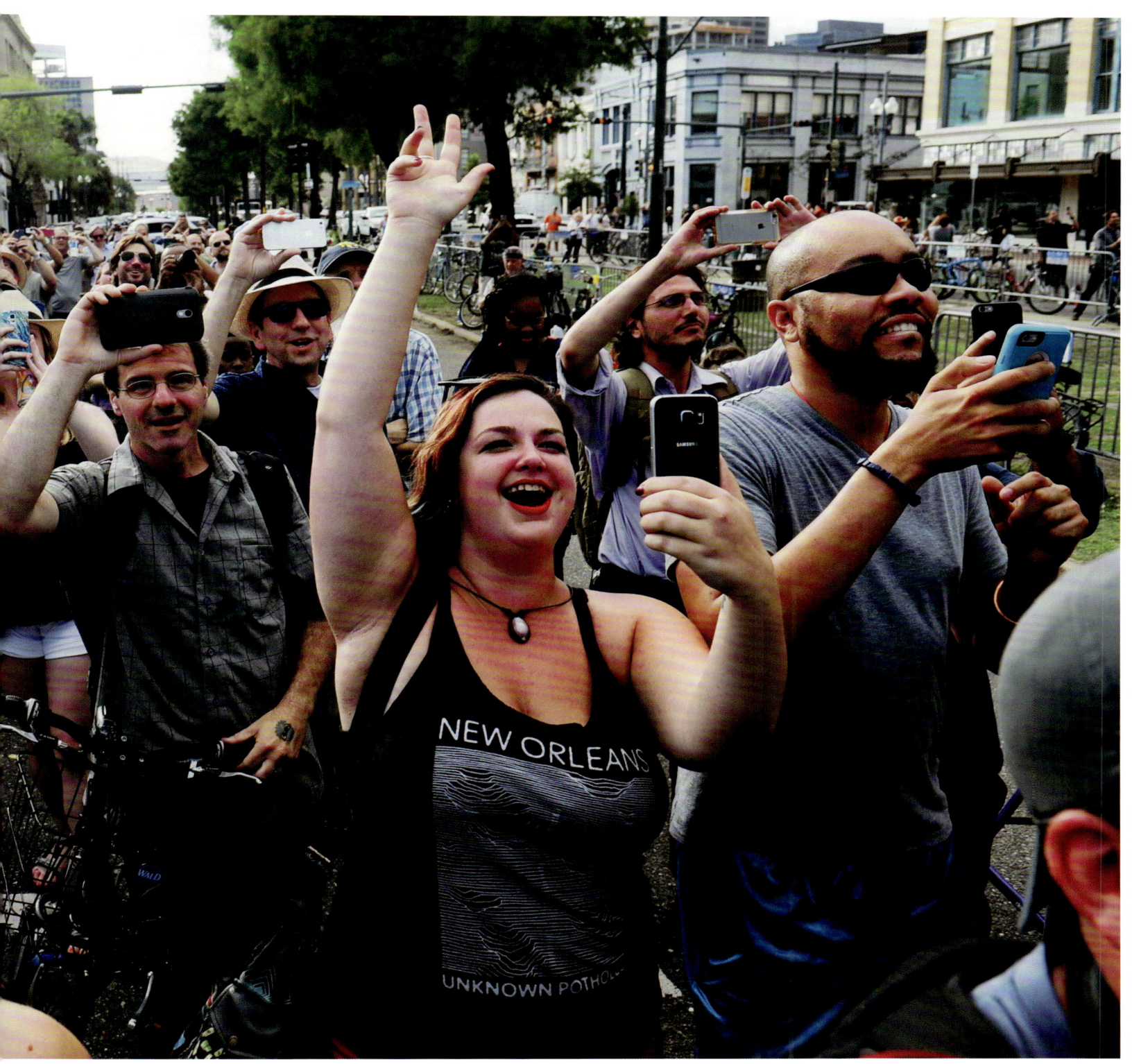

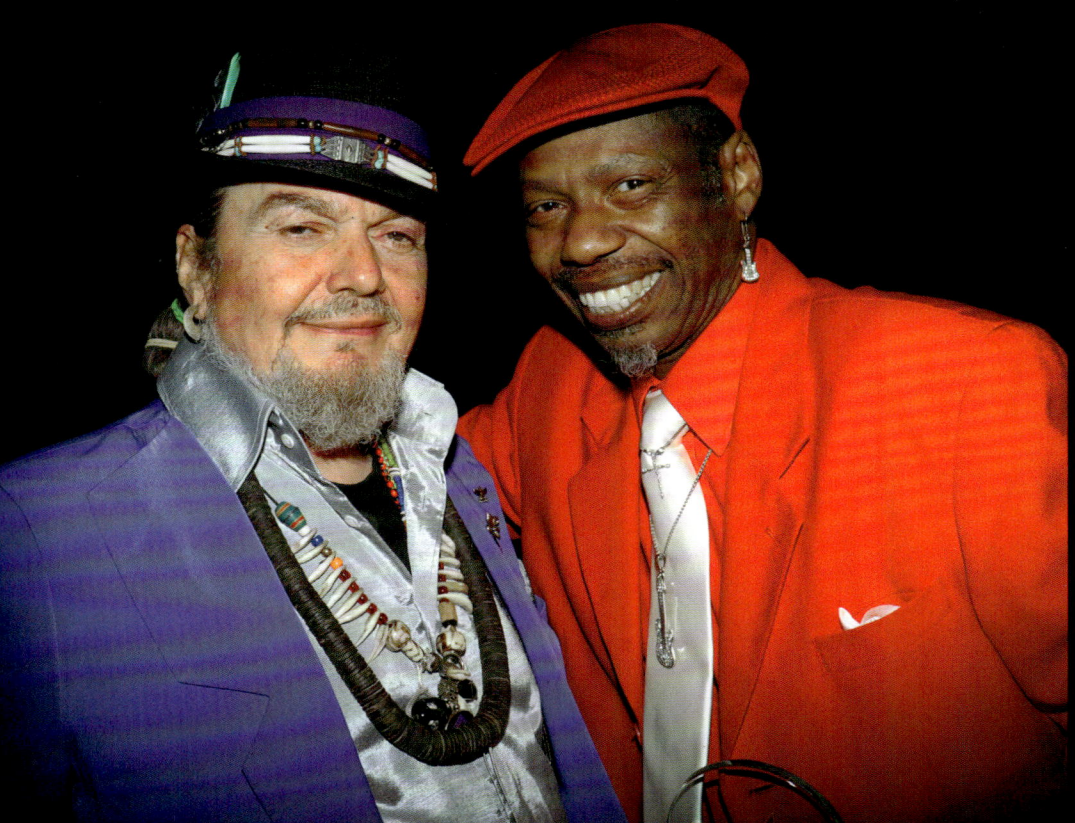

New Orleans music legend Malcolm John Rebennack Jr., known as Dr. John, with bluesman Walter "Wolfman" Washington at the Big Easy Awards, where Washington was honored with the Lifetime Achievement Award, 2012. Dr. John died in 2019 and Washington passed away in late 2022.

You wanna do some livin' before you die?

Do it down in New Orleans.

—FROM "DOWN IN NEW ORLEANS," BY RANDY NEWMAN,

SUNG BY DR. JOHN IN *THE PRINCESS AND THE FROG*

GLOSSARY

Baby Dolls are one of the first women's organizations to mask and perform during Mardi Gras, tracing their origins from Storyville-era brothels and dance halls to their reemergence in post-Katrina New Orleans. Today the Black Masking sisterhood tradition of Baby Dolls is flourishing throughout the city.

Backstreet Cultural Museum, founded in 1999 by Sylvester "Hawk" Francis, is a repository of Black Masking Indian suits, social aid and pleasure club regalia, and photos and recordings honoring Black culture in Tremé. The museum's original location, a former funeral home, was heavily damaged during Hurricane Ida in 2021, and it later reopened in a new location in Tremé. It is now owned and operated by Francis's daughter, Dominique Francis-Dilling.

Tarriona "Tank" Ball is the lead singer of the New Orleans musical group Tank and the Bangas, who skyrocketed to fame after winning NPR's Tiny Desk Contest in 2017.

Jon Batiste is a New Orleans–born singer, songwriter, musician, bandleader, and television personality. He has recorded and performed with artists in various genres of music, released his own recordings, and performed in more than forty countries. He won five Grammy Awards in 2022, including Album of the Year for his LP *We Are,* and Best Music Video for "Freedom," set in New Orleans.

P. G. T. Beauregard was a Confederate general of Creole descent from St. Bernard Parish in Louisiana. His monument was removed from its pedestal in front of City Park in 2017.

Black Lives Matter (BLM) is a political and social movement that seeks to highlight racism, discrimination, and racial inequality experienced by Black people.

Black Masking Indians, sometimes referred to as **Mardi Gras Indians,** originated in the early to mid-nineteenth century. They are African American revelers who dress up for Mardi Gras in elaborate hand-sewn suits that pay homage to Native Americans who aided enslaved people.

Many tribes also parade on St. Joseph's Day (March 19) and the nearest Sunday to that date, better known as **Super Sunday**. **Spy Boy, Flag Boy, Wild Man, Queen,** and **Big Chief** play various roles within a tribe.

Bounce music is an energetic style of New Orleans hip hop music that is said to have originated as early as the late 1980s. Bounce is characterized by a call-and-response style and Black Masking Indian chants. Its dance movements are often hypersexual.

Café du Monde, established in 1872 in the French Market, is open twenty-four hours a day, serving café au lait and beignets, the deep-fried doughy pastry covered in powdered sugar.

Cajuns, also known as Les Acadiens, are descendants of French Canadians who settled along the bayous of South Louisiana. "Cajun" also refers to the culture, music, and food of this ethnic group.

Camellia Brand Red Beans are the signature bean of many households, as well as the Krewe of Red Beans, which celebrates the tradition of cooking red beans on Mondays, historically laundry day.

Carver Theater, built in 1950, is on the National Register of Historic Places. After a post-Katrina renovation, it is used for concerts, funerals, and other community events in Tremé.

Central City is the predominantly African American neighborhood located at the lower end of Uptown, just upriver from the Central Business District. It plays a key role in the city's brass band and Black Masking Indian traditions.

Chewbacchus, a science fiction parade formally known as the Intergalactic Krewe of Chewbacchus, began parading in 2011 as a satiric mashup of Bacchus, the Roman god of wine, and Chewbacca, the Wookie from *Star Wars*.

Congo Square, located in the southern corner of Armstrong Park in Tremé, is an open space where enslaved and free people of color gathered on Sundays for African drumming and singing; it played a significant role in the development of jazz. The tradition of drumming on Sundays continues today.

Harry Connick Jr., born in 1967, is an American singer, pianist, composer, actor, and television host, born and raised in New Orleans. He has earned three Grammy Awards and sixteen nominations.

Creole refers to ethnic groups, individuals, and the culture of those born in New Orleans with European and African, Caribbean, or Hispanic descent.

Jefferson Davis was the president of the Confederate States from 1861 to 1865. His statue was removed from Canal Street in 2017 after 105 years.

Dead Beans Parade, formed in 2018, is a spinoff of the Red Beans parade displaying themes of death; it begins in Bayou St. John and meets up with the Red Beans parade on Lundi Gras in Tremé.

Dr. John (1941–2019), born Malcolm John Rebennack Jr., was a legendary songwriter and musician who combined New Orleans blues, jazz, funk, and rhythm and blues.

Faubourg Marigny is the first suburb east of the French Quarter, founded in the first decade of the nineteenth century by Creole real estate developer and politician Bernard de Marigny. After many years of decline during the mid-twentieth century, the Marigny is now one of the city's most colorful neighborhoods and is home to Frenchmen Street, known for live music.

FestiGals Women's Weekend Experience is New Orleans's first and only women-centric festival. It is held each summer for women to enjoy themselves, be inspired, and become empowered in a safe, festive environment.

Flag Boy is ranked after the Spy Boy in the Black Masking Indian tribe; he carries the "gang flag," a huge staff decorated with feathers and his gang's symbol.

Friday Night Fights, an amateur boxing event created by Central City gym owner Mike Tata, features novelty acts and audience participation.

The Healing Center opened its doors in 2011 in two colorful buildings on St. Claude Avenue. The old furniture store was renovated and repurposed after Katrina by developer Pres Kabacoff and Voodoo Priestess Sallie Ann Glassman to bring "healing" to the community.

Hot 8 Brass Band, formed in 1985, is a Grammy-nominated brass band that blends hip hop, jazz, and funk styles with traditional New Orleans sounds.

Jazz Fest, formally the **New Orleans Jazz & Heritage Festival,** founded in 1970, is an annual seven-day celebration of local music and culture, as well as big-name artists, held at the Fair Grounds Race Course; it attracts hundreds of thousands of visitors to New Orleans each year.

Jazz funerals (traditional funeral processions) begin with a march by family, friends, and a brass band from the home, funeral home, or church to the cemetery. Throughout the march, the band plays somber dirges and hymns; a change in the tenor of the ceremony takes place after either the deceased is entombed or the hearse leaves the procession and members of the procession say their final goodbye and "cut the body loose." The term "jazz funeral" was long used by observers from elsewhere but, until recently, was generally disdained as inappropriate by most New Orleans musicians and practitioners of the tradition.

Krewe is an organization that puts on a parade or ball for the Carnival season.

krewe*delusion*, founded in 2010, is a satirical parade that usually follows Krewe du Vieux.

Krewe de Mayahuel is a Mexican-style carnivalesque walking group that takes its name from the Aztec goddess of fertility and agave. It honors the dead with a rolling altar float in the shape of an ancient pyramid where participants can place photos and belongings of loved ones who have died.

Krewe d'Etat, which had its inaugural parade in 1998, is a Carnival krewe known for its satirical themed floats and parade.

Krewe du Vieux, established in 1987, is a Carnival krewe that parades through the Faubourg Marigny and meanders through the French Quarter. One of the earliest parades on the Carnival calendar, it is noted for wild satirical and adult themes.

Krewe of Spank, formed in 2012, is a subkrewe of the Krewe du Vieux parade. The krewe made its public debut in 2013 and also marches in the Southern Decadence parade.

Robert E. Lee was a Confederate general during the Civil War. Lee's statue was removed from the highest pedestal in New Orleans in 2017, where it had stood since 1884.

Leijorettes, formed in 2014, pay homage to the memory of Princess Leia from the *Star Wars* movie series and march in the Krewe of Chewbacchus parade.

Lundi Gras is the Monday before Fat Tuesday, or Mardi Gras.

Mohawk Hunters is a Black Masking Indian tribe from Algiers on the West Bank.

Hinton Ashley Morris (October 20, 1963–April 2, 2008) was a cultural and political blogger who became popular through a series of post-Katrina blog posts that dealt with the destruction caused by the hurricane and the efforts to rebuild New Orleans. One post in particular, titled "Fuck You You Fucking Fucks," lifted Morris into legendary status and inspired an "FYYFF" T-shirt.

Neutral ground refers to the grassy median between streets that plays a role in the history, culture, and life in New Orleans.

The Neville Brothers band was made up of four brothers—Art, Charles, Aaron, and Cyril Neville. The Grammy Award–winning group recorded their debut album in 1978 and was known for their unique sound of R&B, soul, and funk.

The North Side Skull and Bone Gang is a Black Masking tradition that dates to 1819, in which members dressed as skeletons wearing oversized papier-mâché skulls walk door to door through Tremé on Mardi Gras morning to spread the word that life is fleeting.

Brandan "BMike" Odums is a muralist and multimedia artist renowned for graffiti and murals depicting African Americans. His landmark Studio Be is located in the Faubourg Marigny.

Eva "Tee Eva" Perry helped revive the Baby Dolls, a Black Masking tradition with long roots in New Orleans. She was also known as the "Praline and Pie Lady" for her praline business. Tee Eva died in 2017 at the age of eighty-three.

Phunny Phorty Phellows is a historic Mardi Gras krewe known for its satirical parade that kicks off the Carnival season on January 6 with a ride on the St. Charles Avenue streetcar.

Pigeon Town Steppers is a social aid and pleasure club from the Pigeon Town neighborhood in the Carrollton area that formed in 1994.

Pride Fest is the annual festival and parade celebrating the LGBTQ+ community.

Red Beans Parade, founded in 2009 by the Krewe of Red Beans, honors the red beans and rice culinary tradition on Lundi Gras, the day before Mardi Gras, with elaborate costumes decorated with beans.

Royal Artists, a company founded in 1975 that designs and builds old-line Carnival krewe floats, secured the Rex parade as a client in 2020; it was responsible for many of the elaborately decorated house floats during the pandemic.

Royal Carriages is a company whose mule-drawn carriages have been rolling through the

Faubourg Marigny, where the mules' barns are located, and the French Quarter for more than eighty years.

Second line is a tradition in the brass band parades that are held on most Sundays between October and March. The "first line" is the main section of the parade or the members of the actual club with the parading permit, as well as the brass band; they are followed by the "second line," the revelers who enjoy and dance to the music.

Seventh Ward, Eighth Ward, and Ninth Ward are neighborhoods sometimes called "the back of town"; they are poor or working-class sections that were hit very hard during Katrina and are currently experiencing gentrification.

Shotgun houses are narrow houses arranged with rooms one behind the other to accommodate building codes on narrow lots.

Silence Is Violence is a campaign for peace through community outreach and education, founded in 2007 following the murders of musician Dinerral Shavers and filmmaker Helen Hill.

Social aid and pleasure clubs can be traced back to nineteenth-century benevolent societies that provided health care and burial services for their members. In addition, the clubs encouraged leadership skills and provided a forum for discussing social issues, as well as entertainment in the form of picnics, annual Sunday parades, dinners, and balls.

Société des Champs Elysée (Society of Elysian Fields), founded in 2016 by krewe captain David Roe, is a social aid and benevolent krewe dedicated to the betterment of the neighborhoods along the intersection of Elysian Fields and St. Claude/Henriette DeLille. Krewe members ride the St. Claude/N. Rampart streetcar each year on the night of Epiphany. Even though the streetcar did not run for three years after the track was damaged during the partial collapse of the Hard Rock Hotel, the festivities continued with a second line and ball.

Southern Decadence, founded in 1972, is an annual six-day event held by the LGBTQ+ community during Labor Day Weekend, climaxing with a parade through the French Quarter on the Sunday before Labor Day.

Spirit of Fi Yi Yi and the Mandingo Warriors, led by Big Chief Victor Harris, is a Black Masking Indian tribe from the Seventh Ward. Harris's mentor was Big Chief Tootie Montana, perhaps the most famous Indian. Harris himself has been suiting for well over fifty years, longer than any other Big Chief.

Spy Boy is the first figure in front of a Black Masking Indian tribe, on the lookout for trouble and other tribes, and signals the Flag Boy through chants and sign language.

St. Joseph's Day/Night is a citywide event featuring public and private altars of food and drink commemorating the relief that St. Joseph provided during the famine in Sicily; it is not just celebrated by Italian Americans. Food from the altars is shared with visitors and generally distributed to charities after the altars are dismantled. It is also the day that Black Masking Indians grace neighborhood streets in their splendid suits.

St. Patrick's Day is celebrated throughout the city with major parades in the Irish Channel, Bywater, and French Quarter neighborhoods, including a combined Irish-Italian Parade celebrating both St. Patrick's Day and St. Joseph's Day. In the spirit of Mardi Gras, the Irish Channel parade is famous for throwing onions, carrots, cabbages, potatoes, and other ingredients for making an Irish stew.

Strippers' March, formally known as the Unemployment March, protested the closure of several strip clubs in the French Quarter after they were cited by ATF agents for prostitution and drug violations.

St. Roch is a neighborhood in the Eighth Ward centered along St. Roch Avenue, known for the St. Roch Cemeteries and the St. Roch Market.

Super Sunday is the most significant day for Black Masking Indians other than Mardi Gras Day. The New Orleans Mardi Gras Indian Council usually holds its Indian Sunday on the third Sunday of March, around St. Joseph's Day, which Italians celebrate with food altars. On Super Sunday the Black Masking Indians once again dress in their feathers and beaded suits and take to the streets to meet other "gangs" or "tribes."

Take 'Em Down NOLA is a grassroots organization committed to the removal of all symbols of white supremacy in New Orleans as part of a broader push for racial and economic justice.

Tipitina's live music club was established in 1977 by a group of fourteen music fans and is dedicated to the spirit of the late pianist and musician Professor Longhair. Today, the club is owned and operated by members of the band Galactic.

'tit Rəx, formed in 2008, is the world's first Mardi Gras microkrewe in which members create tiny floats, inspired by the generations-old grade-school tradition of decorating shoebox floats for Mardi Gras. The parade's name is based on the French abbreviation of "petite."

Tremé, pronounced *trə*-MAY, one of the oldest neighborhoods in New Orleans, is directly north and adjacent to the French Quarter. Many free people of color settled there. Despite recent gentrification, Tremé continues to be a racially mixed neighborhood and an important center of the city's African American and Creole culture, especially the modern brass band tradition. HBO aired a four-season television series called *Treme,* created by David Simon, that highlighted post-Katrina New Orleans.

Treme Sidewalk Steppers, a social aid and pleasure club, holds one of the largest annual second lines through the Sixth and Seventh Wards; it has second-lined for thirty years.

Trombone Shorty, whose name is Troy Andrews, is a New Orleans musician, producer, actor, and philanthropist best known as a trombone and trumpet player and a member of the famous Andrews family of musicians.

Undefeated Divas and Gents Social Aid and Pleasure Club (originally the Undefeated Divas), founded by Antoinette and Kevin Devezin, formed their new iteration that includes men right after Hurricane Katrina. It is known for its members' handmade suits and carefully selected footwear. A children's division was later added.

Voodoo, also known as **Vodou,** first came to Louisiana with enslaved West Africans, who merged their religious rituals and practices with those of local Catholics. Its adherents greatly increased in number when followers fleeing Haiti after the 1791 slave revolt settled in New Orleans. Voodoo queens and kings were spiritual and political figures of power in nineteenth-century New Orleans.

Wards are designated areas used in elections and subdivided into precincts. Although the city has not had officials elected to represent wards since 1912, many New Orleanians still identify where they are from by ward number, especially those living in the downtown Sixth, Seventh, Eighth, and Ninth Wards. New Orleans is divided into seventeen wards.

Zulu Social Aid and Pleasure Club, founded in 1916, is a Carnival krewe most famous for its Zulu parade on Mardi Gras morning. Zulu is New Orleans's largest predominantly African American Carnival organization known for its blackfaced krewe members wearing grass skirts and its extremely coveted throws, hand-painted coconuts. (Many are disturbed by Zulu's tradition of blackface, but the organization defends it as their right to express their Black identity, with or without makeup.)